Tanzania

Lake Victoria
p219

Northern Tanzania
p152

Central Tanzania
p210

Northeastern Tanzania
p125

Western Tanzania
p237

Zanzibar Archipelago
p75

◉ **Dar es Salaam**
p50

Southern Highlands
p254

Southeastern Tanzania
p285

THIS EDITION WRITTEN AND RESEARCHED BY

Mary Fitzpatrick,

Stuart Butler, Anthony Ham, Paula Hardy

Contents

NIGEL PAVITT/GETTY IMAGES ©

MAASAI GIRL, NORTHERN TANZANIA, P152

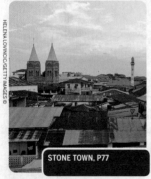

HELENA LOVINCIC/GETTY IMAGES ©

STONE TOWN, P77

Contents

Welcome to Tanzania

Wildlife, beaches, ruins, Mt Kilimanjaro, friendly people, fascinating cultures – Tanzania has all these and more wrapped up in one adventurous, welcoming package.

Wonderful Wildlife

More than almost any other destination, Tanzania is the land of safaris. Wildebeest stampede across the plains. Hippos jostle for space in muddy waterways. Elephants wander along seasonal migration routes and chimpanzees swing through the treetops. Throughout the country, there are unparalleled opportunities to experience this natural wealth. Take a boat safari down the Rufiji River past snoozing crocodiles in Selous Game Reserve. Watch giraffes silhouetted against ancient baobab trees in Ruaha National Park. Sit motionless as waterbirds peck in the shallows around Rubondo Island. Hold your breath while a lion pads past in Ngorongoro Crater.

Idyllic Beaches

It's not just the wildlife that enchants. Tanzania's Indian Ocean coastline is also magical, with tranquil islands and sleepy coastal villages steeped in centuries of Swahili culture. Travel back in time to the days when the East African coast was the seat of sultans and a linchpin in a far-flung trading network extending to Persia, India and beyond. Relax on powdery beaches. Take in pastel-hued sunrises, immerse yourself in languid coastal rhythms, and sit beneath billowing sails on a wooden dhow.

Mt Kilimanjaro

Inland, Mt Kilimanjaro beckons, its graceful, forested flanks rising up to a stately snow-capped summit. It is Africa's highest peak and one of the world's highest freestanding mountains. Climbers by the thousands venture here to challenge themselves on its muddy slopes, rocky trails and slippery scree. The rewards? The thrill of standing at the top of Africa, magnificent views of Kilimanjaro's ice fields, and witnessing the sunrise illuminating the plains far below.

Captivating Cultures

Wherever you go, opportunities abound for getting to know Tanzania's people and cultures. Meet red-cloaked Maasai warriors. Spend time with the semi-nomadic Barabaig near Mt Hanang. Experience the hospitality of a local meal or the rhythms of traditional dance. Watch Makonde carvers bring wood to life. Chat and barter at local markets in the Usambara Mountains. More than anything else, it is Tanzanians themselves – with their characteristic warmth and politeness, and the dignity and beauty of their cultures – who make a visit so memorable. Chances are that you'll want to come back for more, to which most Tanzanians will say *'karibu tena'* (welcome again).

Why I Love Tanzania

By Mary Fitzpatrick, Author

I love Tanzania because of the light, colours and life in almost every scene. Especially at dawn: the rising sun floods the cool grasslands with gold, school children walk along the roadsides and vendors set out their wares. And when nature surrounds you, there is exuberance everywhere: the largest of animals mingle with the most minute; birds of every size and colour soar and sing; trees and plants burst with flowers; landscapes are colourful and diverse. Mostly, though, it's because of the equanimity, charm, dignity and welcome offered by so many Tanzanians.

For more about our authors, see page 416

Above: Dhow, Zanzibar (p77)

Tanzania

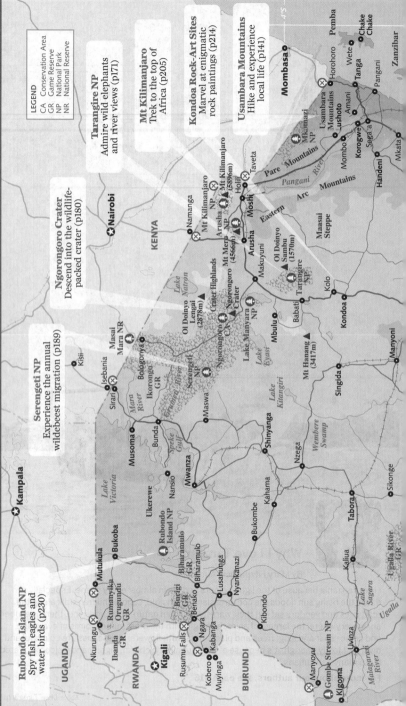

Rubondo Island NP
Spy fish eagles and water birds (p230)

Serengeti NP
Experience the annual wildebeest migration (p189)

Ngorongoro Crater
Descend into the wildlife-packed crater (p180)

Tarangire NP
Admire wild elephants and river views (p171)

Mt Kilimanjaro
Trek to the top of Africa (p205)

Kondoa Rock-Art Sites
Marvel at enigmatic rock paintings (p214)

Usambara Mountains
Hike and experience local life (p141)

LEGEND
CA Conservation Area
GR Game Reserve
NP National Park
NR National Reserve

200 km
120 miles

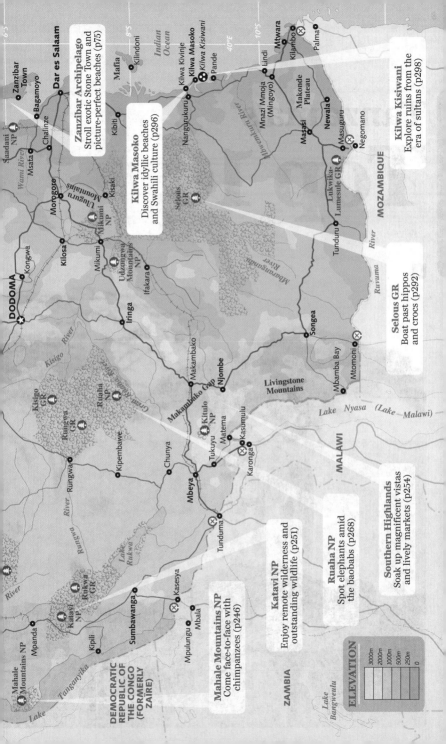

Zanzibar Archipelago
Stroll exotic Stone Town and picture-perfect beaches (p75)

Kilwa Kisiwani
Explore ruins from the era of sultans (p298)

Kilwa Masoko
Discover idyllic beaches and Swahili culture (p296)

Selous GR
Boat past hippos and crocs (p292)

Southern Highlands
Soak up magnificent vistas and lively markets (p254)

Ruaha NP
Spot elephants amid the baobabs (p268)

Katavi NP
Enjoy remote wilderness and outstanding wildlife (p251)

Mahale Mountains NP
Come face-to-face with chimpanzees (p246)

ELEVATION

3000m
2000m
1000m
500m
250m
0

Indian Ocean

DEMOCRATIC REPUBLIC OF THE CONGO (FORMERLY ZAIRE)

ZAMBIA

MALAWI

MOZAMBIQUE

DODOMA

Dar es Salaam

Zanzibar Town

Bagamoyo

Saadani NP

Wami River

Msata

Chalinze

Msata

Kongwa

Morogoro

Kilosa

Kibiti

Kisaki

Kibiti

Mikumi NP

Uluguru Mountains

Mikumi

Udzungwa Mountains NP

Ifakara

Iringa

Selous GR

Kilwa Kivinje

Kilwa Masoko

Kilwa Kisiwani

Kilindoni

Mafia

Pande

Lindi

Mtwara

Kilambo

Palma

Nangurukuru

Mnazi Mmoja (Mingoyo)

Makonde Plateau

Masasi

Newala

Masuguru

Negomano

Mbwemkuru River

Lukwika-Lumesule GR

Tunduru

Ruvuma River

Songea

Mbamba Bay

Mtomoni

Matema

Kasumulu

Karonga

Livingstone Mountains

Lake Nyasa (Lake Malawi)

Kitulo NP

Tukuyu

Makambako Gap

Njombe

Makambako

Chunya

Mbeya

Tunduma

Kipembawe

Rungwa

Ruaha NP

Rungwa GR

Kisigo GR

Kisigo River

Great Ruaha River

Rungwa River

Lake Rukwa

Kaseseya

Sumbawanga

Mpulungu

Mbala

Kipili

Mpanda

Katavi NP

Katavi GR

Rukwa GR

Mahale Mountains NP

Lake Tanganyika

Lake Bangweulu

40°E

6°S

8°S

10°S

Tanzania's
Top 10

Serengeti National Park

1 The sound of pounding hooves on the Serengeti plains draws closer. Suddenly, thousands of animals stampede by in a cloud of dust as the great wildebeest migration – one of earth's most spectacular natural dramas – plays out. Despite the theatrics, time seems to stand still in this superlative park. Lions sit majestically on lofty outcrops, giraffes stride gracefully into the sunset, crocodiles bask on riverbanks. Wildlife watching is outstanding year round. Just allow time to appreciate all the Serengeti (p189) has to offer. Below left: Lioness

Zanzibar's Stone Town

2 Whether it's your first visit or your 50th, Zanzibar's Stone Town (p77) never loses its touch of the exotic. First, you'll see the skyline, with the spires of St Joseph's Cathedral and the Old Fort. Then, as you wander through narrow alleyways, surprises are revealed at every turn. Linger in dusty shops scented with cloves, watch as men wearing white robe-like *kanzu* play a game of *bao*. Admire intricate henna designs on the hands of women clad in *buibui* (black cover-alls). Island rhythms take over as mainland life slips away.

ERICH SCHMIDT/IMAGEBROKER/CORBIS ©

PAUL HARRIS/GETTY IMAGES ©

Ngorongoro Crater

3 On clear days, the magic of Ngorongoro (p180) starts while you're still up on the rim, with chilled air and sublime views over the enormous crater. The descent takes you to a wide plain cloaked in hues of blue and green and covered in an unparalleled concentration of African wildlife. If you're lucky enough to find a quiet spot, it's easy to imagine primeval Africa, with an almost constant parade of animals streaming past against a quintessential East African back-drop. Go as early in the day as possible to maximise viewing time and to take advantage of the morning light.

Mt Kilimanjaro

4 It's difficult to resist the allure of climbing Africa's highest peak, with its snow-capped summit and views over the surrounding plains. Thousands of trekkers complete the climb each year, with a main requirement for success being adequate time for acclimatisation. But there are also other rewarding ways to experience Kilimanjaro (p205). Take a day hike on the mountain's lush lower slopes, learn about local Chagga culture or sip a sundowner from one of many nearby vantage points with the mountain as a backdrop.

CLAUDIA URIBE/GETTY IMAGES ©

Local Life

5 Wildlife galore, a snow-capped peak, fantastic beaches and Swahili ruins are but a backdrop to Tanzania's most fascinating resource – its people. Local culture is accessible and diverse: seek Cultural Tourism Programs to get acquainted with the Maasai, learn about the burial traditions of the Pare and experience a local market day with the Arusha. Hike past Sambaa villages in the Usambaras and watch a Makonde woodcarver at work in Dar es Salaam. Wherever you go, Tanzania's rich cultures are fascinating to discover.
Left: Maasai women

Beaches & Diving

6 With exotic archipelagos, inland lakes and over 1000km of Indian Ocean coastline, you'll be spoiled for choice with Tanzania's beaches. Zanzibar's are developed but lovely, with white sand, palm trees and rewarding diving. To get away from the crowds, head to Pemba (p116), with its placid coves and spectacular diving, or to the mainland near Pangani. To really get away from it all, try the far south, between Kilwa Masoko and the Mozambique border, or inland along the Lake Tanganyika shoreline. Below: Zanzibar (p77)

Chimpanzee Tracking

7 Climbing up steep muddy paths, stumbling over twisted roots and pushing through dense vegetation – chimpanzee tracking is hard work. But the struggle is forgotten as chimpanzees become visible in a clearing ahead. Tanzania's remote western parks – Mahale Mountains (p246) and Gombe Stream (p245) – are among the best places anywhere to see them. Combine chimpanzee tracking with a safari in Katavi National Park or an exploration of the Lake Tanganyika shoreline for an unforgettable adventure well off the beaten track.

Ruins & Rock Art

8 Tanzania offers a wealth of attractions for history buffs. The most impressive of the many coastal ruins are those at Kilwa Kisiwani (p298) – a Unesco World Heritage Site harking back to the days of sultans and far-flung trade routes that linked inland gold fields with Persia, India and China. Standing in the restored Great Mosque, you can almost hear the whispers of bygone centuries. Inland, armed with a sense of adventure and a taste for rugged travel, head for the enigmatic Kondoa Rock-Art Sites, spread throughout central Tanzania's Irangi hills. Above: Great Mosque (p299), Kilwa Kisiwani

Selous Game Reserve

9 Vast Selous (p292), with its tropical climate, profusion of greenery and massive Rufiji River, is completely different to Tanzania's northern parks. Take a boat safari, and as you glide past borassus palms, slumbering hippos and cavorting elephants, watch for the many smaller attractions along the river banks. These include majestic African fish eagles, stately Goliath herons and tiny white-fronted bee-eaters – all part of the daily natural symphony in Africa's largest wildlife reserve. Top right: Leopardess

Ruaha National Park

10 Rugged, baobab-studded Ruaha National Park (p268), together with surrounding conservation areas, is home to one of Tanzania's largest elephant populations. An ideal spot to watch for the giant pachyderms is along the Great Ruaha River at sunrise or sundown, when they head down to the banks to snack or to swim in the company of hippos, antelopes and over 400 different types of birds. A visit here, together with a journey through the Southern Highlands, will be a highlight of your Tanzania travels. Above: Elephant

Need to Know

For more information, see Survival Guide (p363)

Currency
Tanzanian shilling (Tsh)

Languages
Swahili and English

Visas
Required by most travellers and best acquired in advance or at Tanzania's major airports. Proof of yellow-fever vaccination may also be required.

Money
ATMs are in all major towns; most take Visa and MasterCard only. Credit cards are not widely accepted for payment. Most national parks, however, require Visa or MasterCard for entry fees.

Mobile Phones
Local SIM cards can be used in European and Australian phones. Other phones must be set to roaming.

Time
East Africa Time Zone (GMT/UTC plus three hours)

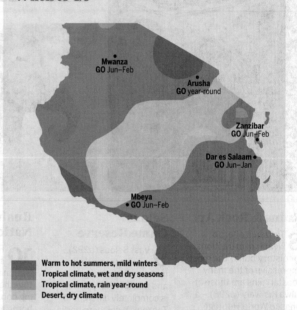

When to Go

Mwanza
GO Jun–Feb

Arusha
GO year-round

Zanzibar
GO Jun–Feb

Dar es Salaam
GO Jun–Jan

Mbeya
GO Jun–Feb

Warm to hot summers, mild winters
Tropical climate, wet and dry seasons
Tropical climate, rain year-round
Desert, dry climate

High Season
(Jun–Sep)

➡ Weather is cooler and dry.

➡ Hotels in popular areas are full, with high-season prices.

➡ Animal-spotting is easiest, as foliage is sparse and animals congregate around dwindling water sources.

Shoulder Season (Oct–Feb)

➡ Weather is hot, especially December through to February.

➡ From late October, the short rains (*mvuli*) fall and the *kusi* (seasonal trade wind) blows.

➡ High-season prices from mid-December to mid-January.

Low Season
(Mar–May)

➡ Heavy rains make secondary roads muddy and some areas inaccessible.

➡ But it seldom rains all day, every day. Landscapes are lush and green.

➡ Some hotels close; others offer discounts.

Useful Websites

Kamusi Project (www.kamusi. org) Living Swahili dictionary.

Lonely Planet (www.lonely planet.com/tanzania) Destination information, hotel bookings, traveller forum and more.

Tanzania Parks (www.tanzania parks.com) Background info on all of Tanzania's national parks.

Tanzania Tourist Board (www.tanzaniatouristboard. com) The TTB's official site.

Zanzibar Tourism (www. zanzibartourism.net) Zanzibar's official tourism site.

SafariBookings (www.safari bookings.com) Excellent resource on Tanzania's parks and wildlife.

Important Numbers

Land-line telephone numbers are seven digits plus area code; mobile numbers are six digits plus a four-digit provider code. Area codes must be used when dialling long distance. There are no central police or emergency numbers.

Country code	✆+255
International access code	✆00

Exchange Rates

Australia	A$1	Tsh1480
Canada	C$1	Tsh1500
Europe	€1	Tsh2158
Japan	¥100	Tsh1582
Kenya	KSh100	Tsh1898
New Zealand	NZ$1	Tsh1339
South Africa	R10	Tsh1526
UK	UK£1	Tsh2722
US	US$1	Tsh1691

For current exchange rates, see www.xe.com.

Daily Costs

Budget: Less than US$50

➡ Camping per person: US$5–10

➡ Bed in a hostel or budget guesthouse: US$15–20

➡ Meal in a local restaurant: US$3

➡ Bus fares: US$5–30

Midrange: US$50–200

➡ Double room in a midrange hotel: US$50–200

➡ Restaurant meal: US$10

➡ Vehicle hire per day: US$200

Top End: More than US$200

➡ Upmarket hotel room: from US$200

➡ Upmarket safari packages per person per day: from US$300

➡ Domestic one-way flights: US$100–350

Opening Hours

Opening hours are generally as follows.

Banks and Government Offices 8am to 3pm Monday to Friday

Restaurants 7am to 9am, noon to 2.30pm and 6.30pm to 9.30pm; reduced hours low season

Shops 8.30am to 6pm Monday to Friday, 9am to 1pm Saturday, often closed Friday afternoon for mosque services

Supermarkets 9am to 6pm Monday to Friday, 9am to 4pm Saturday, 10am to 2pm Sunday

Arriving in Tanzania

Nyerere International Airport, Dar es Salaam (p375) Taxis cost Tsh30,000; one hour to city centre.

Kilimanjaro International Airport (p375) Taxis cost Tsh50,000 to Tsh70,000, airline shuttles Tsh10,000; 45 minutes to Moshi or Arusha.

Zanzibar International Airport (p375) Taxis cost Tsh15,000; 15 minutes to Zanzibar Town

Overland Cross-border bus service to/from Kenya, Uganda, Rwanda and Burundi. Don't change money at borders; arrange visas in advance.

Getting Around

Distances are long in Tanzania; focus on one or two areas rather than trying to fit in too much.

Bus Buses drive dangerously fast and offer minimal comforts. Travel early in the day, and never at night; sit on the shadier side of the bus and keep your luggage with you. Buy tickets the day before and only from a proper office (not from a tout).

Car Rent from reliable companies that are likely to have backup in case of breakdown. Don't drive at night, and don't hesitate to ask your driver to slow down.

Boat & Ferry Scenic and relaxing, but overcrowded, with basic conditions (except for the more modern Zanzibar ferries). Book first-class for lake ferries well in advance.

Train Slow and scenic; delays are common. Bring water and snacks; book cabins in advance.

For much more on **getting around**, see p375

PLAN YOUR TRIP NEED TO KNOW

If You Like...

Wildlife

Serengeti National Park
Outstanding year-round wildlife watching, and the famed great wildebeest migration. (p189)

Ngorongoro Crater The steep walls of this ancient caldera offer a backdrop for abundant, easily spotted wildlife. (p180)

Tarangire National Park Over 3000 elephants and other migrants gather to drink from the Tarangire River during the dry season. (p171)

Selous Game Reserve Sublime riverine scenery, plenty of wildlife and the chance for boat safaris. (p292)

Katavi National Park Hippos, buffaloes and more congregate at dry-season water sources in this remote park. (p251)

Mahale Mountains National Park Verdant mountains soar up from Lake Tanganyika's clear waters while chimpanzee hoots echo through the forest. (p246)

Ruaha National Park Rugged, riverine panoramas and a unique mix of animals including elephants and wild dogs. (p268)

Mikumi National Park Easy-to-reach Mikumi offers year-round wildlife watching. (p259)

Arusha National Park This lush, scenic park makes an easy day trip from Arusha for low-key wildlife experiences. (p166)

Beaches & Islands

Zanzibar The turquoise-hued sea, powdery white sands, island rhythms and intriguing Stone Town work their magic. (p77)

Pangani The coastline running north and south of Pangani is beautiful and uncrowded. (p132)

Mafia A stronghold of Swahili culture, with pampered upmarket getaways plus snorkelling and dhow cruises. (p287)

Lake Tanganyika Remote and stunning, with sandy coves backed by lush, green mountains. (p248)

Masoko Pwani This long, palm-fringed stretch of fine, white sand is one of the southeast's hidden gems. (p296)

Southeastern Coast Sleepy and slow-paced, Tanzania's southern beaches offer a glimpse into traditional coastal life. (p285)

Sange Beach Tucked away between Pangani and Saadani National Park is this magnificent, seldom-visited stretch of sand. (p129)

Lake Nyasa The quiet, mountain-fringed beaches here are ideal for families and those travelling off the beaten track. (p279)

Pemba Hilly, green Pemba holds many surprises, with hidden coves, challenging diving and an intriguing culture. (p116)

Fanjove Private Island Try this Robinson Crusoe–style getaway for coastal culture, relaxation and snorkelling. (p301)

Trekking & Hiking

Mt Kilimanjaro Trek to Africa's roof or explore the mountain's lower slopes. (p205)

Usambara Mountains Hike from village to village through pine forests, maize fields and lovely landscapes. (p141)

Mt Meru Tanzania's second-highest peak is a fine destination in itself, or as a warm-up for Kilimanjaro. (p168)

Crater Highlands Experience the rugged beauty and Rift Valley vistas with a Maasai guide. (p183)

Udzungwa Mountains National Park Forested slopes, rushing streams, tumbling waterfalls and 10 species of primates. (p261)

Mt Hanang Tanzania's fourth-highest peak offers a straightforward climb and an introduction to local Barabaig culture. (p217)

Kitulo National Park There are almost no tourist facilities, but the scenery is outstanding for well-equipped hikers. (p272)

Southern Highlands The areas around Tukuyu, Njombe and Iringa offer many lovely walks. (p254)

Top: Lion, Serengeti National Park (p189)
Bottom: Lake Natron (p187)

Ruins & Rock Art

Kilwa Kisiwani & Songo Mnara Haunting echoes from the days when Kilwa (p298) and Songo Mnara (p300) were the linchpin of far-flung trading networks to Persia and the Orient.

Bagamoyo Ruins at nearby Kaole and a wealth of historical buildings document sleepy Bagamoyo's long history. (p127)

Pangani & Tongoni Crumbling Pangani (p132) and overgrown Tongoni (p137) were once major centres along the Swahili coast.

Mafia The atmospheric ruins on Chole and Juani islands hark back to the Mafia Archipelago's Shirazi-era heyday. (p287)

Kondoa Rock-Art Sites Tanzania's most recently designated Unesco World Heritage Sites. (p214)

Diving & Snorkelling

Zanzibar The north has excellent fish diversity and many pelagics, while Stone Town offers wrecks and reefs. (p82)

Mnemba There is outstanding snorkelling in the waters surrounding this tiny private island, just opposite Zanzibar's Matemwe. (p100)

Pemba Challenging wall and drift dives, or gentler snorkelling around tiny Misali. (p116)

Mafia Island Marine Park Excellent corals, lots of fish and no crowds are the highlights of this marine park. (p290)

Lake Tanganyika Clear, deep waters that are home to many species of colourful cichlids. (p248)

Maziwe Marine Reserve A tiny patch of sand offshore from Pangani that makes a good off-beat snorkelling destination. (p133)

Fanjove Private Island Dive and snorkel in uncharted waters from this low-key island north-east of Kilwa. (p301)

Creature Comforts

Selous Game Reserve The Selous has wonderful lodges, each rivalling the next in setting and ambience. (p292)

Northern Safari Circuit Tanzania's northern parks are awash with fine choices, both within and outside the park boundaries. (p154)

Ngorongoro Crater Try an exclusive lodge overlooking the crater or in the nearby highlands around Karatu. (p180)

Ruaha National Park This park has a fine collection of comfort-able camps and lodges. We can't decide which one we like best – try a few nights at each. (p268)

Mafia Tranquil Mafia has several lovely, unique lodges where you can pamper yourself, enjoy fine dining and take in the beautiful ocean views. (p287)

Zanzibar Archipelago The islands abound in comfortable choices, including Mnemba Island Lodge, offshore from Matemwe, Kisiwa House in Stone Town and Unguja Lodge in Kizimkazi. (p75)

Travelling on a Budget

Travelling on a budget is also a great way to get to know local life.

Usambara Mountains Hike through the hills, following the cycle of local market days. (p141)

Local-Style Dining Sup like a local in a *hoteli* (local eatery) on traditional cuisine. (p360)

Bus Travel Taking the bus costs a fraction of car rental and is an eye-opener into local life. (p383)

Church Singing Sunday ser-vices are long, but the singing is outstanding. (p52)

MV Liemba A sail down Lake Tanganyika on this ageing ferry is one of Africa's classic journeys. (p248)

Cultural Tourism Programs Seek out these community-run ventures for reasonably priced introductions to local life and culture. (p160)

Pare Mountains Spend time here hiking, and learning about burial and other traditions. (p148)

Ruaha Cultural Tourism Program Cattle-herd with the Maasai and take lessons in traditional cooking. (p269)

Southern Tanzania The Southern Highlands (p254) and southeastern coast (p285) are ideal regions to explore on a budget.

Birdwatching

Rubondo Island National Park This tranquil group of islands is an outstanding birding destina-tion, with a wealth of waterbirds. (p230)

Amani Nature Reserve The lush montane forest at Amani is rich with unique bird species. (p141)

Selous Game Reserve The Rufiji River's banks are covered with nests; the river and its tributaries offer outstanding birding. (p292)

Northern Safari Circuit The northern parks host a wealth of avian species, with Lake Manyara a particular birding highlight. (p154)

Udzungwa Mountains This fine destination is home to endemics

including the Udzungwa forest partridge, plus many wetland species. (p261)

Lake Natron With its millions of flamingos, this otherworldly lake is not to be missed. (p187)

Mkomazi National Park Birding is especially rewarding in this off-beat park around Dindera Dam. (p151)

Offbeat Travel

Lake Tanganyika Journey on the MV *Liemba* to Mahale Mountains National Park (p248) or via lake taxi to Gombe Stream National Park (p245).

Western Tanzania Visit Tabora (p239) and safari in Katavi National Park (p251) for an intro-duction to Tanzania's wild west.

Lake Nyasa Laze on the lake-shore, paddle in a dugout canoe or visit a pottery market. (p279)

Southern Highlands Explore the hills around Mbeya and Njombe, hike in Kitulo National Park and relax around Iringa. (p254)

Southeastern Tanzania Immerse yourself in coastal his-tory, with stops in Mafia, Kilwa, Mikindani, Lindi and Mtwara. (p285)

Pangani Relax on lovely beach-es, visit ruins and finish with a boat trip to Zanzibar. (p132)

Saadani National Park Saadani safaris offer the chance to experience bush and beach at the same time. (p129)

Lake Victoria Island-hop at Rubondo Island National Park or explore the lively lakeside towns of Bukoba and Musoma. (p219)

Lake Eyasi Take in Lake Eyasi's stark, other-worldly landscapes and learn about the hunter-gatherer traditions of the local Hadzabe. (p179)

Month by Month

January

The weather almost everywhere is hot, especially along the coast. It's also dry in most areas, including on Kilimanjaro, and this dry, warm season from December into February can be an ideal time to scale the mountain.

February

The weather remains hot, but in parts of the country, the rains are falling, which means green landscapes, flowers and lots of birds.

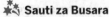 Sauti za Busara

This three-day music and dance festival (www.busaramusic.org) is centred on all things Swahili, both traditional and modern; dates and location vary.

⦿ Wildebeest Calving Season

In one of nature's greatest spectacles, over 8000 wildebeest calves are born each day in the southern Serengeti, although about 40% of these will die before they are four months old.

⦿ Orchids, Kitulo National Park

The blooms of orchids (over 40 species have been identified) as well as irises, geraniums and many other wildflowers carpet Kitulo Plateau in Tanzania's Southern Highlands. It's the rainy, muddy season here, but hardy, well-equipped hikers will be rewarded.

🏃 Kilimanjaro Marathon

This marathon (www.kilimanjaromarathon.com) is something to do around Kilimanjaro's foothills, in case climbing to the mountain's top isn't enough; it's held in February or March, starting and finishing in Moshi, with a half-marathon and a 5km fun run also available.

March

The long rains are in full swing now, although it seldom rains all day or every day. Some hotels close. Those that don't often have low-season discounts, and you'll have many areas to yourself.

🍖 Nyama Choma Festival

Self-described as 'the largest barbecue showcase festival in East Africa', this is the place to try (and try, and try) one of Tanzania's favourite dishes, prepared in infinite variety by master chefs. Held several times annually in Dar es Salaam (www.facebook.com/nyamachomafest).

April

The rains begin to taper off in some areas, although much of the country remains wet. Green landscapes, wildflowers and birds, plus continued low-season prices make this a delightful time to travel, if you can avoid the mud.

☉ Wildebeest Migration

The wildebeest – until now widely scattered over the southern Serengeti and the western reaches of Ngorongoro Conservation Area – begin to form thousands-strong herds that start migrating north and west in search of food.

June

With the ending of the rains, the air is clear and landscapes are slowly beginning to dry out. Temperatures are also considerably cooler.

☉ Serengeti Wildebeest Migration

As the southern Serengeti dries out, vast wildebeest herds continue migrating northwestwards in search of food, crossing the Grumeti River en route. The timing of the crossing (which lasts about a week) varies from year to year, anywhere from May to July.

🏃 Dar es Salaam Charity Goat Races

Tanzania's answer to the Royal Ascot, but here, all proceeds go to charity. Sponsor a goat or three, and come join in the festivities (www.goatraces.com). Dates vary.

July

Cool, dry July marks the start of peak travel season, with higher prices (and crowds) for safaris and lodges. It's an optimal wildlife-watching month, with sparse vegetation and

animals congregating at dwindling water sources.

🎎 Festival of the Dhow Countries

This two-week extravaganza of dance, music, film and literature from Tanzania and other Indian Ocean countries has the Zanzibar International Film Festival (www.ziff.or.tz) as its centrepiece. It's held in early July at various locations in the Zanzibar Archipelago.

☉ Dry Season Wildlife Watching

As rivers and streams dry out, animals congregate around remaining water sources, and it's common to see large herds of elephants and more. Katavi and Tarangire parks are particularly notable for their dry season wildlife watching in July and August.

🎎 Mwaka Kogwa

This sometimes raucous four-day festival in late July marks Nairuzim (the Shirazi New Year). Festivities are best in Makunduchi on Zanzibar.

August

Dry weather continues, as does the Serengeti wildebeest migration. Wildlife watching almost everywhere is at its prime.

☉ Mara River Crossing

By August – often earlier – the wildebeest make their spectacular crossing of the Mara River into Kenya's Masai Mara, before roaming south again in anticipation of the rains.

October

The weather is mostly dry throughout the country, with a profusion of lavender jacaranda blossoms in higher-lying towns and some rain. It's still a fine time for wildlife watching, without the crowds of July and August.

🎎 Makuya Cultural Arts Festival

This lively two-day festival (http://makuyafestival. blogspot.com) showcases traditional dances and drumming of southern Tanzania's Makonde, Makua and Yao tribes. Dates vary, but it's usually held in September or October.

🎎 Bagamoyo Arts Festival

This is a somewhat disorganised but fascinating week of traditional music, dance, drama, acrobatics, poetry reading and more (www.bagamoyofestival. weebly.com), sponsored by the Bagamoyo College of Arts and featuring local and regional ensembles. Dates vary.

🏃 Ruaha Marathon

This marathon in and around Iringa is a good way to test your fitness and to see the Southern Highlands. There are also races for runners with disabilities. Dates vary.

November

Increasing temperatures are mitigated by the arrival of mango season and by the short rains that are

now falling in many areas. It's still a pleasant travel time, before the holiday travel high season.

December

December's holidays and hot but dry weather bring many visitors. It's an ideal time to climb Mt Kilimanjaro and to see the wildebeest in the southern Serengeti.

☉ Swahili Fashion Week

The largest showcase for East African design (www. swahilifashionweek.com), this event is held annually in December; dates vary.

Top: Serengeti wildebeest migration (p194)

Bottom: Women in traditional dress at Mwaka Kogwa (p87), Makunduchi

Itineraries

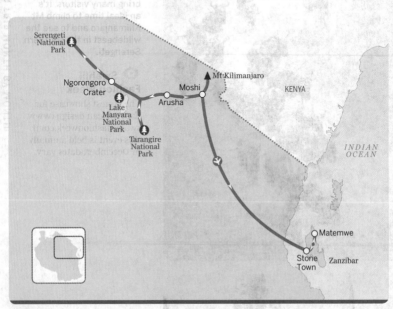

2 WEEKS: Tanzania's Greatest Hits

This route combines wildlife watching or trekking with gorgeous beaches and the alluring 'Spice Islands'. It's a heavily travelled route, with plenty of accommodation and dining choices at all stops.

Fly into Kilimanjaro International Airport. Then, starting at **Arusha**, spend your first week exploring a few of the northern parks. Good wildlife-watching combinations include **Ngorongoro Crater** and **Serengeti National Park** or Ngorongoro plus **Lake Manyara National Park** and **Tarangire National Park**. Alternatively, head from the airport to **Moshi** and embark on a **Mt Kilimanjaro** trek. For either of these options (epic wildlife watching or serious mountain trekking), there are numerous opportunities for hiking and cultural interaction around Arusha and Moshi for any extra days you may have left over.

Give the second half of your adventure over to less energetic pursuits and fly from Moshi or Arusha to **Zanzibar** for a week divided between exploration of **Stone Town** and relaxation on the island's beaches – blissed-out **Matemwe** will meet all your idyllic white-sand needs. Fly out again from Zanzibar, or from nearby Dar es Salaam international airport.

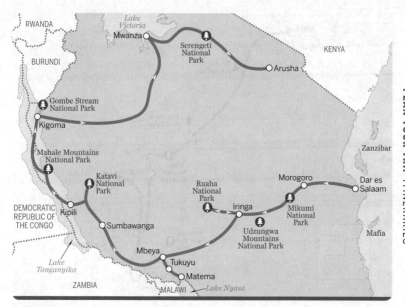

The Southern Highlands & Western Tanzania

6 WEEKS

The Southern Highlands are one of Tanzania's most scenic regions, with particular appeal to adventure-loving travellers who have at least several weeks for exploring. For those with more time and taste for adventure, the region links nicely with remote western Tanzania.

From **Dar es Salaam**, head west to peppy **Morogoro** for cultural tours and hiking, or to **Mikumi National Park**, with its easily spotted wildlife. Next stop: **Udzungwa Mountains National Park**, for several days hiking up the steep, lushly vegetated slopes and exploring the surrounding Kilombero area. Alternatively, continue from Mikumi on to **Iringa**, which makes a relaxing base. From Iringa, a two- or three-night detour to **Ruaha National Park** is well worth the effort, then head on down the Tanzam highway to **Mbeya**. En route are several lovely spots to relax and explore.

While Mbeya town is not as pleasant as Iringa, there is plenty to do in the surrounding area, including hiking in the scenic hills around **Tukuyu** or canoeing, exploring and hiking around Lake Nyasa, using tiny **Matema**, with its picturesque beach, as a base.

Taking your time, it would be easy enough to spend the first three weeks of your itinerary up to this point. With the remaining time, you could return the way you came, with several days left over at the end for a short stay on **Zanzibar** or **Mafia** islands.

For those wanting more adventure, continue northwest from Mbeya via **Sumbawanga** to **Katavi National Park**. This park deserves at least two days, especially in the dry season when wildlife watching is at its best. Double back, and down the escarpment to Lake Tanganyika at **Kipili** for several days relaxing before taking the MV *Liemba* to **Mahale Mountains National Park** and the chimpanzees, or on to **Kigoma** and perhaps an overnight at nearby **Gombe Stream National Park**. From Kigoma, take the train, bus or fly back to Dar es Salaam. Alternatively, continue overland from Kigoma to **Mwanza** and Lake Victoria, from where you could proceed into the **Serengeti** and on to **Arusha**.

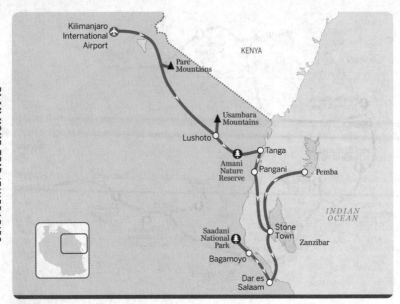

Northeastern Tanzania

Northeastern Tanzania is easily accessible from both Kilimanjaro and Dar es Salaam airports. It has a good array of accommodation options and transport connections for travellers of all budgets, and a delightful mix of beach, culture, historical attractions and bush. It is also conveniently sandwiched between Tanzania's northern circuit wildlife parks and Mt Kilimanjaro to the north and west, and the Zanzibar Archipelago to the east, opening up many possibilities for combining this itinerary with our Tanzania's Greatest Hits itinerary.

From **Kilimanjaro airport**, head southeast to the **Usambara Mountains** around **Lushoto**. It's easy to spend up to a week here hiking, exploring and enjoying the spectacular hill panoramas. Botanists and birders can venture further to **Amani Nature Reserve** in the Eastern Usambaras, with its cool forest walks, night-time symphony of insects, and traditional medicinal display. With extra time and a tolerance for off-the-beaten-track travel, another possible detour before heading to Lushoto is to the **Pare Mountains** for hiking and getting to know local Pare culture.

After the mountains, travel eastwards to enjoy **Tanga**. This coastal town, with its relaxed ambience, wide streets filled with cyclists, nearby beaches and many possibilities for excursions, is one of Tanzania's most pleasant urban areas. It's also the starting point for exploring the **Pangani** area, with its quiet coastline and long history. Many travellers wind up staying here much longer than planned.

Zanzibar is just across the channel from Pangani (from some points, you can see the island's northern tip on clear days) and there are regular boat and plane connections between the two. Get to know **Stone Town**, relax on a beach (or two or three) and perhaps also venture to **Pemba** for a complete change of pace. Once you have finished your exploration of the archipelago, boat and plane connections are easy to **Dar es Salaam**. Allow at least a few days in this crowded, bustling city to see the sights, do some final shopping, enjoy the array of good eateries and perhaps even visit nearby historical **Bagamoyo** or (with a bit more time) tiny **Saadani National Park**.

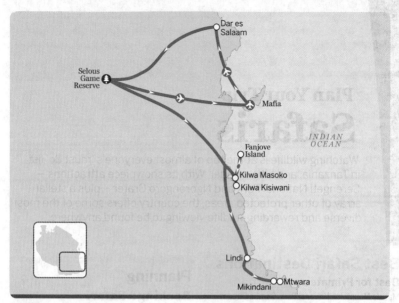

 Selous, Mafia & Beyond
10 DAYS

This itinerary is suited to those wanting to get a glimpse of Tanzania's wildlife and beaches away from the more standard northern circuit–Zanzibar combination. Allow about 10 days for a straight Selous–Mafia combination, and up to four weeks for extended versions taking in Kilwa and Mikindani, further south.

Starting in **Dar es Salaam**, spend a couple of days enjoying the city's restaurants and craft shopping. Wonder Workshop and Mwenge Carvers Market are two highlights. Other possibilities include a museum visit or a cultural tourism tour.

From Dar es Salaam, there are daily bus connections to **Selous Game Reserve**, but it's a long, rough ride. There's also a slow train, and there are daily flights. The Selous is a magnificent reserve – our favourite in Tanzania – and well worth at least three to four days enjoying the fine lodges, the boat safaris, the wildlife and the amazing night sounds, especially hippos grunting in the Rufiji River.

From the Selous, there are daily flight connections on to **Mafia** island, just offshore. Spend the remaining few days of your stay here in one of the lovely island lodges, diving and snorkelling, trying to spot whale sharks or sailing to some of the smaller islands to get a glimpse into the archipelago's fascinating Swahili culture and long history. From Mafia, there are daily flight connections back to Dar es Salaam.

For adventurous travellers with more time and a taste for the offbeat, it's easily possible to continue from Selous Game Reserve (or from the mainland coast opposite Mafia island) south to Kilwa and Mikindani. Tiny, sleepy **Kilwa Masoko** town is an easy spot to pass a day or two, as well as being the springboard to the famed ruins at **Kilwa Kisiwani**, just offshore. Another recommended excursion from Kilwa Masoko is to nearby **Fanjove Island**, which has a lovely lodge, and which is easily combined with both Mafia and Kilwa. Once finished exploring in the Kilwa area, continue by bus southwards via **Lindi** to the **Mtwara** area, where **Mikindani** – with its coconut plantations and long history – is the highlight.

Plan Your Trip

Safaris

Watching wildlife is at the top of almost everyone's 'must do' list in Tanzania, and little wonder. With its showpiece attractions – Serengeti National Park and Ngorongoro Crater – plus a stellar array of other protected areas, the country offers some of the most diverse and rewarding wildlife viewing to be found anywhere.

Best Safari Destinations

Best for Primates
Mahale Mountains National Park, Gombe Stream National Park

Best for Elephants
Tarangire National Park, Selous Game Reserve

Best for Predators
Serengeti National Park, Ruaha National Park

Best Off-Beat Safaris
Katavi National Park, Rubondo Island National Park

Best Birdwatching
Lake Manyara National Park, Serengeti National Park, Rubondo Island National Park, Selous Game Reserve

Best Active Safaris
Lake Manyara National Park, Kilimanjaro National Park, Udzungwa Mountains National Park

Best Dry Season Parks
Katavi National Park, Tarangire National Park, Ruaha National Park, Selous Game Reserve

Best Wet Season Parks
Serengeti National Park, Kitulo National Park

Planning

Booking a Safari

Arusha is the best base for organising visits to the northern parks. Mwanza-based operators also organise safaris into western Serengeti. For the southern parks, there's no comparable hub, although most southern-focused operators have offices in Dar es Salaam. For Gombe Stream and Mahale Mountains, Kigoma is the base for independent and budget travellers, while most upper-end safaris to these parks, and to Katavi, are organised out of Arusha as fly-in packages or – for Mahale and Katavi – as fly-in add-ons to a Ruaha safari. Mwanza and Bukoba are the starting points for Rubondo Island National Park.

Booking and paying for a safari before arriving in Tanzania is recommended if you'll be travelling in popular areas during the high season. While costs may be 5% to 10% higher at the budget level for pre-booked safaris, advance booking enables you to minimise dealings with safari touts. They're not all bad guys, but many are aggressive, slippery or both, and the whole experience can be somewhat intimidating. Pre-booking also minimises the amount of cash that you'll need to carry.

If you wait to book your safari once in Tanzania, allow time to shop around and don't rush into any deals.

Normally, major problems such as vehicle breakdown are compensated for by adding additional time to your safari. If this isn't possible (eg if you have an onward flight), reliable operators may compensate you for a portion of the time lost. However, don't expect a refund for 'minor' problems such as punctured tyres and so on. Park fees are also non-refundable. If you do get taken for a ride, the main avenue of recourse is to file a complaint with both the **Tanzania Tourist Board** (TTB; www. tanzaniatouristboard.com) and the **Tanzanian Association of Tour Operators** (TATO; www.tatotz.org). The police will be of little help, and it's unlikely that you will see your money again.

Costs

Most safari quotes include park entrance fees, accommodation and transport costs to/from the park and within the park, but confirm before paying. Drinks (alcoholic or not) are generally excluded, although many operators provide one bottle of water daily. Budget camping safari prices usually exclude sleeping bag rental (US$5 per day to US$30 per trip).

If accommodation-only prices apply, you'll need to pay extra to actually go out looking for wildlife, either on wildlife drives, boat safaris or walks. There is usually the chance for two of these 'activities' per day (each about two to three hours). Costs range from around US$30 per person per activity up to US$250 per vehicle per day for wildlife drives.

Budget Safaris

Most budget safaris are camping safaris. To minimise costs, you'll likely camp outside national park areas (thereby missing early-morning prime viewing time, but saving on park admission and camping fees) or stay in budget guesthouses. Budget operators also save costs by working with larger groups to minimise per-person

transport costs, and by keeping to a no-frills setup with basic meals and a minimum number of staff. Most budget and many midrange safaris place daily kilometre limits on the vehicles.

Expect to pay from US$150 to US$200 per person per day for a budget safari with a registered operator. To save money, bring drinks with you, especially bottled water, as it's expensive in and near the parks. Snacks, extra food and toilet paper are other worthwhile backpack additions. During the low season, it's often possible to find a lodge safari for close to the price of a camping safari.

Midrange Safaris

Midrange safaris usually use lodges, where you'll have a room and eat in a restaurant. Overall, safaris in this category are comfortable, reliable and reasonably good value. A disadvantage is that they may have somewhat of a packaged-tour or production-line feel, although this can be minimised by selecting a safari company and accommodation carefully, by paying attention to who and how many other people you will travel with, and by avoiding the large, popular lodges during the high season. Midrange lodge safaris cost from US$200 to US$300 per person per day.

Top-End Safaris

Private lodges, luxury tented camps, and sometimes private fly camps, are used in top-end safaris, all with the aim of providing guests with a bush experience as authentic and personal as possible while not foregoing the comforts. For the price you pay (from US$300 up to US$600 or more per person per day), expect a full range of amenities, and high quality guiding. Even in remote settings without running water you will be able to enjoy hot, bush-style showers,

---

TIPPING

Tipping is an important part of the safari experience (especially to the driver/guides, cooks and others whose livelihoods depend on gratuities), and this will always be in addition to the price quoted by the operator. Many operators have tipping guidelines; expect to tip about US$10 to US$15 per group per day to the driver and/or guide, and about US$10 per group per day to the cook – more for top-end safaris or if an especially good job has been done. It's never a mistake to err on the side of generosity while tipping those who have worked to make your safari experience memorable. Whenever possible, give your tips directly to the staff you want to thank.

comfortable beds and fine dining. Expect a good level of personalised attention and an often intimate atmosphere (many places at this level have fewer than 20 beds).

When to Go

Getting around is easier throughout the country in the dry season (late June to October), and in many parks this is when animals are easier to find around waterholes and rivers. Foliage is also less dense, making it easier to spot wildlife. However, as the dry season corresponds in part with the travel high season, lodges and camps become crowded and accommodation prices are at a premium. Some lodges and camps, mainly in Selous Game Reserve and in the western parks, close for a month or so around April and May.

Apart from these considerations, when to go depends in part on what your interests are. For birding, the rainy season months from November/December through to April are particularly rewarding. For walking in wildlife areas, the dry season is best. For general wildlife viewing, tailor your choice of park according to the season. Large sections of Katavi, for example, are only accessible during the dry season, and almost all of the camps close during the rains. Tarangire National Park, although accessible year-round, is another park best visited during the dry season, when wildlife concentrations are significantly higher than at other times of the year. In the Serengeti, by contrast, wildlife concentrations are comparatively low (although still spectacular) during the dry season; it's during the wet season that you'll see the enormous herds of wildebeest massed in the park's southeastern section before they begin their migration north and west in search of food. The dry season, however, is best for lions and other predators. If you are planning your safari around specific events, such as the Serengeti wildebeest migration, remember the timing varies from year to year and is difficult to accurately predict in advance.

Types of Safaris
Vehicle Safaris

In many parks, vehicle safaris are the only option due to park regulations. In the northern parks, vehicle safaris must be done in a 'closed' vehicle, which means a vehicle with closed sides, although there is almost always an opening in the roof that allows you to stand up, get a better view and take photographs. These openings are sometimes just a simple hatch that flips open or comes off, or (better, as it affords some shade) a pop-up style roof. In Selous Game Reserve, some of the southern parks, and Katavi National Park, safaris in open

---

CHECKLIST: WHAT TO BRING

☐ binoculars

☐ good-quality sleeping bag (for camping safaris)

☐ mosquito repellent

☐ rain gear and waterproofs for wet-season travel

☐ sunglasses and sunscreen

☐ camera (and large memory card)

☐ extra contact lens solution and your prescription glasses (the dust can be irritating)

☐ mosquito net (many places have nets, but it doesn't hurt to bring one along)

☐ lightweight, long-sleeved and long-legged clothing in subdued colours, a head covering and sturdy, comfortable shoes (for walking safaris)

☐ field guides (look for: *The Kingdon Field Guide to African Mammals* by Jonathan Kingdon; *The Safari Companion – A Guide to Watching African Mammals* by Richard Estes; *Birds of Kenya and Northern Tanzania* by Dale Zimmerman, Donald Turner and David Pearson; and *Field Guide to the Birds of East Africa* by Terry Stevenson and John Fanshawe)

vehicles are permitted. These are usually high vehicles with two or three seats at staggered levels and a covering over the roof, but open on the sides and back. If you have the choice, open vehicles are best as they are roomier, give you a full viewing range and minimise barriers. The least-preferable option is minibuses, which are sometimes used, especially in the north. They accommodate too many people for a good experience, the rooftop opening is usually only large enough for a few passengers to use at a time and at least some passengers will get stuck in middle seats with poor views.

Whatever type of vehicle you are in, avoid overcrowding. Sitting uncomfortably scrunched together for several hours over bumpy roads puts a definite damper on the safari experience. Most safari quotes are based on groups of three to four passengers, which is about the maximum for comfort in most vehicles. Some companies put five or six passengers in a standard 4WD, but the minimal savings don't compensate for the extra discomfort.

Night drives are permitted in Lake Manyara National Park, in wildlife areas adjoining Tarangire National Park, and inside Tarangire park – the latter only for guests of certain lodges.

Walking Safaris

Places where you can walk in 'big game' areas include Selous Game Reserve, Ruaha, Mikumi, Katavi, Tarangire, Lake Manyara, Serengeti and Arusha National Parks. There are also several parks – notably Kilimanjaro, Udzungwa Mountains, Mahale Mountains and Gombe Stream parks – that can only be explored on foot. Short walks are easily arranged in Rubondo Island National Park.

Most walking safaris offered are for one to two hours, usually done in the early morning or late afternoon and then returning to the main camp or lodge or, alternatively, to a fly camp. Not much distance is covered; the pace is measured and there will be stops en route for observation, or for your guide to pick up an animal's track. Some walking safaris are done within park boundaries, while others are in adjacent areas that are part of the park ecosystem. Multiday walks are possible in Ngorongoro Conservation Area, Serengeti National Park and Selous Game Reserve.

Walks are always accompanied by a guide, who is usually armed. You will need to walk in close proximity to the guide.

Boat & Canoe Safaris

The best place for boat safaris is along the Rufiji River in Selous Game Reserve. They're also possible on the Wami River bordering Saadani National Park, although the wildlife cannot compare. Canoe safaris are possible on the Momella Lakes in Arusha National Park, and sometimes on Lake Manyara (water level permitting).

Itineraries

Don't be tempted to try to fit too much into your itinerary. Distances in Tanzania are long, and at the end, hopping from park to park is likely to leave you tired, unsatisfied and feeling that you haven't even scratched the surface. More rewarding are longer periods at just one or two parks, exploring in depth what each has to offer, and taking advantage of cultural and walking opportunities in park border areas.

Northern Circuit

Arusha National Park (p166) is easily visited as a day trip. Tarangire (p171) and Lake Manyara (p175) parks are frequently accessed as overnight trips from Arusha, although both deserve more time to do them justice. For a half-week itinerary, try any of the northern parks alone (for the Serengeti, it's worth considering flying at least one way, since it's a full day's drive from Arusha), or Ngorongoro Crater together with either Lake Manyara or Tarangire. With a week, you will have just enough time for the classic combination of Lake Manyara, Tarangire, Ngorongoro and the Serengeti, but it's better to focus on just two or three of these. The Serengeti alone, or in combination with Ngorongoro Crater, could easily keep you happy for a week. Many operators offer a standard three-day tour of Lake Manyara, Tarangire and Ngorongoro (or a four- to five-day version including the Serengeti). However, distances to Ngorongoro and the Serengeti are long, and the trip is likely to leave you feeling that you've spent too much time rushing from park to park and not enough time settling in and experiencing the actual environments.

In addition to these more conventional itineraries, there are countless other possibilities combining wildlife viewing with visits to other areas. For example, you might begin with a vehicle safari in the Ngorongoro Crater followed by a climb of Ol Doinyo Lengai (p185), trekking elsewhere in Ngorongoro Conservation Area (p182), relaxing at one of the lodges around Karatu, or visiting Lake Eyasi. Alternatively, combine travel around Lake Victoria and a visit to Rubondo Island National Park (p230) with the western Serengeti.

Southern Circuit

Mikumi (p259) and Saadani National Parks (p129) are good destinations from Dar es Salaam if you only have a couple of nights. Three to four days would be ideal for Selous Game Reserve (p292), or for Ruaha National Park (p268), if you fly. Together, Mikumi and Udzungwa Mountains National Park (p261) offer a potential safari-hiking combination. Recommended week-long combination itineraries include Selous and Ruaha, or Ruaha and Katavi, in the west, both of which allow you to sample markedly different terrain and

SAFARI STYLE

While price can be a major determining factor in safari planning, there are other considerations that are just as important:

➡ **Ambience** Will you be staying in or near the park? (If you stay well outside the park, you'll miss the good early morning and evening wildlife-viewing hours.) Are the surroundings atmospheric? Will you be in a large lodge or an intimate private camp?

➡ **Equipment** Mediocre vehicles and equipment can significantly detract from the overall experience. In remote areas, lack of quality equipment or vehicles and appropriate back-up arrangements can be a safety risk.

➡ **Access and activities** If you don't relish the idea of hours in a 4WD on bumpy roads, consider parks and lodges where you can fly in. Areas offering walking and boat safaris are best for getting out of the vehicle and into the bush.

➡ **Guides** A good driver/guide can make or break your safari. With low-budget operators trying to cut corners, chances are that staff are unfairly paid, and are not likely to be knowledgeable or motivated.

➡ **Community commitment** Look for operators that do more than just give lip service to 'ecotourism' principles, and that have a genuine, long-standing commitment to the communities where they work. In addition to being more culturally responsible, they'll also be able to give you a more authentic and enjoyable experience.

➡ **Setting the agenda** Some drivers feel that they have to whisk you from one good 'sighting' to the next. If you prefer to stay in one strategic place for a while to experience the environment and see what comes by, discuss this with your driver. Going off in wild pursuit of the 'Big Five' means you'll miss the more subtle aspects of your surroundings.

➡ **Extracurriculars** On the northern circuit, it's common for drivers to stop at souvenir shops en route. While this gives the driver an often much-needed break from the wheel, most shops pay drivers commissions to bring clients, which means you may find yourself spending more time souvenir shopping than you'd bargained for. Discuss this with your driver at the outset, ideally while still at the operator's offices.

➡ **Less is more** If you'll be teaming up with others to make a group, find out how many people will be in your vehicle, and try to meet your travelling companions before setting off.

➡ **Special interests** If birding or other special interests are important, arrange a private safari with a specialised operator.

Top: Safari vehicle

Bottom: Watching giraffes, Serengeti National Park (p189)

MICHAL VENERA/GETTY IMAGES ©

TIPS FOR WILDLIFE WATCHING

➡ Your best bet for seeing black rhinos is Ngorongoro Crater. Here they are used to vehicles, while elsewhere in Tanzania they are secretive and occur in remote locations.

➡ Let the vervet monkeys tell you if there's a predator in the neighbourhood. Listen for their screeching alarm calls and look in the direction they're facing.

➡ During the July to October dry season, Tarangire National Park provides outstanding wildlife viewing. Over 3000 elephants and many other migratory animals come here to drink from the Tarangire River.

➡ Hundreds of thousands of flamingos may be seen at Lake Manyara National Park, though they move from lake to lake as water levels and composition change, and their presence is never predictable.

➡ Don't forget a pair of high-quality binoculars. Practise using them at home before departing because some animals, especially birds, don't wait around for you to learn how to aim and focus in the field.

– David Lukas, wildlife expert

wildlife populations. The Ruaha-Katavi combination is increasingly popular given the availability of flights between the two parks. The expanded flight network linking the southern and western parks with the coast has opened up the possibility of longer itineraries combining time on the coast or islands with safaris in Ruaha, Mahale and/or Katavi. Selous and Mafia or Zanzibar is also a recommended safari-beach combination.

Western Parks

For Katavi National Park (p251) alone, plan at least two to three days in the park. For a six- to seven-day itinerary, Katavi and Mahale (p246) make a fine combination, and many fly-in safari schedules are built around this itinerary. Budget in several extra days to relax in between on Lake Tanganyika. Katavi is easily and rewardingly combined with Ruaha, and a Ruaha-Katavi-Mahale grouping is also quite feasible; plan on at least nine or 10 days. For Gombe Stream (p245), budget two days. Adventurous overland travellers can bring Rubondo Island park into a western Tanzania itinerary. At least two days on the island is recommended.

Other Areas

Mkomazi National Park (p151) is an intriguing stop for birders on any itinerary linking Dar es Salaam or the northeastern coast with Arusha and the northern circuit. Kitulo National Park (p272) can be worked into itineraries in the Mbeya-Tukuyu area, or from Iringa. Diving in Mafia Island Marine Park (p290) is easily incorporated into a stay on Mafia island.

Do-It-Yourself Safaris

It's quite feasible to visit the parks with your own vehicle, without going through a safari operator. However, unless you're based in Tanzania or are particularly experienced at bush driving and self-sufficient for spares and repairs, the cost savings will be offset by the ease of having someone else handle the logistics.

For most parks and reserves, you'll need a 4WD. There's a US$40 per day vehicle fee for foreign-registered vehicles (Tsh20,000 for locally registered vehicles). Guides are not required, except as noted in the individual park entries. However, it's recommended that you take one to help you find your way and to find the best wildlife areas.

Carry extra petrol, as it's not available in any of the parks, except (expensively) at Seronera in the Serengeti.

You can rent safari vehicles in Dar es Salaam, Arusha, Mwanza, Karatu and Mto wa Mbu. It's also possible to arrange vehicle hire just outside Katavi National Park. Otherwise, there's no vehicle rental at any of the parks or reserves.

Operators

The following are recommended companies focusing on the northern circuit.

Northern Circuit

Access2Tanzania (www.access2tanzania.com) Budget to midrange. Customised, community-focused itineraries.

Africa Travel Resource (ATR; www.africatravelresource.com) Midrange to top end. A web-based safari broker that matches your safari ideas with an operator and offers excellent background information on its website.

African Scenic Safaris (www.africanscenicsafaris.com) Midrange. Small, family-run operator focusing on customised northern circuit safaris and Kilimanjaro treks.

Anasa Safaris (www.anasasafari.com) Top end. Customised mobile safaris in the northern circuit. It also runs lodges in Mkomazi National Park, Lake Eyasi and Lake Victoria.

Base Camp Tanzania (Map p156; www.basecamptanzania.com) Midrange. Northern circuit safaris and treks.

Duma Explorer (www.dumaexplorer.com) Budget to midrange. Northern Tanzania safaris, Kilimanjaro and Meru treks and cultural tours.

CHOOSING AN OPERATOR

When booking safaris and treks, especially at the budget level, the need for caution can't be overemphasised.

➡ Get personal recommendations, and talk with as many people as you can who have recently returned from a safari or trek with the company you're considering.

➡ Be sceptical of quotes that sound too good to be true. Don't rush into any deals, no matter how good they sound. If others have supposedly registered, ask to speak with them.

➡ Don't give money to anyone who doesn't work out of an office, and don't arrange any safari deals on the spot, at the bus stand or with touts who follow you to your hotel room.

➡ Check the blacklist of the Tanzania Tourist Board (TTB) Tourist Information Centre (p164) in Arusha – although keep in mind that this isn't necessarily the final word. Also check the **Tanzanian Association of Tour Operators** (TATO; ☑027-250 4188; www.tatotz.org) list of licensed operators. TATO isn't the most powerful of entities, but going on safari with one of its members will give you some recourse to appeal in case of problems.

➡ Ask to see a valid, original TALA (Tourist Agents Licensing Authority) licence – it's a government-issued document without which a company can't bring tourists into national parks. For wildlife parks, a tour or safari operator designation on the licence suffices; for Kilimanjaro treks, a TALA mountaineering licence is required. Be sceptical of claims that the original is with the 'head office' elsewhere in the country.

➡ Go with a company that has its own vehicles and equipment. If you have any doubts, don't pay a deposit until you've seen the vehicle (and tyres) that you'll be using and remember that it's not unknown for an operator to show you one vehicle, but then arrive in an inferior one on the day.

➡ Go through the itinerary in detail and confirm what is planned for each stage of the trip. Check that the number of wildlife drives per day and all other specifics appear in the contract. While two competing safari company itineraries may look the same, service can be very different. Beware of client swapping between companies; you can end up in the hands of a company you were trying to avoid.

➡ Watch for sham operators trading under the same names as companies listed in this or other guidebooks. Don't let business cards or websites fool you; they're no proof of legitimacy.

Hoopoe Safaris (Map p156; www.hoopoe.com; India St) Upper midrange. Community-integrated luxury camping and lodge safaris in the northern circuit; also has its own tented camps at Lake Manyara and mobile camps in the Serengeti.

IntoAfrica (www.intoafrica.co.uk) Midrange. Fair-trade cultural safaris and treks in northern Tanzania, including a seven-day wildlife-cultural safari in Maasai areas.

Lake Tanganyika Adventure Safaris (www.safaritourtanzania.com) Midrange. Adventure safaris focusing on Katavi and Mahale Mountains National Parks and Lake Tanganyika.

Maasai Wanderings (www.maasaiwanderings.com) Midrange. Northern Tanzania safaris and treks.

Nature Discovery (www.naturediscovery.com) Midrange. Northern-circuit safaris, and treks on Kilimanjaro, Meru and in the Crater Highlands.

Peace Matunda Tours (www.peacematunda.org) Budget. Cultural walks and tours around Arusha plus northern-circuit wildlife safaris.

Roy Safaris (Map p156; www.roysafaris.com; Serengeti Rd) Upper midrange. Budget and semi-luxury camping safaris in the northern circuit, as well as competitively priced luxury lodge safaris and Kilimanjaro and Meru treks; known especially for their high-quality safari vehicles.

Safari Bookings (www.safaribookings.com) All budgets. A web-based safari planning resource with a large database of operators and a wealth of information on Tanzania's national parks.

Safari Makers (Map p156; www.safarimakers.com) Budget. No-frills northern circuit camping and lodge safaris and treks.

Shaw Safaris (www.shawsafaris.com) Midrange. Northern circuit self-drive safaris.

Summit Expeditions & Nomadic Experience (www.nomadicexperience.com) Upper midrange. Expertly guided Kilimanjaro treks, plus cycling, walks and cultural excursions on the mountain's lower slopes and customised northern circuit wildlife safaris.

Tanzania Journeys (www.tanzaniajourneys.com) Midrange. Northern circuit, community-focused vehicle, active and cultural safaris, including Kilimanjaro treks, day hikes and cultural tours in the Moshi area.

Wayo Africa (www.wayoafrica.com) Top end. Northern-circuit active and vehicle safaris, including Serengeti walking safaris plus visits to Hadzabe areas.

Southern Circuit

The following outifts do southern-circuit safari bookings, and combination itineraries involving Mikumi, Ruaha and Katavi National Parks, Selous Game Reserve, and Zanzibar and Mafia islands.

Afriroots (www.afriroots.co.tz) Runs a Sunday-morning history walk (US$50 per person) around the city centre, exploring Dar's evolution from the Omani sultanate to key ANC and Frelimo hotspots in the struggle for independence. Also excellent is the 'behind-the-scenes' cycle tour ($40 per person) where you'll get to meet locals and hear their stories about living in the city. Proceeds from the tours benefit the communities you visit. Afriroots' community work extends beyond Dar to interesting hiking and cycling safaris.

Authentic Tanzania (www.authentictanzania.com) Midrange. Upmarket camping safaris in southern and western Tanzania, plus safari-coast combination itineraries.

Essential Destinations (Map p56; www.ed.co.tz) Midrange. A long-established outfit with its own fleet of planes, and safari camps and lodges in Ruaha, the Selous and on Mafia island; offers frequent 'last-minute' flight-and-accommodation deals.

Foxes African Safaris (www.foxessafaricamps.com) Top end. Runs lodges and camps in Mikumi, Ruaha and Katavi National Parks, on the coast near Bagamoyo, in the Southern Highlands and in Selous Game Reserve; organises combination itineraries by plane and road vehicle.

Hippotours & Safaris (www.hippotours.com) Midrange to top end. A long-standing operator running customised tours to the southern and western parks and reserves.

Safari Big 5 (0682-077833, 0757-000763; www.safaribig5.com) Midrange. A professional outfit offering midrange itineraries to popular destinations such as Serengeti, Selous and Ngorongoro, as well as smaller parks like Saadani.

Tent with a View (www.saadani.com) Upper midrange. Runs lodges in Selous Game Reserve, Saadani National Park and Zanzibar; midrange and upmarket combination itineraries in these and other areas.

Wild Things Safaris (www.wildthingssafaris.com) Budget & midrange. Udzungwa and Kilombero itineraries, plus southern Tanzania safaris.

Plan Your Trip

Active Tanzania

Tanzania offers many active alternatives to a traditional, sedentary vehicle safari. Options include trekking and hiking, walking safaris in or around wildlife areas, diving, snorkelling, birdwatching, chimpanzee tracking, cycling or fishing. This chapter gives an overview of some of the possibilities.

Trekking & Hiking

Tanzania has rugged, varied terrain and a fine collection of peaks, rolling hills and mountain ranges. Landscapes range from the forested slopes of the eastern Udzungwa Mountains to the sheer volcanic cliffs of the inner wall of Mt Meru's crater, and the final scree-slope ascent of Mt Kilimanjaro. Treks and hikes range from village-to-village walks to bush hikes.

Throughout the country, almost all trekking can be done without technical equipment, by anyone who is reasonably fit. However, most excursions – and all trekking or hiking in national parks and wildlife areas – requires being accompanied by a guide or ranger. This usually also entails adhering to set (sometimes short) daily stages.

Booking

General booking considerations are similar to those for safaris (see p26).

The best places for booking Kilimanjaro treks are Moshi and Marangu, followed by Arusha. Meru treks can be organised independently with park staff at the gate, or booked in Arusha if you'll be going through a trekking operator. Treks in the Crater Highlands and climbs up Ol Doinyo Lengai are best organised in Arusha.

Tanzania's Best...

Trekking & Hiking
Mt Kilimanjaro, Mt Meru, Usambara Mountains, Crater Highlands

Diving & Snorkelling
Zanzibar Island, Pemba Island, Mafia Island Marine Park

Walking Safaris
Selous Game Reserve, Ruaha National Park, Mikumi National Park

Birdwatching
Lake Manyara National Park, Selous Game Reserve, Rubondo Island National Park

Times to Go
Trekking and hiking – June to February

Diving and snorkelling – September to February

Walking Safaris – June to October

Birding – any time, but best from December to June

Costs

Treks on Kilimanjaro and in the Crater Highlands are expensive. Most other treks in Tanzania can be done on a reasonable budget with a bit of effort, and a few are cheap. The following are among the least expensive trekking areas, all of which are accessible via public transport:

Usambara, Pare and Uluguru Mountains All can be done as part of local cultural tourism programs or independently (a guide is recommended); no national park fees.

Mt Hanang and Mt Longido Both can be climbed as part of local cultural tourism programs; no national park fees.

Udzungwa Mountains National Park Main costs will be for park entry and guide fees.

When to Go

The best times for trekking are during the dry, warmer season from mid-December to February, and the dry, cooler season from June to October. The least favourable time is from mid-March to mid-May, when the heaviest rains fall. That said, trekking is possible in most areas year-round, with the exception of the Udzungwa, Usambara, Pare and Uluguru Mountains, where conditions become extremely muddy during the March to May rains.

Types of Treks

Stage-by-stage fully equipped trekking accompanied by guides and porters is the norm for treks on Mt Kilimanjaro and Mt Meru (although climbing Meru doesn't require porters). Ol Doinyo Lengai is also a relatively structured and generally fully equipped venture, given the rugged conditions and difficulties of access, as is most trekking in the Crater Highlands. The Usambaras, and to a lesser extent the Pares, involve comparatively easy village-to-village walks where you can stock up on basic food items as you go along. Most other areas are somewhere in between, requiring that you stock up in advance on basics and have a guide (or a GPS and some basic Swahili), but with flexibility as to routes and guiding.

What to Bring

For Mt Kilimanjaro and Mt Meru, you'll need a full range of waterproof cold-weather clothing and gear. Particularly on Kilimanjaro, waterproof everything, especially your sleeping bag, as things rarely dry on the mountain. In all of Tanzania's mountain areas, expect rain at any time of the year and considerably cooler weather than along the coast. Nights can be very chilly, and a water- and wind-proof jacket and warm pullover are essential almost everywhere. For a checklist of other items to consider, see p28.

MINIMISING COSTS

Organised-trek costs vary considerably and depend on the length of the trek, the size of the group, the standard of accommodation before and after the trek, the quality of bunkhouses or tents, plus the knowledge and experience of guides and trek leaders. To minimise costs:

➡ trek or hike outside national parks (to avoid park entry fees)

➡ carry your own camping equipment (to cut down on rental costs)

➡ avoid treks that necessitate vehicle rentals for access

➡ consider trekking out of season, when you may be able to negotiate discounted rates.

However, it's not worth cutting corners where reliability is essential, such as on Kilimanjaro. Always check that there are enough porters, a cook and an assistant guide or two (in case the group splits or somebody has to return due to illness). Beware of unscrupulous budget companies charging for, say, a five-day trek but only paying mountain and hut fees for four days. And be wary of staff stories about 'running out of money' while on the mountain, as promises of refunds are usually forgotten or denied when you get back to base.

KILI'S TOPOGRAPHY

The Kilimanjaro massif has an oval base about 40km to 60km across, and rises almost 5000m above the surrounding plains. The two main peak areas are Kibo, the dome at the centre of the massif, which dips inwards to form a crater that can't be seen from below, and Mawenzi, a group of jagged pinnacles on the eastern side. A third peak, Shira, on the western end of the massif, is lower and less distinct than Kibo and Mawenzi. The highest point on Kibo is Uhuru Peak (5896m), the goal for most trekkers. The highest point on Mawenzi, Hans Meyer Point (5149m), cannot be reached by trekkers and is only rarely visited by mountaineers.

Kilimanjaro is considered an extinct volcano, although it still releases steam and sulphur from vents in the crater centre.

Guides & Porters

Guides are required for treks on Mt Kilimanjaro, Mt Meru, in the Crater Highlands and in Udzungwa Mountains National Park. Elsewhere, although not essential, a local guide is recommended to show you the way, to provide introductions in remote places, and to guard against occasional instances of hassling and robberies in some areas.

If you decide to hike without a guide, you'll need to know some basic Swahili.

Wherever you trek, always be sure your guide is accredited, or affiliated with an established company. On Kilimanjaro, this should be taken care of by your trekking company, and on Mt Meru and in Udzungwa Mountains National Park, guides are park rangers. The Ngorongoro Conservation Area also has its own guides. In other areas, check with the local tourist office or guide association before finalising your arrangements. Avoid going with freelancers.

Porters are commonly used on Mt Kilimanjaro, and sometimes on Mt Meru, though not elsewhere. In the Crater Highlands, donkeys may be used to carry gear.

Tipping

Tipping for guides and porters is an important budgetary consideration when planning treks on Mt Kilimanjaro and Mt Meru (see boxed text, p169). In other mountain areas, assuming service has been satisfactory, guides will expect a modest but fair tip. A good guideline is about 10% to 15% of your per-day hiking fees.

Trekking Areas

Tanzania's most famous trek is Mt Kilimanjaro, but there are many other options.

Mt Kilimanjaro

Africa's highest mountain (5896m), and Tanzania's most famous trek, Kilimanjaro (p205) offers a choice of routes, all making their way from the forested lower slopes through moorland and alpine zones to the snow- and glacier-covered summit. There are also many walks on Kilimanjaro's lower slopes, with lush vegetation, waterfalls and cultural opportunities centred on local Chagga villages. Marangu and Machame make good bases.

Mt Meru

Although languishing in the shadow of nearby Kilimanjaro, Mt Meru (4566m) is a fine destination in its own right, and considerably less costly than its famous neighbour. It's also worth considering as a preparatory trek for the higher peak and, as part of Arusha National Park (p166), is well suited for safari-trek combination itineraries. The climbing is nontechnical and straightforward, although there's an extremely challenging open ridge walk as you approach the summit that many trekkers feel makes the overall Meru experience even more difficult than scaling Kilimanjaro.

Mt Hanang

Tanzania's fourth-highest peak (3417m), Mt Hanang (p217) offers a comparatively easy trek along well-worn but often overgrown footpaths to the summit. It's also relatively inexpensive to organise, and makes an intriguing destination if you're interested in combining trekking with an introduction to local cultures.

Crater Highlands & Ngorongoro Conservation Area

Together with adjoining parts of the Ngorongoro Conservation Area, the Crater Highlands (p183) offer rugged, rewarding and generally expensive trekking. The spectacular terrain includes steep escarpments, crater lakes, dense forests, grassy ridges, streams and waterfalls, plus the still-active volcano of Ol Doinyo Lengai (p185). This is just north of the Ngorongoro Conservation Area (p182) boundaries and can also be accessed from Lake Natron. Apart from the Maasai people who live here, you'll likely have most areas to yourself.

Usambara Mountains

The western Usambaras (p144) offer village-to-village walks along well-worn footpaths, ranging from a few hours to a week or more. There are enough local guesthouses that carrying a tent is unnecessary. Lushoto is the main base, although there are many other options, including Soni and Mambo. The main centre for hikes in the eastern Usambaras is Amani Nature Reserve (p141), where there is a network of short forest footpaths. Hikes combining the two regions (allow five to six days) are also possible.

Pare Mountains

The Pares (p148) offer relatively short hikes along mostly well-trodden mountain footpaths. There is only minimal tourism development, so hikers should come well prepared, and walk with a guide. Accommodation is generally camping or in very basic local guesthouses.

Udzungwa Mountains

The lush Udzungwas (p261) are fascinating from a botanical perspective, with more unique plant species than almost anywhere else in the region. They are also a prime destination for birders. There is only a handful of fully established trails, ranging from short walks to multiday mountain hikes, for which you'll need a tent and will have to be self-sufficient with food.

RESPONSIBLE TREKKING

➡ Carry out all your rubbish, including sanitary napkins, tampons, condoms and toilet paper (which burns or decomposes poorly).

➡ Take minimal packaging and reusable containers or stuff sacks.

➡ Use toilets where available. Otherwise, bury waste in a small hole 15cm (6in) deep and at least 100m (320ft) from any watercourse. Cover the waste with soil and rocks.

➡ Don't use detergents or toothpaste, even biodegradable ones, in or near watercourses.

➡ For washing, use biodegradable soap and a water container at least 50m (160ft) away from the watercourse. Disperse the waste water widely so the soil filters it fully.

➡ Wash cooking utensils 50m (160ft) from watercourses with a scourer, not detergent.

➡ Stick to existing trails and avoid short cuts; avoid removing the plant life that keeps topsoils in place.

➡ Don't depend on open fires for cooking. Cutting firewood in popular trekking areas can cause rapid deforestation. Cook on a lightweight kerosene, alcohol or Shellite (white gas) stove and avoid those powered by disposable butane gas canisters.

➡ If trekking with a guide and porters, supply stoves for the whole team. In cold areas, see that all members have sufficient clothing so that fires aren't necessary for warmth.

➡ Don't buy items made from endangered species.

Top: Hikers on Mt Kilimanjaro (p206)

Bottom: Scuba diving with glassfish, Zanzibar (p77)

Uluguru Mountains

If you happen to be in the gateway town of Morogoro, it's worth setting aside time for hiking in the densely populated Uluguru (p259) – of interest culturally and botanically. Hikes (most for half a day or a day) range from easy to moderately stiff excursions. Guides are readily organised in Morogoro, and costs are reasonable.

Southern Highlands & Kitulo National Park

Until recently, the rolling hill country in southwestern Tanzania, stretching southwards roughly between Makambako and Mbeya, had little tourist infrastructure. With the recent gazetting of Kitulo National Park (p272) and a slowly expanding network of basic accommodation, this is gradually beginning to change, although you will still be very much on your own in many areas. Short day hikes and excursions can be organised from Mbeya or Tukuyu. For anything longer and for overnight hiking in Kitulo, you will need to be completely self-sufficient and carry a tent and all supplies.

Mahale Mountains

Mt Nkungwe in Mahale Mountains National Park (p246) makes a rugged but scenic two- to three-day trek.

Trekking Operators

Arusha

If you're organising a Kilimanjaro trek in Arusha, look for operators that organise treks themselves rather than subcontracting to a Moshi- or Marangu-based operator.

Dorobo Safaris (www.dorobosafaris.com) Community-oriented treks in and around the Ngorongoro Conservation Area and wilderness treks in Tarangire Park border areas and in the Serengeti.

Kiliwarrior Expeditions (www.kiliwarrior expeditions.com) Upmarket Kilimanjaro climbs and treks in the Ngorongoro Conservation Area.

Summits Africa (www.summits-africa.com) High quality treks and walks in the northern circuit and beyond.

Marangu

Most Marangu hotels organise Kilimanjaro treks. Also worth noting is the 'hard way' option of Marangu Hotel (p205), in which the climber pays park fees, crew fees and transport to the trailhead, plus providing all food and equipment. The hotel will take care of hut reservations and provide the necessary guides and porters.

Moshi

Moshi-based companies focus on Kilimanjaro treks; most can also organise day hikes on the mountain's lower slopes.

Just Kilimanjaro (www.just-kilimanjaro.com) A small, highly regarded operator offering expertly guided Kilimanjaro treks.

Kessy Brothers Tours & Travel (www. kessybrotherstours.com) Kilimanjaro treks.

Moshi Expeditions & Mountaineering (www.memtours.com) Kilimanjaro treks.

Shah Tours (www.kilimanjaro-shah.com) Reasonably priced Kilimanjaro and Meru treks, plus treks in the Ngorongoro highlands and on Ol Doinyo Lengai.

Summit Expeditions & Nomadic Experience (www.nomadicexperience.com) Expertly guided Kilimanjaro treks, plus walks and cultural excursions on the mountain's lower slopes

Tanzania Journeys (www.tanzaniajourneys. com) Kilimanjaro treks plus day hikes and cultural tours in the Moshi area.

Zara Tanzania Adventures (www.zaratours. com) Kilimanjaro treks.

Diving & Snorkelling

Tanzania's underwater marvels are just as amazing as its terrestrial attractions, with a magnificent array of hard and soft corals and a diverse collection of sea creatures, including manta rays, hawksbill and green turtles, barracuda and sharks. Other draws of the local diving scene include: wall dives, especially off Pemba; the fascinating cultural backdrop; and the opportunity to combine wildlife safaris with underwater exploration. On the down side, visibility isn't reliable, and prices are considerably higher than in places such as the Red Sea or Thailand. Another thing to consider – if you're a serious diver and coming to the archipelago exclusively for diving – is that unless you do a live-aboard arrangement, you'll need to travel, often for up to an hour, to many of the dive sites.

RESPONSIBLE DIVING

➡ Never use anchors on the reef, and take care not to ground boats on coral.

➡ Avoid touching or standing on living marine organisms or dragging equipment across the reef. If you must hold on to the reef, only touch exposed rock or dead coral.

➡ Be conscious of your fins. Even without contact, the surge from fin strokes near the reef can damage delicate organisms. Take care not to kick up clouds of sand, which can smother organisms.

➡ Practise and maintain proper buoyancy control. Major damage can be done by divers descending too fast and colliding with the reef.

➡ Take care in underwater caves. Spend as little time within them as possible as your air bubbles may be caught within the roof and thereby leave organisms high and dry. Take turns to inspect the interior of a small cave.

➡ Resist the temptation to collect or buy corals or shells.

➡ Take home all your rubbish. Plastics in particular are a serious threat to marine life.

➡ Don't feed fish.

➡ Never ride on the backs of turtles.

Seasons & Conditions

Diving is possible year-round, although conditions vary dramatically. Late March until mid-June is generally the least favourable time because of erratic weather patterns and frequent storms. July or August to February or March tends to be the best time overall, although again, conditions vary and wind is an important factor. On Pemba, for example, the southeastern seas can be rough around June and July when the wind is blowing from the south, but calm and clear as glass from around November to late February when the monsoon winds blow from the north. The calmest time is generally from around September to November during the lull between the annual monsoons.

Water temperatures range from lows of about 22°C in July and August to highs of about 29°C in February and March, with the average about 26°C. Wetsuits of 3mm are standard; 4mm suits are recommended for some areas during the July to September winter months, and 2mm suits are fine from around December to March or April.

Costs & Courses

Costs are fairly uniform, with Pemba and Mafia island slightly pricier than elsewhere along the coast. Expect to pay up to US$500 for a four-day PADI open-water course and from about US$55 to US$85 for a single dive (with better prices available for multi-dive packages. Most places discount fees by about 10% if you have your own equipment, and for groups. In addition to open-water certification, many operators also offer other courses, including Advanced Open Water, Medic First Aid, Rescue Diver and speciality courses, such as underwater photography.

Most dive operators also offer snorkelling. Equipment rental costs US$5 to US$15; when you're selecting it, pay particular attention to getting a good mask. Most of the best snorkelling sites along the coast are only accessible by boat. Trips average US$20 to US$50 per person per half-day, often including a snack or lunch.

Where to Dive

Generally speaking, Zanzibar (p77)is known for the corals and shipwrecks offshore from Stone Town, and for fairly reliable visibility, high fish diversity and the chance to see pelagics around the island's north and northeast. While some sites are challenging, there are many easily accessed sites for beginning and midrange divers.

Unlike Zanzibar, which is a continental island, Pemba (p116) is an oceanic island located in a deep channel with a steeply dropping shelf. Because of this, diving tends to be more challenging, with an emphasis on wall and drift dives, though there are some sheltered areas for beginners, especially around Misali island. Most dives are to the west around Misali, and to the north around the Njao Gap.

Mafia (p288) offers divers excellent corals, good fish variety (including pelagics), and uncrowded diving, often from motorised dhows.

The far south, in Mnazi Bay-Ruvuma Estuary Marine Park (p309), is offbeat, with still-unexplored areas. Also offbeat is Lake Tanganyika (p248), which offers crystal-clear waters and snorkelling.

Wherever you dive, allow a sufficient surface interval between the conclusion of your final dive and any onward/homeward flights. According to PADI recommendations, this should be at least 12 hours, or more than 12 hours if you have been doing daily multiple dives for several days. Another consideration is insurance, which you should arrange before coming to Tanzania. Many policies exclude diving, so you may need to pay a bit extra – well worth it in comparison to the bills you will need to foot should something go wrong.

Choosing an Operator

When choosing a dive operator, quality rather than cost should be the priority. Consider the operator's experience and qualifications; knowledgeability and competence of staff; and the condition of equipment and frequency of maintenance. Assess whether the overall attitude of the organisation is serious and professional, and ask about safety precautions – radios, oxygen, emergency evacuation procedures, boat reliability and back-up engines, first-aid kits, safety flares and life jackets. On longer dives, do you get a meal, or just tea and biscuits? An advantage of operators offering PADI courses is that you'll have the flexibility to go elsewhere in the world and have what you've already done recognised at other PADI dive centres.

There's a decompression chamber in Matemwe, but otherwise the closest ones are in Mombasa, Kenya (an army facility and not always available to the general public) and in Johannesburg, South Africa. You can also check the **Divers Alert Network Southern Africa** (DAN; www.dansa. org) website, which lists some Tanzania-based operators that are part of the DAN

network. If you choose to dive with an operator that isn't affiliated with DAN, it's highly recommended you take out insurance coverage with DAN.

Other Activities
Birdwatching

Tanzania is an outstanding birding destination, with well over 1000 species, including numerous endemics. In addition to the national parks and reserves, top birding spots include the eastern Usambara Mountains and Lake Victoria. Useful websites include the **Tanzania Bird Atlas** (www.tanzaniabirdatlas.com), **Tanzania Hotspots** (www.camacdonald.com/birding/africatanzania.htm) and **Tanzanian Birds & Butterflies** (www.tanzaniabirds.net).

Boating, Sailing & Kayaking

Local dhow trips are easily arranged along the coast. They are generally best booked for short sails rather than longer journeys. Ask your hotel for recommendations or contact one of the coastal or island hotels, many of which have private dhows that can be chartered for cruises. Catamarans and sailboats can be chartered on Zanzibar, Pemba and in Kilwa, and Dar es Salaam and Tanga have private yacht clubs. Dekeza Dhows (p73) is a good contact for kayaking along the coast south of Dar es Salaam.

Chimpanzee Tracking

Gombe Stream National Park (p245) and Mahale Mountains National Park (p246) have both hosted international research teams for decades, and are outstanding destinations if you are interested in observing chimpanzees at close quarters.

Cycling

Cycling is a seldom-used but fun way to explore Tanzania. When planning your trip, consider the following:

➡ Main sealed roads aren't good for cycling, as there's usually no shoulder and traffic moves dangerously fast. We have heard of several tragedies involving travellers. Secondary roads are ideal.

➡ Distances are long, often with nothing in between. Consider picking a base, and doing exploratory trips from there.

➡ You'll need to carry all basic supplies, including water (at least 4L), food, a water filter, at least four spare inner tubes, a spare tyre and plenty of tube patches.

➡ Throughout the country, cycling is best in the early morning and late afternoon, and in the drier, cooler winter season (June to August/September). Plan on taking a break from the midday heat, and don't count on covering as much territory as you might in a northern European climate.

➡ Mountain bikes are best brought from home, although it's possible to rent good quality ones from some operators. Local rental bicycles (about Tsh500 to Tsh1000 per hour, check at hotels and markets) are usually heavy single speeds or beat-up mountain bikes.

➡ Other considerations include rampaging motorists (a small rear-view mirror is worthwhile), sleeping (bring a tent) and punctures (from thorn trees). Cycling isn't permitted in national parks or wildlife reserves.

➡ In theory, bicycles can be transported on minibuses and buses, though many drivers are unwilling. For express buses, make advance arrangements to stow your bike in the hold. Bicycles can be transported on the Zanzibar ferries and the lake ferries for no additional cost, although this might take some negotiation.

Some useful contacts include:

Afriroots (www.afriroots.co.tz) Budget cycling tours around Dar es Salaam, in southern Tanzania and in the Usambaras.

International Bicycle Fund (www.ibike.org/bikeafrica) Organises cycling tours in Tanzania and provides information.

Summit Expeditions & Nomadic Experience (www.nomadicexperience.com) Cycling excursions on Kilimanjaro's lower slopes.

Summits Africa (www.summits-africa.com) Multiday fully equipped bicycle safaris and combination bike-safari trips in northern Tanzania.

Wayo Africa (www.wayoafrica.com) Upmarket cycling tours around Arusha and in the Lake Manyara area.

Fishing

Mafia, the Pemba channel and the waters around Zanzibar and the Songo Songo Archipelago have long been insider tips in deep-sea fishing circles, and upmarket hotels in these areas are the best places to arrange charters. Other contacts include Mwangaza Hideaway (p298) in Kilwa Masoko and upper-end hotels in most coastal destinations. In Dar es Salaam, anglers can inquire at **Msasani Slipway** (Map p54; ☏022-260 0893; www.slipway.net; off Chole Rd) and at the Dar es Salaam Yacht Club (Map p54).

Inland, Lake Victoria is renowned for its fishing, particularly for Nile perch. Contacts here include Lukuba Island Lodge (p221) and Wag Hill Lodge (p226).

Horse Riding

Riding safaris are possible in the West Kilimanjaro and Lake Natron areas. Contacts include **Makoa Farm** (www.makoafarm.com) and **Equestrian Safaris** (www.safaririding.com).

PLAN YOUR TRIP ACTIVE TANZANIA

Plan Your Trip

Travel with Children

Tanzania could easily seem daunting to families travelling with children – prices for accommodation and park entry fees can be high, road distances are long and vehicle rental is costly. But for those with a sense of adventure, this is a destination with many fantastic attractions for children, most notably its wildlife, beaches, friendly people and almost perpetual good weather.

Best Regions for Kids

Northern Tanzania

Tanzania's north is safari country and Maasai country. It's not cheap, but kids will love seeing the animals, as well as the many colourful cultures. A good selection of child-friendly hotels and restaurants complete the picture.

Zanzibar Island

Zanzibar's gentle beaches alone are enough to make the island the perfect family destination. Many hotels also have swimming pools (ideal for passing time while the tide is out) and spacious grounds, and there's a wide choice of child-friendly cuisine.

Southern Highlands

The highlands offer plenty of space for kids to run around, several wildlife parks, lovely Lake Malawi and family-friendly accommodation.

Northeastern Tanzania

Low-key beaches, family-friendly lodging, historical Bagamoyo and the chance to spot wildlife in Saadani National Park make the northeast a child-friendly choice.

Tanzania for Kids

Wildlife Watching

Tanzania's wildlife areas, especially Serengeti, Tarangire and Ngorongoro Crater, offer almost guaranteed animal spotting, often at very close range. While all parks offer substantially reduced children's entry fees, all fees are valid for only one entry per 24 hours. If staying inside the park, it's a good idea to choose a lodge or safari camp with a pool where the kids can expend their energy between wildlife drives. Alternatively, base yourself outside the park at a hotel with a pool and/or large grounds for running around. Then venture into the park on one well-timed animal-spotting foray, while taking advantage of cultural tours, night drives and other activities outside the park for the remainder of the time.

Beaches

Tanzania's beaches are wonderful, but variable. Depending on the season, the sea can be still and clear with little debris, or cloudy, choppy and with a strong undertow. Sharp, submerged rocks are another consideration. Ask hotel staff about good areas and times to swim safely.

Transport

Renting a vehicle with driver is a good investment for family travel in Tanzania, giving you some control over driving speeds and the chance to stop for bathroom breaks when you'd like. That said, we've met many families happily exploring the country on public transport, particularly the train.

Staying Safe

Tanzania's parks are unfenced, as are the park lodges and camps. The necessity of carefully supervising your children while in camp cannot be overemphasised. Wild animals frequently enter public areas, and a child should not be allowed to walk alone around camp, even for short distances. Exercise particular vigilance in the evenings.

Children's Highlights

Beaches

➡ **Zanzibar** Lovely east coast beaches (p77). In Stone Town, try the Mtoni Marine Centre (p91).

➡ **Pangani** Quiet beaches and sheltered coves, plus many family-friendly resorts, including Peponi (p133) and Fish Eagle Point (p138).

➡ **Lake Nyasa** Matema beach (p280) is wonderful for families, except during the heavy rains (March through May) when waves can be big.

➡ **Mafia Island** Small sections of beach, dhow rides and snorkelling (p287).

Wildlife Areas

➡ Saadani National Park (p129) Beach plus wildlife.

➡ Arusha National Park (p166) Small and manageable; easy day trip from Arusha.

➡ Ngorongoro Crater (p180) Guaranteed wildlife; nearby family-friendly accommodation, including Ngorongoro Farm House (p179).

➡ Southern Safari Circuit (p34) Ideal for older children.

Elsewhere

➡ **Iringa area** (p264) The chance for hiking, exploring nearby Ruaha National Park (p268) and excellent family accommodation.

PLANNING

Planning for family travel takes on a new dimension in the wilds of Tanzania. Following are a few tips and pre-trip considerations to help you get set.

➡ The June through September dry season is best. Mosquitoes tend to be fewer (although anti-malaria precautions should still be taken) and travel overall is easier.

➡ Check with your doctor about recommended vaccinations and malarial prophylactics (see p386). Bring mosquito nets and ensure your children sleep under them.

➡ At beaches, keep in mind the risks of hookworm infestation in populated areas, and watch out for sea urchins while wading in the shallows and snorkelling.

➡ Take care about bilharzia infection in lakes, and thorns and the like in the bush. A fully stocked child-oriented first aid kit is essential.

➡ Street food isn't generally suitable for kids, and 'healthy snacks' are hard to find on the road. Stock up on fresh and dried fruit and juices in major cities. Bring a pocket knife for peeling fruit. Plain yoghurt (*mtindi*) is available in major towns.

➡ Except in five-star hotels, baby changing areas are non-existent.

➡ Processed baby foods, powdered infant milk, disposable nappies, baby wipes and similar items are available in major towns, but not elsewhere.

➡ Child seats for hire cars and safari vehicles are generally not available, unless arranged in advance.

➡ Many wildlife lodges and safari camps have restrictions on accommodating children under 12.

➡ Most hotels and all national parks offer discounted entry and accommodation rates for children, but you'll need to specifically request these, especially when booking through tour operators.

➡ See Lonely Planet's *Travel with Children* for more tips.

Regions at a Glance

Distances between places are long in Tanzania, and it is well worth keeping this in mind when planning your itinerary. One popular two-week combination is northern Tanzania's wildlife parks, followed by a Kilimanjaro trek or relaxation on Zanzibar.

With more time at your disposal, and an adventurous bent, the rest of the country opens up. Head west for chimpanzee trekking and exploring Lake Tanganyika and Lake Victoria. Travel through the Southern Highlands for hiking, lovely hill panoramas and vibrant markets. Southeastern Tanzania is ideal for wildlife (in Selous Game Reserve) and for getting to know traditional Swahili culture (along the coast), while northeastern Tanzania offers hiking, beaches and history. Bustling Dar es Salaam has an international airport and good shopping and dining.

Dar es Salaam

Shopping
Architecture
History

Craft Markets & Chic Boutiques

Whether it's Mwenge carver's market, the weekend craft fair at Msasani Slipway or chic boutiques in upmarket hotels, Dar es Salaam has a wealth of options.

Colonial-Era Architecture

Discover a jumble of architectural styles, from the German-era colonial buildings lining Kivukoni Front, to stately Karimjee Hall, Indian-influenced architecture around Jamhuri St and modern high-rises near the harbour.

Local Museums

History buffs will enjoy the National Museum, with its displays on Oldupai Gorge and the Shirazi civilisation of Kilwa. Head to the Village Museum for an intro to traditional life and cultures.

p50

Zanzibar Archipelago

Beaches
Historical Town
Diving

East Coast Beaches

Zanzibar's combination of powdery white sands, swaying palms, turquoise waters, picturesque dhows and pastel-hued sunrises make its beaches – especially those on the island's east coast – hard to beat.

Old Stone Town

With its maze of alleyways, shops scented with cloves, Arabic-style houses, bustling bazaars, long history and rich cultural melange, this World Heritage Site never loses its appeal.

Diving & Snorkelling

Clear waters filled with colourful corals and fish entice divers of all abilities. There are also fine snorkelling opportunities, especially around Mnemba island.

p75

Northeastern Tanzania

Beaches
Hiking
History

Pangani-Area Beaches

The beaches north and south of Pangani are lovely, dotted with stands of palms and baobabs. They are also almost deserted, compared with those on Zanzibar, just across the channel.

Usambara Mountains

Lushoto and surrounding villages, with their walking trails and hill panoramas, and Amani Nature Reserve, with its many unique plants, are highlights of hiking in this mountainous region.

Historic Towns

Bagamoyo makes a fascinating stop, with its museum, German colonial-era buildings and nearby ruins. Pangani's sleepy streets are also full of history. Just south are the 14th-century Tongoni ruins.

p125

Northern Tanzania

Wildlife
Trekking
Culture

Safari Circuit

Ngorongoro, Serengeti, Tarangire, Lake Manyara: Tanzania's northern safari circuit offers some of the best wildlife watching anywhere on the continent.

Mountain Peaks

Both Mt Kilimanjaro and Mt Meru have challenging treks to the summit for anyone who is reasonably fit and well acclimatised. Other highlights: the Crater Highlands and Ol Doinyo Lengai.

Tribal Peoples

The Maasai are just one of northern Tanzania's tribal groups, but there are many more to get to know. These include the Chagga on Mt Kilimanjaro, the Iraqw around Karatu and the Hadza around Lake Eyasi.

p152

Central Tanzania

Culture
Rock Art
Exploration

Traditional Cultures

The best-known are the semi-nomadic Barabaig around Mt Hanang. Central Tanzania is also home to Maasai, Sandawe, Iraqw and others; visiting the Katesh market gives a fascinating introduction.

Kondoa Rock-Art Sites

The Kondoa Rock-Art Sites are time-consuming to access, but fascinating to explore.

Off the Beaten Track

Few travellers make it to this part of the country, but for those who do, it is fun to discover. Try Dodoma, with its outsized street layout and grandiose buildings, climb Mt Hanang or spend a day in the lively market town of Babati.

p210

Lake Victoria

Birdwatching
History
Islands

Rubondo Island National Park

Lake Victoria offers fine birdwatching opportunities. The highlight is Rubondo Island National Park, with its wealth of waterbirds and migrants.

Sukuma & Nyerere Museums

Two intriguing museums are tucked away near Lake Victoria: the Sukuma Museum outside Mwanza and the Mwalimu Julius K Nyerere Museum in Butiama, near Musoma.

Island Hopping

Choose between tranquil Rubondo Island National Park, tiny Lukuba Island near Musoma, Musira Island near Bukoba or Ukerewe Island, offshore from Mwanza. All are scenic and relaxing, and give glimpses of traditional lakeshore life.

p219

Western Tanzania

Chimpanzees
Exploration
Wildlife

Chimpanzee Trekking

Mahale Mountains and Gombe Stream National Parks offer excellent opportunities to observe chimpanzees up close. Both parks are also highly scenic, and adventurous to reach.

Lake Tanganyika

Clear fish-filled waters, secluded coves, isolated villages and the MV *Liemba* make Lake Tanganyika and its hinterlands a delight to explore. Don't miss Kigoma, Ujiji and inland Tabora.

Katavi National Park

Enjoy superb dry-season wildlife watching at Katavi National Park, with its giant pods of hippos and massive buffalo herds, followed by relaxation on the lakeshore around Kipili.

p237

Southern Highlands

Wildlife
Hiking
Landscapes

National Parks

Both Ruaha and Mikumi National Parks offer outstanding wildlife watching and evocative landscapes. Don't miss Ruaha's elephants and hippos, or Mikumi's zebras and giraffes.

Udzungwa Mountains

Exploring the steep, waterfall-laced slopes of the Udzungwas is a highlight. Other hiking options: guided walks around Mbeya or rugged jaunts on the orchid-laced Kitulo Plateau.

Southern Highlands

The wide swathe from Iringa down to Lake Malawi is beautiful, with rolling hills, wildflower-carpeted valleys, ancient stands of baobabs, vast tea plantations and jacaranda-shaded towns.

p254

Southeastern Tanzania

Coastal Life
Ruins
Wildlife

Mafia Island

With its mangrove-shaded waterways and lively local traditions, Mafia is a delightful intro to Swahili culture. On the mainland, Lindi, Mtwara and Kilwa Masoko also offer glimpses into traditional coastal life.

Kilwa Kisiwani

At these evocative ruins, imagine the days of sultans and monsoon-driven trading networks stretching as far afield as India and China.

Selous Game Reserve

This reserve is a regional highlight, with sublime vistas, boat safaris and many large animals. For something different, discover some offshore 'wildlife', with diving around Mafia Island and Mnazi Bay-Ruvuma Estuary Marine Park.

p285

On the Road

Dar es Salaam

POP 4.36 MILLION

Best Places to Sleep

➡ Alexander's Hotel (p61)

➡ Southern Sun (p60)

➡ Friendly Gecko
Guesthouse (p60)

➡ Ras Kutani (p74)

Best Places to Eat

➡ Oriental (p63)

➡ Mamboz Corner BBQ
(p63)

➡ Terrace (p64)

➡ Black Tomato (p64)

Why Go?

Over the last century, Dar es Salaam has transformed from a sleepy Zaramo fishing village into a thriving, striving, smoke-belching metropolis of over four million people (and growing). Straddling some of the most important sea routes in the world, it is East Africa's second-busiest port and Tanzania's commercial and cultural hub.

At the northern end of the harbour is the Kivukoni Front, with a bustling fish market where dhows dock at dawn to offload the night's catch. There are also excellent craft markets and restaurants and nearby sandy beaches and islands. The city's architecture is a mix of African, Arab, Indian and German, although the quaint colonial Lutheran Church is now dwarfed by towering high-rises that reflect Dar's rising prosperity in the golden-hued sunsets shimmering off their glass exteriors. Many travellers bypass 'Dar' completely; those who stick around will be rewarded by the city's eclectic cultural mix and down-to-earth vibe.

When to Go
Dar es Salaam

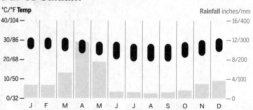

Mar-May Low season, cheaper rates, fewer tourists, but many southern lodges are closed.

Jun-Sep Dry, cool weather and low humidity make this a great time to enjoy the city.

Dec Fashion shows, Christmas, kitesurfing season, and the arrival of migratory birds.

History

In 1862 Sultan Seyyid Majid of Zanzibar alighted on the Zaramo fishing village of Mzizima as the location for his new summer palace. He named it Dar es Salaam, or 'Haven of Peace', a name that reflected its isolated location on a broad natural bay, making it perfect for the new trading depot he envisaged. Yemeni Arabs from the Hadrumat were invited to plant coconuts inland while Indian merchants established the fledgling economy.

Majid's sudden death in 1870 brought an abrupt end to the development, as his succeeding brother, Barghash, had little interest in the new port. So it wasn't until the late 1880s, when the German East Africa Company established a trading station, that the city really began to evolve. By 1887 Dar was the capital of the new German protectorate. The colonial administration was moved from Bagamoyo and the construction of a railway line accelerated the city's growth, facilitating trade with Central Africa via Lake Tanganyika.

As the city grew, social and political awareness grew too. Ironically, World War I was to prove the catalyst for the revival of African institutions such as the Tanganyika African Association, which was sanctioned by the post-war British administration in 1922. This organisation ultimately merged with the Tanganyika African National Union (TANU) to form the basis for the nationalist movement, which achieved independence for the country in 1961. Since then Dar es Salaam has remained Tanzania's undisputed political and economic capital, even though the legislature and official seat of government were transferred to Dodoma in 1973.

In the newly independent Tanzania, Dar fared poorly. President Julius Nyerere favoured a socialist economic model, and one in which urban areas were de-emphasised in favour of rural investment. As Tanzania's primary city, Dar es Salaam languished while a newly nationalised labour market and centralised government spawned Byzantine levels of bureaucracy and corruption. Still, the close ties of friendship between Nyerere and China started to pay dividends when socialism was abandoned in favour of liberalisation in the 1990s. Since then Chinese investment has transformed the city from a quaint colonial backwater into a thrusting, high-rise metropolis. By 2013 direct Chinese investments in Tanzania were $2.1 billion

Dar es Salaam Highlights

1 Meeting woodcarvers, entrepreneurs and performers and finding out what makes the city tick on a **cultural tour** (p53).

2 Discovering Dar's **diverse palate** (p62) savouring dhoklas, barbecued meat, spiced tea and coconut-crusted fish.

3 Heading out to Mbudya and Bongoyo for snorkelling and picnics on pristine **offshore islands** (p71).

4 Joining hardworking locals living it up on **Coco Beach** (p55) at the weekend.

5 Shopping for wonderfully wacky, upcycled souvenirs from **Wonder Workshop** (p65).

6 Immersing yourself in life local style by attending a church service at **Azania Front Lutheran Church** (p52).

7 Getting out on the water by dhow or kayak with **Dekeza Dhows** (p73).

8 Escaping to the luxuriously unspoilt headland of **Ras Kutani** (p74) where turtles come to nest.

and Beijing is now Dar es Salaam's biggest trading partner. Investment is focused on large-scale projects such as roads, bridges, railways, apartments and pipelines. Most notably, though, there is significant investment in the new city of Kigamboni over the bay, where the future of Dar es Salaam lies in a 20-year, US$11.6 trillion project set for completion in 2032.

◉ Sights

Dar es Salaam's centre runs along Samora Ave. Northeast of here is Uzunguni, the old colonial centre where all the sights are located. Southwest are Kisutu and Mchafukoge, the Asian quarter, with its many Indian merchants and traders. It is here that the city is at its most exotic, with dozens of *dukas* (shops) selling everything from lighting fixtures to textiles and spicy samosas. Further west and southwest a jumble of earthy neighbourhoods take over, including Kariakoo, Temeke and Ilala. In these areas – seldom reached by travellers – sandy streets wind past densely packed houses and thriving street markets.

North of the centre, over the Selander Bridge, are the upmarket residential areas of Oyster Bay and Msasani, with their Western-style dining and shopping, and the city's main stretch of sand, Coco Beach.

National Museum & House of Culture
MUSEUM

(Map p56; ☑022-211 7508; www.houseof culture.or.tz; Shaaban Robert St; adult/student Tsh6500/2600; ⊙9.30am-6pm) The National Museum houses the famous fossil discoveries of *zinjanthropus* (nutcracker man) from Oldupai Gorge (although only a copy), along with other archaeological finds. Wander through the History Room and ethnographic collection for insights into Tanzania's past and its mosaic of cultures, including the Shirazi civilisation of Kilwa, the Zanzibar slave trade, and the German and British colonial periods. But despite recent renovations, the museum still has much work to do on appropriate displays and the curation of a coherent narrative.

For vintage auto aficionados, there's a small special collection, including the Rolls Royce used first by the British colonial government and later by Julius Nyerere. The new extension, the House of Culture, provides an educational resource centre and display area for contemporary art.

Botanical Gardens
GARDENS

(Map p56; Samora Ave; ⊙sunrise-sunset) FREE Although in danger of disappearing beneath development, these botanical gardens provide an essential shady oasis in a hot, dusty city. They were established in 1893 by Professor Stuhlman, the first Director of Agriculture, and were initially used as a testing ground for cash crops. They're still home to the Horticultural Society, which tends the indigenous and exotic plants including scarlet flame trees, several species of palm, cycads and jacaranda.

Azania Front Lutheran Church
CHURCH

(Map p56; www.azaniafront.org; Azikiwe St, cnr Sokoine Dr) A striking edifice, with a red-roofed belfry overlooking the water and a rather stern Gothic interior, this is one of the city's major landmarks. The church was built in 1898 by German missionaries and was the centre of the German mission in Tanzania; now it is the cathedral for the diocese and is still in active use for services and choir rehearsals (beautiful – you can sometimes hear the singing from the street).

Services in English are held in the early evening; all other services are in Kiswahili.

St Joseph Cathedral
CHURCH

(Map p56; www.daressalaamarchdiocese.or.tz; Sokoine Dr) The spired, Gothic-style, Roman Catholic cathedral, which is still in use – stop by any Sunday morning to see the standing-room-only overflow from the services and hear the singing – was built at the same time as the Lutheran Church, also by German missionaries. In addition to the striking stained-glass windows behind the main altar (best viewed late in the afternoon), it still contains many of the original German inscriptions and artwork, including the carved relief above the main altar.

Fish Market
MARKET

(Map p56; Kivukoni Front; ⊙6am-sunset) Head down to the Kivukoni fish market at 7am to see fishermen flog their fish to restauranteurs and housewives with all the zeal of Wall St stockbrokers. The market is divided into two main sections, comprising eight zones, one of which is the auction. In other sections fish are cleaned, cooked and resold at marked-up prices. It's colourful and chaotic, and you could walk away with a handsome snapper for as little as Tsh3000.

Some stalls do still sell shells, but the purchase of them is ill-advised for environ-

CULTURAL TOURS

Amid the clamour of Dar's development boom it can sometimes be hard to get a sense of the city's history and culture, so it's well worth taking one of these tours for a glimpse of life at street level.

Afriroots (www.afriroots.co.tz) Runs a Sunday-morning history walk (US$50 per person) around the city centre, exploring Dar's evolution from the Omani sultanate to key ANC and Frelimo hotspots in the struggle for independence. Also excellent is the 'behind-the-scenes' cycle tour ($40 per person) where you'll get to meet locals and hear their stories about living in the city. Proceeds from the tours benefit the communities you visit. Afriroots' community work extends beyond Dar to interesting hiking and cycling safaris; see p34 for details.

Investours (☑0684 504212; www.investours.org; adult/student US$75/50) Offers tours to Mwenge Woodcarvers' Market that give visitors the chance to meet locals, get a glimpse into their lives and invest in their business ideas. Following the tour, all fees are pooled and given to an investor of the visitors' choice as an interest-free microloan to help them expand their business. It operates as a nonprofit organisation and is an excellent way of getting to know the 'real' Dar es Salaam while benefiting the local community. It also has a program in Arusha near the Maasai Market.

Kigamboni Community Centre (☑0788 482684; www.kccdar.com; Kigamboni; ☉Mon-Sat) An impressive locally run centre providing education, talent development and vocational training for Kigamboni-area youth. For visitors, it offers reasonably priced walking and cycling tours (Tsh36,000) as well as a 'day-in-the-village' experience (Tsh70,000). In addition, it can organise traditional dance, drumming, acrobatic, cooking and Swahili lessons. Monday through Saturday afternoon from 5pm to 6pm is the best time to stop by for a visit. With luck, you'll catch one of the free talent shows; call ahead to confirm. To get here, take the ferry to Kigamboni and get a *bajaji* (tuk-tuk) to the centre; it's opposite Kigamboni police station next to Kakala bar.

mental reasons, and the export of them is prohibited.

Village Museum MUSEUM
(☑022-270 0437; cnr New Bagamoyo Rd & Makaburi St; adult/student Tsh6500/2600; ☉9.30am-6pm) The centrepiece of this open-air museum is a collection of authentically constructed dwellings illustrating traditional life in various parts of Tanzania. Each house is furnished with typical items and surrounded by small plots of crops, while 'villagers' demonstrate traditional skills such as weaving, pottery and carving. The idea behind the project is to demonstrate some of the nation's architectural and social traditions, although these days some of the houses are sorely in need of some maintenance. For many, the highlight of the museum is the hour-long tribal dances (adult/child Tsh2000/1000) held in the afternoon.

The museum is 9km north of the city centre; the Mwenge dalla-dalla runs there from New Posta transport stand (Tsh400, 45 minutes).

Nafasi Art Space GALLERY
(☑0716 997254, 0783 245537; www.nafasiart space.org; Western Block, Light Industrial Rd, Mikocheni B) Aiming to be the leading contemporary art centre in Tanzania, Nafasi is a complex of 11 studios housed in an old industrial warehouse in Mikocheni. Fifteen local member artists work there alongside regional and international residencies, all of whom exhibit in the on-site gallery. The centre provides a platform for training and cross-cultural discourse, which it promotes through monthly events; Chap Chap, for example, combines an exhibition and open workshops with evening music, theatre and dance.

🏃 Activities

Bongoyo Boat Trips SNORKELLING
(Map p54; ☑0713 328126; the Slipway, Msasani; adult/child return Tsh36,000/28,000; ☉departures 9.30am, 11.30am, 1.30pm & 3.30pm) If you don't have a car, the quickest and easiest way to enjoy some off-shore island fun is to hop on the ferry to Bongoyo at the Slipway.

Northern Dar es Salaam

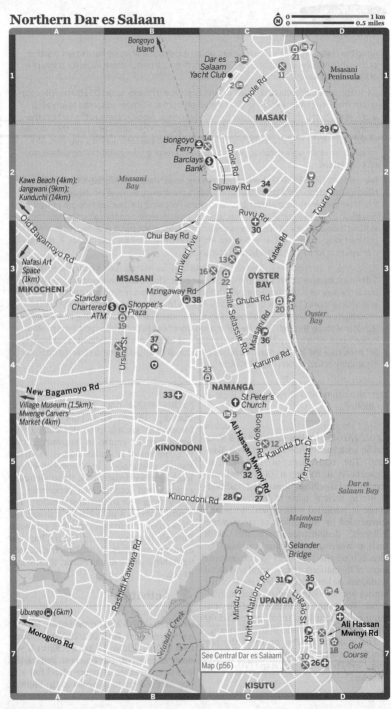

0 — 1 km
0 — 0.5 miles

Bongoyo Island

Dar es Salaam Yacht Club

Chole Rd

Msasani Peninsula

MASAKI

21 7

3

11

2

29

Bongoyo Ferry

14

Barclays Bank

Chole Rd

Slipway Rd

34

17

Toure Dr

Msasani Bay

Kawe Beach (4km);
Jangwani (9km);
Kunduchi (14km)

Ruvu Rd

30

Old Bagamoyo Rd

Nafasi Art Space (1km)

Chui Bay Rd

Kimweri Ave

6

13

16

22

OYSTER BAY

Katoke Rd

MIKOCHENI

MSASANI

Mzingaway Rd

38

Ghuba Rd

20

1

Oyster Bay

Standard Chartered ATM

Shopper's Plaza

19

Haile Selassie Rd

Msasani Rd

36

Ursino St

8

37

Karume Rd

23

New Bagamoyo Rd

Village Museum (1.5km);
Mwenge Carvers'
Market (4km)

33

NAMANGA

St Peter's Church

5

KINONDONI

Ali Hassan Mwinyi Rd

Bongoyo Rd

12

Kaunda Dr

15

32

Kenyatta Dr

Dar es Salaam Bay

Kinondoni Rd

28

27

Msimbazi Bay

Selander Bridge

Rashidi Kawawa Rd

Ubungo (6km)

Morogoro Rd

Selander Creek

Mindu St

United Nations Rd

31

35

4

UPANGA

Lugalo St

24

25

9

18

Ali Hassan Mwinyi Rd

Golf Course

See Central Dar es Salaam
Map (p56)

10

26

KISUTU

Northern Dar es Salaam

DAR ES SALAAM ACTIVITIES

Once there you can snorkel, hike and enjoy simple meals of grilled fish at a shack on the beach. The last boat returns at 5pm and the marine fee is included in the price.

Tanzaquatic FISHING, CRUISE
(☎ 0772 011202, 0756 504987; www.tanzaquatic. com; Shop 17C, the Slipway, Msasani; cruises US$20, glass-bottom boat US$10, island trips per person US$20-30) Enjoy the natural beauty of Msasani Bay on sunset cruises, glass-bottom boat trips, fishing excursions (US$450 per half day for four people) and snorkelling and picnic trips to Bongoyo, Mbudya and Sinda. And, if you really want to splash out, hire its luxury catamaran and strike out for Zanzibar (US$1200 for 18 passengers).

Coco Beach BEACH
(Map p54; Toure Dr) North of the city centre, the Msasani peninsula is fringed with a long stretch of sand and coral rag beach along its eastern side. Swimming is only possible at high tide, but it's a favourite weekend spot for locals, when the beach is dotted with food stalls, coconut stands and beer sellers, particularly the area opposite the Oyster Bay shopping centre. There's also often live music in the evening. Avoid carrying valuables on the beach and steer clear of the quieter stretches.

Taxis charge around Tsh12,000 from the centre of town.

Wildlife Conservation Society of Tanzania BIRDWATCHING
(Map p56; WCST; ☎ 022-211 2518; www.wcs tanzania.org; Garden Ave) The WCST was founded in 1988 with the aim of improving local participation in conservation. Its activities focus on poaching, protection and the preservation of habitat. It also offers twice-monthly bird walks (free, two to three hours), departing from the office at 7.15am on the first and last Saturday of each month.

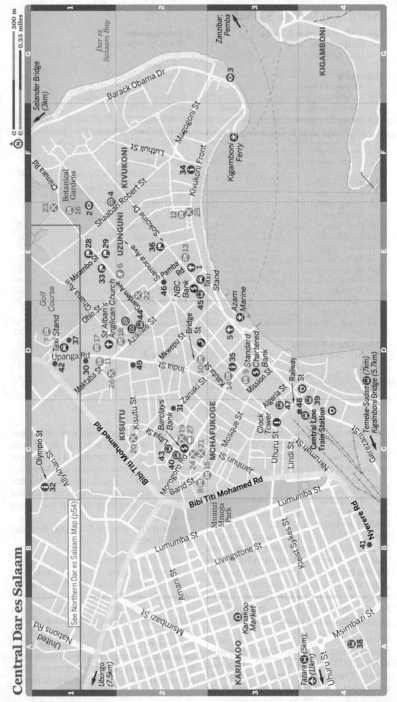

Central Dar es Salaam

0 500 m
0 0.25 miles

See Northern Dar es Salaam Map (p54)

Central Dar es Salaam

◎ Sights
1 Azania Front Lutheran Church	E2
2 Botanical Gardens	E1
3 Fish Market	G3
4 National Museum & House of Culture	F1
5 St Joseph Cathedral	D3

◎ Activities, Courses & Tours
Essential Destinations	(see 30)
6 Wildlife Conservation Society of Tanzania	E2

⊜ Sleeping
7 Dar es Salaam Serena Hotel	D1
8 Econolodge	C2
9 Harbour View Suites	D3
10 Heritage Motel	D2
11 Holiday Inn	D1
12 Hyatt Regency Dar es Salaam	E2
13 Luther House Centre Hostel	E2
14 Rainbow Hotel	D3
15 Safari Inn	C2
16 Southern Sun	E1
17 YMCA	D1
18 YWCA	D2

⊗ Eating
Al Basha	(see 10)
19 Ali's	C2
20 Chapan Bhog	C2
21 Chef's Pride	C2
22 City Garden	E2
23 ex-Holiday Out	E1
24 Mamboz Corner BBQ	C2
25 Oriental	E2
26 Patel Brotherhood	D1

◎ Drinking & Nightlife
27 Akberali Tea Room	C2
Level 8 Bar	(see 12)

❶ Information
28 British High Commission	E1
29 Canadian High Commission	E1
30 Coastal Travels	D1
German Embassy	(see 28)
31 Kearsley Travel	C2
Malawian High Commission	(see 36)
32 Marine Parks & Reserves Unit	C1
33 Mozambique High Commission	E1
Netherlands Embassy	(see 28)
34 Surveys & Mapping Division Map Sales Office	F2
35 Tanzania Tourist Board Information Centre	D3
36 Zambian High Commission	E2

❶ Transport
37 Avis	D1
Coastal Aviation	(see 30)
38 Dalla-dallas to Kisarawe	A4
39 Dalla-dallas to Temeke	C4
40 Dar Express	C2
Fastjet	(see 9)
41 Green Car Rentals	B4
42 Kenya Airways	D1
43 Kilimanjaro Express	C2
44 New Posta Transport Stand	D2
45 Old Posta Transport Stand	E2
46 Precision Air	E2
47 Stesheni Transport Stand	C3
48 Tanzanian Railways Corporation	C4
49 ZanAir	D2

★ Festivals & Events

Goat Races   CULTURAL
(www.goatraces.com; the Green, Kenyatta Dr; adult/child Tsh10,000/5,000) In June have a flutter on Dar's finest racing goats. If your billy goat comes first you get the cash; if not, your money goes to support worthwhile small businesses and charities.

Nyama Choma   FOOD
(www.facebook.com/nyamachomafest; entry Tsh10,000) The largest barbecue block party in East Africa, this festival showcases the skills of Dar's finest pit-masters alongside live bands, soccer matches and a kids' corner. It's held every three months (March, June, September and December).

Swahili Fashion Week   CULTURAL
(www.swahilifashionweek.com) Get ahead on Tanzania's sartorial trends at this December fashion show, which serves as the largest platform for East African designers.

⎙ Sleeping

Dar es Salaam has a reasonable spread of accommodation, although quality midrange hotels are like gold dust. Dozens of budget hotels and hostels cluster downtown. They offer no-frills rooms with air-con. At the top end, hotels are aimed at business travellers or tourists returning from luxury safaris. Here you're looking at US$200-plus for a room with all the comforts of home. The closest places for camping are at Mikadi and Mjimwema on the southern side of the Kurasini Creek.

🛏 City Centre

Most of the reliable budget and midrange lodging is located in Kisutu and Mchafukoge, which are packed with food stalls and restaurants, and are walkable from the ferry terminal. Comfortable high-end accommodation and flagship hotels such as the Hyatt and Serena are located nearby in Uzunguni and Kivukoni.

Safari Inn
HOTEL $

(Map p56; ☎0754 485013, 022-213 8101; www.safari inn.co.tz; Band St; s/d with fan Tsh28,000/35,000, with air-con Tsh35,000/45,000; ❄@) A popular travellers' haunt in Kisutu with English-speaking staff. It has 42 rooms, 10 of which are air-conditioned. All rooms have mosquito nets and a simple continental breakfast is provided.

Econolodge
HOTEL $

(Map p56; ☎022-211 6048, 022-211 6049; econolodge@raha.com; Band St; s/d with fan Tsh25,000/35,000, with air-con Tsh35,000/45,000; ❄) Clean, bland but good-value rooms hidden away in an aesthetically unappealing high-rise. There are no mosquito nets, but rooms have fans for circulation. Payment is in cash only.

YWCA
HOSTEL $

(Map p56; ☎0713 622707; Maktaba St; dm/s without bathroom Tsh10,000/15,000, d Tsh30,000) Located on a small side street between the post office and the Anglican church. Very basic rooms with concrete floors have fans, sinks and clean shared bathrooms. Rooms around the inner courtyard are quieter. Men and women are accepted, and the restaurant serves inexpensive local-style meals.

YMCA
HOSTEL $

(Map p56; ☎0755 066643, 022-213 5457; Upanga Rd; dm/s/d Tsh12,000/25,000/28,000) No-frills rooms in a small compound around the corner from the YWCA, and marginally quieter (though the step up in price from the YWCA isn't justified). There's a canteen with inexpensive meals. Men and women are accepted.

Luther House Centre Hostel
HOSTEL $

(Map p56; ☎022-212 6247, 022-212 0734; luthercentre@yahoo.com; Sokoine Dr; s/d Tsh50,000/65,000; ❄) Rooms here have fans and air-con, and breakfast is available at the restaurant downstairs. The faded state of repair and lack of maintenance makes the price unwarranted, but it does have a fine central location that's just back from the waterfront.

★Holiday Inn
HOTEL $$

(Map p56; ☎0684 885250, 022-213 9250; www. holidayinn.co.tz; India & Maktaba Sts; r excl breakfast US$189-229, ste excl breakfast US$269; P❄@) Undoubtedly the most popular downtown hotel, the Holiday Inn offers spotless modern rooms, courteous service, a handsome buffet breakfast (US$13.50) and a rooftop restaurant. Add to all that a free daily shuttle service to/from Jangwani Sea Breeze Lodge for guests wanting a swim and helpful travel advice booking charter flights to Zanzibar and Pemba, and even helicopter pick-ups to the airport for the hard-pressed business traveller.

Weekend discounts are available.

Heritage Motel
HOTEL $$

(Map p56; ☎022-211 7471; www.heritagemotel. co.tz; cnr Kaluta & Bridge Sts; s/d/tr US$60/80/85; ❄🛜) Good-value rooms in a central location just 15 minutes' walk from the ferry. Rooms are spacious, clean and comfortable with a minifridge, TV and flyscreens at the windows. Next door the Al Basha restaurant serves the hotel breakfast and good Lebanese food.

Rainbow Hotel
HOTEL $$

(Map p56; ☎0754 261314, 022-212 0024; www. rainbow-hoteltz.com; Morogoro Rd; s US$45-55, d US$65-90; ❄🛜) Well located on Morogoro Rd, the Rainbow Hotel distinguishes itself with its friendly staff, good restaurant and great location. Rooms have firm beds, TVs and good air-con and the hotel is within five minutes' walk of the Zanzibar ferry. Taxis are also conveniently located just outside the front door. Two-bedroom apartments are also available for families (US$150).

Harbour View Suites
BUSINESS HOTEL $$

(Map p56; ☎0784 564848; www.harbour view-suites.com; Samora Ave; studio/1-bedroom ste/2-bedroom ste US$160/190/250; ❄@🛜🏊) Well-equipped, centrally located business travellers' apartments with views over the city or the harbour. Some rooms have mosquito nets, and all have modern furnishings and a kitchenette. There's a business centre, a fitness centre, a restaurant and a blues bar. Very popular and often full. Underneath is JM Mall shopping centre, with an ATM and supermarket.

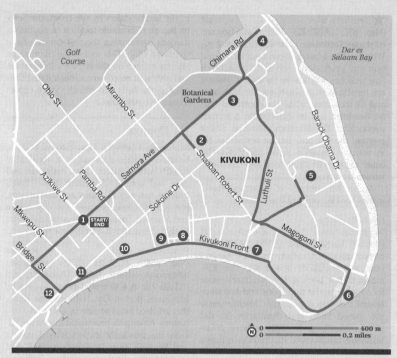

🏃 City Walk
Historic Dar es Salaam

START SAMORA AVE & AZIKIWE ST
END SAMORA AVE & AZIKIWE ST
LENGTH 4.5KM; TWO HOURS

Begin at **1 Askari monument** (Samora Ave & Azikiwe St), a bronze statue dedicated to Africans killed in WWI. Head northeast along Samora Ave to Shaaban Robert St and the **2 National Museum** (p52). Continue eastwards along Samora Ave for half a block. On the right is **3 Karimjee Hall**, the former house of parliament where Julius Nyerere was sworn in as president. Continue eastwards along Samora Ave to Luthuli St. To the northeast is **4 Ocean Rd Hospital**, built in 1897. The small, white, domed building just before is where Robert Koch carried out his pioneering research on malaria and tuberculosis around the turn of the 20th century.

Head south along Luthuli St. On your left is the **5 State House**, originally built by the Germans and rebuilt after WWI by the British. Just southeast on the seafront is the **6 Fish Market** (p52).

From the market, head westwards along Kivukoni Front (Azania Front). To the right are **7 government buildings**, including the Ministry of Foreign Affairs, Ministry of Justice and the Bureau of Statistics, all dating from the German era. To the left is the seafront. Continue straight to the old **8 Kilimanjaro Hotel** (now Hyatt Regency Dar es Salaam).

Just beyond is **9 Azania Front Lutheran Church** (p52), with its landmark red-roofed belfry. The church was built at the turn of the 20th century by German missionaries. Continuing along the waterfront are, first, the **10 Old Post Office** (p67) and then the **11 White Fathers' Mission House**, one of the city's oldest buildings. One block beyond this is **12 St Joseph Cathedral** (p52), another landmark. The cathedral, also built by German missionaries, contains many original German inscriptions and some artwork, including the carved relief above the main altar. From St Joseph's, head one block north along Bridge St to Samora Ave. Follow this eastwards, back to the Askari monument.

★ **Southern Sun**　　　HOTEL **$$$**
(Map p56; ☎022-213 7575; www.tsogosun
hotels.com; Garden Ave; r from US$211; P✴🅿︎❄️)
With its Afro-Islamic decor, popular restau-
rant and professional service, the Southern
Sun punches way above its weight. Rooms
are furnished with plush, comfortable beds
and all mod-cons, while the enormous buf-
fet breakfast can be enjoyed on a terrace
overlooking the Botanical Gardens. Come
evening the bar and Bazara restaurant fill
up with businessmen, expats and locals who
come to enjoy first-rate food and the pretty
garden terrace.

An on-site branch of Kearsley Travel
makes booking onward travel easy.

**Hyatt Regency
Dar es Salaam**　　　LUXURY HOTEL **$$$**
(Map p56; The Kilimanjaro; ☎0764 704704; www.
daressalaam.kilimanjaro.hyatt.com; 24 Kivukoni
Front; r from US$375; P✴🅿︎❄️) 'The Kili-
manjaro' has been a Dar landmark since
its opening in the mid-1960s and has since
hosted a stream of pop stars (Michael Jack-
son stayed here) and dignitaries (so did
Nelson Mandela). In 2006 a huge refur-
bishment transformed its tired decor into a
sleek, marble-clad haven of luxury with ul-
tramodern rooms, two stylish restaurants, a
harbour-view bar and rooftop infinity pool.

Even if you don't stay here, it's worth
dropping by for a drink in the rooftop bar or
a session of pampering in the Anantra spa.

Dar es Salaam Serena Hotel　　　HOTEL **$$$**
(Map p56; ☎0732 123 333, 022-211 2416; www.ser
enahotels.com/serenadaressalaam; Ohio St; r from
US$240; P✴🅿︎❄️) Although overshadowed
in the luxury stakes by the Hyatt, the Sere-
na has an unbeatable location in enormous
gardens overlooking the golf course of the
Gymkana Club. This makes the champagne
Sunday brunch on the terrace a local ritual,
and although rooms are a touch dated they
offer all the bells and whistles you'd expect
from a five-star hotel.

Upanga

Sandwiched between Morogoro Rd and the
Selander Bridge, Upanga is a residential
suburb with a mix of villas, high-rises and
civic and commercial enterprises. There's
little in the way of shops and restaurants,
but it is situated between the city centre
and Msasani. Its location near the Selander
Bridge also makes it a traffic hot spot.

Protea Courtyard　　　HOTEL **$$$**
(Map p54; ☎022-213 0130; www.protea
hotels.com/courtyard; Barack Obama Dr; s/d
US$180/210; P✴🅿︎❄️) Opened in 1948 by
her Royal Begum Om Habibeh Aga Khan,
this art deco hotel preserves a slice of Dar's
history. Among its prominent guests are African independence leaders Jomo Kenyatta
and Kenneth Kaunda. There's a small pool
in the flower-filled courtyard, as well as a
wood-panelled bar, business facilities and a
terrace restaurant serving good Indian food.

Msasani & Kawe Beach

If you have some extra time, don't mind
paying for taxis, or travelling the distance
from the airport (about 20km), the hotels on
Msasani Peninsula and at Kawe Beach offer

SOMETHING DIFFERENT: FRIENDLY GECKO GUESTHOUSE

If you want to stay in Dar a couple of days and connect with an interesting project and
people, consider checking into the Friendly Gecko Guesthouse (☎0759 941848; www.
friendlygecko.com; Africana area; dm US$20, s/d US$45/60; P✴@), which is situated 20km
north of the city centre off the New Bagamoyo Road.

The guesthouse itself comprises a mixture of simple rooms in a large, private house
with a garden and kitchen, but it's the affiliated NGO help2kids (www.help2kids.org) that
makes this a special place to stay. Firstly, because the house is always full of interesting
volunteers, and secondly because 100% of the profits go to support the help2kids or-
phanage and educational outreach programs in local nursery and primary schools.

It's possible to arrange volunteering opportunities through the guesthouse as well as
a host of activities such as market visits to Mwenge and Kariakoo, boat trips to Mbudya
Island, PADI diving courses and day trips (by bus) to Bagamoyo. The less actively in-
clined can just enjoy the pool at the nearby White Sands Resort (p71). Come evening
everyone heads back 'home' for Juliet's Tanzanian dinners (US$5 per person) and a
chance to swap stories.

a break from the urban bustle. If you decide to stay here, bear in mind the traffic bottle-neck over the Selander Bridge, which should be avoided at all costs during rush hour.

CEFA Hostel
HOSTEL **$**

(☏022-278 0425, 022-278 0685; cefahostel@gmail.com; off Old Bagamoyo Rd, Mikocheni B; s/d/tr/q Tsh40,000/60,000/80,000/100,000; **P@☜**) Simple, clean, quiet rooms in a private guesthouse, with good meals available (Tsh10,000). It's popular with volunteers, and often full. It's one block in from Old Bagamoyo Rd (the turn-off is three blocks north of Bima Rd, and about 2km north of Mikocheni B cemetery), and signposted.

★Alexander's Hotel
BOUTIQUE HOTEL **$$**

(Map p54; ☏0754 343834; www.alexanders-tz.com; Mary Knoll Lane; r $185; **✳☜❄**) With its Corbusier-style modernist lines, large roof-top terrace and shady setting, family-run Alexander's is a true boutique hotel. Instead of business blandness there are 17 stylish room with comfortable beds, plump pillows and bright *kikoi* throws and cushions, all of which front the curvaceous, kidney-shaped pool. Breakfast is served in the art- and book-filled dining room, while sundowners and lobster dinners are best taken on the roof terrace.

Mediterraneo Hotel
HOTEL **$$**

(☏0754 812567, 0777 812567; www.mediterraneotanzania.com; Tuari Rd, Kawe; s US$105-115, d US$135-145; **P✳@☜❄**) With its clubby weekend vibe and spacious garden rooms the Mediterraneo is a great family-friendly option. Rooms have wrought-iron beds and colour-washed walls, while the popular open-sided restaurant serves good Italian food overlooking Kawe Beach. Its third Saturday of the month all-night beach party is either to be awaited or avoided, depending on your mindset.

It's about 10km north of the city centre in Kawe, signposted off the Old Bagamoyo Rd. A taxi to the centre of town costs Tsh20,000 and Tsh15,000 to Msasani.

Hotel Slipway
HOTEL **$$**

(Map p54; ☏0713 888301, 022-260 0893; www.hotelslipway.com; Msasani Slipway; s US$120-140, d US$130-150; **P✳☜**) Integrated into the seafront Slipway shopping complex, this apart-hotel offers good-value accommodation. Rooms and apartments are bright and breezy with hand-crafted wooden furniture, bright Indian bed throws, sea-facing balco-

nies and, in the apartments, well-equipped kitchenettes. On your doorstep you also have three standout restaurants, including the hugely popular Waterfront (p64).

Discounted weekly and monthly rates are available. The reception office is near Barclays Bank.

Q Bar & Guest House
GUESTHOUSE **$$**

(Map p54; ☏0754 282474; www.qbardar.com; cnr Haile Selassie & Msasani Rds; dm US$12, s US$50, d US$50-80; **P✳☜**) A Dar institution, the Q Bar has clean, good-value, en suite rooms (several rooms on the upper floors are huge) and some of Msasani's best nightlife. All rooms come with TVs, minifridges and flyscreens in the windows. There's also an eight-bed backpackers' dorm. Food is served downstairs, and there's a bar with live music on Friday evenings and DJs on Thursday and Saturday nights.

Triniti Guesthouse
GUESTHOUSE **$$**

(Map p54; ☏0755 963686, 0769 628328; www.triniti.co.tz; 26 Msasani Rd; r US$65-85; **✳☜**) A unique place in Dar, the Triniti offers informal lodge-like accommodation in 12 detached wooden bungalows set in a mature garden. While rooms are small, they are painted spotlessly white and are decorated with local artworks and colourful soft furnishings. Breakfast is a communal affair with home-baked donuts, fruit and eggs to order. On Friday night the bar hosts a live band and DJ set.

Sea Cliff Hotel
HOTEL **$$$**

(Map p54; ☏022-552 9900, 0764 700600; www.hotelseacliff.com; Toure Dr; r in village US$180-240, r in main bldg US$320-470; **P✳@☜❄**) Sea Cliff has an excellent setting overlooking the ocean at the northern tip of Msasani Peninsula. The hotel is a rather sprawling affair with 93 rooms spread between the main building and the less-appealing and viewless 'village' next door. There are extensive facilities, including a fitness centre, a beauty salon, a casino and restaurants; however, the best feature is the large clifftop garden and pool.

Coral Beach Hotel
HOTEL **$$$**

(Map p54; ☏0784 260192, 022-260 1928; www.coralbeach-tz.com; Coral Lane, Masaki; r US$150-220; **P✳@☜❄**) A quiet hotel (part of the Best Western chain) with front-row views of the sunset over Oyster Bay. Rooms, in new and old wings, are large and comfortable and decorated in a New England style with blue-and-white striped rugs, louvred shutters and coral print throws. Many in the old wing don't have views, so check when you're booking.

Protea Hotel Oyster Bay
HOTEL $$$

(Map p54; ☑0784 666665, 022-266 6665; www. proteahotels.com; cnr Haile Selassie & Ali Hassan Mwinyi Rds; s US$200, d US$230-260, 2-bedroom apt US$315; ⊞❄@🛜🏊) Part of the South African Protea chain, this hotel is styled something like a motel with low-level accommodation units (all with kitchenettes) arranged around an internal garden and pool. Rooms have rather bland, modern decor, but are well furnished and service is friendly and professional. There's also a gym and conference facilities, making this popular with the business crowd.

Ubungo

For travellers passing through the Ubungo bus terminal there's a handful of cheap accommodation (around Tsh25,000 to Tsh35,000) located just west of the terminal or in Ubungo village to the south. Taxis, located just outside the terminal, should cost no more than Tsh5000.

Rombo Green View Hotel
HOTEL $

(☑022-461042; www.rombogreenviewhotel.com; Shekilango Rd; r without bathroom US$20, s US$25, d US$30-40; ⊞❄@) This big, boxy hotel offers well-priced rooms close to the bus station. Rooms are simply furnished with tiled floors, pine beds and rumpled pillows, but the linen is clean, the water hot and the restaurant and bar decent and lively. It's about 500m east of the bus station just off Morogoro Rd.

Moveck Hotel
HOTEL $

(☑0768 688343, 0713 984411; moveckhotel@ gmail.com; Maziwa Rd; s with fan Tsh30,000, d/tr Tsh40,000/50,000; ❄) Located in Ubungo village is this three-storey hotel with basic, serviceable rooms with nets, fans and en suite hot showers. Doubles and triples also have air-con. There's a restaurant next door serving *nyama choma*. It's located 500m south of the bus station in Ubungo.

Other Areas

TEC Kurasini Training & Conference Centre
HOSTEL $

(☑0753 776525, 022-285 1075; www.tec.or.tz; Nelson Mandela Rd; s/d Tsh25,000/50,000, with air-con Tsh50,000/60,000; ⊞@) A church-run place with simple, quiet rooms with fan, and a canteen for meals (Tsh7000). It's southeast of the city centre (about Tsh5000 in a taxi) and 3.5km east of the Temeke Sudan bus stop. Some taxi drivers know it as 'Barazani ya Maaskofu'.

🍴 Eating

Dar es Salaam has a huge array of restaurants catering to the city's cosmopolitan population. They include Indian, Chinese, Ethiopian, Japanese, Mediterranean and Swahili style. Most of the cheaper Tanzanian and Indian restaurants are located in the city centre, with Euro-centric and upmarket seafood restaurants in Msasani. Many of the high-end hotels also offer Sunday lunch buffets and/or brunch; particularly popular are the Bazara Restaurant at Southern Sun (p60) and Kibo Bar at Serena Hotel (p60). Another popular weekend spot is the beachfront Italian restaurant and sushi bar at Mediterraneo Hotel (p61).

Most restaurants in the city centre are closed on Sunday.

✗ City Centre

The area around Zanaki, Kisutu and Jamhuri Sts has many small shops with tasty and inexpensive Indian food and takeaways. Many of them do not serve alcohol.

★ Chapan Bhog
INDIAN $

(Map p56; ☑0685 401417; Kisutu St; meals Tsh2000-10,000; ⊙7am-10pm; 🍴) Chapan's Gujurati *dhoklas* (savory steamed chickpea cakes), south Indian dosas (fermented crepes) and thalis are a vegetarian nirvana in a sea of *nyama choma* (roasted meat). The all-vegetarian menu is extensive and the restaurant has a prime position on temple-lined Kisutu St.

Chef's Pride
TANZANIAN $

(Map p56; Chagga St; meals Tsh1500-6000; ⊙lunch & dinner, closed during Ramadan) This long-standing and popular local eatery serves roasted chicken, biriyani and coconut-crusted fish. In addition, the large menu features fast-food favourites such as pizza, Indian and vegetarian dishes, popular with hungry office workers.

Patel Brotherhood
INDIAN $

(Map p56; Patel Samaj, off Maktaba St; meals Tsh5000-7000; ⊙lunch & dinner; 🍴) This large compound is a favourite evening spot for local Indian families, with good-value Indian veg and non-veg meals (thali, chicken biryani and more). Service can be slow, but there's plenty of local atmosphere to soak up while you're waiting. It's a social club so an additional Tsh2000 per person entry fee is charged to non-members.

From Maktaba St opposite Holiday Inn, make your way through the large parking lot towards the bright blue roof. There's also a children's play area.

ex-Holiday Out
TANZANIAN $

(Map p56; Garden Ave; meals Tsh2500; ⊙7.30am-4pm Mon-Fri) This no-name eatery was formerly dubbed Holiday Out by locals, thanks to its location diagonally opposite the former Holiday Inn hotel (now Southern Sun). Now, there are three adjoining places; the best is to the far right. At each, you can get a plate of *nyama pilau* (meat and seasoned rice), *wali na kuku* (rice and chicken) or other standards, and sit at plastic tables to enjoy it.

City Garden
TANZANIAN $$

(Map p56; Yami Yami; cnr Pamba Rd & Garden Ave; meals Tsh9000-15,000; ⊙lunch & dinner) A lunch buffet (Monday to Friday) and à la carte dining, featuring standards such as grilled fish or chicken and rice. There's a shady outdoor seating area, and it's one of the few places in the city centre open on Sunday.

Al Basha
LEBANESE $$

(Map p56; ☎022-212 6888; Bridge St; meals Tsh8000-9500; ⊙breakfast, lunch & dinner) Dar's best Lebanese restaurant serves a good selection of hot and cold meze dishes, shish kebabs and salads. No alcohol is served but there's a wide selection of fresh juices.

★Oriental
PAN-ASIAN $$$

(Map p56; ☎0764 701234; Hyatt Regency, Kivukoni Front; meals US$30-50; ⊙lunch & dinner) From the high sheen of the marble-tiled floors to the elegant Asian-inspired furnishings, gloved waiters and immaculate sushi bar, the Hyatt's gourmet Asian restaurant aims to seduce and impress. Fortunately with a Thai chef behind the counter, the expertly prepared sushi, bright papaya salads and intensely spiced curries and seafood live up to the opulent surroundings. Booking in advance is recommended.

✕ Upanga

Barbecue House
BARBECUE $

(Map p54; Nkomo St; meals Tsh1500-10,000; ⊙dinner) This quality barbecue place off Ali Hassan Mwinyi St distinguishes itself from the competition with its homemade sides and sauces. Marinated, grilled chicken and fish come with four delicious sauces including green chilli, red chilli and tamarind, and a luscious coconut chutney. Plates of shredded raw cabbage help sop up the sauce, as do sides of fries or *ajam*, a flat bread somewhere between a chapati and a nan.

Delhi Darbar
INDIAN $$

(Map p54; ☎0784-202111; Magore St; meals Tsh15,000-20,000; ⊙lunch & dinner) An upmarket Indian restaurant serving outstanding North Indian cuisine. Expect rich, creamy curries seasoned with chillies,

---

STREET FOOD DAR-STYLE

When dining out in Dar it's worth sampling some of the city's satisfyingly spicy street food. Although you can find carts serving cane juice, coffee and grilled maize throughout the day, most food carts appear around 5pm to cater to the homeward-bound office crowd. Here are three of the best:

Ali's (Map p56; Mwisho St; meals Tsh8,000-12,000; ⊙dinner) Monster beef, chicken and fish *mishkaki* (marinated, grilled kebabs), barbecue chicken and fresh baked garlic nan.

Mamboz Corner BBQ (Map p56; ☎0784 243734; cnr Morogoro Rd & Libya St; meals Tsh4,000-10,000; ⊙dinner) Makers of Dar's best grilled chicken, including spicy gujarr chicken, lemon chicken, chicken *sekela* (with tamarind sauce), dry fried fish and bowls of Zanzibar mix.

Grace Shop (Map p54; Bongoyo Rd; meals Tsh3,000-5,000; ⊙lunch) An informal restaurant and bridal-hire outfit, which you can spot by the Pepsi Cola advert on the door. There's no menu, but the lunchtime meal (ready around noon) includes Tanzanian staples such as ugali, spiced pilau, beans, *mchicha* (a dark green leafy vegetable, similar to spinach), cabbage, fried chicken, fish and goat.

saffron, yoghurt and nuts alongside some good tandoori and kebabs.

Le Bistrot
EUROPEAN $$

(☑0688 687973; Alliance Française, Ali Hassan Mwinyi Rd; meals US$8-20; ☺noon-11pm Mon-Fri, 9am-11pm Sat) Dine at the arty rooftop restaurant of the Alliance Française and enjoy the view over the Gymkana golf course. The menu features a well-executed selection of French, Creole and European dishes such as seafood risotto and *rougaille de saucisses* (sausages in a tomato and garlic sauce with hard-boiled eggs) accompanied by an extensive selection of French wines.

Occasionally the Mauritian chef holds cookery classes (Tsh145,000).

Msasani & Kawe Beach

Village Supermarket
SUPERMARKET $

(Map p54; Seacliff Village, Toure Dr) Pricey but wide selection of Western foods and imported products.

Black Tomato
DELI $

(Map p54; ☑0787 866286; Oyster Bay Shopping Center, Toure Dr; ☺8am-6pm; ☑) Located in the courtyard of the Oyster Bay Shopping Centre, this trendy deli serves salads, sandwiches, smoothies, burgers and brunches. You can count on freshness as the farmers market is also held here. For weekend brunches arrive early or you'll miss out on the sweet corn fritters with crispy bacon. Check out its Facebook page for live music and art exhibits.

Jackie's
TANZANIAN $

(Map p54; Haile Selassie Rd; snacks from Tsh1500; ☺lunch & dinner) *Mishkaki* (marinated, grilled kebabs), plus *chipsi mayai* (omelette mixed with French fries) and other local staples, and a good mix of local and expat clientele in the evenings, when everyone stops by after work.

★ Addis in Dar
ETHIOPIAN $$

(Map p54; ☑0713 266299; www.addisindar.com; 35 Ursino St; meals Tsh10,000-20,000; ☺dinner Mon-Sat; ☑) Addis is decked out with embroidered umbrella lampshades, hand-carved seats and woven tables where food is served communally. Go for one of the combination meals to sample a range of flavours. Everything is served on a large platter covered with *injera* (a sourdough flatbread made of fermented teff flour), which you tear off in pieces and use to scoop up the spicy curries.

Épi d'Or
CAFE $$

(Map p54; ☑0786 669889, 022-260 1663; cnr Chole & Haile Selassie Rds; meals Tsh8,000-12,000; ☺8am-7pm Mon-Sat) This French-run bakery-cafe has a good selection of freshly baked breads, pastries, light lunches, paninis, banana crêpes, and Middle Eastern dishes, plus good coffee.

Rohobot
ETHIOPIAN $$

(Map p54; ☑0774 265126, 0713 764908; Tunisia Rd; meals Tsh12,000-20,000; ☺lunch & dinner Mon-Sat, dinner Sun) This small, informal place consists of some plastic chairs set outside beneath an awning next to the owner-chef's house. Despite its humble appearance the food is tasty and well priced and the owners are very kid-friendly.

Zuane Trattoria & Pizzeria
ITALIAN $$

(Map p54; ☑0766 679600, 022-260 0118; www.zuanetrattoriapizzeria.com; Mzingaway Rd; meals Tsh20,000-50,000; ☺lunch & dinner Mon-Sat) With its luxuriant garden setting this Italian trattoria housed in an old Colonial villa is one of Dar's most atmospheric dining options. The menu features classics such as wood-fired pizzas, *melanzana parmigiana* (an aubergine and parmesan layered bake), pastas, seafood and the ever-popular grilled fillet steak. There's also a children's playground in the garden. Book ahead; it's very popular.

To reach it turn west off Haile Selassie Rd between Shrijee Supermarket and Jackie's.

Waterfront
EUROPEAN $$$

(Map p54; ☑0762 883321; the Slipway, Yacht Club Rd; meals Tsh15,000-35,000; ☺noon-midnight) In the Slipway shopping complex, this is Dar's most popular sundowner spot with westerly views over Msasani Bay. Palm-thatched umbrellas shade tables overlooking the water and happy hour merges seamlessly into dinners of seafood, steaks and oven-fired pizza.

Terrace
INTERNATIONAL, SEAFOOD $$$

(Map p54; ☑0755 706838; the Slipway, Yacht Club Rd; meals Tsh30,000-50,000) Dine beneath a starry night sky on creative, contemporary dishes such as herb-crusted grouper, spicy jerk chicken and tuna carpaccio. The trendy, open-air terrace is dotted with candlelit tables arranged around a luminous swimming pool.

 Drinking & Nightlife

Dar's biggest party nights are Friday, Saturday and Sunday with most bars staying open until the punters leave. On Saturday and

Sunday, Coco Beach (p55) is a popular party venue with local vendors supplying inexpensive beers and snacks. If you decide to hang out here, stay with the main crowd and don't wander off into unlit areas of the beach.

On the third Saturday of every month the Mediterraneo Hotel (p61) hosts a full-moon party.

Akberali Tea Room TEAHOUSE
(Map p56; cnr Morogoro Rd & Jamhuri St; snacks from Tsh200; ⊗lunch) Tea, introduced by the Germans in 1902, is still one of Tanzania's major exports. So take a cup of chai with the locals at this tearoom on Jamhuri St. The most popular style is *chai ya masala*, a strong milky tea spiced with cardamon, sugar and ginger, and accompanied by a samosa or chapati.

Level 8 Bar BAR
(Map p56; ✆0764 701234; 8th fl, Hyatt Regency, Kivukoni Front; ⊗5-11pm Sun-Thu, 5pm-1am Fri & Sat) The Hyatt's sexy rooftop bar has the best views over the harbour, lounge seating and live music some evenings.

Waterfront BAR
(Map p54; ✆0762 883321; the Slipway, Msasani; ⊗noon-midnight) Sundowners with prime sunset views.

George & Dragon PUB
(Map p54; ✆0717 800002; Haile Selassie Rd, Msasani; ⊗4pm-midnight Tue-Fri, 2pm-midnight Sat, 1-11pm Sun) A bonafide English pub where they pull pints, broadcast Premier League games and serve pub grub like fish and chips. There's a DJ in the garden twice a week.

Triniti Bar & Restaurant BAR, RESTAURANT
(Map p54; ✆0784 632967, 0756 181656; www.triniti.co.tz; Msasani Rd; ⊗6pm-late) Happy hours, steak-and-wine Wednesdays, live music on Fridays and big-screen weekend sports. Some events require a Tsh10,000 entry fee.

Q Bar PUB
(Map p54; ✆0754 282474, 022-260 2150; www.qbardar.com; cnr Haile Selassie & Msasani Rds) Happy hour 5pm to 7pm Monday to Friday, live music on Fridays and big-screen sports TV.

☆ Entertainment

Alliance Française DANCE, MUSIC
(Map p54; ✆022-213 1406; www.afdar.com; off Ali Hassan Mwinyi Rd) Traditional and modern dance, live music and more at the month-ly Barazani multicultural nights. It's held on the second or third Wednesday of the month; the schedule is on its website.

Village Museum DANCE
(✆022-270 0437; cnr New Bagamoyo Rd & Makaburi St) *Ngoma* (drumming and dancing) performances from 4pm to 6pm on Saturday and Sunday, plus occasional special afternoon programs highlighting the dances of individual tribes.

Kigamboni Community Centre DANCE
(✆0788-482684, 0753-758173; Kigamboni) Traditional and modern dancing, acrobatics and more on most Saturdays from 5.30pm; call first to confirm.

🛍 Shopping

Most shops in the city centre are closed on Sundays.

★ Wonder Workshop ARTS & CRAFTS
(Map p54; ✆0754 051417; www.wonderwelders.org; 1372 Karume Rd, Msasani; ⊗8am-6pm Mon-Fri, 10am-6pm Sat) ✎ At this excellent workshop, disabled artists create world-class jewellery, sculptures, candles, stationery and other crafts from old glass, metal, car parts and other recycled materials. There's a small shop on the grounds. Crafts can also be commissioned (and sent abroad), and you can watch the artists at work.

Mwenge Carvers' Market ARTS & CRAFTS
(Sam Nujoma Rd; ⊗8am-6pm) This market, opposite the Village Museum, is packed with vendors, and you can watch carvers at work. Take the Mwenge dalla-dalla from New Posta transport stand to the end of the route, from where it's five minutes on foot down

DON'T MISS

DAR BY NIGHT

Dar has a richly textured music scene that remains largely off-limits to travellers due to a dearth of information on popular bands and current hot venues. Bypass the problem on one of Afriroots (p53) new Dar by Night tours (US$50 per person) for an energising insight into some of the city's best foot-thumping, butt-shaking clubs, community centres and bars. The fee includes pick-up and drop-off at your hotel, entrance to clubs and an authentic barbecue dinner.

the small street to the left. The best way to visit Mwenge is with Investours (p53).

Tingatinga Centre
ARTS & CRAFTS

(Map p54; www.tingatinga.org; Morogoro Stores, Haile Selassie Rd; ⊗8.30am-5pm) This centre is at the spot where Edward Saidi Tingatinga originally marketed his designs, and it's still one of the best places to buy Tingatinga paintings and watch the artists at work.

Mnazi Moja Textile Vendors
TEXTILES

(Uhuru St) For *kangas* (printed cotton wraparounds worn by many Tanzanian women) and other colourful textiles, try the vendors and wholesale shops in the Mnazi Moja area.

Slipway
ARTS & CRAFTS

(Map p54; www.slipway.net; Yacht Club Rd, Msasani; ⊗9.30am-6pm) This waterfront shopping centre features upmarket boutiques such as **One Way** leisurewear and **Sandstrom** safari gear, as well as a traditional **craft market**, an ice-cream parlour and children's play area. A great place for unusual souvenirs is the **Green Room** (www.thegreenroomtz.com), where high-quality giftware, home furnishings and artworks are all made from upcycled materials. Coastal Travels (p67) has a branch office here.

Oyster Bay Shopping Centre
SHOPPING CENTRE

(Map p54; Toure Dr; ⊗10am-6pm) Set around a garden courtyard, this small shopping centre is the beating heart of upmarket Oyster Bay. Here you'll find an organic grocer as well as some great craft shops such as kanga-crazy home and giftware from **Moyo Designs** and the **Ngozee** leather shop, as well as the excellent **La Petite Galerie**, where you'll find excellent contemporary art and sculpture.

Sea Cliff Village
MALL

(Map p54; Toure Dr; ⊗9.30am-5.30pm) A high-end shopping mall set around a garden courtyard. There are five restaurants, a supermarket, a secure children's play area and a selection of high-end shops, including a number of jewelers selling Tanzanites. Kearsley Travel (p67) has a branch here.

A Novel Idea
BOOKS

Slipway (Map p54; ☑022-260 1088; www.anovelidea.co.tz; the Slipway, Msasani; ⊗9am-7pm) Dar es Salaam's best bookshop, with classics, modern fiction, travel guides, maps and a kids corner.

ⓘ Information

DANGERS & ANNOYANCES

Dar es Salaam is safer than many other cities in the region, notably Nairobi, though it has its share of muggings and thefts, and the usual precautions must be taken.

Watch out for pickpocketing, particularly at crowded markets and bus and train stations, and for bag snatching through vehicle windows. Stay aware of your surroundings, minimise carrying conspicuous bags or cameras, and leave your valuables in a reliable hotel safe.

At night, always take a taxi rather than taking a dalla-dalla or walking, and avoid walking alone along the path paralleling Barack Obama Drive (previously Ocean Rd), on Coco Beach (which is only safe at weekends, when it's packed with people), and at night along Chole Rd.

With taxis, use only those from reliable hotels or established taxi stands. Avoid hailing taxis cruising the streets, and never get in a taxi that has a 'friend' of the driver or anyone else already in it.

EMERGENCIES

Aga Khan Hospital (Map p54; ☑ 022-211 5151, A&E 022-212 4111, doctor on call 0782 004499; www.agakhanhospitals.org/dar; Barack Obama Dr) A hospital with internationally qualified doctors offering general medical services, specialist clinics and emergency care.

Central Police Station (Sokoine Dr) Near the Central Line Train Station.

Flying Doctors & Amref (Map p54; ☑022-211 6610, flying doctor 0784-240500; www.amref.org; Ali Hassan Mwinyi Rd) For emergency evacuations.

Oyster Bay Police Station (☑022-266 7332; Old Bagamoyo Rd) Opposite the US Embassy.

Traffic Police Headquarters (☑022-211 1747; Sokoine Dr) Near the Central Line Train Station

IMMIGRATION OFFICE

Ministry of Home Affairs (☑022-285 0575/6; www.moha.go.tz; Uhamiaji House, Loliondo St; ⊗visa applications 8am-noon Mon-Fri, visa collections until 2pm) Just off Kilwa Rd, about 3.5km from the city centre.

INTERNET ACCESS

Most hotels, even budget ones, now have either a fixed internet point or wi-fi. Downtown, internet cafes abound; the more professional ones are tucked in commercial centres such as Harbour View Towers and Osman Towers. Most charge between Tsh1000 and Tsh2000 per hour.

Post Office Internet Café (Maktaba St; per hr Tsh1500; ⊗8am-7pm Mon-Fri, 9am-3pm Sat) Terminals inside the post office.

MEDICAL SERVICES

There are good pharmacies at all the main shopping centres including the Slipway, Oyster Bay and Sea Cliff Village.

IST Clinic (Map p54; ☑ 022-260 1308, 022-260 1307, 24hr emergency 0754 783393; www.istclinic.com; Ruvu Rd, Msasani; ☺ 8am-6pm Mon-Thu, 8am-5pm Fri, 9am-noon Sat) A fully equipped Western-run clinic, with a doctor on call 24 hours.

Premier Care Clinic (Map p54; ☑ 0784 254642, 022-266 8385, 022-266 4240; www.premiercareclinic.com; 259 Ali Hassan Mwinyi Rd) Western standards and facilities; next to Big Bite restaurant.

MONEY

Forex bureaus give faster service and marginally better exchange rates than the banks. There are many scattered around the city centre, particularly on or near Samora Ave, where you can easily compare rates. All are open standard business hours.

All the big hotels also offer currency exchange, but their rates are less favourable. The worst rates of exchange are at the Forex Bureau in the arrivals hall at the airport.

There are ATMs all over the city, and in all the major shopping centres.

POST

Main Post Office (Maktaba St; ☺ 8am-4.30pm Mon-Fri, 9am-noon Sat)

TELEPHONE

Starter packs and top-up cards for mobile phone operators are widely available at shops throughout the city.

Telecom Office (Bridge St & Samora Ave; ☺ 7.30am-6pm Mon-Fri, 9am-3pm Sat) Located behind the Extelecoms House. Sells top-up cards for domestic and international calls from any landline phone.

TOURIST INFORMATION

Dar Tourism Airport Information Booth At Julius Nyerere International Airport arrivals area, with city information and maps.

Tanzania Tourist Board Information Centre (Map p56; ☑ 022-212 8472; www.tanzaniatouristboard.com; Samora Ave; ☺ 8am-4pm Mon-Fri, 8.30am-12.30pm Sat) Free tourist maps and brochures, and limited city information.

TRAVEL AGENCIES

For flight and hotel bookings, try the following:

Coastal Travels (Map p56; ☑ 022-211 7959, 022-211 7960; www.coastal.co.tz; 107 Upanga Rd) Especially good for travel to Zanzibar, and for flights linking northern and southern safari circuit destinations (it has its own airline). Also offers reasonably priced city tours, day trips to Zanzibar and Mikumi National Park excursions. It has a branch at Slipway.

Kearsley Travel (Map p56; ☑ 022-213 7713, 022-213 7718; www.kearsleys.com; 16 Zanaki St) One of the oldest travel agencies in Dar. As well as the usual flight, car and hotel bookings it offers well-priced southern circuit safaris. Offices are at Southern Sun (p60) and Sea Cliff Village (p66).

Rickshaw Travels (Map p54; ☑ 0685 082501, 022-260 2303; www.rickshawtravels.com; Buzwagi Rd) Handles all the usual logistics as well as offering tours to the national game parks as well as Kilimanjaro treks. It also has an office in the Serena Hotel (p60).

ⓘ Getting There & Away

AIR

Julius Nyerere International Airport (DAR; ☑ 022-284 2402; www.taa.go.tz) is Tanzania's hub airport. It currently has two terminals, with domestic and international flights departing from Terminal Two, and charters and light aircraft departing from Terminal One. Verify the departure terminal when purchasing your ticket.

A third terminal is currently being constructed to increase capacity to six million arrivals per year. Phase one of the project, which includes the construction of the new terminal building, is scheduled for completion in October 2015. All international flights will then move to Terminal Three, while Terminal Two will serve domestic routes.

Coastal Aviation (Map p56; ☑ reservations 022-284 2700; www.coastal.co.tz; Upanga Rd) Affliated with Coastal Travels (p67), Coastal flies more internal routes than any other airline. Also at Terminal One.

Fastjet (Map p56; ☑ 022-286 6130, 0767-007903, 0685-680533; www.fastjet.com; Samora Ave) Africa's new low-cost airline. Currently offering routes to Johannesburg, Harare, Lusaka, Kilimanjaro, Mbeya and Mwanza, with more on the way. For the best prices book online, in advance. Its desk at the airport isn't always staffed.

Kenya Airways (Map p56; ☑ 0786-390004, 0786-390005; www.kenya-airways.com; Upanga Rd) Scheduled flights to Nairobi and Zanzibar. Some of them transit through Mombasa. Its agent at the airport is Swissport.

Precision Air (Map p56; ☑ 0787 888417, 022-216 8000; www.precisionairtz.com; cnr Samora Ave & Pamba Rd) Affiliated with Kenya Airways, Precision has the largest fleet of aircraft and regular flights to Zanzibar, Kilimanjaro and Mwanza, as well as international flights to Nairobi and Entebbe. Also at Terminal Two.

Tropical Air (☏ 0687 527511, call centre 024-223 2511; www.tropicalair.co.tz; Terminal One) Zanzibari-owned Tropical Air offers frequent services to Zanzibar, Pemba and Mafia as well as occasional services to Tanga and Arusha.

ZanAir (Map p56; ☏ 022-33768, 024-223 3670; www.zanair.com; Haidery Plaza, Kisutu St) A Zanzibari carrier with services to Zanzibar, Pemba, Arusha and Mombasa, Kenya. Also at Terminal One.

BOAT

The main passenger route is between Dar es Salaam and Zanzibar, with some boats continuing on to Pemba.

To/From Zanzibar

The only place at the port to buy legitimate tickets is the tall blue-glass building at the southern end of the ferry terminal on Kivukoni Front. The building is marked 'Azam Marine – Coastal Fast Ferries', and has ticket offices and a large waiting area inside. Avoid the smaller offices just to the north of this building.

Don't fall for touts at the harbour trying to collect extra fees for 'doctors' certificates', departure taxes and the like. The only fee is the ticket price (which includes the US$5 port tax). Also, avoid touts who want to take you into town to buy 'cheaper' ferry tickets, or who offer to purchase ferry tickets for you at resident rates.

Depending on the season, the ferry crossing can be choppy, and most lines pass out seasickness bags at the start of each trip. If you're travelling with the night ferry, it may be worth paying extra for the VIP section, although the fresh air is arguably better than the air-con of VIP.

In addition to Azam's catamarans there are several slow ferries. The main one is *Flying Horse,* which departs daily at 12.30pm (one way US$25) and takes almost four hours.

Azam Marine (☏ 022-212 3324; www.azam marine.com; Kivukoni Front; standard/VIP $35/40) Azam operates four fast catamarans daily between Dar and Zanzibar, departing at 7am, 9.30am, 12.30pm and 3.45pm. All take about two hours, with a luggage allowance of 25kg per person. VIP tickets get you a seat in the air-con hold, but arrive early if you want to sit together.

On Wednesday and Saturday, the two morning services continue to Pemba (standard/VIP $70/80) after a 30-minute transit in Zanzibar.

BUS

Except as noted, all buses currently depart from and arrive at the main bus station at Ubungo, 8km west of the city centre on Morogoro Rd. However, a lot is due to change with the implementation of the new DART (p69) bus network, when all upcountry transport will be switched to Mbezi (past Ubungo on the Morogoro Rd). Ubungo itself will also benefit from a new terminal, which will replace the current sprawling lot and hopefully tame its notorious touts and hustlers.

As always keep an eye on your luggage and your wallet and try to avoid arriving at night. Ask your taxi driver to take you directly to the ticket office window for the line you want to travel with. Avoid dealing with the touts.

Dalla-dallas to Ubungo (Tsh500) leave from New Posta and Old Posta transport stands, as well as from various other spots in town. Taxis from the city centre cost from Tsh30,000. If you're coming into Dar es Salaam on Dar Express or Kilimanjaro Express, you can usually stay on the bus to the town offices on Libya St. Outward bound buses, however, usually depart from Ubungo. Tickets are purchased at Ubungo, and, for Dar Express and Kilimanjaro, at their offices on Libya St. Only buy tickets inside the bus offices.

Following are some sample prices from Dar es Salaam. All routes are serviced at least once daily.

DESTINATION	PRICE (TSH)	DURATION (HR)
Arusha	30,000-35,000	9
Dodoma	25,000	7
Iringa	20,000-25,000	8
Kampala	90,000-100,000	24-29
Mbeya	40,000	12
Mwanza	45,000	15
Nairobi	65,000-70,000	14-18
Songea	45,000	12

Buses to Kilwa Masoko, Lindi and Mtwara depart from south of the city.

Dar Express (Map p56; ☏ 0754 049395; Libya St, Kisutu; ☉ 6am-6pm) Daily buses to Moshi (Tsh30,000, 8½ hours) and Arusha (Tsh30,000, 10 hours) departing every 30 to 60 minutes from 6am to 10am from Ubungo bus station. There's also a daily bus to Nairobi (Tsh65,000, 13 hours) at 6am.

Kilimanjaro Express (Map p56; ☏ 0755 233077; Libya St, Kisutu; ☉ 4.30am-7pm) Hourly buses to Moshi (Tsh33,000, 8½ hours) and Arusha (Tsh33,000, nine hours). The first two early-morning buses depart from outside the office on Libya St; all other buses depart from Ubungo. They're hoping to add a service to Nairobi soon.

TRAIN

Tazara (Tanzanian Zambia Railway Authority; ☏ 0713 225292, 022-286 5187; www.tazara. co.tz; cnr Nyerere & Nelson Mandela Rds; ☉ ticket office 7.30am-12.30pm & 2-4.30pm Mon-Fri, 9am-12.30pm Sat) train station is 6km south-west of the city centre (Tsh10,000 to Tsh12,000 in a taxi). Dalla-dallas to the station leave from either New or Old Posta transport stands, and are marked Vigunguti, U/Ndege or Buguruni. Services run between Dar es Salaam, Mbeya and Kapiri Mposhi (Zambia); see p385.

Tanzanian Railways Corporation train station (Map p56; ☎ 022-211 7833; cnr Railway & St Sokoine Dr) is just southwest of the ferry terminal. Central Line services run between Dar es Salaam and Kigoma (see p385). Commuter trains to Ubungo (Tsh400) also depart from here during rush hour. They are packed and prone to breakdown.

ℹ Getting Around

TO/FROM THE AIRPORT

Dalla-dallas (marked U/Ndege) go to Julius Nyerere Airport from New Posta transport stand. In heavy traffic the trip can easily take one to two hours, and there's no room for luggage. Taxis to central Dar es Salaam cost Tsh30,000 to Tsh35,000 (Tsh35,000 to Tsh40,000 to Msasani Peninsula).

CAR & MOTORCYCLE

Most rental agencies offer self-drive options in town; none offer unlimited kilometres.

Avis (Map p56; ☎ 0754 451111, 022-211 5381; www.avistanzania.com; Amani Place, Ohio St) Not the cheapest prices, but offers a professional service. Has a desk at the Hyatt Regency and the airport, as well as branch offices in Arusha and Stone Town.

Green Car Rentals (Map p56; ☎ 0713 227788, 022-218 3718; www.greencarstz.com; Nyerere Rd) A reputable company with over 20 years' experience. It also has branch offices in Arusha and Zanzibar. You'll find it next to Dar es Salaam Glassworks.

PUBLIC TRANSPORT

Dalla-dallas (minibuses) currently go almost everywhere in the city for Tsh300 to Tsh600. They are invariably packed to overflowing, and are difficult to board with luggage. First and last stops are shown in the front window, but routes vary, so confirm that the driver is going to your destination.

Once the first phase of DART is completed, 2000 dalla-dallas will be assigned new routes as the hybrid buses take over. Other than the terminals at Ubungo and Kivukoni, new city centre bus stops will be at Nyerere Sq, Kisutu and Jangwani. Prices are expected in the same range as dalla-dallas.

Centre city terminals include the following:

New Posta Transport Stand (Map p56; Maktaba St) At the main post office.

Old Posta Transport Stand (Map p56; Sokoine Dr) Down from the Azania Front Lutheran Church.

Stesheni Transport Stand (Map p56; Algeria St) Near the Central Line Train Station; dalla-dallas to Temeke also leave from here; ask for 'Temeke *mwisho*'.

TAXI

Taxis don't have meters. Short rides within the city centre start at Tsh4000. Fares from the city centre to Msasani Peninsula start at Tsh12,000.

ℹ DAR RAPID TRANSIT

With a population growth rate of 8%, oodles of investment and high-rises growing like weeds, Dar es Salaam is projected to become a megacity by 2030. The only problem is all those businesses and people need to get places fast, but with traffic gridlocked for hours every morning and evening the city estimates US$2.5 million a day is being sucked out of the economy.

It's a big problem and one that requires a radical solution. Cue DART (www.dart.go.tz), the Dar Rapid Transit (or BRT/Bus Rapid Transit), a new 137km-network of trunk and feeder roads, 18 terminals, 288 bus stations and pedestrian sidewalks that aim to release the traffic stranglehold, decrease pollution and transform Dar into a pedestrian-friendly city.

Hundreds of new hybrid, high-capacity buses (seating 145 people) will ferry people along segregated bus lanes on seven major routes, the first of which will be the 20km stretch between the Kimara terminal through Ubungo to Kivukoni Front, which is due for completion at the end of 2014. In addition, the city's 9000 dalla-dallas will be slowly phased out of the city centre. Speed limits of 50km/h will be strictly enforced on main routes, as will prohibitions on parking or vending on pedestrian walkways.

The final phase of this huge project won't be completed until 2034, just in time to accommodate Dar's projected seven million-plus population.

Taxi stands include those opposite the Dar es Salaam Serena Hotel, on the corner of Azikiwe St and Sokoine Dr and on the Msasani Peninsula on the corner of Msasani and Haile Selassie Rds.

For a reliable taxi driver, recommended also for airport pick-ups, contact **Jumanne Mastoka** (☎ 0784 339735; mjumanne@yahoo.com). Never get into a taxi that has others in it, and always use taxis affiliated with hotels, or operating from a fixed stand and known by the other drivers at the stand.

AROUND DAR ES SALAAM

Northern Beaches

The beaches, resorts and waterparks 25km north of Dar es Salaam are a popular weekend getaway for families. They are close enough to Dar es Salaam that you can visit for the day (leave early to avoid heavy traffic). The southern section of coast (Jangwani Beach) is broken by frequent stone jetties.

◉ Sights & Activities

Kunduchi Ruins   RUINS
These overgrown ruins include the remnants of a late-15th-century mosque as well as Arabic graves from the 18th or 19th centuries, with some well-preserved pillar tombs. Fragments of Chinese pottery found here testify to ancient trading links between this part of Africa and the Orient. Arrange a guide with your hotel – it's not safe to walk on your own to the ruins, as there have been muggings.

Sea Breeze Marine   DIVING, SNORKELLING
(☎ 0754 783241; www.seabreezemarine.org) Diving around the coral gardens near Bongoyo, Pangavini and Mbudya islands, and diving certification courses (PADI), can be arranged year-round at this long-standing dive outfit. The Discover Scuba option includes a pool session and one shallow open-water dive.

Divers are required to provide proof of certification when booking, and if you haven't been diving for six months you'll need to do the scuba review program.

Kunduchi Kite School   KITESURFING
(☎ 0787 802472, 0719 713620; www.kunduchi-kite-school.com; Kunduchi; 2-person discovery lesson

$210) This is the first kitesurf school on the mainland to take advantage of northeasterly and southeasterly winds that blow between mid-December and February and from April until October. As well as lessons, the school provides the following to experienced kiters: assistance with take-off and landing, lockers, rigging and inflation air, a repair shop and showers.

Follow signs to the Kunduchi Beach Hotel off the New Bagamoyo Rd.

Kunduchi Wet 'n' Wild   WATER PARK
(☎ 0688 058365, 022-265 0050; www.wetnwild.co.tz; Kunduchi; weekday/weekend adult Tsh12,000/14,000, child 2-8yr Tsh10,000/12,000; ⊙ 9am-6pm) This large complex next to the Kunduchi Beach Hotel has multiple pools, 30 water slides, video arcades, a Jungle Gym and an adjoining go-kart track.

🛏 Sleeping & Eating

At all the hotels, it's worth asking about weekend discounts on accommodation. All hotels also charge an entry fee for day visitors on weekends and holidays, averaging Tsh5000 per person.

Jangwani Sea Breeze Lodge   HOTEL $$
(☎ 0786 800960, 022-264 7215; www.jangwaniseabreezeresort.com; Jangwani Beach; s/d US$70/100; 🅿 ❄ @ 🌊) This tidy establishment has 34 comfortable rooms, although most are on the inland side of the road and without beach views. Just opposite is a bougainvillea-draped beachside courtyard, and a restaurant with weekend barbecues and buffets.

Beachcomber   HOTEL $$
(☎ 022-2647772, 022-2647773; www.beachcomber.co.tz; Jangwani Beach; s/d from US$104/122; 🅿 ❄ @ 🛜 🌊) This informal hotel sits on a small plot facing a ragged beach that is unsuitable for swimming. Rooms are rather faded for the price, but adequate. All have small balconies overlooking the pool, if not the beach. If you want to swim in the sea, head to the White Sands resort 500m to the south.

Kunduchi Beach Hotel & Resort   HOTEL $$$
(☎ 0688 915345, 022-265 0050; www.kunduchi.com; Kunduchi Beach; s/d from US$165/190; 🅿 ❄ @ 🌊) This former government hotel is set on the best stretch of beach – a large expanse of clean white sand, with no jetties to mar the view – with a long row of attrac-

tive beach-facing rooms and expansive land-scaped grounds. All the rooms have floor to ceiling windows with balconies, while the restaurant serves a popular Sunday buffet (adult/child Tsh25,000/18,000).

Boat trips can also be arranged to Mbudya (per person/boat $18/72).

White Sands Hotel RESORT $$$
(☑0784 467150, 022-264 7620; www.hotel whitesands.com; Jangwani Beach; s/d US$165/180, 1-/2-bedroom apt US$225/335; ❐❋@❤❄) A large 88-room resort with rooms in two-storey rondavels lined up along the waterfront. All rooms have TVs, minifridg-es and sea views. In addition, there are 28 self-catering apartments – some directly overlooking the beach, others just behind, overlooking a well-tended lawn. There's also a gym and a business centre, and the res-taurant does weekend buffets (per person Tsh25,000).

Waterskiing, laser sailing and windsurf-ing can be arranged. There's a nightclub on most Friday and Saturday nights.

ℹ Getting There & Away

All the Jangwani Beach hotels are reached via the same signposted turn-off from New Baga-moyo Rd. About 3km further north along New Bagamoyo Rd is the signposted turn-off for Kunduchi Beach.

Via public transport, take a dalla-dalla from New Posta transport stand in Dar es Salaam to Mwenge (Tsh400). Once at Mwenge, for Jangwani Beach, take a 'Tegeta' dalla-dalla to Africana Junction (Tsh200), and from there a *bajaji* (tuk-tuk; Tsh2000) or taxi (Tsh3000 to Tsh4000) for the remaining couple of kilo-metres to the hotels. It's also possible to get a direct dalla-dalla from Kariakoo to Tegeta. For Kunduchi Beach, once at Mwenge, take a 'Bahari Beach' dalla-dalla to 'Njia Panda ya Silver Sands'. From here, take a motorcycle or *bajaji* for the remaining distance. Don't walk, as there have been muggings along this stretch of road.

Taxis from Dar es Salaam cost about Tsh60,000 one way. All hotels arrange airport pick-ups.

Driving, the fastest route is along Old Baga-moyo Rd via Kawe.

Offshore Islands

The uninhabited islands of Bongoyo, Mbudya, Pangavini and Fungu Yasini, just off the coastline north of Dar es Salaam,

---

TOP FIVE ACTIVITIES FOR KIDS

➡ Boat trips (p53) to Bongoyo for grilled fish and snorkelling

➡ Drumming or acrobatics classes at Kigamboni Community Centre (p53)

➡ Kunduchi Wet n'Wild (p70) for water park fun

➡ Cycling tours of local neighbourhoods and markets with Afriroots (p53)

➡ Sunset kayaking up Siwatibe Creek with Dekeza Dhows (p73)

---

were gazetted in 1975 as part of the **Dar es Salaam Marine Reserve** (www.marineparks. go.tz). Bongoyo and Mbudya – the two most visited islands, and the only ones with tour-ist facilities – offer attractive beaches backed by dense vegetation. Swimming is possible at any time, unlike on mainland beaches, where swimming is tide-dependent.

The islands are home to coconut crabs, and dolphins can sometimes be spotted in the surrounding waters. There are several nearby dive sites, most off the islands' east-ern sides. Fungu Yasini is a large sandbank without vegetation, while Pangavini has only a tiny beach area. Much of its perim-eter is low coral outcrops, making docking difficult, and it's seldom visited.

There's a fee (adult/child five to 15 years $10/5) to enter the reserve area, including visiting any of the islands. It's included in the price of excursions, and collected before departure.

Bongoyo

Bongoyo, about 7km north of Dar es Salaam, is the most popular of the islands, with a small stretch of beach offering snorkelling and swimming and some short walking trails. Basic grilled fish meals and sodas are available, and snorkelling equipment can be rented.

A **ferry** (☑0713-328126, 022-260 0893; www.slipway.net; the Slipway, Msasani; adult/child Tsh36,000/28,000) departs several times dai-ly (9.30am, 11.30am, 1.30pm and 3.30pm except during the long rains) from Msasani Slipway. The departure and ticketing point is the Waterfront Beach Bar.

DAR ES SALAAM SOUTHERN BEACHES

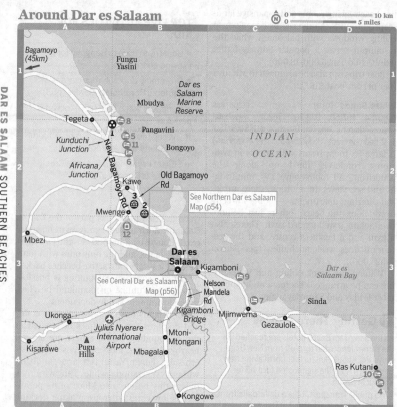

Around Dar es Salaam

0 — 10 km
0 — 5 miles

Bagamoyo
(45km)

Fungu
Yasini

Dar es
Salaam
Marine
Reserve

Mbudya

Pangavini

Tegeta 8

Kunduchi
Junction 5

11

Bongoyo

6

Africana
Junction

Kawe

Old Bagamoyo
Rd

INDIAN
OCEAN

New Bagamoyo Rd

3

2

Mwenge

See Northern Dar es Salaam
Map (p54)

12

Mbezi

**Dar es
Salaam**

Kigamboni

9

Dar es
Salaam Bay

See Central Dar es Salaam
Map (p56)

Nelson
Mandela
Rd

Kigamboni
Bridge

7

Sinda

Ukonga

Mjimwema

Gezaulole

Julius Nyerere
International
Airport

Kisarawe

Pugu
Hills

Mtoni-
Mtongani

Mbagala

Ras Kutani

10

4

Kongowe

Mbudya

Mbudya, north of Bongoyo, and directly offshore from Kunduchi Beach Hotel & Resort, has several beaches (the best and longest one runs along the island's western edge), short walking trails and snorkelling. Near the island's northern end is an old graveyard. Grilled fish and chips are available, as are drinks, and snorkelling equipment can be rented. There are thatched *bandas* for shade and camping (per person with own tent or under open-sided banda Tsh20,000).

The island is best reached from the beaches north of Dar es Salaam; all the hotels organise excursions, and there's a daily ferry (per person US$18) from White Sands Hotel.

Southern Beaches

The coastline south of Dar es Salaam gets more attractive, tropical and rural the further south you go, and makes an easily accessible getaway, far removed – in ambience, if not in distance – from the city. The beach begins just south of Kigamboni, which is opposite Kivukoni Front and reached in five minutes by ferry. About 25km further south are several exclusive resorts.

Kigamboni

The long, white-sand beach ('South Beach') south of Kigamboni, around Mjimwema village, is the closest spot to Dar es Salaam for camping and chilling. It's an easy day trip if you're staying in the city and want some sand and surf.

Around Dar es Salaam

Sights

1 Kunduchi Ruins B2
2 Nafasi Art Space B2
3 Village Museum B2

Activities, Courses & Tours

Kunduchi Wet 'n' Wild ....(see 8)
Sea Breeze Marine ....(see 11)

Sleeping

4 Amani Beach D4
5 Beachcomber B2
6 Jangwani Sea Breeze Lodge B2
7 Kipepeo Beach Village C3
8 Kunduchi Beach Hotel & Resort B2
9 Mikadi Beach C3
10 Ras Kutani D4
Sunrise Beach Resort ....(see 7)
11 White Sands Hotel B2

Entertainment

Village Museum ....(see 3)

Shopping

12 Mwenge Carvers' Market B3

🏃 Activities

Dekeza Dhows SNORKELLING, KAYAKING
(📞0787 217040, 0754 276178; www.dekezadhows.
com; Kipepeo Beach) Dekeza's daily dhow
trips ($35 per person) depart from Kipepeo
Beach to Sinda Island. Boats set off at 10am,
trace the edge of nearby coral reefs for an
hour or so of snorkelling before setting up
lunch on a deserted beach. Fishing trips
aboard the dhows are also possible ($220
for four people), as are sunset cruises ($18
per person).

The same outfit also operates kayak
tours ($15 per person) up the **Siwatibe
Creek**, allowing for the exploration of the
unspoilt mangrove forest behind Kipepeo
Village. The 2½-hour tours set off just before sunset when the trees are filled with
roosting birds.

🛏 Sleeping & Eating

Mikadi Beach BACKPACKERS $
(📞0758 782330; www.mikadibeach.com; campsite per person US$8, d with/without bathroom
US$46/30; 🅿@🐾) This chilled place has a
backpacker-friendly vibe, a convivial bar
with a pool table and 16 thatched beach
bandas on stilts. Two of them are en suite
(with fresh water provided in a drum), the
rest share four showers and toilets. It gets

busy with overland companies between
mid-July and September.

If you fancy heading over to Zanzibar, you
can leave your car here for US$5 per day. A
bajaji to Kigamboni costs Tsh2000.

Sunrise Beach Resort HOTEL $$
(📞0755 400900, 022-282 0222; www.sunrise
beachresort.co.tz; Mjimwema; camping with/with-
out own tent US$10/20, d standard US$33, sea-
view US$60-80, executive US$100; 🅿❄@🛜🐾)
Sunrise has straightforward, closely spaced
rooms just in from the sand plus air-con
'executive' rooms in two-storey brick ron-
davels to the back of the property. There's
also a row of canvas tents on the sand, all
with a mattress, tiny windows and shared
hot-water showers. There's a day-use fee on
weekends of Tsh5000 per person.

A huge selection of activities are also on
offer, from mountain biking to banana boat-
ing. Sinda island boat trips cost US$160 for
four people.

Kipepeo Beach Village LODGE $$
(📞0754 276178; www.kipepeovillage.com; Kipepeo
Village; campsite per person US$9.50, chalet s/d/tr
US$65/85/115; 🅿) Laid-back Kipepeo, locat-
ed 8km south of the ferry dock, has 20 raised
chalets with balconies situated just back
from the beach. Closer to the water, but enclosed behind a fence and a bit of a walk to
the nearest bathroom, are 15 thatched beach
huts without windows, and a camping area.
Its a sand-in-the-toes kind of place and has
a very popular beachside restaurant-bar. Dekeza (p73) dhow tours depart from here.

At weekends there's a Tsh5000 fee for day
use of the beach (the price can be redeemed
at the bar or restaurant).

ℹ Getting There & Away

Take the Kigamboni ferry (per person/vehicle
Tsh200/2000) from Kivukoni Front in Dar es Salaam. Once on the other side, catch a dalla-dalla
heading south and ask the driver to drop you off
at Mjimwema village (Tsh400), from where it's
a 1km walk to Sunrise or Kipepeo. For Mikadi
Beach, it can drop you directly at the entrance.
Bajajis from Kigamboni charge about Tsh4000
to Kipepeo and Sunrise, less to Mikadi Beach.

With your own car, an alternative route
to/from the city is the approximately 35km
stretch via Kongowe, which is about 5km past
Mbagala along the Kilwa Rd. It meets the Kigamboni road at Mjimwema village, just south of the
Sunset/Kipepeo turn-off. The new Kigamboni
bridge should reduce the journey to 20km.

DAR ES SALAAM SOUTHERN BEACHES

KIGAMBONI FERRY

The Kigamboni (Magogoni) ferry makes a good excursion in itself. It runs throughout the day from Kivukoni Front. Although just a five- to 10-minute trip, it offers great views across the water to the rising modern cityscape alongside a small slice of local life as vendors hawk snacks and accessories to city commuters.

In rush hour, however, the ferry can take over an hour to get on board. To alleviate the pressure a new six-lane, cable-stayed bridge is being built across the Kurasini Creek further south, connecting Nelson Mandela Rd in Dar es Salaam with Kibada Rd in Kigamboni. It's due for completion in July 2015, but it won't beat the fun of the ferry.

Ras Kutani

This secluded cape, about 30km south of Dar es Salaam, offers water sports (there's snorkelling but no diving) and the chance for a tropical-island-style getaway without actually leaving the mainland. Nesting sea turtles also favour this section of coast, and both of the following resorts are involved in conservation projects.

🛏 Sleeping

Ras Kutani RESORT $$$
(www.selous.com; Ras Kutani; per person all inclusive from US$250; ☉ Jun–mid-Mar; ☒) Set between the sea and a small lagoon, this resort has spacious natural-style bungalows with beach-facing verandahs. On a rise away from the main lodge are several suites, each with their own plunge pool. Birdwatching, forest walks, horse riding, canoeing in the lagoon and snorkelling can be arranged at the resort.

Amani Beach COTTAGES $$$
(☎ 0782-410033; www.amanibeach.com; Ras Kutani; s weekday/weekend US$140/175, d weekday/weekend US$165/230; P☼@☎☒) The wonderfully peaceful Amani Beach has 10 spacious and well-spaced cottages set on a low cliff directly above the beach and backed by extensive flowering gardens. There's also a beachside swimming pool and delicious, well-prepared cuisine available, as well as birdwatching, forest and beach walks, horse riding and windsurfing opportunities.

Zanzibar Archipelago

Best for Nature

➡ Jozani Forest (p108)

➡ Chumbe Island Coral Park
(p101)

➡ Pemba Flying Foxes (p124)

➡ Misali Island (p120)

Best for Culture

➡ Dhow Countries Music
Academy (p95)

➡ Mrembo Spa (p82)

➡ Sauti za Busara (p87)

➡ Seaweed Center (p110)

Why Go?

Step off the boat or plane onto the Zanzibar Archipelago, and you'll be transported through the centuries – to ancient Persia and tales of Shirazi merchants that inspired *Sinbad the Sailor,* to the court of Swahili princes and Omani sultans, to India, with its heavily laden scents.

For over 2000 years the monsoon winds have shaped the landscape and culture of these islands. Stone Town's Indo-Arabian architecture provides an exotic urban backdrop for elderly men playing *bao* (traditional board game) while women in their *bui-bui* (Islamic cover-alls) pause to chat. On Pemba, clove farms creep up the hillsides and farmers load crates of mangoes onto outbound boats. And, along the coast, village life remains steeped in tradition as fishing dhows set sail on high tides and women farm seaweed off powder-white coral sand. With its tropical tableau and unique culture, the archipelago offers the quintessential Indian Ocean experience.

When to Go
Zanzibar Town

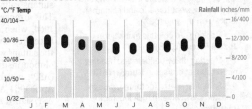

Mar–May *Masika,* the main rains, fall; some hotels close and Zanzibar is crowd-free.

Jul A culture-packed month with the International Film Festival and Mwaka Kogwa.

Jul–Aug Kitesurfing season and summer holidays bring higher prices and hordes of visitors.

Mombasa
(50km)

0   50 km
0   25 miles

Sigi River

A14 • Tanga

Wete

Pemba ③

Pemba

• Tongoni

Chake
Chake

Pangani
River

Pangani

Mkoani

Nungwi

Mkwaja

Tumbatu ⑥

Matemwe
& Mnemba ⑨

• Mligaji

Zanzibar

Saadani
National
Park

Stone
Town ①②

④ Zanzibar

Wani
River

Chumbe
Island ⑧

⑤ East Coast
Beaches ②

Jozani
Forest

⑦ Jambiani

Uzi

• Bagamoyo

INDIAN
OCEAN

A7 • Dar es
Salaam

Zanzibar Archipelago Highlights

① Meeting ghosts and making friends on cultural tours of **Stone Town** (p77).

② Nabbing African print bags, bespoke leather sandals and oyster-shell jewellery on **Gizenga Street** (p95).

③ Diving **Pemba's** underwater mountains, sponge beds and pristine coral gardens (p116).

④ Cycling out to **spice plantations** and discovering what tumeric and cinnamon look like in the wild (p82).

⑤ Tracking red colobus monkeys in **Jozani Forest** (p108).

⑥ Meeting dhow-builders and heading out on sunset cruises in **Nungwi** (p101).

⑦ Sampling *pweza* (octopus), *mhogo* (roasted cassava) and rock lobster in **Jambiani** (p111).

⑧ Sailing to **Chumbe Island** (p101) and seeing what conservation can do for coral gardens.

⑨ Chilling-out in **Matemwe's** luxury lodges (p105) and diving **Mnemba's** crystal-clear waters (p100).

History

The archipelago's history stretches back at least to the start of the first millennium, when Bantu-speaking peoples from the mainland ventured across the Zanzibar and Pemba channels. The *Periplus of the Erythraean Sea* (written for sailors by a Greek merchant around AD 60) makes reference to the island of Menouthias, which many historians believe to be Zanzibar. From around the 8th century, Shirazi traders from Persia also began to make their way to East Africa, where they established settlements on Pemba, and at Zanzibar's Unguja Ukuu.

Between the 12th and 15th centuries trade links with Arabia and the Persian Gulf blossomed. Zanzibar became a powerful city-state, supplying slaves, gold, ivory and wood to places as distant as India and Asia, while importing spices, glassware and textiles. With the trade from the East also came Islam and the Arabic architecture that still characterises the archipelago today.

The arrival of the Portuguese in the early 16th century temporarily interrupted this golden age, as Zanzibar and then Pemba fell under Portuguese control. It was challenged first by the British, and then by Omani Arabs in the mid-16th century. By the early 19th century Oman had gained the upper hand on Zanzibar, and trade on the island again flourished, centred on slaves, ivory and cloves. Trade reached such a high point that in the 1840s the Sultan of Oman relocated his court here from the Persian Gulf.

From the mid-19th century, with increasing European interest in East Africa and the end of the slave trade, Omani rule over Zanzibar began to weaken, and in 1862 the sultanate was formally partitioned. Zanzibar became independent of Oman, with Omani sultans ruling under a British protectorate. This arrangement lasted until 10 December 1963, when Zanzibar gained its independence. Just one month later, in January 1964, the sultans were overthrown in a bloody revolution instigated by the Afro-Shirazi Party (ASP), which then assumed power. On 12 April 1964 Abeid Karume, president of the ASP, signed a declaration of unity with Tanganyika (mainland Tanzania) and the union, fragile from the outset, became known as the United Republic of Tanzania.

Karume was assassinated in 1972 and Aboud Jumbe assumed the presidency of Zanzibar until he resigned in 1984. A succession of leaders followed, culminating in

2000 with the highly controversial election of Aman Abeid Karume, son of the first president.

Today the two major parties in the archipelago are the Chama Cha Mapinduzi (CCM) and the opposition Civic United Front (CUF), which has its stronghold on Pemba. Tensions between the two peaked in the 1995, 2000 and 2005 elections, all marred by violence and allegations of fraud. In 2010, after much wrangling, voters accepted proposals for the incumbent CCM government and the CUF to share power in a new Government of National Unity (GNU), allowing for a gradual rapproachment.

However, little progress has been made at resolving the underlying issues, and with political intrigue over the future structure of the union between Zanzibar and the mainland following the writing of a new constitution in 2014, the survival of GNU is in question. With its pro-secessionist and perceived pro-Islamist stance, support for CUF is rising, placing it in a strong position for the 2015 elections.

ZANZIBAR

POP 900,000

Ringed by some of Africa's best coral beaches and blessed with one of the most mellifluous names in the world, Zanzibar (Unguja) is the archipelago's main island. Sitting at its centre is Stone Town with its quasi-medieval medina, balconied merchants houses and grand House of Wonders.

Drive out of town through the avenue of mango trees – said to be planted over the bodies of past lovers of a 19th-century sultan's daughter – and there's plenty else to explore. To the south, the road cuts through the primeval Jozani forest, home to the rare, red colobus monkey and tiny aders' duiker. Off Kizimkazi, pods of dolphins play, and shoals of luminous fish graze over Chumbe Island's pristine coral garden, while to the east rural villages snake up the coastline from community-minded Jambiani through the surf-and-party hub of Paje to traditional Matemwe, where locals harvest seaweed (most abundant from December to February) and dhows set sail with divers for the lambent coral reef of Mnemba.

At the northern tip of Unguja, Nungwi and Kendwa are the epicenters of tourist activity. Flanked by long, sandy beaches they are well supplied with burgeoning budget and luxury accommodation, restaurants, bars and dance-til-dawn full-moon parties. While there's no denying their buzz or picturesque beauty, choose your spot carefully here as increasing development threatens to mar the area's ineluctable magic and overwhelm fragile community resources.

Stone Town & Ng'ambo (Zanzibar Town)

Zanzibar Town, on the western side of the island, is the heart of the archipelago, and the first stop for most travellers. It is divided into two halves by Creek Road, once a creek that separated Stone Town (Mji Mkongwe) from 'The Other Side' or Ng'ambo, where a small community of slaves once lived and which now accommodates the growing new city with its offices, apartment blocks and slums.

If Zanzibar Town is the archipelago's heart, Stone Town is its soul. Walk through its alleyways overhung with wooden balconies and faces from every shore of the Indian Ocean and you'll easily lose yourself in centuries of history. Each twist and turn brings something new, be it a school full of children chanting verses from the Quran, an abandoned Persian bathhouse or a coffee vendor with his long-spouted pot fastened over coals. Then there are the ghosts. Stone Town was host to one of the world's last open slave markets and stories of cruelty still strike at the conscience.

While the best part of Stone Town is simply letting it unfold before you, it's worth taking one of the recommended tours to really connect with local residents and appreciate its richly textured history.

◉ Sights

Shaped like a triangle, Stone Town sits on a cape, Ras Shangani. It is bounded on two sides by the sea, and along the third by Creek Rd. The harbour and port are located to the north and most of the major sites sit along the seafront opposite. The modern city expands to the east, separated entirely by Creek Rd, the site of the chaotic, daily Darajani Market.

South and north of Zanzibar Town, beyond the heat and hustle, are the wealthy residential area of Mbweni and the northern beaches of Mtoni and Bububu where Omani royalty retired for the weekend.

Zanzibar

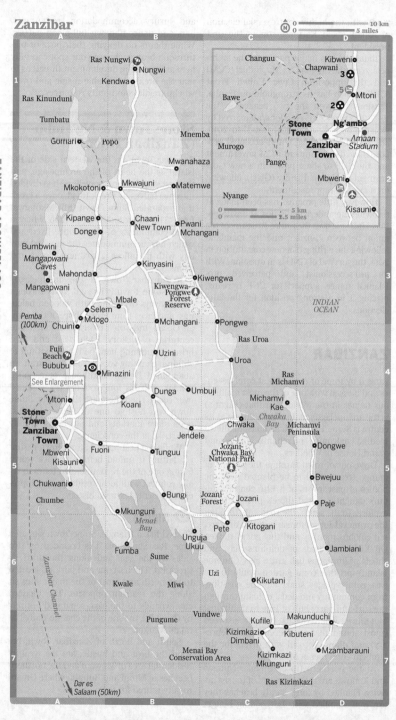

ZANZIBAR ARCHIPELAGO

0 — 10 km
0 — 5 miles

Enlargement (Stone Town / Zanzibar Town area)

Changuu
Kibweni
Chapwani
3
Bawe
5
Mtoni
2
Stone Town
Murogo
Ng'ambo
Zanzibar Town
Pange
Amaan Stadium
Nyange
Mbweni
4
Kisauni

0 — 5 km
0 — 2.5 miles

Main map

Ras Nungwi
Nungwi
Kendwa
Ras Kinunduni
Tumbatu
Gomani
Popo
Mnemba
Mwanahaza
Mkokotoni
Mkwajuni
Matemwe
Kipange
Chaani New Town
Pwani Mchangani
Donge
Bumbwini
Mangapwani Caves
Mahonda
Kinyasini
Kiwengwa
Mangapwani
Kiwengwa-Pongwe Forest Reserve
Mbale
Selem
Mchangani
Pongwe
Pemba (100km)
Chuini
Mdogo
Ras Uroa
Fuji Beach
Bububu
Uzini
Uroa
1 Minazini
Ras Michamvi
See Enlargement
Mtoni
Dunga
Umbuji
Michamvi Kae
Koani
Michamvi Peninsula
Chwaka Bay
Stone Town
Chwaka
Dongwe
Zanzibar Town
Jendele
Mbweni
Fuoni
Jozani-Chwaka Bay National Park
Kisauni
Tunguu
Bwejuu
Chukwani
Bungi
Jozani Forest
Jozani
Paje
Chumbe
Mkunguni
Menai Bay
Pete
Kitogani
Fumba
Unguja Ukuu
Jambiani
Sume
Uzi
Kwale
Miwi
Kikutani
Zanzibar Channel
Pungume
Vundwe
Kufile
Makunduchi
Kizimkazi Dimbani
Kibuteni
Menai Bay Conservation Area
Kizimkazi Mkunguni
Mzambarauni
Ras Kizimkazi
Dar es Salaam (50km)

INDIAN OCEAN

Zanzibar

Old Fort
HISTORIC BUILDING

(Map p84; ⊙9am-10pm) FREE The defining features of the waterfront are the ragstone ramparts of *Ngome Kongwe,* the Old Fort. It was the first defensive structure built by the Busaidi Omani Arabs when they seized the island from the Portuguese in 1698, and did duty as a prison and place of execution until the British transformed it into a ladies tennis club in 1949. Nowadays, the open-air amphitheatre provides a dramatic screening venue for the International Film Festival, while restored rooms house offices for the Zanzibar Cultural Centre.

In the courtyard local artists sell their crafts, and there's a helpful tourist information desk that arranges tours and has schedules for performances.

Forodhani Gardens
GARDENS

(Jamituri Gardens; Map p84) One of the best ways to ease into life on the island is to stop by these formal gardens, originally laid out in 1936 to commemorate the Silver Jubilee of Sultan Khalifa (r 1911–60). In the centre of the grassy plaza is a domed podium where a brass band would play while the marooned ceremonial arch near the waterfront was built to welcome Princess Margaret on a state visit in 1956. Renovated in 2010 by the Aga Khan Trust for Culture, the gardens are now a social hub, with three waterfront cafes, shady benches and an evening food market.

Beit el-Ajaib (House of Wonders)
MUSEUM

(Map p84; Mizingani Rd; adult/child US$4/1; ⊙9am-6pm) Built for ceremonial chutzpah by Sultan Barghash in 1883, the 'House of Wonders' rises in impressive tiers of slender steel pillars and balconies overlooking the Forodhani Gardens. It is the grandest structure in Zanzibar and in its heyday it sported fine marble floors, panelled walls and never-before-seen running water and electricity. Now it houses the **National Museum of History & Culture** with exhibits on the dhow culture of the Indian Ocean and Swahili civilisation.

Aside from the exhibits, the house itself is a wonderful site. Its enormous doors are said to be the largest carved doors in East Africa and outside two bronze canons bear Portuguese inscriptions dating them to the 16th century. In 2012, years of neglected maintenance finally caught up with the palace and a section of balcony on the southeastern corner collapsed, closing the museum to the public. Restoration has since been mired in controversy and the doors remain firmly shut with no date currently set for reopening.

Beit el-Sahel
MUSEUM

(Palace Museum; Map p84; Mizingani Rd; adult/child US$4/1; ⊙9am-6pm) Occupying several blocks along the waterfront, the imposing Palace Museum is a reconstruction of the Sultan Seyyid Said's 19th-century palace home, which was destroyed by the British bombardment of 1896. It was renamed the People's Palace in 1964 when the last sultan, Jamshid, was overthrown. Remarkably, much of the royal paraphernalia – banqueting tables, portraits, thrones and water closets – have survived and now provide the human interest story in this museum dedicated to the Sultanate from 1828 to 1896.

During its day the palace and adjacent harem, **Beit el-Hukm**, were a self-contained ecosystem with raised, private walkways traversing city streets, thus avoiding the need to ever venture outside. Insights into the life of the palace can be gleaned from Princess Salme's fascinating book *Memoirs of an Arabian Princess* (1886), which you can buy in the museum. The youngest of 36 children, Salme was born to a Circassian concubine and herself caused a society scandal when she eloped to Hamburg with a German merchant in 1866. Getting to know the key players, such as her brothers Barghash and Majid, helps bring to life the now dusty displays. Both Barghash and Majid are buried outside in the **Makusurani graveyard**, alongside four other sultans.

ⓘ ETIQUETTE ON THE ARCHIPELAGO

Zanzibar and Pemba are traditional, rural, Muslim societies and attitudes are correspondingly conservative. Avoid getting off to a bad start by observing the following tips:

➡ Dress appropriately in public: locals are deeply offended by revealing clothing. Keep swimwear to the beach, and in towns and villages women should avoid sleeveless tops, plunging necklines and shorts. For men, keep your shirt on when in town, and wear pants or knee-length shorts. Keep a kanga (wrap-around worn by Swahili women) in your bag for any unforeseen circumstances.

➡ Always ask permission before photographing local people.

➡ Non-Muslims should not enter mosques without permission, and then only without shoes.

➡ During Ramadan take particular care with dress, and show respect by not eating or drinking in public places during daylight hours.

Old Dispensary   HISTORIC BUILDING

(Map p84; Mizingani Rd) With its mint-green latticework balconies and sculpted clock tower, the most attractive landmark on the waterfront is this late-19th-century charitable dispensary. It was built by Tharia Topan, a prominent Ismaili Indian merchant who also acted as financial adviser to the sultan and banker to Tippu Tip, Zanzibar's most notorious slave trader. You're free to wander through the interior, which now accommodates offices.

St Joseph's Cathedral   CHURCH

(Map p84; Cathedral St) One of the first sights travellers see when arriving by ferry are the spires of the Roman Catholic cathedral, designed by French architect Berange, who built the cathedral in Marseilles. It was built by local French missionaries between 1893 and 1897 and still serves the local Catholic community of Zanzibaris, Goans and Europeans. It's only open for mass on Sunday.

To reach it follow Kenyatta Rd to Gizenga St, then take the first right to the back gate of the church, which is usually open when the front entrance is closed.

Anglican Cathedral   CHURCH

(Map p84; off New Mkunazini Rd; admission incl slave chambers Tsh6000; ⊙8am-6pm Mon-Sat, noon-6pm Sun) Constructed in the 1870s by the Universities' Mission to Central Africa (UMCA), this was the first Anglican cathedral in East Africa. It was built on the site of the old slave market, the altar reputedly marking the spot of the whipping tree where slaves were lashed with a stinging branch. It's a moving sight, remembered by a white marble circle surrounded by red to symbolise the blood of the slaves.

The driving force behind the construction of the cathedral was Bishop Edward Steere (1874–82), but the inspiration was David Livingstone, whose call to compassion the missionaries answered in 1864 when they settled on the island. One of the stained-glass windows is dedicated to his memory, while the crucifix is made from the tree that grew where his heart was buried in the village of Chitambo in Zambia.

Also worth seeking out is the moving Slave Memorial in the garden. The sculpture, by Swedish artist Clara Sornas, depicts five slaves standing in a pit below ground level. The poignant figures emerge from the rough hewn rock and thus appear hopelessly trapped, shoulders slumped in despair. Around their necks they wear metal collars from which a chain binds them. It's a disturbing and haunting sight.

Services are still held at the cathedral on Sunday mornings.

Slave Chambers   HISTORIC SITE

(Map p84; off New Mkunazini Rd; admission incl Anglican cathedral Tsh6000; ⊙8am-6pm Mon-Sat, noon-6pm Sun) Although nothing of the old slave market remains, some 15 holding cells are located beneath the Anglican Cathedral and St Monica's Hostel. Two of them, beneath St Monica's, are open to the public and offer a sobering glimpse of the appalling realities of the trade. Dank, dark and cramped, each chamber housed up to 65 slaves awaiting sale. Tiny windows cast weak shafts of sunlight into the gloom and it's hard to breathe even when they're empty.

Try to go with a qualified guide who can best illuminate the history.

Darajani Market   MARKET

(Map p84; Creek Rd; ⊙predawn–mid-afternoon) One of the most compelling sights is the main market. Here mountains of spices, sneakers and sandals, meat, fish, live chickens and mobile phones are for sale in a series of covered halls and twisting alleys. The main hall, Estella market, reeks of caged birds, while Kanga St billows with vegetal prints, and wood and fish are auctioned in loud voices in their respective areas. It's hot, heaving and entertaining.

Come in the morning before the heat and the crowds, and dress appropriately. Tourists wandering around in skimpy clothes while locals try to shop is considered the height of rudeness.

Hamamni Persian Baths   HISTORIC BUILDING
(Map p84; Hamamni St; admission Tsh1500) Built by Sultan Barghash in the late 19th century, these were the first public baths on Zanzibar. Although there's no longer water inside, it doesn't take much imagination to envision them in bygone days. Ask the caretaker across the alley to unlock the gate.

Beit el-Amani   HISTORIC BUILDING
(Map p84; cnr Kaunda & Creek Rds) This domed building, formerly the Peace Memorial Museum and now an archive, dates to 1925, when it was inaugurated as a memorial to the accords ending WWI. It was designed by British architect JH Sinclair, who also designed the High Court, further up on Kaunda Rd.

Maruhubi Palace   RUINS
(Map p78) This once-imposing palace, 4km north of Zanzibar Town, was built by Sultan Barghash in 1882 to house his large harem. In 1899 it was almost totally destroyed by fire, although the remaining ruins (primarily columns that once supported an upper terrace, an overhead aqueduct and small reservoirs covered with water lilies) hint at its previous scale. The ruins are just west of the Bububu road and signposted.

Mtoni Palace   RUINS
(Map p78) Built for Sultan Seyyid Said in 1828, Mtoni is the oldest palace on Zanzibar. It was home to the sultan's only legitimate wife, many secondary wives and hundreds of children. Located overlooking the sea, the palace was a beautiful building with a balconied exterior, a large garden courtyard complete with peacocks and gazelles, an observation turret and a mosque. Now only an artful ruin remains with grand, roofless halls and arabesque arches framing glimpses of tropical foliage and an azure sea.

On Tuesday and Friday, nearby Mtoni Marine (p91) hosts a magical candlelit buffet dinner in the roofless halls accompanied by haunting traditional music (Tsh45,000 per person).

To get here head north on the Bububu road, from where the ruins are signposted to the west.

Kidichi Persian Baths   HISTORIC SITE
(Map p78) These baths, 11km northeast of Zanzibar Town, are another construction of Sultan Seyyid Said, built in 1850 for his Persian wife, Scheherezade. It's located among the island's spice plantations, and the royal pair would come here after hunting to refresh themselves in the stylised stucco interiors, which sport typical Persian motifs of birds and flowers. Although poorly maintained you can still make out much of the carving and see the bathing pool and massage tables.

Take dalla-dalla 502 to the main Bububu junction, from where it's a 3km walk east down an unsealed road. Look for the bathhouse to your right.

THE SLAVE TRADE

Slavery has been practised in Africa throughout recorded history, but its greatest expansion in East Africa came with the rise of Islam, which prohibits the enslavement of Muslims. Demands of European plantation holders on the islands of Réunion and Mauritius were another major catalyst, particularly during the second half of the 18th century.

At the outset, slaves were taken from coastal regions and shipped to Arabia, Persia and the Indian Ocean islands. Kilwa Kisiwani was one of the major gateways. As demand increased, traders made their way further inland, ranging as far away as Malawi and the Congo. By the 19th century, with the rise of the Omani Arabs, Zanzibar had eclipsed Kilwa Kisiwani as East Africa's major slave-trading depot. According to some estimates, by the 1860s from 10,000 to as many as 50,000 slaves were passing through Zanzibar's market each year. Overall, close to 600,000 slaves were sold through Zanzibar between 1830 and 1873, when a treaty with Britain finally ended the regional trade.

ZANZIBAR ARCHIPELAGO STONE TOWN & NG'AMBO (ZANZIBAR TOWN)

Mbweni Ruins   HISTORIC SITE

(Map p78) About 5km south of Zanzibar Town, Mbweni was the site of a 19th-century UMCA mission station that was used as a settlement for freed slaves. In addition to the small and still functioning St John's Anglican church, dating to the 1880s, you can see the ruins of the UMCA's St Mary's School for Girls, set amid lush gardens on the grounds of Mbweni Ruins Hotel.

🏃 Activities

With numerous islands within sight of Stone Town, one of the most popular activities is heading out on a dhow for some snorkelling and island-hopping. Diving is also possible.

It's not really advisable to swim in the sea off the town beaches, but if you do fancy a swim Tembo House Hotel (p89) charges Tsh10,000/Tsh5000 per adult/child for pool use.

One Ocean   DIVING

(Map p84; ✆ 024-223 8374; www.zanzibarone ocean.com; off Shangani St) This five-star PADI centre has more than a decade of experience on Zanzibar. In addition to its main office in Stone Town, it has branches at a number of locations along the east coast. It organises dives all around the island, for divers of all levels.

Mrembo Spa   SPA

(Map p84; ✆ 0777 430117, 024-223 0004; www. mrembospa.com; Cathedral St; ⊙10am-6pm) 🍃 Imaginative Mrembo is an authentic Swahili spa housed in an old antique shop. Don't come here looking for sterile suites. Instead, softly spoken Zanzibari therapists lead you to kanga-covered massage tables in colour-washed rooms where you're exfoliated, massaged and manicured with handcrafted scrubs and oils concocted from organically grown ylang ylang, sandalwood and sweet basil.

Other beauty treatments are available, too, including natural henna tattoos accompanied by spiced tea and *kachata* (a local sweet). All the products are available in the excellent shop, where you can find rarely available handmade *udi* (incense) and interesting CDs of local *taarab* music.

Ayda Yoga Zanzibar   YOGA

(Map p84; ✆ 0773 132100; Old Customs House, Mizingani Rd; per person Tsh5000; ⊙5.15pm Mon & Wed) Leave behind the heat and dust of Stone Town and retreat to the breezy top-floor classrooms of the music academy for Ayda's relaxing vinyasa yoga practise. As you move through your *asanas,* synchronising breath and movement, you'll be bathed in light sea breezes through the balcony doors and spoilt with glittering, sunset sea views. It's for women only.

Mnazi Mmoja   FOOTBALL

(Map p84; Creek Rd) Once an area of swampland at the end of the creek, Mnazi Mmoja was reclaimed by the British along with Creek Rd and converted into a sports field. In the 1920s the English Club was located here replete with tennis courts, croquet lawns and a golf course. Now, the grassy flat is used for informal afternoon football matches.

🥗 Courses

Cultural Arts Centre Zanzibar   CRAFT

(Map p84; ✆ 0773 612551; Hamamni St; courses Tsh15,000-25,000) Head down to this friendly cultural arts centre and get to know Stone Town artists while you attempt to fashion your own soap, recycled paper, candles or screen-print T-shirt. The three- to four-hour courses are a lot of fun and a great way to meet an interesting group of locals, although you may be tempted to buy something they made earlier to take home as a souvenir! Courses need to be reserved in advance.

Institute of Swahili & Foreign Languages   LANGUAGE COURSE

(Map p84; ✆ 024-223 0724, 024-223 3337; www. suza.ac.tz; Vuga Rd; per hour/week US$10/200) Zanzibar is regarded as the home of Kiswahili, making this a great place to take some lessons. Experienced teachers and structured courses are offered by the institute along with homestay hook-ups (full board US$20 per person per night) and cultural excursions accompanied by a teacher. Discounts apply to group lessons.

👉 Tours

Numerous travel agencies and tour operators arrange excursions to the spice plantations and ruins north of Zanzibar Town, as well the offshore islands. Most spice tours are arranged on a group formula. If you want a private tour, specify this when booking. Sunset dhow cruises can also be arranged by many midrange and top-end hotels.

SWAHILI BEAUTY SECRETS

In 2006 Stefanie Schoetz opened Mrembo, the island's first Swahili spa. We caught up with her to learn some of the secrets of the trade.

What Inspired Mrembo?

The idea for the spa arose after seeing local women practising their beauty rituals. The more Kiswahili I learnt the greater insight I gained and I combined this with my own passion for plants and spices. One of my good friends here, Damwaju, is a very sophisticated Zanzibari woman who epitomises the Swahili word *mrembo* (a self-conscious beauty). She inspired the name of the spa.

How Did You Source Your Swahili Beauty Secrets?

Damwaju and Bi Kidude (the legendary *taarab* singer who recently passed away) contributed a great deal of knowledge, as did other Zanzibari women at the spa. It's not always easy to source recipes that want to remain hidden, but by cooperating together we create scrubs and oils based on traditional ideas.

What Are Your Favourite Treatments?

The *singo* scrub, which is used by Zanzibari women before their wedding. It's a valuable mixture of spices and flowers, such as ylang ylang, jasmine, rose and mpatchori. We're very proud of this scrub as so much work went into its creation. The *kidonge* clove and spice scrub is also interesting, it is prepared over an open fire with the freshest cloves, which are then pounded and mixed with coconut cream. It's very invigorating.

Do You Use Local Products?

We cultivate all our own herbs and spices, while other herbs and flowers come from nearby gardens. In addition, the essential oils (cinnamon, eucalyptus, camadulensis, lemongrass and clove) come from a local distillery. The only things imported are some perfumes, oud and frankincense, which come from Oman.

What's Your Best Beauty Tip?

Every morning Zanzibari women perfume their clothes with *udi* (perfumed incense) on an *mbao ya chetezo* (wooden burner). The perfume is very subtle and seductive. You should try it out.

Zanzibar Different　　　　CULTURAL TOUR
(☎024-223 0004, 0777 430117; www.zanzibar different.com) Thoughtful, culturally engaging tours exploring the island's fascinating history and rich artisan culture. Unique Stone Town tours explore the role of men and women, children's education, rituals of marriage and mourning and a plethora of handcraft traditions. Tours further afield include the Princess Salme Tour, retracing the fascinating history of this Zanzibari princess by dhow and flower-fringed donkey chariot.

Creative workshops in batik, spice blending and drumming are also available for kids and grown-ups alike. All are arranged in partnership with local experts, including the Dhow Countries Music Academy (p95).

creative tours cover unusual historical and cultural ground. For example, the Ghost Tour looks at the slave trade and revolution through houses and locations believed to be haunted; the Kids Tour engages children in research and allows them to interact with local games; and the Cooking Workshop takes you shopping in the market and into the kitchen of a home cook for a lesson in regional dishes and local spices.

As an extension to your new spicy repertoire, head out on Kawa's cycle tours to the spice plantations and learn to tell your breadfruit from your jackfruit. Or, venture out on the re-cycling adventure and see grassroots projects first hand. A great investment of time, and excellent value.

Kawa Tours　　　　CULTURAL TOUR
(☎0777 488311, 0779 065511; www.zanzibarkawa tours.com; tours US$15-60) Aimed at benefiting and engaging Stone Town residents, these

Eco + Culture Tours　　　　CULTURAL TOUR
(Map p84; ☎024-223 3731, 0755 873066; www.eco culture-zanzibar.org; Hurumzi St) Excursions to Unguja Ukuu, Jambiani village and Stone

ZANZIBAR ARCHIPELAGO

Stone Town

200 m
0.1 miles

Zanzibar Channel

Port & Ferry Ticket Office (150m);
Malindi Area Guesthouses (400m)

Mtoni
(3.6km)

Funguni Rd

Malawi Rd

Ciné
Afrique

Malindi Rd

ZanAir

MALINDI

Majindi St

Kokoni St

Creek Rd

Zanzibar
Tourist
Corporation

Mlandege St

NG'AMBO

Darajani St

Market St

Shamshu
& Sons
Pharmacy

Kiponda St

Kenya
Airways

Jumaa
Mosque

Precision
Air

KIPONDA

Jamatini Rd

Thaira St

Aga Khan
Mosque

Changa Bazaar

Hurumzi St

HURUMZI

Hamamni St

Nyumba ya Moto St

Mizingani Rd

Forodhani
Gardens

Hurumzi St

Gizenga St

NBC

Map numbers: 45 39 50 48 61 22 36 8 68 12 40 32 14 27 71 72 33 13 25 38 4 2 9 20 76 78 28 43 46 66 5 52 6 59 57 74 60 63 35 26 79 80 19 67 51 44

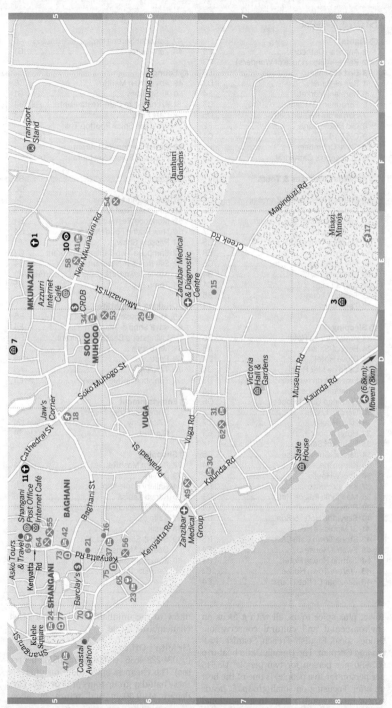

Stone Town

Town, plus spice tours, all with a focus on environmental and cultural conservation. Guides speak English, French, Spanish, Italian and German. The Unguja Ukuu boat trip (US$80 per person for two people, US$45 per person for five people) is one of the best on offer. Focusing on small groups it heads out of this unspoilt village in a traditional dhow to the uninhabited islands of Miwi, Nianembe or Kwale.

Mr Mitu's Office   CULTURAL TOUR
(☎024-223 4636; off Malawi Rd; US$12 per person) The cheapest spice tours on offer are these half-day group tours of 15 people. They depart at 9.30am and return by about

2.30pm. Book a day in advance in high season. The office is signposted just in from Ciné Afrique.

Gallery Tours & Safaris TOUR
(☑ 024-223 2088; www.gallerytours.net) Top-of-the line tours and excursions; it can also arrange Zanzibar weddings, honeymoon itineraries and dhow cruises.

Grassroots Traveller CULTURAL TOUR
(☑ 0772 821725; www.grassroots-traveller.com) Working closely with community-based projects, NGOs and organisations striving for sustainable development, this forward-thinking company helps travellers craft interesting itineraries blending adventure with community engagement to discover that there's more to Zanzibar than sun, sand and sea. It also helps volunteers hook-up successful short- and long-term projects.

Madeira Tours & Safaris TOUR
(Map p84; ☑ 024-223 0406, 0777 415997; www.zanzibarmadeira.com; Baghani St) A large outfit offering tours, cruises, car hire and deep-sea fishing in all price ranges.

Sama Tours TOUR
(Map p84; ☑ 024-223 3543; www.samatours.com; Hurumzi St) Reliable and reasonably priced boat trips and spice tours. Multilingual staff are extremely helpful.

Tropical Tours TOUR
(Map p84; ☑ 0777 413454; Kenyatta Rd) Reliable, budget tour operator. You'll find up-to-the-minute deals on its Facebook page (www.facebook.com/TropicalToursZanzibar).

Zan Tours TOUR
(Map p84; ☑ 024-223 3042, 024-223 3116; www.zantours.com; Migombani St) The largest tour operator in Zanzibar, this professional outfit offers upmarket tours to Zanzibar, Pemba and beyond. It's affiliated with ZanAir, which facilitates easy transfers.

🎎 Festivals & Events

Eid al-Fitr, marking the end of Ramadan, is a particularly fascinating time to be in Stone Town, with lanterns lighting the narrow passageways, families dressed in their best and a generally festive atmosphere. Note that many restaurants close during Ramadan.

The festival of **Mwaka Kogwa**, celebrating the Shirazi New Year (usually in July), is held in several villages but most famously in Makunduchi.

Sauti za Busara CULTURAL
(Voices of Wisdom; www.busaramusic.com; festival pass nonresident US$80-120; ☉ Feb) Showcasing some of the hottest musical talent in Africa, this three-day festival fills the Old Fort and venues across the island with the best *taarab*, jazz, Afro-pop and Bongo Flava.

Zanzibar International Film Festival CULTURAL
(Festival of the Dhow Countries; www.ziff.or.tz; ☉ Jul) Zanzibar's film festival celebrates and nurtures arts from Indian Ocean countries as diverse as India, Iran, Madagascar and the Horn of Africa. For 16 days in July venues around Stone Town host screenings, performing-arts groups, media-related workshops and musical masterclasses.

Jahazi Literary & Jazz Festival CULTURAL
(www.jahazifestival.com; weekend pass Tsh50,000; ☉ Aug) August ends with a long weekend of jazz, blues, poetry and storytelling.

🛏 Sleeping

Stone Town has it all: you can sleep anywhere from the funkiest fleapit to grand medina merchant's houses with lofty views of the harbour. However, rampant development, including the controversial construction of an enormous 67-room Park Hyatt on a piece of prime waterfront property, threatens to mar the character of the old town.

Discounts at budget places may be possible in the rainy seasons from April to May and October to November. To avoid damp ask for rooms on upper floors.

🛏 Stone Town

★ Jambo Guest House GUESTHOUSE $
(Map p84; ☑ 024-223 3779; info@jamboguest.com; off Mkunazini St; s/d/tr without bathroom US$25/40/60; ❄ @) Probably the best budget accommodation in town and extremely popular with backpackers, Jambo runs smooth as clockwork. Nine spick-and-span rooms with Zanzibari beds (carved wooden beds) share four bathrooms, there's complimentary tea and coffee and the atmospheric Green Garden Restaurant provides for an easy dinner opposite.

Garden Lodge GUESTHOUSE $
(Map p84; ☑ 024-223 3298; gardenlodge@zanlink.com; Kaunda Rd, Vuga; s/d/tr US$40/60/70) This efficient, friendly, family-run place offers 18 rooms (two with air con) in a characterful Swahili house fringed with balconies and

STONE TOWN'S ARCHITECTURE

Stone Town's architecture is a fusion of Arabic, Indian, European and African influences. Arab buildings are often square, with two or three storeys. Rooms line the outer walls, allowing space for an inner courtyard and verandahs, and cooling air circulation. Indian buildings, also several storeys high, generally include a shop on the ground floor and living quarters above, with ornate facades and balconies. A common feature is the *baraza*, a stone bench facing onto the street that serves as a focal point around which townspeople meet and chat.

The most famous feature of Zanzibari architecture is the carved wooden door. There are fewer than 250 remaining today in Stone Town, many of which are older than the houses in which they are set. The door, which was often the first part of a house to be built, served as a symbol of wealth and status. While older (Arabian) doors have a square frame with a geometrical shape, 'newer' doors – many of which were built towards the end of the 19th century and incorporate Indian influences – often have semicircular tops and intricate floral decorations.

Many older doors are decorated with carvings of passages from the Quran. Other commonly seen motifs include images representing items desired in the household, such as a fish (expressing the hope for many children) or the date tree (a symbol of prosperity). Some doors have large brass spikes, which are a tradition from India, where spikes protected doors from being battered down by elephants.

decorated with stained-glass windows. Rooms are good value, especially the upstairs ones, which are bright and spacious, and all have hot water, ceiling fans and Zanzibari beds. There's a rooftop breakfast terrace, but otherwise no food.

Coco de Mer Hotel HOTEL $
(Map p84; ☑ 0785 099123, 024-223 0852; coco demer_znz@yahoo.com; Shangani; s/d/tr US$35/55/65) Coco de Mer is conveniently located just off Kenyatta Rd and *very* vaguely reminiscent of the Algarve, with whitewashed walls, green floors and tile work. Avoid the downstairs rooms, many of which have only interior windows; otherwise rooms are fairly good value.

Hotel Kiponda HOTEL $
(Map p84; ☑ 024-223 3052; www.kiponda.com; Nyumba ya Moto St, Kiponda; s/d/tr from US$30/50/65; ☎) A popular, quiet budget place with the feel of the seaside in its whitewashed rooms with blue trim. Ensuite rooms are spread out over several floors, with the more newly renovated ones on upper levels. The breakfast terrace with its open arches and through breeze is a great place to chill out and check wi-fi. The hotel has close links with Sama Tours, which offers a good range of excursions.

St Monica's Hostel HOSTEL $
(Map p84; ☑ 024-223 0773; www.stmonica hostelzanzibar.s5.com; New Mkunazini Rd; s/d

US$40/50, s/d/tr without bathroom US$25/35/50) Built in the late 19th century to accommodate nuns and teachers for UMCA mission, this rambling place next to the Anglican Cathedral has small rooms crowded with beds and friendly staff. All rooms have fans and nets. The restaurant is run by the parish Mother's Union and serves Swahili cuisine (no alcohol).

Flamingo Guest House GUESTHOUSE $
(Map p84; ☑ 024-223 2850; http://flamingo guesthouseznz.com; Mkunazini St; s/d US$17/34, without bathroom US$14/28) The total lack of decor and stark concrete atrium may put some people off, but the Flamingo offers fine, no-frills accommodation at rock-bottom prices. All rooms have fans and mosquito nets and there's a rooftop sitting/breakfast area.

Princess Salme Inn HOTEL $
(Map p84; ☑ 0777-435303; www.princess salmeinn.com; off Funguni Rd, Malindi; d without bathroom US$39, s/d US$35/50, d with air-con US$60; ❄ @) This friendly place has been spruced up a bit with yellow painted walls, white bedding and mosquito nets over the beds and windows. The rooms are basic but clean, with Zanzibari beds and fans, and most sharing two cold-water bathrooms. There's a small rooftop sitting area.

Karibu Inn HOTEL $
(Map p84; ☑ 0777 417392, 024-223 3058; karibuinnhotel@yahoo.com; Shangani; dm US$20,

s/d/tr US$35/50/75; ❄) The Karibu's complete lack of atmosphere and aggressive 'rules' signposted everywhere are compensated for by a very convenient location in the heart of Shangani. Accommodation is in dorms of five to eight beds or basic rooms with soft beds and private bathroom (rooms upstairs are brighter and better ventilated). Towels, linen and hot water all have to be requested at reception. Breakfast is minimal and served in a gloomy hall downstairs.

★**Hiliki House**   GUESTHOUSE $$

(Map p84; ☑0777 410131; www.hilikihouse-zanzibar.com; Victoria St, Vuga; d with/without bathroom US$80/60; ❄🕓) Shhh, don't tell anyone but the six rooms at Hiliki are probably the best-value accommodation in town. From the minute you step inside to be greeted by gentle Aboud to the quiet, elegant rooms furnished with authentic Zanzibari pieces and the wonderful breakfast spread of fruit, pancakes, eggs and honey you'll feel comfortable and cared for. Also at your disposal are the expansive 1st-floor lounge with views over Victoria Gardens, books and an honesty bar.

As if that wasn't enough you can also reserve a room (or the whole house) at Hiliki's three-bedroom beach house, **Pili Pili** (r/house per night US$150/300; 🅿), which is situated on a beautiful, unspoilt beach at Bumbwini.

Zanzibar Coffee House   BOUTIQUE HOTEL $$

(Map p84; ☑024-223 9319; www.riftvalley-zanzibar.com; Tharia St; s US$60-130, d US$85-150; @) Dating from 1885, this building was the home of Tharia Topan, minister to Sultan Bargash and patron of the beautiful Old Dispensary. As you'd expect, his house has elegant proportions which now provide eight individually styled rooms above the first-class coffeeshop. Vintage lamps, antique furniture, old prints and twirling fans all evoke the atmosphere of bygone days, while a top-notch breakfast of homemade pastries and handground coffee is served on the rooftop terrace.

Emerson on Hurumzi   BOUTIQUE HOTEL $$

(Map p84; ☑0779 854225, 024-223 2784; www.emersononhurumzi.com; Hurumzi St; r/ste US$150/175; @🕓) Formerly 236 Hurumzi, this Zanzibar institution is located in two adjacent historic buildings that have been restored along the lines of an *Arabian Nights* fantasy and are full of character. Each of the 15 rooms (most reached by steep staircases) is unique and all are decadently decorated to give you an idea of what Zanzibar must have been like in its heyday.

The popular rooftop restaurant is open Tuesday to Sunday for light lunches and three-course dinners (Tsh40,000) that explore vintage Zanzibari recipes.

Kholle House   BOUTIQUE HOTEL $$

(Map p84; ☑0772 161033; www.khollehouse.com; off Malindi Rd; s US$105-150, d US$130-170; ❄🕓❄) This mini palace was built in 1860 to showcase the finest collectibles of Princess Kholle, society tastemaker and favoured daughter of Sultan Said. Now, after three years of meticulous renovation, it offers 10 rooms with bright tumeric-stained walls, gleaming nutmeg-coloured floors and a mix of Zanzibari and art-deco furniture. The small garden with its delightful plunge pool is a rare luxury in Stone Town and there are views over the port from the rooftop gazebo.

Swahili House   HOTEL $$

(Map p84; ☑0777 510209; www.moivaro.com; Mchambawima St, Kiponda; s/d US$141/156; ❄@❄) This grand Indian merchant's home is over a century old and once accommodated members of the Sultan's family. Restored to its original state it offers 22 vast rooms (some with open bathrooms) furnished Swahili style with handcrafted furniture, Zanzibari beds and colourful cushions and throws. The 5th-floor terrace, one of the highest in Stone Town, offers stunning views, a jacuzzi plunge pool and an excellent bar and restaurant.

Given the very steep staircase, Swahili House isn't suitable for anyone with mobility issues. It's just off Kiponda St.

Zenji Hotel   HOTEL $$

(Map p84; ☑0776 705592, 0774 276468; www.zenjihotel.com; Malawi Rd; s US$35, d with/without bathroom from US$70/50; ❄@🕓) Despite its location on busy Malawi Rd, Zenji is a haven of tranquility with a laid-back downstairs cafe and bright welcoming rooms decorated with batik cushions, traditional furniture and potted plants. An excellent buffet breakfast of homemade pastries and pancakes is served on the roof terrace and downstairs there's a gallery shop showcasing interesting, quality handicrafts from around the island.

Tembo House Hotel   HOTEL $$

(Map p84; ☑0779 413348, 024-223 3005; www.tembohotel.com; Shangani St; s/d/tr from US$110/130/170; ❄@🕓❄) This attractively restored building has a prime waterfront location, including a small patch of beach (but no swimming) and 44 comfortable, excellent-value rooms in new and old wings. Some rooms have sea views. There's a small pool, a restaurant (no alcohol) and a great buffet breakfast on the seaside terrace. It's enormously popular, especially with families.

Beyt al-Salame BOUTIQUE HOTEL $$
(Map p84; ☎0774 444111; www.stonetowninn.com; Kelele Sq, Shangani; s from US$115, d US$130-190; ❉@🖵) This converted teahouse is an atmospheric choice, with just five individually designed rooms, all with period decor. For a splurge, try one of the top-floor Sultan suites, with views to the sea in the distance and raised Jacuzzi-style baths. Downstairs is a good restaurant.

Stone Town Café B&B B&B $$
(Map p84; ☎0778 373737; www.stonetowncafe.com; Kenyatta Rd, Shangani; s US$70, d US$80-90; ❉@) Simple, unpretentious and uncluttered, the Stone Town Café has five rooms with Zanzibari beds dressed in pristine white linens. Black-and-white photos, decorative chests and rugs lend atmosphere, while breakfast smoothies, coffee and avocado toast are served downstairs on the palm-shaded patio.

House of Spices B&B $$
(Map p84; ☎0773 573727, 024-223 1264; www.houseofspiceszanzibar.com; Kiponda St; s/d US$60/90; ❉) True to its name, this 18th-century house was the home of a spice trader with a shop on the ground floor, family accommodation on the 1st floor and two large terraces above used for drying spices. Now there are four individually decorated bedrooms in rich, spicy colours furnished with Zanzibari beds, copper tables and vanity units. A bonus is the excellent restaurant upstairs.

For families or groups all the rooms can be rented as an apartment (US$250 per night).

Africa House Hotel HOTEL $$
(Map p84; ☎0774 432340; www.africahousehotel.com; Shangani; s US$90-125, d US$100-150; ❉@) A colonial classic, the Africa House was formerly the English Club and now has 15 rooms furnished with red-and-gold Shirazi sofas, gilt-framed mirrors and swagged curtains. There's also a perennially popular sunset bar and sheesha lounge, although the restaurant serves rather mediocre fare. Downstairs rooms overlook the road.

Warere Town House HOTEL $$
(Map p84; ☎0782 234564; www.warere.com; off Funguni Rd, Malindi; s US$35-55, d US$55-70; ❉🖵) A well-run hotel with front-room balconies overlooking a flowering garden. Ten rooms come with Zanzibari beds dressed with kanga-lined mosquito nets, blue stucco trim and palm-woven furniture. Laundry and good wi-fi are available and the reception will organise taxis to the beach and local excursions. It's just a few minutes' walk from the port (staff will meet you).

Clove Hotel HOTEL $$
(Map p84; ☎0776 782001; www.clovehotel.com; Hurumzi St; s from US$60, d US$65-85, f US$100-115) Centrally located, the four-storey Clove Hotel has eight snug safari-themed rooms with firm beds, ceiling fans and cool polished-concrete floors. The better rooms are front-facing with balconies over a small

---

ⓘ PAPASI: STREET TOUTS

In Zanzibar Town you will undoubtedly come into contact with street touts. In Swahili they're known as *papasi* (ticks). They are not registered as guides with the Zanzibar Tourist Corporation (ZTC), although they may carry (false) identification cards, and while a few can be helpful, others can be irritating. The main places that you'll encounter them are at the ferry exit and in the Shangani area around Tembo House Hotel and the post office.

If you decide to use the services of an unlicensed tout, tell them where you want to go and your price range. You shouldn't have to pay anything additional, as many hotels pay commission. If they tell you your hotel of choice no longer exists or is full, take it with a grain of salt. Most *papasi* are hoping that your stay will mean ongoing work for them as your guide. If you're not interested in this, explain (politely) once you've arrived at your hotel. If you want a guide to show you around Stone Town, it's better to arrange one with your hotel or a travel agency. For any dealings with *papasi*, if you're being hassled, a polite but firm approach usually works best.

square. Breakfast is served on the roof terrace with sea views.

★ **Kisiwa House**   BOUTIQUE HOTEL $$$
(Map p84; ☑ 024-223 5654; www.kisiwahouse.com; 572 Baghani St, Baghani; r US$180-240; ❀ 🕏) The lovely Kisiwa House has nine spacious rooms and an excellent rooftop restaurant with sea views. Reached via a grand, steep staircase, all rooms have king-size Zanzibari beds, Persian rugs and dark beamed ceilings. A mix of minimalist ethnic and European decor and grand proportions gives the house an understated glamour, making it popular as a honeymoon destination. It's just off Kenyatta Rd.

★ **Emerson Spice**   BOUTIQUE HOTEL $$$
(Map p84; ☑ 0775 046395, 024-223 2776; www.emersonspice.com; Tharia St; r $175-250; ❀ 🕏) With its stained-glass windows, wooden latticework balustrades, tinkling fountains and romantic, soft-hued colour scheme, Emerson Spice is the most atmospheric hotel in Stone Town. Its intimate collection of 11 rooms are carved creatively out of a 19th-century palace and filled with antiques, rich textiles and deep baths. It's hosted celebrities and made the 2012 *Conde Nast* hotlist, and the set-course dinner on its lattice-framed terrace is deeply memorable.

Mashariki Palace Hotel   BOUTIQUE HOTEL $$$
(Map p84; ☑ 024-223 7232; www.mashariki palacehotel.com; Nyumba ya Moto St; r US$320-475) Rising from the ruins of an Omani palace that once housed the sultan's religious counsellor, Mashariki is as regal as it is refined. Soaring proportions make each of the 18 rooms feel palatial, while the use of natural materials – copper, wood, stucco and limestone – keeps things cool and contemporary. Carved four-poster beds, expensive linen sheets, atmospheric lighting and silk-and-wool soft furnishings add a pampered feel. The *coup de grâce* is the rooftop terrace with royal views of the harbour.

Zanzibar Serena Inn   HOTEL $$$
(Map p84; ☑ 024-223 2306, 024-223 3587; www.serenahotels.com; Kelele Sq, Shangani; r US$380-500; ❀ @ 🕏 ☀) Stone Town's most upmarket hotel, with a beautiful setting on the water, plush rooms with all the amenities, and a business centre. It's an undeniably wonderful spot, with a waterfront pool, an English bar and white-suited waiters serving afternoon tea. Still, with the massive

new Park Hyatt nearly next door it remains to be seen whether it can keep up.

Seyyidda Hotel & Spa   BOUTIQUE HOTEL $$$
(Map p84; ☑ 024-223 8352; www.theseyyidazanzibar.com; off Nyumba Ya Moto St; r US$170-290; ❀ @ 🕏) Lighter, brighter and different in style to many Stone Town hotels, the Seyyida is arranged around a verdant courtyard hung with island art. Rooms are modern and styled in neutral tones, and all have satellite TV, and some have sea views and balconies. There's also a rooftop terrace restaurant and a spa.

🛏 Outside Stone Town

★ **Mbweni Ruins Hotel**   LODGE $$
(Map p78; ☑ 024-223 5478; www.proteahotels.com/mbweniruins; Mbweni; s/d US$125/180, ste US$180-250; 🅿 ❀ @ 🕏 ☀) Originally the site of the UMCA mission school for the children of freed slaves, Mbweni Ruins is a tranquil establishment set in lovely, expansive botanical gardens. In addition to well-appointed rooms and a private beach, it has a very good restaurant and a bar with an unimpeded view over stands of mangroves – ideal for bird-spotting.

There's also a private jetty, from which dhow trips to Stone Town can be arranged, and from where Chumbe Island tours (p101) depart; and in the ruined chapel Jo Fox hosts **yoga** (Map p78; ☑ 0773-271942; www.zanzibaryogawithjo.com; ⏰ 5pm Mon, Wed & Fri) sessions twice a week.

You'll find the hotel 5km south of Zanzibar Town and several kilometres off the airport road.

Mtoni Marine Centre   LODGE $$
(Map p78; ☑ 024-225 0140, 0774 486214; www.mtoni.com; Bububu Rd; s US$70-135, d US$85-180, apt $175-240; 🅿 ❀ @ 🕏 ☀) This long-standing family-friendly establishment offers spacious, well-appointed 'club rooms', family apartments and more luxurious 'palm court' sea-view rooms with private balconies. There's a small beach, large gardens, a fantastic 25m infinity pool and a popular waterside bar and restaurant. A branch of Mrembo Spa (p82) is located here, and the lodge arranges a host of activities. One of the best events is the candlelit Swahili dinner held in the ruins of Mtoni Palace (p81) every Tuesday and Friday evening.

It's 3km north of town along the Bububu road.

✖ Eating

When it comes to Zanzibari food, there's no better place to sample it than in Stone Town. Note that during the low season and Ramadan, many restaurants close or operate reduced hours.

✖ Stone Town

★ Luukman Restaurant ZANZIBARI $
(Map p84; New Mkunazini Rd; meals Tsh1500-5000; ⊙7am-9pm) Probably the best local restaurant for quality Zanzibari food. There's no menu, just make your way inside to the 1950s counter and see what's on offer. Servings are enormous and include various biryanis, fried fish, coconut curries and freshly made nan. Occasionally it also serves Zanzibari sweets like *maandazi* (a deep fried, golden brown doughnut slightly sweetened and spiced with cardamon).

Luis Yoghurt Parlour INDIAN $
(Map p84; ☑0765 759579; 156 Gizenga St; meals Tsh10,000-12,000; ⊙10am-3pm & 6-9pm Mon-Sat; ☑) Reserve ahead for a platter of tasty curried pulses with chickpeas or coconut crab curry. Madam Blanche Luis cooks all the Goan specialties herself, offering them up with freshly made nan and creamy lassies (yoghurt drink), fruit smoothies or spiced tea. The restaurant is opposite the Friday mosque.

Passing Show ZANZIBARI $
(Map p84; Malawi Rd; meals Tsh2500-5000; ⊙7am-9pm) Mingle with the locals and enjoy inexpensive pilaus, goat and fish biryani, stewed vegetables and an assortment of deep-fried snacks. To accompany it order a glass of fresh, sweet tamarind juice. If you want to nab a spot on the small shaded patio come early or late to miss the lunch crowd.

New Radha Food House VEGETARIAN $
(Map p84; ☑024-223 4808; thalis Tsh10,000; ⊙8am-9.30pm; ☑) This great little place is tucked away on the small side street just before the Shangani tunnel. The strictly vegetarian menu features thalis, lassis, homemade yoghurt and other dishes from the subcontinent.

Al-Shabany ZANZIBARI $
(Map p84; off Malawi Rd; meals from Tsh3500; ⊙10am-2pm) This is another local favourite, with delicious pilau and biryani, plus chicken and chips. It's on a small side street just off Malawi Rd.

Tamu ICE CREAM $
(Map p84; Kenyatta Rd; 1/2 scoops Tsh2000/3000, tub Tsh30,000; ⊙10.30am-10.30pm) Tamu serves Italian ice cream in traditional and local flavours. Try the baobab or tamarind.

Stone Town Café CAFE $
(Map p84; Kenyatta Rd; meals Tsh8000-15,000; ⊙8am-6pm Mon-Sat) All-day breakfasts, milkshakes, freshly baked cakes, veggie wraps and good coffee.

Archipelago Café-Restaurant CAFE $$
(Map p84; ☑024-223 5668; Shangani St; meals Tsh12,000-18,000; ⊙8am-10pm) An excellent local restaurant with a fine location on a terrace overlooking the sea and a dhow repair yard below. The well-priced menu features coconut curries, orange and ginger snapper, and chicken pilau, topped off by an array of homemade cakes and sweets. There's no bar, but the smoothies are good and you can bring your own alcohol.

Abyssinian Maritim ETHIOPIAN $$
(Map p84; ☑0772 940556; Vuga Rd; meals Tsh5000-18,000; ⊙noon-2pm & 6-11pm) Savour grilled *tibs* (a mix of meat and vegetables) and slurp up spicy curries with wads of *injera* (soft, sour-dough flatbread made from teff flour) at this great little Ethiopian place. Sit outside underneath the pergola sagging beneath an exuberant bougainvillea and wait for enormous platters of food to arrive at your *mesob* (woven table). Spectacular multicoloured fruit smoothies, *tej* (honey beer) and intense, freshly ground coffees complete the feast.

House of Spices Restaurant ITALIAN $$
(Map p84; ☑024-223 1264; www.houseofspices zanzibar.com; Hurumzi St; meals Tsh12,000-15,000; ⊙lunch & dinner Mon-Sat) Laid out on a lantern-lit terrace this Mediterranean restaurant is known for its well-executed seafood dishes and wood-fired pizzas. The seafood platter of grilled lobster, prawns and calamari comes with a choice of five spiced sauces, and there's a good wine list for pairings.

Monsoon Restaurant ZANZIBARI $$
(Map p84; ☑0777 410410; www.monsoon-zanzibar.com; Shangani St; meals Tsh12,000-18,000; ⊙lunch & dinner) The atmospheric Monsoon has traditional-style dining on floor cushions, and well-prepared Swahili cuisine with a Mediterranean twist served to a backdrop of live *taarab* on Wednesday and Saturday evenings.

FORODHANI GARDENS FOOD FEAST

Every evening, starting at about 5pm, Forodhani Gardens (p79) is transformed into a large outdoor dining room. Vendors set up food stalls beneath the banyan trees and locals come out to enjoy the sunset and nibble on island delicacies. Skewers of *mishkaki* sizzle on barbecues (Tsh8000 to Tsh10,000), Zanzibari pizzas (Tsh2000 to Tsh4000) and roti stuffed with minced meat fly off the benches and locals down alarming quantities of achingly sweet, freshly squeezed sugar cane juice (Tsh1000). It's also one of the few places where you can sample delicious *urojo* (fried bhajis and fritters in a coconut curry sauce) and stock up on cassava crisps and Indian mixes.

Locals advise against eating the seafood (freshness is questionable, especially in the dim lighting). And while most prices are reasonable, with some vendors you'll need to bargain. The food fest usually draws to a close around 9pm or 10pm.

Silk Route Restaurant   INDIAN $$
(Map p84; ☑ 024-223 2624; Shangani St; meals Tsh11,000-16,000; ⊙11am-3pm & 6-11pm Tue-Sun, 6-11pm Mon; ☑) A classic Indian restaurant serving spicy curries and spiced rice, which arrive at the table in copper bowls and sit sizzling away on candle heaters. The restaurant rises over three floors. To get a seat on the coveted top floor book ahead or come early.

Green Garden Restaurant   EUROPEAN $$
(Map p84; off Mkunazini St; meals Tsh9000-10,000; ⊙11am-10pm; ☎) A great garden restaurant with two-tier seating in a shady patio and upstairs on an open terrace covered by a *makuti* thatch. Chill-out music sets the tone for light meals of salad, hummus and pita bread and king prawn curries. There's also a wood-fired pizza oven, free wi-fi, smoothies and more.

Lazuli   ORGANIC $$
(Map p84; ☑ 0776 266670; off Kenyatta Rd; meals Tsh8000-10,000; ⊙noon-4pm & 6-10pm Mon-Sat) This Zanzibari–South African place set in a tiny courtyard just off Kenyatta Rd has freshly prepared curries, fresh fruit juices, burgers, chapati wraps, salads, smoothies, pancakes and more. Service can be extremely slow, but it's all healthy and delicious, and the owners, Bonita and Fahmi, are welcoming.

Café Foro   CAFE $$
(Map p84; Forodhani Gardens; meals Tsh10,000-15,000; ⊙8am-10pm) A lovely waterfront pavilion in Forodhani Gardens serving a simple menu of burgers, wraps, salads and grilled fish. Its location near the children's play area makes this an ideal spot for a family pit stop.

Sambusa Two Tables
Restaurant   ZANZIBARI $$
(Map p84; ☑ 024-223 1979; meals US$15; ⊙by advance arrangement) For sampling authentic Zanzibari dishes, it's hard to beat this restaurant in a family house just off Kaunda Rd, where the proprietors bring out course after course of delicious local delicacies. Advance reservations (preferably the day before) are required; 15 guests can be accommodated.

★Emerson Spice
Rooftop Tea House   FUSION $$$
(Map p84; ☑ 024-223 2776; www.emerson spice.com; Tharia St; prix fixe dinner menu US$30; ⊙7-11pm Fri-Wed) Perched on top of a Swahili mansion in an intricately carved wooden gazebo, Emerson's Tea House screams 'date night'. Enjoy expertly made cocktails with 360-degree views over Stone Town. Mojitos are followed by multicourse dinners with an emphasis on seafood, spices and island fruit. Try the delicate passionfruit ceviche or the prawns with grilled mango, and refreshing sorbets of custard apple and a hint of saffron.

La Taverna   ITALIAN $$$
(Map p84; ☑ 0776 650301; http://lataverna zanzibar.com; New Mkunazini Rd; meals Tsh15,000-30,000; ⊙11am-11pm) Bringing a dash of Italian brio to Stone Town, La Taverna has a romantic screened patio and a warm terracotta tiled interior with the requisite checked tablecloths. Seafood takes pride of place with lightly battered calamari *fritti*, grilled lobster and seafood pasta alongside classic regional dishes such as Milanese cutlets and marinated beef fillet. The wood-fired pizza oven was imported from Italy, making this the town's most popular takeout choice.

LouLou's
EUROPEAN $$$

(Map p84; ☏ 024-224 0170; www.loulou zanzibar.com; Kenyatta Rd; meals US$12-16; ☺11am-10pm Mon-Sat) With a Belgian chef behind the menu, LouLou's offers European dining in a stylish, contemporary restaurant. Expect your carrots and courgettes to come diced, your crabs to come in pancakes with béchamel and your desserts to be heavy on Belgian chocolate. No credit cards.

Outside Stone Town

Mtoni Marine
EUROPEAN $$$

(Map p78; ☏ 024-225 0117; meals Tsh15,000-38,000; ☺lunch & dinner) Mtoni Marine's waterfront restaurant has a range of seafood and meat grills, and waterside barbecues several times weekly, sometimes with a backdrop of traditional music.

Raintree Restaurant
EUROPEAN $$$

(Map p78; ☏ 024-223 5478; Mbweni Ruins Hotel; meals Tsh15,000-30,000) The Raintree has elegant dining in a lovely setting overlooking the surrounding gardens and the water, including delicious seafood grills and salads. It also has a free shuttle service from Stone Town.

Drinking & Nightlife

Stone Town isn't known for its nightlife, but there are a few popular spots.

Zanzibar Coffee House
CAFE

(Map p84; ☏ 024-223 9319; snacks Tsh5000-12,000) East African coffee is some of the finest in the world, and the top spot in Zanzibar for a serious cup is this charming cafe. It's affiliated with Utengule Coffee Estate in Mbeya, from where much of the coffee is sourced, and coffee beans are available for sale. Besides coffee (and a range of smoothies and milkshakes), you can nibble on sweet and savory crepes, salads, sandwiches and toasted bruschetta topped with prawns, vegetables and seafood.

Kaya Shop & Tearoom
CAFE

(Map p84; ☏ 0748 901937; Mkunazini St) Tucked away on a busy shopping street in this thriving local neighbourhood, Kaya is a good place to stop for an unhurried cup of spiced tea and a piece of cake. While you enjoy it, you can browse the pan-African crafts in the shop.

Livingstone Beach Restaurant
BAR

(Map p84; ☏ 0779 701472; off Shangani St; meals Tsh17,000-32,000; ☺10am-2am) This worn but popular place in the old British Consulate building has seating directly on the beach – perfect for sundowners and lovely in the evening, with candlelight. While the restaurant chaotically serves some mediocre food it's a wonderful place for a drink and hosts regular live music.

Post
BAR, TAPAS

(Map p84; ☏ 0778 933144, 0778 809009; Shangani St; ☺10am-10pm; ☏) Located above the historic Post Office, this contemporary wine bar serves a long list of wines and beer accompanied by tapas plates of prawns, *patatas bravas* (spicy potatoes) and cheesy croquettes. The friendly staff, indoor-outdoor seating and rowdy scene, especially on big football nights, have made it a popular local hangout.

Mercury's
PUB

(Map p84; ☏ 024-223 3076; Mizingani Rd; ☺9.30am-midnight) A very popular place for waterside sundowners watching local football matches on the beach. International football is also screened here and there's live music on Saturday evenings until 1am. Food is served and consists of crowd-pleasers such as pizza, pasta and seafood grills. During Ramadan opening hours are 6pm to midnight.

Africa House Hotel
BAR

(Map p84; www.theafricahouse-zanzibar.com; Shangani St) With an enviable front-row view of the sunset, the terrace bar of the Africa House Hotel – once the British Club – is a perennially popular place for sundowners.

Tatu Pub
BAR

(Map p84; ☏ 0778 672772; Shangani St; ☺10-1am) This place has a well-stocked pub on the 1st floor, a pub-style restaurant on the 2nd floor (meals Tsh8,000 to 20,000), and a rooftop cocktail lounge on the 3rd floor where you can soak in ocean views.

Mcheza Bar
BAR

(Map p78; ☏ 024-225 0117; www.mtonirest aurant.com; Mtoni Marine, Bububu Rd) Mtoni Marine's beachside sports bar draws mainly an expat crowd. Six satellite TVs, two of them big screens, broadcast an endless diet of football accompanied by cold beers, burgers and South African steaks.

TAARAB MUSIC

No visit to Zanzibar would be complete without spending an evening listening to the evocative strains of *taarab*, the archipelago's most famous musical export. *Taarab*, from the Arabic *tariba* (roughly, 'to be moved'), fuses African, Arabic and Indian influences, and is considered by many Zanzibaris to be a unifying force among the island's many cultures. A traditional *taarab* orchestra consists of several dozen musicians using both Western and traditional instruments, including the violin, the *kanun* (similar to a zither), the accordion, the *nay* (an Arabic flute) and drums, plus a singer. There's generally no written music, and songs – often with themes centred on love – are full of puns and double meanings.

Taarab-style music was played in Zanzibar as early as the 1820s at the sultan's palace, where it had been introduced from Arabia. However, it wasn't until the 1900s, when Sultan Seyyid Hamoud bin Muhammed encouraged formation of the first *taarab* clubs, that it became more formalised.

One of the first clubs founded was Akhwan Safaa, established in 1905 in Zanzibar Town. Since then other clubs have sprung up, including the well-known Culture Musical Club. In traditional clubs, men and women sit separately, with the women decked out in their finest garb and elaborate hairstyles. Audience participation is key, and listeners frequently go up to the stage to give money to the singer.

☆ Entertainment

Entertainment Zanzibari-style centres on traditional music and dance performances.

Dhow Countries Music Academy   TAARAB
(Map p84; ☎0777 416529; www.zanzibar music.org; Old Customs House, Mizingani Rd; concerts Tsh10,000; ⊙9am-6pm) Zanzibar's celebrated music genre, *taarab* is a form of mellifluously sung poetry. The tradition is kept alive by this dynamic academy, which trains next-generation masters and hosts weekly *taarab* concerts as well as a lively program of Afro-jazz and fusion bands. If you like what you hear you can always take a lesson. Concerts start at 7pm and CDs are on sale.

Old Fort   DANCE
(Map p84; admission Tsh6000) On Tuesday, Thursday and Saturday evenings from 7pm to 10pm there are traditional *ngoma* (dance and drumming) performances at the Old Fort.

Shopping

Mall shopping can't compare with treasure hunting in Stone Town's medina. All those kiosks hawking Kenyan sculptures are just there to throw less dedicated shoppers off the scent of major scores such as painstakingly woven *ukili* (plaited date palm leaves) bags, cool, contemporary jewellery and African designer fashion. Shopping here is also a great way to make a sizeable contribution to the local economy and support traditional handicrafts.

In terms of bargaining, there are no hard and fast rules. Traders in the market and in smaller tourist shops will offer bigger or smaller bargains depending on how slow trade is. As a rule of thumb start negotiations at half of the offered price and work your way up. In Western-style shops, or shops supporting local co-operatives, prices are fixed.

A good place to start is Gizenga St, which is lined with small shops and craft dealers.

Doreen Mashika   FASHION
(Map p84; ☎0767 369777; www.doreenmashika. com; 267 Hurumzi St) For Zanzibari high fashion head to this store on Hurumzi St. Trained in Switzerland, Doreen's signature style effortlessly combines African prints and materials (horn, beads, leather, silk and silver) with European designs. Her beaded collars and cuffs, printed pencil skirts, horn-and-silver necklaces and Chanel-style bags in loud African prints are sure to steal the show back home.

Any outfit can be made to measure within two to three days, and an online shop is in the offing.

Upendo Means Love   CLOTHING
(Map p84; ☎0772 744086; www.upendomeans love.com; off Kenyatta Rd) This unique interfaith women's project aims to build bridges between Zanzibar's minority Christians and the largely Muslim population, through its

multifaith sewing school and fashionable boutique. The result: stylish, pared-down ladies' and children's summerwear in funky kanga and *kikoi* fabrics, and cross-cultural friendships and economic independence. Resident Danish fashion students help keep the line fresh and full of on-trend ideas.

Fahari
ACCESSORIES

(Map p84; ☎0714 541537; www.fahari-zanzibar. com; 62 Kenyatta Rd) ✐ Fashionable Fahari combines the cutting-edge expertise of accessories designer Julie Lawrence and traditional Zanzibari skills in weaving, sewing and leatherwork. The result is eye-catching bags in leather and *ukili,* delicate oyster-shell jewellery (sourced from Menai Bay) and floating kaftans fit for a spice island honeymoon. All design and manufacture are carried out in the workshop, which you can peak in as you browse; and the more you buy the better you'll feel as employees enjoy a share of the profits.

Sasik
HANDICRAFTS

(Map p84; ☎0773 132100; Gizenga St) The bold applique cushions, coverlets and throws in Sasik are the work of self-taught Saada Abdullah Suleiman and a team of over 45 Zanzibari women. Their intricate vegetal designs in bright primary colours are influenced by typical Swahili and Arabian patterns, many of them originating in the carved doors around Stone Town. Buy off the shelf or order bespoke designs and colour schemes.

Surti & Sons
ACCESSORIES

(Map p84; ☎0777 472742; http://surtiandsons. wordpress.com; Gizenga St) For over 30 years, Parvin Surti and his family have been shoeing Zanzibaris in beautiful, durable leather sandals (US$25 to US$35) in a range of understated styles in soft, natural colours. All the sandals are handstitched and made from good-quality leather, and great attention is shown to comfort and customer satisfaction. Belts and bags are also available.

Zenji Boutique
ARTS & CRAFTS

(Map p84; ☎0777 247243; www.zenjizanzibar.com; Malawi Rd; ⏰8am-8pm) ✐ A well-curated showcase of eclectic Zanzibari and Tanzanian crafts displayed with details of their provenance and production. Kit yourself out with upcycled beach bags made out of rice sacks or dhow sails, metalwork sculpture, pretty 'bead' jewellery made from recycled plastics or paper and more. It's all beautifully displayed in a dedicated gallery beside the Zenji Cafe.

Moto Handicrafts
HANDICRAFTS

(Map p84; www.motozanzibar.wordpress.com; Hurumzi St) ✐ This island-wide handicraft co-operative aims to support the island's rural economy by providing a platform for the sale of handcrafted *ukili* bags, sun hats, baskets, mats and other woven products. The cooperative itself is based in Pete, where it also has a small shop selling bright batik wraps in vegetable dyes.

For a greater insight into the skill involved in *ukili* and batik printing, take its Craft & Culture Tour (US$25 per person for groups of two, $15 per person for groups of four).

Saifa
CLOTHING

(Map p84; http://sites.google.com/site/saifashop/; Kelele Sq) Owned by tailor Omar Mrisho, Saifa is a one-stop shop for T-shirts, fabric bags, wallets and accessories, all made out of African fabrics such as kanga, *kitenge* or batik.

Zanzibar Gallery
SOUVENIRS

(Map p84; ☎024-223 2721; http://zanzibargallery.net; cnr Kenyatta Rd & Gizenga St; ⏰9am-6.30pm Mon-Sat, to 1pm Sun) This long-standing gallery has a fine collection of souvenirs, textiles, woodcarvings, antiques and more.

Kanga Kabisa
CLOTHING

(Map p84; www.kangakabisa.com; off Kenyatta Rd) If you're crazy for the bright and colourful kanga-wraps worn by Swahili women then head to this one-stop shop for adult and children's clothing fashioned out of kanga cloth. Styles are simple and vaguely retro, and perfect for beachwear. Diagonally opposite Africa House Hotel.

Gallery Bookshop
BOOKS

(Map p84; 48 Gizenga St; ⏰9am-6pm Mon-Sat, to 2pm Sun) A large selection of books and maps, including travel guides.

❶ Information

DANGERS & ANNOYANCES

While Zanzibar remains a relatively safe place, robberies and muggings do occur, notably in Zanzibar Town. The most high-profile incident to hit the international headlines was an acid attack on two volunteer teachers, which took place in August 2013. So far no one has been arrested and the motives for the attack are unclear as both girls were wearing full-length clothes and no jewellery.

Follow the normal precautions: avoid isolated areas, especially isolated stretches of beach, and leave your valuables in a hotel safe. At night in Zanzibar Town, take a taxi or walk in a group. Should your passport be stolen, get a written report from the police. Upon presentation of this report, immigration will issue you a travel document that will get you back to the mainland.

If you've rented a bicycle or motorcycle, be prepared for stops at checkpoints, where traffic police may demand a bribe. Assuming your papers are in order, the best tactic is respectful friendliness.

INTERNET ACCESS

Most hotels, and some cafes and restaurants, now offer wi-fi. It doesn't always work well in historic buildings due to the thick walls and weak signal.

Azzurri Internet Café (Map p84; New Mkunazini Rd; per hr Tsh1000; ☺8.30am-8.30pm) Around the corner from the Anglican cathedral.

Shangani Post Office Internet Café (Map p84; Kenyatta Rd; per hr Tsh1000; ☺8am-4.30pm Mon-Fri, 8am-12.30pm Sat) Also international telephone calls.

MEDICAL SERVICES

There are several private medical centres in Zanzibar Town (consultations US$30 to US$50) and top-end hotels usually have an internationally trained doctor on call for a fee, but anything serious should be treated in Dar es Salaam.

Shamshu & Sons Pharmacy (Map p84; ☎0715 411480, 024-223 2199; Market St; ☺9am-8.30pm Mon-Thu & Sat, 9am-noon & 4-8.30pm Fri, 9am-1.30pm Sun) Convenient, reasonably well stocked pharmacy behind the Darajani Market.

Zanzibar Medical & Diagnostic Centre (Map p84; ☎0777 750040, 024-223 1071; off Vuga Rd; ☺24hr emergency) The best private clinic on the island.

Zanzibar Medical Group (Map p84; ☎024-223 3134; Kenyatta Rd) Private clinic in the centre of town; slightly cheaper than Zanzibar Medical & Diagnostic Centre.

MONEY

There are several ATMs in Stone Town (though none elsewhere), mostly located on Kenyatta Rd, New Mkunazini Rd and Shangani St; all accept Visa and MasterCard. There are also numerous forex bureaus (most open until 8pm) where you can change cash. Rates for US dollars are better than those for British pounds and euros. Officially, accommodation on Zanzibar must be paid for in US dollars, and prices are quoted in dollars, but especially at the budget places it's

rarely a problem to pay the equivalent in Tanzanian shillings.

POST & TELEPHONE

Shangani Post Office (Map p84; Kenyatta Rd; ☺8am-12.30pm & 2-4.30pm Mon-Fri, to 12.30pm Sat) Operator-assisted calls from Tsh1500 per minute; Skype Tsh2000 per hour.

TOURIST INFORMATION

Mambo Magazine (www.mambomagazine.com) has lots of background and events info for the Zanzibar Archipelago.

Zanzibar Tourist Corporation (ZTC; Map p84; Creek Rd; ☺8am-5pm) About 200m north of Darajani Market on the same side of the road, with tourist information and standard tours.

TOUR OPERATORS & TRAVEL AGENCIES

Tour operators and agencies can help with island excursions and plane and ferry tickets. Only make bookings inside the offices, and not with anyone outside claiming to be staff.

❶ Getting There & Away

AIR

Coastal Aviation and ZanAir have daily flights connecting Zanzibar with Dar es Salaam (US$70), Arusha (US$265), Pemba (US$95), Selous Game Reserve and the northern parks. Coastal Aviation goes daily to/from Tanga via Pemba (US$120), and has good-value day-excursion packages from Dar es Salaam to Stone Town. Tropical Air flies daily between Zanzibar and Dar es Salaam, and Precision Air has connections to Nairobi (Kenya).

Coastal Aviation (Map p84; ☎024-223 3489, airport 024-223 3112; www.coastal.cc) At the airport, with a booking agent next to Zanzibar Serena Inn.

Kenya Airways (Map p84; ☎024-223 4520/1; www.kenya-airways.com; Bububu Rd, Mlandege) Just north of town in the Muzamil Centre.

Precision Air (Map p84; ☎0786 300418, 024-223 5126; www.precisionairtz.com; Bububu Rd, Mlandege) Located in the Muzamil Centre, north of Zanzibar Town

ZanAir (Map p84; ☎024-223 3678, 024-223 3670; www.zanair.com; Migombani St) Located with affiliated ZanTours.

BOAT

You can get tickets at the port (the ticket office is just to the right when entering the main port gate), or through travel agents. The departure and arrivals areas for the ferry are a few hundred metres down from the port gate along Mizingani Rd. If you leave Zanzibar on the night ferry, take care with your valuables, especially when the boat docks in Dar es Salaam.

Dhows link Zanzibar with Dar es Salaam, Tanga, Bagamoyo and Mombasa (Kenya). Foreigners are not permitted on dhows between Dar es Salaam and Zanzibar.

Azam Marine (☑ Dar es Salaam 022-212 3324, Zanzibar 024-223 1655; www.azammarine. com) Operates the most reliable scheduled service between Dar es Salaam, Zanzibar and Pemba aboard a fleet of fast, modern catamarans. There are four daily services from Dar to Zanzibar (VIP/adult/child US$40/35/25) and two weekly services from Zanzibar to Pemba (VIP/adult/child US$40/35/25).

Scheduled departures on all routes are subject to weather conditions and can change with little notice.

ⓘ Getting Around

TO/FROM THE AIRPORT

The airport is about 7km southeast of Zanzibar Town. A taxi to/from the airport costs Tsh15,000. Dalla-dalla 505 also does this route (Tsh500, 30 minutes), departing from the corner opposite Mnazi Mmoja hospital. Many Stone Town hotels offer airport pick-ups for confirmed bookings for a fee. For hotels elsewhere on the island, transfers usually cost about US$25 to US$50, depending on the location.

CAR & MOTORCYCLE

It's easy to arrange car, moped or motorcycle rental and prices are reasonable, although breakdowns are fairly common, as are moped accidents. Considering how small the island is, it's often not that much more expensive to work out a good deal with a taxi driver.

You'll need either an International Driving Permit (IDP; together with your home licence), a licence from Kenya (Nairobi), Uganda or South Africa, or a Zanzibar driving permit; there are police checkpoints along the roads where you'll be asked to show one or the other. Zanzibar permits can be obtained on the spot from the traffic police (located at the corner of Malawi and Creek Rds). If you rent through a tour company, it'll sort out the paperwork.

Daily rental rates average from about US$25 for a moped or motorcycle, and US$40 to US$55 for a Suzuki 4WD, excluding petrol. Full payment is required at the time of delivery, but don't pay any advance deposits.

Asko Tours & Travel (Map p84; ☑ 024-223 4715, 0777 411854; www.askotours.com; Kenyatta Rd) Offers reasonable rates for car hire.

DALLA-DALLAS

Open-sided dalla-dallas piled with people link all major towns on the island. For most destinations, including the beaches, there are several vehicles daily, with the last ones back to Stone Town departing by about 3pm or 4pm. None of

the routes cost more than Tsh2000, and all take plenty of time (eg between one and 1½ hours from Zanzibar Town to Jambiani). All have destination signboards and numbers. Commonly used routes include the following:

ROUTE NO	DESTINATION
116	Nungwi
117	Kiwengwa
118	Matemwe
206	Chwaka
214	Uroa
308	Unguja Ukuu
309	Jambiani
310	Makunduchi
324	Bwejuu
326	Kizimkazi
501	Amani
502	Bububu
505	Airport ('U/Ndege')

PRIVATE MINIBUS

Private tourist minibuses run daily to the north- and east-coast beaches and are cheaper than hotel transfers and taxis, which routinely cost US$50. Book through any travel agency the day before you want to leave, and the minibus will pick you up at your hotel in Stone Town at 8am. Travel takes from one to 1½ hours to most destinations, and costs Tsh10,000 per person. Return buses depart Nungwi at 9.30am and Paje, Bwejuu and Jambiani at 10am.

TAXI

Taxis don't have meters, so you'll need to agree on a price with the driver before getting into the car. Town trips cost from Tsh3000, more at night.

Offshore Islands

Popular day trips and snorkelling excursions are possible to most of the offshore islands within view of Stone Town. They cost roughly US$25 to US$30 per person for a half-day excursion with lunch included with a licensed tour operator. Boats depart every morning (weather permitting) from the beach by the Big Tree on Mizingani Rd and outside the Tembo House Hotel. If you choose to visit the islands with unlicensed operators who tout for business along the waterfront, bear in mind that safety equipment is likely to be inadequate and boats may be overloaded. Also, if anything goes wrong there is no way to get your money back.

All the islands within reach of Stone Town also have exclusive island lodges, although if you base yourself here, keep in mind that it's not possible to travel between Stone Town and the islands after dark, and factor in the costs of transport to/from Stone Town.

Islands that are further afield, such as Chumbe, Tumbatu and Mnemba, are reached from Mbweni, Mkokotoni and Matemwe respectively.

Changuu

Also known as Prison Island, Changuu lies about 5km northwest of Zanzibar Town. It was originally used to detain 'recalcitrant' slaves and later as a quarantine station. Changuu is also known for its large family of giant tortoises, who were brought here from Aldabra in the Seychelles around the turn of the 20th century. There's a small beach and a nearby reef with snorkelling, as well as the former house of the British governor, General Lloyd Matthews. While day trippers are confined to the ruins and the tortoise sanctuary, guests at the island lodge have the run of nature trails snaking through the forest and a small beach.

Day trips to visit the tortoises cost about US$30 per person including lunch and island entry fee, but excluding boat transfer costs from Stone Town (usually around US$60 to US$70 for a boat).

🛏 Sleeping

Changuu Private Island Paradise   LODGE $$$
(📞0773 333241; www.privateislands-zanzibar.com; Changuu Island; full board per person US$350; ❄) Fifteen rustic-deluxe thatched cottages make up this island lodge. All are brightly decorated and sport small verandahs and outdoor showers. The restaurant is in General Matthews' restored colonial house and serves fancy four-course dinners; there's also a pool and a floodlit tennis court in the forest.

Rates include airport transfers.

Chapwani

This tiny, privately owned island (also known as Grave Island, thanks to its small cemetery and the tombs of colonial-era British seamen) is about 4km north of Zanzibar Town. It has a white-sand beach backed by indigenous forest which is home to some fruit bats and duikers. The island can only be visited if you're staying or dining at the lodge. Advance bookings are required for both. As

Chapwani is a waterless island, all fresh water must be pumped in from Zanzibar.

🛏 Sleeping

Chapwani Island Lodge   LODGE $$$
(www.chapwaniisland-zanzibar.com; half-board per person US$176-198; ☉ Jun-Mar; ❄) Eleven simple, whitewashed cottages are set just back from the beach and offer a laid-back escape from Stone Town. Guests spend their days dreaming on day beds or exploring the barnacle-clad reef and bird-filled forest. To break up this paradisal monotony there's a free daily shuttle to Zanzibar Town.

Bawe

Tiny Bawe, about 7km west of Zanzibar Town and several kilometres southwest of Changuu, offers a beach and snorkelling. For years marketed as a day out from Stone Town, it's now privately owned, and while snorkelling in the surrounding waters is possible, the island itself can only be visited by guests of Bawe Tropical Island Lodge (📞0773 333241; www.privateislands-zanzibar.com; Bawe Island; full board per person US$400; ❄).

Tumbatu

The large and seldom-visited island of Tumbatu, just off Zanzibar's northwest coast, is populated by the Tumbatu people, one of the three original tribal groups on the archipelago. Although Tumbatu's early history is unknown, ruins of a mosque have been found at the island's southern tip that may date to the early 11th century. As recently as the last century, there were no water sources on Tumbatu and villagers had to come over to the mainland for supplies.

There's no accommodation, but Tumbatu can be visited as a day trip from Kendwa or Nungwi. Alternatively, local boats sail throughout the day between Tumbatu and Mkokotoni village, which lies just across the channel on Zanzibar, and which is known for its bustling fish market. The trip takes from 30 minutes to three hours, depending on the winds, and costs about Tsh200. Residents of Tumbatu aren't used to tourists (they are actually notorious for their lack of hospitality) so if you're heading over on your own, it's best to get permission first from the police station in Mkokotoni, or from the *she-he* (village chief) in Nungwi, who will probably request a modest fee. There's at least one bus daily between Mkokotoni and Stone

Town. Once on Tumbatu, the main means of transport are bicycle (ask around by the dock) and walking.

Mnemba

Tiny Mnemba island, just northeast of Matemwe, is the ultimate tropical paradise for those who have the money to enjoy it, complete with white sands, palm trees and turquoise waters. While the island itself is privately owned, with access restricted to guests of Mnemba Island Lodge, the surrounding coral reef can be visited by anyone. It's one of Zanzibar's prime **diving** and **snorkelling** sites, with a huge array of fish, including tuna, barracuda, moray eels, reef sharks and lots of colourful smaller species.

🛏 Sleeping

Mnemba Island Lodge   LODGE $$$
(☑ 027-252 4199; www.andbeyond.com/mnemba-island/; Mnemba Island; full board per person US$1200-1600; ⊗ mid-May–Mar) This exclusive island lodge is a playground for the rich and famous, and is often rented out in its entirety.

Other Islets

Just offshore from Zanzibar Town are several tiny islets, many of which are ringed by coral reefs. These include **Nyange**, **Pange** and **Murogo**, which are sandbanks that partially disappear at high tide, and which offer snorkelling and diving (arranged through Stone Town dive operators).

Bububu (Fuji Beach)

This modest, undistinguished stretch of sand, 10km north of town in Bububu, is the closest place to Zanzibar Town for swimming, though if you're after a beach holiday, it's better to head further north or east. It's accessed via the small track heading west from just north of the Bububu police station.

🛏 Sleeping

★ Mangrove Lodge   LODGE $$
(☑ 0777 436954, 0777 691790; www.mangrovelodge.com; Chiuni; s US$40-50, d US$80-100; 🐾) One of only four eco-accredited lodges on the island, lovely Mangrove is owned by former guide Haji and his Italian partner Paola. Their gentle life philosophy imbues the idyllic spot on the edge of the Chuini Bay where Sultan Barghash once spent his weekends. Sandy lanes lead through tropical gardens to 10 spacious bungalow rooms with double-aspect windows, comfortable beds and large, tiled bathrooms. The *makuti*-thatched lounge overlooking the bay is the focus of lodge life, that and lazy days spent on unspoilt Mwawimbini beach.

Haji and Paola are heavily invested in the locale; their staff come from Chuini, where they have funded a dispensary, and they encourage friendly interaction with bike rides to nearby spice plantations and fishing trips with local fishermen. They also encourage guests to 'Pack for a Purpose' (www.packforapurpose.org).

It's 14.5km north of Stone Town, several kilometres west off the main road just north of Bububu. Transfers can be arranged.

Mangapwani

The small and unremarkable beach at Mangapwani is notable mainly for its nearby caves, and is frequently included as a stop on spice tours.

The caves are located about 20km north of Zanzibar Town along the coast, and are an easy walk from Mangapwani beach. There are actually two locations. The first is a large **natural cave** with a freshwater pool that is rumoured to have been used in connection with the slave trade. North of here is the sobering **slave cave**, a dank, dark cell that was used as a holding pen to hide slaves after the legal trade was abolished in the late 19th century.

To get to the beach, follow the main road north from Zanzibar Town past Bububu to **Chuini**, from where you head left down a dirt road for about 8km towards Mangapwani village and the beach. Dalla-dallas also run between Stone Town and Mangapwani village, from where it's a short walk to the beach. Just before the Serena Club, there's a small sign for the caves, or ask locals to point the way.

🍴 Eating

Mangapwani Serena Beach Club   SEAFOOD
(☑ 024-223 3051; set lunch with round-trip transport US$50; ⊗ lunch) There are no facilities at Mangapwani other than the Serena Beach Club, with a bar and a set grilled seafood lunch. Loungers are located under the palms for post-prandial snoozes.

WORTH A TRIP

CHUMBE ISLAND CORAL PARK

The uninhabited island of Chumbe, about 12km south of Zanzibar Town, has an exceptional shallow-water coral reef along its western shore that abounds with fish life. Since 1994, when the reef was gazetted as Zanzibar's first marine sanctuary, the island has gained widespread acclaim, including from the UN, as the site of an impressive ecotourism initiative centred on an ecolodge and local environmental education programs. It's now run as **Chumbe Island Coral Park** (www.chumbeilsand.com), a private, nonprofit nature reserve.

The fine state of Chumbe's reef is due largely to the fact that from the 1960s it was part of a military zone and off limits to locals and visitors. In addition to nearly 200 species of coral, the island's surrounding waters host about 370 species of fish and groups of dolphins who pass by to feed on the abundant fish life. The island also provides a haven for hawksbill turtles, and more than 50 species of birds have been recorded, including the endangered roseate tern.

Chumbe can be visited as a day trip, although staying overnight in one of the **eco-bungalows** (☑024-223 1040; www.chumbeisland.com; Chumbe Island; full board per person $280; @) ✈ is recommended. Each bungalow has its own rainwater collection system and solar power, and a loft sleeping area that opens to the stars. Advance bookings are essential. Day visits (also by advance arrangement only) cost US$90 per person. Boats depart from Mbweni Ruins Hotel (p91) at 10am.

Nungwi

This large village at Zanzibar's northernmost tip is a dhow-building centre and one of the island's major tourist destinations. Nungwi is also where the traditional and modern knock against each other with full force. Fishing and dhow-building are the centuries-old trade here, yet you only need to take a few steps back from the waterfront to enter another world, with blaring music and a motley collection of guesthouses, interspersed with five-star hotels. For some travellers it's the only place to be on the island (and it's one of the few places you can swim throughout the day); others will probably want to give it a miss.

◉ Sights & Activities

Other than diving, snorkelling, fishing and an array of other watersports activities, you can watch the dhow-builders, take a guided village tour, extend your yoga practice and visit the aquarium. The lighthouse, which dates to 1886, is still in use and not open to the public.

Mnarani Aquarium AQUARIUM
(☑0777 496569; admission US$5; ⊙9am-6pm) Traditionally Zanzibar's turtles have been hunted for their meat but in 1993, with the encouragement of conservationists, the villagers of Nungwi opened this sanctuary in a natural tidal pool near the lighthouse. Now

fishermen who end up with a turtle in their net are paid a small fee to bring them here, while nests on Nungwi beaches are monitored and protected. A logbook is kept and every year hatchlings are released into the sea in February.

Proceeds from the entrance fees are reinvested into the scheme and the village, hopefully demonstrating the benefits of turtle conservation. On weekends, children from schools in Matemwe, Kiwengwa and Uroa (where turtles are still hunted) are brought to the aquarium as part of an outreach program.

Cultural Village Tour CULTURAL TOUR
(per person US$15) Adjacent to the aquarium you can sign up for village tours, which last two hours and are a great way to see the village, its dhow-builders and thriving fish market. Best of all, the volunteer who accompanies you offers interesting insights into local life and answers questions about the skills and techniques used in the dhow-building. Note, most dhow-builders don't like their picture being taken so always ask permission first.

Nungwi Cycling Adventures CULTURAL TOUR
(☑0778 677662; www.zanzibarcyclingadventures. com; per person US$25-40) Get away from the beach with these off-road tours to rural villages, Portuguese ruins and coral caves filled with stalactites. One tour visits the blacksmiths in Kilimani while another traverses

rice plantations to lunch on beaches known only to locals. A minimum of three people is required.

ZanziYoga YOGA
(☑0776 310227; www.yogazanzibar.com; per person US$20) Centre yourself with morning (8am) and evening (5.15pm) yoga practice with Marisa van Vuuren at Flame Tree Cottages. The Hatha Yoga practise is suitable for all levels and focuses on breathing techniques, posture and reiki. Recently Marisa has joined forces with Divine Diving (www.scubazanzibar.com) at Amaan Bungalows, combining the efficient breathing practise of yoga with diving.

Spanish Dancer Dive Centre DIVING
(☑0777 417717; www.spanishdancerdivers.com; 2/6 dives US$132/320) Based in a breezy rondaval at the southern end of the beach, Spanish Divers is a big, friendly five-star PADI outfit with five instructors teaching courses in a dedicated classroom in seven languages. Fast boats whisk divers to Mnemba, Tumbatu and, weather permitting, to waters just south of Pemba. There's also a live-aboard diving option in *Julia*, a gorgeous 50ft catamaran (six to eight people maximum).

East Africa Diving & Water Sport Centre DIVING
(☑0777 420588; www.diving-zanzibar.com; 2/4 dives US$110/190) Nungwi's oldest diving outfit is located on the beach in front of Jambo Brothers Bungalows. It's five-star PADI accredited, and has two fast, inflatable boats carrying a maximum of 14 divers with two instructors. Mnemba, Tumbatu and Hunga are all frequent dive sites. Tanks are smaller here, which may suit female divers better.

Zanzibar Watersports DIVING
(☑0773 235030; www.zanzibarwatersports.com; 2/6 dives US$100/295) This long-term Nungwi PADI outlet is located at Paradise Beach Bungalows. Dive sites are predominantly on the western side of the island and boats accommodate up to 20 divers. Snorkelling, kayaks, dhow cruises and wakeboarding are also offered.

Kiteboarding Zanzibar KITEBOARDING
(☑0779 720259; www.kiteboardingzanzibar.com) Nungwi's only kitesurfing centre is IKO certified and equipped with Cabrinha, Dakine and NPX kit. It also has a kite mobile to transfer surfers to Matemwe. The best wind conditions are between January and February and June and July. Proof of certification is required.

Zanzibar Parasailing WATER SPORTS
(www.zanzibarparasailing.com; solo/tandem US$80/120) Offers solo and tandem flights along with other thrill-seeking watersports such as waterskiing, wakeboarding and banana-boating.

🛏 Sleeping & Eating

Most hotels and the centre of all the action are just north and west of Nungwi village, where it gets quite crowded and there's plenty of activities. If partying isn't your scene, there are some lovely, quiet stretches of sand on Nungwi's eastern side where swimming is more tidal. Most of Nungwi's hotels have restaurants, and in the village there are several shops with basics.

🛏 West Nungwi

Safina Bungalows GUESTHOUSE $
(☑0777 415726; www.newsafina.com; s/d/tr from US$30/50/70) Safina is a decent budget choice, with no-frills bungalows around a small garden, just in from the beach in the centre of Nungwi, and meals in a double-storey pavilion. Seven of the 25 rooms have air-con.

Baraka Beach Bungalows BUNGALOW $
(☑0777 422910, 0777 415569; http://barakabungalow.atspace.com; s/d US$35/50) Small and friendly, Baraka has nine no-frills stone-and-thatch cottages with ensuite bathrooms around a tiny well-kept garden. There's also a restaurant, serving pizza and curries, where you can bury your toes in the sand.

Nungwi Guest House GUESTHOUSE $
(☑0772 263322; http://nungwiguesthouse.tripod.com; Nungwi village; d/tr US$35/40) A good budget option in the village centre, with simple, clean ensuite rooms around a small garden courtyard, all with fans. There's no food. Spot it by the walls painted with light-blue fish.

Union Beach Bungalows BUNGALOW $
(☑0776 583412; http://unionbungalow.atspace.com; s/d from US$40/50; ❄🖥📶) Very simple no-frills bungalows plus rooms in a two-storey block, some with air-con and fridge. Meals are available at the Blue Wimbi restaurant.

Paradise Beach Bungalows   HOTEL **$$**
(📞 0773 203786, 0778 677691; www.nungwi
paradisebungalows.com; dm US$20, s/d/tr
US$35/60/75) This large, busy two-storey
block has 19 plain rooms, including some
dorm beds. All have fans and hot water, and
there's a restaurant. Only consider staying
here if you want to be in the thick of things,
as it's next to a noisy restaurant and there's
nowhere to chill.

Langi-Langi Beach Bungalows   HOTEL **$$**
(📞 0733 911000, 024-224 0470; www.langilangi
zanzibar.com; s US$90 d US$100-180; ❄@🐾) A
flashpackers place with 32 comfortably furnished rooms in a neat multistorey complex
overlooking the beach. There's a small pool
in a flowering courtyard, a massage deck, an
internet cafe and a well-regarded restaurant
serving Swahili dishes and excellent curries.
If you like what you eat you can even take a
cookery course.

Flame Tree Cottages   B&B **$$**
(📞 0777 479429, 024-224 0100; www.flametree
cottages.com; s/d US$120/170; ❄🛜🐾) The
cosy Flame Tree offers simply but thought-
fully furnished cottages in a flowering gar-
den with a small pool. It's a perfect secluded
spot for families or romancing couples in a
quieter spot on the northeastern edge of
Nungwi. Breakfast is served on your veran-
dah; dinner can be arranged with advance
order. In the evenings ZanziYoga (p102)
takes place on one of the flat roofs overlook-
ing the beach.

Smiles Beach Hotel   HOTEL **$$**
(📞 0774 444334, 0773 444105; www.smilesbeach
hotel.com; s/d/tr US$110/140/180; ❄🛜) Smiles,
at the quieter edge of west Nungwi, has
well-maintained, well-appointed rooms in
somewhat stern-looking two-storey blocks
overlooking a patch of beach. They're good
value, all with small sea-facing balconies,
and with more space and quiet than at some
of the other central hotels.

Amaan Bungalows   HOTEL **$$**
(📞 0775 044719, 024-550 1152; www.amaanbunga
lows.com; s US$70-150, d US$80-160; ❄@) This
large, efficient place is at the centre of the
action. There are 86 rooms of varying size,
ranging from small garden-view with fan to
nicer, spacious sea-view rooms with air-con
and small balconies. All have hot water. Also
in the crowded complex is a waterside bar-
restaurant, internet access, moped rental,
diving and fishing outfits and a travel agency.

Z Hotel   BOUTIQUE HOTEL **$$$**
(📞 0774 266266; www.thezhotel.com; s/d from
US$170/220; ⊙mid-Jun–mid-Mar; ❄@🛜🐾)
This boutique hotel is the most upmarket
choice by far in this part of Nungwi (rivalled
only by the less-atmospheric Hilton Double-
tree). Rooms, all beautifully appointed, are in
a three-storey block overlooking an infinity
pool and the water. There's a spa, a boutique
and a branch of East Africa Diving on-site, as
well as a popular waterside restaurant.

While everything is very comfortable, the
compound lacks a feeling of space, and it's
hard to escape into a pampered five-star
mentality given the surrounding crush of
budget places.

🛏 East Nungwi

Mnarani Beach Cottages   LODGE **$$**
(📞 0777 415551, 024-224 0494; www.light
housezanzibar.com; east Nungwi; half board
s US$80-107, d US$130-200; ❄@🛜🐾) The
Mnarani is the first place you come to on the
eastern side of Nungwi, just after the light-
house (the name means 'at the lighthouse' in
Swahili). It's set on a small rise overlooking
the sea, with easy access to the narrow beach
below. Accommodation is in pleasant cottag-
es, larger family rooms or the two-storey
Zanzibar House. It is well suited to couples
and families, and has a surprising feeling of
space despite the fact that it is often fully
booked.

Sazani Beach Hotel   BUNGALOW **$$**
(📞 0776 668681, 0774 271033; www.sazanibeach.
com; s/d/tr US$80/130/160; @🛜) Sazani is a
quiet, quirky place with 10 agreeably rustic
cottages on a somewhat overgrown hillside
overlooking the sea. It's on the eastern side
of Nungwi, past Mnarani Beach cottages.
The area immediately in front is popular for
kitesurfing.

★**Ras Nungwi Beach Hotel**   HOTEL **$$$**
(📞 024-223 3767; www.rasnungwi.com; east Nung-
wi; r garden US$125-210/sea view US$175-305;
⊙Jun-Mar; ❄@🐾) This beautifully situated,
upmarket place has long been a standout in
Nungwi, with a low-key ambience, luxurious
sea-view chalets in mature tropical gardens,
and less-expensive rooms in the main lodge.
The hotel can organise fishing and water-
sports, and there's a dive centre and a spa. It's
the last (for now) hotel down on Nungwi's
eastern side, and has managed to retain an
atmosphere of quiet charm.

ℹ Information

There's an internet cafe and forex bureau at Amaan Bungalows.

Because of the large number of tourists in Nungwi, it's easy to overlook the fact that you're in a traditional, conservative environment. Be respectful, especially with your dress and your interactions with locals, and ask permission before snapping photos. Also, don't walk along the beach alone or with valuables, particularly at night.

ℹ Getting There & Away

Bus 116 runs daily between Nungwi and Zanzibar Town (Tsh2000) along a tarmac road.

Kendwa

About 3km southwest of Nungwi is Kendwa. It's a long, wonderfully wide stretch of sand, although the once-quiet ambience is now gone, thanks to a rash resort development and an almost nonstop party vibe. That said, there is more space than at Nungwi, and amenable tidal patterns mean that there is swimming at all hours.

🏃 Activities

The scene in Kendwa is all about the beach, with volleyball nets, snorkelling and dive outlets dotted along the beach. Dhow cruises, boat trips to Tumbatu and Nungwi and diving can be arranged through most hotel receptions.

★ Scuba Do DIVING
(📞 0777 417157; www.scuba-do-zanzibar.com; 2/6 dives US$120/330) Tammy and Christian's five-star Gold Palm dive center has been operating for more than 12 years and is one of the most forward-thinking and ecofriendly outfits on the island. Both are dive masters and Christian is the only Emergency First Response Instructor in Tanzania, while Tammy spearheads beach and underwater clean-up projects. Committed to the local community, they have a well-trained, professional crew of 10 dive masters and offer excellent courses and excursions.

Groups of no more than 12 dive a range of 20-plus reef sites including Mnemba, which is reached in 30 minutes in their high speed inflatables. Snorkelling trips visit both Tumbatu and Mnemba (US$45 to US$85), and they also offer budget and multiday cruises on their four-cabin catamaran.

You can find them on the beach at Sunset Kendwa.

🛏 Sleeping

Kendwa Rocks BUNGALOW $$
(📞 0777 415475; www.kendwarocks.com; dm US$17, bandas without bathroom s US$30-40, d US$40-70, bungalows s US$55-70 d US$65-115; ❄) A Kendwa classic, although it has considerably expanded from its humble beginnings. Accommodation is in no-frills beach *bandas* sharing toilets, nicer self-contained bungalows on the sand, cool stone garden cottages and suites and rooms up on the cliff top. Full-moon parties are an institution.

Sunset Kendwa BUNGALOW $$
(📞 0777 414647; www.sunsetkendwa.com; s US$65-85, d US$85-98; ❄) This long-standing place has a mix of rooms on the beach and on the cliff top, some with air-con and all with bathrooms with hot water, plus some cliff-top rooms in two-storey blocks. There's a resident dive operator and a popular beachside restaurant-bar with evening bonfires on the beach.

Les Toits du Palme BUNGALOW $$
(📞 0777 851474; www.lestoitsdepalme.com; d US$50-80, with air-con & hot water US$100; ❄) Three basic wooden beach bungalows on the sand, and six more rooms up on a small cliff. Everything's no-frills, but it's one of the few backpackers' chill spots left at Kendwa, although for how much longer is unknown as they were in discussions to sell at the time of research.

La Gemma del'Est RESORT $$$
(📞 024-224 0087; www.diamonds-resorts.com; full board per person from US$265; 🅿❄@☎≋) Kendwa's quietest, most family-friendly re-

---

TOP ZANZIBAR BEACHES

Almost all of Zanzibar's beaches would be considered superlative if they were located anywhere else, but a few stand out, even here:

Matemwe For its powdery, white sands and village life.

Kendwa Wide, white and swimmable around the clock.

Pongwe For its crystal waters and lack of crowds.

Jambiani For the otherworldly turquoise shades of its waters.

sort, with large grounds, a good beach, several restaurant-bars (including one on a jetty over the water), a gym, a spa and a huge pool.

ℹ️ Getting There & Away

You can walk to Kendwa from Nungwi at low tide in about 25 to 30 minutes, but take care as there have been some muggings. Alternatively, you can arrange boats with hotels in both Nungwi and Kendwa.

Via public transport from Stone Town, dalla-dalla 116 or bus 14 can drop you at the Kendwa turn-off, from where it's about a 2km walk to the beach. If you're driving, this access road has been graded, and is passable in 2WD, with some care needed over the rocky patches.

Matemwe

The long, idyllic beach at Matemwe has some of the finest sand on Zanzibar. In the nearby village, life moves at its own pace, with women making their way across the shallows at low tide to harvest seaweed, strings of fish drying in the sun, and chickens wandering across the road – all thousands of miles from the world of ringing mobile phones and traffic jams that most of Matemwe's visitors have left behind.

🏃 Activities

Matemwe is a quiet, traditional village and other than hanging out at the beach and watching fishermen offload their catch there aren't any sights or activities. This is a place to really switch off. It's also the best base for diving and snorkelling in the spectacular coral gardens of the **Mnemba Island Conservation Area** (p100), which lies 2.5km offshore. Other than Pemba, this is the best dive site in the archipelago and you're guaranteed to see a wonderful variety of marine life including green turtles, bottlenose dolphins and shoals of batfish, trigger fish and humpback snappers. During the migration, it's even possible to spot humpback whales.

One Ocean   DIVING
(www.zanzibaroneocean.com; Matemwe Village; 2/6 dives US$120/325; ⊙ Jun–mid-Apr) This experienced five-star PADI dive outfit is located at Matemwe Beach Village. Aside from a range of courses, it offers excellent dive trips to Mnemba with a maximum of nine divers or 16 divers and snorkellers per group. Snorkelling trips cost US$45 per person.

DADA   COOKING COURSE
(📱 0777 466304; http://dadazanzibar.wordpress.com; per person in group of 2/4 US$25/15) Stir yourself from the sunbed and head into the village for a cooking masterclass with Matemwe's *dadas*. Learn to make the perfect tomato sauce balanced with coconut and cassava leaves, or mould and mix perfect date balls and baobab jam. Classes run from 10am to 1pm and consist of a maximum of four people.

🛏 Sleeping

Key's Bungalows   BUNGALOW $
(📱 0777 411797; www.allykeys.com; s/d US$40/50) This quirky backpackers' place on the beach at the north end of Matemwe village has a chilled beach bar arranged around a dhow bar and a dart board. Nine simple rooms are located in a two-storey block. Meals are also available.

Mohammed's Restaurant & Bungalows   BUNGALOW $
(📱 0777 431881; http://mohammedsbungalows.wordpress.com; s/d/tr US$35/50/60) This establishment has four very basic ensuite bungalows, each with two large beds, in Mohammed's small garden just back from the beach. Grilled fish and other local meals can be arranged.

Matemwe Beach Village   LODGE $$
(📱 0777 437200, 0777 417250; www.matemwebeach.net; half-board per person r US$90-110, ste US$130-150; P ❋ @ 🛜 ❄) This recommended beachfront place has a low-key ambience and good-value bungalows with small verandahs. Most are on the beach, with a few more set back about 100m on a low rise. There's also a private beachfront honeymoon suite with its own plunge pool and a huge open lounge area padded with colourful pillows.

Beside the pool you'll find One Ocean dive centre.

Panga Chumvi   LODGE $$
(📱 0777 862899; www.pangachumvi.com; garden/sea view s US$110/140, d US$150/180; ⊙ Jun-Apr; @) 🕐 Lovely Panga Chumvi was the family home of Rebecca, Abdulla and Othman for many years before they converted it into this unpretentious beach haven set on a large seafront plot shaded by tall palms. Fifteen rooms are spread about the property in separate *makuti*-thatch bungalows featuring nutmeg-coloured concrete floors and

elegant coconut wood furnishings. For two months of the year an artist in residence works with villagers and guests on inspiring creative projects.

Zanzibar Retreat Hotel BOUTIQUE HOTEL $$
(☑ 0776 108379; www.zanzibarretreat.com; d garden/sea view US$135/240; ☉ Jun-Apr; ✳ @ 🛜 ☲) A well-located place on the beach with just seven smallish rooms, all well appointed and with Zanzibari beds. The main attractions, besides the lovely beachside setting, are the common areas, all with polished hardwood floors, and including an upstairs bar overlooking the beach.

Sele's Bungalows BUNGALOW $$
(☑ 0776 931690; http://selesbungalows.wix.com/zanzibar; d with/without bathroom from US$70/45, f US$120; ☉ May-Feb) This friendly, no-frills place has seven simple cottage-style rooms in a dhow-themed garden on the beach. The two family rooms (each with two double beds) are upstairs, open on one side and sharing a toilet. The others (all doubles) have private bathroom, and all have fans. There's also a small restaurant and a bar.

Green & Blue BOUTIQUE HOTEL $$$
(☑ 0774 411025; www.greenandblue-zanzibar.com; d garden US$300-306, sea view US$490-600; ☉ Jun-Apr; @ 🛜 ☲) A gorgeously designed lodge nestled in luxuriant green gardens on a rocky bluff facing off with Mnemba. Fourteen independent cottages are styled in a turquoise-and-yellow colour scheme and come with indoor and outdoor showers, and private verandahs with hammocks and plunge pools. The communal areas are just as photogenic, with a two-storey bar, restaurant and pool area projecting over the beach, and dining here is as refined as the surroundings would suggest.

In its own secluded corner, the Tulia Spa has professionally trained massage therapists and beauticians and its own private pool.

Sunshine Hotel HOTEL $$$
(☑ 0774 388662; www.sunshinezanzibar.com; s US$130-150, d US$170-230; @ 🛜 ☲) This immaculate place on a curve of white sand has 12 rooms in two-storey blocks, all with louvered doors, sunshine-yellow soft furnishings and cleverly concealed moulded bathrooms. All look over the lush garden and tempting infinity pool towards the beach. There are also two suites, a garden apartment and an excellent restaurant.

Matemwe Lodge LODGE $$$
(www.asiliaafrica.com/matemwe; ste full board US$680-1340; ☉ Jun-Easter; @ ☲) Matemwe Lodge, on the northern edge of the village, is a relaxing, upmarket place with a dozen spacious and impeccably decorated seaside bungalow suites. It has a pampered, upmarket atmosphere and receives consistently positive reviews. All the bungalows have their own verandah and hammock. Snorkelling, dhow cruises, diving, fishing, in-room massages and reef walks can all be arranged.

ℹ Information

Hyperbaric Chamber (☑ 0777 788500; www.sssnetwork.com) The island's only decompression chamber. Dr Henrik Friis Juhl serves as the medical officer.

ℹ Getting There & Away

Matemwe village is located about 25km southeast of Nungwi and is reached via a tarmac road branching east off the main road by Mkwajuni. Dalla-dallas travel here daily from Stone Town (Tsh1500). Early in the day they continue as far as the fish market at the northern end of the beach (this is where you can catch them as well). Otherwise, the start/terminus of the route is at the main junction near Matemwe Beach Village hotel.

Kiwengwa

Kiwengwa village is spread out along a fine, wide beach, and is the locus of Zanzibar's package-tourism industry. Hidden behind high walls in lushly planted gardens, most of the Italian-run resorts are all-inclusive, with guests seldom leaving the grounds. By contrast the village is poor and dusty, highlighting an uncomfortable lack of social and environmental awareness. Few resorts allow visitor access so unless you're pre-booked there's little reason to come here.

🏃 Activities

★**Maisha Mazuri**
Horse Riding Club HORSE RIDING
(per hour US$45) This well-maintained stable with 13 sleek-looking horses offers a truly unique chance to get out and experience the natural tranquility and beauty of the interior of the island. Five-hour hacks through waving rice fields, dank coral caves and tropical scrub cost US$200. Shorter rides along the beach at Kiwengwa are also possible.

🍴 Sleeping & Eating

Kiwengwa is the heart of Zanzibar's all-inclusive package-holiday industry. Lining the pristine beach, a glut of gated Italian resorts are hidden behind high walls. You won't be allowed access without a reservation or lunch booking.

Waikiki RESORT **$$**
(📞 0779 401603; www.waikikiafrica.com; r US$70-90; ☺ mid-Jun–Apr; ❄ 🛜) Run by the ebullient Flavio and his wife Sarah, Waikiki is a fun and friendly resort with 15 rooms. Flavio's Italian background means good coffee, great food (including pizza and Italian ice-cream) and a legendary Friday party (until 3am) during the summer months. There are dozens of chill-out zones, an onsite kite school, a popular beach bar and a lovely stretch of beach where, even at low tide, you can wallow in deep tidal pools. The cheapest rooms don't have air-con.

Shooting Star Lodge BOUTIQUE HOTEL **$$$**
(📞 0777 414166; www.shootingstarlodge.com; s/d garden view US$130/200, sea-view cottages US$170/300; ❄ @ 🛜) This intimate small lodge is recommended both for its location on a low cliff overlooking a beautiful, quiet beach, and for its service and cuisine. The closely spaced, impeccably decorated rooms range from three garden-view 'lodge rooms' to 11 spacious sea-view cottages and two honeymoon suites. There's also a salt-water infinity pool, and a raised beachside bar.

Bluebay Beach Resort RESORT **$$$**
(📞 024-224 0240/1; www.bluebayzanzibar.com; s/d with half-board from US$190/300; 🅿 ❄ @ 🛜) Quieter than many of its neighbours, enormous Bluebay has a large range of rooms and an expansive freshwater swimming pool. The grounds are expansive, green and serene and there is a host of activities on offer from sailing and tennis to windsurfing. There's also a spa and a fitness centre and One Ocean Dive Centre has a base here.

ℹ️ Getting There & Away

Dalla-dalla 117 runs daily between Kiwengwa village and Stone Town (Tsh1500) along the tarmac road.

Pongwe

Pongwe's quiet arc of beach is dotted with palm trees and backed by dense vegetation, and is about as close to the quintessential tropical paradise as you can get. Thanks to its position in a semi-sheltered cove, it also has the advantage of having less seaweed than other parts of the east coast. Just inland is the **Kiwengwa-Pongwe Forest Reserve** (☺ 8am-5pm) protecting indigenous coral rag forest, red colobus and other monkeys, a wealth of bird and plant species, deep coral caves and water reservoirs. There are a few short nature trails, and it's possible to enter some of the caves. Visits can be organised with Stone Town tour operators, or with Pongwe- and Kiwengwa-area hotels.

To the southeast, around the headland of Ras Uroa, is the small fishing village of **Uroa** and another stretch of Italian-owned resorts. As with the resorts at Kiwengwa they are aimed at the package-holiday market and don't permit public access without prior booking.

🍴 Sleeping & Eating

Seasons Lodge LODGE **$$**
(📞 0776 107225; www.seasonszanzibar.com; r US$165-195; @ 🛜) Eschewing palm and thatch for bungalows of coral rag and *chokaa* limestone, Seasons offers a level of comfort above many beachside hotels. Each of the seven bungalows is lined with windows with a deck over the beach and sparkling, modern bathrooms with claw-foot tubs. Thoughtful touches include torches, *kikoi*, mosquito spray and free mountain bikes and kayaks, and meals include vegetables and fruit from the garden.

★ Pongwe Beach Hotel HOTEL **$$$**
(📞 0784 336181, 0773 000556; www.pongwe.com; r US$176-250, ste US$230-300; ☺ Jun-Apr; 🅿 @ 🛜) The intimate and unassuming Pongwe Beach Hotel has 20 bungalows among the palms on a wonderful, deep arc of bleached white beach. Most rooms are sea-facing (three are garden view), spacious and breezy, the restaurant is excellent, and when you tire of the turquoise panoramas at your doorstep, there's an infinity pool, fishing and excursions to Stone Town. It's justifiably popular and often fully booked.

ℹ️ Getting There & Away

Dalla-dallas to Pongwe depart from Zanzibar Town's Mwembeladu junction; take dalla-dalla 501 from Darajani towards Amani stadium and ask to be dropped Mwembeladu (Tsh300, 10 minutes), from where you can get dalla-dalla 233 to Pongwe-Pwani (Tsh1500, one hour), and then walk the last stretch. Likewise dalla-dalla 214 runs between Mwembeladu and Uroa several times daily. A taxi or hotel transfer costs US$50.

Jozani-Chwaka Bay National Park

This cool and shady patch of green is the largest area of mature, indigenous forest left on Zanzibar. Situated inland from Chwaka Bay on low-lying land, the area is prone to flooding, which nurtures a unique swamp forest of moisture-loving trees and lush, feathery ferns. The forest is located 35km southeast of Zanzibar Town off the road to Paje, and is best reached via bus 309 or 310, by chartered taxi or with an organised tour.

Also along the main road is the entrance to the butterfly centre and, near the village of Pete, the Moto Handicrafts (p96) workshop where it hosts its Craft & Culture workshop.

◉ Sights

Jozani Forest   PARK

(☑0777 488350; adult/child with guide US$10/5; ☺7.30am-5pm) Living among Jozani's tangle of vines and branches are populations of the endangered red colobus monkey, as well as Sykes monkeys, bushbabies, Ader's duikers and more than 40 species of birds. There's a nature trail in the forest, which you can follow with an information sheet (it takes about 45 minutes to walk), and to the south a boardwalk extends deep into a creek where you can walk through wild mangroves.

When observing the monkeys, take care not to get too close (park staff recommend no closer than 3m) both for your safety and the safety of the animals. In addition to the risk of people being bitten, there's considerable concern that if the monkeys were to catch a human illness it could rapidly wipe out the already threatened population.

Tour groups visit around 9.30am and 3pm or 4pm so if you want to avoid them arrive early or late, which are also good times to see the monkeys when they are active. Drinks and simple meals are available at the on-site cafe-restaurant.

**Zanzibar
Butterfly Centre**   WILDLIFE SANCTUARY

(☑0774 224472; www.zanzibarbutterflies.com; Pete; per adult/child US$6/3; ☺10am-5pm) Along the main road about 1km before the Jozani Forest entrance is this butterfly centre, one of the largest butterfly enclosures in East Africa, with a netted garden and tours where you can see the life cycle stages of the butterfly, including some beautiful cocoons. Profits support local conservation and community projects.

Michamvi Peninsula

Curling around Chwaka Bay like a long bony finger, the 10km stretch of beach along the eastern side of the Michamvi Peninsula is the stuff of advertising posters. Fine, white, coral sand offsets a sea of extraordinary colours, merging from blue to green and the deepest sapphire. So far, hotels are spaciously strung out along the peninsula with lots of dense vegetation between them, but development has started to gather pace here, too. Luxury options can be found just north of Bwejuu, while up at the tip of the headland you'll find some spectacular midrange places.

🛏 Sleeping & Eating

Sagando Hostel   HOSTEL $

(☑0773 193236; http://sagandohostel.com; s/d/tr US$25/45/60) Just back from the beach, this is an amenable budget option, with a handful of single- and two-storey bungalows on the sand in a small, enclosed garden and meals on order.

Hotel Ras Michamvi   HOTEL $$

(☑0777 413434; www.rasmichamvi.com; s US$105-145, d US$130-180; ▣@❄) Occupying one of the most scenic locations on the island at the tip of the peninsula, Ras Michamvi sits on a bluff with expansive views. Idyllic, deserted beaches flank both sides and can be accessed via steep staircases although the views from the infinity pool are mesmerising enough. After a candlelit dinner of roast guinea fowl or grilled fish, retire to one of the thatched bungalows and dream of impossibly blue seas and coral gardens.

Kae Funk   BUNGALOW $$

(☑0777 222346, 0777 439059; www.kaefunk.com; s US$50-100, d US$70-120; @) This chilled place has a large reggae bar decorated in lots of beach flotsam, loft swings and eight double rooms perched up cliff. They're nicely decorated with simple furniture and African print fabrics and just manage a peak at the sea over the high wall that a developer has built in front of the plot. In season, the bar is a cool place to hang out, with all-day music, sundowners and spicy curry lunches (pre-booking required).

Breezes Beach Club & Spa   RESORT $$$
(✆ 0774 440883; www.breezes-zanzibar.com; half-board per person US$130-228; ❊ @ 🕾 ☃) On the east side of the peninsula near Bwejuu, this place receives consistently good reviews. Accommodation is in well-appointed rooms and suites in lovely gardens. There's diving, a gym and other activities. Advance bookings only – you won't get by the tight gate security without one.

Michamvi Sunset Bay   RESORT $$$
(✆ 0777 878136; www.michamvi.com; half-board per person US$170-210) Formerly Michamvi Watersports, this large, South African-owned resort just north of Kae village and overlooking Chwaka Bay has an array of comfortable rooms with the standard amenities, a restaurant, and – uniquely for Zanzibar's east coast – sunset views over the water.

Rock   SEAFOOD $$
(✆ 0777 835515; www.therockrestaurantzanzibar. com; Tsh15,000-25,000; ⏰ 10am-10pm) Zanzibar's most photogenic restaurant is perched on a coral outcrop in the middle of the sea just off Kijiweni Beach. At low tide you can walk out to it, otherwise you can swim or catch the boat from the beach. Unsurprisingly the menu offers a variety of fresh prawns, lobster, crab and fish. Book ahead in high season. It's opposite Upendo Beach Villa, which is signed from the road.

Upendo Beach Villa   INTERNATIONAL $$$
(✆ 0777 244492, 0777 770667; www.upendozanzibar.com; meals US$8-25) This sexy beachside bar and restaurant is the brainchild of Trish Dhanak and sits on a beautiful stretch of beach opposite the Rock. Behind the bar, Zaru, the island's best barman, mixes delightful daquiris and mocktails, while sunstunned diners lounge on turquoise *barazas* (stone benches) and beanbags around the pool. The menu is a mix of comfort classics such as burgers and beef tacos, alongside spicy curries, Indian snacks and immense seafood platters.

Set back from the restaurant, a fabulous private villa can be rented either as a whole house or as individual rooms (rooms US$200 to US$370).

❶ Getting There & Away

Dalla-dallas travel regularly from Stone Town (Tsh2000). There's also at least one dalla-dalla between Michamvi village (on the northwestern side of the peninsula) and Makunduchi (Tsh1500). Local boats cross between Mi-

chamvi village to Chwaka. Hiring one will cost from about Tsh30,000 for a sailboat (about Tsh50,000 for a motorboat).

Bwejuu

The large, dusty village of Bwejuu sits back from the beach 4km north of the main junction to Zanzibar Town. It's quieter than the party hub of Paje and the beach is nicely shaded by palms with women going about their seaweed gathering on the blistering white beach.

🍴 Sleeping & Eating

Mustapha's Place   BUNGALOW $
(✆ 0776 718808, 024-224 0069; www. mustaphasplace.com; dm US$15, r per person US$20-25) Rasta-run Mustapha's has a variety of creatively decorated rooms, some with their own bathroom and all with their own theme. Meals are taken family style, and staff can assist with bike rental, drumming lessons and other diversions. It's south of Bwejuu village, and just across the road from the beach.

⭐ **Bellevue Bungalows**   BUNGALOW $$
(✆ 0777 209576; www.bellevuezanzibar.com; s US$50-90, d US$60-100; @ 🕾) Lovely Bellevue is deservedly popular not only for its creatively decorated rooms, terrific sunrise terraces and bountiful breakfasts of local honey, pancakes and spiced juices, but also for its laid-back atmosphere and engaging hosts Melanie and Dim. Dim runs Kite Centre Zanzibar (p110) in Paje (free transfers and 10% discounts apply if you stay at Bellevue) while Melanie is the driving force behind Jenga (p110), a social enterprise enabling artisans and producers to sell their work.

Excellent food, including barbecues, sushi and Swahili dinners, and a range of unusual tours such as crab-catching with chef Chulla, make this a standout place to stay.

Upepo Boutique Beach Bungalows   BUNGALOW $$
(✆ 0784 619579; www.zanzibarhotelbeach.com; s/d/tr US$45/70/90) This neat, friendly place is owned by a Zanzibari-Canadian couple who work hard to maintain the homey feel of the place. Two simple bungalows house spacious rooms with comfortable beds, beamed ceilings and lazy ceiling fans. All have small terraces and views over the garden to the glorious beach. The thatched restaurant-bar is the most popular on the

beach, serving pasta, curries and fish with jugs of sangria.

Robinson's Place
GUESTHOUSE $$

(📞0777 413479; www.robinsonsplace.net; s US$30, d US$60-80) An extension to the family home of Ann and Ahmed, this *Robinson Crusoe*–style getaway has a small collection of brightly styled, quirky rooms directly on the beach. The two-storey Robinson House has an upstairs tree-house double, open to the sea and the palms. Some rooms have their own bathroom, and the shared *makuti*-thatch bathroom is spotless.

Twisted Palms Lodge
BUNGALOW $$

(📞0776 130275; www.twistedpalms.zanzibarone. com; d on hill US$35-55, on beach US$60-70) Twisted Palms offers five clean, bright cottages up on a hill just behind the road, each with one double and one twin bed. Directly on the beach are five more beachside cottages (two quads, two triples, one double). There's a dhow for excursions and seafood meals are served in its restaurant up on stilts over the water.

Kilimani Kwetu
BUNGALOW $$

(📞024-224 0235; www.kilimani.de; s/d US$45/65) Conceived as a community development project between five Germans and the villagers of Bwejuu, this is a chilled place with four simple rooms in a half-acre of sand dunes and gardens. The place is managed by Wadi and a friendly team of villagers, who also whip up good Swahili food (cookery lessons are possible). But it's not all sun and fun; previous successful funding projects have helped with the completion of a library and an adult education centre.

JENGA

Jenga (http://jengazanzibar.com) Jenga is a social enterprise aiming to offer Zanzibari entrepreneurs a platform (both online and in-store) from which to sell their handmade products. And, what products they are: vibrant clutches in colourful graphic fabrics, laptop cases made from kite sails, beaded bracelets, natural beauty products and more. It has a store opposite the Rock, next to Upendo Beach Villa, on the Michamvi Peninsula, and it hopes to open one in Paje next.

🛈 Getting There & Away

Bus 324 goes daily between Stone Town and Bwejuu, and will drop you along the main road, from where it's about 500m down to the beach.

Paje

Paje has a wide, white beach at the junction where the coastal road north to Bwejuu and south to Jambiani joins with the road from Zanzibar Town. It's quite built up, with a cluster of small-scale places on the beach and a party atmosphere. Paje is also Zanzibar's main kitesurfing centre; during the season, between December and June, the sea is filled with surfers, often so much so that it can be difficult to find a quiet spot to swim.

🏃 Activities

⭐ Seaweed Center
CULTURAL TOUR

(📞0777 107248; www.seaweedcenter.com; tour US$10) 🏴 This social enterprise enables the women of Paje to not only harvest their seaweed – which is the island's second-biggest export – but also make a healthy living out of transforming it into desirable organic soaps, scrubs and essential oils. Head to the centre in the village for a fascinating tour of their farms and the processing centre where they dry and make the soaps. You can also have a go at making soap, while recharging with a surprisingly sweet-tasting seaweed smoothie.

Bestselling take-home gifts include Pemba honey and citrus scrub, clove soap and bottles of pure coconut oil.

Kite Centre Zanzibar
KITESURFING

(www.kitecentrezanzibar.com; board & kite rental per day/week US$100/370; ⊗mid-Dec–mid-Mar & mid-Jun–mid-Oct) Affiliated with Bellevue Bungalows, this IKO-accredited outfit offers branded kites, experienced instructors and excellent courses catering to all abilities.

Airborne Kite Centre
KITESURFING

(📞0715 548464; www.airbornekitecentre.com; board & kite rental per day US$115) Offers IKO-accredited courses and private tuition for beginners up to would-be instructors. Full-moon trips and kite-surfing at Mnemba are also possible.

Harakakite
KITESURFING

(📞0777 244416; www.zanzibarkiteschool.com; ⊗Dec-Mar & mid-May-Oct) IKO-accredited courses for adults and children over the age of nine, including a beginner's discovery course for US$100.

Buccaneer Diving
DIVING, SNORKELLING

(www.buccaneerdiving.com; single dive US$50) This large five-star PADI dive center, based in the Arabian Nights hotel, offers well-structured courses in a classroom and pool. Three experienced instructors and a dive master speak six languages between them. Snorkelling at Mnemba Island is also offered (US$90).

🛏 Sleeping

Demani Lodge
LODGE $

(📞0777 460079, 0772 263115; www.demanilodge. com; dm/s/d/tr US$17/20/39/67; @⚑) Calling backpackers and beach-lovers of all stripes, this lodge is setting new standards for budget accommodation in Paje with a mix of neatly constructed *bandas* and cabins lined with *makuti*. Three of the 17 rooms are ensuite while the rest share a spotless shower block tiled in fashionable mosaic (towels require a US$10 deposit). White dressed beds, kanga curtains, a small pool and a sociable bar with a cool soundtrack make for instant success.

The only drawback: Demani is not on the beach. To get there take the road south to Jambiani and you'll see it signposted to the right of the main road.

Jambo Beach Bungalows
BUNGALOWS $

(📞0774 529960, 0772 271401; jambo.booking@ hotmail.com; dm/s/d/tr US$20/25/45/65) Run by the friendly Saidi Simba, Jambo is located on the beach just north of the village. Eight thatched bungalows and two dorm rooms (sleeping eight people) have a mix of sand and concrete floors, rustic wooden furniture, fans and mosquito nets. There's also a beach bar and simple restaurant. Even better, Jambo is located in front of Dhow Inn so when the going gets tough you can pop over and use its laundry (open to the public), and have a top-notch meal and a swim.

Kilimani Kidogo
GUESTHOUSE $$

(📞0777 201088; www.kilimakidogo.com; s/d/f US$70/180/$270; ✳🛜⚑) This fully staffed villa can either be rented in its entirety or rooms can be booked individually. Either way the friendly house-party atmosphere is a highlight, as are the well-equipped communal rooms (games, jigsaws, books, pool table), colourful ensuite bedrooms and pretty flower-filled garden and pool. The house is slightly south of Paje, on the road to Jambiani.

Kitete Beach Bungalows
HOTEL $$

(📞0772 361010; www.kitetebeach.com; s/d/tr US$60/90/110) This good-value place on the beach has 17 spacious, whitewashed rooms in double-storey bungalows on a small plot, all with ceiling fans and ocean views. It's aimed mainly at the kitesurf crowd, with equipment lockers, a pool table and a terrace restaurant overlooking the beach. Diving, snorkelling, sailing and deep-sea fishing can also be arranged.

Paje by Night
LODGE $$

(📞0777 880925; www.pajebynight.net; s/d from US$70/85; ☽ Jun–mid-Apr; ✳@🛜⚑) Located in the thick of things in the centre of Paje, this noisy place is known for its party atmosphere and has a crowded mix of no-frills standard and more spacious rooms, plus several four-person rustic 'jungle bungalows'. Air-con is available only in the larger rooms and jungle bungalows. There's a restaurant with a pizza oven and an on-site kitesurf centre, Paje by Kite.

Dhow Inn
BOUTIQUE HOTEL $$$

(📞0777 525828; www.dhowinn.com; d US$150–250; P✳🛜⚑) With its 28 architect-designed bungalows clustered around three pools and set amid sculptural gardens of bright-red canna flowers and palms, Dhow Inn is a vision of style amid Paje's rough-and-ready hotel scene. Beige-on-white interiors soothe heat-weary travellers, while the main clubhouse offer a games room, a laundry (Tsh10,000 per load), a spa, a TV room and an excellent boutique stocked with local crafts and own-brand clothes.

There's also a separate washdown area for kites and secure storage facilities, and the beach bar and grill restaurant is a popular local dining spot.

🛈 Getting There & Away

Dalla-dalla 324 runs several times daily between Paje and Stone Town (Tsh1200) en route to/ from Bwejuu. The Makunduchi–Michamvi dalla-dalla also stops at Paje.

Jambiani

Jambiani is a long village on a stunning stretch of coastline. The village itself, a sun-baked and somnolent collection of thatch and coral-rag houses, is stretched out over more than a kilometre starting just south of Paje. The sea is an ethereal shade of turquoise and is usually dotted with *ngalawa* (outrigger canoes), while on the beach women tend seaweed farms. It's quieter than Paje and Nungwi, and the village benefits from fairly good services – there's a post office, a bakery, a nursery, a primary and secondary school, and a tourism training institute – which creates a noticeable sense of community spirit. Eco + Culture (p83) also has a branch here, and offers village tours. In fact, this is probably one of the best places on the island to gain an insight into village life.

More recently coastal erosion and declining fish populations have initiated co-operation between JAMABECO (Jambiani Marine & Beach Conservation) and Marine Cultures (www.marinecultures.org) to promote conservation, create an artificial reef and explore new aquaculture projects such as sponge and sea cucumber farms. With support and sustained education Jambiani will hopefully be able to pioneer more sustainable fishing and tourism practises, which will ultimately benefit the island as a whole.

Many of the hotels contribute to the quality of life in the village, hosting local-friendly events such as free football screenings during major tournaments and festivals such as the **Water Sports Festival** (19–21 September), where proceeds go back into village projects.

🛏 Sleeping

Jambiani is pleasantly devoid of any large resorts and instead is served by a host of small-scale budget and midrange guesthouses.

⭐ **Mango Beach House**   GUESTHOUSE $
(📱 0773 498949, 0784 405391; www.mango-beach-house.com; s US$25-45, d US$35-60, house US$60-100) With only three bedrooms and a shared dining table in Kiddo's Café, Mango Beach House is a sociable place. Rooms are simple

with king-size beds, artful decor and colourful fabrics collected from Lisa's journeys around the island. The real action happens in the open-plan living area, which is like a lounge on the beach with day beds and furniture made out of driftwood.

Self-catering applies to whole house rental. And you'll need to book for lunch and dinner at Kiddo's Cafe.

Garden Bungalows   BUNGALOW $
(📱 0773 551613; www.gardenbungalows-zanzibar.com; dm US$20, s/d $35/45) These beautifully constructed bungalows with terraces and *makuti*-thatch roofs are a steal at this price. They're also located right on the beach in a tranquil spot and presided over by the creative owner, Dula. The popular bar serves pina coladas as well as *dafu* (young coconuts), fresh juices and shakes; and there's some wonderful Swahili cuisine on offer from coconut crusted fish to *pili pili* prawns (spicy prawns). Bike hire can be arranged (US$10 per day).

Jambiani Guesthouse   GUESTHOUSE $
(📱 0774 532424; www.zanzibar-guesthouse.com; d US$50, house US$150-200) Blink and you might miss this tiny bungalow with a sandy, fenced front yard and five simple double rooms (one ensuite). It's great as a house rental for groups (sleeps seven to 10) although rooms are also rented individually. It runs like a house, too, with a public access kitchen and a small sitting room. Rama manages the house and helps organise activities, while Mohammed can whip up Zanzibari feasts if required.

Al Hapa Hotel   HOTEL $
(📱 0773 048894, 0777 485842; www.alhapazanzibar.n.nu; s/d/tr $50/65/85) A simple place consisting of five beachside bungalows, a two-storey house and large beach bar. Rooms

---

SEAWEED FARMING IN ZANZIBAR

You may be forgiven for thinking that seaweed farming is a traditional island trade, so regular are the farms along Zanzibar's eastern beaches. But the practise wasn't introduced until the late 1980s, when commercial companies, in conjunction with the University of Dar es Salaam, promoted the activity on the island as a means of providing employment and promoting sustainable resource management.

However, this wasn't just a charitable endeavour: seaweed is a valuable natural product containing carrageenan, which acts as a natural gelling agent used in any number of products from toothpaste, perfume and shampoo to yoghurt, milkshakes and medicine. In fact, Zanzibar's seaweed, an estimated 12,000 tons of it in 2013, finds its way to China, Korea, Vietnam, Denmark, Spain, France and the USA, and is second only to tourism in terms of foreign-exchange earnings.

sport 1950s floor tiles, bright yellow walls, firm beds and kanga curtains, and are equipped with mosquito nets, fans and hot water. Outside hammocks are slung between palms and locals hang out at the laid-back beach bar.

★ Red Monkey Lodge   BUNGALOW $$

(🖉 0777 713366; www.redmonkeylodge.com; s/d US$72/104; 🕾) 🖋 An inspiring place run by the charming Angelo, Red Monkey has nine minimal-chic rooms overlooking the beach at the southern end of the village. It has an ethical, environmentally friendly outlook with furniture made from recycled dhows, soaps supplied by the Seaweed Centre in Paje and a free water dispenser in the restaurant. It's surrounded by protected forest and, if you're lucky, you'll see the monkeys commute along the beach while you breakfast.

There's also tons to do. There's a kitesurf school on-site and diving, snorkelling and village tours are easily arranged.

Coral Rock   HOTEL $$

(🖉 024-224 0154; www.coralrockzanzibar.com; r US$110-160; 🌐@🕾🛪) The aptly named Coral Rock is on a large coral rock jutting out into the sea at the southern end of Jambiani. Thatched bungalows have smart ethnic furnishings and air-con, while the meandering beachfront is dotted with terraces and chill-out zones as well as a gorgeous infinity pool. There are free kayaks, paddle skis and windsurf boards, and kite-surfing can be arranged with Red Monkey next door.

Blue Oyster Hotel   HOTEL $$

(🖉 0787 233610, 024-224 0163; www.blueoyster hotel.com; s US$60-110, d US$70-120; 🅿🕾) Personable and professional, Blue Oyster continues to offer good-value accommodation in Jambiani with locally furnished rooms in two-storey villas overlooking the sea. Loungers dot the beach in front and there's an open-air terrace restaurant serving plates of coconut curry and mango kingfish. You can also arrange diving excursions and tours onsite with affiliated operators.

Casa Del Mar Hotel   HOTEL $$

(🖉 024-224 0400; www.casa-delmar-zanzibar.com; d downstairs/upstairs US$96/118; 🛪) Colourful Casa del Mar brings a dash of design to Jambiani with 14 rooms in two double-storey houses set amid tropical gardens full of papaya, guava and fragrant frangipani. All the furniture and artworks were made in Jambiani and many of the staff come from the vil-

lage. Good food and conversation are to be had in the beachside restaurant where you'll find detailed information on local activities.

✗ Eating

With its strong sense of community and impressive entrepreneurial streak, Jambiani has a lively and diverse local restaurant scene.

Kim's Restaurant   ZANZIBARI $

(🖉 0777 457733; meals Tsh2000-14,000; ☺lunch & dinner) Dig your toes into the sandy floor of this palm-thatched restaurant and dig into spicy fish samosas, whole grilled fish and octopus curry. It's best to order in advance and with time to spare. Eating here is a leisurely experience. It's signposted from Blue Oyster Hotel.

Sea Horse Restaurant   SEAFOOD $

(meals Tsh5000-12,000; ☺lunch & dinner) Decorated with garlands of found shells and bright blue-and-yellow tablecloths, the Sea Horse is a jolly beachside place serving grilled fish and lobster and tasty coconut curries and calamari. In the evening lanterns cast a romantic glow over dewy-eyed honeymooners.

Kiddo's Cafe   ZANZIBARI $

(☺10am-6pm; 🖋) Sit beneath suspended dhow sails downstairs or climb to the treehouse-style upper bar decorated with interesting flotsam and bright soft furnishings. Gourmet juices are similarly colourful, combining pineapple, mango, passionfruit and coconut milk, and are accompanied by light snacks of pancakes, omelettes, salads and grilled fish. Affiliated with Mango Beachhouse; you'll need to book ahead for dinner.

Alibi's Well   INTERNATIONAL $

(🖉 0786 231988; www.handsacrossborderssociety. org; meals Tsh3000-14,000; ☺11.30am-6pm daily, 6-9pm Fri) Let Jambiani's tourism students practise their skills on you at the restaurant of the Jambiani Tourism Training Institute. It's not such a hardship when you gaze over the beach from the raised terrace restaurant and munch on thin-crust pizza, grilled fish or stir-fried chicken.

❶ Getting There & Away

Dalla-dalla 309 runs several times daily to Jambiani from Darajani Market in Stone Town. The Makunduchi–Michamvi dalla-dalla also stops at Jambiani. South of Jambiani the coastal road deteriorates to become a sandy, rocky track. All public transport uses the new tarmac road.

Makunduchi

The main reason to come to Makunduchi is for the village's colourful celebration of Mwaka Kogwa, a four-day festival held in late July. During the festivities villagers from the north and south symbolically beat one another with banana leaves in order to settle old scores and clean the slate for the new year. In addition, a house is usually burnt down, a practice thought to originate in Zoroastrianism. Otherwise, Makunduchi is remarkable mainly for its 1950s high-rise apartment blocks and a seaweed-strewn stretch of coast.

The only accommodation is at a large, lonely gated resort, La Madrugada, that was undergoing renovation at the time of research. Otherwise, during the festival, it shouldn't be too hard to arrange accommodation with locals as it's considered an unfavourable omen if you don't have at least one guest.

Bus 310 runs to Makunduchi on no set schedule, with plenty of additional transport from both Zanzibar Town and Kizimkazi during Mwaka Kogwa. A tarmac road connects Makunduchi with Jambiani and Paje, but there's no regular public transport.

Kizimkazi

This small village – at its best when the breezes come in and the late-afternoon sunlight illuminates the sand – actually consists of two adjoining settlements: Kizimkazi Dimbani to the north and Kizimkazi Mkunguni to the south. It has a small, attractive beach broken by coral rock outcrops. However, the main reason people visit is to see the dolphins in nearby Menai Bay.

Kizimkazi Dimbani is also the site of a Shirazi mosque (2km north of the village) dating from the early 12th century and thought to be one of the oldest Islamic buildings on the East African coast, although much of what is left today is from later restorations. Inside, in the mihrab, are inscribed verses from the Quran dating to 1107 and considered to be among the oldest-known examples of Swahili writing. If you want to take a look, ask for someone to help you with the key. You'll need to take off your shoes, and you should cover up bare shoulders or legs. The mosque is just north of the main beach area.

 ## Activities

Most Kizimkazi hotels organise tours to view the dolphins, as does Cabs Restaurant in Kizimkazi Dimbani (US$50 per boat including snorkelling equipment). You can also arrange trips through tour operators in Stone Town, with Safari Blue in Fumba or with some of the hotels at Paje and Jambiani from Tsh20,000 per person.

While the dolphins are beautiful, the tours, especially those organised from Stone Town, can be quite unpleasant, due to the hunt-and-chase tactics used by some operators, and they can't be recommended. If you do go out, the best time is early morning when the water is calmer and the sun not as hot. Late afternoon is also good, although winds may be stronger.

Sleeping & Eating

Karamba   LODGE $$
(☑0777 418452, 0773 166406; www.karamba resort.com; Kizimkazi Dimbani; s US$60-95, d US$70-120; @☀) Karamba, on the northern end of the beach in Kizimkazi Dimbani, has a string of 23 rooms in whitewashed cottages lined up along a small cliff overlooking the sea. They're simple and in need of a bit of maintenance. There's a restaurant, and a beachside chill-out bar with throw pillows, and a small pool.

Swahili Beach Resort   LODGE $$
(☑0777 416614, 0777 844442; www.swahili beachresort.com; Kizimkazi Mkunguni; s/d/tr from US$100/120/140; ☉Jun-Mar; ✿@☀) This place, with stone cottages set around manicured grounds, is lacking in shade and atmosphere, but the accommodation is comfortable and good value, and it works with a dive centre in Paje.

★**Unguja Lodge**   LODGE $$$
(☑0774 477477; www.ungujalodge.com; Kizimkazi Mkunguni; half-board per person US$210-262; P@☞☀) ✐ This secluded, low-key lodge has 12 organically designed two-storey villas shaded by thick indigenous forest. They're impeccably decorated by owner Elies, with gorgeous coconut wood furniture, found-art objects and woven rugs, and all have either sea views or private plunge pools. A stretch of private beach, an infinity pool, an on-site dive centre (the only one in the area) and an excellent restaurant mean it is regularly booked out.

WATCHING THE DOLPHINS

To enjoy watching the dolphins in their natural habitat, heed the advice posted on the wall of the Worldwide Fund for Nature (WWF):

➡ As with other animals, viewing dolphins in their natural environs requires time and patience.

➡ Shouting and waving your arms around will not encourage dolphins to approach your boat.

➡ Be satisfied with simply seeing the dolphins; don't force the boat operator to chase the dolphins, cross their path or get too close.

➡ If you decide to get in the water with the dolphins, do so quietly and calmly and avoid splashing.

➡ No one can guarantee that you will see dolphins on an outing, and swimming with them is a rare and precious occurrence.

ℹ Getting There & Away

To reach Kizimkazi from Zanzibar Town take bus 326 (Kizimkazi) direct (Tsh2000), or take bus 310 (Makunduchi) as far as Kufile junction, where you'll need to get out and wait for another vehicle heading towards Kizimkazi, or walk (about 5km). As you approach from Stone Town go right at Kufile junction (ie towards Kizimkazi) and then right again at the next fork to Kizimkazi Dimbani. Kizimkazi Mkunguni is to the left at this last fork.

Menai Bay

At 470 sq km (180 sq miles), Menai Bay is Zanzibar's largest protected marine environment. It is framed by the sleepy villages of Fumba to the west and Unguja Ukuu to the east, and is home to an impressive assortment of corals, fish and mangrove forests, some idyllic sandbanks and deserted islets, and a sea-turtle breeding area. Since 1997 it's been protected as part of the Menai Bay Conservation Area, and under the authorship of the Institute of Marine Sciences and the Pwani Project (http://lulufumba.wix.com/thepwaniproject) work continues on nurturing sustainable aquaculture and ethical dolphin tourism. The main reasons to visit are to enjoy the untouristy ambience, to take advantage of some good sailing, and for the chance to see dolphins.

Across the bay, Unguja Ukuu is notable as the site of what is believed to be the earliest settlement on Zanzibar, dating to at least the 8th century, although there is little remaining today from this era.

🏃 Activities

★ Safari Blue
CRUISE

(☑ 0777 423162; www.safariblue.net; Fumba; adult/child 6-14yr $65/35) Safari Blue organises group-based (maximum 20 people) day excursions on well-equipped dhows around Menai Bay. The excursions, which leave from Fumba at 9.30am, include a seafood lunch, plus snorkelling equipment and time to relax on a sandbank. Before booking, check weather conditions, as some months, notably April/May and July/August, can get quite windy or rainy.

Transfers from Stone Town to Fumba cost an additional $60 per vehicle.

🛏 Sleeping

Menai Beach Bungalows
COTTAGES $$

(☑ 0777 772660, 0777 4068009; www.visitzanzibar.se; Unguja Ukuu; s/d/f $40/60/75; P) Marooned on a broad sandy beach beneath the palms and mangroves that make up the shoreline of Unguja Ukuu, these five independent bungalows offer a unique opportunity to see a corner of the island that is so far unaffected by tourism. Comfortable, white-washed rooms open onto an empty beach, hammocks rock in the breeze and each evening fish bought from the local fishermen makes its way to the barbecue.

With a background in education, owners Kina and Erik are involved in various educational projects in the village. Contact them for further information on volunteering.

Fumba Beach Lodge
LODGE $$$

(☑ 0777 860504; www.fumbabeachlodge.com; Fumba; s/d half-board from US$217/366; P 🔊 ≊) Set on a secluded peninsula on Menai Bay,

Fumba Beach has 26 spacious cottages set in expansive grounds. The feel is more safari camp than beach hotel, with rooms spread out amid the vegetation with decks overlooking the water. There's also a small pool and a resident dive operator. Although the beach at Fumba isn't picture-perfect and has a considerable amount of coral rock, the setting is beautiful and uncrowded.

It's 18km south of Zanzibar Town next to Fumba village.

PEMBA

POP 407,000

Although separated by only 100km of sea, Pemba and Zanzibar are very different. Unlike Zanzibar, where tourist infrastructure is well developed, Pemba remains largely 'undiscovered'. Much of the coast is lined with mangroves and lagoons; however, there are stretches of sand and some idyllic uninhabited isles. The healthy coral reefs, the steeply dropping walls of the Pemba Channel and an abundance of fish provide the best diving in East Africa. Inland, unlike flat, sandy Zanzibar, Pemba's terrain is hilly and fertile,

Pemba

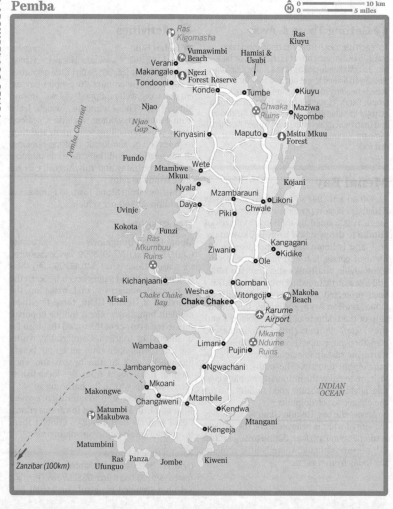

lushly planted with fruit and spice trees. In the days of Arab traders, the island aptly bore the name *Jazirat al Khuthera*, the Green Island. Surprisingly, very few tourists cross the channel. Those who do, however, are seldom disappointed.

Throughout much of the history of the Omani Sultanate, it was Pemba, with its extensive plantations and agricultural base, that provided the foundation for the archipelago's dominance. Cloves cover the island and 75% of Zanzibar's crop originates here, contributing over 30% of the archipelago's foreign-exchange earnings. This has made the island's post-independence poverty and marginalisation – per capita income is the lowest in Tanzania and most clove farmers are tenants to the government – a bitter pill to swallow and has promoted strong support for the main opposition party, Civic United Front (CUF).

ⓘ Getting There & Away

AIR

Pemba-Karume Airport is 6km east of Chake Chake. ZanAir and Coastal Aviation both offer two daily flights from Dar es Salaam to Pemba via Zanzibar. Both charge about US$95 from Pemba to Zanzibar (US$140 to Dar es Salaam). Auric Air also flies from Pemba to Zanzibar (US$100) three times daily. The cheapest service, however, is with Flightlink, which flies Pemba–Zanzibar (US$60) and Pemba–Dar es Salaam (US$90). Flights to Tanga are also possible with Coastal (US$100) and Auric (US$65).

BOAT

Ferries to/from Zanzibar and Dar es Salaam dock in Mkoani.

Azam Marine (p98) offers the most reliable service twice a week from Dar es Salaam (VIP/adult/child US$80/70/50), departing at 7am on Wednesday and Saturday and transiting through Zanzibar (around 9.30am to 10am) to arrive in Pemba around 1pm. Zanzibar–Pemba tickets cost US$40/35/25.

Otherwise, the *Royal* also runs twice a week from Dar es Salaam via Zanzibar (adult/child US$75/40), returning on Thursday and Sunday morning at 7.30am. Other ferries such as the *Maendeleo* and *Serengeti* also run, but their seaworthiness and safety record are questionable. Dhows also run from Wete to Tanga and Mombasa, Kenya, but foreigners are prohibited from sailing on them.

Tickets for all companies can be booked commission-free at various businesses in Chake Chake, Wete and Mkoani. Buying in advance ensures a seat.

An immigration officer usually checks passports on arrival. If you don't see them at the port and you aren't coming from Zanzibar, you're required to go to the immigration office and sign in.

ⓘ Getting Around

Crowded dalla-dallas plod down the main roads, most of which are sealed, but for many places you'll have to get off at the nearest junction and walk, wait for a lift or try to negotiate an additional fee with the bus driver to deliver you. There are few taxis.

Few tourists rent cars on Pemba as it's hard to organise in advance and roads are poorly signed. For many people the easiest way to get around is to hire a car and a driver (roughly $70 per day including petrol). In Chake Chake, vehicles and drivers can be found near the clock tower; in Mkoani and Wete they congregate near the fish markets.

Cycling is another good alternative; distances are short and roads are lightly travelled.

Chake Chake

Lively Chake Chake, set on a ridge overlooking mangrove-filled Chake Chake Bay, is Pemba's main town and the best base for visiting the island's southern half, including Misali. There's no equivalent of Stone Town here, but it's an appealingly scruffy city whose compact core is packed tight with small shops and makes for an interesting walk.

◉ Sights & Activities

Pemba Museum   MUSEUM
(adult/student US$5/3; ⊙8.30am-4.30pm Mon-Fri, 9am-4pm Sat & Sun) Filling what's left of an 18th-century Omani-era **fort**, which was probably built on the remains a 16th-century Portuguese garrison, this is a small but well-executed museum with displays on island history and Swahili culture. You'll enjoy your visit to Ras Mkumbuu, Mkame Ndume and Chwaka ruins much more if you stop here first.

Pemba Essential Oil Distillery   TOUR
(tour Tsh3000; ⊙8am-3.30pm Mon-Fri) Visitors to this out-of-town factory can see the tanks where clove stems, cinnamon leaves, eucalyptus leaves, lemongrass and sweet basil are turned into essential oils. Check in at the office and someone will show you around. From July to February locals deliver their clove stems here. The tour may be a little lackadaisical, but the process is fascinating

Chake Chake

Chake Chake

and many of the essential oils are for sale. To reach the factory, head 10 minutes northeast out of town towards Machomani or take dalla-dalla 316.

Clove buds are bought and sold in town at the **Zanzibar State Trading Corporation** (Mkoani Rd) warehouse, a short walk southeast of town just past the post office. Both places are best visited in combination with a spice tour, which can be arranged through all travel agencies.

Umoja Children's Park   AMUSEMENT PARK

Kiwanja cha Kufurahishia Watoto ('Fairgrounds for Making Children Happy') is a relic from Pemba's socialist days. Surprisingly, most of the remaining rides still work. It's now opened only twice a year: around Eid al-Fitr and Eid al-Kebir.

👉 Tours

Coral Tours   TOUR

(📞 0777 437307; tours_travelpemba@yahoo.com; Main Rd; ⊗ 8am-5pm) Headed up by the charming and energetic Nassor Haji, Coral Tours can fix you up with knowledgeable guides for island tours (to Misali, Ngezi, Kidike and the spice plantations) at wallet-friendly prices. A half/full-day tour with a driver typically costs US$70/120, while a car alone costs US$50/70. The office also sells ferry and plane tickets and can help you with bike hire and small tourism maps.

🛏 Sleeping

Le Tavern   HOTEL $

(📞 0777 429057; Main Rd; s/d US$20/30) The cheapest rooms in town are simple and clean, if a little dusty, and they could all do with a lick of paint. Still, they have mosquito nets and fans and there are cold-water showers.

Pemba Island Hotel   HOTEL $

(📞 0777 490041; pembaislandhotel@yahoo.com; Wesha Rd; s/d/tw US$40/60/80; ❄🖥📶) Clean rooms with cable TV, air-con, nets and hot water, plus a rooftop restaurant serving good homecooked meals such as *samaki na uali* (fish and rice) with spicy kachumbari salad. Nothing special, nothing wrong.

Hifadhi Hotel   HOTEL $$

(📞 0777 245777, 024-2542775; http://hifadhihotel. com; Tibirinzi St; s/d/ste US$90/110/150; ❄@📶🏊) This glass-fronted hotel brings a shock of modernity to Chake Chake with 14 turquoise rooms with swagged curtains, Zanzibari beds, mini-fridges and bathroom toiletries. It also has the only pool in town and two Swahili restaurants.

Pemba Misali Sunset Beach   RESORT $$

(📞 0775 044713; www.pembamisalibeach.com; Wesha Rd; s/d US$90/120; ❄@📶) 🐾 Out amid the mangroves just before Wesha, 7km from Chake Chake, this resort is quite reasonably priced for Pemba. Its most expensive bungalows sit on the white-sand beach, and diving, snorkelling and canoe trips through the mangroves are available. The restaurant sits on a deck looking out towards the sunset.

Eating

There's a small town-centre **night market** where you can get grilled *pweza* (octopus) and *maandazi* (doughnuts) and experience a slice of Pemban life.

Samail Modern Hotel & Restaurant
ZANZIBARI $

(☎0776 627619; meals Tsh4000-6000) A welcome addition to Chake Chake's restaurant scene, Samail serves marinated chicken with rice, as well as grilled fish and biriyani. The ice cream, cakes and fresh fruit juice are a bonus.

Balloon Brothers
SNACKS $

(Market St; snacks from Tsh100; ☺lunch) This is a local haunt which offers snacks such as samosas, sugar-coated *ubuyu* (baobab fruit) and bungo juice, the latter being very popular on Pemba. For something more substantial the *mishkaki* (marinated meat skewers) are good.

Ahaabna
TANZANIAN $

(Le-Tavern; Main Rd; meals Tsh5000-6000; ☺dinner) Located on the top floor of Le Tavern, this restaurant offers just one meal a day, either pilau or biryani with a choice of green bananas, chicken or fish.

Nabahani
TANZANIAN $

(Misufuni St; meals Tsh1500-3000) Typical local dishes such as beans and rice, chicken and dumplings, ugali (a staple made from maize and/or cassava flour) and fish.

Chake-Chake Needs
SELF-CATERING $

(Wete Rd; ☺8am-4.30pm & 5-9pm) This dishevelled little grocery stocks exotic items such as peanut butter, pasta and cornflakes.

Pemba Misali
Sunset Beach
EUROPEAN, TANZANIAN $$

(Wesha Rd; meals Tsh8000-16,000; ☺lunch & dinner) Dine seaside on a mix of local (coconut curry with prawns) and international (macaroni and cheese) food. It's 7km west of Chake Chake in Wesha.

ⓘ Information

Since the closure of Barclays Bank there are no ATM facilities on Pemba. A few local banks and bureau de change will change money (preferably US dollars), although all have unfavourable rates. To be safe, be sure to bring enough cash with you.

Dira Hospital (☎0777 424418; Wete Rd, Machomane; ☺7am-9pm) A private clinic with pharmacy.

Tawazul Internet (Main Rd; per hr Tsh1000; ☺8am-9pm) Conveniently located with the most reliable service.

ⓘ Getting There & Away

Most buses depart from points along Main Rd rather than the bus stand. Mkoani (Tsh1500, 1½ hours) dalla-dallas park near Coral Tours. Wete (Tsh1400, 1½ hours), Konde (Ths2000, two hours) and Vitongoji (Tsh500, 30 to 45 minutes) dalla-dallas park near PBZ bank, while much less frequent ones for Wesha (Tsh500, 30 minutes) are around the corner on Wesha Rd. Pujini (Tsh1000, one hour) is the only notable destination that uses the bus stand.

ⓘ PEMBA PECULIARITIES

Tourism in Pemba is different from anywhere else in the country, even Zanzibar. Keep the following in mind.

➡ Despite the scarcity of tourists, prices are as high as (and sometimes higher than) those in Zanzibar.

➡ Most businesses operate from 8am to 3pm and many reopen from 7pm to 9pm. Outside Chake Chake few stores open on Sundays. Many also shut down for a few minutes at 1pm so the men can pop over to the mosque for prayers.

➡ Other than local brews (the most common of which is *nazi*, a fermented coconut wine), there's little alcohol available on the island once away from the expensive resorts.

➡ Unmarried couples are not allowed to share a room in most hotels in towns (no problems at the resorts) and you may be asked to produce a marriage certificate as proof.

MISALI

A little patch of paradise surrounded by crystal waters and some of the most stunning coral reefs in the archipelago: a trip to Misali never disappoints. There are underwater and terrestrial nature trails, and you can arrange guides at the visitor centre. On the northeast of the island is **Mbuyuni Beach**, with fine, white sand and a small visitor centre. About a 10-minute walk south of the visitor centre is **Bendera Cave**, believed to be inhabited by the spirits of ancestors and used by some Pembans for traditional rituals. To the west are the larger **Mpapaini Caves**. Nesting turtles and breeding seabirds favour the beaches on its western side, which have been set aside just for them. There are no permanent settlements, though the island is in active use by local fishermen. Camping is not permitted for tourists.

The island is part of the **Pemba Channel Conservation Area** (PECCA; adult/student US$5/3) which covers Pemba's entire west coast. All divers, snorkellers and beachgoers to Misali or any other place here must pay the admission fee.

You can get to Misali on your own from Wesha, but it's easier, and not much more expensive, to arrange excursions through hotels or travel agencies. Coral Tours in Chake Chake, Ocean Panorama Hotel in Mkoani and Sharook Guest House in Wete all charge under US$110 for two people including lunch and entry fees.

ℹ️ Getting Around

TO/FROM THE AIRPORT

Dalla-dallas from Chake Chake to Furaha will drop you off at the airport (Tsh500, 20 minutes), but they don't come there to pick people up. They're quite infrequent, so leave early. A taxi to town costs Tsh15,000 to Tsh20,000.

CAR & MOTORCYCLE

There are a few taxis around Chake Chake, and cars and motorbikes can be hired through travel agencies. Prices are fairly standard: US$40 to Mkoani and US$70 to Ras Kigomasha.

Around Chake Chake

If you're staying in Chake Chake there are a number of interesting sights within easy reach by either bike or taxi.

⊙ Sights

Ras Mkumbuu Ruins   RUINS
(adult/student $5/3) Ras Mkumbuu is the long, thin strip of land jutting into the sea northwest of Chake Chake. At its tip are the ruins of a settlement believed to be Qanbalu, the oldest known Muslim town in Africa. It was founded in the 8th century, and by the early 10th century it was one of the major cities along the East African coast. The main ruins, consisting of a large mosque, some tombs and houses, date from around the 14th century, and several walls are still standing.

During the rainy season you'll likely be able to drive no further than Kichanjaani (Depu), leaving about a 3.5km walk. You could also go by boat from Wesha.

Makoba Beach   BEACH
The shore near Vitongoji town has several small attractive baobab-dotted coves with some weirdly eroded rocks and a little sand. Most beaches are notable for scenery rather than swimming (though you can take a dip among the rocks at high tide if you want). The top spot is Makoba Beach, 7km east of Chake Chake. Take the left junction at the end of the paved road after Vitongoji; the other road leads to smaller **Liko La Ngezi Beach**.

The nearest dalla-dallas will get you is to Vitongoji town (Tsh500, 30 to 45 minutes), which is 2km away from Makoba, but you might be able to convince the driver to deliver you for Tsh2000. It's an easy bike ride from Chake Chake.

Mkame Ndume (Pujini) Ruins   RUINS
These atmospheric ruins (late 15th to early 16th centuries) were either a fort or a palace of the infamous Mohammed bin Abdul Rahman, who ruled Pemba prior to the arrival of the Portuguese. Locally, Rahman is known as Mkame Ndume (Milker of Men), and for Pembans his name is synonymous with cruelty. The primary feature is a large stone staircase that led from the kilometre-long channel (now dry) connecting this site to the ocean, and while only a few small walls are

left standing, the remains of the ramparts give an indication of Pujini's power in its heyday.

The ruins are located 10km southeast of Chake Chake, near Pujini. Dalla-dallas to Pujini (Tsh1000, one hour) are infrequent and the ruins are poorly signposted. A taxi from Chake Chake costs about Tsh30,000 return.

Wambaa

Just south of Chake Chake, through a landscape thick with banana trees, jackfruit and papaya, where cloves lie out on roadside mats drying during the season, you'll reach the tiny village of Wambaa. Nearby is the palm-backed Wambaa Beach and the island's most exclusive property, Fundu Lagoon.

🛏 Sleeping

Fundu Lagoon　　　　　LODGE $$$
(📞0774 438668; www.fundulagoon.com; r full board hillside US$750-880, beachside US$830-980; ⊙mid-Jun–mid-Apr; @🏊) Set on a low hillside overlooking the sea, Fundu's luxurious tents are tucked away amid the vegetation and each have their own plunge pool. Particularly notable is the fabulous bar, set over the water on a long jetty. There's a spa and a PADI five-star dive operator here, primarily operating around Misali and off Pemba's southern tip, plus plenty of other aquatic excursions from paddling through mangroves to sunset dhow cruises.

Rates include all nonmotorised activities such as kayak tours and dhow cruises, and discounts apply to longer stays. No children under 12.

Mkoani

Although it's Pemba's major port, Mkoani has managed to fight off all attempts at development and remains a small and uneventful town. There's one good guesthouse and dining options are limited to street stands by the port, which serve night and day.

Immigration is 500m up the main road from the port in the town proper and the Chinese-run Abdalla Mzee Hospital, Pemba's best, is up the next hill in Uweleni.

Buses run regularly to Chake Chake (Tsh1500, 1½ hours), Wete (Tsh3000, two hours) and Konde (Tsh3500, 2½ hours) from in front of the port.

🛏 Sleeping

Zanzibar Ocean Panorama　　　HOTEL $
(📞0773 545418, 024-245 6166; www.zanzibar oceanpanorama.com; Mkoani; dm/s/tw US$20/35/50; ❄@) The welcoming Ocean Panorama is set up on a hill overlooking the sea and has bright, clean rooms with decks and Zanzibari beds. Manager Ali has lots of information on Pemba and arranges good-value trips, including dhow cruises and snorkelling at Misali or the old wreck (between about October and March) at Ras Ufunguo. Head left when exiting the port and walk 700m up the hill. Lunch and dinner (meals US$15) need to be pre-booked.

Kiweni Island

Tranquil Kiweni Island, marked as Shamiani on some maps, is just off Pemba's southeastern coast. It's a remote and tranquil place surrounded by mangroves and long stretches of sand which provide a nesting ground for sea-turtle colonies. Off-shore is some good snorkelling. Until recently tourism was unknown on the island, where villagers get by on fishing and farming. Now, the Pemba Lodge brings adventurous souls for a truly off-the-beaten track experience.

🛏 Sleeping

Pemba Lodge　　　　　LODGE $$
(📞0777 415551; www.pembalodge.com; per person full board US$165) 🌿 Taking its lead from highly successful Chumbe, Pemba Lodge is designed to offer a Robinson Crusoe castaway experience with light footprints. Its five stilted bungalows are constructed from natural materials, sport recycled dhow furniture and have rainshowers, solar-powered lights and composting toilets. Dinner is seafood bought from the local fishermen, and kayaks and snorkelling tours are included in the price. The lodge is also heavily involved in turtle conservation.

Transfers cost US$30 from Mkoani and US$60 from the airport. It's also possible to sail here on a catamaran or a dhow from its sister hotel, Mnarani Beach Cottages (p103) in Nungwi.

Wete

The rundown town of Wete is Pemba's second-largest port, situated on an inlet on the northwest coast of the island. It is a good

Wete

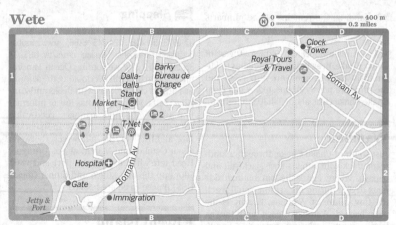

Wete

🛌 Sleeping

❌ Eating

base for exploring northern Pemba. It's also the easiest place to see Pemba flying foxes, with a large colony hanging from some trees just uphill from the port.

🛏 Sleeping & Eating

Pemba Crown Hotel HOTEL $
(☑ 0777 493667; www.pembacrown.com; Bomani Ave; s/d US$30/40; ❄) This large, white-washed and balconied hotel is Wete's best accommodation option, with 15 rooms sporting firm beds, air-con and simple furnishings. There's no restaurant, but a simple breakfast is provided.

Sharook Guest House GUESTHOUSE $
(☑ 0777 431012; www.pembaliving.com; Wete; s/d US$35/50) Run by the Sharook brothers, this four-bedroom guesthouse is the homiest option in town. The friendly English-speaking owners know much about travel on the island, and can recommend good-value excursions to the off-shore Mtambwe Mkuu ruins (US$5 per person), Fundo Island (US$30 for the boat) and the Ngezi Forest (US$35 per person), as well as organising car, bike and

motorcycle rental. There's no restaurant, but pre-ordered dinners can be served in the TV room.

Sharook Riviera Grand Lodge GUESTHOUSE $
(☑ 0777 431012; www.pembaliving.com; dm US$20, s/d US$30/50; ❄) Bigger and better than the original, but less cosy, this so-called 'grand lodge' has eight simple, ensuite rooms with Zanzibari beds, nets and air-con. There's a nice narrow view of the bay from the rooftop restaurant.

Hill View Inn GUESTHOUSE $
(☑ 0776 338366; s/d US$20/30, r without bathroom US$15) This small establishment up behind the ugly grey apartments has no-frills, clean rooms; the ones upstairs are better since they catch some breezes. There's satellite TV in the lounge and meals, which need to be pre-ordered, and hot water are available on request.

Times Restaurant TANZANIAN, EUROPEAN $
(Bomani Ave; meals Tsh6000; ⊙ breakfast, lunch & dinner) An attempt to add some class to work-a-day Wete, this white-tablecloth restaurant's menu promises prawn curry, tandoori chicken and pizza. Though if you plan to order any of these, it's best to let the cook know several hours in advance.

ℹ Information

Barky Bureau de Change (Bomani Ave; ⊙8.30am-3.45pm Mon-Sat, 8.45am-12.30pm Sun) Best place in town to change money.
T-Net (Bomani Ave; per hr Tsh1500; ⊙8.30am-3pm & 7-9pm) Pemba's best internet cafe.

Royal Tours & Travel (📞 0777 429244; royal tours@live.com; Bomani Ave; ⏰ 8am-3pm Mon-Sat, 8am-noon Sun) Books plane and ferry tickets, hires vehicles and leads tours.

ℹ Getting There & Away

There are two dalla-dalla routes (both use 606) between Wete and Chake Chake (Tsh1400, 1½ hours). Most vehicles use the faster eastern 'new' road (these are labelled in green), while some (red) travel via Ziwani along the 'old' road, which features more forest and some ocean vistas. There are also frequent dalla-dallas to Konde (Tsh1500, one hour).

A shuttle bus from Wete to Mkoani (Tsh3000) is timed to connect with most ferry departures and arrivals. It picks up passengers at various points around town and leaves Wete three hours before the boat departure.

Tumbe

The large village of Tumbe lies on a sandy cove on the northern coast fringed by dense mangroves. The beach north of the village is the site of Pemba's largest fish market, and if you're in the area it's well worth a stop to watch the bidding. Tumbe is also one of the places (Chwale, Pujini and Kidike are others) where you still can see Pemba's light-hearted 'bull fights', said to date back to the days of Portuguese influence on the island. They're usually done after the rice harvest, at New Year and sometimes for Tourism Day (27 September).

There's no accommodation in Tumbe or nearby Konde. Dalla-dallas from Chake Chake to Konde pass Chwaka and Tumbe (Tsh2000, two hours). From Wete, you'll have to change vehicles in Konde for the final leg.

◉ Sights

Chwaka Ruins   RUINS
(adult/child US$5/3) Beginning about 1.5km southeast of Tumbe, spread out amid palm trees and cassava fields, are the Chwaka Ruins dating back to the 9th century. The main destination is the Haruni Site, with remnants of a town that existed from the 11th to 15th centuries and grew to perhaps 5000 people. It's named after Harun, son of Mkame Ndume and, according to local tradition, just as cruel as his father. Legend says the pillared structure next to the semi-intact Friday Mosque is his tomb.

Ngezi Forest Reserve

The dense and wonderfully lush forest at Ngezi is one of the last remaining areas of primary forest that once covered western Pemba. It's notable in that it resembles the highland rainforests of East Africa more than the lowland forests found on Zanzibar. The 1476-hectare reserve (admission/transit fee US$5/2; ⏰ 7.30am-3.30pm) is a true double canopy with an upper layer of mgulele, mwavi, mtondoo and mvule trees towering up to 40m high with lianas snaking between them providing swings for raucous monkeys. You'll find the visitor centre 4km west of Konde on the road to Ras Kigomasha.

Two nature trails tunnel beneath the tropical canopy, and off-trail walks are allowed. All visits must be done with a naturalist guide, some of whom speak English. Most visitors follow the Josh Trail (Tsh6000 per person), which takes under an hour and is good for spotting birds and red colobus monkeys (in the early morning and late afternoon). A highlight of the Toofik Trail (Tsh10,000), which normally takes five to seven hours, is the snake pond, home to several slitherers, including spitting cobra. Night walks (Tsh10,000) are also available; most participants are hoping to see Pemba flying foxes and scops owls, one of the island's four endemic bird species.

A taxi from Konde (ask around) costs Tsh5000. Kervan Saray (p124) will deliver its guests here for free.

Kigomasha Peninsula

North of the Ngezi Forest, thick trees give way to scrub as you wend your way up the remote Kigomasha Peninsula to the headland with its winking lighthouse (admission US$5) and sweeping views back across the island. Curving around the eastern side of the peninsula is the stunning, 4km-long Vumawimbi Beach. You may need to rub your eyes to check that you haven't died and gone to heaven, so idyllic is the view with fishermen mending nets and *ngalawas* bobbing on the surf. It's an isolated spot so come with company and a picnic.

Verani Beach on the western side of the peninsula suffers unfairly by comparison but is hardly less beautiful. At its northern end you'll find the Pango Ya Watoro (Cave of the Fugitives). At low tide you can walk the length of the beach to the lighthouse

PEMBA FLYING FOXES

Pemba's only endemic mammal is a large and critically endangered bat *(Pteropus voeltzkowi)* called *popo* in Swahili. They spend their days in trees rather than caves and the island's biggest roosting site, home to some 4000 bats, is at **Kidike Sanctuary** (☏ 0777 472941; adult/student/child US$5/3/1; ⊙9am-6pm) about 10km northeast of Chake Chake. There's a large population here due to the proximity of a local burial site, which meant the colony was undisturbed. Now this local-government initiative can be visited as a day trip encompassing other cultural activities such as cooking classes, fishing and even bull fights (with advance notice). Outside peak season, ring ahead to check that someone is there. Kidike is 3.5km off the Chake–Wete road. Some people at the junction will hire their bicycles or you can wait for a lift.

Popo can also be easily seen in **Wete**. There are several colonies in **Ngezi Forest Reserve** but they're all very far from the trails.

(not advisable on your own), but check when the tide comes in so you don't get stranded.

Offshore, spectacular **dive sites** include the Swiss Reef sea mountains, the sponge-covered Edge, which plunges into the Pemba Channel, and the Njao Gap, with its walls, mountains and coral gardens. Dolphins, large manta rays and whales are also regular visitors.

🏃 Activities

Swahili Divers
DIVING
(www.swahilidivers.com) This five-star PADI Dive Centre is located at Kervan Saray and has been operating on the island since 1999. It offers good-value dive packages; for example, its seven-night package includes accommodation, meals, transfers, dive gear and 10 dives, plus a kayak and walking excursion, for US$1865 per person.

🛏 Sleeping & Eating

A couple of accommodation options sit on Verani Beach, opposite the dive sites.

Matango Beach Resort
RESORT $$
(☏ 0777 009315, 0777 481629; www.matango beachresort.com; Makangale; d/f US$100/160; ❄ ⛱) A welcome addition to Verani Beach is this well-priced new resort with neatly constructed beach chalets with thatched roofs, small decks and private barbecues. Rooms are huge, air-conditioned and situated just back from the beach so you can watch the sun go down from your deck.

Kervan Saray Beach Lodge
LODGE $$
(☏ 0773 176737; www.kervansaraybeach.com; dm full board US$55, s/d US$160/250; Ⓟ @ 🛜 ⛱) The almost luxurious Kervan Saray is a lovely, relaxing lodge on the shore (there's a

beach only half the year) near Makangale village. Accommodation is in a vaguely Arabian-themed high-roof bungalow or a six-bunk dorm, and the restaurant serves a daily set menu (nonguests US$15). Swahili Divers is based here and diving, naturally, is the main activity, but snorkelling and kayaking are also offered, as is camping on deserted isles.

Airport pick-up costs US$90 per vehicle.

Manta Resort
RESORT $$$
(☏ 0776 718853, 0776 718852; www.themanta resort.com; full board d garden US$495-595, seafront US$745; ❄ @ 🛜 ⛱) Superbly situated on Verani Beach, the Manta Resort rests on a breezy escarpment with perfect ocean views. Accommodation is in a mix of seafront and garden cottages with private terraces, polished concrete floors and comfy king-sized beds. Pride of place goes to its new wacky but wonderful floating suite (US$1500 per night) with a sun- and star-gazing roof deck, a dining deck and an underwater bedroom, with surreal views of cruising manta rays, dancing octopus and tropical fish.

The rest of the resort has a barefoot luxury vibe with a pool, a beach bar and a terrace fronting truly memorable sunsets. Spa treatments, kayaks and dhow cruises are free; and diving (it's a PADI five-star centre) and fishing charters are possible.

Airport transfers cost US$90 per person. No children under seven years.

ⓘ Getting There & Away

The only dalla-dallas on this road leave Makangale for Konde (Tsh1000, one hour) at 7am and return at 1pm. Sometimes a second truck follows a short time later.

Northeastern Tanzania

Best for Nature

➡ Amani Nature Reserve
(p141)

➡ Saadani National Park
(p129)

➡ Maziwe Marine Reserve
(p133)

Best for Culture

➡ Usambara Mountains
(p141)

➡ Pare Mountains (p148)

➡ Bagamoyo Arts Festival
(p128)

Why Go?

Northeastern Tanzania's highlights are its coastline, its mountains and its cultures. These, combined with the area's long history, easy access and lack of crowds, make it an appealing focal point for a Tanzania sojourn.

Visit the moss-covered ruins at Kaole and Tongoni, step back to the days of Livingstone in Bagamoyo, relax on palm-fringed beaches around Pangani or explore Saadani, a seaside national park. Inland, hike forested footpaths in the Usambaras while following the cycle of market days of the local Sambaa people. Learn about traditions of the Pare, or experience the bush in seldom-visited Mkomazi National Park.

Most of the northeast is within a half-day's drive or bus ride from Dar es Salaam or Arusha, and there are good connections to Zanzibar. Main roads are in decent condition and there is a wide range of accommodation.

When to Go
Lushoto

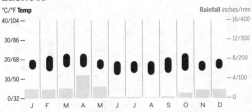

Mar–May The Usambara and Pare mountains get muddy; hiking is slippery but vistas are green.

Oct Drumming, dancing and other cultural displays are the highlights at the Bagamoyo Arts Festival.

Jun–Nov The beaches are relaxing and the mountains are refreshingly cool.

Northeastern Tanzania Highlights

1 Lazing on the long, white beaches around **Pangani** (p132), while getting a taste of Swahili history and culture.

2 Hiking along winding footpaths in the scenic **Usambara Mountains** (p141).

3 Snorkelling around **Maziwe Marine Reserve** (p133).

4 Stepping back into history in the former colonial capital of **Bagamoyo** (p127), with its carved doorways and old buildings.

5 Relaxing on the beach and watching wildlife in and near **Saadani National Park** (p129).

6 Getting acquainted with local culture in the **Pare Mountains** (p148)

7 Exploring the bush in **Mkomazi National Park** (p151).

LEGEND
MR   Marine Reserve
NP   National Park
NR   Nature Reserve
FR   Forest Reserve

KENYA

History

For at least 2000 years, northeastern Tanzania has been attracting visitors. In the 1st century AD, the author of the mariners' chronicle *Periplus of the Erythraean Sea* mentions the existence of the trading outpost of Rhapta, which is thought to have been somewhere around present-day Pangani. Several centuries later, a string of settlements sprang up along the coast with links to ports in Arabia and the Orient. Today, traces of this history are best seen along the coast at Kaole, Tongoni, Pangani and Bagamoyo.

Bagamoyo

Strolling through Bagamoyo's narrow, unpaved streets, or sitting at the port watching dhows (ancient Arabic sailing vessels) get loaded, takes you back to the mid-19th century. This is when the town was one of the most important settlements along the East African coast and the terminus of the trade caravan route linking Lake Tanganyika with the sea. Slaves, ivory, salt and copra were unloaded before being shipped to Zanzibar and elsewhere, and many European explorers, including Richard Burton, Henry Morton Stanley and David Livingstone, began and ended their trips here. In 1868 French missionaries established Freedom Village at Bagamoyo as a shelter for ransomed slaves, and for the remainder of the century the town served as a way station for missionaries travelling from Zanzibar to the interior.

From 1887 to 1891 Bagamoyo was the capital of German East Africa, and in 1888 it was at the centre of the Abushiri Revolt, the first major uprising against the colonial government. In 1891 the capital was transferred to Dar es Salaam, sending Bagamoyo into a slow decline from which it has yet to recover. Bagamoyo's unhurried pace and long history make it an agreeable day or weekend excursion from Dar es Salaam. At the southeastern edge of town are beaches with high-tide swimming. Almost every worthwhile sight has an admission fee, making a Bagamoyo visit a rather expensive endeavour. Both the Catholic Museum (p127) and the Caravan Serai Museum (p128) offer tourist information and guides.

◉ Sights & Activities

Bagamoyo Town   HISTORIC SITE
(adult/child Tsh20,000/10,000) With its cobwebbed portals and crumbling German-era colonial buildings, central Bagamoyo, or *Mji Mkongwe* (Stone Town) as it's known locally, is well worth exploration. The most interesting area is along Ocean Rd. Here you'll find the old German boma (a fortified living compound; in colonial times, an administrative office), built in 1897, and Liku House, which served as the German administrative headquarters. There is also a school, which dates to the late 19th century and was the first multiracial school in what is now Tanzania.

On the beach is the German Customs House (1895), Bagamoyo's port, where you can watch boat builders at work, and a busy fish market (on the site of the old slave market), with lively auctions most afternoons. Northwest of here are several small streets lined with carved doors similar to those found elsewhere along the coast. Further south is the mid-19th-century Old Fort. The ridiculously steep fee levied to walk around the old town is payable at the Antiquities branch office at the Old Fort, where you can also get a guide.

Catholic Museum   MUSEUM
(☑023-244 0010; Tsh10,000; ⊙10am-5pm) About 2km north of town and reached via a long, mango-shaded avenue is the Catholic mission and museum, one of Bagamoyo's highlights. In the same compound is the chapel where Livingstone's body was laid before being taken to Zanzibar Town en route to Westminster Abbey. The mission dates from the 1868 establishment of Freedom Village and is the oldest in Tanzania.

Kaole Ruins   RUIN
(adult/child Tsh20,000/10,000; ⊙8am-4pm Mon-Fri, 9am-5pm Sat & Sun) Just south of Bagamoyo are these atmospheric ruins. At their centre are the remains of a 13th-century mosque, which is one of the oldest in mainland Tanzania and also one of the oldest in East Africa. It was built in the days when the Sultan of Kilwa held sway over coastal trade, and long before Bagamoyo had assumed any significance. Nearby is a second mosque, dating to the 15th century, and about 22 graves, many dating to the same period.

Among the graves are several Shirazi pillar-style tombs reminiscent of those at Tongoni, but in somewhat better condition, and a small museum housing Chinese pottery fragments and other remnants. Just east of the ruins, past a dense stand of mangroves, is the old harbour, now silted, that was in use during Kaole's heyday.

The easiest way to reach the ruins on foot is by heading south for about 5km along the road running past Chuo cha Sanaa to the signposted Kaole turn-off at the southern end of Kaole village. Walk with a guide and don't carry valuables. A *bajaji* (tuk tuk) from town costs around Tsh5000 (Tsh10,000 for a taxi).

College of Arts   ARTS CENTRE

(Chuo cha Sanaa; www.tasuba.ac.tz) Located about 500m south of Bagamoyo along the road to Dar es Salaam is this renowned theatre and arts college, home of the national dance company. When school is in session there are occasional performances, and it's usually possible to arrange drumming or dancing lessons.

The annual highlight is the Bagamoyo Arts Festival, usually held around late September or October. The festival features traditional dance and drumming performances, acrobatics displays, drumming workshops and much more. It's not the most organised – advance information on schedules is rarely available – but it is a good way to meet Tanzania's up and coming artists and performers, and to get introduced to local talent and culture.

Caravan Serai Museum   MUSEUM

(Tsh20,000; ⊙9am-6pm) This undistinguished museum has a small display documenting the slave trade. It's at the town entrance, just past and diagonally opposite CRDB bank.

WILDLIFE IN THE NORTHEAST

On the coast is **Saadani National Park** (p129) with a lovely beach plus hippos, crocodiles, many birds, giraffes and elephants. Inland, on the Kenya border and known for its black-rhino conservation project, is **Mkomazi National Park** (p151). Tiny **Amani Nature Reserve** (p141) is a fine destination for ornithologists and botanists, with many endemic bird and plant species. **Maziwe Marine Reserve** (p133) has white sands, clear waters and snorkelling.

Tours

The coast around Bagamoyo is full of waterbirds and mangrove ecosystems, and there are a few uncrowded stretches of sand. Most hotels can arrange excursions to **Mbegani lagoon**, the **Ruvu River delta** and **Mwambakuni sand bar**, all nearby. Expect to pay from US$25 to US$30 per person with four people.

Sleeping

Funky Squids B&B   B&B $

(☑ 0755 047802, 0778 227276; the.funky.squids@gmail.com; s/d Tsh50,000/65,000; P🅿🛜) This newish place has seven clean, modest rooms and a large beachfront bar-restaurant. It's at the southern end of town, next door to (and immediately south of) the Bagamoyo College of Arts (Chuo cha Sanaa).

New Bagamoyo Beach Resort   LODGE $$

(☑ 0783 261655; www.facebook/newbagamoyobeachresort.com; camping US$9, bandas per person without bathroom US$20, s/d US$75/88; P❄🛜) This seaside place is fine, friendly and very relaxed, with adequate rooms in two blocks (ask for the one closer to the water). It also has a few no-frills budget *bandas* (thatched-roof huts) on the beach that have just a bed. The cuisine is French-influenced and tasty. It also has a boat for excursions.

Travellers Lodge   LODGE $$

(☑ 0754 855485, 023-244 0077; www.travellerslodge.com; camping US$12, s/d cottages from US$60/80; ❄) With its relaxed atmosphere and reasonable prices, this is among the best value of the beach places. Accommodation is in clean, pleasant cottages scattered around expansive grounds, some with two large beds. There's a restaurant and a children's play area. It's just south of the entrance to the Catholic mission.

Livingstone Beach Resort   HOTEL $$

(☑ 0756 224539, 0712 198308; www.livingstonebeachresort.co; s/d/tr US$80/150/225; P❄🛜🏊) This beachside place has modest whitewashed stone and thatch bungalows (some with a double bed, others with a double and a single), scattered around expansive palm-tree-studded grounds. In front is a tiny, mangrove-fringed beach. Kayaking and snorkelling can be arranged, and there's a restaurant.

✕ Eating

Poa Poa TANZANIAN $
(light meals Tsh7000-10,000; ⊘8am-10pm Mon-Sat) Coffees, spiced tea, milkshakes, chapati wraps, pizza and local-style meals are among the offerings at this small place in the old town centre. It's several blocks back from the dhow port and customs house.

New Top Life Inn TANZANIAN $
(meals Tsh5000) This scruffy but popular local haunt has been around for ages, serving chicken and beef, plus chips or *ugali* (a staple made from maize or cassava flour, or both). It's two blocks north of Caravan Serai Museum.

**Funky Squids Beach
Bar & Grill** TANZANIAN, EUROPEAN $$
(📱0755 047802, 0778 227276; the.funky.squids@gmail.com; meals Tsh7000-12,000; ⊘lunch & dinner; 🛜) This large, beachfront bar-restaurant serves a good selection of tasty meat and seafood grills.

ℹ Information

MONEY
CRDB At the town entrance; ATM.

ℹ Getting There & Away

BOAT
Nonmotorised dhows to Zanzibar cost around Tsh5000 (around Tsh10,000 to Tsh15,000 for motorised boats) and take around four hours with a good wind. You'll need to register first with the immigration officer in the old customs building, which is also the departure point. Departure times vary, and are often around 1am, arriving in Zanzibar sometime the next morning if all goes well. There is no regular dhow traffic direct to Saadani or Pangani.

BUS
Dalla-dallas (minibuses) from 'Makumbusho' (north of Dar es Salaam along the New Bagamoyo road, and accessed via dalla-dalla from New Posta) head to Bagamoyo (Tsh2200, two hours) throughout the day. The transport stand in Bagamoyo is about 700m from the town centre just off the road heading to Dar es Salaam. Taxis to the town centre charge from Tsh2000. There is also a daily dalla-dalla to Saadani village via Msata on the main Arusha highway, departing Bagamoyo at about 10am (Tsh10,000, three hours).

CAR
Bagamoyo is about 70km north of Dar es Salaam and an easy drive along good tarmac. The best route for drivers is via Old Bagamoyo Rd through Mikocheni and Kawe. It's also possible to reach Bagamoyo from Msata (65km west on the Dar es Salaam to Arusha highway, north of Chalinze) on a good, paved 64km road.

Saadani National Park

About 70km north of Bagamoyo along a lovely stretch of coastline, and directly opposite Zanzibar, is tiny Saadani National Park (www.saadanipark.org; adult/child US$30/10), a 1000-sq-km patch of coastal wilderness. Unpretentious and relaxing, it bills itself as one of the few spots in the country where you can enjoy the beach and watch wildlife at the same time. It's easily accessed from both Dar es Salaam and Zanzibar as an overnight or weekend excursion and is a good choice if you don't have time to explore further afield, although it cannot compare with Tanzania's better-known parks and reserves. About 25km north of Saadani's northern Madete Gate is the long, mostly deserted and stunningly beautiful Sange beach, with several places to stay.

To the south of the reserve is the languidly flowing Wami River, where you'll see hippos, crocodiles and many birds, including lesser flamingos (in the delta between July and October), fish eagles, hamerkops, kingfishers and bee-eaters. The best way to explore is on the boat safaris offered by most lodges.

While terrestrial wildlife-watching opportunities are modest, animals are definitely present. In addition to hippos and crocs, it's quite likely that you'll see giraffes, and elephant spottings are increasingly common (we saw a herd of 50-plus on one visit). With luck, you may see Lichtenstein's hartebeests and even lions, although these are more difficult to spot. Birding is very good.

✗ Activities

Boat trips along the Wami River, wildlife drives (in open-sided vehicles), bush walks and village tours can be arranged through most camps and lodges. Guides (optional for vehicle safaris, required for walking safaris) cost US$20 per day, per group.

Walking Safaris
Walking safaris are a good way to get a taste of the bush and of Saadani's more subtle attractions. They are available in dry season only. The cost is US$20 per person, plus a guide fee of US$20 per group.

🛈 SAADANI NATIONAL PARK

Why Go To enjoy the long, mostly deserted coastline plus some wildlife; ease of access from Dar es Salaam for those without much time.

When to Go June to February; black cotton soil is a problem in many areas during heavy rains from March through May.

Practicalities Drive, bus or fly in from Dar es Salaam; bus from Bagamoyo; drive from Pangani. Entry points are Mvave Gate (at the end of the Mandera road, for visitors from Dar es Salaam); Madete Gate (for those coming from Pangani along the coastal road); and Wami Gate (for those coming from Bagamoyo). Entry fees are valid for 24 hours, single entry only. Entry, camping, guide, walking and boat-safari fees can be paid with Visa, Mastercard or cash at Mvave Gate, and with cash only at Madete and Wami Gates. All entry gates are open from 6am to 6pm; exiting the park is permitted up to 7pm. **Park Headquarters** (☏0785 555135; www.tanzaniaparks.com; ⊕8am-5pm) are at Mkwaja, at Saadani's northern edge.

Budget Tips There's no vehicle rental at the park. Your best budget bet is to get a group together and arrange a day safari with one of the lodges outside Saadani.

Boat Safaris

Boat safaris (US$50 per person) are very relaxing and enjoyable. There is a chance you may spot hippos, crocs and many birds, and it's interesting to watch the vegetation along the Wami River's banks change with the decreasing salinity of the water as you move upstream. In some sections there are also marked variations between the two banks, with areas of date palms and lush foliage on one side, and whistling thorn acacias reminiscent of drier areas of the country on the other.

Wildlife Drives

All the lodges offer vehicle safaris. You'll likely need to explore off main routes for the best wildlife watching; during the rains, take care not to drive throgh Saadani's notorious black cotton soil when detouring. A park guide costs US$20 per group.

🛏 Sleeping & Eating

🛏 Inside the Park

Saadani Park Resthouse & Bandas   BANDA $$
(☏0689 062346, 0785 555135; saadani@tanzaniaparks.com; banda/resthouse per person US$40/50) Saadani's nice new park *bandas* and resthouse are just back from the beach near Saadani village, in an area that elephants seem to like. The resthouse has three singles and a suite; the *bandas* have spacious double- and single-bedded rooms. Both have cold-water showers and self-catering kitchens. Bottled water is available in Saadani village; otherwise, bring all food and drink.

Saadani Park Campsites   CAMPGROUND $$
(camping US$30) Public campsites are available in a good location directly on the beach just north of Saadani village, and also along the Wami River at Kinyonga, both with basic ablution facilities, but no food or drink.

Saadani Safari Lodge   LODGE $$$
(☏0756 316815; www.sanctuaryretreats.com; per person all inclusive US$356-508; ⊕Jun-Mar; 🅿🛜🌊) This upmarket retreat is the only lodge within the park. It has a natural, overgrown but luxurious feel, a row of comfortable cottage suites directly on the beach, an open-style restaurant, a beachside pool and a sundowner deck. Excursions include boat safaris on the Wami River, bush walks and snorkelling excursions to a nearby sandbank. Children under 12 years old are not allowed.

🛏 Outside the Park

The coastal lodges and camps in Sange, about 25km north of Saadani's northern Madete Gate, also make good bases for exploring Saadani National Park.

Saadani River Park   GUESTHOUSE $
(☏0788 397780; r Tsh25,000-30,000) This unmissable (look for the towering *makuti* – thatched roof of palm leaves) local guesthouse in Saadani village, just down from the bus stand, has a few very basic rooms in

the main building plus one in a separate cottage, all with bathroom (sometimes bucket showers), mosquito net and fan. Meals are available on order.

Kisampa — TENTED CAMP $$
(☑ 0769 204159; www.afrikaafrikasafaris.com; per person full board US$180) ✈ For genuine bush adventure, it's difficult to beat this unique, family-friendly camp. Set off on its own about a two-hour drive from Saadani in a private nature reserve, Kisampa is integrated with the surrounding community, and offers many ways for guests to get involved. Accommodation is in rustic bungalows. Saadani safaris, bush walks, beach camping and other activities fill the days.

Very favourable package deals are also offered for children, making it an ideal destination for a family bush adventure.

Tent With a View Safari Lodge — LODGE $$$
(☑ 0713 323318, 022-211 0507; www.saadani. com; s/d full board US$355/550, s/d all inclusive US$655/750; ℙ) ✈ This hideaway has raised tree-house-style *bandas* on a lovely stretch of deserted, driftwood-strewn beach, just north of the Saadani park boundary. All have verandas and hammocks. Excursions include safaris in the park and boat trips on the Wami River. The same management runs a lodge in Selous Game Reserve, and combination itineraries can be arranged.

ℹ Information

Saadani Tourist Information (☑ 0689 062346, 0785 555135; infosaadani@tanzania parks.com) This information office, just west of Saadani village, can help with booking park *bandas*, resthouses and campsites. It can also arrange walking tours of Saadani village.

ℹ Getting There & Away

AIR
There are airstrips in the north near Mkwaja headquarters and in the south near Saadani village. Flights from Dar es Salaam (one way US$140) and Zanzibar (US$75) can be booked with Coastal Aviation (p67).

BOAT
Local fishing boats sail regularly between Saadani and Zanzibar, but the journey is known for being rough and is not recommended. It's better to arrange a boat charter with one of the Saadani lodges or with lodges near Pangani.

BUS
There's a daily bus from Dar es Salaam's 'Standi ya Shamba' transport stand, just after Ubungo main station near Tanesco, departing Dar between 11am and 1pm, and Saadani at 5am (Tsh10,000, five to six hours). There are plans to move departures for this bus to Mbezi transport stand (further west from Ubungo along the Morogoro road).

From Bagamoyo, there's a vehicle daily via Msata on the main Chalinze–Arusha road, departing Bagamoyo at about 10am and Saadani village at 6am (Tsh10,000, three hours)

If you've arrived in the park via public transport, there's no vehicle rental in the park for a safari, unless you have arranged something in advance with the lodges. The Saadani Tourist Information office can help you arrange a motorcycle or (sometimes) vehicle transfer from Saadani village to the nearby park campsite and park *bandas*.

CAR
Several lodges provide road transport to and from Dar es Salaam from about US$200 per vehicle, one way. Allow four to five hours for the journey.

From Dar es Salaam, the main route is via Chalinze on the Morogoro road, and then north to Mandera village (about 50km north of Chalinze on the Arusha highway). At Mandera bear east along a good gravel road and continue about 60km to Saadani. It's also possible to reach Saadani from Dar es Salaam via Bagamoyo. From Bagamoyo town, head north for 44km along a mostly rough road to the Wami entry gate and the Wami River. Except during heavy rains, the river is bridged; check with park headquarters or the camps about the bridge's status before venturing up. Once at the bridge, it's 21km further to Saadani village.

Coming from Pangani, take the ferry across the Pangani River, then continue south along a reasonably good, scenic road past stands of

SAADANI VILLAGE

This tiny, scruffy village, just south of the main park area, doesn't look like much today, but it was once a major local port. You can still see the crumbling walls of an Arab-built fort that was used as a holding cell for slaves before they were shipped to Zanzibar. During German colonial times the fort served as the customs house. Short walking tours with local guides can be arranged at the Saadani Tourist Information Office, opposite the village.

cashew, sisal and teak to the reserve's northern Madete Gate. (At the large signboard for Mkwaja, continue straight, then take the right fork at the next 'Y' junction.) Transfers can be arranged with Saadani or Pangani (Ushongo) lodges from about US$150 per vehicle each way (1½ to two hours).

Although Saadani officially stays open year-round, roads within the park get very muddy and difficult to pass during the rains and you'll probably be limited to the area around the beach and the camps. When driving away from the main park routes during the rains, be careful to avoid getting your vehicle stuck in the area's treacherous black cotton soil.

Pangani

About 55km south of Tanga is the small and dilapidated Swahili outpost of Pangani. It rose from obscure beginnings as just one of many coastal dhow ports to become a terminus of the caravan route from Lake Tanganyika, a major export point for slaves and ivory, and one of the largest ports between Bagamoyo and Mombasa. Sisal and copra plantations were established in the area, and several European missions and exploratory journeys to the interior began from here. By the end of the 19th century, focus had shifted to Tanga and Dar es Salaam, and Pangani again faded into anonymity.

Today, the sleepy town makes an intriguing step back into history, especially in the area within about three blocks of the river, where you'll see some carved doorways, buildings from the German colonial era and old houses of Indian traders. More of a draw for many travellers are the beaches running north and south of town, which are lovely, with stands of coconut palms alternating with dense coastal vegetation and the occasional baobab. The beaches are also the best places to base yourself.

Pangani's centre, with the market and bus stand, is on the corner of land where the Pangani River meets the sea. About 2km north is the main junction where the road from Muheza joins the coastal road. This is where you should get off the bus if you're arriving from Muheza and staying at the beaches north of town.

History

Compared with Tongoni, Kaole and other settlements along the coast, Pangani is a relatively modern settlement. It rose to prominence during the mid-19th century, when

THIS OPEN SORE OF THE WORLD

David Livingstone, the famous explorer and missionary, was born in 1813 in Scotland. After a childhood spent working at a local cotton gin, followed by medical studies and ordination, he sailed for South Africa, arriving in 1841. Over the next two decades, Livingstone penetrated some of the most inaccessible corners of the continent on a series of expeditions, making his way north into the Kalahari, west to present-day Angola and the Atlantic coast, and east along the Zambezi River to Victoria Falls. In 1866, he departed from the Mikindani area in southeastern Tanzania for what was to be his final expedition, seeking to conclusively solve the riddle of the Nile's source. He reached as far as Ujiji, where he was famously 'found' by the American journalist Henry Morton Stanley.

After exploring parts of Lake Tanganyika with Stanley and spending time near Tabora, Livingstone set off again on his quest. He died in 1873 in Chitambo, in present-day Zambia. After cutting out and burying his heart, his porters carried his embalmed body in an epic 1500km journey to Bagamoyo and the sea, from where it was then taken to England.

During his travels, Livingstone was tormented by the ravages of the slave trade that surrounded him. On his trips back to Europe, he spoke and wrote ceaselessly against it in an effort to expose its horrors and injustices to the rest of the world. These efforts, combined with the attention attracted by his well-publicised funeral, the establishment of Freedom Village in Bagamoyo and reports from other missionaries, marked a point of no return for the slave trade. British attempts to stop the trade were mobilised, and it finally ground to a halt in the early 20th century.

In 1874, Livingstone was buried with full honours in London's Westminster Abbey. Today a plaque memorialises his efforts with what were purportedly his last written words: 'All I can add in my solitude, is, may heaven's rich blessing come down on every one, American, English or Turk, who will help to heal this open sore of the world.'

it was a linchpin between the Zanzibar sultanate and the inland caravan routes, and it was during this era that the riverfront slave depot was built. Pangani's oldest building is the old *boma,* which dates to 1810 and was originally the private residence of a wealthy Omani trader. More recent is the Customs House, built a decade later. Probably several centuries older is the settlement at Bweni, diagonally opposite Pangani on the southern bank of the river, where a 15th-century grave has been found.

In September 1888, Pangani was the first town to rebel against the German colonial administration during the Abushiri Revolt.

◎ Sights & Activities

Staff at the Pangani Cultural Tourism Program office (☉8am-5pm) in the yellow building at the bus stand (not to be confused with the similarly named cultural-tourism office diagonally opposite the ferry dock), organise town tours (per person US$10), river cruises (US$70 for up to three people), full-day bicycle trips to Ushongo (per person Tsh40,000) and excursions to Maziwe Marine Reserve (US$40 per person). All the hotels south of Pangani also organise Maziwe trips and other activities around Pangani, often more reliably and at more economical rates than the cultural tourism program office.

Tanga Coelacanth Marine Park   PARK
(adult/child US$20/10) The goal of this recently declared 'park' is to protect the local population of prehistoric coelacanth fish. Temporary headquarters are in Kigombe village, about 20km north of Pangani. At the time of research, no fees were being collected, and the park was existing in name only.

Maziwe Marine Reserve   SNORKELLING
(adult/child US$10/5) About 10km offshore is this tiny sand island with snorkelling in the surrounding crystal-clear waters. Dolphins favour the area and are frequently spotted. Maziwe can only be visited at low tide; there's no food or drink, but a picnic lunch is included in most excursions. Most hotels organise these for about US$35 to US$45 per person.

Kasa Divers   DIVING
(☑0784 134056; kasadivers@gmail.com; Ushongo Beach) A good contact for snorkelling, diving and excursions, including to Maziwe island. It's at the northern end of Ushongo beach, next to Emayani Beach Lodge (p134).

Pangani River Boat Trips

Meandering along the southern edge of town, the muddy Pangani attracts waterbirds, crocodiles and other animals. It's best explored on a river cruise via local dhow, which can be arranged with any of the hotels. Expect to pay about US$70 for up to three people.

🛏 Sleeping & Eating

🛏 Town Centre

Seaside Community Centre Hostel   GUESTHOUSE $$
(☑0755 276422; s/d/tr US$20/30/60, with aircon US$30/50/75; ℗ �) This church-run place has spotless, pleasant rooms with fans and verandas, and meals on order. Its motto: 'Lovely and tenderly service is our joy and mission'. It's about 1km from the bus stand (Tsh2000 in a taxi).

As you enter Pangani from Tanga, shortly after the tarmac begins, a small road branches right to the bus stand and left to the hostel; watch for the small signpost. After turning, continue 300m straight, then go right. The hostel is about 50m along, to the left, down a small lane.

🛏 North of Pangani

Peponi Holiday Resort   CAMPGROUND, BANDAS $$
(☑0784 202962; www.peponiresort.com; camping US$6.50, s/d half board US$75/98; ℗ @ glyph glyph) Relaxing Peponi is set in expansive palm-studded grounds on the beach 20km north of Pangani. There's a shady beachfront campsite, simple, breezy double and family bungalows, a restaurant and bar, a small pool and a handcrafted dhow for snorkelling excursions. It's an ideal spot for families and campers. Buses running along the Pangani–Tanga road will drop you at the gate.

Capricorn Beach Cottages   BOUTIQUE HOTEL $$
(☑0784 632529; www.capricornbeachcottages.com; s/d US$82/120; ℗ glyph glyph) This classy place on the beach 19km north of Pangani has three lovely, spacious self-catering cottages set in large grounds dotted with baobab trees. Each cottage has a hammock and a veranda. There's a clothing boutique, pizza oven, a deli selling homemade bread and other gourmet essentials, and the possibility for catered dinners under the stars. Wonderfully relaxing.

Mkoma Bay
LODGE $$

(☑ 0786 434001, 0784 283565; www.mkomabay.com; s/d luxury tents from US$90/155, 4-8-person house from US$320; P @ 🛜 🗷) The highlights at this stylish lodge are the magnificent views over Mkoma Bay and the subdued, comfortable ambience. Accommodation is in seven raised, well-appointed tents of the sort you find in upmarket safari camps, set around expansive grounds on a low cliff overlooking the beach. There is also a four-bedroom self-catering house and a good restaurant. This is excellent value.

Swimming in the bay and beach walking are wonderful, and kayaks are available to use. It's 3km north of the Pangani–Muheza road junction.

Bahari Pori
LODGE $$

(☑ 0754 073573, 0713 917754; www.baharipori.com; s/d/tw US$50/88/88, 6-person cottage US$230; P 🛜 🗷) On a small cliff set well back from the water, Bahari Pori has pleasant, Zanzibari-bedded safari-style tents set around lovely manicured grounds overlooking the mangroves and the sea in the distance. There's an Italian restaurant and a pizza oven. A footpath leads about 10 minutes down the escarpment and through the mangroves to a small swimming beach.

It's about 7km north of the Pangani–Muheza road junction.

🛏 Ushongo Beach

The beaches get more beautiful the further south you go. Lovely Ushongo beach is a beautiful, long arc of fine white sand about 15km south of the Pangani River.

Beach Crab Resort
CAMPGROUND, COTTAGES $

(☑ 0784 543700, 0767 543700; www.thebeachcrab.com; camping US$6, s/d/tr beach huts US$23/36/54, s/d/tr bungalows US$70/100/120; P 🛜) 🌴 This backpacker- and family-friendly place is at the southern end of Ushongo beach. It has beachside camping, spotless, good-value backpacker huts sharing clean ablution blocks with the campsite, plus simple, comfortable and airy double and family bungalows. It also has a large, beachside bar-restaurant, windsurfing, kayaks, beach volleyball, snorkelling excursions and a raised tree-house lounge.

The ambience is natural and relaxed, the setting lovely and the owners are very helpful. Pick-ups can be arranged from the Pangani ferry.

Emayani Beach Lodge
LODGE $$

(☑ 0782 457668, 027-264 0755; www.emayanilodge.com; s/d half board US$115/180) On the northern end of Ushongo beach, Emayani has a row of pleasant, rustic bungalows strung out along a fine stretch of sand. The ambience is very natural – all bungalows are made entirely of thatching and open to the breezes – and the cuisine is tasty. Kayaks and windsurfing equipment are available to rent.

There's a nearby outfitter for snorkelling, diving and other excursions.

Tides
LODGE $$$

(☑ 0784 225812; www.thetideslodge.com; s/d half board from US$245/340; P @ 🗷) The beautiful Tides has a prime seaside location on a wonderful stretch of beach, delightful, spacious, upmarket cottages directly on the sand and excellent cuisine. The cottages have huge beds surrounded by billowing mosquito nets, large bathrooms and stylish decor. There are also several family cottages and a private honeymooners' luxury suite, plus a beachside bar and restaurant.

The lodge arranges honeymooners' snorkelling trips to Maziwe, complete with a waiter, cool box, champagne and all the trimmings.

🛏 Sange Beach

Lovely, long and almost-deserted Sange beach is about midway between Pangani town and the northern border of Saadani park. Many new lodges are under construction, but only a few were open at the time of research.

★ Tembo Kijani
LODGE $$

(☑ 0687 027454, 0785 117098; www.pangani-ecolodge.com; d tree house/cottage full board US$160/215; P) 🌴 This small ecolodge on a wonderful stretch of beach has four completely open-sided tree-house *bandas* nestled into the bush just back from the sea, two comfortable ground-level beach cottages and delicious, healthy cuisine. The owners have made great efforts to minimise the lodge's footprint and maximise sustainability. The overall results are impressive, with the lodge running on solar and wind power.

Saadani safaris, bush walks and other cultural excursions can be arranged, including visits to nearby Maangati cattle herders and tastings of the local coconut beer. Baboons,

THE ABUSHIRI REVOLT

Although the Abushiri Revolt, one of East Africa's major colonial rebellions, is usually associated with Bagamoyo, Pangani was its birthplace. The catalyst came in 1884, when a young German, Carl Peters, founded the German East Africa Company (Deutsch-Ostafrikanische Gesellschaft or DOAG). Over the next few years, in an effort to tap into the lucrative inland caravan trade, Peters managed to extract agreement from the Sultan of Zanzibar that the DOAG could take over the administration of customs duties in the sultan's mainland domains. However, neither the sultan's representative in Pangani nor the majority of locals were amenable to the idea. When the DOAG raised its flag next to that of the sultan, simmering tensions exploded. Under the leadership of an Afro-Arab trader named Abushiri bin Salim al-Harth, a loosely organised army, including many of the sultan's own guards, ousted the Germans, igniting a series of fierce power struggles that continued in other port towns along the coast. The Germans didn't subdue the revolt until more than a year later, after the arrival of reinforcements, the imposition of a naval blockade and the hanging of Abushiri. In the wake of the revolt, the DOAG went bankrupt and the colonial capital was moved from Bagamoyo to Dar es Salaam.

dik-diks and other small wildlife are frequent visitors at camp.

Kijongo Bay Resort LODGE $$$
(📞0787 055572; www.kijongobayresort.com; s/d half board from US$230/340; 🅿🛜🏊) Kijongo Bay's highlights (apart from the long, lovely beach stretching in front) are its seven spacious, airy two-storey villas. They're all set in a large, sandy compound, and each can sleep up to six, including on an upper open-air terrace. There's a motorised boat for river trips and excursions. It has a restaurant, and there are plans for a spa.

ℹ Information

The closest banks and ATMs are in Tanga.

ℹ Getting There & Away

AIR

There are daily flights connecting Mashado airstrip (just south of Pangani town, on the south side of the river) with Dar es Salaam (US$160 one way), Zanzibar (US$110), Kilimanjaro airport (US$230) and Arusha (US$250) with Coastal Aviation (p67) and Auric Air (p381).

BOAT

Dhows sail regularly between Pangani and Mkokotoni, on the northwestern coast of Zanzibar. Better and safer is the fast MV *Ali Choba*, which sails three times weekly between Ushongo (south of Pangani), Pangani and Zanzibar. The trip takes about 90 minutes, and costs US$290 per boat for up to five passengers, or US$55 per person for five or more passengers between Ushongo and Zanzibar (US$310 per boat or US$60 per person between Pangani and Zanzibar). Book through your hotel or Emayani

Beach Lodge. Another option is to contact the reliable **Mr Wahidi** (📞0784-489193), who offers motorised dhow transfers between Pangani town and either Nungwi or Kendwa on Zanzibar for US$150 per boat for up to four people, plus US$35 per additional person. Allow about four hours for the trip.

BUS

The best connections between Pangani and Tanga are via the rehabilitated coastal road, with about five buses daily (Tsh2500, 1½ hours). The first departure from Pangani is at about 6.30am, so you can connect with a Tanga–Arusha bus. There's at least one daily direct bus between Pangani and Dar es Salaam (Tsh13,000). It's also possible to reach Pangani from Muheza (Tsh2500), from where there are connections to Tanga or Korogwe, but the road is worse and buses are sporadic.

There's also a daily bus between Tanga and Mkwaja (at the northern edge of Saadani National Park) that passes Mwera village (6km from Ushongo) daily at about 7am going north and 3.30pm going south. It's then usually possible to hire a motorcycle to take you from Mwera to Ushongo.

CAR & MOTORCYCLE

For Ushongo and the beaches south of Pangani, all the Ushongo hotels do pick-ups from both Bweni (the village just across the river from Pangani town) and Tanga.

The vehicle ferry over the Pangani River from Pangani to Bweni village runs regularly between about 6am and 10pm daily (Tsh200 per person, Tsh5000 per vehicle). From Bweni, you can arrange a taxi in advance with the Ushongo hotels (about Tsh30,000 per taxi for up to three passengers). Otherwise, motorcycles charge about Tsh10,000 to the Ushongo hotels.

Tanga

POP 273,300

Tanga, a major industrial centre until the collapse of the sisal market, is Tanzania's second-largest seaport and its fourth-largest town behind Dar es Salaam, Mwanza and Arusha. Despite its size, it's a pleasant place with a sleepy, semicolonial atmosphere, wide streets filled with cyclists and motorcycles, intriguing architecture and faded charm. It makes an amenable stop en route to or from Mombasa, and is a springboard to the beaches around Pangani.

The town centre is along the waterfront and easily covered on foot. About 1.5km south of here (Tsh2000 in a taxi), and south of the railway tracks in the Ngamiani section, is the bus station. About 2km east of town, reached by following Hospital Rd (which runs parallel to the water) is the quiet, residential Ras Kazone section, with several hotels and eateries.

History

Although there has probably been a reasonably sized settlement at Tanga since at least the Shirazi era, the town first came into its own in the early to mid-19th century as a starting point for trade caravans to the interior. Ivory was the main commodity traded, with a turnover of about 70,000lb annually in the late 1850s, according to explorer Richard Burton who visited here. The real boom, however, came with the arrival of the Germans in the late 19th century. They built up the town and harbour as part of the construction of a railway line linking Moshi and the Kilimanjaro region with the sea. The Germans also introduced sisal to the area, and Tanzania soon became the world's leading producer and exporter of the crop, with sisal the centre of local economic life. In WWI, Tanga was the site of the Battle of Tanga (later memorialised in William Boyd's novel, *An Ice-Cream War*), in which poorly prepared British troops were soundly trounced by the Germans.

As the world sisal market began to collapse in the 1970s, Tanga's economy spiralled downward. Today, much of the town's infrastructure has been abandoned and the economy is just a shadow of its former self, although vast plantations still stretch westwards along the plains edging the Usambara Mountains.

◉ Sights & Activities

The most interesting areas for a stroll are around Jamhuri Park overlooking the harbour. Here you'll find the old German-built clock tower, and the park and cemetery surrounding the Askari Monument at the end of Market St.

Urithi Tanga Museum
MUSEUM

(☑0784 440068; Independence Ave; ⊙9am-5pm Mon-Sat, 10am-2pm Sun) **FREE** Tanga's old *boma* has been rehabilitated, and now houses this small but worthwhile museum, with historical photos and artefacts from the area.

Toten Island
HISTORIC SITE

Directly offshore from Tanga is this small, mangrove-ringed island ('Island of the Dead') with the overgrown ruins of a mosque dating at least to the 17th century and some 18th- and 19th-century gravestones. Pottery fragments from the 15th century have also been found, indicating that the island may have been settled during the Shirazi era. Toten Island's apparently long history ended in the late 19th century, when its inhabitants moved to the mainland.

While the ruins are less accessible and less atmospheric than those at nearby Tongoni, the island is worth a look if you have extra time. Excursions can be organised through the Tatona Tourist Information Centre (p139) for about US$65 per person including motorboat transfer and guided tour.

Tanga Yacht Club
SWIMMING

(☑027-264 4246; www.tangayachtclub.com; Hospital Rd, Ras Kazone; day admission Tsh3000) This place has a small, clean beach, showers and a restaurant-bar area overlooking the water. It's a pleasant place to relax and, especially on weekend afternoons, it's a good spot to meet resident expats and get the lowdown on what's happening in town.

⊨ Sleeping

⊨ Central Tanga

ELCT Mbuyukenda Tumaini Hostel
GUESTHOUSE $

(☑0763 410059; mbuyukendahostel@elct-ned.org; Hospital Rd; s Tsh20,000, d in old/new wing from Tsh25,000/30,000; ℗) Rather faded overall, but the newer rooms (all doubles) are decent value for the price. It's in a quiet compound just southwest of Bombo Hospital, and diagonally opposite Katani House. Meals can be arranged with advance notice. Taxis charge Tsh5000 from the bus stand.

Motel Sea View
HOTEL $

(Bandarini Hotel; ☑ 0713 383868, 027-264 5581; motelseaviewtang@hotmail.com; Independence Ave; r Tsh35,000; P) In a colonial-era building opposite Jamhuri Park, this place is faded and scruffy but atmospheric. The double-bedded rooms have fans but no mosquito nets, and a few have verandas overlooking the harbour. The in-house restaurant serves breakfast and dinner only.

Central City Hotel
HOTEL $

(☑ 0718 282272, 027-264 4476; centralcityhotel ltd@yahoo.com; Street No 8, Ngamiani; r Tsh45,000-60,000; P✳) This bland but reliable budget choice is the closest hotel to the bus stand that we can recommend. Rooms have fans, hot water, a minifridge and a double bed. There is also a restaurant. From the bus stand, go right onto Taifa Rd ('Double Rd') to the roundabout. At the roundabout, go right onto Street No 8; Central City is 600m down on your left.

Regal Naivera Hotel
HOTEL $

(☑ 0765 641464, 027-264 5669; regalnaivera hotel@yahoo.com; r Tsh45,000-100,000; P✳🛜) This large, pink edifice is in a quiet location

two blocks in from Hospital Rd and behind Katani House. It has clean, modern rooms in varying sizes, all with a double bed, fan, air-con and minifridge. It also has a restaurant.

CBA Hotel
HOTEL $

(☑ 0689 444000; www.cbahotel.com; Ras Kazone Hotel; s/d Tsh50,000/55,000; P✳🛜) CBA has a quiet setting in a large garden. It has clean, modest rooms with mosquito nets that are reasonable value for money. It also has a restaurant. It's directly opposite Tanga Yacht Club.

Nyumbani Hotel
HOTEL $$

(☑ 027-264 5411; www.nyumbanihotels.com; Independence Ave; s/d Tsh70,000/95,000; P✳🛜✉) Modern rooms, efficient service, a restaurant, a small pool and a central location are the main selling points of this otherwise un-distinguished high-rise hotel.

Mkonge Hotel
HOTEL $$

(☑ 027-264 3440; mkongehotel@kaributanga. com; Hospital Rd; s/d US$80/90, with sea view US$90/100; P✳🛜✉) The imposing Mkonge Hotel, in a lovely setting on a vast, grassy lawn overlooking the sea, has reason-ably comfortable rooms (worth the extra money for a sea view), lackadaisical service, a restaurant and wonderful views. The pool costs Tsh5000 for nonguests.

NORTHEASTERN TANZANIA TANGA

WORTH A TRIP

PLACE OF RUINS

Tongoni Ruins (adult/child Tsh10,000/5000; ⊘ 8am-5pm) About 20km south of Tanga, just off the coastal road, the Tongoni Ruins are set picturesquely between baobabs over-looking the mangrove-lined coast. They include the crumbling remains of a mosque and about 20 overgrown Shirazi pillar-style tombs, the largest collection of such tombs on the East African coast. Both the mosque and the tombs are estimated to date from the 14th or 15th century.

Tongoni's heyday was in the 15th century, when it had its own sultan and was an inad-vertent port of call for Vasco da Gama, whose ship ran aground here. By the early 18th century the settlement had declined to the point of nonexistence, due to Portuguese dis-ruption of local trade networks and the fall of Mombasa. In the late 18th century, it was resettled by Shirazis fleeing Kilwa (who named it Sitahabu, or 'Better Here Than There'), and experienced a brief revival, before declining completely shortly thereafter.

Although most of Tongoni's pillars have long since toppled to the ground, you can still see the recessed areas on some where decorative porcelain vases and offering bowls were placed. There are also about two dozen more recent, and largely unremarkable, tombs dating from the 18th or 19th century.

To get here, take any vehicle heading towards Pangani along the coastal road and get out at the turn-off (marked by a signboard). The ruins are about 1km further east on foot, on the far edge of the village (ask for 'magofu'). It's worth getting an early start, as finding a lift back in the afternoon can be difficult. Taxis from town charge from about Tsh15,000 for the round trip.

Tanga

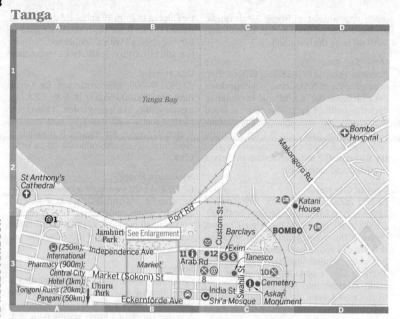

Tanga

Majuba's B&B   B&B $$

(graberh1@gmail.com; Raskazone Rd; d US$100;
Ⓟ❋🛜🏊) This B&B offers two quiet, spa-
cious and beautifully decorated luxury rooms,
each with a minifridge and satellite TV.

🛏 Outside Tanga

Meeting Point Tanga   LODGE $$
(☏0716 666617; www.meetingpointtanga.net;
Tanga International Conference Centre; s/tw from
US$55/75, 4- or 5-person bungalows US$190-
200; @) This large compound, located on a
mangrove estuary south of town, has simple
twin-bedded rooms sharing ablutions and
spacious self-catering waterside bungalows.
There's a small swimming area in the estuary, a dhow, Swahili language courses and
drumming instruction.

The centre is involved in various community projects, and makes a good base for
anyone wanting to explore the Tanga area in
greater depth. Go about 6km along the Pangani road to the signposted turn-off (shortly
after the tarmac ends); the lodge is around
4km away.

Fish Eagle Point   LODGE $$
(☏0784 346006; www.fisheaglepoint.com; per
person full board US$90-144; Ⓟ🏊) 🌿 Fish
Eagle Point, on a mangrove-fringed cove,
has spacious beachfront cottages in varying
sizes, a dhow, snorkelling, sea kayaking, fish-
ing and birding. It's ideal for families. Fol-
low the Horohoro road north from Tanga for
38km to the signposted right-hand turn-off,
from where it's 10km further.

✕ Eating

Tanga Fresh   DAIRY $
(yoghurt & milk from Tsh500; ⊗6.30am-4pm)
Tanga is the home of Tanga Fresh, which
produces delicious, fresh yoghurt and milk
that is sold throughout the region. The
outlet is at the end of the small dirt road
opposite the Tanesco building; look for the
big gate to the left.

SD Supermarket   SUPERMARKET $
(Bank St; ⊗9am-1.30pm & 3-6pm Mon-Fri, 9am-
2pm Sat) A good stop for self-caterers; it's
behind the market.

Food Palace   INDIAN $
(☑027-264 6816; Market St; meals Tsh7000;
⊗7.30am-4pm daily & 7-10pm Fri-Sun) Offers
tasty Indian snacks and meals, including
some vegetarian selections, and good local
ambience.

Pizzeria d'Amore   ITALIAN $$
(☑0715 395391, 0683 171356; Hospital Rd; meals
Tsh10,000-18,000; ⊗11.30am-2pm & 6.30-11pm
Tue-Sun) A small garden restaurant with
tasty pizzas, pasta and continental fare. It
has an upstairs, breezy terrace for dining
and a bar.

Tanga Yacht Club   EUROPEAN $$
(☑027-264 4246; www.tangayachtclub.com; Hos-
pital Rd, Ras Kazone; admission Tsh3000, meals
from Tsh9000; ⊗lunch & dinner Wed-Mon) Seafood and mixed grill dishes, overlooking the
water.

ℹ Information

DANGERS & ANNOYANCES
The harbour area is seedy and best avoided.
In the evenings, take care around Port Rd and
Independence Ave near Jamhuri Park.

INTERNET
Click On-Line (Custom St; per hour Tsh2000;
⊗8.30am-6pm Mon-Sat) Internet cafe.

MEDICAL SERVICES
International Pharmacy (☑0713 237137;
Street No 7) Well-stocked pharmacy.

MONEY
Barclays (Independence Ave) ATM.
Exim (Independence Ave) Next to Barclays;
ATM.
NBC (cnr Bank & Market Sts) Just west of the
market. Changes cash; ATM.

TOURIST INFORMATION
Tatona Tourist Information Centre (www.
tangatourism.com; ⊗8am-4.30pm Mon-Fri,
to 1pm Sat) The helpful staff at Tatona can
provide information on nearby attractions,
and advice for accommodation and transport
options. They will also link you up with Tatona-
approved (ie reliable) tour agencies and guides
for excursions. Stop in here first, before visiting
any of the other 'tourism offices' in town.

Its office is diagonally opposite the post office
in the small white gazebo.

ℹ Getting There & Away

AIR
There are daily flights on **Coastal Aviation**
(☑0778-242966, 0658-777762; pembaaviation
tanga@gmail.com; Independence Ave) and Auric
Air (p381) one way between Tanga and Dar es
Salaam US$190, Zanzibar US$120 and Pemba
$US95). Auric Air's Tanga booking agent is the
Tatona Tourist Information Centre. The airstrip
is about 3km west of town along the Korogwe
road (Tsh4000 by taxi).

BUS
Buses for Dar es Salaam depart daily every few
hours from 6.30am to 2pm in each direction
(Tsh12,000 to Tsh18,000, six hours).

To Arusha, there are at least three departures
daily between about 6am and 11am (Tsh12,000
to Tsh17,000, seven to eight hours). To Lushoto

(Tsh7000, four hours), several direct buses daily depart from 7am.

To Pangani (Tsh2500, 1½ hours) there are several larger buses and many dalla-dallas throughout the day along the coastal road.

All transport leaves from the main bus stand on Taifa Rd ('Double Rd'), at the corner of Street No 12.

ⓘ Getting Around

There are taxi ranks at the bus station, and at the junction of Usambara and India Sts. Tatona Tourist Information Centre (p139) can help with bicycle rental. Occasional dalla-dallas run along Ocean Rd between the town centre and Ras Kazone.

Amboni Caves

Long the subject of local legend, these limestone caves (per adult/child Tsh20,000/10,000) are one of the most extensive subterranean systems in East Africa and an intriguing excursion for anyone with an interest in spelunking. Now home to thousands of bats, they were traditionally believed to house various spirits, and continue to be a place of worship and ritual.

The caves were originally thought to extend 200km or more, and are said to have been used by the Kenyan Mau Mau during the 1950s as a hideout from the British. Although a 1994 survey concluded that their extent was much smaller – with the largest of the caves studied only 900m long – rumours of them reaching all the way to Mombasa persist.

It's possible to visit a small portion of the cave network, which is quite interesting, once you get past the litter at the entrance. Bring along a torch and wear closed shoes to avoid picking bat droppings off your feet afterwards.

The caves are about 8km northwest of Tanga off the Tanga–Mombasa road, and best accessed via bicycle arranged through Tatona Tourist Information Centre (p139) (US$45 per person including entry fee, bicycle rental and guide).

Alternatively, take a dalla-dalla towards Amboni village and get off at the turn-off for the caves, near the forestry office. From here, it's 2.5km on foot to Kiomoni village; the caves stretch west of Kiomoni along the Mkulumuzi River.

Galanos Sulphur Springs

If bending and crawling around the caves has left you feeling stiff in the joints, consider finishing the day with a visit to these green, odorous and rather underwhelming sulphur springs (Tsh5000 per person) nearby. (They are included with most Amboni Cave tours.) The springs take their name from a Greek sisal planter who was the first to recognise their potential for relaxation after the rigours of a long day in the fields. Now, although still in use, they are quite unappealing despite their purportedly therapeutic properties.

The unsignposted turn-off for the springs is along the Tanga–Mombasa road, about 2km north of the turn-off for the caves, just after crossing the Sigi River. From here, it's about 2km. Dalla-dallas from Tanga run as far as Amboni village, from where you'll need to continue on foot.

Muheza

Muheza is a scrappy junction town where the roads to Amani Nature Reserve and to Pangani branch off the main Tanga highway. Although well inland, it's culturally very much part of the coastal Tanga region, with a humid climate, strong Swahili influences and surrounding landscapes marked by extensive sisal plantations broken by stands of palms. Muheza's main market and trading area, dominated by rows of rickety wooden market stalls and small corrugated metal-roofed houses, is about 1km uphill from the main highway.

🛏 Sleeping & Eating

GK Lodge   GUESTHOUSE

(r Tsh13,000) This local guesthouse has clean, basic rooms but no food. It's 1.2km from the bus stand: follow signs to Amani Nature Reserve; after crossing the railroad tracks, continue along the Amani road for 500m to the signposted right-hand turn-off.

ⓘ Getting There & Away

Transport to Amani leaves from the bus stand just off the Tanga road. There are two buses daily to and from Amani, departing Muheza about 2pm (Tsh3500, two hours), and Amani at 6am. There are connections to Tanga (Tsh2000, 45 minutes) throughout the day, and direct daily buses in the morning to Lushoto (Tsh4000, three hours).

WORTH A TRIP

LUTINDI CULTURAL TOURISM

Lutindi Cultural Tourism Project (☎0763 695541, 027-264 1040; lutindi-hospital@elct.org) About 20km northwest of Korogwe at Msimbazi village is the signposted turn-off for Lutindi and the Lutindi Cultural Tourism Project. Lutindi is the site of the first mental hospital in East Africa, and you can arrange a tour through the compound, visit the workshops where some residents are employed at craft making, walk in the surrounding tea plantations and gain insights into a side of local life far removed from general tourism.

There's a simple guesthouse (per person Tsh25,000), with breakfast, lunch and dinner available (Tsh3000 to Tsh7000). Take a dalla-dalla from Korogwe for about 6km to Welei village. You'll need to walk the remaining 7km from here. Taxis from Korogwe to Lutindi charge about Tsh35,000.

Korogwe

Korogwe is primarily of interest as a transport junction. In the western part of town, known as 'new' Korogwe, are the bus stand and several accommodation options. To the east is 'old' Korogwe, with the now-defunct train station. Southwest of town, a rough road branches down to **Handeni**, known for its beekeeping and honey production, and its hospital.

Sleeping & Eating

Motel White Parrot MOTEL $
(☎0758 989243; motelwhiteparrot@gmail.com; Main Hwy; camping Tsh15,000, s/d from Tsh40,000/50,000; P ❄) This roadside rest stop has a collection of plastic animals at the entrance, clean, decent rooms, an adjoining, grassy campsite with hot-water showers and cooking area, and a restaurant. If you need to break your journey, it's a soulless but efficient place to stop.

USAMBARA MOUNTAINS

With their wide vistas, cool climate, winding paths and picturesque villages, the Usambaras are one of northeastern Tanzania's delights. Rural life revolves around a cycle of bustling, colourful market days that rotate from one village to the next, and is largely untouched by the booming safari scene and influx of 4WDs in nearby Arusha. It's easily possible to spend at least a week trekking from village to village or exploring with day walks.

The Usambaras, which are part of the ancient Eastern Arc chain, are divided into two ranges separated by a 4km-wide valley. The western Usambaras, around Lushoto, are the most accessible. The better road network here means they get a lot of tourists. The eastern Usambaras, around Amani, are less developed. Both ranges are densely populated, with an average of more than 300 people per sq km. The main tribes are the Sambaa, Kilindi, Zigua and Mbugu.

Although the climate is comfortable year-round, paths get too muddy for trekking during the rainy season. The best time to visit is from June to November, after the rains and when the air is clearest.

Amani Nature Reserve

The often overlooked **Amani Nature Reserve** (adult/child US$10/5 per visit, not per day) is located west of Tanga in the heart of the eastern Usambaras. It's a peaceful, lushly vegetated patch of montane forest humming with the sounds of rushing water, chirping insects and singing birds. It is also exceptionally rich in unique plant and bird species – a highly worthwhile detour for those ornithologically or botanically inclined. Among the unique bird species you may see are Amani sunbirds, banded green sunbirds and the green-headed oriole.

History

Although Amani was only gazetted as a nature reserve in 1997, research in the area began a century earlier when the Germans established a research station and botanical gardens here. Large areas of forest were cleared and numerous new species introduced. Within a few years the gardens were the largest in Africa, totalling 304 hectares and containing between 600 and 1000 different species of plants, including many endemic species. Soon thereafter, exploitation of the surrounding forest began and the gardens began to decline. A sawmill was

CHIEF KIMWERI

Kimweri, chief of the powerful Kilindi (Shambaa) kingdom during the first half of the 19th century, is one of the Usambara region's most legendary figures. From his capital at Vuga (on the main road between Mombo and Lushoto), he ruled over an area stretching from Kilimanjaro in the north to the Indian Ocean in the east, levying tributes on towns as distant as Pangani. The extent of his dominion in the coastal regions soon brought him into conflict with Sultan Seyyid Said of Zanzibar, who also claimed sovereignty over the same areas. Ultimately, the two leaders reached an agreement for joint governance of the northeastern coast. This arrangement lasted until Kimweri's death in 1869, after which the sultan assumed full authority.

Tradition holds that Kimweri had magical powers, including control of the rain and the ability to call down famines upon his enemies. His kingdom was highly organised, divided into subchiefdoms ruled by his sons and districts ruled by governors, prime ministers and local army commanders. It was Kimweri to whom the missionary Johann Ludwig Krapf went to request land to build his first church for the Anglican Church Missionary Society.

Following the death of Kimweri, interclan rivalries caused the kingdom to break up, and fighting over who was to succeed him continued until the Germans arrived in the region.

started and a railway link was built connecting Zigi, about 12km below Amani, with the main Tanga–Moshi line to transport timber to the coast.

During the British era, research shifted to Nairobi, and the railway was replaced by a road linking Amani with Muheza. Many of the facilities at Amani were taken over by the nearby government-run malaria research centre and the gardens fell into neglect.

More recently, thanks to funding from the Tanzanian and Finnish governments and the EU, projects have been underway to promote sustainable resource use by local communities. Local guides have been trained and visitor access to the eastern Usambaras has improved thanks to a trail network.

◉ Sights & Activities

There's a visitor centre at the old Station Master's House at Zigi with information about the area's history, animals and medicinal plants.

Walking Trails

For getting around, there's a network of short walks along shaded forest paths that can be done alone or with a guide (per person per day US$15). Most trails take between one and three hours. They are detailed in the booklet *A Guide to Trails and Drive Routes in Amani Nature Reserve*, on sale at the information centre at Zigi and at the reserve office in Amani.

🛏 Sleeping & Eating

Zigi Rest House CAMPGROUND, GUESTHOUSE $
(☑ 027-264 0313, 0784 587805; www.amaninature.org; camping US$30; s/d Tsh15,000/30,000; breakfast/lunch/dinner Tsh3000/6000/6000) Rooms here have bathrooms, three twin beds and are quieter and marginally more comfortable than those at Amani Conservation Centre Resthouse. There is hot water for bathing and meals are available, though it's a good idea to bring fruit or snacks as supplements. Camping is possible; bring all supplies. It is located at the main reserve gate.

**Amani Conservation Centre
Rest House** CAMPGROUND, GUESTHOUSE $
(☑ 027-264 0313, 0784 587805; www.amaninature.org; camping US$30; s/d Tsh15,000/30,000; breakfast/lunch/dinner Tsh3000/6000/6000; ℗) The setting and rustic atmosphere here are better than at Zigi Rest House, but rooms aren't as comfortable and they can be less peaceful. There is also a small area to pitch a tent, a supply of hot water and simple meals available. Continue straight past the main fork in Amani to the reserve office. The guesthouse is next to the office.

Amani Forest Camp CAMPGROUND, COTTAGES $
(Emau Hill; ☑ 0782 656526; www.amaniforestcamp.com; camping US$7, s/d/tr tented bandas US$74/98/132, s/d/tr cottage US$94/128/177; ☉ mid-Jun–Mar; ℗) 🌿 This rustic place has good camping, comfortable permanent tents sharing ablutions and the four-person Turaco cottage with bathroom. All are in a wooded

setting with fine birding and walking trails. Continue 1.5km past Amani on the Kwamkoro road to the signposted turn-off, from where it's 3km further along a narrow bush track. Half- and full-board options are also available.

ℹ Information

Entry and guide fees are payable at the Zigi entrance gate.

ℹ Getting There & Away

Amani is 32km northwest of Muheza along a dirt road which is in fair condition, except for the last 7km, where the road is rocky and in bad shape (4WD only). There's at least one truck daily between Muheza and Amani (Tsh3500, two hours), continuing on to Kwamkoro, 9km beyond Amani. Departures from Muheza are between about 1pm and 2pm. Going in the other direction, transport passes Amani (stopping near the conservation centre office) from about 6am.

In the dry season, you can make it in a 2WD as far as Zigi (25km from Muheza), after which you'll need a 4WD. Allow 1½ to two hours between Muheza and Amani, less in a good car with high clearance. There's also a walking trail from Zigi up to Amani (2½ to three hours). Driving from Muheza, the route is straightforward and signposted until the final junction, where you'll see Bulwa signposted to the right; Amani is 2km further to the left.

Mombo

Mombo is the scruffy junction town at the foot of the Usambara Mountains where the road to Lushoto branches off the main Dar es Salaam–Arusha highway. There's no recommended accommodation in Mombo. Most buses from either Arusha or Dar pass at a reasonable hour, so you should have no

ℹ MARKET DAYS

Local villages are especially colourful on market days, when traders come on foot from miles around to peddle their wares:

Bumbuli Saturday, with a smaller market on Tuesday

Lushoto Sunday, with a smaller market on Thursday

Mlalo Wednesday

Soni Tuesday, with a smaller market on Friday

Sunga Wednesday, very colourful

trouble getting a dalla-dalla up to Soni or Lushoto to sleep.

Soni

Tiny Soni has essentially no tourist infrastructure, but makes an amenable stop if you're staying longer in the Usambaras. Guides for all hiking routes from Soni are best arranged in nearby Lushoto, or at Maweni Farm. Among Soni's attractions are Kwa Mungu Mountain, about 30 minutes on foot from Soni village centre, and the small Soni Falls, which you can see to the left along the road coming up from Mombo. Soni is also the starting point for several wonderful walks, including a two- to three-day hike to the Mazumbai Forest Reserve and Bumbuli town, and a three- to five-hour return walk to pine-clad Sakharani, a Benedictine mission that sells locally produced wine. There's also a lovely, longer walk from Maweni Farm up to Gare Mission and on to Lushoto. The area around Gare (one of the first missions in the area) was reforested as part of erosion-control efforts, and it's interesting to see the contrast with some of the treeless, more eroded surrounding areas. After Gare, and as a detour en route to Lushoto, stop at the village of Kwai, where there's a women's pottery project. Kwai was also an early research post for soil science and erosion-control efforts.

🛏 Sleeping & Eating

Maweni Farm   LODGE $$
(☏ 0784 279371, 0784 307841; www.maweni.com/lodge; d US$60-80, without bathroom US$50; ℗ 🛜) This is an atmospheric old farmhouse set in lush, rambling grounds against a backdrop of twittering birds, flowering gardens and a water lily-covered pond, with Kwa Mungu mountain rising up behind. The rooms (some in the main house and some in a separate block) are straightforward and spacious. Meals (with advance notice) and guides can be arranged.

Maweni is 2.9km from the main Soni junction along the dirt road leading past the weekly market.

ℹ Getting There & Away

Soni is about 20km uphill from Mombo along the road to Lushoto (which is 12km further on). It's easy to reach via dalla-dalla from either destination (Tsh1500 from Lushoto, Tsh1500 from Mombo).

Lushoto

This leafy highland town is nestled in a fertile valley at about 1200m, surrounded by pines and eucalyptus mixed with banana plants and other tropical foliage. It's the centre of the western Usambaras and makes an ideal base for hikes into the surrounding hills.

Lushoto is also the heartland of the Wasambaa people (the name 'Usambara' is a corruption of Wasambaa or Washambala, meaning 'scattered'). Local culture is strong. In Muheza and parts of the Tanga region closer to the coast, Swahili is used almost exclusively. Here however, Sambaa is the language of choice for most residents.

History

During the German era Lushoto (then known as Wilhelmstal) was a favoured holiday spot for colonial administrators, a local administrative centre and a mission station. It was even slated at one point to become the colonial capital. Today, thanks to a temperate climate, it's best known for its bustling market – liveliest on Sundays – and its superb walking opportunities. In addition to a handful of colonial-era buildings – notably the German-built churches, the prison and various old country estates – and the paved road from Mombo, the Germans left a legacy of homemade bread and cheeses, now produced by several missions in the area.

Due in part to the high population density of the surrounding area and the resulting deforestation, erosion has long been a serious concern for this region. Erosion-control efforts were first initiated during the British era and today various projects are underway.

Activities

Hiking

The western Usambaras around Lushoto offer wonderful walking. Routes follow well-worn footpaths that weave among villages, cornfields and banana plantations, and range from a few hours to several days. It's possible to hike on your own but you'll need to master basic Swahili phrases, carry a GPS, get a map of the area and plan your route via the handful of villages where local guesthouses are available. However, occasional robberies of solo hikers means that hiking with a guide is recommended.

Most Lushoto hotels can recommend guides and routes, and the tourist informa-

tion centres also organise hikes. Don't go with freelancers who aren't associated with an office or a reliable hotel. Rates vary depending on the hike and have become very costly. Expect to pay Tsh30,000 per person for a half-day hike to Irente Viewpoint. You'll pay up to Tsh125,000 per person per day on multiday hikes, including camping or accommodation in very basic guesthouses, guide fees, forest fees for any hikes that enter forest reserves (which includes most hikes from Lushoto) and food. If you're fit and keen on covering some distance, most of the set stages for the popular hikes are quite short, and it's easy to do two or three stages in a day. However, most guides will want to charge you the full price for the additional days, so you'll need to negotiate an amicable solution. A basic selection of vegetables and fruits is available along most routes and bottled water is sold in several of the larger villages. If you're hiking on your own, carry a filter.

Lushoto can get chilly and wet at any time of year, so bring a waterproof jacket.

Sleeping & Eating

In & Near Town

Tumaini Hostel HOSTEL $
(☑027-264 0094; tumaini@elct-ned.org; Main Rd; d/ste/f Tsh30,000/40,000/50,000, s without bathroom Tsh17,000; ℗) This good-value place run by the Lutheran church offers clean, twin-bedded rooms and hot-water showers in a two-storey compound overlooking tiny gardens. A restaurant is attached. It's directly in the town centre, near the Telecom building. Profits support church-run community projects in the area.

St Eugene's Lodge GUESTHOUSE $
(☑0784 523710, 027-264 0055; www.usambara-st-eugene.com; s/tw/tr/ste US$25/45/54/60) Run by an order of sisters, the unpretentious St Eugene's has pleasant rooms with balconies and views over the surrounding gardens. Tasty meals are served, and homemade cheese and jam are for sale. St Eugene's is along the main road, about 3.5km before Lushoto, on the left coming from Soni. Ask to get dropped at the Montessori Centre.

Rosminian Hostel GUESTHOUSE $
(☑0785 776348, 0684 116688; d Tsh30,000; ℗) This small church-run place has straightfor-

ward double-bedded rooms overlooking a tiny compound. All have hot-water showers, mosquito nets and TVs; meals are available with advance order. It's 1.8km before town, and about 300m off the main road to the left when coming from Soni. Ask the bus driver to drop you at the turn-off.

Lushoto Highland Park HOTEL $

(☑ 0789 428911, 0716 112132; lushotohighlandpark hotel@yahoo.com; s/d/ste US$35/40/50; ℗) Just uphill from the post office, and just below the old District Commissioner's residence, this modern-looking place has reliable although somewhat cluttered and overfurnished rooms. Some have a balcony, all come with mosquito nets and there's a restaurant.

St Benedict's Hostel GUESTHOUSE $

(☑ 0712 369174; camping Tsh7000, s/d/tr Tsh20,000/30,000/45,000) St Benedict's offers one larger double plus several smaller rooms. The rooms are no-frills and rather dark and gloomy, but the location is convenient. Meals are available with advance order. It's next door to and run by the Catholic church.

Lawn's Hotel LODGE $$

(☑ 0784 420252, 0754 464526; www.lawnshotel. com; camping US$12, s/d/tr US$45/55/70; ℗🗟) This Lushoto institution is faded but full of charm, with vine-covered buildings and extensive gardens. It has spacious, slightly dilapidated wooden-floored rooms with fireplaces, plus newer doubles and twin-bedded bungalows, a bar and a restaurant. Turn left at the traffic circle at the town entrance, following the unpaved road up and around to the right through the pine trees to the hotel.

Tumaini Cafe & Makuti African
Restaurant TANZANIAN, EUROPEAN $

(☑ 027-264 0027; Main Rd; meals from Tsh6000; ◷7am-10pm) Tumaini Cafe – on the main road next to the Telecom building – offers cheap snacks, breakfasts and meals, including banana milkshakes, freshly-baked rolls and well-prepared continental fare. In the same compound and under the same management, is Makuti African Restaurant, which is open for lunch and dinner only and serves tasty local food.

🛏 Outside Town

Irente Biodiversity Reserve GUESTHOUSE $

(Irente Farm; ☑ 0784 502935, 0788 503002; www. irentebiodiversityreserve.org; camping Tsh8000,

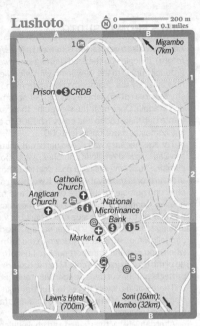

Lushoto

s/d/tr from Tsh30,000/50,000/95,000, 4-/6-person house Tsh200,000/175,000; ℗) ✎ This rustic, church-run place in a quiet setting 4.5km from town has camping, two small double rooms (one sharing ablutions) and accommodation in converted farm buildings, including a six-person self-catering cottage. Rates include a farm breakfast. Irente Farm also prepares picnic lunches for Tsh8000 per person with advance order and sells homemade cheese, jams and bread.

HIKES FROM LUSHOTO

An easy walk to get started is to Irente Viewpoint (6km, allow two to three hours return). It begins on the road running southwest from the Anglican church and leads gradually uphill to the viewpoint, with wide views on clear days. It's impressive to see how abruptly the Usambaras rise up from the plains below. En route is Irente Biodiversity Reserve (p145), where you can get accommodation, or buy fresh cheese, yoghurt and granola. Once near the viewpoint, there are two paths; the better one goes through Irente Cliff View Lodge and costs Tsh2000 to the viewpoint, including a soda. The adjoining 'container route' costs Tsh1000.

For another easy walk, head north out of Lushoto along the road running between the Catholic and Anglican churches. After about five minutes, bear sharply left and start climbing, following the road past scattered houses and small farm plots. About 35 minutes further is the royal village of Kwembago, the traditional seat of the local Sambaa chief and notable for its large open field and handful of old double-storey, balconied houses. Continue uphill, bear right at the junction, and follow the path around and then down again to the other side of the Lushoto valley, where it joins with the tarmac road leading to Migambo. For a longer variant, head left at the large junction after Kwembago, and follow footpaths steeply down to the former mission hospital station of Bumbuli, where you can find transport back to Lushoto via Soni. From Bumbuli, it's a scenic, gentle climb up and into the cool Mazumbai Forest Reserve, which at its higher levels protects patches of dense upper montane forest.

There's also a lovely three- to four-day hike – ideal for scenery and local culture – from Lushoto to Mtae or Mambo through stands of pine, patches of wild asters, cornfields and villages.

Alternatively try the rugged and challenging six-day walk to Amani Nature Reserve. The tourist information centres have wall maps detailing some of the routes. Nearby villages with accommodation include Bumbuli (with rooms at the old Lutheran mission hospital guesthouse), Lukozi (local guesthouse rooms), Rangwi (basic rooms in a lovely setting at the local convent), Mtae (local guesthouses) and Mambo View Point Eco Lodge & Mambo Cliff Inn. In Mazumbai Forest Reserve, there is good accommodation in the middle of the forest at university-run guesthouses.

Swiss Farm Cottage
LODGE $$

(📞 0714 970271, 0784 700813; www.swiss-farmcottage.co.tz; per person half board in standard/luxury bungalow US$50/65; 🅿) This tranquil spot, complete with cows grazing on the hillsides, does a good job of mixing Tanzania with Switzerland. There are standard family rooms, and a bungalow with two doubles sharing a sitting area with a fireplace. The rooms are comfortable and there's hiking at your doorstep.

It's 15km from Lushoto past Migambo village, and a good option for those with private transport.

Mullers Mountain Lodge
LODGE $$

(📞 0784 500999, 0782 315666; www.mullers mountainlodge.co.tz; camping US$10, s/d US$45/60, q without bathroom US$90, cottage US$120; 🅿) This old family homestead is set in sprawling grounds, with rooms in the main house or, for more privacy, in nearby cottages (with two rooms sharing a sitting room). There are also a few less appealing cement huts with shared bathroom, a camping area and a restaurant. It's about 17km from Lushoto past Migambo village, and signposted.

Irente Cliff View Lodge
LODGE $$

(📞 027-264 0026; www.irenteview.com; s/d/ste from US$50/65/120; 🅿) Stunning views over the plains below on clear days from all the rooms compensate for the somewhat overfurnished interior at this lodge, which is built on the edge of a cliff about 1.5km beyond Irente Farm at Irente Viewpoint. Just below is a grassy camping ground (camping US$6) with hot-water showers.

ℹ️ Information

GARAGE
Rosmini Garage (St Patrick's VTC) About 1.5km before town on the Mombo road.

INTERNET ACCESS

Bosnia Internet Café (Main Rd; per hour Tsh2000; ⊙8.30am-6pm Mon-Fri, 9am-2pm Sat) At the southern end of town.

Mt Usambara Communications Centre (per hour Tsh2000; ⊙7.30am-5.30pm) Near the market.

MEDICAL SERVICES

Afro-Medics Duka la Dawa (Main Rd; ⊙8am-1pm & 2-8pm Mon-Sat, 11am-1pm Sun) Near the market.

MONEY

CRDB (Main Rd) ATM; at the Western Union building, diagonally opposite the prison.

National Microfinance Bank (Main Rd; ⊙8am-3pm Mon-Fri) Changes cash only.

TOURIST INFORMATION

Friends of Usambara Society (www.usambara travels.com) Just down the small road running next to NMB bank, with hikes and cycling tours (bring your own bicycle).

SED Tours (☑0784 689848; www.sedadven tures.com; Main Rd) Reliable hikes and cultural tours; on the main road opposite the park.

❶ Getting There & Away

Dalla-dallas go throughout the day between Lushoto and Mombo (Tsh3000, one hour), the junction town on the main highway.

Daily direct buses travel from Lushoto to Tanga (Tsh6000, four hours), Dar es Salaam (Tsh12,000 to Tsh15,000, six to seven hours) and Arusha (Tsh12,000 to Tsh13,000, six hours), with most departures from 7am. To get to the lodges near Migambo, take the road heading uphill and north-east of town to Magamba, turn right at the signposted junction and continue for 7km to Migambo junction, from where the lodges are signposted.

Mlalo

Set in a valley cut by the Umba River, Mlalo is an incongruous place with a Wild West feel, a modest selection of basics and accommodation. Nearby is Kitala Hill, home of one of the Usambara subchiefs. The walk between Mlalo and Mtae (five to six hours, 21km) is beautiful, passing terraced hillsides, picturesque villages and patches of forest. There are no recommended sleeping or eating options.

Buses run daily between Dar es Salaam and Mlalo via Lushoto, departing Lushoto by about 1pm, and Mlalo by about 5am (Tsh4000 between Mlalo and Lushoto). There are also sporadic dalla-dallas.

Mtae & Mambo

Tiny Mtae is perched on a cliff about 55km northwest of Lushoto, with fantastic 270-degree views over the Tsavo Plains and down to Mkomazi National Park. Mambo is just a few kilometres southwest, also with views, and with better sleeping and eating options. The area makes a fine destination if you only have time for one hike from Lushoto. En route is Sunga village, with a colourful market on Wednesdays. Just to the southeast is Shagayu Peak (2220m), one of the highest in the Usambara Mountains. In addition to many walking paths, the area is also known for its traditional healers.

🛏 Sleeping & Eating

Mambo Viewpoint Eco Lodge & Mambo Cliff Inn LODGE, CAMPGROUND $
(☑0785 272150, 0769 522420; www.mambo viewpoint.org; camping US$8-10, s/d in Cliff Inn US$20/35, s/d in Viewpoint from US$60/85; Ⓟ🖥) ✎ This place, reached via the signposted lefthand fork at the junction 3km before Mtae, has stunning views, comfortable cottages and permanent tents. Just a few minutes walk downhill is the affiliated Mambo Cliff Inn, with clean, good-value backpacker accommodation in stone and thatch rondavels. The owners offer information on the area, and can organise hikes, village stays and more.

Overall, it's a great base for exploring the Usambaras. Meals are available at both Mambo Viewpoint (continental fare) and Mambo Cliff Inn (local dishes).

❶ Getting There & Away

The road between Lushoto and Mtae is full of turns and hills, and is particularly beautiful as it

---

GREETINGS IN KISAMBAA

As you're hiking in the Usambaras, you'll likely hear more of the local Sambaa language spoken than Swahili. Following are a few phrases in KiSambaa to get you started.

➡ *Onga maundo* Good morning

➡ *Onga mshee* Good afternoon

➡ *Niwedi* I'm fine (in response to *Onga maundo* or *Onga mshee*)

➡ *Hongea (sana)* Thank you (very much)

winds its way up the final 7km to Mtae. If travelling by public transport you'll need to spend at least one night in Mtae as buses from Lushoto (Tsh7000, four hours) travel only in the afternoons, departing Lushoto by about 1pm. The return buses from Mtae to Lushoto depart between 4am and 5am en route to Dar es Salaam. A taxi from Lushoto costs about Tsh70,000. For Mambo, negotiate with the driver to take you all the way, or get dropped at the Mtae–Mambo junction, from where it is just a short walk to Mambo village and Mambo Cliff Inn.

PARE MOUNTAINS

The lovely and seldom visited Pare Mountains, divided into northern and southern ranges, lie southeast of Kilimanjaro and northwest of the Usambara range. Like the Usambaras, they form part of the ancient Eastern Arc chain, and their steep cliffs and forested slopes host a number of unique birds and plants. Also like the Usambaras, the Pares are densely populated, with many small villages linked by a network of paths and tracks. The main ethnic group here is the Pare (also called the Asu). While there are some historical and linguistic differences among various Pare groups, socially they are considered to be a single ethnic entity.

The Pare Mountains are not as developed for tourism as the Usambaras, and you'll be mostly on your own when exploring. Thanks to the relative isolation, the traditions and folklore of the Pare have remained largely untouched. Unlike the Usambaras, there is no major developed infrastructure base from where you can take a series of hikes. The best way to begin exploration is to head to Same and then up to Mbaga (for the south Pares) or to Usangi (for the north Pares). From both Usangi and Mbaga there are hikes ranging from half a day to three days or more, and English-speaking guides can be arranged.

Same

Same (*sah*-may) is a lively market town and the largest settlement in the southern Pares. You'll need to pass through here to get to Mkomazi National Park and Mbaga, a centre for hikes in this area. Same has little tourist infrastructure and the town is more suitable as a starting point for excursions into the Pares rather than as a base. If you want to

stay a few days before heading into the villages, there are walks into the hills behind town, although for most of the better destinations you will need to take local transport at least part of the way. Sunday is the main market day, when traders from all over the Pares come to trade their wares.

The **Catchment Office** (for paying forest reserve fees) is at the end of town, on the main road past the market.

National Microfinance Bank (go left out of the bus stand, up one block, then left again) changes cash. There's no ATM.

🛏 Sleeping & Eating

Elephant Motel MOTEL $
(☑0754 839545, 027-275 8193; www.elephant motel.com; camping US$10, s/tw/tr US$35/40/50; ℗) Elephant Motel has simple, pleasant rooms, a cavernous restaurant serving up decent meals, a TV, a children's playground and a campground. It's on the main highway 1.5km southeast of town, and is a popular overnight stop for self-drivers en route to the coast from points west. It can help with car hire for Mkomazi safaris.

Amani Lutheran Centre GUESTHOUSE $
(☑0784 894140, 027-275 8107; tw/d Tsh25,000/30,000; ℗) This modest place offers a handful of clean, pleasant, newly renovated rooms in a quiet compound, plus meals on order. It's along the main road about 500m north of the highway, and about five minutes' walk from the bus stand. It can help arrange vehicle rental for Mkomazi safaris through the nearby Lutheran diocese offices.

❶ Getting There & Away

Buses on the Dar es Salaam–Arusha highway stop at Same on request. There's also a direct bus from Arusha to Same, departing Arusha at around 8am (Tsh6000, 2½ hours). To Mbaga, there are one or two vehicles daily, departing Same between 11am and 2pm (Tsh5000, two to three hours).

Mbaga

Mbaga (also known as Mbaga-Manka), in the hills southeast of Same at about 1350m, is a good base for hikes deeper into the surrounding southern Pare mountains. You can walk from here in two or three days to the top of Shengena Peak (2462m), the Pares' highest point. Mbaga, an old Lutheran mission station, has long been an influential town because of its location near the centre of the Pares, and even today it is in many respects a more important local centre than Same.

A popular three-day circular route is from Mbaga to Chome village, where you can spend a night before ascending Shengena Peak on the second day and then returning to Mbaga.

Sleeping & Eating

Hill-Top Tona Lodge LODGE
(☏0754 852010; http://tonalodge.org; camping US$10, r per person without bathroom US$15; P) The rustic Hill-Top Tona Lodge is the former mission house of Jakob Dannholz. It is an amenable base with basic, no-frills cottages, meals and views. It can provide hiking guides. Traditional dancing performances can be arranged. Transport from Same to the lodge can be organised with the owner for about Tsh100,000 to Tsh150,000 per vehicle (worth negotiating for smaller groups).

Getting There & Away

There are one or two uncomfortable vehicles daily around midday from Same to Mbaga, departing Same between about noon and 2pm (Tsh5000, two to three hours, 40km). Coming from Moshi, you'll need to get a bus by 8am in order to reach Mbaga the same day. Coming from Dar es Salaam, you'll probably need to stay overnight in Same. From Mbaga to Same, departures are at 4am. It's also possible to catch one of several daily dalla-dallas from Same to Kisiwani, and then walk about 5km uphill to Mbaga.

If you're driving to Mbaga, there is an alternate route via Mwembe, which can be reached by following the Dar es Salaam–Arusha highway 5km south to the dirt road leading off to the left.

Mwanga & Around

This district capital sprawls across the plains at the foot of the Pares 50km north of Same on the Dar es Salaam–Arusha highway. Once away from the scruffy central junction and old market area, it's a shady, pleasant town with wide, unpaved roads, swathes of green and stands of palm. It's of interest primarily as a transport junction for changing vehicles to Usangi, the starting point for excursions in the northern Pares.

About 10km south of Mwanga is **Nyumba ya Mungu (House of God) Reservoir**, home to Luo fishing communities that originally migrated here from the Lake Victoria area.

❶ PARE MOUNTAINS

Lodging and food in the Pares are, for the most part, very basic. With the exception of Hill-Top Tona Lodge in Mbaga and Mhako Hostel (p150) in Usangi, most accommodation is with villagers or camping. Prices for both average Tsh5000 to Tsh15,000 per person per night. For all destinations, except Mbaga and Usangi, it's a good idea to bring a portable stove.

The best places to arrange guides are Lomwe Secondary School (p150) in Usangi and Hill-Top Tona Lodge in Mbaga. For organised treks, expect to pay per person about Tsh20,000 per day for guide fees, Tsh3000 per day for village fees and about Tsh5000 per meal. There's a US$30 per person per visit forest fee (Tsh5000 for Tanzania residents) for any walks that go into forest reserves, including walks to Shengena Peak. The forest fees are payable at the Catchment Office in Same or through your guide. For any hikes with guides, the stages are generally short (two or three can usually be easily combined if you are reasonably fit) although your guide will still expect you to pay for the same number of days.

The Pares can be visited comfortably at any time of year, except during the March through May long rains, when paths become too muddy.

Sleeping & Eating

Anjela Inn GUESTHOUSE
(d Tsh15,000, in newer annex Tsh25,000; P❄) ✉ Anjela Inn has clean, noisy doubles in the main building and similar but larger, quieter rooms next door, plus meals. It's 10 minutes on foot from the highway and bus stand; follow the main road towards the 'new' market, turn left down a wide, tree-lined lane at the small clutch of signboards, then keep straight on.

Getting There & Away

Buses go daily between Moshi and Mwanga (Tsh3000 to Tsh4000, one hour), departing in the morning. From Mwanga, there are dalla-dallas in the mornings to Usangi.

Usangi

Usangi, lying in a valley ringed by mountains about 25km east of Mwanga, is the centre of the northern Pares and the best base for exploring the region.

The place to arrange hikes and guides is at Lomwe Secondary School; ask for the school director. Even if school isn't in session, someone will be around to help.

In addition to short walks, a long day-hike is possible through **Kindoroko Forest Reserve** (which begins about 7km south of Usangi village) to the top of Mt Kindoroko (2113m), the highest peak in the northern Pares. From the upper slopes of Mt Kindoroko, you can see over the Maasai Steppe to the west and to Lake Jipe and into Kenya to the northeast.

🛌 Sleeping & Eating

Lomwe Secondary School   CAMPGROUND $
(lomwesec@googlemail.com; camping Tsh3000; r per person Tsh7000) There's a basic guesthouse and camping at this local secondary school at the top end of Usangi. If you sleep at the school, you can prepare your own meals (bring your own stove, equipment and ingredients), or you can arrange to eat meals prepared by school staff. Follow the main road, bearing right at the fork.

Mhako Hostel & Restaurant   GUESTHOUSE $
(☑027-275 7642; s/ste with bathroom Tsh25,000/35,000, s/d without bathroom Tsh13,000/25,000) This cheery place has clean, pleasant rooms and good, inexpensive meals. Some of the non-self-contained rooms only have interior windows; it's worth paying a little more for the nicer ones with toilets and balconies. Mhako is along the main road to the right as you enter Usangi.

ℹ Getting There & Away

Dalla-dallas run several times daily along the unpaved but good road winding up from Mwanga to Usangi (Tsh2000, 1½ hours) from around 8am. Hiring a taxi costs from Tsh35,000. From both Arusha (Tsh6000, four hours) and Moshi (Tsh4000 to Tsh5000, two hours), there are several direct buses daily to Usangi departing in the morning. Ask to get dropped at Lomwe Secondary School. Allow at least two to three days for an excursion to Usangi, including time to get here and organise things.

PARE CULTURE

The Pare (locally, Wapare) hail from the Taita Hills area of southern Kenya, where they were herders, hunters and farmers. It was the Maasai, according to Pare oral tradition, who pursued them into the mountains, capturing and stealing their cattle. Today, many Pare are farmers, cultivating plots of vegetables, maize, bananas, cassava and cardamom. Thanks to significant missionary activity, the Pare distinguish themselves as being among Tanzania's most educated groups. During the 1940s, leading Pares formed the Wapare Union, which played an important role in the independence drive.

Traditional Pare society is patrilineal. Fathers are considered to have great authority during their lifetime as well as after death, and all those descended from a single man through male links share a sense of common fate. Once a man dies, his ghost influences all male descendants for as long as the ghost's name is remembered. After this, the dead man's spirit joins a collectively influential body of ancestors. Daughters are also dependent on the goodwill of their father. Yet, since property and status are transmitted through the male line, a father's ghost only has influence over his daughter's descendants until her death.

The Pare believe that deceased persons possess great powers, and thus have developed elaborate rituals centred on the dead. Near most villages are sacred areas where the skulls of tribal chiefs are kept, although you're unlikely to see these unless you spend an extended period in the mountains. When people die, they are believed to inhabit a netherworld between the land of the living and the spirit world. If they are allowed to remain in this state, ill fate will befall their descendants. The prescribed rituals allowing the deceased to pass into the world of the ancestors are of great importance.

For more about Pare culture, read *The Shambaa Kingdom* by Steven Feierman (1974) and the intriguing *Lute: The Curse and the Blessing* by Jakob Janssen Dannholz, who established the first mission station at Mbaga.

MKOMAZI NATIONAL PARK

Wild and undeveloped **Mkomazi National Park** (☑027-275 8249; adult/child US$30/10) spreads along the Kenyan border in the shadow of the Pare Mountains, its dry savannah lands contrasting sharply with the moist forests of the Pares. The reserve, which is contiguous with Kenya's Tsavo West National Park, is known for its black rhinos, which were introduced into the area from South Africa for breeding in a project spearheaded by Tony Fitzjohn, the force behind conservation work in Mkomazi. The rhinos are within a heavily protected 45-sq-km enclosure built around Hafino Mountain in north-central Mkomazi, and not viewable as part of general tourism.

In addition to the rhinos, there are wild dogs (also reintroduced and, as part of a special endangered species program, also not viewable as part of general tourism). Animals that you're more likely to spot include oryx, eland, dik-dik, the rarely seen gerenuk, kudu and Coke's hartebeest. The huge seasonal elephant herds that once crossed regularly between Tsavo and Mkomazi are beginning to come back, after reaching a low point of just a dozen elephants in the area in 1989, although elephants still are not commonly spotted in Mkomazi.

With more than 400 species, Mkomazi is a birder's delight. Species to watch for include various weaver birds, secretary birds, crowned and bateleur eagles, helmeted guinea fowl, various hornbills, storks and the pygmy falcon.

The main reasons for visiting the park, apart from enjoying Babu's Camp (p151), are for birding and to appreciate the evocative nyika bush landscapes studded with baobab and thorn acacia and broken by low, rocky hills. Despite its relative ease of access, Mkomazi is still well off the beaten track. Walking safaris can be arranged at Zange main gate (US$20 guide fee, plus US$20 to US$25 walking tour fee).

Sleeping & Eating

Mkomazi Park Campsites CAMPGROUND $$
(camping in public campsite US$30, special campsite US$50) Park campsites include a scenic spot at Dindera Dam (special campsite), about 45km in from Zange entry gate, as well as public campsites at Zange Gate, Ibaya (about 15km from Zange Gate) and Maore. All have only basic facilities. The Zange Gate campsite is the best bet for those arriving without transport, as it's just behind park headquarters.

Babu's Camp TENTED CAMP $$$
(☑0784 402266, 027-254 8840; www.anasa safari.com; per person full board from US$270) This classic safari-style camp is the only permanent camp in the park. Its five tents are set amid baobabs and thorn acacias in the northern part of the reserve looking towards the Gulela Hills. The cuisine is tasty, staff are attentive and the surrounding landscapes are wide and lovely. Wildlife drives, walks and night drives can be arranged.

Getting There & Away

Dalla-dallas between Same and Mbaga can drop you at Zange Gate, 5km east of Same, from where you can arrange guides and begin a walking safari. Vehicles for Mkomazi safaris can be arranged in Same at Elephant Motel (p148) and through Amani Lutheran Centre (p148) for about US$150 per vehicle per day.

MKOMAZI NATIONAL PARK

Why Go Excellent birding; dry, savannah wilderness scenery; eland, oryx and gerenuk.

When to Go June until February for wildlife, year-round for birding. Much of Mkomazi's secondary road network is impassable during the rains; main routes are all-weather.

Practicalities Drive in from Same on the Dar es Salaam–Arusha highway to Zange main entry gate (open 7am to 6pm). Park entry, guide and walking-safari fees are payable here with Visa, MasterCard or cash (when the credit-card machines are broken). There's another exit point at Njiro Gate to the southeast, which makes a circuit drive possible.

Budget Tips Take a dalla-dalla or taxi from Same to Zange Gate; camp and do a walking safari.

Northern Tanzania

Why Go?

To paraphrase that well-known quote about Africa, we envy those who've never been to northern Tanzania because they have so much to look forward to.

This is a land of superlatives, from Africa's highest mountain to arguably the greatest wildlife spectacle on the planet. But Mt Kilimanjaro and the Serengeti plains are merely starting points to so many journeys of a lifetime. Mt Meru is Kilimanjaro's rival in both its beauty and the challenge of climbing it, while the Crater Highlands rank among Africa's most haunting landscapes. When it comes to wildlife, there's Tarangire's elephant kingdom, Lake Manyara's tree-climbing lions and the massed flamingos of Lake Natron. It all converges in Ngorongoro: venturing into its crater can feel like returning to earth's first morning.

But this, too, is a journey among the Maasai and the Hadzabe whose presence here makes this one of Africa's most stirring and soulful destinations.

Best for Culture

➡ Experience cultural tourism programs (p160)

➡ Hunt with the Hadzabe at Lake Eyasi (p180)

➡ Take a coffee tour (p199)

➡ Visit a Maasai village (p160)

Best for Nature

➡ Serengeti National Park (p189)

➡ Mt Kilimanjaro National Park (p205)

➡ Ngorongoro Crater (p180)

➡ Ol Doinyo Lengai (p185)

➡ Tarangire National Park (p171)

➡ Lake Natron (p187)

When to Go
Arusha

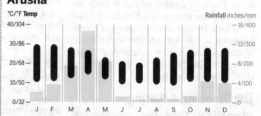

Jan–Mar The wildebeest migration is in the southern Serengeti.	**Apr–May** Rain turns roads muddy making travel mostly miserable.	**Sep–Oct** The best time to travel. Animals gather around the last of the water.

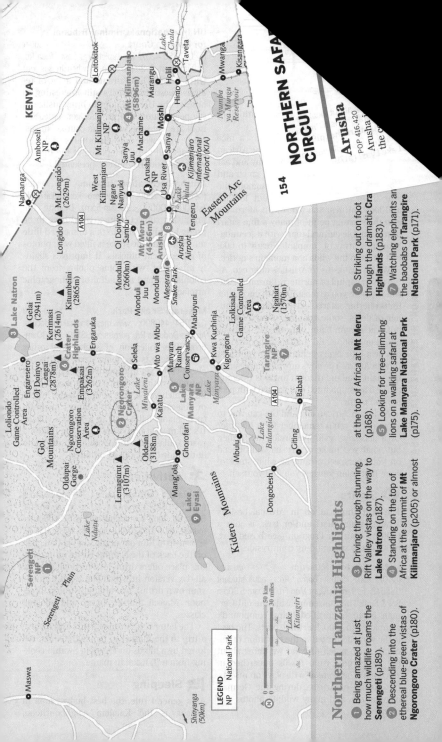

Arusha

POP 416,420

Arusha i
the c

Northern Tanzania Highlights

1 Being amazed at just how much wildlife roams the **Serengeti** (p189).

2 Descending into the ethereal blue-green vistas of **Ngorongoro Crater** (p180).

3 Driving through stunning Rift Valley vistas on the way to **Lake Natron** (p187).

4 Standing on the top of Africa at the summit of **Mt Kilimanjaro** (p205) or almost at the top of Africa at **Mt Meru** (p168).

5 Looking for tree-climbing lions on a walking safari at **Lake Manyara National Park** (p175).

6 Striking out on foot through the dramatic **Crater Highlands** (p183).

7 Watching elephants an the baobabs of **Tarangire National Park** (p171).

NORTHERN TANZANIA ARUSHA

...s a large, sprawling city with all of ...ntradictions that brings.

On the one hand, Arusha offers a nice break from the rigours of life on the African road – it has excellent places to stay and eat and, for the most part, it is lush, green and enjoys a temperate climate throughout the year thanks to its altitude (about 1300m) and location near the foot of Mt Meru. It's also the starting point of many a fine safari or memorable cultural tour, with a seemingly endless array of companies ready to take you out into the wilds at a moment's notice.

Which brings us to Arusha's alter ego. As the safari capital of northern Tanzania, Arusha is where you're most likely to encounter touts offering safaris, souvenirs and all manner of deals, some genuine, many of them not. Their main haunts are the bus stations and along Boma Rd and their persistence can be a little overwhelming if it's your first time in Africa. The city's downtown area and the main road out of town towards Dodoma are also noisy, polluted and packed with people and traffic.

A vibrant African city and the gateway to experiences you'll remember for a lifetime? Or a necessary evil? We prefer the former, but what you make of Arusha will depend on your perspective and at what stage of your Tanzanian journey you find yourself.

◉ Sights

The best thing to do in Arusha, besides arrange your safari and/or trek, is join a Cultural Tourism Program (see boxed text, p160) in the surrounding countryside.

Natural History Museum MUSEUM
(☏027-250 7540; Boma Rd; adult/student US$5/2; ☺9am-5.30pm Mon-Fri, 9.30am-5.30pm Sat & Sun) This museum inside the old German *boma* (a fortified living compound), completed in 1900, has three parts. The best is the wing dedicated to the evolution of humans, since much of what we know about the topic came from fossils unearthed in Tanzania. There are also displays on insects, the history of Arusha during the German colonial era, and many wildlife photos and mounts.

UN International Criminal Tribunal for Rwanda Court COURT
(☏027-250 4207; www.unictr.org; East Africa Rd; ☺9am-noon & 2-5pm Mon-Fri when in session) **FREE** There's little drama and a lot of tedious questions, but it's still interesting to observe the UN's attempt to bring justice to the perpetrators of Rwandan genocide. Visitors are welcome when the court is in session – there were only a handful of trials and appeals still to be completed at the time of writing. Photo ID must be presented.

Arusha Declaration Museum MUSEUM
(☏027-250 7800; Makongoro Rd; adult/child Tsh8000/4000; ☺9.30am-5pm) Despite the promising subject matter, you'd have to be pretty bored to come to this unfocused little museum. Half the space is filled with photos of government officials. It improves slightly after that, with some photos from the colonial era and a handful of ethnographic artefacts.

Meserani Snake Park ZOO, MUSEUM
(☏0754 440800; www.meseranisnakepark.com; Arusha-Dodoma Rd; admission US$10; ☺7.30am-6pm) The collection of snakes and other reptiles here is the main draw, but there's also a corny yet informative Maasai cultural museum with mock-ups of home and bush life, which you'll visit with a Maasai warrior. You can also take a 30-minute camel ride (per person Tsh15,000) to a Maasai village. It's 25km west of Arusha along the Dodoma road. Dalla-dallas to Monduli can drop you at the gate (Tsh1500, 45 minutes).

🏃 Activities

★Via Via Cultural Tours CULTURAL TOUR
(☏0754 038981; www.viaviacafe.com/en/arusha; Boma Rd; 1hr/1 day drum lesson US$20/50, city/market tour US$20/40, cooking class US$30; ☺9am-4pm) Run out of the Via Via Cafe, just off the back of the Natural History Museum, this place offers drum lessons (including an all-day version in which you learn to make your own drum), two-hour city tours, three-hour 'Maasai Market Tours', and cooking classes.

The latter run for three hours and involve a trip to the market to buy ingredients, followed by a hands-on lesson in Swahili cooking from a 'Tanzanian mama'.

🛏 Sleeping

As a general rule, the best budget area in Arusha is the Kaloleni neighbourhood, north of Stadium St and east of Colonel Middleton Rd (a 10-minute walk from the bus stand), followed by the the busy central market area south of the stadium. Things are slightly quieter around the Clock Tower. For mid-range and top end places, head to leafy eastern Arusha.

The places outside the city combine a semi-rural setting with easy transport into town and most do cultural walks. See also Arusha National Park, since some of those lodges are easy drives to town.

City Centre & Clock Tower

Kitundu Guesthouse GUESTHOUSE $
(☑027-250 9065; Levolosi Rd; s/d Tsh25,000/30,000, with shared bathroom Tsh15,000/20,000) A decent, reliable choice. It's worth paying extra for a room with an attached bathroom. Avoid the claustrophobic ground-floor rooms and go for the far better, light-filled rooms up on the first or second floors where there are Mt Meru views from the shared landing. All rooms have mosquito nets.

Raha Leo GUESTHOUSE $
(☑0753 600002; Stadium St; s/d Tsh25,000/30,000, with shared bathroom Tsh20,000/25,000) Undistinguished although adequate double and twin rooms, some along the corridor, others around an open-air lounge. With hot water and cable TV it's one of the best-value options in town, and the location is central but quieter than most.

Arusha Centre Tourist Inn HOTEL $
(☑0764 294384, 027-250 0421; atihotel@habari.co.tz; Livingstone Rd; s/d US$25/30; @🖾) Unremarkable but clean and fairly spacious rooms are on offer here – they're just about fine for the price (ask for a discount anyway), but be prepared for an early morning wake-up call from the neighbouring mosque. The three storeys ring a courtyard, and there's a restaurant at the front with OK food and plenty of Maasai men staring at the TV.

Arusha Backpackers BACKPACKERS $
(☑0773 377795; www.arushabackpackers.co.tz; Sokoine Rd; dm/s/d with shared bathroom US$10/12/20; @) There's a buzz about this place in more ways than one – it's popular with those looking to hook up with other travellers, but the absence of mosquito nets may deter some. Shared bathrooms have an institutional feel. Unless you're looking for travel buddies, look elsewhere.

New Safari Hotel HOTEL $$
(☑0787 326122, 027-254 5940; www.thenewsafarihotel.com; Boma Rd; s/d/tr US$100/125/180; ❄@) Once the favourite of white hunters and their tall tales from the African bush, the New Safari was reborn in 2004 and is the pick of the city-centre mid-range options. Rooms are generally large, have tiled floors and a touch of class in the decor. It's also within walking distance of just about anything in the city centre.

Arusha Naaz Hotel HOTEL $$
(☑0744 282799, 027-257 2087; www.arushanaaz.net; Sokoine Rd; s/d/tr from US$45/60/75; ❄🖾) Naaz is short on atmosphere, but otherwise OK value, with comfortable 1st-floor rooms in a convenient location by the Clock Tower; the main reason to stay here (as opposed to Eastern Arusha) is to be within walking distance of the city centre. Rooms are not all the same, so check out a few first; we think those around the triangular courtyard are best.

Eastern Arusha

★**Ujamaa Hostel** HOSTEL $
(☑0753 960570; www.ujamaahostel.com; Fire Rd; dm half board plus laundry US$18) Focusing on volunteers, but open to all, Ujamaa is the most communal spot to lay your head in Arusha. Besides the clean dorms with shelves, lockable drawers and hot-water baths, there's a TV lounge, book exchange, plenty of travel advice and a quiet backyard. It can also hook you up with a variety of volunteer opportunities (minimum two-week commitment) in Arusha.

★**Blues & Chutney** B&B $$
(☑0658 127380, 0732 971668; www.bluesandchutney.com; House No 2 Olorien, Lower Kijenge; s/d US$120/160; 🖾) An intimate and sophisticated boutique B&B on a quiet street southeast of the centre, Blues & Chutney has the feel of a tranquil enclave for people in the know. The decor is white-wood and classy, the atmosphere refined, and four out of the six light-and-airy rooms have large private balconies. The restaurant serves home-style cooking and there's a small bar.

Themi Suites Hotel APARTMENT $$
(☑0732 979621, 0732 979617; www.themisuiteshotel.com; Njiro Hill Rd; 2-/3-bedroom apt US$150/180; ❄🖾) This excellent place is ideal for families or for those who want their own spacious serviced apartments with kitchen, dining and lounge area. They come

Arusha

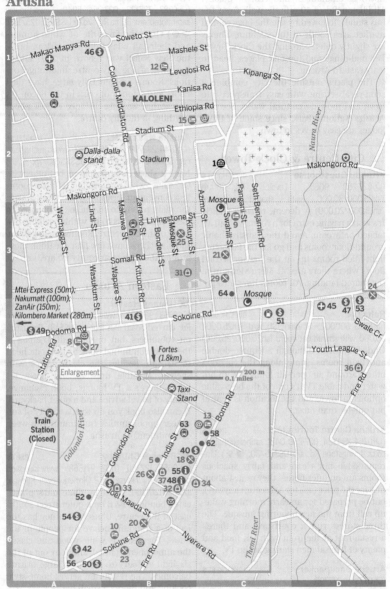

with attractive wrought-iron furnishings, as well as flat-screen TVs, microwaves and washing machines. The two-bedroom apartments fit four, the three-bedroom ones can accommodate six. There's also a good on-site restaurant.

Outpost Lodge   LODGE $$
(☎0754 318523; www.outposttanzania.net; Serengeti Rd; s/d/tr US$62/81/94; @🎧🔅) The rooms here are nothing special, but come with attractive stone floors, and the lush grounds and communal poolside

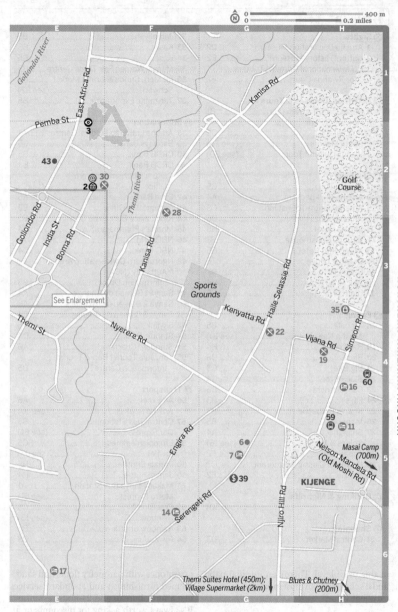

restaurant-lounge with couches, board games and fresh-squeezed juices make for a decent overall package. It's in a quiet residential area off Nyerere Rd.

Spices & Herbs GUESTHOUSE **$$**
(axum_spices@hotmail.com; Simeon Rd; s/d US$40/50; @🛜) The 19 rooms behind this popular Ethiopian restaurant are simple but warm, with woven grass mats and wooden wardrobes adding character not often found

Arusha

at this price level. There's an internal patio and it's cheaper than most in eastern Arusha – excellent value.

Impala Hotel   HOTEL **$$**
(☏0774 878679, 027-254 3082; www.impala hotel.com; Simeon Rd; s/d/tr US$100/130/175; 🅿❄@🛜🏊) Filling a gap between the small family-run guesthouses and the big luxury hotels, the nothing-special Impala offers adequate rooms (be sure you get one of the newer ones with parquetry floors and safari-themed furnishings) and abundant services like a forex bureau and 24-hour restaurant. It's always worth asking for discounts or an upgrade to a better room.

★**African Tulip**   BOUTIQUE HOTEL **$$$**
(☏0783 714104, 027-254 3004; www.theafrican tulip.com; Serengeti Rd; s/d/tr US$190/230/300, ste US$310-500; 🅿❄@🛜🏊) 🍃 Marketing itself as a luxury boutique hotel, the deserv-

edly popular African Tulip inhabits a green, quiet side street and successfully combines an African safari theme with a genteel ambience. The large rooms are supremely comfortable havens from Arusha's noise. There's a whimsical baobab tree in the restaurant, carved wood around the common areas and a small garden around the swimming pool at the back.

There are two bars and a gift shop, and a percentage of proceeds from the hotel goes towards charitable projects.

Outside Arusha

Meserani Snake Park   CAMPGROUND $
(027-253 8282; www.meseranisnakepark.com; camping incl snake park admission US$10; P) This overlander-oriented place has good facilities, including hot showers, a bar-restaurant with cheap meals and a vehicle repair shop. It's 25km west of Arusha along the Dodoma road.

★ Karama Lodge   LODGE $$
(0754 475188; www.karamalodge.com; s/d/tr US$104/138/199; P @ 🛜 🏊) Truly something different, on a forested hillside in the Suye Hill area just southeast of town, Karama offers 22 rustic and rather lovely stilt bungalows, each with a verandah and views to both Kilimanjaro and Meru on clear days. It's signposted north of Old Moshi Rd.

There are short walking trails nearby and a creative restaurant that caters to vegetarians. Massage and yoga are also possibilities. Rates drop significantly outside high season.

★ Onsea House   B&B $$$
(0787 112498; www.onseahouse.com; s/d US$250/300; P 🛜 🏊) Run by a Belgian chef whose eye for the little things is what really makes this lovely bed and breakfast such a great place. The rooms each have their own themes, plus there's the Machweo Wellness Retreat and Fine Dining, a fabulous spa and yoga centre with a top-notch restaurant. Very tranquil and very classy. It's about 1km off the Moshi road on the edge of town.

Kigongoni   LODGE $$$
(0732 978876; www.kigongoni.net; s/d/tr incl guided walks from US$170/198/315; P @ 🛜 🏊) Kigongoni's tranquil hilltop perch, about 5km past Arusha, gives it an almost wilderness feel. Spacious cottages, all with porches, fireplaces and wide views, are scattered around the forest, some quite a hilly walk from the cosy common areas. It's about 5km beyond Arusha towards Moshi.

A portion of the lodge's profits go to support the Sibusiso Foundation (www.sibusiso. com), which helps mentally disabled children in the region.

Arusha Coffee Lodge   LODGE $$$
(027-250 0630; www.elewana.com; s US$263-375, d US$350-500; P @ 🛜 🏊) Set smack in the middle of a shade-grown coffee plantation and elegant through and through, this is one of the most talked about properties in Arusha. The gorgeous standard rooms have split-level floors making them feel like suites and the restaurant has few peers. The only downside is that traffic noise is loud. It's along the highway just west of town.

Eating

Decent hotel restaurants include Arusha Coffee Lodge, African Tulip, Karama Lodge and Onsea House.

City Centre & Clock Tower

★ Khan's Barbecue   BARBECUE $
(Mosque St; mixed grill from Tsh7500; ⊙ from 6.30pm Mon-Fri, from 4.30pm Sat & Sun) This Arusha institution is an auto-spares store by day and the best known of many earthy roadside barbecues around the market area by night. It lays out a heaping spread of grilled, skewered meat and salad. If you want to feel like a local, this is a fine place to begin.

Big Bite   INDIAN $
(Swahili St; mains Tsh5000-12,000; ⊙ noon-2.30pm & 6-9.30pm Wed-Mon; 🖉) One of the oldest and most reliable Indian restaurants in Arusha. Don't let the modest premises or fast-food-esque name fool you.

Universal Classic Restaurant   TANZANIAN $
(0753 830050; off Swahili St; meals Tsh2500-5500; ⊙ 6am-8pm Sun-Fri) A bigger than average selection of simple but hearty local foods with chicken curry, beef pilau and ugali roast beef among the options.

ℹ️ DANGERS & ANNOYANCES

At night, take a taxi if you go out. It's not safe to walk after dusk, except around the market, where the streets remain crowded for a few hours after dark. But even here, be wary and don't carry anything valuable.

CULTURAL TOURISM PROGRAMS

Numerous villages around Arusha (and elsewhere in the country) run 'Cultural Tourism Programs' that offer an alternative to the safari scene. Most usually centre on light hikes and village activities.

Although the line is sometimes blurred between community empowerment and empowering the enterprising individuals who run them, these programs nevertheless provide employment for locals and offer an excellent chance to experience Tanzania at the local level. Most have various 'modules' available, from half a day to several nights. Transportation, sometimes by dalla-dalla and sometimes by private vehicle, is extra. Overnight tours are either camping or homestays; expect conditions to be basic. Payments should be made on-site; always ask for a receipt.

All tours in the Arusha area (and elsewhere) can be booked through the Tanzania Tourist Board (TTB) Tourist Information Centre (p164), which has brochures and a thick binder with detailed information (including prices) about most of them. The office can also outline the best transport options. Most should be booked a day in advance, but some guides wait at the TTB office on standby each morning.

If you have further questions, the **Cultural Tourism Program office** (☑ 0786 703010, 027-205 0025; www.tanzaniaculturaltourism.com; Natural History Museum, Boma Rd), at the back of the Natural History Museum in Arusha, may (or may not) be able to assist. Either way, check out its website. You can also contact many of the places directly to make the necessary arrangements.

Ilkiding'a (☑ 0732 978570, 0713 520264; www.ilkidinga.com) Walks (ranging from half-day strolls to a three-day 'cultural hike' sleeping in homes along the way) and the chance to experience the traditional culture of the Wa-arusha people are the main attractions in this well-organised program around Ilkiding'a, 7km north of Arusha.

Ilkurot (☑ 0784 459296, 0713 332005; kinyorilomon@yahoo.com) A good choice for those interested in Maasai culture. Stops on their village and trekking tours (using donkeys or camels, if you wish) include a *boma*, herbal doctor, midwife and other community members. Overnighters have the choice of camping or sleeping in a guesthouse or *boma*. The village is 25km north of Arusha off the Nairobi Rd.

Longido (☑ 0787 855185, 0715 855185; touryman1@yahoo.com) This program centres on the 2637m-high Mt Longido and the large Maasai village of the same name. In addition to the climb itself (eight to 10 hours return), Longido makes a good introduction to Maasai life, including a visit to some *bomas* and the Wednesday cattle market.

The village is easily reached by dalla-dalla. The mountain and village lie just east of the main road between Arusha and Namanga (on the Tanzania–Kenya border), 80km north of Arusha.

Mirapot TANZANIAN $
(India St; meals Tsh6000-15,000; ☺6.30am-8pm Mon-Sat) Recently taken a touch upmarket by Mama Mrambo, this place serves local fish dishes, traditional beef stew, or chicken in coconut sauce, as well as burgers, sandwiches and decent local coffee.

Shanghai CHINESE $
(☑0756 659247; Sokoine Rd; meals Tsh4000-14,000; ☺noon-3pm & 6-10.30pm; ☑) Very good Chinese-owned restaurant with fast service and 'Far East meets the Wild West' decor – let's face it, when did a Chinese restaurant in Africa ever win a style award? It's hidden behind the post office.

Arusha Naaz Hotel TANZANIAN $
(☑027-257 2087; Sokoine Rd; buffet Tsh10,000; ☺buffet noon-6pm) This place has an all-you-can-eat lunch buffet and large snack counter.

Café Barrista CAFE $
(☑0754 288771; www.cafebarrista.com; Sokoine Rd; meals Tsh4000-10,000; ☺7.30am-6.30pm Mon-Sat, 8am-5pm Sun; ☎☑) A recent move a little upmarket has done nothing to dimin-

Mkuru (☎0784 724498, 0784 472475; www.mkurucamelsafari.com) The Maasai village of Mkuru, 14km off the Nairobi road north of Mt Meru and 60km from Arusha, hosts the region's pioneering camel camp. You can take a short camel ride around the village or multi-day safari as far away as Mt Kilimanjaro and Lake Natron. There's a simple tented camp in the village or you can pitch your own tent. Rides can also be combined with various cultural activities, a baboon cave safari, or a two-hour climb up Ol Doinyo Landaree (Mountain of Goats).

Monduli Juu (☎0786 799688, 0787 756299; mpoyoni@yahoo.com) Monduli Juu (Upper Monduli) comprises four small villages along the Monduli Mountains, northwest of Arusha in Maasai country. You can visit traditional doctors, see a school or eat a meaty meal in a bush *orpul* (Maasai camp where men go to eat meat). Many people come to trek along the escarpment for views over the Rift Valley plains.

Most activities begin in Emairete village (9km from Monduli town), where there are several simple spots to camp (bring everything with you from Arusha) and some Maasai *bomas* that take overnight guests.

Mulala (☎0784 747433, 0784 499044; agapetourism@yahoo.com) Set on the southern slope of Mt Meru about 30km northeast of Arusha, this program is completely run by women. Tours focus on farming and daily life and include visits to a women's cooperative and cheese makers. Camping is possible if you have camping gear, though with an early start, you could do this tour as a day trip from Arusha.

Ng'iresi (☎0754 320966, 0754 476079; lotisareyo@yahoo.com) One of the most popular programs, the primary tours at Ng'iresi village (about 7km northeast of Arusha on the slopes of Mt Meru) include visits to Wa-arusha farms, houses and a school. There is also a traditional medicine tour, along with several waterfalls and a hike up a small volcano. There's no public transport here; arrange it as part of your booking.

Oldonyo Sambu (☎0784 694790, 0784 663381; msaiboma@yahoo.com) Oldonyo Sambu's trekking and camping trips offer the option of riding donkeys, horses or camels. Cultural activities in the village are also on offer. The village is 35km north of Arusha off the Nairobi road and can be easily reached by dalla-dalla.

Peace Matunda (☎0787 482966; www.peacematunda.org) Near Kimundo, around 15km northeast of Arusha, this place offers half- to three-day hiking, camping and mountain-biking tours, visits to local families and to coffee and banana plantations, as well as volunteer programs with a focus on underprivileged kids.

Tengeru (☎0756 981602, 0754 960176; www.tengeruculturaltourism.org) The site of the bi-weekly Tengeru Market, about 10km east of Arusha and signposted off the main highway, the Tengeru program includes visits to a coffee farm and a local school, and an introduction to the life of the Meru people. Homestays can be arranged.

ish the appeal of this friendly place. Try their chocolate croissant, or fill up with sandwiches, salads and wraps, as well as great coffee. There's also an internet cafe and wi-fi (free with meal purchases).

⭐**Fifi's** INTERNATIONAL, BAKERY **$$**
(☎0786 487727, 027-254 4021; Themi St; breakfasts Tsh3000-17,000, mains Tsh14,000-18,000; ☺7.30am-10pm Mon-Fri, 8.30am-10pm Sat & Sun) As good for breakfast or a quiet afternoon coffee as for a more substantial meal, this sophisticated bakery has free wi-fi and serves

up exciting dishes such as beef fillet with blue-cheese sauce. A very cool place.

Via Via CAFE **$$**
(☎0782 434845; www.viaviacafe.com/en/arusha; Boma Rd; mains Tsh10,000-16,000; ☺9am-10pm Mon-Sat) Cultured and laid-back, with the best soundtrack of any restaurant in Arusha, this place along the river behind the Natural History Museum is a popular meeting spot. They serve coffee, salads and sandwiches plus more substantial meals such as pasta and grilled fish. There's a decent bar and live music.

Africafé
CAFE $$

(Boma Rd; breakfast Tsh5200-10,800, mains Tsh9000-18,000; ☺7am-9pm) A fine refuge from the Boma Rd touts, this classy place has European-cafe vibes with prices to match. The menu is heavy on sandwiches, with other dishes such as grilled meats, burgers, and the fine grilled Nile perch with garlic and butter. There's also a good bakery.

Self-Catering

Village Supermarket
SUPERMARKET $

(Njiro Hill Rd; ☺9am-9pm) Part of the Njiro Hill Shopping Complex southeast of the centre, this place is Arusha's best-stocked supermarket. There's a decent open-air food court outside the door and a cinema complex in the same building.

Nakumatt
SUPERMARKET $

(Dodoma Rd; ☺8.30am-10pm Mon-Sat, 10am-9pm Sun) On the edge of the city centre, this is the largest supermarket in central Arusha.

Biashara
SUPERMARKET $

(Clock Tower roundabout; ☺8.30am-9.30pm Mon-Sat, 10am-2.30pm Sun) Aka the Clock Tower Supermarket, this small place has a big wine selection.

Eastern Arusha

★ Blue Heron
INTERNATIONAL $$

(☏0785 555127; www.blue-heron-tanzania.com; Haile Selassie Rd; mains Tsh13,000-23,000; ☺9am-4pm Mon-Thu, to 10pm Fri, 10am-10pm Sat) Our pick of the garden restaurants that are a recurring theme out in Arusha's east, the Blue Heron gets the tricky combination of lounge bar and family restaurant just right. Sit under the leafy verandah or out on the lawn tables to enjoy a menu that ranges from paninis and soups up to beef tenderloin and creative specials like fried rice-and-broccoli balls with curry ratatouille.

There's a children's menu, a carefully chosen selection of South African wines and a steady stream of expats looking for a quiet place to pass an afternoon.

Spices & Herbs
ETHIOPIAN, EUROPEAN $$

(☏0685 313162, 0754 313162; Simeon Rd; mains Tsh8000-18,000; ☺10.30am-10.30pm; ☏🖋) Unpretentious al fresco spot serving two menus: Ethiopian and Continental. Ignore the latter and order *injera* (Ethiopian bread) soaked in beef, chicken or lamb sauce, or *yegbeg tibs* (fried lamb with Ethiopian butter, onion, green peppers and rosemary). The service is good and there's plenty of art on the walls.

TapaSafari
SPANISH, INTERNATIONAL $$

(☏0757 009037; www.tapasafari.co.tz; Kanisa Rd; small/large tapas from Tsh3000/5000, mains Tsh10,000-35,000; ☺11am-10pm; ☏🖋) With a semi-outdoor setting, this restaurant and wine bar ticks many boxes. There are snacks, grills, pizza and pasta, but the real stars are the Spanish tapas and extensive list of South African wines to choose from. Sundays are especially popular with a four-course set menu (Tsh22,000).

SCHOOL OF ST JUDE

He's the patron saint of hopeless cases, but St Jude would definitely be smiling at what has been achieved in his name in a school just outside Arusha. To score a place in Australian Gemma Sisia's pioneering establishment you have to meet two very different requirements. First, you've got to be extremely bright – only the smartest kids get to sit the entrance exam and only the best results get a place – and second, you've got to be very poor. If you do get in, you pretty much get a free ride all the way through to graduation.

The School of St Jude kicked off in 2002 with three students and one teacher. Ten years later the school had expanded to three campuses, 350 staff and 1500 students. Has Gemma's plan for 'fighting poverty through education' worked? It's hard to argue with the results: St Jude students' exam scores are outranked only by the most expensive Tanzanian private schools. The huge pride that St Jude parents have in their kids and the fierce competition to get a place underline the school's impact even more effectively.

The school welcomes visitors Monday to Friday during term time, though you'll need to make an appointment: see the 'Visit Us' page of the school website (www.schoolofstjude.org) for more information. There are opportunities for long-term volunteers and donations are appreciated.

Tony Wheeler, co-founder of Lonely Planet

★ Bay Leaf
EUROPEAN **$$$**

(☎ 027-254 3055; www.bayleaftz.com; Vijana Rd; mains Tsh11,000-37,000; ◷ 8am-11pm; 🛜) Arusha's poshest menu features dishes such as figs primavera (parma-wrapped brie and stuffed figs with sticky balsamic toffee), slow-cooked West Kili lamb shanks, and Wellington of game birds (wrapped in 'ethereal' filo pastry). It also offers a great wine list (by the glass and bottle), as well as separate lunch, dinner and Indian menus. Book ahead.

✖ Outside Arusha

★ River House
INTERNATIONAL **$$**

(☎ 0689 759067; www.shanga.org; Dodoma Rd; 4-course lunches US$18; ◷ 9.30am-4.30pm) 🖉 An offshoot of the inspiring Shanga project, diners at River House are greeted with champagne and then served a huge and delicious four-course lunch in gorgeous gardens – it's part buffet, although the soup and dessert are served to your table. It's an event as much as a meal. It's on the Burka Coffee Estate, 3km west of the Nakumatt supermarket; reservations are required.

🍷 Drinking & Nightlife

Via Via
CAFE

(Boma Rd; ◷ 9am-4am Mon-Sat) This cafe is a good spot for a drink and one of the best places to find out about upcoming cultural events, many of which are held here. On Thursday nights there's karaoke and a live band. Things get started at 9pm and admission is a steep Tsh7000.

Masai Camp
CLUB

(Old Moshi Rd; admission Tsh5000; ◷ 9pm-dawn Fri & Sat) Arusha's loudest and brashest club is an institution on the Arusha party scene. The music is a mix of African and Western.

🛍 Shopping

★ Shanga
HANDICRAFTS

(☎ 0689 759067; www.shanga.org; Dodoma Rd; ◷ 9am-4.30pm) 🖉 What started out as a small enterprise making beaded necklaces has branched into furniture, paper, clothing and many other products, mostly using recycled materials and made by disabled workers. Their products are sold around the world, and a visit to their workshop and store just out of town (3km west of Nakumatt) is quite inspiring.

It's on the Burka Coffee Estate and plantation tours can be arranged.

DON'T MISS

ARUSHA MARKETS

The **Central Market** (Soko Kuu) in the heart of the city and the larger **Kilombero Market** (Dodoma Rd), just to the west, are worth an hour or two of strolling time. There are many more colourful local markets around the region including **Ngaramtoni Market**, 12km northwest of town on the Nairobi road, on Thursday and Sunday, which draws Maasai from miles around, and the **Tengeru Market**, 10km east towards Moshi, on Wednesday and Saturday. Mind your pockets and bags at all of them.

★ Schwari
HANDICRAFTS, HOMEWARES

(Haile Selassie Rd; ◷ 9am-5pm Mon-Thu & Sat, to 8pm Fri) Fabulous handicrafts and classy homewares, children's toys and national parks maps – Schwari has picked the best of local crafts to produce one of the loveliest collections on offer in Arusha. It's attached to the equally lovely Blue Heron (p162).

Maasai Women Fair Trade Centre
HANDICRAFTS

(☎ 0784 210839, 027-254 4290; www.maasaiwomentanzania.org; Simeon Rd; ◷ 9am-4pm Mon-Sat) 🖉 A project of Maasai Women Development Organisation (MWEDO), this small shop raises money for education and other projects. It has expensive but high-quality beadwork (and a few other crafts), including some items seldom sold elsewhere, like Christmas ornaments. There's an on-site coffee shop.

Jamaliyah
HOMEWARES

(☎ 0754 592721; Boma Rd; ◷ 9am-5pm Mon-Fri, to 1pm Sat) This original little place makes and sells picture frames made of dhow wood.

Mt Meru Curios & Crafts Market
MARKET

(Fire Rd; ◷ 7am-7pm) Souvenirs (and a few high-quality items) are found at Mt Meru Curios & Crafts Market, often incorrectly called the Maasai Market. Hard bargaining is required, but it's worth persisting as it has the widest selection in central Arusha.

Tanzanite Experience
JEWELLERY

(☎ 0767 600990; www.tanzaniteexperience.com; 3rd fl, Blue Plaza, India St; ◷ 8am-5pm Mon-Fri, 9am-1pm Sat) One of many shops selling tanzanite. This one has set up a little museum about this rare gem, which is mined almost exclusively in the Kilimanjaro area.

Cultural Heritage
SOUVENIRS, HANDICRAFTS

(Dodoma Rd; ⊙9am-5pm Mon-Sat, to 2pm Sun) The large and unmissable Cultural Heritage craft mall on the western edge of Arusha has all the usual souvenirs with some less common items. Shopping is hassle-free, but prices are higher. There's a DHL office here.

Kase
BOOKS

(✐027-250 2640; Boma Rd; ⊙9am-5.30pm Mon-Fri, to 2pm Sat) Best bet for national park books and maps. If the Boma Rd shop doesn't have what you want, try the other **branch** (✐027-250 2441; Joel Maeda St; ⊙9am-2pm & 5-8pm Mon-Fri, 9am-2pm Sat) around the corner.

ℹ Information

GARAGE
Fortes (✐027-250 6094; www.fortes-africa.com; off Factory Rd) Arguably Arusha's most reliable vehicle repairs.

Meserani Snake Park (✐027-253 8282; www.meseranisnakepark.com) Twenty-five kilometres west of town on the Dodoma Rd, this is the mechanic of choice for overland trucks.

IMMIGRATION
Immigration Office (East Africa Rd; ⊙7.30am-3.30pm Mon-Fri) Near the Makongoro Rd junction.

INTERNET ACCESS
There are many internet cafes around the market and Clock Tower areas. The normal rate is Tsh1000 per hour.

Café Barrista (Sokoine Rd; per hour Tsh1000; ⊙7.30am-6.30pm Mon-Sat, 8am-5pm Sun) Has computers and wi-fi (the latter is free if you buy a meal).

Internet Cafe (Boma Rd; per hour Tsh1000; ⊙9am-6pm Mon-Fri, 9.30am-6pm Sat & Sun) Inside the grounds of the Natural History Museum.

New Safari Hotel (Boma Rd; per hour Tsh1000; ⊙24hr) In the hotel lobby.

MEDICAL SERVICES
Arusha Lutheran Medical Centre (✐027-254 8030; www.selianlh.habari.co.tz; Makao Mapya Rd; ⊙24hr) The best medical facility in the region, but for anything truly serious, get yourself to Nairobi.

Moona's Pharmacy (✐0754 309052; Sokoine Rd; ⊙8.45am-5.30pm Mon-Fri, to 2pm Sat) Well-stocked pharmacy, west of NBC bank.

MONEY
Forex bureaus are clustered along Joel Maeda St, India St, and Sokoine Rd between the Nakumatt supermarket and the Clock Tower. Sanya

Bureau de Change, with several locations along Sokoine Rd, is open 7am to 7pm daily, including public holidays.

TOURIST INFORMATION
The bulletin boards at the Tourist Information Centre and Cafe Barrista are good spots to find safari mates.

Ngorongoro Conservation Area Authority (NCAA) Information Office (✐027-254 4625; www.ngorongorocrater.org; Boma Rd; ⊙9am-5pm Mon-Fri, to 1pm Sat) Has free Ngorongoro booklets and a cool relief map of the conservation area.

Tanzania National Parks Headquarters (Tanapa; ✐027-250 3471; www.tanzaniaparks.com; Dodoma Rd; ⊙9am-5pm Mon-Fri, to 1pm Sat) Just west of town, this office has info on Tanzania's national parks.

Tanzania Tourist Board Tourist Information Centre (TTB; ✐027-250 3842, 027-250 3843; www.tanzaniatouristboard.com; Boma Rd; ⊙8am-4pm Mon-Fri, 8.30am-1pm Sat) Knowledgeable and helpful staff have information on Arusha, Northern Circuit parks and other area attractions. They can book Cultural Tourism Program tours and provide a good free map of Arusha and Moshi. The office also keeps a 'blacklist' of tour operators and a list of registered tour companies.

TRAVEL AGENCIES
Skylink (✐0755 351111, 027-250 9108; www.skylinktanzania.com; Goliondoi Rd) Domestic and international flight bookings.

ℹ Getting There & Away

AIR
Most flights use **Kilimanjaro International Airport** (JRO; ✐027-255 4707, 027-255 4252; www.kilimanjaroairport.co.tz), about halfway between Moshi and Arusha, while small planes, mostly to the national parks, leave from **Arusha Airport** (✐027-250 5920; www.taa.go.tz; Dodoma Rd), 8km west of town along the Dodoma Rd. Verify the departure point when buying your ticket.

Air Excel (✐027-254 8429; www.airexcelonline.com; 2nd fl, Subzali (Exim Bank) Bldg, Goliondoi Rd) Flights from Arusha to various Serengeti airstrips and Lake Manyara National Park.

Coastal Aviation (✐0752 059650, 027-250 0343; www.coastal.co.tz; Arusha Airport) Arusha to Lake Manyara, Serengeti and Ruaha National Parks, as well as West Kilimanjaro and Zanzibar.

Ethiopian Airlines (✐027-250 4231; www.ethiopianairlines.com; Boma Rd; ⊙8.30am-12.30pm & 2-5pm Mon-Fri, 8.30am-1pm Sat)

International services to Kilimanjaro International Airport from Addis Ababa.

Fastjet (☑ 0783 540540; www.fastjet.com/tz; 2nd fl, Blue Plaza, India St; ☺ 8am-6pm Mon-Sat) Good for low-cost domestic and other African destinations, with direct Kilimanjaro International Airport to Dar es Salaam flights and onward connections.

Precision Air (☑ 0756 979490; www.precision airtz.com; Boma Rd) Flies to Dar, Mwanza and Zanzibar from both Kili International and Arusha Airports. Also handles Kenya Airways bookings.

Regional Air (☑ 0784 285753; www.regional tanzania.com; Great North Rd) Connects Arusha Airport with Serengeti and Lake Manyara airstrips, as well as Zanzibar.

RwandAir (☑ 0732 978558; www.rwandair.com; Swahili St) Twice weekly Kigali to Kili International service.

ZanAir (☑ 027-254 8877; www.zanair.com; Summit Centre, Dodoma Rd) Connects Arusha with Dar es Salaam, Pemba and Zanzibar.

BUS

Arusha has two bus stations. If you want to avoid the bus stations altogether, most buses make a stop on the edge of town before going to the stations. Taxis will be waiting at that location.

When leaving Arusha, the best thing to do is book your ticket the day before, so that in the morning when you arrive with your luggage you can get straight on your bus. For predawn buses, take a taxi to the station and ask the driver to drop you directly at your bus.

Despite what you may hear, there are no luggage fees (unless you have an extraordinarily large pack).

Central Bus Station Arusha's biggest bus station is intimidatingly chaotic in the morning and is popular with touts. If you get overwhelmed head straight for a taxi, or duck into the lobby of one of the hotels across the street to get your bearings.

Makao Mapya Bus Station (Wachagga St) The Makao Mapya bus station (aka Dar Express bus station), situated a little to the northwest, handles most of the luxury buses to Dar es Salaam.

Dar es Salaam

The best companies (all four-across seating and relatively new air-conditioned buses) to/from Dar es Salaam (eight to 10 hours) are listed here. If you take an early departure, with luck you *might* be able to catch the last ferry to Zanzibar. Super luxury means there's a toilet on board.

In addition to the following services, less reliable options depart early morning from the central bus station. They're sometimes cheaper, but you get what you pay for. Ordinary buses (Tsh18,000) depart 5.30am to 11am.

 THE NAIROBI SHUTTLE

The fastest, most comfortable and most reliable services between Arusha and Nairobi are the minibus shuttle services. Rainbow Shuttle, Impala Shuttle and Jamii Shuttle are among the most reliable operators (see p377).

Dar Express (☑ 0784 946155, 0754 525361; Wachagga St; luxury/full luxury Tsh25,000/30,000) Generally the best company, Dar Express has buses departing Makao Mapya bus station from 5.50am to 8am.

Metro Express (Wachagga St; luxury/full luxury Tsh33,000/36,000) Metro Express has two early morning services to Dar from Makao Mapya bus station.

Other Destinations

The following services depart from the Central Bus Station unless otherwise stated.

Babati, Kolo and Kondoa The buses of **Mtei Express** (☑ 0742 941707; Wachagga St) depart the central bus station, but also stop at their own office on Kilobero Rd, 300m north of Nakumatt, where you won't have to deal with touts. They leave hourly to Babati (Tsh6000, three hours) between 6am and 4pm. Their 6am bus continues on to Kondoa (Tsh15,000, seven hours) via Kolo (Tsh14,000, 6½ hours).

Dodoma Early morning buses (Tsh25,000, 11 hours) with Mtei Express, among other companies.

Lushoto Buses (Tsh12,000 to Tsh13,000, six hours) depart daily at 6am and 6.45am. It's often more comfortable (although more expensive) to take an express bus towards Dar as far as Mombo, and then get local transport from there to Lushoto.

Moshi Buses and minibuses (about Tsh3000, 1½ hours) run up to 8pm. It's pricier (US$10) but more comfortable to take one of the Arusha–Nairobi shuttles.

Mwanza Most buses to Mwanza (Tsh28,000 to Tsh38,000, 12 hours) leave the central bus station (some use Makao Mapya), between 6am and 7.30am; all travel via Singida.

Musoma Various companies have buses (Tsh33,000, 11 to 12 hours) leaving at 6am, passing through Serengeti National Park and Ngorongoro Conservation Area. Foreigners must pay the park entry fees (US$100) to ride this route.

Tanga Buses (Tsh16,000, seven hours) depart between 6am and noon. Otherwise, take any Dar es Salaam bus and transfer at Segera junction, although waits can be lengthy.

NORTHERN TANZANIA ARUSHA

ℹ Getting Around

TO/FROM KILIMANJARO INTERNATIONAL AIRPORT

The starting price for taxis from town to KIA is US$50. Some drivers will go for less, but many others will only go for more.

TO/FROM ARUSHA AIRPORT

Taxis from town charge from Tsh17,000. Any dalla-dalla heading out along the Dodoma road can drop you at the junction, from where you'll have to walk about 1.5km.

CAR

Parking anywhere in the city centre costs Tsh1000 per day – an attendant with tickets is likely to be lurking not far from where you park.

For any serious safari, you'll need a large 4WD (ie Toyota Landcruiser) with a pop-top roof for wildlife viewing. It's worth shopping around as quoted prices can vary significantly. We were quoted US$250 per day including driver, fuel and 200km free per day, but this dropped to US$130 per day with 120km free, although fuel wasn't included. Do your sums carefully as extra kilometres are charged at a steep US$0.68 per kilometre.

You can get smaller and cheaper RAV4-style 4WDs, but they're not ideal for wildlife viewing, although they're generally fine during the dry season. Expect to pay around US$600 per week with around 100km free per day.

Drivers are included in the price. Book as early as possible because demand is high.

Arusha Naaz (☑ 0786 239771, 027-250 2087; www.arushanaaz.net; Sokoine Rd; ⊙ 9am-5pm)

ℹ ARUSHA NATIONAL PARK

Why Go Climbing Mt Meru; canoe and walking safaris; fine birding; easy day-trip from Arusha

When to Go Year-round

Practicalities Drive in from Arusha or Moshi. The main park entrance is at the southern Ngongongare gate. The northern Momella gate is 12km further north near park headquarters, which is the main contact for making campsite reservations. Entrance fees can be paid in cash or credit card at the main Ngongonare gate.

Budget Tips Join a pre-arranged safari or charter a dalla-dalla for the day with other travellers in Arusha; if not climbing Mt Meru, visit on a day trip to avoid camping fees.

Fortes (☑ 027-250-6094; www.fortescarhire.com; off Factory Rd) Excellent and experienced operator that also allows self-drive.

Rainbow (☑ 0765 046006; www.rainbowcarhire.com; New Safari Hotel, Boma Rd)

LOCAL TRANSPORT

Dalla-dallas (Tsh400) run along major roads from early until late. There are taxi stands all around the city centre and some park in front of most hotels, even many budget ones. A ride across town, from the Clock Tower to Makao Mapya bus station, for example, shouldn't cost more than Tsh3500. Motorcycle taxi drivers will almost always tell you Tsh2000 for a ride in the city centre, but will go for Tsh1500 if you insist.

Arusha National Park

Arusha National Park (☑ 0767 536136, 0689 062363; www.tanzaniaparks.com/arusha.html; adult/child US$45/15; ⊙ 6.30am-6.30pm) is one Tanzania's smallest (552 sq km) but most beautiful and topographically varied northern circuit parks. It's dominated by **Mt Meru**, an almost perfect cone with a spectacular crater. Also notable is **Ngurdoto Crater** (often dubbed Little Ngorongoro) with its swamp-filled floor. Wildlife is present, but for the most part it's a sideshow to the scenery and the trekking and climbing possibilities.

Activities

Climbing Mt Meru

Trekking the Momella Route to the summit of Mt Meru is one of the country's most underrated activities. See p168 for more.

Wildlife Drives

Just north of Ngongongare gate is Serengeti Ndogo (Little Serengeti), a small patch of open grassland that almost always has zebras and other plains animals. Here the road divides: Outer Rd, to the west, has great Meru views, but the eastern Park Rd is the better route for wildlife. Both are good all-year roads passable in 2WD cars, as are most other tracks through the park. Park Rd leads past the road up Ngurdoto Crater and then to Momella Lakes, both beautiful attractions as well as good wildlife-spotting areas.

The park's altitude, which varies from 1400m to more than 4500m, has a variety of vegetation zones but most of the park is forested and the dense vegetation reduces visibility. Animal life is also far less abundant than in other northern Tanzanian parks.

Arusha National Park

NORTHERN TANZANIA

Map labels:

5 km
2.5 miles

N

Ngurdoto Crater

Momella Lakes

Kinandia Swamp

Lake Longil
Lake Jembamba
Senato Pools

Park Rd

Lendruga Swamp

Arusha National Park

Lokia Swamp

Ngurdoto Museum

NGURDOTO

Ngongongare Hill

Ngongongare (grassland)

Mto Wa Chui River

Meru View Lodge & Ngurdoto Lodge (700m);
Arusha (30km)

Ngongongare Gate

Serengeti Ndogo

Park Rd

Outer Rd

MOMELLA

Ngare Nanyuki (8km)

Hatari Lodge

Park Headquarters

Momella Gate

Camp Sites

Outer Rd

Kiboko Lodge

Waterfall

Momella Route

Tululusia Hill

Fig Tree Arch

Mato Falls

Itikoni Clearing

Mirakamba Hut (2514m)

Topela Mbogo

Kitoto Hill

Kitoto Camp (disused)

Momella Route

Jekukumia River

Ngare Nanyuki River

Little Meru (3820m)

Saddle Hut (3570m)

Mgongo Wa Tembo

Rhino Point (3814m)

Ash Cone

Meru Crater

Lengusa River

Njeku Camp (disused)

Falls

Njeku Viewpoint

Meru Summit (4566m)

Nevertheless you can be fairly certain of sighting zebras, giraffes, waterbucks, bushbucks, klipspringers, dik-diks, buffaloes and hippos. There are also elephants, leopards, red duikers and black-and-white colobus (most often sighted near the Ngurdoto Museum). There are no lions or rhinos due to poaching.

CLIMBING MT MERU

At 4566m, Mt Meru is Tanzania's second-highest mountain. Although overshadowed by Kilimanjaro in the eyes of trekkers, it's a spectacular volcanic cone with one of East Africa's most scenic and rewarding climbs, involving a dramatic walk along the knife edge of the crater rim.

Mt Meru starts its steep rise from a circular base some 20km across at 2000m. At about 2500m some of the wall has broken away so the top half of the mountain is shaped like a giant horseshoe. The cliffs of the inner wall below the summit are more than 1500m high: among the tallest in Africa. Inside the crater, more recent volcanic eruptions have created a subsidiary peak called the Ash Cone that adds to the scenic splendour.

Momella Route

The Momella Rte is the only route up Mt Meru. It starts at Momella gate on the eastern side of the mountain and goes to the summit along the northern arm of the horseshoe crater. The route can be done comfortably in four days (three nights). Trekkers aren't allowed to begin after 3pm, which means that if you travel to the park by bus you'll almost certainly have to camp and wait until the next day to start climbing.

While Meru is small compared with Kilimanjaro, don't underestimate it: because of the steepness, many have found that Meru is almost as difficult a climb. And it's still high enough to make the effects of altitude felt, so don't try to rush up if you're not properly acclimatised.

Stage 1: Momella gate to Miriakamba Hut (10km, four to five hours, 1000m ascent) There are two routes, one long and one short, at the start of the climb. Most people prefer taking the mostly forested long route up and the short route down, so that's how the trek is described here. And do watch out for buffaloes...

From Momella gate, the road winds uphill for an hour to Fig Tree Arch, a parasitic wild fig that originally grew around two other trees, eventually strangling them. Now only the fig tree remains, with its distinctive arch large enough to drive a car through. After another hour the track crosses a large stream, just above Maio Falls and one hour further you'll reach Kitoto Camp, with excellent views over the Momella Lakes and out to Kilimanjaro in the distance. It's then one final hour to Miriakamba Hut (2514m). From Miriakamba you can walk to the Meru Crater floor (a two- to three-hour return trip) either in the afternoon of Stage 1 or during Stage 4 (there is time to do it on the morning of Stage 2, but this is a bad idea as it reduces your time for acclimitisation), but you need to let your guide know you want to do this before starting the climb. The path across the floor leads to Njeku Viewpoint on a high cliff overlooking a waterfall, with excellent views of the Ash Cone and the entire extent of the crater.

Stage 2: Miriakamba Hut to Saddle Hut (4km, three to five hours, 1250m ascent) From Miriakamba the path climbs steeply up through pleasant glades to reach Topela Mbogo (Buffalo Swamp) after 45 minutes and Mgongo Wa Tembo (Elephant Ridge) after another 30 minutes. From the top of Mgongo Wa Tembo there are great views down into the crater and up to the main cliffs below the summit. Continue through some open grassy clearings and over several stream beds (usually dry) to Saddle Hut (3570m).

From Saddle Hut a side trip to the summit of Little Meru (3820m) takes about an hour and gives impressive views of Meru's summit, the horseshoe crater, the top of the Ash Cone and the sheer cliffs of the crater's inner wall. As the sun sets behind Meru, casting huge jagged shadows across the clouds, the snow on Kili turns orange and then pink as the light fades.

Stage 3: Saddle Hut to Meru Summit and return (5km, four to five hours, 816m ascent, plus 5km, two to three hours, 816m descent) This stage, along a very narrow ridge between the outer slopes of the mountain and the sheer cliffs of the inner crater, promises some of

Birdwatching

Birdlife is abundant with around 400 species recorded in the park. Raptors are common at higher altitudes. Like many in the Rift Valley, the seven spring-fed Momella Lakes are shallow and alkaline and attract a wide variety of wader birds, including year-round flamingos. Due to their varying

the most dramatic and exhilarating trekking anywhere in East Africa. During the rainy season, ice and snow can occur on this section of the route, so take care. If there's no mist, the views from the summit are spectacular.

If you're looking forward to watching the sunrise behind Kilimanjaro, but you're not keen on attempting this section in the dark, the views at dawn are just as impressive from **Rhino Point** (3814m), about an hour from Saddle Hut, as they are from the summit – perhaps even more so because you'll also see the main cliffs of the crater's inner wall being illuminated by the rising sun.

Stage 4: Saddle Hut to Momella gate (5km, three to five hours, 2250m descent)

From Saddle Hut, retrace the Stage 2 route to Miriakamba. From Miriakamba, the short path descends gradually down the ridge directly to Momella gate. It goes through forest some of the way, then open grassland, where giraffes and zebras are often seen.

Practicalities

Costs Trekking companies in both Arusha and Moshi organise treks on Mt Meru. Most charge from US$450 to US$750 for four days. That said, you can do things quite easily on your own for around US$380 for a four-day, three-night trek. You'll also need to add in the costs of food (which you should get in Arusha, as there's nowhere to stock up near the park), and of transport to and from the park.

The following are the minimum per-person costs:

➡ park entrance fee US$45 per day

➡ hut fees US$30 per day

➡ rescue fee US$20 per trip

➡ guide fees US$15 per day.

Tipping Park rangers receive a fixed monthly salary for their work, and get no additional payment from the park for guiding, which means that tips are much appreciated. It happens rarely, but rangers and porters here occasionally expect the big tips demanded by their Kilimanjaro counterparts. If this happens and you're already on the trail, work out an arrangement to keep going, and then report them to headquarters when you get down the mountain.

For a good guide who has completed the full trek with you, plan on a tip of about US$50 per group. Cook and porter tips should be around US$30 and US$20 respectively. Tip more with top-end companies.

Guides and porters A ranger-guide is mandatory and can be arranged at Momella gate. Unlike on Kilimanjaro, guides on Meru are regular park rangers whose purpose is to assist (and protect) you in case you meet some of the park's buffaloes or elephants, rather than to show you the way, although they do know the route. If there's a shortage of rangers, which is often, you may end up in a larger group than you hoped for.

Optional porters are also available at Momella gate. The charge is US$10 per porter per day and this is paid directly to them at the end of the trek. They come from one of the nearby villages and are not park employees so you'll also need to pay their park entrance (Tsh1500 per day) and hut (Tsh2000 per night) fees at Momella gate before starting to trek. Porters will carry rucksacks weighing up to 20kg (excluding their own food and clothing).

Accommodation There are two blocks of four-bed bunkhouses ('huts') spaced for a four-day trek. Especially during the July–August and December–January high seasons, they're often full, so book ahead. It's also a good idea to carry a tent (though if you camp, you'll still need to pay hut fees). Each bunkhouse has a cooking and eating area; bring your own stove and fuel.

PEOPLES OF NORTHERN TANZANIA: THE MAASAI

The Maasai are pastoral nomads who have actively resisted change, and many still follow the same lifestyle they have for centuries. Their traditional culture centres on their cattle, which along with their land, are considered sacred. Cows provide many of their needs: milk, blood and meat for their diet, and hides and skins for clothing, although sheep and goats also play an important dietary role, especially during the dry season.

Maasai society is patriarchal and highly decentralised. Maasai boys pass through a number of transitions during their life, the first of which is marked by the circumcision rite. Successive stages include junior warriors, senior warriors, junior elders and senior elders; each level is distinguished by its own unique rights, responsibilities and dress. Junior elders, for example, are expected to marry and settle down; somewhere between the age of 30 and 40. Senior elders assume the responsibility of making wise and moderate decisions for the community. The most important group is that of the newly initiated warriors, *moran,* who are charged with defending the cattle herds.

Maasai women play a markedly subservient role and have no inheritance rights. Polygyny is widespread and marriages are arranged by the elders, without consulting the bride or her mother. Since most women are significantly younger than men at the time of marriage, they often become widows; remarriage is rare.

mineral content, each lake supports a different type of algal growth, which gives them different colours. Birdlife also varies quite distinctly from one lake to another, even when they're only separated by a narrow strip of land.

Canoeing

Wayo Africa (p34) offers 2½ hour Momella Lake canoe safaris (US$65 per person plus a US$20 canoeing fee paid at the park gate) in the morning and afternoon.

🛏 Sleeping

The park has three **public campsites** (camping US$30) in the vicinity of Momella gate (including one with a shower). More wide-ranging sleeping options are found outside the park boundary.

Kiboko Lodge LODGE $$
(☎ 0784 652260; www.wfkibokolodge.com; s/d half board from US$75/130) 🌿 Most employees at this nonprofit, charity-run lodge are former street kids who received training at the Watoto Foundation's vocational training school. But it's not just a feel-good project, it's a great place to stay. The spacious and attractive stone cottages have fireplaces, hot water and safes, and the thatched-roof lounge is almost homey. It's 5km down a 4WD-only road east of Ngongongare gate.

Meru View Lodge LODGE $$
(☎ 0784 419232; www.meru-view-lodge.de; s/d US$100/140; @ 🛜 🌊) This unassuming place

has a mix of large and small (all priced the same) cottages set in quiet grounds just 1km south of Ngongongare gate. They also run the nearby **Ngurdoto Lodge**, which has the same prices and similar facilities.

★**Hatari Lodge** LODGE $$$
(☎ 0752 553456, 027-255 3456/7; www.hatarilodge.com; s/d full board US$480/640) The most atmospheric and upmarket of the park lodges – the property was originally owned by Hardy Kruger, of *Hatari!* film fame – with 'modern retro' room decor, a prime location on large lawns frequented by giraffes, and views of Meru and Kilimanjaro on clear days. It's on the edge of the park, about 2km north of Momela gate.

Rooms are spacious, with large windows, and there's a fireplace and top-notch cuisine.

Rivertrees Country Inn LODGE $$$
(☎ 0732 971667, 027-255 3894; www.rivertrees.com; s/d/tr from US$180/220/290, 2-room River House US$1000; 🅿 @ 🛜 🌊) With a genteel old-world ambience and excellent cuisine served family-style around a large wooden dining table, Rivertrees is a perfect postnational park stop. A variety of rooms and cottages, some wheelchair accessible, are spread throughout vast natural gardens with huge trees along the Usa River. It's east of Usa River Village, set back off the Moshi Hwy.

Meals are superb, as are the cultural tours (to local villages and coffee farms) and spa treatments.

ℹ Information

The best map of the park is the Maco *Arusha National Park* map, widely available in Arusha. The Veronica Roodt *Arusha National Park – The Tourist Map* is also reasonable.

ℹ Getting There & Away

Arusha National Park is 25km outside Arusha, and Ngongongare gate is 6.5km north of the Arusha–Moshi road. From the northern entrance, by Momella gate, it's possible to continue via a rough track that joins the main Nairobi highway near Lariboro.

There are four daily buses between Arusha and Ngare Nanyuki village (6km north of Momella gate) that depart Arusha from 1.30pm to 4pm and Ngare Nanyuki between 7am and 8am. Buses stop at Ngongongare gate (Tsh4000, 1½ hours). A taxi from Arusha should cost about Tsh50,000.

Tarangire National Park

Welcome to one of Africa's most underrated parks. Thanks to its proximity to the Serengeti and Ngorongoro, Tarangire National Park (☎ 0767 536139, 0689 062248, 025-31280/81; www.tanzaniaparks.com/tarangire.html; adult/child US$45/15; ☉ 6am-6pm) is usually assigned only a day visit as part of a larger northern circuit safari. We think it deserves a whole lot more, at least in the dry season. It's a place where elephants dot the plains like cattle, and where lion roars and zebra barks fill the night, all set against a backdrop of constantly changing scenery.

Tarangire has the second-highest concentration of wildlife of any Tanzanian national park (after Serengeti) and reportedly has the largest concentration of elephants in the world. The Tarangire ecosystem, with the park as its heart and soul, also has more than 700 resident lions, and sightings are common. Less visible, but nonetheless present, are leopards and cheetahs. What sustains them are large herds of zebras, wildebeest, giraffes, buffaloes and other herbivores. With more than 450 bird species, some say that Tarangire is the best bird-watching destination in Tanzania.

But this is one place where the wildlife tells only half the story. Dominating the park's 2850 sq km, the great stands of epic baobabs should be reason enough to come here, but there are also sun-blistered termite mounds in abundance, as well as grassy savannah plains and vast swamps. And cleaving the park in two is the Tarangire River, its meandering course and (in some places) steep riverbanks providing a dry-season lure for so many stirring wildlife encounters.

Come the short rainy season, and the park changes completely, as its wild inhabitants disperse across the Maasai Steppe, over an area 10 times larger than the park. This, too, is a Tarangire speciality: one of the park's greatest rewards is the chance to discern and tune into the seasonal rhythms of wild Africa.

◉ Sights & Activities

Wildlife Drives

The northern triangle bordered by the park boundaries to the northeast and west, and by the Tarangire River and Tarangire Safari Lodge in the south, offers the most easily accessible as well as some of the most rewarding wildlife areas of the park. Amid a varied habitat of open plains and light woodland, you'll find elephants, zebras and wildebeest in abundance in this baobab-rich region, with predators, particularly lions, also a possibility.

Further south, wildlife draws near to the water all along the Tarangire River valley that cuts the park in two, while the swamps of Silale, Lormakau and Ngusero Oloirobi are alive with possibility as predators lie in wait in the shallows whenever herbivores come to drink. This chain of swamps runs north–south through the park, beginning just west of the Tarangire Sopa Lodge. Gurusi Swamp, in the park's southwestern bulge, is another rich wildlife area.

ℹ TARANGIRE NATIONAL PARK

Why Go Excellent dry season wildlife watching, especially elephants and lions; evocative baobab-studded landscapes.

When to go June to October

Practicalities Drive in from Arusha; entrance fees can be paid in cash or by credit card at both the main gate and Boundary Hill gate.

Budget Tips Join a pre-arranged safari or charter a dalla-dalla with other travellers; stay outside the park to avoid camping fees.

Tarangire National Park

0 ————————— 20 km
0 ————————— 10 miles

Tarangire National Park

Sleeping

1	Boundary Hill Lodge	B2
2	Maramboi Tented Lodge	A1
3	Oliver's Camp & Little Oliver's Camp	B3
4	Osupko Lodge	A1
5	Public Campsite	A1
6	Roika Tarangire Tented Lodge	A1
7	Sanctuary Swala	A3
8	Tarangire River Camp	A2
9	Tarangire Safari Lodge	A1
10	Tarangire Sopa Lodge	B2
11	Tarangire Treetops Lodge	B2
12	Zion Campsite	A1

Some of the lodges inside the park (and all of them outside the park) can arrange **night drives** for guests.

Walking Safaris

Three-hour walking safaris (US$20 per person plus US$20 per group) can be organised from the park gate (though the armed rangers are simply security and haven't had much training about wildlife). Most of the lodges can organise walks with their own trained guides, but only for their own guests.

🛏 Sleeping

Staying in the park gets you right into the heart of the action from the moment you wake up. Outside, the closer you are to the gate the better if you don't want to miss that crucial first hour or two inside the park.

A further option is the Tarangire Conservation Area (TCA), a remote region outside the park to the northeast, with animals aplenty from November to March, but fewer in other months. If staying in the TCA, park access is through the Boundary Hill gate.

🛏 Inside the Park

Public Campsite CAMPGROUND **$**
(camping US$30) A public campsite is a short drive into the park near the northwestern tip. It has a good bush location but simple cold-water facilities. Bring supplies from Arusha.

★Tarangire Safari Lodge LODGE, TENTED CAMP **$$$**
(✆0784 202777, 027-254 4752; www.tarangire safarilodge.com; s/d full board US$250/400; 🅿🛜❄) A fabulous location overlooking the Tarangire River, excellent service, good food and well-priced accommodation make this lodge our pick of the in-park options. The sweeping vistas are such that there's no need to go elsewhere for a sundowner, while the accommodation includes stone bungalows or standard ensuite safari tents; the latter have good views from their doorsteps. It's 10km inside the park gate.

★Sanctuary Swala TENTED CAMP **$$$**
(✆027-250 9817; www.sanctuaryretreats.com; s/d full board US$1106/1622; ☉Jun-Mar; 🅿@🛜❄) Arguably the most refined safari experience inside Tarangire, this premier-class camp nestles in a grove of acacia trees and overlooks a busy water hole in the southwestern part of the park by Gurusi Swamp. Each of the 12 lovely tents has a big deck and its own butler. It's in a great wildlife-watching location with lots of lions.

Oliver's Camp &
Little Oliver's Camp
TENTED CAMP $$$

(http://oliverscamp.asiliaafrica.com; s/d full board US$930/1330; ☺mid-May–Mar; P) Notable for its fine location near Silale, deep in the heart of the park; comfortable and spacious, the 10 tents have an agreeably rustic style and the whole camp has a personal ambience. Excellent guides lead walking safaris, night drives (sometimes using night-vision equipment) and fly camping, making this an ideal spot for adventurous travellers. No direct bookings; contact a travel agent.

Just 1km away, sibling-property Little Oliver's has five similarly luxurious tents and the same prices.

Tarangire Sopa Lodge
LODGE $$$

(☑027-250 0630; www.sopalodges.com; s/d/tr full board US$370/650/829; P 🛜 🍽) Tarangire's Sopa Lodge is a fairly standard evocation of the Sopa brand. Rooms are large (effectively suites), the carpets have been mercifully removed, but facilities are ageing, some of the rooms are dark and most lack line-of-sight thanks to the overgrown brushwood, although elephants often come right up to the window. The location, close to the middle of the park, is good.

Before the Park Gate

Zion Campsite
CAMPGROUND $

(☑0754 460539; camping US$10; P) A bare and unkempt compound 6km before the park gate it may be, but it's cheaper than camping inside the park, and the showers are warm. Bring your own food.

Maramboi Tented Lodge
TENTED CAMP $$$

(☑0784 207727; www.tanganyikawilderness camps.com; s/d/tr full board US$250/375/510; P @ 🛜 🍽) Unlike any other lodge around Tarangire, Maramboi sits amid palms and savannah on Lake Manyara's southeastern shore, 17km from Tarangire's entrance. The 20 large, airy tents with wooden floors all have decks looking out towards the lake, Rift Valley Escarpment and sunset. Staff are friendly. The turn-off to the lodge is 6km south of Kigongoni.

Tarangire River Camp
LODGE $$$

(☑0737 206420, 0732978879; www.mbalimbali. com; ☺closed Apr; P) With good views from its hilltop perch overlooking a river valley and lovely open-sided thatched huts, Tarangire River Lodge is a fine choice set away in a private, Maasai-run concession north-west of the park – it's around 30 minutes by road from the main park gate.

Roika Tarangire
Tented Lodge
TENTED CAMP $$$

(☑0754 001444, 027-250 9994; www.tarangire roikatentedlodge.com; camping US$30, s/d US$225/350; P @ 🛜 🍽) Though it's set off from the park, 5km southwest of the gate, Roika sits in the bush and is visited by lots of wildlife, especially elephants. The 21 widely spaced tents sit on elevated platforms under thatched roofs and have animal-shaped bathtubs. Maasai village visits and night drives are available. The campsite has hot showers and a kitchen is planned.

Osupuko Lodge
LODGE $$$

(☑0754 657737, 0787 925353; www.osupukolodges. com; s/d full board US$230/360; P 🍽) Near the seasonal Minjingu River, this place has 10 rather unsightly rondavels, but each has big windows and indoor/outdoor showers. Views, including of elephants and other wildlife in season, are impressive, and the camp is overall reasonable value. Cultural walks in the surrounding Maasai areas and a special candlelit dinner for two inside a baobab tree can be arranged.

In the Tarangire Conservation Area

Boundary Hill Lodge
LODGE $$$

(☑0787 293727; www.tarangireconservation.com; r per person full board US$550; P @ 🍽) 🌿 Widely praised for its commitment to the environment and the Maasai community (it owns a 50% stake), Boundary Hill has eight large individually designed hilltop rooms with balconies peering out over Silale Swamp in the park.

Tarangire Treetops Lodge
TENTED CAMP $$$

(☑027-250 0630; www.elewana.com; s/d full board US$1120/1690; P @ 🛜 🍽) Not your ordinary tented camp, this pampered place has 20 huge suites set on stilts or built treehouse-style around the baobabs. It's almost an hour's drive to the Boundary Hill gate, but it's ideal if you're looking for more of a luxury-in-the-wilderness experience.

❶ Information

Maco puts out the best Tarangire map, available in Arusha and at the park gate. The hand-drawn *New Map of Tarangire National Park*, available in Arusha and elsewhere, is outstanding, with different versions for wet and dry seasons.

❶ Getting There & Away

Tarangire is 130km from Arusha via Makuyuni (the last place for petrol and supplies). At Kigongoni village there's a signposted turn-off to the main park gate, which is 7km further down a good dirt access road. The only other entrance is Boundary Hill gate along the northeast border, which provides access to some lodges located in the area. The park doesn't rent vehicles.

Coastal Aviation (p164) and Air Excel (p164) sometimes stop at Tarangire's Kuro airstrip on request on their flights between Arusha and Lake Manyara.

Manyara Ranch Conservancy

Occupying an important wildlife dispersal area northwest of Tarangire National Park, the privately run, 140-sq-km Manyara Ranch Conservancy (www.manyararanch. com) is a critical cog in the ecosystem of northern Tanzania's Maasai Steppe.

The conservancy began life as a colonial cattle ranch that later fell into disuse. Thanks to the African Wildlife Foundation (www.awf.org), which runs the conservancy, the vegetation is recovering and wildlife is returning to the area. Already there are fairly reliable year-round populations of elephants, lions (two small resident prides), leopards, hyenas (striped and spotted), giraffes, zebras and other herbivores. More than 300 bird species have also been recorded here.

True to the conservancy model, the project is not just about protecting wildlife, and AWF works closely with neighbouring Maasai communities to ensure that these communities receive some benefits from the wildlife that lives within their midst.

◎ Sights & Activities

Walking safaris and day or night wildlife drives (watch for striped hyenas and aardwolfs on the latter) are all possible and usually included as part of accommodation packages. Other possibilities include cultural visits to nearby Maasai villages or halfday horseback safaris (per person US$125).

⌂ Sleeping

Manyara Ranch
Tented Camp   TENTED CAMP$$$
(☎ 0683 918888, 027-254 5284; www.manyara ranch.com; s/d full board US$715/1160; ℗) ✐ In the heart of the conservancy, this stun-ning tented camp has spacious and beautifully furnished tents, each set in their own secluded stand of bush and with private verandahs and reclining couches. The interiors are a classic and refined combination of canvas and wood. Sundowners are served by the campfire with a view of the surrounding plain.

From your nightly accommodation rate, US$40 per person goes to the ranch's conservation activities.

❶ Getting There & Away

There's no public transport to the conservancy. If self-driving, from Makuyuni head south along the road towards Tarangire. After 10km, opposite a building with red and blue walls, a stone sign on the right-hand (western) side of the road says 'Manyara Ranch Conservancy'. Take the turn, veering right then follow the dirt road and the signs for 6.6km into the camp.

Mto wa Mbu

Mto wa Mbu is the busy gateway to Lake Manyara, which is fed by the town's eponymous 'River of Mosquitoes'. Over the years, this diverse place – by some estimates, all of Tanzania's 120 tribal groups are present here – has evolved into something of a travellers centre with plenty of lodges, campsites, hole-in-the-wall eateries, petrol stations, moneychangers, souvenir stalls and just about anything else that could tempt a passing safari vehicle to disgorge its inhabitants.

🏃 Activities

Mto wa Mbu Cultural Tourism
Program   CULTURAL TOUR
(☎ 0784 606654, 027-253 9303; http://mtocultural programme.tripod.com; day trip from US$30; ⊙ 8am-6.30pm) ✐ The local Cultural Tourism Program offers tours to surrounding villages, markets, and a nearby waterfall, with an emphasis on farming and hiking along the escarpment. Most day trips can be done by mountain bike rather than walking. Home stays and meals with local families can also be arranged. The office is in the Red Banana Restaurant, close to the main bus stop.

⌂ Sleeping & Eating

There are many cheap guesthouses in Mto wa Mbu. The best area to look in is south of the main road behind the market.

Maryland Resort
GUESTHOUSE **$**

(📞 0754 299320; camping Tsh10,000, s/d from Tsh35,000/45,000, d with shared bathroom Tsh25,000; 🅿️) Signposted off the main road just before Lake Manyara National Park gate, this bright peach building is meticulously maintained by the friendly owner who lives on-site. Most of the nine rooms are on the small side, but with hot water and cable TV, they're priced right. Meals are available by request and there's a kitchen.

Njake Jambo Lodge & Campsite
CAMPGROUND **$$**

(📞 027-250 5553; www.njake.com; Arusha-Karatu Rd; camping US$10, s/d US$90/120; 🏊) A base for both independent travellers and large overland trucks, there's a shaded and well-maintained grassy camping area, plus 16 good rooms in double-storey chalet blocks.

Twiga Campsite & Lodge
BACKPACKERS **$$**

(📞 0713 334287; www.twigacampsitelodge.com; Arusha-Karatu Rd; camping US$10, r US$40-140; 🅿️@🏊) This popular place is a real travellers' hub with simple but well-kept standard rooms, bungalows and a decent campsite. It's a good place to hook up with other safarigoers, and bike hire is available.

Blue Turaco Pizza Point
PIZZERIA **$**

(Arusha-Karatu Rd; pasta Tsh5000-7000, pizzas Tsh10,000-16,000; ⏰ noon-9pm) The Blue Turaco Pizza Point, unmissable along the main road, makes good wood-fired pizzas in a casual streetside setting.

ℹ️ Information

There's an ATM (by Twiga Campsite & Lodge, but don't count on it working) and a handful of slow internet cafes in town.

ℹ️ Getting There & Away

BUS
Buses and dalla-dallas run all day from Arusha (Tsh5500 to Tsh6500, two hours) and Karatu (Tsh2500, one hour) to Mto wa Mbu. You can also come from Arusha on the minibuses that run to Karatu. All vehicles stop along the main road in the town centre.

CAR
Car hire for trips to Lake Manyara National Park (including fuel and driver US$150) is available in Mto wa Mbu through the Cultural Tourism Program office and Twiga and Njake Jambo campsites.

The rough track north to Lake Natron begins here.

Lake Manyara National Park

Lake Manyara National Park (📞 0767 536137, 0689 062294, 025-39112; www.tanzaniaparks.com/manyara.html; adult/child US$45/15; ⏰ 6am-6pm) is one of Tanzania's smallest parks and although many safari itineraries skip it, we strongly recommend you make the detour. The dramatic western escarpment of the Rift Valley forms the park's western border. To the east is the alkaline Lake Manyara, which covers one-third of the park, but shrinks considerably in the dry season. During the rains the lake hosts millions of flamingos (best seen outside the park on the lake's east shore) and other birdlife.

While Manyara lacks the raw drama of other northern circuit destinations, its vegetation is diverse, ranging from savannah to marshes to evergreen forest (11 different ecosystems in all) and it supports one of the highest biomass densities of large mammals in the world. Elephants, hippos, zebras, giraffes, buffaloes and wildebeest are often spotted. Leopards and hyenas are also here. Lake Manyara is also home to a famous population of tree-climbing lions. Lions climb trees in other parks, too, but it's a real speciality here – scientists speculate that they may have developed the habit to escape a nasty biting fly that devastated the Ngorongoro Crater lion populations back in the 1960s. Tracking them down can be tricky, but worth the effort.

NORTHERN TANZANIA LAKE MANYARA NATIONAL PARK

ℹ️ LAKE MANYARA NATIONAL PARK

Why Go Excellent birding; tree-climbing lions; dramatic Rift Valley Escarpment scenery

When to Go Year-round. June to October is best for large mammals, November to June is best for birds.

Practicalities Stay in Mto wa Mbu, atop the escarpment or inside the park; bring binoculars to optimise wildlife watching over the lake. Entrance fees can be paid in cash or credit card at the main gate.

Budget Tips Stay in Mto wa Mbu to avoid camping fees; charter a dalla-dalla for the day.

ⓘ LOCAL MARKETS

Consider timing your arrival in the area around the Crater Highlands, Lake Natron and Mto wa Mbu to coincide with one of the region's weekly markets. They're very much social as well as commercial events, and, with the partial exception of Mto wa Mbu, almost entirely local affairs.

Monday Engaruka Juu

Wednesday Selela

Thursday Engaresero, Engaruka Chini and Mto wa Mbu

The Marang Forest Reserve, a 250-sq-km reserve of highland forest off the park's southwestern boundary has recently been added to the park, although tracks for wildlife drives are yet to be developed.

◉ Sights & Activities

Wildlife Drives

Just inside the park's main gate, the **northern woodland** is dense, green and overrun by baboon troops; sightings of blue monkeys are also possible. There's also a **hippo pool** at the lake's northernmost tip. Between the water's edge and the steep Rift Valley walls, the **floodplains** host wildebeest, buffaloes, zebras and Lake Manyara's much-studied elephants, while the thin **acacia belt** that shadows the lake shore is where you're most likely to see arboreal lions. Most drives are either self-drive or part of an organised safari through your lodge or operator.

Night Drives

This is the only northern circuit park where anybody can do night drives, unlike Tarangire National Park where you must be sleeping at the particular camp that offers them. The Lake Manyara night drives are run by Wayo Africa (p34) from 8pm to roughly 11pm (US$55 to US$77 per person depending on group size, plus US$50/25 park fee per adult/child). Park fees must be paid directly to the park before 5pm. Advanced booking (and usually advance payment) is required.

Walking Safaris

The park allows two- to three-hour walking safaris (per person US$20, plus US$20 per group up to eight people) with an armed ranger along three trails. Reservations are required and the park has no vehicles to take hikers to the trailheads.

The **Msara Trail**, the nearest path to the gate (11km away), follows its namesake river along the Rift Valley Escarpment through great birdwatching territory up to a viewpoint. The **Lake Shore Trail** starts 38km into the park near the *maji moto* (hot springs). It crosses acacia woodland and savannah and is the path where walkers are most likely to meet large mammals and find flamingos. The **Iyambi River Trail**, 50km from the gate, is wooded and rocky with good birdwatching and a chance of viewing mammals.

Walking safaris with Wayo Africa (p34) go down the escarpment from the Serena lodge. If there's enough water (usually there's not), Wayo also include canoe safaris on the lake.

🛏 Sleeping

There are only a handful of options within the park boundaries, but they come with the advantage that you can be out among the wildlife from dawn, unlike those who have to drive into the park from elsewhere. Staying atop the escarpment does, however, generally mean sweeping views. Mto wa Mbu is another good base for visiting the park, especially for budget travellers.

🏨 In the Park

Public Campsite No. 1 CAMPGROUND $
(☑ 025-39112; camping US$30) One of two public campsites in the park, Campsite 1 is close to park headquarters and the park gate, with toilet and shower.

Public Campsite No. 2 CAMPGROUND $
(☑ 025-39112; camping per person US$30) Shaded Campsite 2 ('Riverside' or 'Endabash' campsite), set amid sausage trees and other vegetation near the Endabash River about an hour's drive from the gate, has relatively new toilet and shower facilities, and tank water for cooking (and, if treated, for drinking).

★ Lake Manyara Tree Lodge LODGE $$$
(☑ 028-262 1267; www.andbeyond.com; ste per person all inclusive US$1205; ⊘ closed Apr; P 🛜 ⛱) This lovely, luxurious place is one of the most exclusive lodges in all of Tanzania, and the only permanent camp inside the park. The 10 gorgeous stilted treehouse suites with private decks and views from the bathtubs and outdoor showers are set in a

mahogany forest at the remote southern end of the park. The food is excellent and the rooms have butler service.

Lemala Manyara
TENTED CAMP $$$

(☑ 027-254 8966; www.lemalacamp.com; s/d all-inclusive US$575/850; ☻ Jun-Mar; ℗) Situated far into the park, near the Endabash River and hot springs, Lemala has nine tents (one family sized) overlooking the lake from a stand of acacias. It makes the most of its bush setting, but don't let the prices fool you – it's not a luxury camp. Tents have wood floors and furnishings, but we reckon they're a touch overpriced, a recent drop in prices notwithstanding.

Guests here can do night drives in the park.

Atop the Escarpment

★**Panorama Safari Campsite**
CAMPGROUND $

(☑ 0784 118514; camping Tsh10,000; ℗) The first accommodation you reach going up the hill is hot and dusty with run-down warm-water ablutions, but the price is great and the views are as wonderful as any of the luxury lodges up here. Dalla-dallas from Mto wa Mbu heading to Karatu pass the entrance (Tsh750).

The campsite has small no-frills tents and igloo-like structures right up against the cliff, and sunset views are just a short walk away. Mattresses are on the thin side. It serves drinks, but no food.

Escarpment Luxury Lodge
LODGE $$$

(☑ 0767 804864; www.escarpmentlodge.co.tz; s/d all-inclusive US$800/990; ℗@☒) The wood-floored chalets at this relatively new place are the height of luxury – plenty of space, wonderfully deep bathtubs, leather sofas, tasteful recycled furnishings, wide verandahs, the finest linens and big windows. Views of the lake are as expansive as you'd expect from up here on the escarpment.

Lake Manyara Serena Safari Lodge
LODGE $$$

(☑ 027-254 5555; www.serenahotels.com; s/d full board US$308/519; ℗@☎☒) A large complex with shady grounds, the 67 well-appointed rooms are in appealing two-storey conical thatched bungalows. Nature walks and village visits are available, as is massage; fine views come at no extra cost. It lacks the intimacy and naturalness of other properties up here on the escarpment, but is nevertheless a justifiably popular choice.

Below the Escarpment

There are a few camps east of Mto wa Mbu.

Migunga Tented Camp
TENTED CAMP $$$

(☑ 0754 324193; www.moivaro.com; camping US$10, s/d/tr full board US$247/348/450; ℗@) The main attraction of this place (still often known by its previous name, Lake Manyara Tented Camp) is its setting in a grove of enormous fever trees (*migunga* in Swahili) that echoes with bird calls. The 21 tents ringing large, grassy grounds are small but quite adequate and fairly priced. There's also a great rustic dining room. It's 2km south of the main road.

The adjacent campsite has good hot-water facilities. Village tours and mountain-bike hire are available.

Ol Mesera Tented Camp
TENTED CAMP $$$

(☑ 0784 428332; www.ol-mesera.com; s/d full board US$135/245; ℗@) Run by a spritely Slovenian pensioner, this personalised place, in a bush setting amid baobab and euphorbia trees, has four straightforward safari tents and is an ideal spot to do cultural walks, cooking classes or just relax for a few days. It's 14km up the Lake Natron road.

Public transport towards Engaruka or Lake Natron can drop you at the turn-off, from where it's an easy 1.5km walk.

Manyara Wildlife Safari Camp
LODGE $$$

(☑ 0712 332211; www.wildlifecamp.co.tz; s/d full board US$275/350; ℗☒) Tastefully furnished safari tents and stilted cottages with tiled floors and four-poster beds, all on the plains close to Lake Manyara, make this place a good choice if being close to the lake is a priority. It's a 15-minute drive to the park gate, and signposted off the main road.

❶ Information

The hand-drawn *New Map of Lake Manyara National Park*, available in Arusha and elsewhere, has different versions for wet and dry seasons, but doesn't include the Marang Forest Reserve that has recently been added to the park.

❶ Getting There & Away

Air Excel (p164), Coastal Aviation (p164) and Regional Air (p165) offer daily flights between Arusha and Lake Manyara. The airstrip is atop the escarpment near the Serena.

Karatu

POP 26,620

Roughly halfway between Lake Manyara National Park and Ngorongoro (it's 14km southeast of Lodoare gate), this charmless town makes a convenient base for visiting both. Many camping safaris out of Arusha overnight here to avoid paying the camping fees in Ngorongoro. Services are basic, but include several banks that change cash and have ATMs, a few internet cafes, petrol stations, and several minisupermarkets (although it's better to stock up in Arusha).

⊙ Sights & Activities

Market   MARKET

The seventh day of each month is Karatu's *mnada* (market) day – worth making some time for if you happen to be passing through.

Ganako-Karatu Cultural Tourism Program   CULTURAL TOUR

(☑ 0767 612980, 0787451162; www.kcecho.org) The Ganako-Karatu Cultural Tourism Program has an office down the hill from the east edge of town. Its main trips are to nearby coffee plantations and Iraqw (Mbulu) villages. Many of its half- and full-day trips are done by mountain bike.

🛏 Sleeping

🛏 In Karatu

The Bwani neighbourhood, south of the Hai petrol station and supermarket, has many good guesthouses where owners haven't yet learned the phrase 'nonresident price', plus many local restaurants and bars. This is where most safari drivers sleep.

Vera Inn   GUESTHOUSE $

(☑ 0754 578145; Milano Rd, Bwani, Karatu; s/d Tsh30,000/40,000) One of the best guesthouses in Karatu, Vera Inn has rooms that are small but sparkling clean and have hot-water showers and cable TV.

★ Eileen's Trees Inn   LODGE $$

(☑ 0754 834725, 0783 379526; www.eileenstrees. com; s/d full board US$100/150; P@🕲🏊) This place gets consistently good reports from travellers and it's easy to see why – the rooms are large and come with wooden four-poster beds (with mosquito nets) and wrought-iron furnishings in some bath-

rooms. But the food and friendly service are what really elevate this place above others in its price range in Karatu.

Country Lodge   LODGE $$

(☑ 0789 582982, 027-253 4622; www.country lodgekaratu.com; s/d/tr US$100/160/200, half board US$115/195/255; P@🕲) Signposted off the main road just north of Karatu, this excellent place offers 22 simple but quiet and tidy rooms in 11 cottages arrayed around five acres of greenery. The cottages have verandahs, and there's a restaurant serving good food made from locally sourced ingredients.

🛏 Around Karatu

Octagon Safari Lodge & Irish Bar   LODGE $$

(☑ 027-253 4525; www.octagonlodge.com; camping with own/hired tent US$15/30, s/d half board US$85/150; @🕲) The unexpectedly lush and lovely grounds at this Irish-Tanzanian-owned lodge mean you'll soon feel far away from Karatu. The cottages are small but comfortable, and by Karatu standards the rates are excellent. The restaurant and Irish bar round out the relaxing vibe. It's 1km south of the main road on the west side of town.

Cultural walks can be arranged, as can Ngorongoro safaris.

★ Gibb's Farm   LODGE $$$

(☑ 027-253 4397; www.gibbsfarm.net; s/d/tr half board US$562/850/1175; P@🕲) The long-standing Gibb's Farm, filling a 1920s farmstead, has a rustic highland ambience, a wonderful setting with views over the nearby coffee plantations, a spa, and beautiful cottages (a few standard rooms, too) set around the gardens. The lodge gets consistently good reviews, as does the cuisine, which is made with home-grown organic produce. It's about 5km north of the main road.

★ Plantation Lodge   LODGE $$$

(☑ 0784 260799, 027-253 4405; www.plantation-lodge.com; s/d half board US$275/400, ste from US$600; P@🕲🏊) A place that makes you feel special, this relaxing lodge fills a renovated colonial farmstead and the decor is gorgeous down to every last detail. The uniquely decorated rooms spaced around the gardens have large verandahs and crackling fireplaces to enhance the highland ambience. Excellent home-grown food, too. It's west of Karatu and about 2.5km north of the highway.

Rhotia Valley Tented Lodge   TENTED CAMP $$$
(📱0784 446579; www.rhotiavalley.com; s half
board US$155-280, d US$250-390; 🅿 @ 📶 ⚐) ✐
Right up against the Ngorongoro Conserva-
tion Area, this refreshingly unpretentious
hilltop lodge has 15 large tents (two are fam-
ily sized) with either forest or valley views,
the latter offering a peek at Lake Manyara
and even Mt Meru and Mt Kilimanjaro on a
clear day. Good meals are served under the
big thatch roof. It's 10km northeast of Kara-
tu, well signposted off the highway.

Cultural tours and nature walks are avail-
able, and rates include a 20% donation to the
school-orphanage the owners (two Dutch
doctors who live on-site) opened nearby.

Ngorongoro Farm House   LODGE $$$
(📱0736 502471, 0784 207727; www.tanganyika
wildernesscamps.com; s/d/tr full board
US$250/375/510; 🅿 @ 📶 ⚐) This atmos-
pheric place, 4km from Lodoare gate, is set
in the grounds of a 500-acre working farm
that provides coffee, wheat and vegetables
for this and the company's other lodges. The
50 well-appointed rooms, some a long walk
from the restaurant and other public areas,
are huge. Farm tours and coffee demonstra-
tion are available, as is massage.

✕ Eating

Bump's Café   TANZANIAN, EUROPEAN $
(📱0783 116694; Arusha Rd; meals Tsh4500-8500;
🕘7am-7pm; 📶) A simple (but fancy by Karatu standards) American-Maasai-owned restaurant on the west end of town with a mix
of local and Western meals, this is a good
spot to order lunch boxes. The menu is limited after lunchtime. There's also an internet
cafe costing Tsh1000 per hour.

❶ Getting There & Away

There are several morning buses between Karatu and Arusha (Tsh6000, three hours), some
continuing to Moshi (Tsh9000, 4½ hours). There
are also more comfortable nine-seater minivans
to/from Arusha (Tsh8000, three hours) that
depart throughout the day. Transport leaves
from several spots along the main road.

Lake Eyasi

Uniquely beautiful Lake Eyasi lies at 1030m
between the Eyasi Escarpment in the north
and the Kidero Mountains in the south.
Like Lake Natron far to the northeast, Eyasi makes a rewarding detour on a Ngorongoro trip for anyone looking for something
remote and different. The lake itself varies
considerably in size depending on the rains
and supports a mix of water birds, including
huge breeding-season (June to November)
populations of flamingos and pelicans. In
the dry season, it's little more than a parched
lakebed, contributing to the rather otherworldly, primeval ambience of the area.

The presence of the traditional Hadzabe
lends a soulful human presence to the region. Also in the area are the Iraqw (Mbulu), a people of Cushitic origin who arrived
about 2000 years ago, and Datoga, noted
metalsmiths whose dress and culture is
quite similar to the Maasai.

PEOPLES OF NORTHERN TANZANIA: THE HADZABE

The area close to Lake Eyasi in Tanzania is home to the Hadzabe (also known as Hadzapi,
Hadza or Tindiga) people who are believed to have lived here for nearly 10,000 years. The
Hadzabe are often said to be the last true hunter-gatherers in East Africa and of the around
1000 who remain, between one-quarter and one-third still live according to traditional ways.

Traditional Hadzabe live a subsistence existence, usually in bands or camps of 20
to 30 people and there are no tribal or hierarchical structures within Hadzabe society.
Families engage in communal child-rearing, and food and all other resources are shared
throughout the camp. Camps are often moved, sometimes due to illness, death or the
need to resolve conflicts, while camps may even relocate to the site of a large kill such as
a giraffe; one enduring characteristic of Hadzabe society is that their possessions are so
few that each person may carry everything they own on their backs when they travel.

The Hadzabe language is characterised by clicks and may be distantly related to that
of Southern Africa's San, although it shows only a few connections to Sandawe, the
other click language spoken in Tanzania, and genetic studies have shown no close link
between the Hadzabe and any other East African peoples.

Academic studies of the Hadzabe abound, but there is no finer treatment of the group
than in the final chapter of Peter Matthiessen's *The Tree Where Man Was Born*.

◉ Sights & Activities

Ghorofani Market   MARKET

Ghorofani, Lake Eyasi's main village, lies a few kilometres from the lake's northeastern end. Its *mnada* (market), held on the fifth day of the month, attracts shoppers and traders from around the lake region.

Lake Eyasi Cultural Tourism Program   CULTURAL TOUR

(✆ 0764 295280; rangergotz@yahoo.co.uk; ◷ 8am-6pm) This Cultural Tourism Program, centred on Lake Eyasi, is at the entrance to Ghorofani. You can hire English-speaking guides (US$30 per group, up to 10 people) to visit nearby Hadzabe (an extra US$20 per group) and Datoga communities or the lake. One option is to join the Hadzabe on a hunting trip with traditional weapons, for which you'll need to depart before dawn. Canoeing and fishing expeditions are also possible.

⛌ Sleeping

There are three very basic guesthouses in Ghorofani; basic supplies are sold in the village, but it's better to stock up in Karatu. The campgrounds will cook meals if you order in advance.

Eyasi-Nyika Campsite   CAMPGROUND $

(✆ 0762 766040; camping US$10; ℗) One of Eyasi's best campgrounds, Eyasi-Nyika has seven widely spaced grassy sites, each under an acacia tree, and you can cook for yourself. It's in the bush, 3km outside Ghorofani, signposted only at the main road: after that, just stick to the most travelled roads and you'll get there.

Eyasi Datoga Campsite   CAMPGROUND $

(✆ 0762 921573, 0752 224128; www.eyasidatoga campsite.com; camping with own/hired tent US$10/20; ℗) Close to Ghorofani, this place has simple campsites, most of which are sheltered with semi-permanent structures made from local wild palm.

Kisima Ngeda   TENTED CAMP $$$

(✆ 027-254 8715; www.anasasafari.com/kisima-ngeda; camping US$10, s/d half board US$335/445; ℗⛱) Kisima Ngeda roughly translates as 'spring surrounded by trees', and there's a natural spring at the heart of this lakeside property creating an unexpectedly green and lush oasis of fever trees and doum palms. The seven tents are plenty comfortable and the cuisine (much of it locally produced, including dairy from their own cows) is excellent. It's signposted 7.5km from Ghorofani.

There's basic camping 2km past the main lodge (the only camping on the lakeshore), with a toilet and shower and the same awesome scenery.

Tindiga Tented Camp   TENTED CAMP $$$

(✆ 0754 324193, 027-250 6315; www.moivaro.com; s/d full board US$247/348) Just under 2km from the lakeshore, Tindiga Tented Camp has rustic tents that sit nicely with the overall Lake Eyasi experience – comfortable, but with a sense of being far from civilisation.

ℹ Information

All foreigners must pay a US$10 village tax at the Lake Eyasi Cultural Tourism Program office at the entrance to Ghorofani.

ℹ Getting There & Away

Two daily buses connect Arusha to Barazani passing Ghorofani (Tsh11,500, 4½ to five hours) on the way. They leave Arusha about 5am and head back about 2pm and you can also catch them in Karatu (Tsh4500, 1½ hours to Ghorofani). There are also several passenger-carrying 4WDs to Karatu (Tsh5500; they park at Mbulu junction) departing Ghorofani and other lake towns during the morning and returning throughout the afternoon.

Ngorongoro Crater

Pick a superlative – amazing, incredible, breathtaking – they all apply to the stunning ethereal blue-green vistas of the **Ngorongoro Crater** (crater services fee per vehicle per entry per 24hr US$200). But as wonderful as the views are from above, the real magic happens when you get down inside and drive among an unparalleled concentration of wildlife, including the highest density of both lions and overall predators in Africa. Put simply, this is one of Africa's premier attractions and this world-renowned natural wonder is deservedly a Unesco World Heritage Site.

◉ Sights & Activities

◉ Crater Floor

At 19km wide and with a surface of 264 sq km, Ngorongoro is one of the world's largest unbroken calderas that isn't a lake. Its steep, unbroken walls soar 400m to 610m and provide the setting for an incredible natural drama as prey and predators graze and stalk their way around the open grasslands, swamps and acacia woodland on the crater floor. It's such an impressive sight that, other vehicles aside, you'll wonder whether you've descended into a wildlife paradise.

There are plenty of hippos around the lovely **Ngoitoktok Springs picnic site**, and **Lake Magadi** attracts flocks of flamingos to its shallows in the rainy season. **Lerei Forest** (also known as Lereal Forest, which has a less appealing picnic site, and is the starting point for the Lerai Ascent Road) is good for elephants, of which there are around 200 to 300 in the crater. Predators include around 600 spotted hyenas, 55 lions (at last count) and both golden and black-backed jackals. These predators are sustained by large numbers of resident herbivores, with wildebeest, zebras, buffaloes and Grant's gazelles the most common. Less commonly seen are elands, warthogs, hartebeests, bushbucks, waterbucks and Bohor's reedbucks. Around 20% of the wildebeest and zebras migrate annually between the crater and the Serengeti. Another huge drawcard is the chance to see the critically endangered black rhino – around 30 inhabit the crater floor, and they're most often seen between the Lerei Forest and the Lemala ascent-descent road.

The reason for all this abundance is the presence of water, from both the permanent springs that sustain the swamps and the permanent streams and rivers fed by run-off from the crater rim forests.

The main route into the crater is the Seneto descent road, which enters the crater on its western side. To come out, use the Lerai ascent road, which starts south of Lake Magadi and leads to the rim near headquarters. The Lemala road is on the northeastern side of the crater near Ngorongoro Sopa Lodge, and is used for both ascent and descent.

The gates open at 6am and close for descent at 4pm; all vehicles must be out of the crater before 6pm. Officially, you're only allowed to stay down in the crater for a maximum of six hours, but this is rarely enforced – when we drove out of the crater on the Lerai ascent road, there was no one checking vehicles. Self-drivers are supposed to hire a park ranger (US$20 per vehicle) for the crater where the descent begins, but are sometimes let in without one.

ⓘ NGORONGORO CRATER

Why Go Extraordinary scenery and fabulous wildlife watching

When to Go Year round

Practicalities Usually visited en route to Serengeti from Arusha via Karatu. It can get *very* cold on the crater rim, so come prepared. All fees, including those for the crater, are paid at **Lodoare gate** (☏ 027-253 7031; ⊘ 6am-6pm), just south of Ngorongoro Crater on the road from Arusha, or Naabi Hill gate on the border with Serengeti National Park. Should you wish to add days or activities to your visit, you can pay fees at the headquarters (p183).

Budget Tips Stay outside the park to avoid camping fees: visit as part of a larger group to reduce your portion of the crater services fee. Even though the US$200 fee to enter the crater is per vehicle, the guards check the number of passengers against the permit, so it's not possible to join up with people you meet at your campsite or lodge once inside the Ngorongoro Conservation Area (NCA).

⊙ Crater Rim

A sealed road encircles all but the northern section of the crater rim and there are stunning views through the trees at various points along the way. Apart from the vantage points offered by the various lodges, the best views are from the head of the Seneto descent road above the crater's western end, and where the road reaches the rim after climbing up from Lodoare Gate.

There's wildlife outside the crater, but not as abundantly as in most other parks. Still, you might see elephants and leopards along the rim road.

Unlike national parks where human residents were evicted, the Ngorongoro Conservation Area (NCA) remains part of the Maasai homeland and over 40,000 Maasai live here with grazing rights. You'll see them out tending their cattle and goats, as well as selling necklaces and knives alongside the road. Many children wait along the road to pose for photos, but note that most of them are skipping school or shirking their chores, so it's best not to stop. There are cultural *bomas*, too, which charge US$50 per vehicle.

NGORONGORO CONSERVATION AREA IN A NUTSHELL

Lying within the boundaries of the 8292 sq km Ngorongoro Conservation Area (Map p184; NCA; ☑ 027-253 7006; www.ngorongorocrater.org; adult/child 5-16 yr old US$50/10, crater services fee per vehicle per 24hr US$200; ⊘ 6am-6pm) are the Ngorongoro Crater, Oldupai Gorge and much of the Crater Highlands (although not Ol Doinyo Lengai and Lake Natron).

The main NCA gates are Lodoare (the main park entrance if you're coming from Arusha) and Naabi Hill (well outside the NCA boundaries and shares premises with the Naabi Hill entrance to Serengeti National Park).

Other important things to note:

➡ If you're transiting through Ngorongoro en route to the Serengeti, you still have to pay the NCA entrance fee.

➡ Entry fees apply for a 24-hour period. If you enter the NCA at, for example, 10am and you're staying overnight, then you must leave before 10am the next morning to avoid incurring an additional day's fee.

➡ In theory all entry, camping and crater fees should be paid in advance at a bank, but in practice you can pay at the gate. Although credit cards are accepted, cash is preferred.

🛏 Sleeping & Eating

There are three special campsites around the crater rim: Simba B (camping US$50), just up the road from Simba A; and Tembo A (camping US$50) and Tembo B (camping US$50) north of Sopa Lodge. None of them have facilities and should be reserved as far in advance as possible.

Simba A Public Campsite   CAMPGROUND $

(camping US$30) The only public campsite is Simba A, up on the crater rim not far from headquarters. It has basic facilities and can get very crowded, so hot water sometimes runs out. Even so, it's a fine location and far and away the cheapest place to stay up on the rim.

If you're not self-catering, try Mwahingo Canteen at park headquarters; there are also several small restaurants and bars in Kimba village.

Kitoi Guesthouse   GUESTHOUSE $

(☑ 0754 334834; r without bathroom Tsh8000; ℗) This unsigned place is the best of four guesthouses in Kimba village, near the crater. The ablution block is out the back, and so are awesome views of Oldeani. On request someone will cook food or heat water for bucket showers. Officials at the park gate may insist you pay the camping fee upon entering the park, even if you plan to sleep in this village.

★ Ngorongoro Crater Lodge   LODGE $$$

(☑ 028-262 1267; www.andbeyond.com; r per person all inclusive US$1550; ℗ @ 🛜) Few luxuries are spared at this eclectic rim-top lodge, self-described as 'Versailles meets Maasai'. There are actually three separate lodges here, and few spaces lack crater views (yes, even the toilets have them). The rooms are sophisticated and intimate, with abundant use of wood. This is the place to go for the full Ngorongoro experience of knock-out views and no-expenses-spared luxury.

Rhino Lodge   LODGE $$$

(☑ 0768 578856, 0762 359055; www.ngorongoro. cc; s/d with full board US$150/270; 🛜) This small, friendly lodge, run by Italians in conjunction with the Maasai community, is the cheapest place in the NCA. The rooms are simple and tidy, and the balconies have fine forest views, often with bushbucks or elephants wandering past. It's arguably the best-value place up here, as long as you don't need a crater view. The communal areas are as good as any up on the rim.

Lemala Ngorongoro Tented Camp   TENTED CAMP $$$

(☑ 027-254 8952, 027-254 8966; www.lemala camp.com; s/d full board US$865/1270) Beautiful wood-floored safari tents and an attractive bush setting close to the Lemala ascent-descent road make this place an excellent choice. Although some of the other mobile tented camps move with the seasons, this one is reliably stable and gets you closer to nature than you'll get in the bricks-and-mortar lodges.

Ngorongoro Serena Safari Lodge
LODGE **$$$**

(☏ 027-254 5555; www.serenahotels.com; s/d full board US$625/805; P @ 🛜) The popular Serena sits unobtrusively in a fine location on the southwestern crater rim near the main descent route. It's comfortable and attractive (though the cave motif in the rooms is kind of kitschy) with good service and outstanding views (from the upper-floor rooms), though it's also big and busy.

Ngorongoro Wildlife Lodge
LODGE **$$$**

(☏ 027-254 4595; www.hotelsandlodges-tanzania. com; r per person full board US$220/440; P @ 🛜) The rooms here are tired and in desperate need of an overhaul, the service can be dysfunctional and wi-fi costs a ridiculous US$10 per hour. But (and it's a big but), the crater views here (from the rooms, from the bar...) are the best on the rim. In fact, the views are so good that they may just outweigh all of the lodge's shortcomings.

Ngorongoro Sopa Lodge
LODGE **$$$**

(☏ 027-250 0630; www.sopalodges.com; s/d full board US$370/650; P @ 🛜 ✱) This 98-room lodge is well located on the eastern crater rim (the sunset-watching side) – it's convenient for Empakaai and the Crater Highlands, less so if you're heading to the Serengeti. The rooms are spacious but plain and many lack views or have only limited sight lines: request the top floor. There's hot water only in the morning and evening.

Mwahingo Canteen
TANZANIAN **$**

(meals from Tsh2000; ⊙ 11am-9pm) Almost all visitors eat at their lodge or campground, but Mwahingo Canteen, at headquarters, does chicken, pilau, and beans and rice.

ⓘ Information

The crater falls within the Ngorongoro Conservation Area Authority (NCAA), which has its **headquarters** (☏ 027-253 7006; www. ngorongorocrater.org; ⊙ 8am-4pm) at Park Village at Ngorongoro Crater and an information centre (p164) in Arusha. Ignore the signs for a tourist information office at the park headquarters – even they couldn't explain to us what their purpose was.

ⓘ Getting There & Around

Only 4WDs are allowed into the crater. If you aren't travelling on an organised safari and don't have your own vehicle, the easiest thing to do is hire one in Karatu, where most lodges charge about US$160 per day including fuel for a 4WD with a pop-up top.

Driving is not allowed before 6am or after 7pm. Petrol is sold at headquarters, but it's cheaper in Karatu.

The Crater Highlands

The hauntingly beautiful Crater Highlands is where the Rift Valley really gets interesting. The highlands warp along numerous extinct volcanoes, calderas (collapsed volcanoes) and the dramatic Rift Valley Escarpment on the park's eastern side. The peaks include Oldeani (3216m), Makarot (Lemagurut; 3107m), Olmoti (3100m), Loolmalasin (3648m), Empakaai (also spelled Embagai; 3262m), Ngorongoro (2400m) and the still-active Ol Doinyo Lengai (2878m). The different peaks were created over millions of years by a series of eruptions connected with the birth of the Great Rift Valley, and the older volcanoes have since collapsed, forming the striking 'craters' (really, they're calderas) that give the range its name.

◉ Sights

Olmoti Crater
VOLCANO

Although it lacks the drama of Ngorongoro and Empakaai, Olmoti Crater, 13km north of the Lemala ascent-descent road, is worth visiting on your way north into the Highlands. It's also the starting point for a two-day trek to Empakaai Crater. Olmoti's crater floor is shallow, haired with grass and crossed by the Munge River. To reach the rim, it's a one-hour return walk from where the 4WD track ends on the crater's eastern side. From here, a short trail leads to the Munge Waterfall.

Empakaai Crater
VOLCANO

Lake-filled Empakaai Crater, 23km northeast of Olmoti Crater, may not be as famous as Ngorongoro, but many travellers consider it to be its match in beauty. The lake, which draws flamingos and other waterbirds, fills most of the crater floor, which is surrounded by steep-sided, forested cliffs at least 300m high. The view from the crater rim is one of our favourites in northern Tanzania, but hiking down into the crater is a wonderful experience as well.

The road from Ol Doinyo Lengai runs along part of the eastern crater rim, which varies in altitude from 2700m to 3200m, and a steep, well-kept trail descends from the road through montane forest rich in

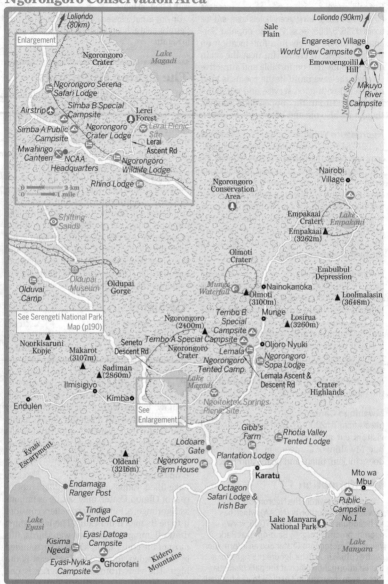

birdlife; also keep an eye out for hyenas, buffaloes, blue monkeys and even elephants. En route to the crater floor, watch for views of the turquoise lake down below and the perfect volcanic cone of Ol Doinyo Lengai away to the northeast. Count on around 30 minutes down to the lake shore, and an hour for the climb back up. It is possible to circumnavigate the lake on foot, which will take at least four hours.

If you're planning on hiking, you are, in theory, required to pick up an armed ranger

Lake Natron

0 — 20 km
0 — 10 miles

Lake Natron Tented Camp

Gelai ▲
(2941m)

Gelai-Lumbwa ◉

Ol Doinyo ▲
Lengai
(2878m)

▲ Kerimasi
(2614m)

Kitumbeini ▲
(2865m)

Engaruka Ruins
Campsite

◉ Engaruka Chini
⊗ Engaruka Juu

Engaruka
Ruins

Engaruka
Basin

◉ Selela

Ol Mesera
Tented Camp

Burko ▲
(1797m)

▲
Losiminguri
(3216m)

Engaruka
RUINS

(adult/child Tsh10,000/5000) Halfway to Lake
Natron, on the eastern edge of the Ngorongoro Conservation Area, lies this 300- to
500-year-old ruin of a farming town that
developed a complex irrigation system with
terraced stone housing sites. Although the
ruins are historically significant, casual visitors are likely to be more impressed with the
up-close views of the escarpment than the
vaguely house-shaped piles of rocks.

Archaeologists are unsure of Engaruka's
origins, although some speculate that the
town was built by ancestors of the Iraqw
(Mbulu) people, who once populated the area
and now live around Lake Eyasi. Others
propose it was the Sonjo, a Bantu-speaking
people.

Knowledgeable English-speaking guides
(no set prices) for the ruins or other walks
in the area, including a one-day climb of
nearby Kerimasi, can be found at Engaruka Ruins Campsite, or arranged in advance
through the Tanzania Tourist Board (TTB)
Tourist Information Centre (p164) in Arusha. It's also worth contacting the **Engaruka
Cultural Tourism Program** (☑0754 507939,
0787 228653; www.tanzaniaculturaltourism.go.tz/
engaruka.htm), which arranges visits to local
Maasai villages and other local attractions,
and climbs up Kerimasi and Ol Doinyo Lengai.

The ruins are unsigned above the village
of Engaruka Juu. Turn west at Engaruka
Chini, a smaller village along the Lake Natron road, and follow the rough track 4.5km
until you reach Engaruka Juu Primary
Boarding School.

Ol Doinyo Lengai
VOLCANO

Ol Doinyo Lengai (2878m), 'Mountain of
God' in the Maasai language, is one of the
most beautiful mountains in Africa. The
northernmost mountain in the Crater Highlands, it's an almost perfect volcanic cone
with steep sides rising to a small flat-topped
peak. It's also the youngest volcano in the
Crater Highlands, and still active, with the
last eruptions in 2008. Climbing to the summit is one of the most popular Crater Highland treks.

At the peak, you can see hot steam vents
and growing ash cones in the north crater.
With a midnight start, a trek from the base
village of Engaresero at Lake Natron is possible in one long day. Although the number
of climbers scaling Ol Doinyo Lengai has
grown in recent years, the loose ash along

(US$20) from the ranger post at Nainoka-
noka (next to Olmoti Crater) en route to
Empakaai.

To get here, count on a 90-minute drive
from the Lemala ascent-descent road.

TREKKING THE CRATER HIGHLANDS

The best way to explore the Crater Highlands is on foot, although because of the logistics and multiple fees involved, trekking here is expensive: from US$350 and up (less if you have a large group) for overnight trips. Treks range from short day jaunts to excursions of up to two weeks or more. For all routes, you'll need to be accompanied by a guide, and for anything except day hikes, most people use donkeys or vehicle support to carry water and supplies (though vehicles can't go everywhere the donkeys can).

Nearly all visitors arrange treks through a tour company. Many Arusha-based companies can take you up Ol Doinyo Lengai (just outside the NCA boundaries) as can many of the accommodation places in Lake Natron or Engaruka.

Alternatively, you can contact the NCA directly to arrange your trek. However, this requires advance notice, usually winds up costing about the same as going through a tour company, and you'll need to provide all camping equipment and supplies, including water for yourself and the ranger. For most hikes you'll also need to hire a vehicle to deliver you to the starting point and collect you at the end; few routes are circuits. The NCA will then take care of arranging the campsites, guides and donkeys.

There are no set routes, and the possibilities are numerous. Good two-day trips include the **Ngorongoro Crater rim**, **Olmoti to Empakaai**, and **Empakaai to Lake Natron**. These three can be strung together into an excellent four-day trip: start at Nainokanoka to make it three days or extend it one day to climb **Ol Doinyo Lengai**.

If you base yourself at Ngorongoro Crater or Karatu, there are some good day hikes that let you experience the area on a lower budget, such as climbing **Makarot** or **Oldeani**, or walking along the **Empakaai Crater** or **Olmoti Crater**. Apart from transport costs, these involve only the US$50 NCA entry fee and US$20 per group guide fee. Oldeani is the least complicated option, since the climb starts at headquarters. From Oldeani, it's possible to camp and continue on down to Lake Eyasi where there's public transport.

most of the path makes it a difficult climb and an even tougher, often painful, descent. Ol Doinyo Lengai, like most active volcanoes, is a constantly changing landform, and lava flows in 2013 had, at the time of our visit, all but filled the crater created during the 2007–08 eruption. As a result, views down into the crater from the rim or summit were more limited than in previous years.

🛏 Sleeping

Apart from a few rudimentary campsites out here and options around Ol Doinyo Lengai and Lake Natron, you'll need to carry in your own supplies. There are two special campsites around the rim of Empaakai Crater and a further 15 out on the western plains. Camping at each costs US$50 per person and reservations should be made through the NCA as far in advance as possible.

Engaruka Chini has an unnamed, unsigned bucket-shower guesthouse (single/double without bathroom Tsh6000/12,000). It's the green-fronted building right near the entrance gate into town.

Engaruka Ruins Campsite CAMPGROUND $
(camping US$10; 🅿) Engaruka Ruins Campsite in Engaruka Juu is dusty but shady with acceptable ablutions. You can use its tents for free and meals are available on request. It's handy for arriving buses and the Engaruka Cultural Tourism Program.

Jerusalem's Campsite CAMPGROUND $
(price by negotiation) This basic campsite sits right by the Engaruka Ruins. There are toilets and little else.

ℹ Information

District fees (ie tourist taxes) must be paid at three gates along the way: Engaruka Chini (US$10), 7km before Engaresero (US$10), and at Engaresero (US$15).

ℹ Getting There & Away

There's a daily bus to Arusha (Tsh8000, four to five hours) via Mto wa Mbu (Tsh4500, 1½ hours) leaving Engaruka at 6am and turning around for the return trip shortly after arrival. There's no public transport between here and Ngorongoro Crater.

Lake Natron

Shimmering amid the sun-scorched Kenyan border northeast of Ngorongoro Conservation Area, this 58km-long, but just 50cm-deep, alkaline lake should be on every adventurer's itinerary. The drive from Mto wa Mbu is remote, with a desolate, otherworldly beauty and an incomparable feeling of space and ancientness. The road traces the Rift Valley Escarpment through untrammelled Maasai land with small *bomas* and big mountains always in view on this almost treeless plain. Plenty of zebras, giraffes, wildebeest and ostriches graze in the near distance. From June to November at the lake itself, upwards of three million flamingos gather here – it's one of East Africa's most stirring wildlife spectacles.

🏃 Activities

The base for visits is the small oasis of Engaresero (also spelled Ngare Sero; 'impermanent water' in Maasai) on the southwestern shore.

Engaresero Cultural Tourism Program
CULTURAL TOUR

(📞027-205 0025; www.tanzaniaculturaltourism.go.tz/engaresero) 🏄 Drawing together a whole host of activities around Engaresero and Lake Natron, this Maasai-run cultural tourism program offers a range of activities, including guided walking trips to the lake, to hot springs, to a nearby waterfall and to a set of recently discovered 120,000-year-old human footprints preserved in volcanic ash. It also offers biking tours, village visits, 'ethno-botanical' tours and trekking to the summit of Ol Doinyo Lengai.

You could also try contacting the Engaresero Association of Guides (emolo88@yahoo.com; ⊙8am-6.30pm), which has an office at the village council, just north of town.

🍴 Sleeping & Eating

There are several budget campsites clustered around the southwestern end of the lake, and Engaresero village has some small restaurants and grocery stores.

Mikuyo River Campsite
CAMPGROUND $

(camping US$10) The closest camp to town has simple amenities, but a nice shady location. There are no cooking facilities.

World View Campsite
CAMPGROUND $

(📞0786 566133; www.worldviewcampsite.com; camping US$10, full board in own tent US$25; P) A few kilometres south of town along the escarpment and amid several Maasai *bomas,* there are unbeatable views of Ol Doinyo Lengai, and good ones of the lake, too. It's a grassy area with a little shade, a lot of wind, and clean bathroom facilities with sit-down toilets. A luxury lodge is planned, but the owner says budget camping will remain.

Lake Natron Tented Camp
CAMPGROUND, TENTED CAMP $$

(📞0754 324193; www.moivaro.com; camping US$10, s half board US$157-242, d US$203-343; P🏊) Near the village with a view of the lake. The tents, some with both indoor and outdoor showers, and pleasant grass-roofed cottages (called 'Maasai rooms' and 20% cheaper) are in shady grounds near the river. There's a large and sometimes busy campground with good facilities next door, and campers can use all lodge amenities, including the restaurant and swimming pool.

ℹ️ Getting There & Away

The road from Mto wa Mbu is part sandy, part rocky. During the rainy season you may have to wait a few hours at some of the seasonal rivers

---

LAKE NATRON IN TROUBLE?

For a number of years, Tanzania's government has pushed aggressively for the construction of a soda ash mine on the lake. Such a project will, they say, produce 1.5 million tonnes of soda ash per year, lead to profits of US$480 million and create 1000 jobs in an otherwise impoverished corner of the country. Conservationists and many locals disagree, disputing the projected profit estimates and warning that any mine would devastate the flamingo population to a level from which it may never recover. Festo Semanini, Head of the BirdLife International Office in Tanzania, has warned that if the factory goes ahead, it would be the 'greatest ecological mistake Tanzania has ever committed'. Scared off by negative publicity, India's TATA company has withdrawn from the project, although as of 2014, the Tanzanian government was still actively seeking foreign investment for the mine.

before you're able to cross. The road past the lake to Loliondo and into the Serengeti is in better shape because it's used far less. Those continuing this way should carry extra supplies of petrol since the last proper station is in Mto wa Mbu, though some people sell expensive petrol from their homes.

A rickety, crowded bus runs between Arusha and Loliondo, stopping in Engaresero (Tsh23,000, nine hours). It departs Arusha 6.30am Sunday and passes back through Engaresero on Thursday around 10am. Trucks run between Mto wa Mbu and Engaresero pretty much daily (sometimes including 4WDs operating as public transport), but it's not unheard of to have to wait two days to find a ride, especially in the rainy seasons.

If driving from Ngorongoro, you'll need to set out early and count on an entire day to reach Lake Natron – ask at the NCA headquarters and Nainokanoka ranger post about track conditions.

Oldupai Gorge & Western Ngorongoro

Standing near the western rim of the Ngorongoro Crater and looking out towards the west is like contemplating eternity. Table-flat plains stretch towards the Serengeti with the forbidding Gol Mountains away to the north. Within this landscape, Maasai eke out a subsistence existence from the dust of plains where wildlife is wary but present nonetheless – wildebeest, eland, topi, gazelle and zebra herds come here between January and March on the southern stretch of their endless migration.

But there is more to these plains than meets the eye. Slicing its way through up to 90m of rock and two million years of history, Oldupai (Olduvai) Gorge on the plains northwest of Ngorongoro Crater is a dusty, 48km-long ravine sometimes referred to as the cradle of humankind. Thanks to its unique geological history, in which layer upon layer of volcanic deposits were laid down in an orderly sequence up until 15,000 years ago, it provides remarkable documentation of ancient life, allowing us to begin turning the pages of history back to the days of our earliest ancestors.

⊙ Sights & Activities

Good easy day-trek spots in the western reaches of the NCA include Makarot, Little Oldupai and Lake Ndutu.

THE PROBLEM WITH THE NGORONGORO LIONS

In 1962, unusually heavy rains led to a plague of stomoxys, a biting fly that caused a crash in the crater's lion population – just nine females and one male survived. Seven males migrated into the crater by 1965, but no further lions made their way into the crater for the almost three decades that followed. Although the crater's lion numbers rebounded to as many as 125 by 1975, the result was a genetic bottleneck that continues to haunt Ngorongoro's lion population to this day.

The current lion population in the crater stands at 55, and studies have shown that sperm abnormalities are common among Ngorongoro males, with signs that the fertility of females lions may also be affected. Until very recently, one lion researcher told us, so small was the genetic pool that fathers were mating with their daughters, and sisters with their brothers. Many lions left the crater over the years, but very few came here from elsewhere. The recent arrival into the crater of an unknown coalition of male lions brought a much-needed injection of new genes into the population, but the level of inbreeding remains critical.

In an attempt to facilitate the interchange of lions between Ngorongoro and the Serengeti, the Ngorongoro Lion Project (www.lionresearch.org), an offshoot of the Serengeti Lion Project, has begun a pilot program that deploys traditional Maasai warriors into areas where conflict between lions and Maasai herders is greatest and charges them with the not-inconsiderable task of protecting lions and protecting Maasai herds into the bargain. Where this program differs from other similar projects elsewhere in East Africa is in the additional plan to pay local communities for the lions with which the Maasai share the land, turning more common compensation programs on their head by paying the Maasai for live lions rather than dead cows. If successful, the plan may enable lions to move along a human-dominated corridor between the Serengeti and Ngorongoro, replenishing the gene pool in the crater in the process.

Oldupai Museum
MUSEUM

(adult/child Tsh27,000/13,000; ⊙ 7.30am-4.30pm)
The small Oldupai Museum on the rim of
Oldupai Gorge stands on one of the most
significant archaeological sites on earth.
It was here in 1959 that Mary Leakey discovered a 1.8-million-year-old ape-like skull
from an early hominin (human-like) now
known as *Australopithecus boisei*. This
discovery, along with fossils of over 60 early hominids (including *Homo habilis* and
Homo erectus), forever changed the way we
understand the dawn of human history.

The museum documents the foundation
of the gorge, fossil finds and the legacy of
Mary Leakey and her husband, Louis. You're
allowed to visit the museum on your own
(a series of explanatory panels guide you
through the exhibits), whereafter a guide
will give a short lecture. The guide will
then take you down into the gorge (where
international archaeological teams are still
at work) or out to the **shifting sands**, a
9m-high, 100m-long black dune of volcanic
ash that has blown across the plain from Ol
Doinyo Lengai.

You'll need a minimum of 45 minutes
to do the museum justice and listen to the
lecture, more if you go down into the gorge
or visit the shifting sands. And yes, you did
read that entrance fee correctly – the admission fee increased ninefold overnight with
the stroke of a bureaucrat's pen in 2012. It's
still worth it.

The turn-off to the museum is 27km
northwest of the Seneto descent road, and
from the turn-off it's a further 5.5km along a
rutted track to the museum.

ᨰᨧ Sleeping

Ndutu Safari Lodge
LODGE $$$

(☑ 027-253 7015; www.ndutu.com; s/d full board
US$297/493) This good-value place has a
lovely setting in the far western part of NCA,
just outside the Serengeti. It's well located
for observing the enormous herds of wilde-
beest during the rainy season, and watching
for genets who lounge in dining room raft-
ers. The 34 Lake Ndutu–facing cottages lack
character, but the lounge is attractive and
the atmosphere relaxed and rustic.

Olduvai Camp
TENTED CAMP $$$

(☑ 0782 993854; www.olduvai-camp.com; ℗) An
intimate, remote camp in wonderful opposition to the large corporate lodges on the crater rim, Olduvai is built around a kopje with
postcard views of Makarot, and it makes a
fine spot to watch wildebeest during the
rainy season. The 17 tents are attractive if
sparse, but the dining room and lounge
are lovely. It's 3.5km off the Serengeti road
(which is unsigned).

Maasai-led cultural walks in the savannah and nearby gorge are recommended.
All accommodation bookings must be made
through a safari company; direct bookings
are not encouraged – staff wouldn't even tell
us a price for independent travellers.

Serengeti National Park

Few people forget their first encounter with
Serengeti National Park (☑ 0689 062243,
0767 536125, 028-262 1515; www.tanzaniaparks.
com/serengeti.html; adult/child US$60/20;
⊙ 6am-6pm). Perhaps it is the view from the
summit of Naabi Hill at the park's entrance,
from where the Serengeti's grasslands appear to stretch to the very ends of the earth.
Or maybe it's a coalition of male lions stalking across open plains, their manes catching
the breeze. Or it may be the epic migration
of animals in their millions, following the
ancient rhythm of Africa's seasons. Whatever
it is, welcome to one of the wildest places –
one of the greatest wildlife-watching destinations on earth.

It's here on the vast plains of the Serengeti
that one of earth's most impressive natural

> ### ❶ SERENGETI NATIONAL PARK
>
> **Why Go** Wildebeest migration; excellent
> chance of seeing predators; overall high
> wildlife density; fine birdwatching; stun-
> ning savannah scenery
>
> **When to Go** Year round; July and August
> for wildebeest migration across Mara
> River; February for wildebeest calving;
> February to May for birdwatching.
>
> **Practicalities** Drive in from Arusha or
> Mwanza, or fly in. To avoid congestion,
> spend some time outside the central
> Serengeti and Seronera area. Entrance
> fees can be paid in cash or by credit
> card at the Naabi Hill, Ndabaka, Klein's
> and Bologonya gates.
>
> **Budget Tips** Catch the Arusha–
> Musoma bus and hope to see something
> along the way; stay in the public camp-
> sites; book a budget safari from Arusha.

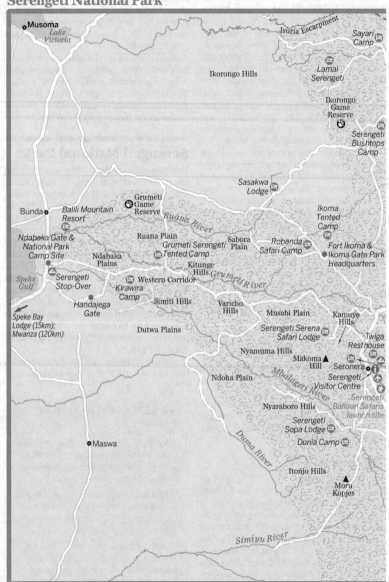

Musoma
Lake Victoria
Isuria Escarpment
Sayari Camp
Lamai Serengeti
Ikorongo Hills
Ikorongo Game Reserve
Serengeti Bushtops Camp
Sasakwa Lodge
Grumeti Game Reserve
Ikoma Tented Camp
Bunda
Balili Mountain Resort
Ruana River
Ruana Plain
Ndabaka Gate & National Park Camp Site
Ndabaka Plains
Grumeti Serengeti Tented Camp
Sabora Plain
Robanda Safari Camp
Fort Ikoma & Ikoma Gate Park Headquarters
Speke Gulf
Serengeti Stop-Over
Kirawira Camp
Western Corridor
Kitunge Hills
Grumeti River
Speke Bay Lodge (15km); Mwanza (120km)
Handajega Gate
Simiti Hills
Varicho Hills
Musabi Plain
Kamuyo Hills
Dutwa Plains
Serengeti Serena Safari Lodge
Twiga Resthouse
Nyamuma Hills
Makoma Hill
Seronera
Ndoha Plain
Mbalageti River
Serengeti Visitor Centre
Serengeti Balloon Safaris launch site
Nyaraboro Hills
Serengeti Sopa Lodge
Maswa
Dunia Camp
Duma River
Itonjo Hills
Moru Kopjes
Simiyu River

cycles has played out for aeons as hundreds of thousands of hoofed animals, driven by primeval rhythms of survival, move constantly in search of fresh grasslands. The most famous, and numerous, are the wildebeest (of which there are some 1.5 million) and their annual migration is the Serengeti's calling card. There are also resident wildebeest populations in the park and you'll see these smaller but still impressive herds yearround. In February more than 8000 wildebeest calves are born each day, although

cially its lions. Hunting alongside the lions are cheetahs, leopards, hyenas, jackals and more. These feast on zebras, giraffes, buffaloes, Thomson's and Grant's gazelles, topis, elands, hartebeests, impalas, klipspringers, duikers and so many more. It's an incredible birdwatching destination, too, with over 500 species.

⊙ Sights

⊙ Seronera & the South

Visiting or staying in Seronera, at the heart of the park and readily accessed from both Arusha and Mwanza, involves something of a trade-off. On the one hand, this is wildlife central, with sightings of lions (around 300 live in the park's south alone), leopards and cheetahs almost guaranteed. At the same time, such abundance comes at a price – you may find yourself among a pack of 20 vehicles jostling to look at a single lion.

Southeast of Seronera is a prime base for wildlife watching during the December–April wet season, when it's full of wildebeest. This corner of the Serengeti also has year-round water and a good mix of habitats. Most Seronera safaris concentrate along the **Seronera River** and with good reason – the trees along the riverbank are home to one of the world's densest concentration of leopards, while lion sightings are common. Lion sightings are also probable around the **Maasai Kopjes**, **Simba Kopjes**, **Moru Kopjes**, **Gol Kopjes** and **Barafu Kopjes**, and around **Makoma Hill**. The vast plains south of the Seronera River, often known simply as the **Serengeti Plains**, are particularly good for cheetahs. The plains that rise towards the **Kamuyo Hills** west of the Seronera River (draw a line west of the Seronera Wildlife Lodge) are particularly good for elephants, spotted hyenas and cheetahs.

⊙ Grumeti & the Western Corridor

The migration usually passes through the Serengeti's Western Corridor, and the contiguous **Grumeti Game Reserve**, sometime between late May and early July. The crossing of the **Grumeti River** may not rival that of the Mara River further north, but it's still one of the migration's great spectacles.

During the rest of the year, lions and leopards are prevalent along the forest-fringed Grumeti River, which also has hippos and

about 40% of these will die before reaching four months old. A few black rhinos in the Moru Kopjes area offer a chance for the Big Five, although they're very rarely seen.

The 14,763 sq km Serengeti National Park is also renowned for its predators, espe-

LAETOLI & GOL MOUNTAINS

About 45km south of Oldupai Gorge at remote Laetoli (adult/child Tsh10,000/5000; ⊙7.30am-4.30pm) is a 27m-long trail of 3.7-million-year-old hominid footprints, probably made by *Australopithecus afarensis*. Discovered by Mary Leakey's team in 1976 and excavated two years later, it's an extraordinarily evocative and remote site. A long-planned (and still under construction) EU-funded museum is planned, but there's a small temporary museum on the site. There are cast copies of the prints in Oldupai Museum (p189).

An extremely rough, 4WD-only track connects the Oldupai Museum with Laetoli via Noorkisaruni Kopjo and Endulen. A far better road runs to Endulen from Kimba on the Ngorongoro Crater Rim along the southern side of Makarot. Coming from either route, Laetoli lies 9km west of Endulen.

There are some places that are so far off well-travelled routes that there are no tracks other than those left by wildlife and traditional herders. The remote and rarely visited Gol Mountains, northwest of Ngorongoro but still within the boundaries of the Ngorongoro Conservation Area, is just such a place. This remains one of the most traditional corners of Tanzania, home to Maasai who still kill lions as their rite of passage into warriorhood, and who still live outside cash society.

Travelling out here is a major, multi-day undertaking and one that is best organised through a professional Arusha-based safari company or the NCA.

giant crocodiles. North of the river, try the Kitunge Hills, Ruana Plain and just about anywhere in the Grumeti Game Reserve, while south of the river concentrate on the Ndabaka Plains, Simiti Hills, Dutwa Plains, Varicho Hills and down to the Mbalageti River.

These western reaches of the Serengeti are most easily reached from Mwanza. If driving from the Ndabaka Gate, count on at least half a day to reach Seronera, more if you stop along the way.

Central Serengeti

Except when the migration passes through (usually in November and December), this is not the Serengeti's most prolific corner when it comes to wildlife. Its mix of light woodland, acacia thorn and open plains can also be dispiriting during the heat of the day, which, given the lack of lodges in the area, is when most people pass through as they travel between the north and south of the Serengeti. This is also one area of the park experiencing a growing problem with local communities encroaching into the park, with a concomitant effect on wildlife numbers. In other words, you're more likely to visit here on your way elsewhere, rather than for its own sake.

Even so, there are some fine vistas along this north–south route through the park, not to mention a blissfully remote feel to much of the countryside around here. If nothing else, the park's central area is worth passing through to gain a deeper appreciation of just how vast the Serengeti ecosystem really is.

Northern Serengeti

Compared with Seronera and the south, the Serengeti's north receives relatively few visitors. It begins with acacia woodlands, where elephants congregate in the dry season, then north of Lobo stretches into vast open plains. The migration usually passes through the western side during August and September and comes down the eastern flank in November.

North of the Grumeti River, the Bologonya Hills, Bologonya River, Nyamalumbwa Hills and Mara River are all outstanding. If you're driving from the Mara River to Seronera, allow the best part of a day.

Outside the park, the little-visited Ikorongo Game Reserve, which shadows the northwestern boundary of the park, is wild and worth visiting. Away to the east, the Loliondo Game Controlled Area, just outside the Serengeti's northeastern boundary, offers the chance for Maasai cultural activities, walking safaris, night drives and off-road drives. A loop east across Loliondo and then down through the Crater Highlands or Ngorongoro is a wonderfully remote alternative to driving back down through the park.

🏃 Activities

Wildlife Drives

A wildlife drive in the Serengeti – either self-drive, as part of an organised safari, or as operated by your Serengeti lodge – is one of the most enjoyable things you can do in Africa. Exploring the Serengeti's four major areas – Seronera and the South, Grumeti and the Western Corridor, Central Serengeti and the Northern Serengeti – requires careful planning; an understanding of what each has to offer and at which time of the year will determine how you experience this wonderful place.

Walking Safaris

One new development in the Serengeti is the introduction of walking safaris. Led by Wayo Africa (p34), multiple-day camping trips are available in the Moru Kopjes and Kogatende (by the Mara River) regions and can be as relaxing or as adventurous as clients like.

Balloon Safaris

Serengeti Balloon Safaris   SAFARIS
(☏ 0784 308494, 027-254 8077; www.balloonsafaris.com; per person US$539) There's no better way to see the Serengeti than by spending an hour floating over the plains at dawn, followed by an 'Out of Africa' full English breakfast in the bush under an acacia tree. You'll rise to 1000m for a vast view, then drop down to treetop level. To be sure of a spot, reserve well in advance.

There is a booking office at the Serengeti Visitor Centre (p196). Pick-up from your camp or lodge is at 5.30am, and you're back by 9.30am.

🛏️ Sleeping & Eating

There are nine public campsites (camping US$30) in the Serengeti: six around Seronera, one at Lobo and one each at Ndabaka and Ikoma gates. All have flush toilets, while Pimbi and Nyani (two of the Seronera campsites) have kitchens, showers and solar lighting.

There are also dozens of special campsites (camping US$50), although many are occupied on a semi-permanent basis by mobile or more sedentary camps. The others should be booked well in advance.

If you're camping and don't want to cook for yourself, there are two local restaurants (meals around Tsh5000) and three little groceries at staff quarters, close to Twiga Resthouse, while anyone can dine at the latter.

🏠 Seronera & the South

Twiga Resthouse   GUESTHOUSE $$
(☏ 028-262 1510; serengeti@tanzaniaparks.com; r per person US$30; ☐) Simple but decent rooms with electricity and hot showers, and satellite TV in the lounge. Guests can use the kitchen or meals can be cooked for you if you order way in advance. There's a well-stocked little bar and a bonfire at night. If Twiga is full, there might be room at the similar Taj Resthouse, used mostly by visiting park officials.

Dunia Camp   TENTED CAMP $$$
(http://dunia.asiliaafrica.com; s/d all inclusive US$1060/1590; ☐) Unlike the large impersonal lodges that predominate in Seronera, this is an intimate eight-tent camp with a classic safari ambience.Comfortable, with great service, it's essentially a mobile camp that stays put. Set below the Nyaraboro Hills, but at the end of a long rise, Dunia has both distant views and up-close encounters with wildlife. Highly recommended if you want a bush atmosphere.

Serengeti Serena
Safari Lodge   LODGE $$$
(☏ 027-254 5555; www.serenahotels.com; s/d full board US$391/651; ☐ @ 🛜 🏊) Maasai-style bungalows boast well-appointed rooms with lovely furnishings and views. The top-floor rooms are best. Guides lead short nature walks around their hill and the Maasai do a dance show at night. It's a good location for those who want to explore several parts of the park but not have to switch accommodation, and the hilltop location offers fine views when the migration's in town.

Serengeti Sopa Lodge   LODGE $$$
(☏ 027-250 0630; www.sopalodges.com; s/d/tr full board US$370/650/829; ☐ @ 🛜 🏊) Though architecturally unappealing and with less-inspired rooms than you might expect for the price, the Serengeti Sopa Lodge is removed from the Seronera scrum in a valley of yellow acacia trees. As is the Sopa style, the 73 rooms are spacious, with small sitting rooms and two double beds, and some even come with views. It's 45 minutes south of Seronera.

Grumeti & the Western Corridor

Serengeti Stop-Over CAMPGROUND $
(☑028-262 2273; www.serengetistopover.com; campsite/banda per person US$10/35; P) Just 1km from Ndabaka gate along the Mwanza–Musoma road, this sociable place has camping with hot showers and a cooking area, plus 14 simple rondavels, and a restaurant-bar. Safari vehicle rental is available and Serengeti day trips are feasible. It also offers trips on Lake Victoria with local fishermen, visits to a traditional healer, and other Sukuma cultural excursions.

Balili Mountain Resort TENTED LODGE $$
(☑0754 710113, 0764 824814; www.bmr.co.tz; camping with own/hired tent US$15/20, s/d/tr US$50/70/90, day entry US$5; P) Neither a mountain nor a resort, but 'no-frills tented lodge on a big rocky hill' doesn't have the same ring to it. It's perfectly comfortable, but its main draws are the views of Lake Victoria and the Serengeti. It's up above Bunda, north of Ndabaka gate, reached by a roller-coaster of a road.

★**Grumeti Serengeti Tented Camp** TENTED LODGE $$$
(☑028-262 1267; www.andbeyond.com; tents per person all-inclusive US$595-1245; ◎closed Apr; P ⬤ ⬤) Instead of taking to the hills for panoramic views, Grumeti gets down into the thick of the action along the Kanyanja River; a prime spot during the migration when you can watch crocs catch wildebeest as you lounge in the swimming pool. It mixes its wild location with chic pan-Africa decor and the 10 tents are superluxe; only three have unobstructed river views.

Kirawira Camp TENTED LODGE $$$
(☑027-254 5555; www.serenahotels.com; s/d full board US$971/1534; P @ ⬤ ⬤) Kirawira, ringing a low hill, works a colonial theme with plenty of antiques and polished wood floors. The tents have big porches and very un-tent-like bathrooms. Guests rave about the food.

FOLLOW THE MIGRATION

You've come to see the wildebeest migration, but how can you be sure to be there when it happens? The short answer is that you can't, and making the decision of when to go where always involves some element of risk. What follows is a general overview of what usually happens, but it's a guide only:

January–March During the rains, the wildebeest are widely scattered over the southern and southwestern section of the Serengeti and the western side of Ngorongoro Conservation Area.

April Most streams dry out quickly when the rains cease, nudging the wildebeest to concentrate on the few remaining green areas, and to form thousands-strong herds that begin to migrate northwest in search of food.

May–early July In early May, the herds cross northwest towards the Western Corridor and the crossing of the crocodile-filled Grumeti River usually takes place between late May and early July, and lasts only about a week.

Mid-July–August By the second half of July, the herds are moving north and northwest into the northern Serengeti and Kenya's Masai Mara. As part of this northwards push, they make an even more incredible river crossing of the Mara River.

September–October In early September, the last stragglers leave the Serengeti and most will remain in the Masai Mara throughout October.

November–December The herds usually begin moving south again in November in anticipation of the rains, crossing down through the heart of the Serengeti and to the south in December.

Exceptions to these guidelines are common. In November 2013, for example, it began raining in the Masai Mara when the herds had already crossed into Tanzania, prompting the wildebeest to return en masse to the Mara. There they remained for three weeks before resuming their southwards push. And in June 2014, unseasonal rains in the southern Serengeti prompted the herd to split in two – most continued north as usual but a significant number of zebras and wildebeest occupied the plains south of Seronera into July.

Sasakwa Lodge
LODGE $$$

(www.singita.com; r per person all inclusive US$1850; P 🛜 ≋) ✈ One of a trio of exclusive lodges in a private concession in the Grumeti Game Reserve; in addition to their tourism focus, conservation dominates much of what they do here, from running a private anti-poaching unit to facilitating the reintroduction of the black rhino to the western corridor of the Serengeti ecosystem. Offers horseback rides.

Robanda Safari Camp
TENTED CAMP $$$

(📞 0754 324193; www.moivaro.com; s/d $247/373; P) A refreshingly small budget (by Serengeti standards) camp on the plains near Robanda village just outside Ikoma gate with seven no-frills tents covered by a thatched roof. You can do guided walks and night drives here, if you have your own vehicle.

Ikoma Tented Camp
TENTED CAMP $$$

(📞 0754 324193, 027-250 6315; www.moivaro.com; s/d full board US$287/433; P) Just outside the Ikoma Gate and handy for just about anywhere in the park, this relatively simple tented camp combines a closeness to the local community with excellent prices and high levels of comfort.

🛏 Northern Serengeti

★Serengeti Bushtops Camp
LODGE, TENTED CAMP $$$

(www.bushtopscamps.com; s/d all inclusive US$1300/1980; P @ 🛜 ≋) In a remote corner of the northern Serengeti, close to the boundary with the Ikorongo Game Reserve, this remarkable camp has large permanent tents with expansive wood floors and decks with a spa bath, perfectly placed sofas and fabulous views. Many Serengeti lodges are luxurious, but this place is simply magnificent. The food is similarly excellent.

★Serengeti Migration Camp
TENTED CAMP $$$

(📞 027-250 0630; www.elewanacollection.com; s/d full board US$1118/1490; P 🛜 ≋) One of the most highly regarded places in the Serengeti with 20 large, stunning tents with decks, and a plush lounge, around a kopje by the Grumeti River. The blend between a tent's immersion in the surrounds and the luxury of permanence is perfectly executed here. There are great views and front-row seats during the few weeks the migration passes through. Walks are also possible.

Klein's Camp
LODGE $$$

(📞 028-262 1267; www.andbeyond.com; r per person all inclusive US$995; P 🛜 ≋) This classic Serengeti camp is exclusive and strikingly situated (the views are awesome) on a private concession just outside the northeastern park boundary, with 10 luxurious stone-and-thatch cottages, and the chance for bush walks, night wildlife drives or a relaxing massage.

Sayari Camp
TENTED CAMP $$$

(http://sayaricamp.asiliaafrica.com; s/d all inclusive US$1260/1990; ☉ Jun-Mar; P 🛜 ≋) Deep in the far north, near the Mara River, this wonderfully remote camp has an understated elegance and genuine style. The 15 tents have wooden floors and decks, are large yet cosy, and the pool is built into the boulders. Short bush walks and spa treatments are both available, and if you're lucky with the timing it's the perfect place for the wildebeest river crossing.

Lamai Serengeti
LODGE $$$

(📞 0784 208343; www.nomad-tanzania.com; s/d all-inclusive US$1570/2150; ☉ Jun–mid-Mar; P 🛜 ≋) Built on a kopje near the Mara River in far northern Serengeti, Lamai blends into its surroundings so well it's nearly invisible. There are two lodges, one with eight rooms and another with four, each with its own dining areas and swimming pools. All rooms have African-themed decor, soothing earth tones and are open-fronted with great views.

🛏 Mobile Camps

Mobile camps are a great idea, but something of a misnomer. They do move (though never when guests are in residence), following the wildebeest migration so as to try to always be in good wildlife-watching territory, but with all the fancy amenities people expect on a luxury safari, relocating is a huge chore and most only move two or three times a year.

★Wayo Green Camp
TENTED CAMP $$$

(📞 0784 203000; www.wayoafrica.com; per person all inclusive from US$300) These 'private mobile camps' combine the best aspects of both tented camps and budget camping safaris and are the best way possible to get a deep bush experience in the Serengeti. They use 3m x 3m dome tents and actual mattresses (off the ground) and move from site to site every couple of days. Wayo also runs excellent walking safaris.

Serengeti Safari Camp
TENTED CAMP $$$

(☎ 0784 208343; www.nomad-tanzania.com; s/d all inclusive US$1120/1550) One of the original mobile camps and now one of the most exclusive, it has six tents and some of the best guides in the Serengeti.

Serengeti Savannah Camp
TENTED CAMP $$$

(☎ 027 254 7000; www.serengetisavannahcamps.com; s/d/tr full board US$335/520/780; ⊙ Jun-Mar) A little less luxurious than others of its kind, but a lot more reasonably priced. It moves just twice a year between Ndutu and Seronera.

Olakira Camp
TENTED CAMP $$$

(☎ 0736 500156; www.asilaafrica.com; s/d US$1060/1590) A match for many of the more permanent camps dotted around the Serengeti, Olakira moves between the far south (roughly December to March) and far north of the park.

ⓘ Information

Serengeti Visitor Centre (☎ 0732 985761; serengeti_tourism@yahoo.com; ⊙ 8am-5pm) The Serengeti Visitor Centre at Seronera has an excellent self-guided walk through the Serengeti's history and ecosystems, and it's well worth spending time here before exploring the park. There's a coffee shop with snacks and cold drinks.

ⓘ Getting There & Around

The park has four main entry and exit points, plus two lesser-used gates at Handajega and Fort Ikoma.

Naabi Hill gate (⊙ 6am-6pm) The main (and most heavily trafficked) access gate if coming from Arusha; 45km from Seronera.

Ndabaka gate (⊙ 6am-6pm) Main gate for the Western Corridor; a 1½-hour drive from Mwanza and 145km from Seronera. Last entry at 4pm.

Klein's gate (⊙ 6am-6pm) In the far northeast, it allows a loop trip combining Serengeti, Ngorongoro and Lake Natron, the latter just two to three hours from the park. Last entry at 4pm.

Bologonya gate This gate would be on the route to/from Kenya's Masai Mara National Reserve, but the border is closed and unlikely to open any time soon.

AIR

Air Excel (p164), Coastal Aviation (p164) and Regional Air (p165) have daily flights from Arusha to the park's seven airstrips, including Seronera and Grumeti.

BUS

Although not ideal, shoestring travellers can do their wildlife watching through the window of the Arusha–Musoma buses that cross the park, but you'll need to pay US$110 in entrance fees for Serengeti and Ngorongoro. The buses stop at the staff village at Seronera, but you're not allowed to walk or hitchhike to the campsites

---

ROAD ACROSS THE SERENGETI?

In 2010, Tanzania's president announced that the government planned to build a road across Serengeti National Park to connect Mto wa Mbu with Musoma. The government argued that the road was necessary to bring economic development to this remote and often-neglected corner of the country. Conservationists were appalled. The impact of increased traffic (including freight trucks) upon wildlife and the natural environment within the park, they countered, could be catastrophic. They also pointed out that any such road would run counter to Tanzania's international obligations to protect and preserve this Unesco World Heritage-listed site.

In June 2014 the East African Court of Justice ruled that a tarmac road would be unlawful. In response, the government declared the ruling to be meaningless, 'because the government had long decided not to build the road across the Serengeti'. One NGO representing Maasai communities in the Ngorongoro and Loliondo areas complained that the decision would perpetuate the isolation of many Maasai from economic opportunities in the rest of the country.

Despite the ruling, conservationists remain concerned that the government, under pressure from the local authorities in Arusha, may be planning to take the tarmac portion of the road to the borders of the Serengeti, with an upgraded but unpaved 50km gravel road across the park still on the agenda. In October 2014 the Tanzanian government announced plans to appeal the regional court's ruling, arguing that the court had no jurisdiction to forbid the construction of the road.

or resthouses, and the park has no vehicles for hire, so unless you've made prior transport arrangements it's nearly pointless getting off here.

CAR

Driving is not permitted in the park after 7pm, except in the visitor centre area where the cut-off is 9pm. Petrol is sold at Seronera. Almost everyone explores the park in 4WDs, but except during the heaviest rains 2WDs will have no problems on the main roads and can even manage some of the secondary ones.

KILIMANJARO AREA

Moshi

POP 184,290

The noticeably clean capital of the densely populated Kilimanjaro region sits at the foot of Mt Kilimanjaro and makes a good introduction to the splendours of the north. It's a low-key place with an appealing blend of African and Asian influences and a self-sufficient, prosperous feel, due in large part to it being the centre of one of Tanzania's major coffee-growing regions. Virtually all visitors are here to climb Mt Kilimanjaro or to recover after having done so.

◉ Sights & Activities

Even inside the city, **Mt Kilimanjaro** is the main attraction and you'll probably be continually gazing north trying to catch a glimpse. Most of the time it will be hidden behind a wall of clouds, but nearly every evening after 6pm it emerges from the mist to whet your appetite for altitude. From December through June it's usually visible during the mornings too and usually topped by much more snow. For an even better view, look around town for flyers advertising **scenic flights**.

🛏 Sleeping

🛏 Central Moshi

AA Hill Street Accommodation   GUESTHOUSE $

(☏ 0784 461469, 0754 461469; azim_omar @hotmail.com; Kilima St; s/d/tr Tsh20,000/ 30,000/40,000) Walk past the seamstresses plying their trade just off Kilima St, and climb the stairs to this quiet, friendly place that's ideal for those looking for an alterna-

tive to the busy backpacker scene. Don't be put off by the list of restrictions (no alcohol, no shared rooms for nonmarried couples) – if those things matter, go elsewhere.

Rooms are simple, tidy and we especially liked Room 202, which is large and has a balcony, but can be noisy.

Haria Hotel   HOTEL $

(☏ 0752 328042; Mawenzi Rd; d US$27, dm/d with shared bathroom US$12/24; ☎) This laid-back, switched-on place has a devoted following and it's not hard to see why. The rooms are nothing special, but they're large and come with a friendly overall feel, thanks to the predominantly female staff. It's worlds better than other, better-known and more expensive places nearby and the restaurant serves a limited menu of local meals at fair prices. Breakfast costs Tsh3000.

Kindoroko Hotel   HOTEL $

(☏ 0757 369628; www.kindorokohotels.com; Mawenzi Rd; s/d/f US$25/35/50; @☎) Rooms here are small and sit somewhere between basic and simple, but they come with cable TV and hot water. The main reason to stay is the guests-only rooftop bar, an excellent meeting place with fine Kilimanjaro views. As their promotional material says, the hotel 'leaves you in no doubt that you are in Africa' – make of that what you will.

Buffalo Hotel   HOTEL $

(☏ 0756 508501; New St; s/d/tr/ste US$30/35/45/50; ❄) The long-popular Buffalo Hotel has straightforward rooms; all have private bathrooms thanks to a recent overhaul. Avoid the ground-floor rooms and head up the stairs; there's no elevator. The lack of wi-fi lets it down a little, but there's an internet cafe next door and it's generally a good deal.

Lutheran Umoja Hostel   GUESTHOUSE $

(☏ 027-275 0902; Market St; s/d Tsh30,000/ 40,000, with shared bathroom Tsh15,000/25,000; P@) The cheapest place in the city centre has clean, no-frills rooms around a small (mostly) quiet courtyard. It's popular with volunteers.

Bristol Cottages   HOTEL $$

(☏ 027-275 5083; www.bristolcottages.com; 98 Rindi Lane; s/d US$60/70, cottage s/d/ tr US$70/80/100, ste s/d/tr US$80/100/120; P❄☎) This place exudes a sense of peace upon entering – the leafy compound is an attractive counterpoint to busy Moshi

NORTHERN TANZANIA MOSHI

streets – and the rooms are well-presented; the suites are particularly spacious. For all this talk of peace, however, early morning noise can be a problem. Even so, it's probably our midrange pick in the downtown.

Parkview Inn HOTEL $$
(☎0754 052000, 027-2750711; www.pvim.com; Aga Khan Rd; s/d/ste US$70/80/120; P❋@☎☎) No one would ever call this centrally located place attractive, but the modern (though ageing) rooms and swimming pool make it a good post-climb rest spot at the

midrange level. Rooms at the back are quieter and generally preferable.

Nyumbani Hotel HOTEL $$
(☎0767 123487, 027-275 4432; www.nyumbani hotels.com; Rengua Rd; s/d from US$80/110; ❋@☎☎) A good midrange choice in the heart of town and with a modern business feel. Rooms are large, and the cheapest, standard rooms have balconies. It doesn't have a huge amount of charm, but it's a good deal nonetheless.

Kilimanjaro Crane Hotel
HOTEL **$$**

(☑0763 399503, 027-275 1114; www.kilimanjaro
cranehotel.com; Kaunda St; s/d with air-con
US$50/60, d/tr without air-con US$50/60, ste
US$110; ✦@☎☎) This long-standing mid-
range option has tired but adequate rooms
with safari colours of the kind you'll see fad-
ing in the sun at roadside furniture show-
rooms. It's a touch cheaper than others in
this category and rooms have cable TV and
large beds backing a small garden. There are
great Kili views from the rooftop.

Outside the City Centre

★Hibiscus
B&B **$**

(☑0768 146589, 0766-312516; www.thehibiscus
moshi.com; off Taifa Rd; s/tw US$25/40; ☎) This
cosy B&B has six spotless, impeccably deco-
rated rooms, all with fan and most with pri-
vate bathroom, plus a delightful garden and
meals on request. Highly recommended. It's
in a quiet residential area just northwest of
the town centre.

Honey Badger
GUESTHOUSE **$**

(☑0767 551190, 0787 730235; www.honeybadger
lodge.com; dm from US$15, s/d from US$50/70;
P@☎☎) A large family-run place with
shady gardens and a variety of rooms. Dorm
dwellers must pay US$3 to use the large
pool. It offers a variety of tours and lessons
(drumming, cooking etc) and volunteer op-
portunities can be arranged. The restaurant
serves gourmet pizzas from its stone oven
from Thursday to Sunday. It's 7km from
town off the Marangu road.

★AMEG Lodge
LODGE **$$**

(☑0754 058268, 027-275 0175; www.ameglodge.
com; off Lema Rd; s/d from US$70/94, s/d ste
US$127/149) This friendly place wins plaudits
from travellers for its lovely setting in 4.5
acres of manicured gardens with palm trees
and frangipanis, 4km northwest of the town
centre. Attractive rooms with broad verandahs and plenty of space lie dotted around
the compound, the service is friendly, and
the overall feel is that of a rural oasis on the
fringe of the city.

You'll need your own wheels, but there's
an on-site bar and restaurant.

Sal Salinero Villa
HOTEL **$$**

(☑0784 683605, 027-275 2240; www.salsalinero
hotel.com; off Lema Rd, Shanty Town; s/d
US$100/150; P✦☎☎) In a secure com-
pound in the Shanty Town area northwest
of the city centre, Sal Salinero offers 27 large

rooms in a mock-Italian villa with hardwood
flooring plus 20 more modern-feeling cot-
tages under palm trees. Rooms are comfort-
able rather than luxurious.

✕ Eating & Drinking

★Kaliwa
THAI **$**

(☑0762 620707; Arusha Rd; mains Tsh7000-9000;
⊙11am-11pm; ☎) This welcome addition to
Moshi's rather limited eating scene sits at
the southwestern end of Uhuru Park with
a stylish outdoor eating area and fragrant
Thai dishes such as basil beef. Wines, good
coffee and a sophisticated vibe have attract-
ed a well-to-do local crowd from the start
and its popularity shows no sign of waning.

Milan's
INDIAN **$**

(Mankinga St; meals Tsh5000-6500; ⊙11am-
9.30pm; ☑) This colourful all-vegetarian spot
is our favourite Indian restaurant, and not
only because the prices are so low: it's really
delicious.

Sikh Club
INDIAN **$**

(☑027-275 2473; Ghala St; mains Tsh5000-9000;
⊙noon-3pm & 6-10pm Tue-Sun; ☑) There are
fancier choices elsewhere, but ask most In-
dians in town where they eat out and the
majority will direct you to this plastic-chair
place overlooking a dirt football pitch. Ser-
vice is slow because everything's prepared to
order. The menu runs the full gamut from
tandoori to a mean *malai kofta*.

The Coffee Shop
CAFE **$**

(☑027-275 2707; Kilima St; mains Tsh6500-9000;
⊙7.30am-9.30pm Mon-Sat; ☎) ✐ A cafe with
garden seating, good coffee and homemade
breads, cakes, yoghurt, breakfast, soups

COFFEE TOURS

With the most popular coffee tour
in town, **Kahawa Shamba Coffee
Tours** (☑0784 324121, 0754 461376;
www.kilimanculturaltourism.com; per
person Tsh30,000, transport from Moshi
Tsh50,000) is a laudable community-run
venture that not only shows you how
beans are grown, picked and roasted,
but offers insight into the lives of the
Chagga coffee farmers who live on
Kilimanjaro's lower slopes. Meals with
local families can be arranged, as can
additional village and waterfall walks. It's
easiest to book at Union Café.

Moshi

N 0 ———————— 200 m
0 ———————— 0.1 miles

Kilimanjaro Christian
Medical Centre (3.5km);
Mt Kilimanjaro (40km)

Marangu Rd

Honey
Badger
(6km)

Hibiscus
(170m)

Taifa Rd

Shah Tours (300m);
AMEG Lodge (2.3km);
Olpopongi Maasai Cultural
Village Booking Office (450m);
Sal Salinero Villa (3km)

Kibo Rd

Old Moshi Rd

Kilimanjaro
International (45km);
Arusha (80km)

Horombo Rd

Rengua Rd

35

28
29

40
41 12
33
10
42
46

Boma Rd

36
37

26

7

45

13

31 32

Taxi
Stand

15

Rindi La

30

Station Rd

Aga Khan Rd

11

2

18

14

Arusha Rd

Kaunda St

4

Killma (Hill) St

Taxi
Stand

39

Mosque

43

KENYATTA St

Selous St

44

22
1

Sikh
Temple

Mankinga St

17
19

Hindu
Temple

Mawenzi (Nyerere) Rd

Ghala St

38
23

School St

16

3

34

Chagga St

KIUSA

Kiusa St

Kawawa St

Lindi St

27 5

8

24 20

21

Market

Market St

Liwali St

Masjid
Riadha

9

Viwanda St

Riadha St

Bodeni St

New St

Swahili St

Mission St

Mafuta St

Kibo Rd

Mill Rd

25

Chunya St

Moshi (2km)

NORTHERN TANZANIA

Moshi

and low-priced light meals. Of the latter, the local dishes (choose a sauce with ugali or chapati) are generally preferable to the Chinese-inspired selections. Proceeds go to a church project.

Pamoja Cafe TANZANIAN, INTERNATIONAL $
(New St; mains Tsh3500-8000; ⊙8am-10pm Mon-Sat, 10am-9pm Sun; 🛜) Following a time-honoured tradition of budget-traveller hangouts the world over, Pamoja Cafe is basic but gives the punters what they want with free wi-fi, a funky musical soundtrack, Western snacks (burgers and sandwiches) and cheap local cuisine, such as *nyami mchuzi* (beef stew with rice, ugali or chapati). There's also a nightly barbecue from 5.30pm.

Nile Springs TANZANIAN $
(New St; mains from Tsh6000; ⊙7am-11pm) Funny place this. The dark interior is home to waiters watching the TV, and the service is otherwise somewhere between unwilling and dysfunctional. But the roadside terrace is a good place to try local dishes without worrying about the hygiene. There's chicken with coconut or *samaki wa kuchemsa* (boiled fish with ugali).

★**Kilimanjaro Coffee Lounge** CAFE $$
(📋0754 610892; Station Rd; meals Tsh7000-13,000; ⊙8am-9pm Mon-Sat, 10am-8pm Sun; 🛜) A recent move opposite the Nakamutt Supermarket has done this place the world of good. The semi-garden setting is away from the road, bringing a semblance of peace, and the food ranges from pizza and Mexican dishes to salads, sandwiches, burgers and steaks, alongside excellent milkshakes and juices. Throw in free wi-fi and you've all the makings of a travellers' classic.

★**Union Café** CAFE $
(📋0784 590184, 027-275 2785; Arusha Rd; ⊙7.30am-8.30pm; 🛜) 🍴 The Kilimanjaro Native Cooperative Union, which represents tens of thousands of small-holding coffee farmers, runs this stylish shop. Although it also serves good pizzas, pastas and burgers (meals Tsh7000 to Tsh15,000), it's all about the coffee – the cooperative's own beans are roasted on-site. It also has a generator, reliable wi-fi and an atmosphere that's at once trendy and carries echoes of colonial Africa.

VOLUNTEERING IN MOSHI

While most travellers who visit Moshi come to climb Mt Kilimanjaro, a significant proportion also come to volunteer. As a general rule, volunteering works best for both traveller and the organisation in question if you treat it as a genuine commitment rather than as simply a fun extension of your trip. It's also preferable if you have a particular skill to bring to the experience, especially one that cannot be satisfied by local people.

In Moshi, and to a lesser extent Arusha, many groups looking for help post flyers on notice boards around town. Alternatively, Honey Badger (p199), Hostel Hoff (☑0787 225908; www.hostelhoff.com; dm US$19) and the less cosy Foot2Afrika (Hosetl Foot Prince; ☑0/84 828835; www.foot2afrika.com; dm US$23) will set you up with a project that fits your skills and desires as long as you sleep at their hostels. In most cases they require a minimum stay (at least two weeks, but rules vary) and may include breakfast, dinner and laundry. In Arusha, Ujamaa Hostel (p155) is a similar set-up.

It is also worth remembering that, officially, volunteering in Tanzania requires a special immigration permit, known as a permit 'C' or a 'CTA' permit. These are not always easy to obtain and immigration in Moshi is regarded as one of the most 'difficult' in the country when it comes to such matters. If in doubt, ask your hostel or whoever arranged your volunteering for assistance.

Self-Catering

Abbas Ali's Hot Bread Shop   BAKERY $
(Boma Rd; ⊙9am-6pm Mon-Fri, to 5pm Sat) Moshi's best bakery.

Nakumatt   SUPERMARKET $
(Station Rd; ⊙8.30am-10pm Mon-Sat, 10am-9pm Sun) Moshi's largest supermarket.

Aleem's   SUPERMARKET $
(Boma Rd; ⊙8.45am-1pm & 2-5pm Mon-Fri, 8.45am-1pm & 2-4pm Sat) Small, reasonably well-stocked grocery store.

Kilimanjaro Star   SUPERMARKET $
(Mawenzi Rd; ⊙8.30am-10pm) Marginally the pick of the grocery stores in the city centre.

🛍 Shopping

I Curio   HANDICRAFTS
(Viwanda St; ⊙9am-6pm) Better than the ordinary craft shops, and with fixed prices. Also stocks a small selection of national park maps and books.

Shah Industries   LEATHER
(☑0754 260348; www.kiliweb.com/shah; Mill Rd; ⊙9am-5pm Mon-Fri, to 2pm Sat) 🕮 Lots of interesting leatherwork, some of it made by people with disabilities.

ℹ Information

IMMIGRATION

Immigration Office (Boma Rd; ⊙7.30am-3.30pm Mon-Fri)

INTERNET RESOURCES

Kiliweb (www.kiliweb.com) Privately run tourist website for Moshi.

MEDICAL SERVICES

Jaffery Charitable Medical Services (☑027-275 1843; Ghala St; ⊙8.30am-5pm Mon-Fri, to 1pm Sat) Moshi's most reliable laboratory.

Kemi Pharmacy (☑027-275 1560; Rengua Rd; ⊙7am-7pm Mon-Sat) One of numerous pharmacies dotted around the city centre.

Kilimanjaro Christian Medical Centre (☑027-275 4377/80; www.kcmc.ac.tz; Sokoine Rd; ⊙24hr) Around 4.5km north of the centre.

TOURIST INFORMATION

There's no tourist office in Moshi. The Coffee Shop, Kilimanjaro Coffee Lounge and Union Café restaurants have message boards. People seeking climbing partners sometimes post requests on them.

TRAVEL AGENCIES

Zara Tours (☑0754 451000, 027-275 4240; www.zaratours.com; Rindi Lane; ⊙8.30am-1pm & 2-5pm Mon-Fri, 8.30am-1pm Sat) Airline bookings.

ℹ Getting There & Away

AIR

Kilimanjaro International Airport (KIA) is 50km west of town, halfway to Arusha. There's also the small Moshi airport just southwest of town, along the extension of Market St, which handles occasional charters.

Precision Air (☑0787 800820, 027-275 3495; www.precisionairtz.com; Old Moshi Rd; ⊙8am-

5pm Mon-Fri, 9am-1pm Sat & Sun) Flies from KIA to Dar, Zanzibar and Mwanza.

Coastal Aviation (☑ 0785 500445, 0785 500729; www.coastal.co.tz; Arusha Rd) Flies daily from Moshi airport (if there are enough passengers) on their Arusha–coast circuit, and possibly also to the northern national parks.

Fastjet (☑ 0685 680533; www.fastjet.com) Flights between KIA and Dar es Salaam with onward connections across Tanzania and East Africa.

BUS

Buses and minibuses run throughout the day to Arusha (Tsh3000, 1½ hours) and Marangu (Tsh2000, 1½ hours).

The chaotic bus station is conveniently located in the middle of the city. There are many touts and arrivals can be quite annoying if you're new to this sort of thing. This is one good reason to travel with the companies that have their own offices. It's best to buy tickets the day before you plan to travel.

All of the following buses use their own offices rather than the bus station. Ordinary buses (Tsh20,000) and a few less-reliable luxury companies use the bus station.

Dar Express (☑ 0759 942550; Boma Rd) Eight daily departures to Dar (Tsh36,000, seven to eight hours) from 7am to noon aboard full luxury buses (with air-con and toilets). The 7am bus sometimes arrives early enough for you to catch the afternoon ferry to Zanzibar, but don't count on it.

Metro Express (☑ 0715 113344; Selous St) Two daily departures (luxury/full luxury Tsh32,000/36,000) for Dar at 8am.

Kilimanjaro Express (☑ 0715 213231; Rengua Rd) Four morning departures to Dar aboard luxury buses (Tsh33,000).

Mtei Express (☑ 0759 613563; Boma Rd) Buses to Dar (Tsh28,000) as well as to Babati (Tsh9000, four to five hours) and Dodoma (Tsh28,000, 12 to 14 hours) via Arusha (Tsh3000, 1½ hours).

ⓘ Getting Around

Parking anywhere in the city centre costs Tsh1000 per day – an attendant with tickets is likely to be lurking not far from where you park.

TO/FROM THE AIRPORT

Taxi drivers are tough negotiators; try for US$30, but expect to pay more.

TAXI & DALLA-DALLA

There are taxi stands near the Clock Tower and at the bus station, plus you can find taxis by most hotels. The bus station to a city-centre hotel should cost Tsh2500 and it's Tsh3500 to Shanty Town. Motorcycle taxi drivers expect

Tsh1000, even for a very short ride. Dalla-dallas run down main roads from next to the bus station.

Machame

The rather ill-defined and spread-out village of Machame lies 25km northwest of Moshi on Mt Kilimanjaro's lower slopes, surrounded by dense vegetation and stands of banana. Most visitors only pass through briefly en route to the trailhead for the popular Machame Rte.

🛏 Sleeping

⭐**Kaliwa Lodge** LODGE $$ (☑ 0762 620707; www.kaliwalodge.com; s/d US$80/160; ℙ) At an altitude of 1300m and close to Machame gate, this new German-run place opened in 2012 and has a refreshingly contemporary Bauhaus architectural style with soothing grey cube-like structures. Rooms have abundant glass, the colour scheme is muted but very modern, and the setting amid palm trees and lush gardens is as lovely as the rest of the place.

Makoa Farm FARM, GUESTHOUSE $$$ (☑ 0754 312896; www.makoa-farm.com; rates vary with packages; ℙ) This restored 1930s farmstead and working farm is primarily a base for horse-riding safaris that range across Tanzania's north for experienced riders, but its guest cottages make a pleasant break for nonriding partners who want to stay behind and relax. It's about 17km from Moshi, off the Machame road and unsignposted – ask for directions when booking.

Meals at the property are made with farm produce and served family-style together with the owners and an assorted menagerie of pets in the main farmhouse.

Marangu

Nestled on the lower slopes of Mt Kilimanjaro, 40km northeast of Moshi, amid dense stands of banana and coffee plants, is the lively, leafy market town of Marangu. It has an agreeable highland ambience, cool climate and good selection of hotels, all of which organise treks. While you'll generally get slightly better budget deals in Moshi, Marangu makes a convenient base for Kili climbs using the Marangu or Rongai routes, and it's an enjoyable stop in its own right.

Marangu is also the heartland of the Chagga people, and there are many possibilities for walks and cultural activities. *Marangu* means 'place of water' and the surrounding area is laced with small streams and waterfalls (most with a small entry charge) to visit.

◉ Sights & Activities

Both Banana Jungle Lodge and Kilimanjaro Mountain Resort have authentic models of traditional Chagga houses. At Kilimanjaro Mountain Resort, there's also the **Chagga Live Museum** (adult/child US$3/2; ⊙10am-5pm), a small outdoor museum illustrating traditional Chagga life.

Most hotels can also provide English-speaking guides (US$10 to US$15 per person per day) to other attractions in the area, including rather claustrophobic 'caves' (actually dugout holes and tunnels) that were used by the Chagga for hiding during the era of Maasai raids about 200 years ago, a sacred tree, local blacksmiths' workshops and waterfalls. About 6km southwest of Marangu is **Ngangu Hill**, with views and the small, old Kilema mission church nearby.

Day hikes as far as Mandara Hut (10km one way; allow around three hours up and 1½ hours back) in Mt Kilimanjaro National Park can also be arranged.

🛏 Sleeping

Coffee Tree Campsite CAMPGROUND $
(☑0754 691433; www.coffeetreecampsite.com; campsites per person US$10, rondavels/chalets

LAKE CHALA SAFARI CAMP

If you're looking for something remote and relaxing, **Lake Chala Safari Camp** (☑0753 641087, 0786 111177; www.lakechalasafaricamp.com; camping with own/hired tent US$10/30, s/d half board US$150/200, day visit US$5; P 🛜), an ecocamp overlooking its namesake caldera lake by the Kenyan border, could be perfect. It has attractive facilities (including a restaurant and cooking area) and a lovely location, ideal for walks, birdwatching or just doing nothing. With the recent construction of an upmarket (but still reasonably priced) tented camp, there's something to appeal to most budgets.

per person US$15/18; @) ⬦ This place has expansive, trim grounds, hot-water showers, tents for hire, double rondavels and four- to five-person chalets. It's 700m east of the main road, signposted near Nakara Hotel. There's no food, but there are several eateries nearby. The owner is committed to slowing the environmental destruction of Kilimanjaro, and is a good source of information on local conservation efforts.

Bismarck Hut Lodge GUESTHOUSE $
(☑0754 318338; camping US$5, r per person without bathroom US$10-15; P) Along the road to the park gate and shortly before the turn-off to Capricorn Hotel, the no-frills Bismarck has a few clean, basic rooms, a small camping area, two large, old resident tortoises and meals on order.

Babylon Lodge LODGE $$
(☑027-275 6355; www.babylonlodge.com; s/d/tr US$40/60/80; P @ 🛜) Friendly Babylon has simple and clean twin- and double-bedded rooms clustered around small, attractive gardens. It's often somewhat more flexible than other properties on negotiating Kili trek packages. It's 700m east of the main junction.

Kibo Hotel LODGE $$
(☑0754 038747; kibohotel@myway.com; camping US$5, s/d/tr US$50/65/85; P) Kibo is where Hans Meyer stayed before starting his famous first ascent of Kilimanjaro. (Another prominent guest in more recent times was Jimmy Carter.) Now the hotel is well past its prime, but the wooden flooring, large-paned windows and surrounding gardens lend atmosphere. It's 1.5km west of the main junction. Meals are available.

Banana Jungle Lodge LODGE $$
(☑0754 270947, 027-275 6565; camping per student/nonstudent US$5/10, s/d/tr US$50/60/75; P) Accommodation at this family homestead is in bungalow-style rooms or modernised Chagga huts, all surrounded by dense plantings of banana and other vegetation. It's a good choice for learning about Chagga life. There's a reproduction of a traditional Chagga house and a small working farm. It's about 5km east of Marangu in Mamba (off the road leading to the Rongai Route trailhead).

To get here, head east at Marangu's main junction, go 2km to the Mamba Lutheran church, turn left at the signboard and then follow the signboards 2.5km further.

Kilimanjaro Mountain Resort   LODGE $$$

(☑0754 693461; www.kilimountresort.com; camping with own/hired tent US$17/30, s/d/tr US$133/200/293; P@☎) This stately old-style building is surrounded by gardens and forest 3km west of the main junction. It has spacious, well-appointed rooms (some with enormous beds), a restaurant (meals US$18) and the adjoining Chagga Live Museum.

Marangu Hotel   LODGE $$$

(☑0754 886092, 027-275 6594; www.marangu hotel.com; campsites per person US$6.50, s/d/tr half board US$105/160/215; @☎☎) This long-standing hotel is the first place you reach coming from Moshi. It has an appealingly faded British ambience, pleasant rooms in expansive grounds, lovely gardens and a campground with hot-water showers. Low season rates (doubles US$110) apply if you join one of the hotel's fully equipped climbs.

❶ Getting There & Away

Minibuses run throughout the day between Marangu's main junction (Marangu Mtoni) and Moshi (Tsh2000, 1½ hours). Once in Marangu, there are sporadic pick-ups from the main junction to the park gate (Tsh1500), 5km further. For the Holili border, change at Himo junction.

Mt Kilimanjaro National Park

Since its official opening in 1977, Mt Kilimanjaro National Park (☑0767 536134, 0689 062309, 027-56605; www.tanzaniaparks.com/kili. html; adult/child US$70/20; ☺6.30am-6.30pm) has become one of Tanzania's most visited parks. Unlike the other northern parks, this isn't for the wildlife, although it's there. Rather, coming here is all about gazing in awe at a mountain on the equator capped with snow, and to climb to the top of Africa.

At the heart of the park is the 5896m Mt Kilimanjaro, Africa's highest mountain and one of the continent's most magnificent sights. It's also one of the highest volcanoes and the highest freestanding mountain in the world, rising from cultivated farmlands on the lower levels, through lush rainforest to alpine meadows, and finally across a barren lunar landscape to the twin summits of Kibo and Mawenzi. (Kilimanjaro's third volcanic cone, Shira, is on the mountain's

---

❶ MT KILIMANJARO NATIONAL PARK

Why Go? The chance to climb Africa's tallest mountain.

When to Go Year-round, but best late June to October and late December to February

Practicalities Park entry gates include Machame, Marangu (the site of park headquarters), Londorosi and several other points; trekkers using the Rongai Route should pay their fees at Marangu gate. There are six routes to the summit: Machame, Marangu, Umbwe, Rongai, Shira Plateau and Mweka. Requirements have recently changed and you must pay at least six days worth of park fees for all routes except Marangu (five-day minimum).

Budget Tips Climb the Marangu route, but don't try and skimp on supplies and other essential elements that may compromise your safety.

---

western side.) The lower rainforest is home to many animals, including buffaloes, elephants, leopards and monkeys, and elands are occasionally seen in the saddle area between Kibo and Mawenzi.

A trek up Kili lures around 25,000 trekkers each year, in part because it's possible to walk to the summit without ropes or technical climbing experience. But don't be fooled by the number of people who climb Kilimanjaro – this is a serious undertaking. While many thousands of trekkers reach Uhuru Peak without major difficulty, many more don't make it because they suffer altitude sickness or simply aren't in good enough shape. And every year some trekkers and porters die on the mountain. Come prepared with appropriate footwear and clothing, and most importantly, allow yourself enough time. If you're interested in reaching the top, seriously consider adding at least one extra day onto the 'standard' climb itineraries: accepted medical advice is to increase sleeping altitude by only 300m per day once above 3000m – which is about one-third of the daily altitude gains above 3000m on the standard Kili climb-routes offered by most operators.

🏃 Trekking Mt Kilimanjaro

When to Climb

Mt Kilimanjaro can be climbed at any time of year, though weather patterns are notoriously erratic and difficult to predict. Overall, the best time for climbing the mountain is in the dry season, from late June to October, and from late December to February or early March, just after the short rains and before the long rains. During November and March/April, it's more likely that paths through the forest will be slippery, and that routes up to the summit, especially the Western Breach, will be covered by snow. That said, you can also have a streak of beautiful, sunny days during these times.

Climbing Conditions & Equipment

Don't underestimate the weather on Kilimanjaro. Conditions on the mountain are frequently very cold and wet, and you'll need a full range of waterproof cold-weather clothing and gear, including a good-quality sleeping bag. It's also worth carrying some additional sturdy water bottles. No matter what the time of year, waterproof everything, especially your sleeping bag, as things rarely dry on the mountain. It's often possible to rent sleeping bags and gear from trekking operators. For the Marangu Route, you can also rent gear from the Kilimanjaro Guides Cooperative Society stand just inside Marangu gate, or from a small no-name shop just before the gate. However, especially at the budget level, quality and availability can't be counted on, and it's best to bring your own.

Apart from a small shop at Marangu gate selling a limited range of chocolate bars and tinned items, there are no shops inside the park. You can buy beer and soft drinks at high prices at huts on the Marangu Rte.

Costs

Kilimanjaro can only be climbed with a licensed guide and we recommend organising your climb through a tour company. No-frills four-night, five-day treks up the Marangu Route start at about US$1300, including park fees, and no-frills six-day budget treks on the Machame Rte start at around US$1600. Prices start at about US$1300 on the Rongai Route, and about US$1700 for a seven-day trek on the Shira Plateau Route. For other routes, their starting points are further from Moshi and transport costs can be significant, so clarify whether they're included in the price. A proposed hike in government taxes may soon send prices even higher.

Most of the better companies provide dining tents, decent-to-good cuisine and various other extras to both make the experience more enjoyable and maximise your chances of getting to the top. If you choose a really cheap trip you risk having inadequate meals, mediocre guides, few comforts, and problems with hut bookings and park fees. Also, remember that an environmentally responsible trek usually costs more.

Whatever you pay for your trek, remember that the following park fees are not negotiable and should be part of any quote from your trekking operator:

➡ National park entry fees – US$70 per adult per day

➡ Huts/camping fees – US$60/50 per person per night

➡ Rescue fee – US$20 per person per trip

YOHANI KINYALA LAUWO

The first Tanzanian to scale Kilimanjaro was Yohani Kinyala Lauwo, whose memory is still revered in his home town of Marangu. Lauwo was only 18 in 1889 when he was appointed by Chief Marealle I to be the guide for Hans Meyer (the first Westerner to reach Uhuru Peak). In those days the route was not defined, climbing equipment was rudimentary and wages were much lower. During his trek, Lauwo earned just Tsh1 per day.

Following this successful ascent, Lauwo remained in Marangu, where he spent much of the remainder of his life leading foreign trekkers up the mountain and training new guides. In 1989, at the 100th anniversary celebration of the first ascent of Kilimanjaro, Lauwo was the only person present who had been around a century earlier; he died in 1996 at the claimed age of 125. His family still lives in Marangu.

POSSIBLE KILI SCAMS

Paying park fees

For anyone paying directly at the gate, all entry, hut, camping and other park fees must be paid with either Visa or MasterCard and your PIN. One scam involves the relevant officer billing you for less than you owe (eg Tsh100 instead of US$100). After your trek and upon exiting the park, they point this out to you and ask you to pay the difference in cash. The cash, of course, goes into the pockets of whoever is collecting it. Check carefully the amount (*and* currency) before entering your PIN and keep all receipts at least until after you've left the park.

Disreputable guides

While most guides are dedicated, professional, properly trained and genuinely concerned with making your trip safe and successful, there are exceptions. Although it doesn't happen often, some guides leave the last hut deliberately late on the summit day to avoid going all the way to the top. Going with a reputable company, preferably one who hires full-time guides (most don't) is one way to prevent bad experiences. Also, insist on meeting the guide before signing up for a trip, familiarise yourself with all aspects of the route, and when on the mountain have morning and evening briefings so you know what to expect each day. The night before summiting talk to other climbers to be sure your departure time seems realistic (though note that not everyone leaves at the same time), and if not, get an explanation from your guide. Should problems arise, be polite but firm.

Other costs will vary depending on the company, which should handle food, tents (if required), guides and porters, and transport to/from the trailhead, but not tips.

TIPPING

Most guides and porters receive only minimal wages from the trekking companies and depend on tips as their major source of income. As a guideline, plan on tipping about 10% of the total amount you've paid for the trek, divided up among the guides and porters. Common tips for satisfactory service are from about US$10 to US$15 per group per day for the guide, US$8 to US$10 per group per day for the cook and US$5 to US$10 per group per day for each porter.

Guides & Porters

Guides, and at least one porter (for the guide), are obligatory and are provided by your trekking company. You can carry your own gear on the Marangu Rte, although porters are generally used, but one or two porters per trekker are essential on all other routes.

All guides must be registered with the national park authorities. If in doubt, check that your guide's permit is up to date. On Kili, the guide's job is to show you the way and that's it. Only the best guides, working for reputable companies, will be able to tell you about wildlife, flowers or other features on the mountain.

Porters will carry bags weighing up to 15kg (not including their own food and clothing, which they strap to the outside of your bag), and your bags will be weighed before you set off.

Maps

Topographical maps include *Map & Guide to Kilimanjaro* by Andrew Wielochowski and *Kilimanjaro Map & Guide* by Mark Savage. The hand-drawn *New Map of the Kilimanjaro National Park* is evocative for an overview, but no real use for trekking detail.

Trekking Routes

There are six main trekking routes to the summit. Trekkers on all but the Marangu Rte must use tents.

Officially a limit of 60 climbers per route per day is in effect on Kilimanjaro. It's not always enforced, except on the Marangu Rte, which is self-limiting because of maximum hut capacities. When this limit is enforced, expect the advance time necessary for booking a climb to increase, with less flexibility for last-minute arrangements.

➡ **Marangu Rte** A trek on this route is typically sold as a four-night, five-day return package, although at least one

THE (MELTING) SNOWS OF KILIMANJARO

Since 1912, when they were first measured, Kilimanjaro's glaciers, estimated to be over 10,000 years old, have lost 85% of their ice and the loss has accelerated over the last decade. If nothing changes, they'll disappear by 2030. Kili's northern ice field, the mountain's largest, recently split into two and has lost 29% of its ice volume and 32% of its surface area since 2000 – that's four million cubic metres of ice.

The main factors are believed to be an increase in the Indian Ocean's temperature and a loss of forest cover on the mountain's lower slopes: fewer trees means less moisture in the air, which means the ice sublimates (turns from ice directly to vapour) faster.

For now, perhaps the only certain thing is that if you want to see the top of Kilimanjaro draped in snow, you shouldn't wait long to book your trek.

extra night is highly recommended to help acclimatisation, especially if you've just flown in to Tanzania or arrived from the lowlands.

➡ **Machame Rte** This increasingly popular route has a gradual ascent, including a spectacular day contouring the southern slopes before approaching the summit via the top section of the Mweka Route.

➡ **Umbwe Rte** Much steeper, with a more direct way to the summit, Umbwe is very enjoyable if you can resist the temptation to gain altitude too quickly. Although the route is direct, the top, very steep section up the Western Breach is often covered in ice or snow, which makes it impassable or extremely dangerous. Many trekkers who attempt it without proper acclimatisation are forced to turn back. An indication of its seriousness is that until fairly recently, the Western Breach was considered a technical mountaineering route. Only consider this route if you're experienced and properly equipped, and travelling with a reputable operator. Reliable operators will suggest an extra night for acclimatisation.

➡ **Rongai Rte** Growing in popularity, this route starts near the Kenyan border and goes up the northern side of the mountain.

➡ **Shira Plateau Rte** Also called the Londorosi Route, this attractive route is somewhat longer than the others, but good for acclimatisation if you start trekking from Londorosi gate (rather than driving all the way to the Shira Track trailhead), or if you take an extra day at Shira Hut.

➡ **Mweka Rte** For descent only, and often used as part of the Machame, Umbwe and (sometimes) Marangu routes.

West Kilimanjaro

West Kilimanjaro is often overlooked in the rush to climb Mt Kilimanjaro or visit the northern safari parks. That's a real shame, because it encompasses the Maasai lands running north of Sanya Juu village up to the Kenyan border, and is a region of savannah bush lands and impressive wildlife populations – this is an important dispersal area for lions from southern Kenya, while it's also part of an elephant corridor linking Kenya's Amboseli National Park with Mt Kilimanjaro National Park. Other draws include opportunities for walks, cultural activities and horse riding.

◉ Sights & Activities

For horse-riding safaris, Makoa Farm (p203) in Machame runs eight- to 10-day riding safaris in the West Kilimanjaro area.

Kilimanjaro Conservancy   WILDLIFE CONSERVANCY
(✆ 0754 333550, 027-250 2713; www.thekili conservancy.org) ✎ Centred on 44-sq-km Ndarakwai Ranch and set up in 2001, this private conservancy is one of very few such projects in Tanzania. Like similar places in Kenya, the former colonial cattle ranch, which includes grassy plains and woodland, has been artfully converted into a protected area that blends conservation with community development.

The conservancy has been significant in allowing wildlife populations to recover in this important area that connects the Amboseli ecosystem in southern Kenya with Mt Kilimanjaro and Arusha National Parks and beyond. The conservancy has also set a private anti-poaching force. There are now more than 70 mammal species and around 350 bird species. Elephants, zebras, cheetahs, warthogs and lesser kudus are either resident or pass through on a regular basis, while lions and buffaloes are rare but increasing. At the same time, the conservancy is supporting the local school and helping to build fences to prevent crop damage caused by elephants.

Olpopongi Maasai
Cultural Village   CULTURAL TOUR
(☑0756 718455; www.olpopongi-maasai.com; tours per person for day/overnight visit US$59/95, with pick-up & transport from Moshi US$139/169, from Arusha US$169/190) Olpopongi Maasai Cultural Village is a good stop for anyone wanting to spend a night in an authentically constructed Maasai *boma* (a fortified living compound) or learn about Maasai traditions. There's a small, informative museum, medicinal walks, lessons in spear-throwing techniques, and more. It's an excellent destination for families with children. They have a booking office in Moshi.

🛏 Sleeping

Olpopongi Maasai Cultural Village offers a night in a Maasai *boma* as part of its overnight tour package.

★Ndarakwai Ranch   TENTED CAMP **$$$**
(☑0784 550331, 0754 333550, 027-250 2713; www.ndarakwai.com; s/d half board with wildlife drives US$487/772; P🛜) 𝄃 Ndarakwai Ranch, a lovely 15-tent camp run by the Kilimanjaro Conservancy, makes a comfortable base for safaris and walks. The sophisticat-

ed and spacious permanent tents inhabit a lovely woodland area close to the banks of the Ngare Nairobi River amid stands of yellow-barked acacias. Accommodation rates include US$45 per person per night conservancy fees.

Shu'mata Camp   TENTED CAMP **$$$**
(www.shumatacamp.de; s/d full board US$735/ 1270) By the same people who brought you Hatari Lodge (p170) in Arusha National Park, this permanent tented camp has Kilimanjaro at its back and sweeping, big-sky views down into the Amboseli ecosystem of southern Kenya. The camp's decor is modelled on Hemingway's love for a classic safari camp blended with Maasai colours, and the sense of luxury and blissful isolation make this a fabulous experience.

Combined packages with their Arusha National Park property are possible.

ℹ Getting There & Away

There is no public transport to either Olpopongi or the Kilimanjaro Conservancy, although both can arrange pick-ups from Moshi and elsewhere (for a fee, of course).

If driving, turn off the Arusha–Moshi highway at Boma Ng'ombe (23km west of Moshi). Continue 27km along a mostly sealed road to Sanya Juu, from where a poorly signposted track continues 25km further to Olpopongi. For the conservancy and Ndarakwai Ranch, follow the directions for Olpopongi; the Ndarakwai turn-off is signposted a few kilometres before it.

Central Tanzania

Best for Culture

➡ Kondoa Rock-Art Sites (p214)

➡ Cultural Tourism Programs (p217)

➡ Katesh's *mnada* (market) (p217)

Best for Nature

➡ Kondoa Rock-Art Sites (p214)

➡ Mt Hanang (p217)

➡ Lake Singidani (p218)

Why Go?

Central Tanzania lies well off most tourist itineraries and that's just the way we like it. Exceptional and enigmatic, the Unesco World Heritage–listed Kondoa Rock-Art Sites, scattered across remote hills along the Rift Valley Escarpment, are the region's premier attraction. Not far away, Mt Hanang soars well over 3000m and is a worthy climb, both for its own sake and for the chance to summit all on your own. Both attractions also serve as gateways to the world of the colourful Barabaig and other tribes whose traditional lifestyles remain little touched by the modern world.

And then there's Dodoma, Tanzania's legislative capital, an intriguing relic of nationalist ambition with interesting architecture and the region's best facilities. Travel here isn't always easy – transport and accommodation can be a little rough around the edges – but it's a window into a Tanzania very few visitors ever get to see.

When to Go
Dodoma

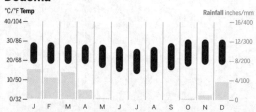

Apr–Nov During the dry season it's dusty, but temperatures are refreshingly cool.

Dec–Mar During the rainy season many roads are difficult to travel.

Apr–Aug Flamingos reside in some lakes.

Dodoma

POP 410,960

Dodoma was a nice idea at the time. Like all custom-built capitals – think Abuja or Yamoussoukro in Africa, Brasilia or Canberra elsewhere – Dodoma never really caught on and lacks a certain authenticity and the atmosphere that goes with it. Although the town was located along the old caravan route connecting Lake Tanganyika and Central Africa with the sea, Dodoma was of little consequence until 1973 when it was named Tanzania's official capital.

According to the original plan, the entire government was to move to Dodoma by the mid-1980s and its population was to live in smaller independent communities set up along the lines of Nyerere's *ujamaa* (familyhood) program. The plans proved

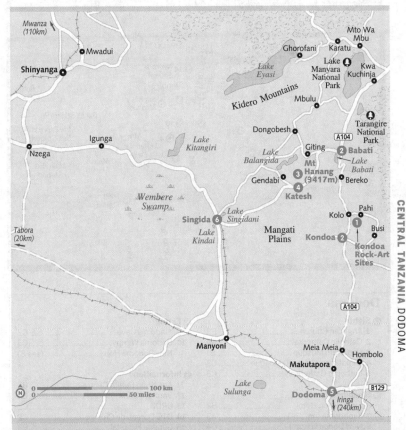

Central Tanzania Highlights

1 Visiting a mysterious Unesco World Heritage–listed attraction and having it all to yourself at the **Kondoa Rock-Art Sites** (p214).

2 Getting to know the Barabaig, Sandawe and other traditional tribes of Central Tanzania on a cultural tour out of **Babati** (p216) or **Kondoa** (p214).

3 Summiting (and sleeping atop overnight) Tanzania's seldom-climbed fourth-highest peak, **Mt Hanang** (p217).

4 Experiencing a colourful *mnada* (market), especially the one at **Katesh** (p217).

5 Admiring the religious and political architecture of **Dodoma** (p211).

6 Relishing travel completely off the beaten path in **Singida** (p218).

Dodoma

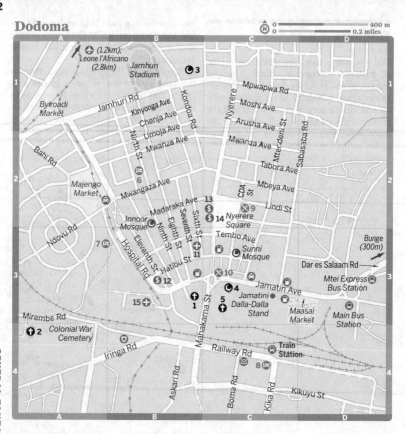

Dodoma

⊙ Sights
1 Anglican Church............................... B3
2 Catholic Cathedral........................... A4
3 Gaddhaffi Mosque B1
4 Jamatkhana (Ismaili) Mosque C3
5 Lutheran Cathedral C3

🛏 Sleeping
6 Kidia Vision Hotel............................ B2
7 Kilondoma Inn A3
8 New Dodoma Hotel C4

✕ Eating
9 Aladdin's Cave C2
10 Dodoma Wimpy C3
New Dodoma Hotel .... (see 8)

ℹ Information
11 Aga Khan Health Centre.................... B3
12 Barclays Bank B3
13 CRDB... C2
14 DTC Bureau de Change C2
15 General Hospital B3

unrealistic for a variety of reasons and although the legislature meets here, Dar es Salaam remains the unrivalled economic and political centre.

Though there has been slow growth over the years, its grandiose street layout and the imposing architecture of many church and government buildings sharply contrasting with the slow-paced reality of daily life, makes Dodoma feel as though it's dressed in clothes that are several sizes too big.

Because Dodoma has so many government buildings, be careful taking photos.

◉ Sights

Anglican Church   CHURCH
(Hospital Rd) In an interesting swapping of styles, the domed Anglican church in the town centre looks like something straight out of the Middle East.

Jamatkhana (Ismaili) Mosque   MOSQUE
(Cnr Mahakama St & Jamatin Ave) This mosque sits across the road from the Anglican Church. Built in 1954 and used exclusively by Dodoma's Indian community, it has a distinctly British neoclassical design.

Lutheran Cathedral   CHURCH
(Mahakama St) Next door to the Jamatkhana (Ismaili) Mosque, the Lutheran Cathedral is Dodoma's finest example of modernist architecture.

Catholic Cathedral   CHURCH
(Mirembe Rd) West of the centre, the enormous Catholic cathedral has Roman-style mosaics showing some saints, including the Ugandan Martyrs.

Gaddhaffi Mosque   MOSQUE
(Jamhuri Rd) Funded by the toppled Libyan dictator and opened in 2010, the pink Gaddhaffi Mosque north of the centre is one of East Africa's largest mosques. It can hold 4500 worshippers.

Bunge   NOTABLE BUILDING
(Dar es Salaam Rd) The home of Tanzania's parliament is an African-influenced round building. It's only open to visitors during sessions (bring your passport), but well worth a look from the outside at other times. Photography is strictly prohibited.

⊨ Sleeping

Water supplies are erratic, so be prepared for bucket baths at the cheapest hotels. Also, hotels fill up fast whenever parliament is in session, so you may need to try several before finding a room.

Kilondoma Inn   GUESTHOUSE $
(✐0745 477399; www.kilondoma.blogspot.com; off Ndovu Rd; d Tsh20,000; P❋🛜) We're not sure how this new place can offer so much (rooms have air-conditioning, cable TV, fans and hot water) for so little. Even if the price rises a bit it would still be one of the best-value properties in Dodoma. Double beds are just barely big enough for two.

Kidia Vision Hotel   HOTEL $
(✐0784 210766; Ninth St; d Tsh30,000-45,000, ste Tsh70,000-80,000; P🛜) Well-managed and, unlike most other hotels in its class, well maintained, this is a very solid choice at this level. Rooms are comfy and clean, though you don't get much extra as the price rises.

New Dodoma Hotel   HOTEL $$
(✐026-232 1641; www.newdodomahotel.com; Railway Rd; s/d with fan US$50/70, with air-con from US$70/95; P❋@🛜⊠) The former Railway Hotel's flower-filled courtyard is a lovely oasis and the rooms have some style. The suites face the main street and are noisier than the standard rooms. There's a gym, good dining and a not-so-clean swimming pool.

✕ Eating

Aladdin's Cave   SWEETS, EUROPEAN $
(CDA St; snacks from Tsh350, meals Tsh2500-8000; ⊙9.30am-1pm daily & 3.30-5.30pm Tue-Sat; ✐) Dodoma's version of an old-fashioned candy store and soda fountain. It also serves veggie burgers and pizzas.

Dodoma Wimpy   FAST FOOD $
(Jamatin Ave; snacks from Tsh350, mains Tsh2000-5000; ⊙7am-10pm) Not a real Wimpy, but it does have greasy burgers along with the usual assortment of local meals and snacks, most of them of Indian origin like *bhaji* and chicken *biryani*.

★ Leone l'Africano   ITALIAN $$
(✐0754 073573, 0788 629797; Mlimwa Rd; meals Tsh8500-14,000; ⊙5-10pm Tue-Fri, noon-3pm & 5-10pm Sat & Sun) Tasty Italian food, including one of Tanzania's better pizzas, served in the shadow of Lion Rock. You can try local wines or play it safe with a European vintage. There's a playground and a 12-hole minigolf course.

New Dodoma Hotel   INTERNATIONAL $$
(Railway Rd; meals Tsh5000-16,000; ⊙7am-10pm) The menu here goes global with choices such as pizza, fish and chips, *dhal tadka* and fajitas. The Indian and local dishes are the most reliable and the outdoor Barbeque Village grills up all kinds of meat at dinnertime. The Chinese-owned restaurant within the hotel is a lucky dip, since dishes can be both good and awful.

CENTRAL TANZANIA DODOMA

TANZANIA'S WINE INDUSTRY

Dodoma is the centre of Tanzania's tiny wine industry, originally started by Italian missionaries in the early 20th century. Most of what is produced is for church use, and the commercially available vintage won't win awards any time soon, but you can sample it at restaurants around town and various small grocery stores sell it. If you're willing to make a day of it, you can visit the vineyards at the Italian-owned **Cetawico** (Central Tanzania Wine Company; ☑ 0786 799010; www.cetawico.com), which bottled its first product in 2005 and is now one of Dodoma's most successful vintners. It's 50km northeast of Dodoma at Hombolo.

---

❶ Information

Aga Khan Health Centre (☑ 026-232 1789; Sixth St; ☺ 8am-8pm Mon-Sat) First destination for illnesses. Has a good pharmacy.

Dodoma Guide (www.dodoma-guide.com) Moderately useful privately run website.

General Hospital (Hospital Rd; ☺ 24hr)

❶ Getting There & Away

AIR

The airport is just north of the city centre (Tsh4000 in a taxi).

Flightlink (☑ 0787 845200, 0754 972173; www.flightlinkaircharters.com) Flightlink has a daily service between Dodoma and Dar es Salaam with onward connections to Pemba, Zanzibar and Arusha.

BUS

The following bus services leave from the **main bus station** unless otherwise stated. For local destinations, use the **Jamatini dalla-dalla stand** west of the bus stand.

Arusha and Moshi Mtei Express has the best buses to Arusha (Ts25,000, 11 hours) and Moshi (Tsh28,000, 12 to 14 hours). All leave at 6am.

Dar es Salaam Shabiby has 'full luxury' (four-across seating and toilets) buses (Tsh24,000, six to seven hours) that leave from its own terminal across the roundabout from the main bus terminal. Other buses (Tsh12,000 to Tsh20,000) depart Dodoma frequently from 6am to 1pm. Buses that started their trip to Dar in Mwanza pass through in the afternoon and you can usually get a seat.

Iringa The route to Iringa (Tsh12,000, four hours) is now around three-quarters paved.

Kondoa Buses (Tsh7000, three hours) depart 6am, 6.30am, 10.30am and noon: they use a section of the old Great North Rd connecting Cape Town and Cairo. If you take the morning bus you may be able to get a connection to Babati the same day.

Mwanza Buses (Tsh36,000, eight hours) via Singida (Tsh16,000, three hours) leave Dodoma between 6am and 7.30am, and Mwanza-bound buses from Dar es Salaam pass through around midday.

Kondoa Rock-Art Sites

The district of Kondoa, especially around the tiny village of Kolo, lies at the centre of one of the most impressive collections of ancient rock art on the African continent. It's also one of Tanzania's least-known and most underrated attractions. If you can tolerate a bit of rugged travel, this is an intriguing and worthwhile detour.

To visit independently, stop at the **Antiquities Department** (☑ 0752 575096; ☺ 7.30am-6pm) office along Kolo's main road to arrange a permit (per adult/child Tsh27,000/13,000) and mandatory guide (free, but tips expected), some of whom speak English. There's a good little museum here covering not only archaeology, but also the culture of the Irangi people.

⊙ Sights

There are 186 known sites (and surely many more), of which only a portion have been properly documented. If you base yourself in Kolo or Kondoa you can comfortably see three of the best sites in a day, four if you really rush.

Fenga Rock-Art Complex ROCK ART
One of the most impressive of the Kondoa rock-art sites is the excellent Fenga complex, whose dominant feature is a painting of people who appear to be trapping an elephant. It's around 20km north of Kolo and just a bit off the Arusha–Dodoma Rd, followed by a hilly 1km walk.

Thawi Rock-Art Site ROCK ART
The most varied, and thus best overall collection of rock paintings in the Kondoa area,

is at Thawi, about 15km northwest of Kolo and reachable only by 4WD.

Kolo Rock-Art Site
ROCK ART

The most visited, though not the best, the Kolo sites (B1, B2 and B3) are 9km east of Kolo village and a 4WD is required. You'll need to climb a steep hill at the end of the road to see them. The most interesting figures here are humans with what are either wild hairstyles or masks.

Pahi Rock-Art Site
ROCK ART

East of the Kolo sites, on the back side of the same mountain east of Kolo, are the mostly white (ie modern) Pahi sites. These can be reached by 2WD vehicles. Buses from Arusha and Babati going to Busi pass the nearby village of Pahi.

 Tours

While very few safari operators have Kondoa on their itineraries, some will tack a day in Kondoa onto their longer safaris. The Kondoa Irangi Cultural Tourism Program (p217) in Kondoa regularly brings people here (US$60 per person, minimum two people).

🛏 Sleeping & Eating

Kolo has some tea rooms serving chapati, beans and rice, and sometimes chicken.

Amarula Campsite
CAMPGROUND $

(☑0754 672256; www.racctz.org; camping with own/hired tent US$10/20) This work in progress, 6km east of Kolo on the road to Pahi, has beautiful scenery and simple facilities.

Mary Leakey Campsite
CAMPGROUND $

(camping Tsh7500) Managed by the Department of Antiquities, there's nothing here but quiet isolation and year-round water. It's along the Kolo (Hembe) River bed halfway to the Kolo Sites.

New Planet
GUESTHOUSE $

(☑0787 907915; s/d Tsh18,000/23,000; Ⓟ) In Kondoa, about a five-minute walk north of the bus stand, this clean and quiet place is the best the district has to offer. Rooms are fairly large and have fans and TV; buckets of hot water are available on request. Meals at the restaurant hidden in the back are reasonable.

KONDOA ROCK ART

Although several archaeologists, most prominently Mary Leakey, have studied these sites, the history of most remains shrouded in mystery, with little known about either their artists or even their age. Some sites are still used by local rainmakers and medicine men.

Rock art experts divide the Kondoa paintings into two distinct styles or eras. The oldest are the so-called Red Paintings, which are also the most sophisticated. Some experts maintain that the oldest paintings date back around 7000 years, perhaps even older. The Red Paintings (often ochre or orange) usually contain stylised depictions of humans, sometimes hunting with bows and arrows or dancing and playing musical instruments, while many are drawn with skirts, strange hairstyles and body decoration. Large animals, notably giraffes and antelopes, are also common, and geometric shapes also appear.

The Red Paintings are thought to have been made by the Sandawe, who are distantly related linguistically to South Africa's San, a group also renowned for its rock art, or the Hadza people, who now live around Lake Eyasi in northern Tanzania. Whoever they were, the makers sometimes used hands and fingers, but also brushes made of reeds or sticks. Some of the colours were probably made by mixing various pigments with animal fat to form crayons.

The second category is known as the Late White Paintings. Far simpler (even crude) when compared to the Red Paintings, the Late White Paintings mostly date from the last 1500 years and were painted by Bantu-speaking peoples who migrated into the area. The better ones resemble wild or mythical animals, human figures and patterns using dots, circles and rectangles, but many of these more recent works take on unintelligible form, largely because most were painted using fingers rather than brushes.

For more information, contact the Trust for African Rock Art (www.africanrock-art.org) or pick up a copy of the excellent *African Rock Art* by David Coulson and Alec Campbell.

ℹ️ Information

Kondoa has internet access, but no banking services for travellers.

ℹ️ Getting There & Away

Kolo is 80km south of Babati. Buses to Kolo (Tsh7500, 3½ hours) depart Babati at 7am and 8.30am. From Arusha, Mtei Express buses to Kondoa, leaving at 6am, pass Kolo (Tsh11,500, 6½ hours). The last bus north from Kondoa leaves at 9am. There are only buses to Dodoma (Tsh8500, three hours) from Kondoa, not Kolo. They leave at 6am, 10am and 12.30pm. Catching a bus in Kondoa means you'll get a seat; wait for it to pass Kolo and you'll need to stand.

It could be possible to visit as a day trip from Babati (or as a stop en route to Dodoma) using public transport if you're willing to hitchhike after visiting the Kolo sites; there are *usually* some trucks travelling this road in the afternoon.

It is possible to hire motorcyles in Kolo and these can reach all the sites detailed earlier, but you'll have to get off and walk up some hills. Hiring motorcycles is very expensive if done through the Antiquities Department (Tsh25,000 just to the Kolo sites, for example), but you can try to get a better price with locals or hire a vehicle in Kondoa, 25km south of Kolo.

Babati

POP 93,110

The dusty market town of Babati, about 175km southwest of Arusha in a fertile spot along the edge of the Rift Valley Escarpment, has a frontier feel. It's only notable as a jumping-off point for Mt Hanang, 75km southwest. Stretching south from the city is the tranquil Lake Babati, fringed by tall reeds and home to hippos and water birds. If you're here on the 17th of the month, don't miss Babati's monthly mnada (market) about 5km south of town.

🛏️ Sleeping & Eating

There are dozens of cheap and largely indistinguishable guesthouses, as well as a couple of small grocery stores scattered around town.

Kahembe's Modern
Guest House
GUESTHOUSE $

(☑ 0784 397477; www.kahembeculturalsafaris. com; Sokoine Rd; s/d Tsh25,000/30,000; 🛜) Home of Kahembe's Culture & Wildlife Safaris, this friendly place just northwest of the bus stand has decent twin- and double-bedded rooms with TVs and reliable hot-water showers. Their full breakfast, complete with sausages, cornflakes, fruit, toast and eggs, is included in the price, not to mention a great way to start the day.

White Rose Lodge
GUESTHOUSE $

(☑ 0784 392577; www.manyarawhiterose.blogspot. com; Ziwani Rd; d Tsh25,000; 🅿️🛜) A good-value spot set somewhat inconveniently (unless you're driving) off the Singida Rd south of town. Rooms are similar in standard to other Babati cheapies, only much newer.

Royal Beach Hotel
CAMPGROUND, BANDAS $

(☑ 0785 125070; camping with own/hired tent Tsh15,000/18,000, bandas Tsh35,000; 🅿️) On a peninsula in Lake Babati, the Royal Beach has an attractive bar and restaurant area, and a wood, stone and thatch disco (Friday and Saturday) that would make Gilligan proud. Boat trips to see hippos can be arranged. The rock *bandas* are set away from the lake with no views and are quite ordinary inside. It's 3km south of Babati.

Ango Bar & Restaurant
TANZANIAN $

(Arusha–Dodoma Rd; buffet breakfast Tsh6000, lunch or dinner Tsh8500; ⊗ 7am-9.30pm) Behind a petrol station near the bus stand, this unexpectedly colourful place offers local fare, always including a few veggie dishes.

ℹ️ Information

There are slowish internet connections at a couple of well-signposted places around town. **NBC** (Arusha–Dodoma Rd) Changes cash and has an ATM.

ℹ️ Getting There & Away

The Babati–Dodoma Rd is still rough in parts, but quite passable. For the final section before Dodoma you need to go in a security convoy if travelling after 4pm.

If travelling from Babati to Arusha (Tsh9000, four to five hours), the first departures in both directions are at 5.30am and the last leave at 4pm, though dalla-dallas go until 6pm. Other destinations include Kondoa (Tsh8500, 3½ hours), Mwanza (Tsh29,000 to Tsh35,000, 10 hours) and Singida (Tsh8500, four hours, last departure from Babati around 10am).

For Mto wa Mbu, catch an Arusha bus and change in Makuyuni. There's no direct bus to Dodoma (Tsh17,000) although you may be sold a Dodoma ticket; you'll have to change at Kondoa, although it's usually faster to travel on the paved road via Singida.

CULTURAL TOURISM IN CENTRAL TANZANIA

Babati and Kondoa districts are home to a colourful array of tribes, many of whom have changed their lifestyle little over the past century. Many villages welcome visitors, but, unlike those around Arusha, none are geared towards tourism. The most famous (and most visited) tribe is the Barabaig, who still follow a traditional semi-nomadic lifestyle and are recognisable by the goatskin garments still worn daily by many women. Unrelated to the tribes around them, the Sandawe are one of the oldest peoples of Tanzania and they may have been the ones who painted the early rock art around Kondoa. They speak a click language and still hunt with bow and arrow.

Kahembe's Culture & Wildlife Safaris (☑0784 397477; www.kahembeculturalsafaris. com; Sokoine Rd) In Babati, this reliable and knowledgeable outfit has been offering cultural tours in the region since 1992. Besides village visits, it's the main operator organising Mt Hanang climbs.

Kondoa Irangi Cultural Tourism Program (☑0784 948858; www.tanzaniacultural tours.com) The Kondoa Rock-Art Sites are the bread and butter of this company in Kondoa town, but director Moshi Changai also leads Barabaig, Sandawe and Irangi village visits by bicycle or car. Overnight stays in local homes are possible.

Mt Hanang

One of Tanzania's most rewarding mountain treks is also one of its least known. The volcanic Mt Hanang (3417m), Tanzania's fourth-highest mountain, rises steeply above the surrounding plains between Babati and Singida and you'll likely be the only climber on the satisfying trek to the summit.

The principal path to the top is the **Jorodom Route**, which begins in the town of Katesh on the mountain's southern side and *can* be done in one long day (usually 10 hours) with an additional day necessary for making arrangements, although overnighting at the top is more enjoyable. While a guide isn't strictly essential, the trail can be hard to follow so we definitely recommend hiring one. This is best arranged through Kahembe's Cultural & Wildlife Safaris in Babati. With a group of two, the climb costs US$128 per person, including food, guide, lodging in Katesh the nights before and after the climb, and the US$30 per person forest reserve fee and Tsh2800 per person village fee. Transport is extra.

If you're trekking independently, register and pay at the **forest cachement office** (☑0784 456590) in room 15 of the Katesh municipality building (Idara ya Mkuu wa Wilaya) on the hill above Katesh. It's best to call ahead since the staff is sometimes out of the office. Guides can be hired here for Tsh12,000 per day, but you'll be responsible for your own food and water. Don't go with any freelancers who hang around Katesh (many of whom will say they're with Kahembe's). Some are legit, but there have been instances of these guides taking climbers part way up the mountain and then robbing them.

Regardless of how you do the trip, carry plenty of water since there's none to be found during the climb.

Katesh is also known for its large **mnada** held on the 9th, 10th and 28th of each month. Maasai, Barabaig, Iraqw and other peoples from a wide surrounding area converge to buy and sell cattle and trade their wares.

🛏 Sleeping

Summit Hotel GUESTHOUSE $
(☑0787 242424; r from Tsh20,000; ℗) This bright-green place up the hill just east of the municipality office is Katesh's best lodging, and the most convenient for climbing Mt Hanang.

Colt Guesthouse GUESTHOUSE $
(☑027-253 0030; s/d Tsh12,000/15,000, without bathroom Tsh6000/8000; ℗) This older place northwest of the bus stand by the market is simple but clean and provides hot-water buckets on request.

ℹ Getting There & Away

Buses between Singida (Tsh6500, 1½ hours) and Babati (Tsh7000, 2½ hours), which includes all Arusha–Mwanza buses, pass through Katesh all morning. After lunch, you'll probably need to hitch.

Singida

POP 150,380

There's no compelling reason to do more than pass through Singida en route between Mwanza and Dodoma, but there is a pretty lake and a dusty museum if you find yourself with an hour or two to kill.

◉ Sights

Lake Singidani LAKE
Lake Singidani is one of three saline lakes just west of town. With green waters and plenty of rocky spots along the shore it's quite beautiful, even when it's completely dried up, which happens during some dry seasons. The lake attracts plenty of water birds, including pelicans and sometimes flamingos. Singidani begins 600m past the post office.

Regional Museum MUSEUM
(Makumbusho ya Mkoa; ⊙9am-5pm) FREE This museum at the Open University of Tanzania is mostly lacking labels, but the little collection of weapons, jewellery and other items from the region's tribes is quite good.

🛏 Sleeping & Eating

Lutheran Centre Lodging GUESTHOUSE $
(☑026-250 2936; Boma Rd; r from Tsh15,000, with shared bathroom Tsh10,000; @) With cable TV and hot water, this small, quiet place, part of a complex with a restaurant and internet cafe, is the best value in town.

Stanley Motel Annex HOTEL $$
(☑0754 476785; www.stanleygroupofhotels.com; camping US$5, s/d US$15/20) Spread over three properties, this well-run place has pretensions to grandeur, but is, in the end, a fairly simple establishment that's good value for money. Go for the Stanley Annex, which was built in 2013.

The restaurant, at the older version of the hotel, one street down from the rocky hill, offers its unique take on various world cuisines, including chow mein, moussaka, Hawaiian fish (made with peanut butter, pineapple and curry) and pizza.

Razaki Munch Corner TANZANIAN $
(meals Tsh2500-5500; ⊙7am-9pm Mon-Sat, to 3pm Sun) This brilliantly named restaurant has a big menu of local foods, from goat pilau to chicken and chips. It's alongside the market, just west of the Ismaili Mosque's onion-shaped minaret-clocktower.

ⓘ Information

Thanks to its status as regional capital, Singida has reasonably good infrastructure, including some internet cafes and banks (changing cash at poor rates), with ATMs along Boma Rd (aka Sokoine Rd and Arusha Rd).

ⓘ Getting There & Away

Singida's bus stand is 2.5km outside of town (Tsh3000 in a taxi). Buses depart to Arusha (Tsh15,000, seven hours, between 6am and 9am) and Mwanza (Tsh15,000, five hours, between 6am and 8am); Mtei Express is the best company to Arusha. Buses running between Arusha and Mwanza arrive in Singida later in the morning, but there may not be seats available.

The Arusha-bound buses stop at Katesh (Tsh6500, 1½ hours) and Babati (Tsh8500, four hours). There are also several buses and coastals going to Dodoma (Tsh16,000, three hours) throughout the morning and two buses, originating in Arusha, going to Tabora (Tsh21,000, six hours).

Lake Victoria

Best for Culture

➜ Ukerewe Island (p229)
➜ Kiroyera Tours (p224)
➜ Sukuma Museum (p229)
➜ Musira Island (p232)

Best for Nature

➜ Rubondo Island National Park (p230)
➜ Jiwe Kuu (p223)
➜ Lukuba Island (p221)

Why Go?

Tanzania's half of Africa's largest lake sees few visitors, but the region holds many attractions for those with a bent for the offbeat and a desire to immerse themselves in the rhythms of local life beyond the tourist trail. The cities of Musoma and Bukoba have a quiet waterside charm while most villagers on Ukerewe Island follow a subsistence lifestyle with little connection to the world beyond the shore.

Mwanza, Tanzania's second-largest city, is appealing in its own way and it's the perfect launching pad for a Serengeti–Lake Natron–Ngorongoro loop. And if you add the forest of idyllic Rubondo Island National Park, deep in the lake's southwest reaches, you will have a well-rounded safari experience.

If you have the time you can be sure to leave this little corner of Tanzania with new experiences and wonderful memories.

When to Go
Mwanza

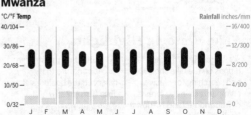

Jun Move with the groove at the Bulabo Dance Festival near Mwanza.

Jun–Sep During dry season there are clear days and high temperatures.

Dec This is the best time to catch and eat *senene* (grasshoppers).

Musoma

Little Musoma, capital of the Mara region, sits serenely on a Lake Victoria peninsula with both sunrise and sunset views over the water. It's one of those African towns with nothing special on offer other than an inexplicable appeal.

There are banks and internet cafes along and just off Mukendo Rd.

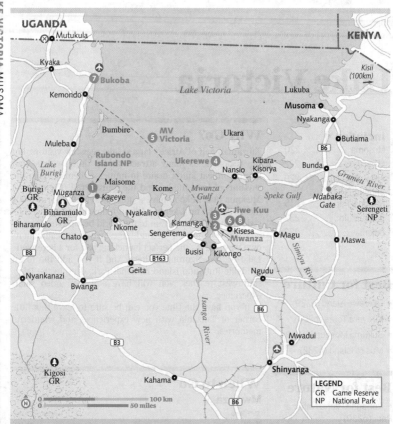

Lake Victoria Highlights

❶ Watching birds and hippos on the lake shore, and searching for elusive chimpanzees in the forests of **Rubondo Island National Park** (p230).

❷ Soaking up the sights, sounds and smells as you stroll Temple St and Makoroboi in central **Mwanza** (p222).

❸ Pondering the strange forces of nature that balanced the boulders at **Jiwe Kuu** (p223).

❹ Biking through the villages and farms of **Ukerewe** (p229).

❺ Crossing the lake between Mwanza and Bukoba on the historic **MV Victoria** (p236).

❻ Watching traditions defy time at the **Bulabo Dance Festival** at the Sukuma Museum (p229).

❼ Exploring the Haya heartland in the seldom-travelled Kagera region on a cultural tour from **Bukoba** (p232).

❽ Learning about Sukuma culture at the **Sukuma Museum** (p229).

⊙ Sights

Matvilla Beach
BEACH

The best thing to do in Musoma is visit Matvilla Beach at the tip of the peninsula (follow Mukendo Rd, Musoma's main street, north of downtown for 1.5km) with its pinky-grey granite boulders. It's prime sunset-watching-with-a-beer territory – and there are bars there to help you with that.

Mwigobero Market
MARKET

Mwigobero Market is on the city's eastern shore. Small lake boats to nearby islands and villages load and unload passengers and cargo here.

German Boma
NOTABLE BUILDING

History buffs may enjoy the tower of the old German *boma* (a fortified living compound; in colonial times, an administrative office), now part of the Musoma District Commissioner's Office. It's past the post office behind Mukendo Hill.

🛏 Sleeping

Most guesthouses are in the city centre, east of Mukendo Rd.

★ Tembo Beach Club
CAMPGROUND, GUESTHOUSE $

(☑028-262 2887; camping Tsh15,000, r Tsh45,000; P🛜) It has a sociable bar-restaurant (mains Tsh3000 to Tsh5000) and a reasonable camping area that's often busy with the clients of overland truck tours. Best of all, it has some recently tarted-up rooms with African art on the walls. They are far enough from the bar that you can be lulled to sleep by waves rather than kept awake by music.

Mlima Mukendo Hotel
HOTEL $

(☑0768 065003; Mukendo Rd; s/d Tsh20,000/30,000) A bright green tower of a hotel on the main road (take a room at the back). It offers the best town-centre accommodation with smart, well cared for rooms with wardrobes, desks and big bathrooms.

King's Sport Lodge
GUESTHOUSE $

(☑028-262 0531; Kusaga St; r without breakfast Tsh16,000) Near Mwigobero Market, this simple place has spotless rooms, a quiet town-centre location and low prices, making it an easy choice for backpackers. The rooms have school desks instead of normal tables.

WORTH A TRIP

LUKUBA ISLAND LODGE RESORT

Lukuba Island Lodge Resort (☑Arusha 027-254 8840; www.anasasafari.com; s/d full board incl transfer from Musoma US$380/690; 🌊) An awesome island getaway, this lovely remote resort has a laid-back ambience and is highly recommended. There are five cosy stone-and-thatch bungalows and three safari tents with outdoor baths along the pretty beach. Nearby is an enormous flat-topped boulder, perfect for sunset watching. It's 17km from Musoma and one hour by boat. Advance bookings are required.

Afrilux Hotel
HOTEL $

(☑028-262 0031; Mwigobero Rd; s/d Tsh35,000/45,000; P🌀🛜) Something of a Musoma institution, the Afrilux has decent hot showers, helpful staff, good wi-fi and a relaxed courtyard bar-restaurant. On the negative side there's zero sound insulation in the rooms.

Matvilla Beach & Lodge
CAMPGROUND, BUNGALOW $$

(http://matvillabeach.co.tz; Matvilla Beach; camping Tsh10,000, bungalows s/d US$40/50; P🛜) Out at the tip of the peninsula, 1.5km from the centre, this is a gorgeous multipurpose spot amid the rocks. There are hot showers for campers and new stone bungalows that are calm, quiet and blend into giant, granite boulders.

There's a very popular bar-restaurant making it noisy for campers. There are also two beaches; one has a volleyball net and sun loungers.

New Peninsula Hotel
HOTEL $$

(☑0756 505081; Mwisenge Rd; r Tsh45,000-75,000, ste Tsh100,000; P🌀🛜🌊) The long-standing Peninsula, about 1.5km from the town centre, has faded but reasonable rooms. The best feature is a somewhat quieter setting than the other more central hotels in this category.

There is a beach but it is filthy and you cannot swim in it due to the threat of bilharzia. There is also a pool up the road, but at the time of research it was 'out of order' (in other words, empty).

MWALIMU JULIUS K NYERERE MUSEUM

Mwalimu Julius K Nyerere Museum (Butiama; admission Tsh8000; ⊙9am-5pm) Julius Nyerere, the first President of Tanzania, was born in the otherwise insignificant little town of Butiama. This small museum inside the family compound celebrates his life and work. It contains a few stools, shields and other gifts he was given. Boxes of Nyerere's personal effects, including his diaries, a handwritten Swahili translation of part of Plato's Republic and collections of his poetry are also here. Although these are not on display, you can ask the staff to see them.

In the family compound next to the museum you can see his two homes (admission Tsh1000; 8am to 6pm), still occupied by his wife and son; his father's house; and the graves of Nyerere and his parents. His mother's house, where he was born, along with the houses of his father's 21 other wives no longer exist.

The museum itself is only really worth a visit for dedicated Nyerere fans but the journey to the town and the interest your presence will generate is fun.

There are frequent dalla-dallas (pick-up trucks or minibuses) to Butiama (Tsh3000, one hour) from Musoma.

✖ Eating & Drinking

Matvilla Beach & Lodge　　TANZANIAN $
(meals Tsh5000-7000) With its lakeside setting, Matvilla Beach is everyone's favourite place for fried fish or chicken and a beer. Staff will arrange taxis to take you back to town. There are no set opening hours – according to staff it's open all the time.

Afrilux Hotel　　TANZANIAN, EUROPEAN $
(Mwigobero Rd; meals Tsh5000-10,000; ⊙7am-11pm) The restaurant at this four-storey building with round windows serves the usual hotel dishes including grilled tilapia (Nile perch), vegetable curry and something resembling pizza. It's a good social place to eat.

Mara Dishes　　BUFFET $
(Kivukani St; buffet Tsh5000; ⊙9am-10pm) Mara Dishes, east of CRDB bank, has a relatively large buffet and masses of locals piling in for a good feed.

Free Park Bar　　BAR
(Mukendo Rd; meals Tsh4000-5000; ⊙10am-11pm) This humble beer garden of sorts is one of the most popular and most sociable drinking spots in town.

ⓘ Getting There & Away

BUS
The bus terminal is 6km out of town at Bweri, though booking offices remain in the town centre. Dalla-dallas (pick-up trucks or minibuses; Tsh4000; 20 minutes) go frequently to/from the city centre and a taxi costs Tsh10,000. Frequent buses connect Musoma and Mwanza (Tsh8000, four hours). Mohammed Trans has good service (5am and 1pm) and its buses depart from its ticket office east of CRDB bank. To get to Ukerewe Island, take a dalla-dalla to Bunda (Tsh3000, between 5.30am and 4pm, one hour) and from there take a bus or dalla dalla to Naniso (the 'capital' of the island) for Tsh6000. Between Coast Line, Kimotco and Manko there's a direct bus to Arusha daily (Tsh35,000, 11 to 12 hours) at 6am, passing through Serengeti National Park (using Ikoma Gate) and Ngorongoro Conservation Area. However, you have to pay an exorbitant $110 in park fees to ride this route. Better to fly.

Mwanza

POP 706,500

Tanzania's second-largest city, and the lake region's economic heart, Mwanza is set on Lake Victoria's shore, surrounded by hills strewn with enormous boulders. In addition to being notable for its strong Indian influences, Mwanza is a major industrial centre and busy port. Yet, despite its rapidly rising skyline, Mwanza manages to retain a casual feel. In addition to being a stop on the way to Rubondo Island National Park, Mwanza is a great starting or finishing point for safaris through Ngorongoro and the Serengeti, ideally as a loop by adding Lake Natron.

◉ Sights

Rock City

The surrounding hills and boulders give Mwanza its 'Rock City' nickname and make it one of Africa's most beautiful cities.

Bismarck Rock
LANDMARK

Mwanza's icon, Bismarck Rock, is a precariously balanced boulder atop the lovely jumble of rocks in the lake next to the Kamanga ferry pier. The little park here is a brilliant sunset spot.

Jiwe Kuu
LANDMARK

One of the more interesting rock formations around Mwanza is Jiwe Kuu (Big Rock), which some people call the Dancing Rocks. Many round boulders sit atop this rocky outcrop north of town and have managed to last eons without rolling off. Dalla-dallas to Bwiru run west down Nyerere Rd; their final stop leaves you within a 1.5km walk.

Robert Koch Hill
HILL

Smack in the city centre is Robert Koch Hill, with an attractively decrepit German-built mansion at the top. Several Maasai now live here, but if you introduce yourself and give them a small donation (Tsh5000 should be okay), you can look around. To get here, push through the bustling market, and take the trail through the beer garden and past all the piles of rubbish. You shouldn't go up there late in the day and single women shouldn't go alone.

Saa Nane National Park
PARK

(028-254 1819; office on Capri Point; adult/child US$30/15; 6.30am-6.30pm, last entry 5pm) The rocky island 500m off Capri Point is Saa Nane National Park. Even though it's only 0.76 sq km and home to only monkeys and impalas, visiting costs more than some huge wildlife-filled national parks. With 70 bird species it does make a worthwhile short excursion for birders.

In addition to the entry fees add US$35 for the return boat trip (which can seat 20). You can check out the old bones and some rather sorry looking stuffed animals in the office for free.

Markets & Temples

Central Mwanza along Temple St and west to Station Rd has an oriental feel due to its many temples (both Hindu and Sikh) and mosques, as well as Indian trading houses lining the streets. The street-side market and ambience continue west through the Makoroboi area, where the namesake scrap-metal workshop is hidden away in the rocks. Kerosene lamps (*makoroboi* in Swahili), ladles and other household goods are fashioned from old cans and other trash.

East of Temple St, the huge and confusing Central Market is fun to explore.

Mwaloni Market
MARKET

Mwaloni Market, under the roof with the giant Balimi ad, is quite a spectacle. The city's main fish market also has lots of fruits and vegetables, most shipped in on small boats from surrounding villages, and there are almost as many marabou storks as vendors. Photography is prohibited because some scenes in the controversial documentary film *Darwin's Nightmare* (2004) were shot here.

Maasai Market
MARKET

Mwanza has a Maasai Market, with a couple of dozen Maasai selling beaded jewellery and medicines on both sides of the footbridge.

Tours

Several travel agencies in town hire 4WDs and can organise complete safaris to Serengeti and Rubondo Island national parks. While Mwanza's operators are not as good as the best agencies in Arusha, we're unaware of any in town that will blatantly rip you off. It's not easy to meet other travellers in Mwanza, but you can ask the agencies whether they have other clients interested in combining groups to save money, or try posting a notice at Kuleana Pizzeria (p227).

ℹ️ LAKE VICTORIA FACTS

➡ 69,484 sq km, about half of which is in Tanzania

➡ The world's second-largest freshwater lake by surface area after Lake Superior in North America

➡ Infested with bilharzia in many shoreline areas (swimming isn't recommended)

➡ Once home to some 500 cichlid species. Populations started to crash in the 1960s due to pollution, overfishing and the introduction of ever hungry Nile Perch. Today there are signs that the cichlid population is recovering. New species and hybrid species, perhaps better able to withstand the modern pressures placed on them, are now emerging.

Mwanza

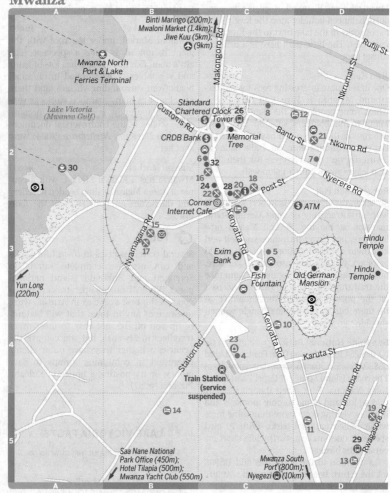

Fortes Africa SAFARIS
(☎028-250 0561; www.fortes-africa.com; Station Rd) The most upmarket, reliable and professional company. There's also a branch inside Ryan's Bay hotel.

Fourways SAFARIS
(☎028-254 0653; www.fourwaystravel.net; Kenyatta Rd) Also books plane tickets.

Kiroyera Tours SAFARIS
(☎0784 568276; www.kiroyeratours.com) Can generally beat others for car-rental rates (and the vehicles and drivers they use are recommended). There's no walk-in office.

Masumin Tours & Safaris SAFARIS
(☎028-250 0192; www.masuminsafaris.com; Kenyatta Rd) Also books plane tickets.

Serengeti Expedition SAFARIS
(☎028-254 2222; www.serengetiexpedition.com; Nkrumah Rd) One of the cheaper operators in Mwanza. Also books plane tickets.

Serengeti Passage SAFARIS
(☎028-250 0061; www.serengeti-passage.com; Uhuru St) Low-cost safari specialist.

Machemba Rd

are no mosquito nets, but the rooms are sprayed daily.

Traffic noise drifts up to the rooms, but that's common with all city-centre hotels.

Isamo Hotel
HOTEL $

(☏ 028-254 1616; Rwagasore St; r Tsh25,000-50,000; ﹟ 🛜) There's a lot of street noise seeping into the rooms here but grab a pair of ear plugs and enjoy one of the cheapest and best deals in town. The well-kept rooms are a good size and some have little balconies overlooking the chaos.

Cheaper rooms are fan only.

Kantima Hotel
HOTEL $

(☏ 0754 093048; Kenyatta Rd; r Tsh18,000-25,000; P ﹟) This cheery and friendly place has bright and clean rooms, but the hot-water bathrooms, which are very small and not all that inviting, really let the side down. Some of the rooms have maps of the world on the wall so you can plan your next adventure – or imagine being somewhere with better bathrooms.

Kishamapanda Guesthouse
GUESTHOUSE $

(☏ 0755 083218; Kishamapanda St; d with/without bathroom Tsh15,000/13,000, tw Tsh20,000) This tidy little place is down a tiny alley behind the less-appealing New Geita Lodge. It's one of the best budget places in Mwanza. The shared bathrooms have ceiling fans and Western toilets.

Mwanza Yacht Club
CAMPGROUND $

(☏ 0762 891280; Capri Point; camping Tsh10,000) This is where the big overland tourist trucks stop. It has a great lakeside location, hot showers and security.

Ryan's Bay
RESORT $$

(☏ 028-254 1702; www.ryansbay.com; Capri Point; s/d from US$110/140; P ﹟ 🛜 ☲) The flashest place in Mwanza has lake views and large, well-appointed rooms with acacia-tree murals on the walls. It's a bit resort-like but there's a great pool complex (guests only) and one of the best Indian restaurants in town (mains Tsh10,000 to Tsh17,000).

Hotel Tilapia
HOTEL $$

(☏ 0784 700500, 028-250 0517; www.hoteltilapia. com; Capri Point; s/d/ste US$100/120/150; ﹟ 🛜 ☲) The ever-popular Tilapia, on the city side of Capri Point, has a variety of rooms, most of which are dated but decent and look out at the lake. It also has rooms on a historic boat. Though they are smaller

🛏 Sleeping

Most of the very inexpensive guesthouses in Mwanza's commercial centre are by-the-hour businesses.

★ Midland Hotel
HOTEL $

(☏ 0718 431255; www.midlandhotel.com.tz; Rwagasore Rd; s Tsh50,000-60,000, d Tsh60,000-90,000; ﹟ 🛜) This eye-catching blue tower is solid all round with well-equipped rooms (free wi-fi reaches most), good service, a rooftop bar and a proper breakfast buffet. Best of all, it will sometimes discount. There

Mwanza

and a little off-kilter, their special character makes them fun.

JB Belmont Hotel   HOTEL $$

(☎028-250 5057; www.jbbelmonthotel.biz; Kenyatta Rd; s/d from US$60/80; ❋ 🖥) A smart and welcoming city-centre hotel that verges on having business suaveness. The standard rooms are very small but they've made the most of the restricted space. The beds are some of the most comfortable you'll find in western Tanzania. It's quite discreet with just a small entrance in a large mirrored tower block.

It can get noisy on a Wednesday and Saturday night, as a band plays in a hotel nearby.

Gold Crest Hotel   HOTEL $$

(☎028-250 6058; Post St; s US$95-110, d US$125-140; 🅿❋🖥🏊) A solid business-class standard in the heart of town with attractive, comfortable rooms, all with balconies. Those on upper floors facing north have postcard-quality lake views; those on the south face the car park. It's very noisy on Wednesday and Saturday nights when a band at a neighbouring hotel rocks the city till late.

Wag Hill Lodge   LODGE $$$

(☎0754 917974; www.waghill.com; s/d all-inclusive US$236/413; 🅿🏊) The intimate and beautiful Wag Hill, on a small wooded peninsula

outside Mwanza, is an excellent post-safari cool down. It has just five double bungalows with screened walls and great wooden furniture; all but one are perched on rocks for lake views. Power is all solar.

Kayaks, fishing gear and guided walks are available, and there are plenty of birds, monkeys and other local wildlife to keep you company. The half-hour transfer is by boat or 4WD depending on the conditions. There are cheaper rates for self-caterers.

To get here, head out of town on the road running past the St Augustine University and follow the dirt roads, asking for directions all the way.

✕ Eating & Drinking

Sizzlers Restaurant   INDIAN $

(Kenyatta Rd; mains Tsh8000-12,000; ⊙noon-3pm & 6-11pm) Quiet during the day, this cheap Indian joint transforms into a hive of buzzing activity in the evenings, when people grab a streetside table and tuck into the chicken tikka which sizzles on the hot coals of the outdoor barbecue. It also does a range of other Indian meals.

Mayi   TANZANIAN $$

(Rwagasore St; meals Tsh7000-20,000; ⊙7am-9pm) Pricey for local food, but the food tastes great and the portions are generous. The little thatch huts and lack of traffic noise all help to make this one of the most pleasant dining spots in Mwanza's centre. It's below the bright-green Mayi Hotel.

DVN Restaurant
TANZANIAN $

(Nyamagana Rd; meals Tsh3000-4000; ⊙7am-5pm) Excellent local is fare served fast and cheap in this church-run place with a cute, old-fashioned cafe look and feel. It's behind the post office and quite hidden with just a small sign above a tucked-away door. You might need to ask for someone to point it out.

Salma Cone
SNACKS $

(Bantu St; snacks Tsh500-1500; ⊙9am-10pm) *Sambusas* (Indian pastry snacks stuffed with curried meat or vegetable), ice cream and juice are all pleasers here but it's the smell of barbecuing meat that will draw you in for a kebab. Its plastic outdoor tables make this a fun corner to lounge during the evening.

Burger Point & Cafe
BURGERS $

(Post St; mains Tsh4500-5000; ⊙9am-5.30pm) Plastic tables and chairs, a semi-open-air environment, and loads of burgers, fried chicken and chips make this a popular local lunch stop.

Binti Maringo
INTERNATIONAL $

(Balewa Rd; meals Tsh7500, pizzas Tsh12,000; ⊙8am-8pm) 🍴 Sandwiches, pizzas and the classic meat stew get dished up in this simple open-air spot. Profits support the Kuleana Center for Children's Rights, which houses and educates street children. To get there go out of town a hundred metres. Take the first right after the dirty stream and it's 30 metres down on your right.

Hotel Tilapia
INTERNATIONAL $$

(Capri Point; meals Tsh12,000-19,000; ⊙7am-midnight; 🛜) The hub of Mwanza's expat population and a magnet to passing tourists, the restaurant of the Hotel Tilapia has an attractive terrace overlooking the lake. You can choose everything from Japanese tepanyaki to Indian or continental.

Diners
INDIAN $$

(Kenyatta Rd; meals Tsh8000-12,000; ⊙11am-3pm & 6-11pm; 🍴) This odd timewarp serves some of Mwanza's best Indian food, though Chinese decorations and menu items are holdovers from its previous incarnation as a Chinese restaurant.

New Mwanza Hotel
INDIAN, INTERNATIONAL $$

(Post St; meals Tsh10,000-12,000; ⊙12.30-3pm & 7.30-11pm; 🛜🍴) This 1st-floor, open-air restaurant has little in the way of character, but is known for producing decent Indian food. There are also Chinese, continental and Swahili dishes, including several styles of tilapia. The Jambo Stars play live and loud on Saturday nights (Tsh5000) starting at 10pm.

Yun Long
CHINESE $$

(Nasser Dr; mains Tsh15,000; ⊙noon-11pm) The food is exceptionally ordinary (unless you can convince the Chinese chefs to cook you something authentic), but we love this place anyway because of its leafy lakeside garden overlooking Bismarck Rock. If you don't feel like eating here then at least go for a sunset drink with a watery backdrop.

Kuleana Pizzeria
INTERNATIONAL $$

(☎028-256 0566; Post St; pizzas Tsh10,000-12,000; ⊙7am-9pm; 🍴) 🍴 Don't expect Italian-class food, but this is a relaxed and popular place for pizzas and snack-style food (omelettes, sandwiches and breads) with a good mix of locals and expats. The friendly owner feeds many street children.

🛍 Shopping

Bookspot
BOOKS

(Kenyatta Rd; ⊙9am-1pm & 2-5.30pm) New and used books in English, and national-park maps. Also has traditional masks and carvings on display.

ℹ Information

DANGERS & ANNOYANCES

Mwanza is generally a fairly safe city to stroll about with few touts or security issues, but we have been approached a couple of times by people claiming to be undercover police (complete with fake ID cards) asking to see our papers. Ignore them, walk away immediately and do not give them your passport or other papers.

INTERNET ACCESS

Corner Internet Cafe (Kenyatta Rd; per hour Tsh1500; ⊙8am-7pm Mon-Sat, 10am-4pm Sun) Central internet cafe.

MEDICAL SERVICES

Aga Khan Health Centre (☎028-250 2474; www.agakhanhospitals.org; Miti Mrefu St; ⊙24hr) For minor illnesses.

Bugando Hospital (☎028-250 0513; www.bugandomedicalcentre.go.tz; Wurzburg Rd) The government hospital has a 24-hour casualty department.

MONEY

All the major banks have ATMs and most change cash.

TRAVEL AGENCIES

Several agencies in town book 4WD rental and organise safari tours of the Serengeti and Rubondo Island national parks. Most also sell air tickets.

TOURIST INFORMATION

Tourist Office (www.tanzaniatourist.gov.tz; New Mwanza Hotel, Post St; ⊙9am-1pm & 2-5.30pm Mon-Sat) There's a small tourist-office branch inside the lobby of the New Mwanza Hotel, but don't expect overly knowledgeable staff.

USEFUL WEBSITES

The **Mwanza Guide** website (www.mwanza-guide.com) has useful tourist information.

❶ Getting There & Away

AIR

Precision Air (☑028-250 0819; www.precision airtz.com; Kenyatta Rd) flies to Dar es Salaam, Kilimanjaro, Bukoba and, internationally, to Nairobi. Auric Air (p381) has flights to Bukoba, Kigoma and Mpanda. **Air Tanzania** (☑0782 737730; www.airtanzania.co.tz; Kenyatta Rd) flies to Dar es Salaam five days a week. **Fastjet** (☑0756 7540543; www.fastjet.com; Kenyatta Rd) also flies to Dar.

Coastal Aviation (☑0752 627825; www. coastal.cc; airport) has a daily flight to Arusha airport stopping at various Serengeti National Park airfields. It also flies to Dar es Salaam, Zanzibar and, internationally, to Kigali. Flight schedules and destinations constantly change so it pays to check each airline's website for the latest.

Auric and Coastal both do charters.

BOAT

Ferries connect Mwanza with Bukoba and Ukerewe Island.

BUS

Nyegezi Bus Station, about 10km south of town, handles buses to all points east, south and west including Dar es Salaam (Tsh45,000, 15 hours). **Mohammed Trans** (off Miti Mrefu St), departing for Dar at 6am, has good service and its buses conveniently begin at its city-centre ticket office before heading to the bus terminals. **NBS** and many other companies go to Tabora (Tsh15,000, six hours) during the morning.

Jordan has the best buses to Arusha (Tsh28,000, 12 hours). It leaves its city-centre office at 5am and the bus station at 6am and travels via Singida, as do all other Arusha-bound buses. Buses to Bukoba (Tsh20,000, six to seven hours), departing between 6am and 1pm, mostly use the Busisi ferry, but if they're redirected to the Kamanga ferry in central Mwanza, you can meet them there.

Adventure is the best of four companies departing daily at 5.30am to Kigoma (Tsh31,000, 10 hours).

Buses for Musoma (Tsh8000 to Tsh10,000, three to four hours, last bus 4pm) and other destinations along that road depart from **Buzuruga Bus Station** in Nyakato, 4km east of the centre.

There's no need to travel to the bus stations to buy tickets since numerous ticket agencies are stationed at the old **City-Centre Bus Terminal** (now a car park). They don't charge an official commission, but have been known to overcharge.

TRAIN

Mwanza is the terminus of a branch of the Central Line and trains run to Tabora (Tsh26,900/22,700/11,800 in 1st/2nd/3rd class) on Thursday and Sunday at 4pm.

---

❶ CROSSING MWANZA GULF

Travelling west from Mwanza along the southern part of Lake Victoria entails crossing the Mwanza Gulf. There are two ferries, each with advantages.

The **Kamanga Ferry** (passenger Tsh1000, vehicle Tsh7200) docks right in town. It departs Mwanza hourly between 7am and 6.30pm, except Sunday when departures are every two hours from 8am to 6pm. If you're travelling to Bukoba or anywhere along that highway, ask which ferry the bus will use; you may be able to save a trip to the bus station by boarding the bus here.

The government-run **Busisi Ferry** (aka Kigongo ferry; passenger Tsh400, vehicle Tsh8000), 30km south of Mwanza, has the advantage of the road west being paved. It also sails more often (every 30 minutes from 7am to 10pm) but there are often delays. Many trucks use this boat and government officials sometimes call and tell the pilots to wait for them.

SUKUMA DANCING

The Sukuma, by far Tanzania's largest tribal group with nearly 15% of the country's population, are renowned nationwide for their pulsating dancing. Dancers are divided into two competing dance societies, the Bagika and the Bagulu, that compete throughout Sukumaland (the Sukuma homeland around Mwanza and southern Lake Victoria). The culmination is the annual **Bulabo Dance Festival** held at the Sukuma Museum in June. The most famous of the dozens of dances are those using animals, including the Bagulu's *banungule* (hyena and porcupine dance) and the Bagika's *bazwilili bayeye* (snake dance). Before beginning, the dancers are treated with traditional medicaments to protect themselves from injury. And the animals, too, are given a spot of something to calm their tempers.

ℹ Getting Around

TO/FROM THE AIRPORT

The airport for Mwanza is located 10km north of town (Tsh10,000 in a taxi). Dalla-dallas to the airport (Tsh400) follow Kenyatta and Makongoro roads.

BUS & TAXI

Dalla-dallas (labelled Buhongwa) to Nyegezi bus station run south down Kenyatta and Pamba roads. The most convenient place to find a dalla-dalla (labelled Igoma) to Buzuruga bus station is just northeast of the clock tower, where they park before running down Uhuru St.

There are taxi stands all around the city centre. Unless it's an exceptionally short trip, taxi fares are Tsh5000 within the centre. You can get a taxi to Buzuruga (Tsh7000) and Nyegezi (Tsh12,000) bus stations. Motorcycle taxis are everywhere and charge Tsh1000 within the centre.

Around Mwanza

Sukuma Museum

Located in Bujora village, **Sukuma Museum** (☑ 0765 667661; admission Tsh15,000, video Tsh200,000; ⊙ 9am-6pm Mon-Sat, 10am-6pm Sun) is an open-air museum where, among other things, you'll see traditional Sukuma dwellings, the grass house of a traditional healer, blacksmith's tools and a rotating cylinder illustrating different Sukuma words for counting from one to 10. In the past these were used by various age-based groups as a secret language of initiation. Each group used its own words among its members and these could not be understood by others. The museum is 18km east of Mwanza.

Also on the grounds is the **Royal Drum Pavilion**, built in the shape of a king's stool, holding a collection of royal drums that are still played on church feast days, official government visits and other special events.

The **Round Church** was built here in 1958 by David Fumbuka Clement, the Québecois missionary priest who founded the museum. It has many traditional Sukuma stylings. English-speaking guides are available.

On request, the museum can organise on-the-spot performances of **traditional drumming and dancing** for Tsh80,000 (for up to nine people) per performance.

Sunday opening times change depending on when mass finishes.

🛏 Sleeping & Eating

The centre has no-frills *bandas* (thatched-roof hut; per person with meals Tsh30,000) in the style of Sukuma traditional houses and a **campground** (camping Tsh15,000). The accommodation is rarely used and you'll need to let them know in advance. There's a little bar and you can use the kitchen.

ℹ Getting There & Away

Bujora is 18km east of Mwanza off the Musoma road. Take a dalla-dalla (Tsh500, 30 minutes) to Kisesa from Uhuru Rd north of the market in Mwanza. From Kisesa, motorcycle taxis cost Tsh1000. Or walk a short way along the main road and turn left at the sign, following the small dirt road for 1.7km. A taxi from Mwanza, with waiting time, will cost Tsh45,000 to Tsh50,000.

En route from Mwanza, just past Igoma on the left-hand side of the road, is a graveyard for victims of the 1996 sinking of the Lake Victoria ferry MV *Bukoba*.

Ukerewe

With its simple lifestyle and rocky terrain broken by lake vistas and tiny patches of forest, Ukerewe Island, 50km north of

Mwanza, makes an intriguing, offbeat diversion. There are a few sights, including what's claimed to be sub-Saharan Africa's first **Cotton Ginnery** (1904), now shuttered and home to scores of vervet monkeys, in Murutunguru (don't miss the little forest reserve behind it). **Ikulu** ('White House') is the modest 1928 European-style palace of the island's former king, signposted just behind the market in Bukindo. The real attraction, however, is the deeply rural life between these sights. Ukerewe is unusual in its highly successful farming techniques, centuries of stable population, and the fact that every patch of land and every tree is individually owned. There's a fascinating account of how this all works in John Reader's brilliant book *Africa: A Biography of the Continent*.

Nansio, the main town, has internet access (when the island's electricity is working) but no internationally linked ATMs. Shared taxis and dalla-dallas connect Ukerewe's few sizable villages.

☞ Tours

Ukerewe Tourist Information Centre
GUIDED TOUR

(☏ 0783 864006; guidemwala@gmail.com) Paulo Faustine runs this centre from his computer/mobile-phone repair shop next to La Bima Hotel (look for the green 'i' sign). He is a friendly and reliable guide for tours around Ukerewe and surrounding islands. Other potential guides with lower prices and less English may meet you at the dock.

He can organise interesting half-day walking tours of the island (per person Tsh25,000) and half-day bike tours (per person Tsh40,000).

🛏 Sleeping & Eating

La Bima Hotel
GUESTHOUSE $

(☏ 0732 515044; s/tw Tsh20,000/25,000; ℗) Despite cramped rooms (some with hot water) and peeling paint, this OK place is Nansio's best lodging. It has the top restaurant too.

ℹ Getting There & Away

The passenger ferry MV *Clarius* sails daily from Mwanza North Port to Nansio (adult/child Tsh5000/3050, 3½ hours) at 9am weekdays and 10am on weekends; it returns at 2pm. Two other ferries (3rd-class/1st-class/car Tsh5000/6000/7000, three hours) dock at Kirumba, north of Mwanza's centre near the giant Balimi ad. The MV *Nyehunge* departs Mwan-

za at 9am and Nansio at 2pm and the MV *Samar III* departs Mwanza at 2pm and Nansio at 8am.

It's also possible to reach Nansio from Bunda, a town on the Mwanza–Musoma road, which means that you can go from Mwanza to Ukerewe and then on towards Musoma or the Serengeti without backtracking. If using public transport, take a Mwanza–Musoma bus and disembark at Bunda. Here buses (and sometimes dalla-dallas) head to Nansio (Tsh6000, five to six hours) daily at 10am and 1pm using the Kisorya ferry (passenger/car Tsh400/5000, 40 minutes), which crosses four times daily in each direction. In the reverse direction, vehicles to Bunda leave Nansio at 8am and 10am. After these buses depart there are no vehicles direct to Nansio, but you can take a dalla-dalla to Kisorya and catch another on the island. The last ferry to Ukerewe sails at 6.30pm. The last ferry leaving Ukerewe is at 5pm, but don't use it unless you have your own vehicle or are willing to try hitching part of the way to Bunda.

Rubondo Island National Park

Alluring for its tranquillity and sublime lakeshore scenery, **Rubondo Island National Park** (adult/child US$30/10) is one of Tanzania's best-kept secrets. There may be days when you're the only guests on the 240-sq-km island. **Birdwatching**, particularly for shore birds (there are many migrants in November and December), brings the most visitors, but **walking safaris** (half-day walks US$25 per person) and **boat rides** (US$25 per person) can also be rewarding. Officially children under 12 cannot go on walking safaris but there's usually some flexibility in this. Elephants, giraffes, black and white colobus and chimpanzees were long ago introduced alongside the island's native hippo, bushbuck and sitatunga, an amphibious antelope that hides among the marshes and reeds along the shoreline. Rubondo is probably the best place in Tanzania to see it.

Rubondo's chimps are not yet habituated, but research experts were just getting started in late 2014 on the long process of getting them used to human company. This could take up to four or five years but sightings will probably increase as the chimps lose their fear of humans. In the meantime, fascinating chimp walks can take you in search of them, although there may not be actual sightings.

Though the beaches look inviting, there are enough crocodiles and hippos that swimming is prohibited.

🛏 Sleeping

Rubondo Park Bandas & Resthouse
CAMPGROUND, BANDA $

(camping US$30, r per person US$30) The *bandas* facing the beach at Kageye on Rubondo's eastern shore are some of the better national park–run *bandas* in Tanzania. Each has a comfortable double and single bed, hot-water bathroom, and privacy afforded by surrounding jungle trees. There's also a resthouse in the same location with similar quality rooms, but with TVs.

All rooms have electricity in the mornings and evenings. There are fully equipped kitchens for cooking, and staff can be hired to cook for you; a free meal for them should be payment enough. A tiny shop 10 minutes' walk north of the *bandas* sells a few basics such as rice, eggs and potatoes, and there's a cool little bar on the shore right by the *bandas*.

★ Rubondo Island Camp
TENTED CAMP $$$

(☑0736 500515; http://rubondo.asiliaafrica.com; s/d all-inclusive US$1090/1650; ⊗closed Apr–May; 🛜❄) 🏊 Recently taken over by the very upmarket Asilia group, this is a wonderful lakeside perch with stunning safari tents. Well, we say tents, but these 'tents' have three solid walls, fine furnishings, bathrooms to splash in and deliciously comfortable beds. There's a fabulous wooden bar and restaurant area hanging onto a low cliff with lake views.

Activities on offer include chimp walks (for the moment you're very, very unlikely to see the chimps but you'll certainly see their night nests and other clues to their presence), birdwatching trips and fishing. It can also do game drives but that's not the best way to see the island.

ℹ Getting There & Away

AIR
Auric Air (p381) makes a Rubondo (US$325 return) diversion on its Mwanza–Bukoba flights. This requires a two-night stay if flying return out of Mwanza since arrival is in the late afternoon and departure in the early morning. **Coastal Aviation** (☑0752 627825; www.coastal.co.tz) also flies to the park by request. A charter flight with Auric costs around US$3000.

BOAT
There are two ways to reach Rubondo by park boat (up to seven passengers); both should be arranged in advance. Fishermen are prohibited from delivering people to the island because of complaints in the past of tourist scams.

The park recommends using Kasenda, a small port about 5km from Muganza (Tsh1500 on a motorcycle taxi and Tsh5000 in a taxi). From here it's 20 to 30 minutes by boat to Rubondo Island and another 15 minutes by park vehicle to drive across the island to Kageye. This costs US$100 return per boat. Muganza is just off the main Mwanza–Bukoba road. Public transport is frequent but buses normally drop you at the junction on the main road where the turn-off for Muganza is. There are plenty of motorbikes willing to whizz you into the town or Kasenda. All buses between Bukoba (Tsh12,000, two hours) and Mwanza (Tsh12,000, four hours) pass through, as do Bukoba–Dar es Salaam buses. Dalla-dallas run to nearby destinations such as Biharamulo (Tsh5000, two hours).

The second option is Nkome, at the end of a rough road north of Geita, where the boat costs US$100 to Kageye and takes about two hours. Expect choppy water on this crossing. The warden's office, where you get the boat, is located outside Nkome, Tsh500 by *piki-piki* (motorbike) or Tsh2000 by taxi from where the final dalla-dalla stops. Two buses go direct from Mwanza to Nkome (Tsh12,000, four to five hours). They leave Mwanza at 10am, but you can meet them at the Kamanga ferry. Alternatively, it is possible to take a bus to Geita where there are frequent dalla-dallas to Nkome (Tsh5000, two hours).

ℹ RUBONDO ISLAND NATIONAL PARK

Why Go The tranquil setting and lovely lakeshore scenery; fine birding; and a chance to see sitatungas and chimpanzees (chimps are currently being habituated to humans).

When to Go June to early November.

Practicalities Start from Bukoba or Mwanza, travel to the nearest port and continue by park boat. Alternatively, arrive by charter flight. Book accommodation and transport through park headquarters. If the phones are down, staff at the Saa Nane/Tanapa office in Mwanza (☑028-254 1819, on Capri Point) can help.

Budget Tips This is generally a good park for budget travellers. Access to the island is by taking a bus to the nearest lakeshore town and then taking an (expensive) boat ride out to the island. Once there the park *bandas* offer excellent cheap accommodation and self-catering possibilities. Safaris are taken on foot.

Biharamulo

The old German administrative centre of Biharamulo is a small nowhere town that some travellers find inexplicably appealing. It certainly has a remote 'lost in Africa' feel.

Heading north from Biharamulo, the road passes between the 1300-sq-km **Biharamulo Game Reserve** and the 2200-sq-km **Burigi Game Reserve**, the latter long discussed as a new national park, but so far nothing has come of it. Neither has particularly significant tourist facilities, although animal populations, particularly in swampy Burigi, have revived after suffering severely from the refugee influxes during the 1990s. Roan and sable antelopes, eland, sitatungas, elephants, giraffes, zebras, lions and more are present. Arrangements to visit should be made in Dar es Salaam, but can also be made at the game-reserve office in Biharamulo.

🛏 Sleeping

German Boma   HISTORIC HOTEL $

(✆0766 477065; r per person Tsh10,000; ℗) The 1902–05 German *boma* on the hill above town has a good guesthouse with well-kept rooms in little rondavels (circular African buildings) in the courtyard. They have hot water but no fans. There's no food, so you'll need to eat down near the bus station. Two rooms in the *boma* hold a few old photos and weapons.

❶ Getting There & Away

There are two or three dalla-dallas and a bus (6am) that depart early each morning direct to Mwanza (Tsh10,000, six hours) and Bukoba (Tsh10,000, two hours). The Bukoba bus leaves at 8am. There's one dalla-dalla a day to the Rwandan border (Tsh11,000; 8am; two hours).

To travel to Mwanza later in the day take one of the frequent shared taxis to Nyankanazi (Tsh5000, one hour) and wait for a bus there. For Bukoba, catch a connection in Muleba (Tsh8000, 1½ hours).

Bukoba

Bustling, green-leafed Bukoba has an attractive waterside setting and amenable small-town feel. Everyone who comes to visit here seems to like it, even though it's a little hard to put your finger on exactly why. The town traces its roots to 1890, when Emin Pasha (Eduard Schnitzer), a German doctor and inveterate wanderer, arrived on the western shores of Lake Victoria as part of efforts to establish a German foothold in the region. Since then, the second-largest port on the Tanzanian lakeshore has flourished thanks to the income generated by coffee and vanilla farming.

The surrounding Kagera region is the home of the Haya people, known for their powerful kingdoms that once held sway in this area. Prior to the rise of the Haya kingdoms, Kagera was at the heart of an advanced early society known for its iron production.

◉ Sights & Activities

Musira Island   ISLAND

The big chunk of rock in front of Bukoba was a prison island in the days of the kings and now it offers an intriguing getaway. Upon arrival introduce yourself to the chairman and pay the island fee of Tsh3000. Ask him to show you the path to the summit, which passes the Orthodox church and several homes made from elephant grass.

KIROYERA TOURS

Kiroyera Tours (✆028-222 0203; www.kiroyeratours.com; Shore Rd) This is a well-informed agency leading cultural tours in Bukoba and the Kagera region, and is an essential stop for travellers in Bukoba. Its half- and full-day tours include visiting ancient rock paintings and walking in Rubale Forest. If you liked your Zanzibar spice tour, consider a Kagera vanilla and coffee tour (US$80).

Kiroyera also runs half-day bike tours (US$15); sells bus, boat and plane tickets; supplies boats to go to Musira Island (one person US$60, two people US$100); and organises visits to national parks in Tanzania and gorilla tracking in Uganda. In addition to making local culture readily accessible to visitors, Kiroyera has established several community projects and won awards for promoting community development through tourism.

Bukoba

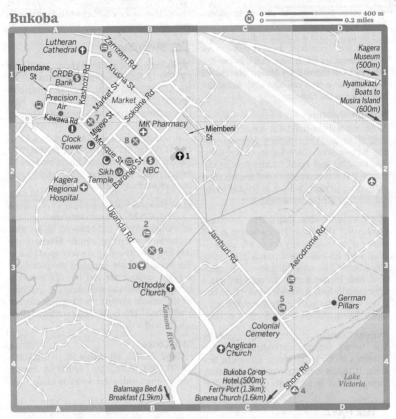

Bukoba

Sights
1 Mater Misericordiae Cathedral B2

Activities, Courses & Tours
Kiroyera Tours ....(see 4)

Sleeping
2 CMK Lodge B3
3 ELCT Bukoba Hotel C3
4 Kiroyera Campsite.................................. D4

Eating
5 Lake Hotel C3
6 New Banana Hotel.................................. B1

Eating
7 ELCT Tea Room...................................... A1
8 New Rose Café.. B2
9 Victorius Perch B3

Drinking & Nightlife
10 Lina's Night Club B3

Crowded passenger boats (Tsh2000) depart Nyamukazi, near the museum, but with these you don't get the chance to see the cliffs and caves (where traditional healers used to be buried) on the backside so it makes sense to hire a boat for the trip or take a tour. Kiroyera Campsite (p235) charges US$60 for a boat for one person and US$100 for two.

Kagera Museum   MUSEUM
(admission Tsh2000; ⊙ 9.30am-6pm) This small but worthwhile museum mixes a collection of local tribal items with photographs of wildlife from the Kagera region. A guide (which is more or less compulsory) charges Tsh3000. Attached to the museum is the **Bukoba Disabled Assistance Project** (BUDAP) workshop where men and woman

with polio make *ngoma* drums, handbags and jewellery.

The museum is across from Bukoba's airport in the Nyamukazi area. If taxi drivers or motorcycle-taxi drivers don't know the museum, tell them 'Peter Mulim' and they'll know the area. You can also walk along the lakeshore to the museum.

Notable Buildings

Most colonial-era buildings are at the lake end of town. When filming *Mogambo* in the Kagera area, Clark Gable, Grace Kelly, Ava Gardner and Frank Sinatra (not in the movie, but accompanying Gardner, his then wife) enjoyed many a drink at the Lake Hotel, built by the Germans in 1901.

Mater Misericordiae Cathedral   CATHEDRAL
(Jamhuri Rd) This landmark cathedral in the centre of town certainly draws attention to itself with its huge see-through, glass steeple. It looks like something from a B-grade sci-fi film. Unfortunately the entrance gates are normally locked outside service time but if you come past in the early morning there's more chance of them being open.

Bunena Church   CHURCH
The town's original cathedral, the 1914 Bunena Church is the oldest church in Bukoba. It paints a pretty picture when seen from Bukoba Beach, but isn't much up close. The rocky cliff below it, however, is very attractive.

🛏 Sleeping

⭐ **Balamaga Bed & Breakfast**   B&B $
(☑0789 757289; www.balamagabb.com; s/d Tsh55,000/85,000, s/d without bathroom Tsh50,000/70,000; 🅿) High up in the hills overlooking the lake, this great-value homey place has four spacious, comfortable rooms (two self-contained and two sharing a bathroom) decorated with artistic photos. The garden is so gorgeous and full of birds you'll forget you're in Bukoba. It's a world away from most cheap Tanzanian hotels.

ELCT Bukoba Hotel   HOTEL $
(☑0754 022682; www.elctbukobahotel.com; Aerodrome Rd; s/tw/ste US$40/45/60; 🅿 @) This Lutheran conference centre between the lake and the city centre is a very good choice. The rooms in this rambling complex have a slight sanatorium feel but it's impeccably maintained and well-run. The gardens, which include a tree of roosting pelicans, are a real treat. The hotel sign promises 'Tranquility' and it delivers.

CMK Lodge   HOTEL $
(☑0682 265028; off Uganda Rd; r Tsh25,000-35,000; 🅿) Plain, but sparkling rooms and a quiet side-road location make this

---

THE HAYA

Bukoba is the heartland of the Haya people, one of Tanzania's largest tribes and a prominent player in the country's history. The Haya had one of the most highly developed early societies on the continent and by the 18th or 19th century was organised into eight different states/kingdoms. Each was headed by a powerful and often despotic *mukama* (king) who ruled in part by divine right. It was the *mukama* who controlled all trade and who, at least nominally, owned all property, while land usage was shared among small, patrilineal communes. Order was maintained through a system of appointed chiefs and officials, assisted by an age-based army. With the arrival of the colonial authorities, this political organisation began to erode. The various Haya groups splintered and many chiefs were replaced by people considered more malleable and sympathetic to colonial interests.

In the 1920s, in the wake of growing resentment towards these propped-up leaders and the colonial government, the Haya began to regroup and in 1924 founded the Bukoba Bahaya Union. This association was initially directed towards local political reform but soon developed into the more influential and broad-based African Association. Together with similar groups established elsewhere in the country, notably in the Kilimanjaro region and Dar es Salaam, it constituted one of Tanzania's earliest political movements and was an important force in the drive towards independence.

Today the Haya receive as much attention for their dancing (characterised by complicated foot rhythms, and traditionally performed by dancers wearing grass skirts and ankle rattles) and for their singing as for their history. Saida Karoli, a popular female singer in the East African music scene, comes from Bukoba.

ANCIENT KATURUKA

Katuruka Heritage Site (adult/child Tsh10,000/3000; ⊙9am-5pm Tue-Sun) preserves the oldest-known iron-smelting furnace in East, Central and Southern Africa (from 500 BC; long before equivalent techniques were known in Europe). While the site itself is essentially just old bricks and some small nuggets, there are interesting shrines to King Rugomora (r 1650–75AD) and Mugasha, the god of storms and water. Your guide will tell you some fascinating legends about them.

A replica of the king's thatch burial house holds a small archaeological museum.

The trip here is a chance to see deeply rural Tanzania. From Bukoba, take a Maruka-bound dalla-dalla to Katuruka (Tsh1500, 45 minutes). The ticket booth is 200m off the road.

near-downtown hotel one of Bukoba's best value. On top of that you get a warm welcome for free.

Kiroyera Campsite　　CAMPGROUND $
(✉0784 568276; www.kiroyeratours.com; Shore Rd; camping with own/hired tent Tsh8000/11,500, banda with/without bathroom Tsh30,000/25,000; ℗) A great backpackers' spot on the beach (very crowded on weekends) and the most original rooms in this half of Tanzania: three genuine Haya *msonge* (grass huts) with beds, electricity and shared bathrooms, and one with its own bathroom.

If you don't stay here, you should at least stop for a drink and some fried fish and rice (around Tsh8000) in the chilled beach-shack restaurant.

New Banana Hotel　　HOTEL $
(✉028-222 0892; Zamzam Rd; r Tsh20,000) Run-down, but in a good location and bright and cheery. There's hot water, and fresh flowers in the rooms show that management cares. Outside is a pleasing little bar-cafe.

Bukoba Co-op Hotel　　HOTEL $
(✉028-222 1251; Shore Rd; s/d/tw Tsh20,000/25,000/30,000; ℗) Fair value, but slightly aged rooms with TVs, ceiling fans and minifridge, but the best feature is its location at the end of Bukoba Beach. Rooms on the 2nd floor have limited lake views and the restaurant is one of Bukoba's best.

Lake Hotel　　HOTEL $
(✉0765 876240; r Tsh20,000-30,000, without bathroom Tsh10,000; ℗) This historic hotel near but not at the lake lacks any elegance it may have once had (in fact, some rooms are downright shabby), but it still clings to a hint of historical charm.

✖ Eating & Drinking

Menus throughout Bukoba almost always feature grilled fish and usually *ndizi* (cooked plantains; called *matoke* in the Haya language).

Bukoba Co-op Hotel　　INTERNATIONAL $
(Shore Rd; meals Tsh8000; ⊙7am-10pm) The beach setting makes this a popular gathering spot. The grilled tilapia, pizzas and curries are pretty good.

Victorius Perch　　INTERNATIONAL $
(Uganda Rd; meals Tsh10,000; ⊙6am-midnight) The most ambitious menu in town features Chinese, Indian, European and even tries for Italian, though many items aren't always available.

New Rose Café　　TANZANIAN $
(Jamhuri Rd; meals Tsh2000-5000; ⊙8am-7pm Mon-Sat) A wonderful and unassuming Bukoba institution that feels like a cross between a grocer and a little cafe-restaurant.

ELCT Tea Room　　TANZANIAN $
(Market St; breakfast Tsh4000, lunch Tsh5000-7000; ⊙8am-5pm Mon-Sat) Popular all-you-can-eat buffet, right in the town centre, serving all your Tanzanian favourites at low prices.

Lina's Night Club　　CLUB
(Uganda Rd; ⊙24hr) *The* nightclub in Bukoba is open 24 hours but the bar only gets busy in the evening, and the club from Friday to Sunday.

❶ Information

MEDICAL SERVICES
Kagera Regional Hospital (Uganda Rd)
MK Pharmacy (Jamhuri Rd; ⊙8.30am-7pm Mon-Sat, 10am-2pm Sun)

MONEY

NBC (Jamhuri Rd) Changes cash. The ATM works with Visa and MasterCard.

ℹ Getting There & Away

AIR

There are daily flights to and from Mwanza on **Auric Air** (www.auricair.com) and Dar es Salaam via Mwanza with **Precision Air** (☎ 0782 351136; www.precisionairtz.com; Kawawa Rd). Auric also continues onwards to Kampala, Uganda.

BOAT

There's a passenger-ferry service between Bukoba and Mwanza on the historic MV *Victoria*. Tickets for all classes are sold at the port at the window labelled 'Booking Office 3rd Class'. Boats (1st-class/2nd-class/3rd-class Tsh36,000/24,000/17,500) leave at 9pm on Monday, Wednesday and Friday. They take about nine hours. Kiroyera Tours (p232) can often find tickets even when the booking office says they're sold out. If not, they can arrange for you to sleep in the Assistant Captain's cabin.

BUS

All bus companies have ticket offices at or near the bus stand. The staff at Kiroyera Tours can also buy tickets for you; for a small fee.

There are buses to:

Mwanza (Tsh20,000, six to seven hours) via Muganza (Tsh12,000, two hours). Frequent departures between 6am and 1pm; Mohammed Trans and Bunda are two of the better companies.

Kigoma (Tsh27,000; 6am; 13 to 15 hours) with Visram.

Dar es Salaam (Tsh52,000 to Tsh60,000, 21 hours) All buses leave at or before 6am. The route goes through Muganza, Kahama, Singida and Dodoma. Some buses continue to Dar es Salaam in a single trip, including Mohammed Trans and Sumry, the two best companies, while others overnight in Morogoro to avoid reaching Dar in the wee hours.

Western Tanzania

Best for Culture
➜ MV *Liemba* (p248)
➜ Katonga (p241)
➜ Kipili (p249)
➜ Livingstone's Tembe (p239)

Best for Nature
➜ Mahale Mountains
National Park (p246)
➜ Katavi National Park
(p251)
➜ Gombe Stream National
Park (p245)
➜ Lake Tanganyika (p248)
➜ Kalambo Falls (p252)

Why Go?
Western Tanzania is rough, remote frontier land, with vast trackless expanses, minimal infrastructure and few visitors: not much different to when Stanley found Livingstone here. The west serves a sense of adventure now extinct in the rest of the country. This is precisely what attracts a trickle of travellers, many of whom plan their itineraries around the schedules of the MV *Liemba,* which sails down Lake Tanganyika, and the Central Line train, which crosses the country.

But it's wildlife watching that brings most people. Gombe Stream, Jane Goodall's former stomping grounds, and Mahale Mountains National Parks are two of the world's best places for chimpanzee encounters, while the vast floodplains of rarely visited Katavi National Park offer an almost primeval safari experience.

Unless you charter a plane as part of a tour, you'll need plenty of time and patience to travel here. But, for that certain sort of traveller, Tanzania's west is Tanzania's best.

When to Go
Kigoma

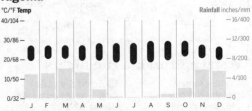

Dec–Apr Rains bring washed-out roads along with brilliant lightning displays.

May–Nov Dry-season travel is easiest, but the forests turn leafless.

May–Jun This is when chimpanzees are most likely to be seen in large groups.

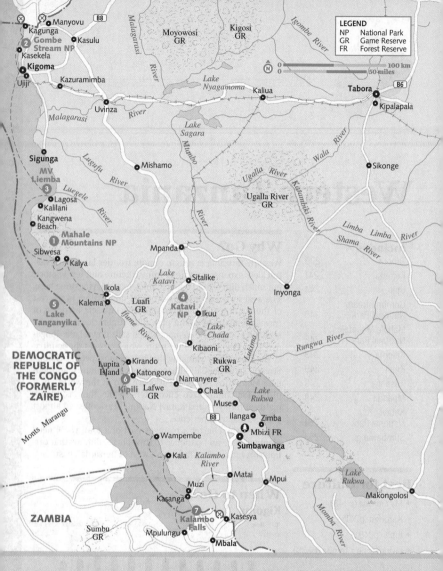

Western Tanzania Highlights

1 Visiting **Mahale Mountains National Park** (p246), the ultimate 'get-away-from-it-all' destination.

2 Mingling with the chimps at **Gombe Stream National Park** (p245).

3 Sailing down Lake Tanganyika aboard the **MV Liemba** (p248).

4 Experiencing the primeval rhythms of nature in **Katavi National Park** (p251).

5 Diving and snorkelling amid the kaleidoscopic cichlids in **Lake Tanganyika** (p248).

6 Kicking back on the shore of Lake Tanganyika at **Kipili** (p249).

7 Standing in the spray of the seldom-visited **Kalambo Falls** (p252).

Tabora

Leafy Tabora was once the most important trading centre along the old caravan route connecting Lake Tanganyika with Bagamoyo and the sea, and several other minor slave-trading routes converged here. The region, known in those days as Kazeh, was the headquarters of many slave traders, including the infamous Tippu Tib. A string of European explorers passed through its portals, most notably Livingstone and Stanley, who both spent many months here. Stanley noted in 1871 that it contained 'over a thousand huts and *tembes* (house with a flat earthen roof), and one may safely estimate the population…at five thousand people'. By the turn of the 19th century the Germans had made Tabora an administration and mission centre, and following construction of the Central Line railway Tabora became the largest town in German East Africa. It also became a regional education centre and many large schools are located here.

Today, it's primarily of interest to history buffs and rail fans, who'll have to wait here if taking a branch line to Mpanda or Mwanza.

◎ Sights

There are many buildings dating back to the German era. Notably attractive ones include the Catholic **cathedral**, with concrete inner walls painted to look like wood and marble, and the old **boma**, now an army base so you can't take photos.

Livingstone's Tembe   HISTORIC SITE
(admission Tsh10,000; ◎ 8am-4pm) This deep maroon-coloured, flat-roofed Arabic-style home, built in 1857, is the main attraction in these parts. It was Livingstone's residence for part of 1871. Later that year, Stanley waited three months here hoping that the Arabs would defeat Mirambo, famed king of the Nyamwezi (People of the Moon) tribe, and reopen the trail to Lake Tanganyika. When Mirambo was victorious, Stanley had to travel to Ujiji via Mpanda. Stanley and Livingstone returned here together the next year.

The large building was undergoing restoration at the time of research (but was still open to the public). It is now a museum and has some original Zanzibar carved doors, a few Livingstone letters and some slave-trading information. It's 8km southwest of town in Kwihara. Occasional dalla-dallas

(Tsh500) heading to Kipalapala from a stop just southwest of the new bus stand (near the public toilet) can drop you at Etetemia. From there it's a 2.5km walk straight down the road: if in doubt, just ask for 'Livingstone'. Taxis from town should cost about Tsh15,000 return and motorbikes Tsh3000, but there is a good chance you'll pay more.

⊨ Sleeping

John Paul II Hostel   GUESTHOUSE $
(☑ 0755 344128; Jamhuri St; r without bathroom Tsh10,000; r with breakfast Tsh20,000; ℗) Spotless, quiet, secure and cheap. You can't really go wrong at this church-run place where the foundation stone was laid by John Paul II himself. The entrance to the quiet compound is in the back. If the cathedral gate is closed, you'll have to walk around to the east; it's at the back of the big yellow building.

Golden Eagle Hotel   GUESTHOUSE $
(☑ 026-260 4623; Market St; tw without bathroom Tsh15,000, tw Tsh20,000-25,000; ℗) Thanks to the friendly owner (plus the central location and good, cheap restaurant), this 1st-floor place is the most traveller-friendly spot in town. Rooms are old, though tidy, and have TVs, hot water and ceiling fans. It can be a bit noisy though.

Frankman Palace Hotel   HOTEL $
(☑ 0768 683068; d Tsh75,000-85,000; ℗ ✳ ⊛) With glitter walls and frilly ribbons the rooms here are certainly eye-catching, but it's also one of the town's smarter offerings. It has wi-fi, but the manager describes it as 'too slow'. It's the green-roofed building behind the bus station next to the stadium.

Orion Tabora Hotel   HISTORIC HOTEL $$
(☑ 026-260 4369; Station Rd; s Tsh65,000-90,000, d Tsh85,000-105,000; ℗ ⊛) The old railway hotel, originally built in 1914 by a German baron as a hunting lodge, has been restored and provides unexpected class in this out-of-the-way region. The atmosphere fades inside the rooms but it outshines anything else in town. Ask for a room in the Kaiser Wing, with screened porches looking out onto the gardens.

It also has the town's best restaurant and a well-stocked bar. It's rather loud Fridays through to Sundays when the live band plays in the outdoor bar. Camping is allowed, but you'll have to negotiate a price with the manager.

Tabora

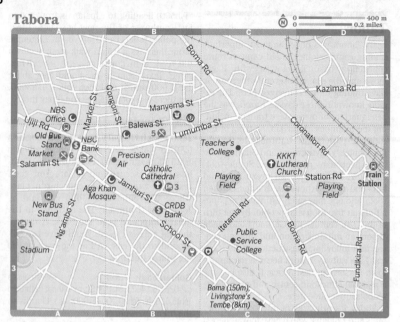

Tabora

🍴 Eating & Drinking

Mayor's Fast Food TANZANIAN $
(snacks from Tsh300, buffet per plate from Tsh2500; ⏰ 7am-11pm) It offers samosas and other snacks, plus a good buffet. The price depends on the meat you choose. There are two branches: one on Lumumba St and the other, called **Mayor's Hotel**, in the market.

Golden Eagle Hotel INDIAN, TANZANIAN $
(Market St; meals Tsh3000-8500; ⏰ 7am-10pm; 📶) Good food and low prices; the vegetarian *thali* (mixed curries and rice) is just

Tsh5000 and a fried tilapia (Nile perch) is Tsh8500.

Orion Tabora Hotel TANZANIAN, EUROPEAN $$
(Station Rd; meals Tsh5000-15,000; ⏰ breakfast, lunch & dinner) Tabora's top dining spot has a mix of local and continental food, with pizza and Indian available for dinner. There's dining indoors and in the outside bar area, which has a pool table, and there is a live band on Friday, Saturday and Sunday.

However, we must warn that we got serious food poisoning from the chicken *tikka masala* so maybe don't order that one!

Mauwa Bar BAR
(School St; ⏰ 3pm-1am) Busy and noisy bar with tables and a pool table outside under the trees. It's opposite the police station.

ℹ Getting There & Away

AIR
Air Tanzania (📞 026-260 4401; www.airtanzania.co.tz) flies on Monday and Thursday to both Kigoma and Dar es Salaam.

BUS
NBS, mostly offering four-across seating, is the top company operating out of Tabora. Some NBS buses depart from its office at the **'old' bus stand**. All other buses use the nearby

'new' bus stand. Several buses depart daily between 6am and 10am to Mwanza (Tsh15,000, six hours). Buses also go to the following:

Dodoma (Tsh40,000; 6am; eight hours)

Kigoma (Tsh25,000; 7am; eight hours)

Mpanda (Tsh20,000; 7am; eight hours)

Arusha (Tsh30,000; 6am; 10 to 11 hours) 6am departure via Singida (Tsh20,000, four hours) and Babati (Tsh25,000, six hours)

Mbeya (Tsh35,000; 6am; 12 hours) Sasebossa and Sabena have departures several times a week.

For all buses, arrive 30 minutes before departure.

TRAIN

Tabora is an important train junction. Trains go to:

Dar es Salaam (Tsh54,900/40,600/20,400 in 1st/2nd/3rd class)

Kigoma (Tsh31,700/24,900/12,500 in 1st/2nd/3rd class; 9pm Wednesday & Saturday)

Mpanda (Tsh27,500/21,200/11,100 in 1st/2nd/3rd class; 9pm Monday, Wednesday & Saturday)

Mwanza (Tsh29,600/22,700/11,800 in 1st/2nd/3rd class; 10pm Wednesday & Saturday)

Kigoma

This agreeable little town is the regional capital and only large Tanzanian port on Lake Tanganyika. It's also the end of the line for the Central Line train and a starting point for the MV *Liemba* and visits to Gombe Stream National Park. Kigoma is hardly a bustling metropolis, but it feels that way if you've slogged across Western Tanzania by road to get here.

Other than a few scattered buildings dating to the German colonial era, including the train station and what some call Kaiser House (now the home of the Regional Commissioner), Kigoma has no real attractions, but several villages and beaches around town could easily occupy a few days.

◉ Sights

Jakobsen's (Mwamahunga) Beach   BEACH
(admission Tsh5000) Jakobsen's is actually two tiny, beautiful sandy coves below a wooded hillside. The overall setting is idyllic, especially if you visit during the week when few people are around; you could forgive yourself for thinking you were in the Caribbean. There are some *bandas* for shade, and soft drinks and water are sold at the guesthouse.

It's 5km southwest of town, signposted off the road to Katonga. Dalla-dallas to Katonga can drop you at the turn-off, from where it's about a 20-minute walk. A taxi is Tsh10,000.

Katonga   VILLAGE
This large and colourful fishing village is quite a spectacle when the 200-plus wooden boats pull in with their catch. During the darkest half of the moon's cycle they come back around 8am after they've spent the night on the lake fishing by the light of lanterns. Dalla-dallas (Tsh400) come here frequently.

Kibirizi   VILLAGE
There are many fishermen at Kibirizi, 2km north of town by the oil depots. The early afternoon loading of the lake taxis is impressive in a noisy, colourful and rather chaotic kind of way. You can walk here by following the railway tracks or the road around the bay.

☞ Tours

Mbali Mbali   SAFARIS
(☏ 028-280 4437; www.mbalimbali.com) Western Tanzania–focused safari operator based at Kigoma Hilltop Hotel. It does boat and air charters.

⊨ Sleeping

Jakobsen's Guesthouse   GUESTHOUSE $
(☏ 0753 768434; www.kigomabeach.com; camping with own/hired tent Tsh15,000/20,000, r per person Tsh40,000, cottage Tsh240,000; ℗) This comfortable guesthouse has a lovely clifftop perch above Jakobsen's Beach, while the two shady campsites with bathrooms, lanterns and grills are down near the lake. It's good value and a wonderful spot for a respite, but there is no food available so you'll need to self-cater.

You can rent kayaks (per day Tsh25,000), sailboats (Tsh50,000) and snorkelling gear (Tsh10,000). Water and soft drinks are available.

Gombe Executive Lodge   GUESTHOUSE $
(☏ 0758 891740; r Tsh10,000-30,000; ❋) This is the standout cheapie in town. It's on a quiet and dusty side road and has a real homely feel to it, with spotless rooms, attached hot-water bathrooms and air-con. Breakfast is Tsh3000 extra.

Coast View Resort   HOTEL $
(☏ 0713 491570, 028-280 3434; r Tsh30,000-60,000; ℗❋@) The highest hotel in town

Kigoma

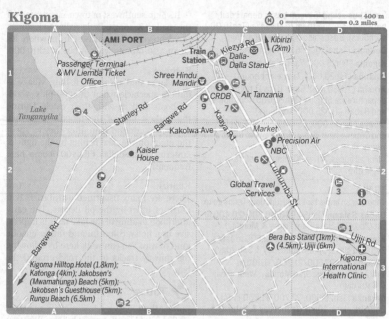

Kigoma

Sleeping

Eating

Information

doesn't have rooms with views, but you can see everything from the restaurant's gazebo tower. The limited sightlines are the only shortcoming here; rooms and service are solid.

Amini Lodge   GUESTHOUSE $
(☑ 0768 371213; Lumumba St; r without/with aircon Tsh17,000/20,000; P﹡) Half-a-dozen small and tidy rooms set in a quiet courtyard just off the main road into town. There's a little restaurant serving meals if you don't want to walk to town.

New Mapinduzi Guest House   GUESTHOUSE $
(☑ 0753 771680; Lumumba St; s/d Tsh12,000/ 14,000, s/d without bathroom Tsh6000/8000) This guesthouse down a tiny alley is a good choice if you want to be right in the centre of town. The basic, self-contained rooms have TVs and fans. There is no food available.

Kigoma Hilltop Hotel   HOTEL $$
(☑ 028-280 4437; www.mbalimbali.com; s/d/ste US$90/140/225; ﹡☎﹡) This hotel is atop an escarpment overlooking the lake. The double and twin cottages are within a large walled compound roamed by zebras. Rooms have all the mod-cons and are easily the best in town. The pool (nonguests Tsh10,000) is large, but not as clean as it could be.

Snorkelling, jet-skiing and fishing trips are available. It's owned by Mbali Mbali, which has lodges in all the western circuit national parks. Wi-fi is available but you'll be charged a whopping US$5 per hour.

Lake Tanganyika Hotel   HOTEL $$
(☑ 028-280 3052; www.laketanganyikahotel.com; s/d from US$85/105; P﹡☎﹡) This is a decent enough place right on the beach. The

rooms have lake views, but they are on the small side and the staff are rather lacklustre. The gardens are pleasing and nonguests can use the pool (Tsh5000).

✕ Eating & Drinking

Sun City
TANZANIAN $

(Lumumba St; meals Tsh3000-5000; ☺7am-8pm) A clean and almost artistic spot for *wali maharagwe* (rice and beans) and other local meals. There's also chicken biryani on Sunday.

Coast View Resort
TANZANIAN, ITALIAN $$

(mains Tsh10,000-12,000; ☺7am-9pm) Assuming you can score a table with a view, it's worth the trip up here for dinner or sundowners. The menu is mostly local, but has some Italian too.

Kigoma Catering
INTERNATIONAL $$

(Lumumba St; mains Tsh3000-13,000; ☺8am-7pm) The biggest and broadest menu in town, with Indian, Chinese, European and local dishes. Though it won't wow you, the food is pretty good.

❶ Information

CONSULATES

Burundian Consulate (☑0739 22849; Bangwe Rd; ☺9am-3pm Mon-Fri) Most Western nationalities can have a two-week tourist visa issued while they wait. It costs US$40 (they only accept US dollars) and requires one passport photo.

Democratic Republic of Congo Consulate (☑0765 947249; Bangwe Rd; ☺9am-4pm Mon-Fri) Visiting the Democratic Republic of the Congo (DRC; formerly Zaire) is often an exercise in patience, and the fun and games start the moment you enter a Congolese embassy or consulate. If you want a Congolese tourist visa, you must get it in advance from your home country. A visa issued here may be refused at the border.

The embassy here is more helpful than most (especially if you speak French). But if you're just planning on visiting Virunga National Park and Goma then so-called Virunga Visas are easily issued via the Visit Virunga website (www.visit-virunga.org).

IMMIGRATION

Formalities for those riding the MV *Liemba* are handled by an officer who boards the boat in Kasanga. If you're headed to Burundi or DRC, there are immigration offices at Ami Port and Kibirizi.

INTERNET ACCESS

Baby Come & Call (Lumumba St; per hour Tsh1500; ☺8am-8pm Mon-Sat) Internet access just up from the train station.

MEDICAL SERVICES

Kigoma International Health Clinic (☑0715 491995; Ujiji Rd; ☺24hr) For minor medical issues. It's 1km beyond Bero petrol station.

MONEY

CRDB (Lumumba St) Changes US dollars, euros and British pounds. The ATM accepts MasterCard and Visa.

NBC (Lumumba St) ATM. Accepts MasterCard and Visa.

TOURIST INFORMATION & TRAVEL AGENCIES

Gombe/Mahale Visitors Information Centre (☑028-280 4009; gonapachimps@yahoo.com; ☺9am-4pm) It's signposted off Ujiji Rd near the top of the hill; turn left at the T-junction. The staff know plenty about Gombe, but seem quite misinformed about Mahale.

❶ Getting There & Away

AIR

Precision Air (☑028-280 4720; www.precision airtz.com) flies daily to Dar es Salaam via Mwanza. **Air Tanzania** (☑0782 7377321; www.airtanzania.co.tz) flies to Tabora on Monday and Thursday, and to Dar es Salaam daily except Tuesday and Saturday. Air travel to Kigoma is in a constant state of flux, so expect this information to change.

Global Travel Services (☑0759 896711; Lumumba St) sells tickets for most airlines in Kigoma and elsewhere.

The airport is about 5km east of the town centre. A taxi costs Tsh5000.

BOAT
Ferry

The MV *Liemba* (p248) between Kigoma and Mpulungu (Zambia) via Lagosa (for Mahale Mountains National Park) and other lakeshore towns departs from the passenger terminal, north of the Lake Tanganyika Hotel. Services are on alternate weeks.

Cargo ships to Burundi and DRC also take passengers. They depart from Ami Port near the train station.

Lake Taxi

Lake taxis are small, wooden motorised boats, piled high with people and produce that connect villages along the entire Tanzanian lakeshore. They're inexpensive, but offer no toilets or other creature comforts, little if any shade, and can be dangerous when the lake gets rough. Nights are very cold. Lake taxis going north depart from Kibirizi. Boats to the south leave from Ujiji.

BUS

All buses depart from the dusty streets behind the unsigned Bero petrol station (coming from Kigoma, look for the large, white petrol station with an NBC ATM). The bus station is unusually organised with all the bus companies having little ticket offices with destinations clearly signed in a long row. Other bus ticket offices are scattered around the Mwanga area just to the west.

Buses go to:

Mwanza (Tsh31,000, 6am, 10 to 12 hours). Via Nyankanazi (Tsh20,000, seven hours). The best services are provided by Adventure and NSL Express.

Bukoba (Tsh27,000, 6am, 12 hours). Via Biharamulo (Tsh25,000, eight hours). This service is operated by Ya-Alli and Takbir.

Tabora (Tsh23,000, 6am, eight hours) The best service is provided by NBS and Sasebosa.

Mpanda (Tsh20,000, 6am, eight hours). Operated by Adventure.

Uvinza (Tsh5000, four hours) Any bus to Tabora or Mpanda will pass through Uvinza.

TRAIN

Kigoma station is the end of the line and as far west as you can ride a train in Tanzania. Trains go from Kigoma to Tabora (Tsh31,700/24,900/12,500 in 1st/2nd/3rd class) at 5pm on Thursday and Sunday.

ℹ Getting Around

Dalla-dallas (Tsh400) park in front of the train station and run along the main roads to Bera bus stand, Kibirizi, Katonga and Ujiji.

Taxis between the town centre and Bera bus stand or Kibirizi charge Tsh2000 to Tsh3000.

Don't pay more than Tsh1000 for a motorcycle taxi anywhere within the city.

Ujiji

Tiny Ujiji, one of Africa's oldest market villages, earned its place in travel lore as the spot where explorer-journalist Henry Morton Stanley uttered his famously casual 'Dr Livingstone, I presume?'

As a terminus of the old caravan route to the coast, Ujiji grew prosperous on the back of the slave and ivory trade and during Livingstone's time it was the main settlement in the region; a status it lost after the train station was built at Kigoma. Burton and Speke also stopped here in 1858 before setting out to explore Lake Tanganyika. Despite its distinguished past, little remains today of Ujiji's former significance except that some buildings away from the main road show Swahili traits.

Ujiji is 8km south of central Kigoma; dalla-dallas (Tsh400, 20 minutes) run between the two towns throughout the day. The Livingstone site is down a cobblestone street about 1km off the main road. The port and the beach are 300m further on from there. Just ask for Livingstone and the dalla-dalla driver will drop you off at the right place.

⊙ Sights

Livingstone Memorial Museum   MUSEUM, MONUMENT
(admission Tsh20,000; ⊘8am-6pm) The site where the immortal words, 'Dr Livingstone, I presume?' were uttered by Stanley on meeting Livingstone in 1871 is commemorated by a stark grey, half-collapsed monument inside a chain-link fence. The two mango trees here (two others have died) are said to have been grafted from the original tree that shaded the two men during their encounter.

Down below, and part of the same complex, the Livingstone Memorial Museum

---

TRAVELLING IN THE WEST

Travelling in western Tanzania has long been the preserve of the determined. You had to put up with atrocious roads and be ready to rough it on the backs of trucks. The roads were so bad that buses simply couldn't get through.

Today things are changing fast and almost all the main routes are being upgraded and paved. This is reducing journey times and allowing buses to replace trucks. In fact, if you stick to the main routes it's very unlikely you will need to ride in anything other than a bus.

Despite this, road conditions are more challenging here than in much of Tanzania and journey times are often long. Many people take to the skies instead. There is an increasing range of internal flights linking towns and parks in western Tanzania.

holds little more than a few prints about the East African slave trade, a few paintings by local artists and papier-mache replicas of the two men. The steep admission fee makes the complex only worth a visit if you really love the Livingstone and Stanley story.

Port

PORT

Many people find Ujiji's beach and small dhow port more interesting than the Livingstone and Stanley razzmatazz. They don't use power tools to build the boats, so the construction methods have been the same for generations.

Gombe Stream National Park

With an area of only 52 sq km, Gombe Stream National Park (☑Kigoma 028-280 4009; adult/child US$100/20, trekking fee US$20) is Tanzania's smallest national park, but its connection to Jane Goodall has given it world renown. Many of Gombe's 100-plus chimps are well habituated and though it can be difficult, sweaty work traversing steep hills and valleys, if you head out early in the morning sightings are nearly guaranteed. As well as chimp tracking you can see Jane's old chimp-feeding station, the viewpoint on Jane's Peak and Kakombe Waterfall. In addition to walking in the forest, it's possible to swim in the lake (no hippos or crocodiles, though bilharzia may be a risk) or hike along the shore.

🛏 Sleeping & Eating

Accommodation rarely fills up completely, but it's best to book rooms in advance through the visitor centre (p243) in Kigoma.

Tanapa Resthouse GUESTHOUSE $
(☑Kigoma 028-280 4009; r/camping US$20/30) Next to the visitor centre at Kasekela, this quite comfortable place has six simple rooms with electricity during morning and evening. Two overflow facilities have rooms of lesser quality and toilets at the back. The restaurant's prices are high (breakfast US$10, lunch US$15, dinner US$15) but you can bring your own food and use the kitchen for free.

Gombe Forest Lodge TENTED CAMP $$$
(☑0732 978879; www.mbalimbali.com; s/d all-inclusive except drinks US$800/1250; ⊙May-Feb) Gombe's only private lodge has a shady, waterside location with just seven tents that

> **ⓘ GOMBE STREAM NATIONAL PARK**
>
> **Why Go** Thanks to the work of Dr Jane Goodall, this is arguably the most famous chimpanzee reserve in the world – and one of the best places to see chimps up close.
>
> **When to Go** Any time other than March and April when the lodge is closed, and rains can make walking the trails hard work.
>
> **Practicalities** The chimps are a long walk from the two accommodation options. The only way here is by boat. All tourism activities are organised and paid for at Kasekela, on the beach near the centre of the park (this is where lake taxis drop you).
>
> **Budget Tips** Apart from the high entry fees it's possible to visit Gombe on a budget: take a lake taxi to and from the park, stay in the Tanapa Resthouse and self-cater.

offer a certain class and sophistication in the jungle. The tents are luxurious without being ostentatious.

ⓘ Information

If you arrive late in the afternoon, park officials won't start the clock on your visit until the following morning. This means that for a two-night stay and one day of chimp tracking, you'll only be charged one 24-hour entry (if you leave for Kigoma early in the morning). While this policy has been in place for some time, it's always possible it will change, so confirm before you go. Children aged under 16 are not permitted to enter the forest, though they can stay at the resthouse. Visitors are limited to one hour with each group of chimps but you are allowed to go and find another group after your hour is up for no extra cost.

ⓘ Getting There & Away

Gombe is 26km north of Kigoma and the only way there is by boat.

At least one lake taxi to the park (Tsh4000, three hours) departs from Kibirizi around noon. Returning, it passes Kasekela as early as 7am.

You can also hire boats at Kibirizi; hiring requires hard bargaining, but the price will be a little cheaper than the charter options (around US$250 return to charter a fishing or goods boat). You may have to pay in advance for petrol, but don't pay the full amount until you've arrived back in Kigoma. Some boat owners may try to tell you there are no lake taxis in an effort to get business.

It's safer and more comfortable (in part because there will be a sun shade) to arrange a charter with an established company. Chartering the Tanapa boat costs US$300 return plus US$20 for each night you spend at Gombe. Organise it through the park information office (p243) in Kigoma. A boat is also available through the Lake Tanganyika Hotel (US$450, US$50 per night overnight charge) in Kigoma. Mbali Mbali, also in Kigoma, charges US$655 return for those not staying at the lodge in Gombe and US$350 return for lodge guests. There's no overnight charge. All these boats take 1½ to two hours.

Day trips are possible on a chartered boat, but you should leave very early as late starts reduce your chances of meeting the chimps.

Mahale Mountains National Park

It's difficult to imagine a more idyllic combination: clear, blue waters and white-sand beaches backed by lushly forested mountains soaring straight out of Lake Tanganyika, as well as some of the continent's most intriguing wildlife. And, because of the unrivalled remoteness, visitor numbers to Mahale Mountains National Park (☏0789 045090; www.mahalepark.org; ☺6am-6pm) are very low (though steadily rising). There's a chance you might have the entire 1613-sq-km park all to yourself. The rainforest blanketing Mahale's western half is, in essence, a small strip of the Congo. It's most notable as a chimpanzee sanctuary, and there are around 900 of our primate relatives split into 14 groups residing in and around the park, along with leopards, blue duikers,

---

WILDLIFE IN THE WEST

Gombe Stream (p245) and Mahale Mountains National Parks offer the chance to observe habituated chimpanzees at close range. During the dry season Katavi National Park (p251) presents abundant numbers of most other wildlife that visitors to Tanzania hope to see; and all without another 4WD in sight. And don't forget the opportunity to dive or snorkel with cichlids off Kipili on Lake Tanganyika.

---

red-tailed monkeys, red colobus (a favourite snack of chimps), giant pangolin and many Rift Valley bird species not found elsewhere in Tanzania. There are also hippos, crocs and otters in the lake and lions, elephants, buffaloes and giraffes roaming the savannah of the near-impossible-to-reach eastern side of the mountains.

There are no roads in Mahale; walking and boating along the shoreline are the only ways to get around.

🏃 Activities

Mahale has excellent snorkelling and swimming off its powder-white beaches, but unfortunately humans aren't the only ones to enjoy such beachside beauty – a large crocodile population here means that swimming and snorkelling are now banned.

No matter what you do or where you go in the forest, guide fees are US$20 per group (up to six people). Porters cost US$15 per day. If you stay at one of the lodges the guide fees will be included in your package.

Chimpanzee Tracking

The main reason most people make the considerable effort to visit Mahale is to see chimps. Kyoto University researchers have been studying chimps here since 1965 and their 'M' group is well habituated to people. Mahale's size and terrain mean chimp tracking can take time, and it requires steep, strenuous walking, but almost everyone who visits has a successful sighting. Mahale is widely regarded as one of the best places in the world to see wild chimpanzees.

Only one group of up to six people are allowed with the chimps at any one time. This means that you might have to wait several hundred metres back from the chimps before you get a turn. Each group is allowed only one hour a day with the chimps and this is strictly enforced (with calls of '10 minutes remaining', 'five minutes remaining'). If one hour is not enough (and most people find it is) then it's possible to pay an extra US$100 for a 'photographer's experience' and get three hours with the chimps. You'll also have to pay a negotiable extra fee to your guide.

Face masks (provided) must be worn at all times when in the presence of the chimps. Children under the age of 12, and anyone suffering from a cold, flu or other illness is not allowed to visit the chimps. A few years ago the park lost five chimps after they caught the flu from a park visitor.

During June and July the chimps come down to feed around the lodges almost daily.

Hiking

Climbs of **Mt Nkungwe** (2462m), Mahale's highest peak, must be accompanied by an armed ranger. The usual arrangement is two days up and one down, camping midway and again near the peak. Trekkers must bring their own camping gear and food. The climb requires a reasonable degree of fitness, but the trail is in decent shape. A two-day option requires a willingness to scramble and hack your way through the bush.

🛏 Sleeping

There are three lodging options, each with its own beach, spread out along the lake. You can also **bush camp** (per person US$50, per group US$20) with a park ranger.

Mango Tree Bandas   BUNGALOW $$
(☑0789 045090; per person US$40) The lovely Mango Tree *bandas* are some of the better park-run *bandas* in Tanzania. They're set about 100m in from the shore and while they lack the lake views of the private camps, their position in the forest means the night sounds are wonderful.

The problem is that you have to be completely self-sufficient with food and drink, and bring everything you might need with you. Given the problems with access, this is not a simple task. The kitchen is well-equipped.

Kungwe Beach Lodge   TENTED CAMP $$$
(☑0732 978879; www.mbalimbali.com; s/d all inclusive excl alcohol US$890/1430; ☺mid-May–mid-Feb; ☞) This is a wonderfully low-key and enjoyable luxury camp with beautifully appointed safari tents (think big four-poster beds, weathered storage chests and piping-hot showers) hidden under beach-fringed trees. The centrepiece of the camp is the dhow-shaped dining area. The price includes daily chimp tracking and a boat safari.

Greystoke Mahale   LODGE $$$
(www.nomad-tanzania.com; s/d all inclusive US$1670/2350; ☺Jun-Mar) Situated on a beautiful sandy bay, this is a real Robinson-Crusoe-in-his-hippy-years kind of place where all the rooms are made of knocked-together, weathered, old ship timber. There's a gorgeous multilevel clifftop bar for the essential evening drinks and a tame pelican.

❶ MAHALE MOUNTAINS NATIONAL PARK

Why Go Up-close encounters with chimpanzees; stunning scenery with mountains rising up from the lakeshore.

When to Go Open year-round, but March to mid-May is too wet to enjoy it. June through October are the easiest (driest) months for hiking up the steep slopes.

Practicalities There are no roads to the park. Most visitors fly, but a variety of boats, including the historic MV *Liemba*, go from Kigoma, Kipili and other lakeshore towns.

Budget tips By catching the MV *Liemba* ferry to Mahale, staying in the park *bandas* and self-catering you can have a cheap and fun chimpanzee experience. If your schedule doesn't match the *Liemba's* you can also get there via lake taxis. Keep in mind that these are very slow, very uncomfortable and not all that safe.

As nice as it is, the rates are extraordinarily high even by East African standards. Prices include chimp tracking.

❶ Getting There & Away

There are many ways to reach Mahale; most are either expensive or difficult.

AIR
Safari Airlink (www.flysal.com) and **Zantas Air** (☑0778 434343) fly to Mahale twice-weekly, the former starting in Dar es Salaam and the latter in Arusha, when there are enough passengers (usually four) to cover costs. Zantas continues to Kigoma, but doesn't fly in the other direction. All flights stop at Katavi National Park en route, and thus the parks are frequently visited as a combination package. Expect to pay approximately US$930 one way from Dar, US$825 one way from Arusha and US$360 one way between Mahale and Katavi National Parks.

If you've booked with one of the lodges, a boat will meet your flight. Otherwise, arrange a boat in advance with park headquarters.

CHARTER BOAT
In Kigoma, Mbali Mbali (p241) charges US$2950 return for a speedboat (four to five hours).

LAKE TAXI

Lake taxis head south from Ujiji to Kalilani (Tsh7000), 2km north of park headquarters, on most days anytime from 5pm to 6pm (sometimes later). The trip often takes more than a day. Generally they depart from Kalilani around noon. Park staff know what's happening with the boats, so they can advise you on days and times.

One option to make the journey more bearable is to take a Saratoga bus from Kigoma to Sigunga (Tsh7000, 11am, six to seven hours) and wait for the lake taxi there. Sigunga to Kalilani usually takes seven to eight hours. You could also have the park boat pick you up in Sigunga; it's two hours to headquarters. Sigunga has a basic guesthouse.

A couple of weekly boats head north from Kalema (Tsh20,000) or nearby Ikola each evening for an even choppier journey than the one from Kigoma. It can take anywhere from 12 to 36 hours depending on the winds. They head south from Kalilani at around 3pm.

MV LIEMBA

It's hard to beat the satisfyingly relaxing journey to Mahale via ferry. The MV Liemba stops at Lagosa (also called Mugambo) to the north of the park (US$35/30/25 in 1st/2nd/economy class), about 10 hours from Kigoma. Under normal scheduling, it reaches Lagosa around 3am whether coming from the north (Thursday) or south (Sunday), but with the frequent delays, southern arrivals present a good chance of passing the park during daylight, which makes for a very beautiful trip. It has often been out of service, though hopefully things will be better after the substantial overhaul it received in 2014. Services are on alternate weeks.

You can arrange in advance for a park boat (holding eight people with luggage) to meet the Liemba. It's one hour from the Liemba to the bandas, including a stop to register and pay at headquarters. The cost is expensive: Tsh240,000. Chartering a fisherman's boat for the trip will cost only a little less. Lagosa has a basic guesthouse where you can wait for the Liemba after leaving the park.

TANAPA BOAT

With a bit of luck you can travel for free on the park boat. Park staff travel to Kigoma several times a month and if space is available they'll take passengers. This is usually only possible when leaving the park, as on the return trip from Kigoma the boat carries supplies. The Gombe/Mahale Visitors Information Centre (p243) in Kigoma knows when boats are travelling.

ROAD

Saying you can get to Mahale by 'road' is a bit misleading, because there is no road and certainly no public transport – for the moment. However it is possible to get to Lagosa and the park airstrip by private 4WD (and it has to be a serious 4WD) from both Kigoma and Katavi National Park. The easier route is from Kigoma. A reasonable road runs from Kigoma to Sigunga, leading to a very bumpy track on to Lagosa. Allow six to seven hours for this journey. The route from Katavi is one of the roughest, slowest and most jarringly painful you can make in East Africa. Allow 10 to 12 hours. If you arrive in Lagosa after dark you'll have to overnight there. A jeep hired in either Kigoma or the Katavi area will cost around US$300 with fuel per day (and remember it will take the driver a day to get back home again).

At the time of research, both routes were under construction. In the future, overland access might become easier and cheaper.

LAKE TANGANYIKA

Lake Tanganyika is the world's longest (660km), second-deepest (more than 1436m) and second-largest (by volume) freshwater lake. At somewhere between nine and 13 million years old, it's also one of the oldest. Thanks to its age and ecological isolation it's home to an exceptional number of endemic fish, including 98% of the 250-plus species of cichlids. Cichlids are popular aquarium fish due to their bright colours, and they make Tanganyika an outstanding snorkelling and diving destination. Not all of the lake is bilharzia free, so it's best to check locally before diving in.

Kigoma is the only proper town on the Tanzanian shore, though small, rarely visited settlements line the shore. They offer a fascinating look at local life, while the rolling countryside around the villages is beautiful and ideal for day treks. Besides the services of the MV Liemba, lake taxis travel the shoreline at least every two or three days. Getting around can be difficult, and sometimes expensive, but with perseverance you can, eventually, get to all lakeside towns and villages overland by a mix of some of the world's most overcrowded buses or by a variety of boats.

Kalema

Kalema (Karema) is the first almost-major lakeshore centre south of Mahale Mountains. It is a functioning Catholic mission station, originally established in 1885. Parts of the main compound – with brick arches that give it an Italian ambience – were originally a Belgian fort before being handed over to the White Fathers (also known as the Missionaires of Africa; an international Christian missionary group so named after the colour of their robes) in 1889. The large church built the following year is still in use, but it feels modern after extensive changes.

There are two simple guesthouses in town and it's worth enquiring at the mission to see if they have rooms available.

Buses connect Kalema with Mpanda (Tsh7000, four to five hours).

Kipili

Kipili, snoozing on the shores of Lake Tanganyika, is another old mission station. It is reached by a beautiful road through the Lafwe Game Reserve. The hilltop ruins of the 1880s church, 3km north of town, are very evocative and surrounded by dreamy lake views of the many islands just offshore. The islands have many rocky points, ideal for snorkelling with clouds of cichlids. The experience is akin to snorkelling in a coral reef in the Red Sea, only without the salt.

🛏 Sleeping

St Benedict Mission HOTEL **$**
(r Tsh15,000; 🅿) Just past the village and on the lakeshore is the guesthouse of the St Benedict Mission. The small and fairly clean rooms have cold-water-only showers.

★ Lake Shore Lodge & Campsite LODGE **$$$**
(📞 0763 993166; www.lakeshoretz.com; camping US$14, banda s/d full board US$160/240, chalet s/d full board US$345/490; 🅿🛜) The universally praised Lake Shore Lodge & Campsite has chalets with a lovely open 'African Zen' design incorporating shells, sand, ropes, flowers and sun-bleached wood – it's a place of barefoot luxury. If this is outside your budget it also has *bandas,* which are a low-key version of chalets, and camping with spotless bathrooms.

There are enough activities to keep you busy for days: kayaking on the lake, quad biking, mountain biking, diving (it's the only PADI-certified operation on the lake in Tanzania), snorkelling, village tours, island dinners and more. It is great to combine a trip to the lodge with a trip to Katavi and/or Mahale Mountains National Parks. Staff can take you to both using their own trucks and boats.

ℹ Getting There & Away

From Sumbawanga catch a bus towards Kirando and get off at Katongoro (Tsh10,000, 11am Monday to Saturday, five hours). Katongoro is 5km from Kipili. Next either walk, wait for a passing vehicle or ride on a motorbike (Tsh7000). Lake Shore Lodge will pick up its guests at Katongoro for US$5. From Mpanda go to Namanyere (Tsh15,000, four hours), where you can catch a passing vehicle heading to Kipili.

Kasanga

The sprawling village of Kasanga is the MV *Liemba's* last (or first) stop in Tanzania, and the port is being upgraded to serve as an export-import hub for DRC. The Germans founded it as Bismarckburg and the ruins of the old *boma* sit at the tip of the peninsula, 2km from the town, just behind the jetty. You can't visit or photograph it as it's now a military base. Kalambo Falls is within striking distance.

Simple rooms are available in town.

ℹ Getting There & Away

One or two buses a day travel from Sumbawanga to Kasanga (Tsh8000, noon, five to six hours) via Matai. The MV *Liemba* usually arrives from the north first thing on a Friday morning (every second week).

Mpanda

This small and somewhat scruffy town is a major transit point. Historically it was a significant trade hub and there are still many Arab businessmen living here.

The post office has reliable internet and the CRDB bank has an internationally linked ATM.

🛏 Sleeping & Eating

Mpanda has many hotels, but few good ones.

New Super City Hotel HOTEL **$**
(📞 0763 728903; d or tw Tsh15,000-18,000; 🅿) The hottest place in town has huge rooms

with sofas, as well as some wear and tear, instant hot showers and an okay in-house restaurant. It's at the southern roundabout.

Baraka Guesthouse GUESTHOUSE $
(☑ 0783 672424, 025-820 0485; r Tsh25,000, without bathroom Tsh15,000; Ⓟ) This quiet place west of the centre has tidy rooms with TV and occassional hot water. It's nothing special, but Mpanda being what it is, Baraka's rooms are up there with the best.

Moravian Hostel GUESTHOUSE $
(☑ 0785 006944; s/tw without bathroom & breakfast Tsh7000/9000; Ⓟ) This church-run place is friendly and good enough for the price, quieter than the competition (most other cheapies have attached bars), and conven-

ient for early-morning buses. The common bathrooms do leave a little to be desired though (an air-freshener would help).

ⓘ Getting There & Away

AIR
Auric Air (www.auricair.com) Auric Air flies on Thursday afternoons to Mwanza.

BUS
Mpanda's bus station is east of the Sumbawanga road near the southern roundabout. Most companies have ticket offices near the half-built Moravian church in the town centre, and their buses actually start there before going to the station.

Sumry serves Sumbawanga (Tsh15,000, 6am, 8am and 2pm, five to six hours) via Sitalike

---

TANZANIA'S CHIMPANZEES

Western Tanzania is the easternmost limit of chimpanzee habitat and their most famous residence due to the work of Jane Goodall. Hired in 1957 as Louis Leakey's secretary, Goodall had no formal scientific training, but Leakey was impressed by her detailed work habits in the field and love of animals. In 1960 he chose her to study wild chimp behaviour at Gombe Stream Chimpanzee Reserve, now Gombe Stream National Park.

Her research was so groundbreaking that it redefined the relationship between humans and other animals. During her first year she was the first person to see chimps make and use tools (they stripped leaves off a stem and used these to fish termites out of their mounds) and hunt and eat meat. She also documented their elaborate social behaviour, showing that they sometimes kill (and sometimes eat) each other, engage in long-term warfare, adopt orphans, form family bonds that last a lifetime and practise occasional monogamy. Goodall not only expanded our knowledge of primates, she revolutionised the entire field of ethology (animal behaviour). She gave the animals she observed names (David Greybeard, Mike, Frodo, Fifi, etc) instead of numbers and insisted that they had personalities, minds and feelings. This seems logical to a layperson, but defied scientific convention. The research continues today, making it one of the longest-running studies of a wild animal population. Less famous, but also important, Toshida Nishida of Kyoto University began research at Mahale the following year. That work also continues.

While Pan troglodytes schweinfurthii (Eastern chimpanzee), one of four chimp subspecies, was once common across western Tanzania, it's now endangered. Around 2800 remain, all along Lake Tanganyika and Rubondo Island where some were released in the 1960s and 1970s after being rescued from zoos and circuses. Many organisations are working to protect Tanzania's chimps, but three quarters of them live outside protected areas. Also, loss of habitat (due to logging for wood and charcoal, and expanding farming) is accelerating.

Both Gombe Stream and Mahale Mountains National Parks have chimpanzee communities that are fully habituated to humans and visiting them is an awesome experience. Viewing time is limited to one hour and you aren't allowed to approach closer than 10m, though guides routinely flout the latter rule and chimps happily break the rule themselves. Remember that chimpanzees are susceptible to human diseases, so if you have a cold, you won't be allowed to track them, and at Mahale, everyone must wear a surgical-style mask. Additionally, don't eat, drink, smoke, shout, point, use a camera flash or wear perfume anywhere near the chimps. The minimum age for tracking is 12 at Mahale and 16 at Gombe. Tracking is allowed year-round, but during rainy season the mud makes the trails treacherous and the chimps spend much of their time in trees.

(Tsh3000, 45 minutes). If you're going to Sitalike they sometimes try to charge you the full fare to Sumbawanga. Whether or not you pay the lower fare depends on the mood of the people in the ticket office.

NBS and **Air Bus** go to Tabora (Tsh20,000, 6am, eight hours).

Adventure goes to Kigoma (Tsh20,000, 6am and 3pm, eight to 10 hours) via Uvinza (Tsh20,000, four to five hours).

TRAIN

A branch of the **Central Line** connects Mpanda with Tabora (Tsh27,500/21,200/11,100 in 1st/2nd/3rd class) via Kaliua at 4pm on Tuesdays, Thursdays and Sundays.

Katavi National Park

Thrity-five km southwest of Mpanda, **Katavi National Park** (adult/child US$30/10; ⊘ 6am-6pm) is Tanzania's third-largest national park (together with two contiguous game reserves the conservation area encompasses 12,500 sq km) and one of its most unspoiled wilderness areas. Though it's an isolated alternative to more popular destinations elsewhere in Tanzania (Serengeti National Park receives more visitors per day than Katavi does all year), the lodges are just as luxurious as anywhere else. For backpackers it's one of the cheapest and easiest parks to visit, if you're willing to take the time and effort to get there.

Katavi's dominant feature is the 425-sq-km Katisunga Plain, a vast grassy expanse at the heart of the park. This and other floodplains yield to vast tracts of brush and woodland (more Southern African than Eastern), which are the best areas for sighting roan and sable antelopes: together with Ruaha National Park, Katavi is one of the few places you have a decent chance of spotting both. Small rivers and large swamps support huge populations of hippos and crocodiles and Katavi has more than 400 bird species. The park really comes to life in the dry season, when the floodplains dry up and elephants, lions, zebras, giraffes, elands, topis and many more gather at the remaining waters. The park's hippos are the standout; up to a thousand at a time can gather in a single, muddy pool at the end of the dry season (late September to early October is the best time) and its buffaloes. Katavi is home to some of the largest remaining buffalo herds in Africa and it's not unusual to see over a thousand of these steroid-fuelled bovines at any one time.

The park no longer hires vehicles but **Riverside Camp** in Sitalike charges US$200 per day for a 4WD with a pop-up roof.

All payments must be made at **park headquarters** located 1km south of Sitalike or the **Ikuu Ranger Post** near the main airstrip. If you fly in, rangers will be waiting at the airstrip for park admission fees. Anyone staying in the park has to pay the camping fee, but this will be included in the overall package if staying in one of the top-end camps.

🏃 Activities

Walking safaris with an armed ranger and bush camping (US$50 per person, plus guided walking fee per group US$20 for short walk, $US25 long walk) are permitted throughout the park. This makes it a great park for budget travellers. The road to Lake Katavi, another seasonal floodplain, is a good walking destination. The road begins at the headquarters so a vehicle is not needed.

Some top-end camps no longer allow their guests to go on walking safaris. There have been reports of some serious incidents involving undertrained park staff leading walking safaris resulting in injury to the tourists. This is also one of the most tsetse-fly-infested parks in Africa.

ⓘ KATAVI NATIONAL PARK

Why Go Outstanding dry-season wildlife watching. Rugged and remote wilderness ambience.

When to Go August through October is best for seeing large herds of wildlife. From February to May it's very wet, so getting around the park can be almost impossible and all the top-end camps close. It's a good time for birdwatching though.

Practicalities Drive in or bus from Mpanda or Sumbawanga; fly in from Ruaha National Park or Arusha.

Budget tips Katavi is one of Tanzania's more budget-friendly parks. By taking a bus to Sitalike, staying in one of the cheap options there and then setting out on a walking safari, you can see Katavi cheaply. You can also camp in the park.

WORTH A TRIP

KALAMBO FALLS

Variously reported as anywhere from 211m to 250m high, and often misrepresented as Africa's second-tallest waterfall (as far as uninterrupted drops go, it does crack the top 10), Kalambo Falls plunges impressively down the Rift Valley Escarpment along the Zambian border. The gorge is famous in archaeological circles since evidence of human activity dating from the early Stone Age right through to the Iron Age have been found here.

Liemba Beach Lodge in Kasanga charges about US$100 for a boat to the mouth of the Kalambo River, from where it's a long climb. If you're prepared to camp and hike, you can also use lake taxis.

In the dry season it's possible to drive (4WD only; look for the 'Kalambo Falls 16km' sign in Kawala village on your way to Kasanga) to within a few minutes' walk of the falls. In the rainy season a good driver can usually make it to Kapozwa village, about a 20-minute walk away. In Sumbawanga, 4WD drivers ask for Tsh200,000 for the 250km return trip. Saloon-car drivers charge less, but they must stop far from the falls.

🛏 Sleeping & Eating

🛏 In the Park

Besides bush camping, there are two public campsites (US$30); one at Ikuu near Katisunga Plain and the other 2km south of Sitalike. Both have a lot of wildlife passing through. Bring all your food and drink with you.

All park lodges are located around the Katisunga Plain in the vicinity of the Ikuu Airstrip.

Katavi Park Bandas　　BUNGALOWS $$
(katavi@tanzaniaparks.com; r per person US$30; P) This is 2km south of the village and within park boundaries (so you need to pay park entry fees when staying here). The rooms are big, bright and surprisingly good. Zebras, giraffes and other animals are frequent visitors.

★ Katavi Wildlife Camp　　TENTED CAMP $$$
(Foxes; ☑ 0754 237422; www.kataviwildlifecamp.com; s/d all inclusive except drinks US$675/1150; ◎ Jun-Feb; P) ✐ This comfortable, well-run camp has a prime setting overlooking Katisunga making it the best place for in-camp wildlife watching. The six tents have large porches with hammocks and are down-to-earth comfortable without being over the top. The quality guides round out the experience. It's owned by Foxes African Safaris, who offer some excellent combination itineraries with southern parks. The price includes a wildlife drive.

Chada Katavi　　TENTED CAMP $$$
(www.nomad-tanzania.com; s/d all inclusive US$1120/1550; ◎ Jun-Jan; P) Set under big trees in a prime location overlooking the Chada floodplain, this place promotes a classic safari ambience. It's at its most Hemingway-esque in the dining tent. This is a good spot for walking safaris – it has excellent guides – and fly camping can be arranged with advance notice. The price includes a wildlife drive.

Katuma Bush Lodge　　TENTED CAMP $$$
(☑ 0732 978879; www.mbalimbali.com; s/d all inclusive except drinks US$710/1070; ◎ mid-May–mid-Feb; P🐾🎏) With stunning views over the grasslands, the large safari tents here have four-poster beds, carved wooden showers and plenty of privacy. The defining feature is the relaxing lounge fronted by a deck with a small swimming pool. The price includes a wildlife drive.

🛏 Sitalike

Most backpackers stay at this little village at the northern edge of the park. There are a couple of small restaurants and grocery stores here.

Kitanewa Guesthouse　　GUESTHOUSE $
(☑ 0767 837132; s/d Tsh15,000/16,000; P) This fair-value spot by the bus-truck stop has adequate concrete-cube rooms with bucket showers and squat toilets. It only has electricity at night for the first few hours.

Riverside Camp BUNGALOWS, CAMPGROUND **$$**
(📞 0767 754740; camping US$10, s/d US$30/60;
P) Aimed at park visitors, hence the high prices. Its best feature is the resident pod of hippos, but the *bandas* are decent enough and the owner is a trustworthy guy who can rent out a jeep for a safari. It only has electricity in the first few hours of the night.

ℹ Getting There & Away

AIR

Safari Airlink (www.flysal.com) and **Zantas Air** fly twice a week to Ikuu Airstrip and the lodges will often let nonguests fly on their planes if space is available. All lodges provide free pick-up at Ikuu Airstrip for their guests. If you aren't staying at a lodge, arrange a vehicle or a ranger for walking *before* you arrive. If you are flying in, it is good to combine a trip to Katavi with a trip to Mahale Mountains National Park.

BUS

Buses and trucks between Mpanda and Sumbawanga can pick you up and drop you off in Sitalike or at park headquarters. Transport is frequent in the mornings, but after lunch you may have to wait several hours for a vehicle to pass. Two dalla-dallas depart Sitalike for Mpanda (Tsh3000, 45 minutes) at dawn and return at noon and 4pm. If you're driving, the only petrol stations are in Mpanda and Sumbawanga.

Sumbawanga

While there's little reason to make the peppy and pleasant capital of the Rukwa region a destination in itself, anyone travelling through the west is likely to pass through; and most enjoy their time here. This is the last stocking-up spot for those headed north to Katavi National Park. There are two ATMs on the main road and some internet cafes.

The surrounding Ufipa Plateau, which lies at 2000m, is home to an ecologically important mix of forest and montane grassland, with many endemic plants. It has also been declared an 'Important Bird Area' by BirdLife International. The bird-rich **Mbizi Forest Reserve**, a couple of hours' walk from Sumbawanga, is a closer place to meet feathered friends.

Down below the Mbizi Escarpment is the vast, shallow **Lake Rukwa**, which can be accessed from many villages near its meandering shoreline. Ilanga, served by frequent

4WDs (Tsh5000, two hours) throughout the day, provides the easiest access.

🛏 Sleeping & Eating

Most of Sumbawanga's guesthouses are in the fun and lively neighbourhood around the bus station. The area around the station is full of simple bars and restaurants.

Libori Centre HOTEL **$**
(📞 0757 494225; r Tsh15,000-25,000; P) This church-run place has rooms that are essentially clean and are very quiet and secure. Besides the addition of a chair, we couldn't see any discernible difference between the cheapest and most expensive rooms. A very basic breakfast is included. It's close to the bus station.

Holland Hotel HOTEL **$**
(📞 0786 553753; r Tsh45,000; P) Unexpectedly swish for such a dusty little place, the Holland Hotel, which is close to the bus station, offers big, airy, bright rooms with desks and, unfortunately, an awful lot of noise. The downstairs restaurant might not be the best place to eat in town, but it's certainly the nicest. Secure parking is available.

Ikuwo Lodge HOTEL **$**
(📞 025-280 2393; Nyerere Rd; r Tsh30,000) If all you want is a place to crash in the centre of the market district, then this aquarium-blue, all-glass block will do nicely. There are instant hot showers and plenty of street noise.

ℹ Information

Bethlehem Tourism Information Centre
(📞 0784 704343; charlesnkuba450@hotmail.com; Mpanda Rd; ⏱7am-10pm) A one-stop tourist information and local tour service operated by the enthusiastic and helpful Charles. He can help with onward transport, and organises local walking tours and trips further afield to destinations such as Lake Rukwa.

ℹ Getting There & Away

Numerous bus companies operate out of Sumbawanga and most ticket offices are located just outside the bus stand. Most buses depart between 7am and 9.30am. Buses go to:
Mbeya (Tsh16,000 to Tsh17,000, seven hours) via Tunduma.
Mpanda (Tsh15,000, five to six hours).

To get to Kasesya on the Zambian border there's a dalla-dalla (Tsh10,000; four to five hours) at 8am and 4pm.

Southern Highlands

Why Go?

Tanzania's Southern Highlands officially begin at Makambako Gap, about halfway between Iringa and Mbeya, and extend southwards into Malawi. Here, the term encompasses the entire region along the mountainous chain running between Morogoro in the east and Lake Nyasa and the Zambian border in the west.

The Highlands are a major transit route for travellers to Malawi or Zambia, and are an important agricultural area. They are also wonderfully scenic and a delight to explore, with rolling hills, lively markets, jacaranda-lined streets, lovely lodges and plenty of wildlife. Hike in the Udzungwa Mountains, watch wildlife in Mikumi or Ruaha National Parks, get to know the matrilineal Luguru people in the Uluguru Mountains, or head well off the beaten track to Tanzania's southwesternmost corner. Here, wild orchids carpet sections of Kitulo National Park and verdant mountains cascade down to the tranquil shores of Lake Nyasa.

Best for Nature

➡ Ruaha National Park (p268)

➡ Udzungwa Mountains National Park (p261)

➡ Mikumi National Park (p259)

➡ Kitulo National Park (p272)

Best for Culture

➡ Lake Nyasa (p279)

➡ Uluguru Mountains (p259)

➡ Tukuyu (p278)

➡ Iringa (p264)

When to Go
Mbeya

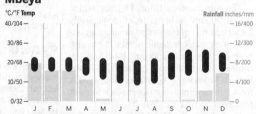

Jul–Sep Ruaha National Park is at its best, with 'sand rivers' and elephants.

Oct–Nov Jacarandas everywhere; wonderful wildlife viewing and hiking.

Dec–Mar Kitulo National Park's flower display is in full bloom; peak birding season in Ruaha NP.

Morogoro

POP 286,000

Morogoro would be a fairly scruffy town were it not for its setting at the foot of the Uluguru Mountains, which brood over the landscape from the south. The surrounding area is one of the country's breadbaskets, home to the prestigious Sokoine University (Tanzania's national agricultural institute), and a major educational and mission station. While there are few attractions, Morogoro offers a good introduction to Tanzanian life outside Dar es Salaam, plus the chance for cultural tours and hikes in the nearby Ulugurus.

🛏 Sleeping

Princess Plaza Lodge & Restaurant   GUESTHOUSE $

(☑0754 319159; Mahenge St; d Tsh30,000; ✳🛜) Princess is a basic guesthouse with small no-frills rooms, all with hot water, air-con, fan and free wi-fi access. Some have interior windows only. There are no mosquito nets, but rooms are sprayed daily. Downstairs is an inexpensive local-style restaurant. It's one block in from the main road, and a five minute walk from the dalla-dalla (minibus) stand in the town centre.

Amabilis Centre   HOSTEL $

(☑0716 880717, 0719 348959; amabilis. conferencecentre@yahoo.com; Old Dar es Salaam Rd; s Tsh20,000, s/tw without bathroom Tsh15,000/20,000; 🅿) This church-run place on the northeastern edge of town offers small, spotless rooms in a multistorey building surrounded by gardens. All rooms have fan, net and hot water, and meals are available with advance order. Dalla-dallas heading towards Bigwa will drop you in front, or take a taxi from Msamvu bus stand (Tsh5000).

Mama Pierina's   GUESTHOUSE $

(☑0786 786913; Station St; tw with fan/air-con Tsh25,000/45,000; 🅿✳) The ageing Mama Pierina's is long past its prime, with lackadaisical plumbing and faded facilities, but the welcome is warm and the central location is convenient. The no-longer new 'newer' rooms to the back of the compound are worth the extra money and are reasonable value for a double. The restaurant serves undistinguished but filling meals.

Hotel Oasis   HOTEL $$

(☑0754 377602, 023-261 4178; hoteloasistz@moro goro.net; Station St; s/d/tr from US$50/60/80; 🅿✳🛜❄) Oasis has acceptable albeit faded rooms that are redeemed by generally good service, a decent restaurant, convenient central location, small gardens and a sparkling, recently renovated swimming pool. All rooms come with fan, air-con, TV and fridge.

Morogoro Hotel   HOTEL $$

(☑023-261 3270, 023-261 3271, 023-261 3272; www.morogorohotel.com; Rwegasore Rd; s/d/ste from US$50/70/140; 🅿✳❄) This Morogoro institution has decent twin- and double-bedded rooms in detached bungalows set in spacious green grounds 1.5km off the main road and opposite the golf course. It's popular for weddings on weekends, which can mean loud music until late. Its restaurant and pool are popular for whiling away a Sunday afternoon.

Windows are all screened – a nice touch if you don't want to use the air-con.

New Acropol Hotel   B&B $$

(☑0754 309410; newacropolhotel@morogoro. net; Old Dar es Salaam Rd; s/d/tr US$55/65/75; 🅿✳🛜) This eccentric B&B-style hotel has six mostly spacious and somewhat heavily furnished rooms around a tiny cement courtyard. All have TV, fridge, fan and nets, and there is a good restaurant-bar.

Mbuyuni Farm Retreat   B&B $$$

(☑0784 601220, 023-260 1220; www.kimango. com; s/d US$115/190, 4-person self-catering cottage US$140; 🅿❄) This quiet place consists of three roomy, lovely cottages in the private gardens of a farm just outside Morogoro overlooking the Uluguru Mountains. Meals are available; self-catering is also possible. Turn north off the main highway 12km east of Morogoro at the end of Kingolwira village

---

CHILUNGA CULTURAL TOURISM PROGRAM

Chilunga Cultural Tourism (☑0754 477582, 023-261 3323; www.chilunga. or.tz; Rwegasore Rd) Organises day and overnight excursions around Morogoro, including village visits, hikes and Mikumi NP safaris. Its programs are a good introduction to local life. Prices run from US$25 per person per day for short excursions up to about US$75 per person per day for multi-day hikes, including transport, guide, and village and forest fees.

Southern Highlands Highlights

1 Spotting elephants amid the baobabs in wild and rugged **Ruaha National Park** (p268).

2 Tracking snorting wildebeest, grazing buffaloes and skittish impalas in lovely and easy-to-access **Mikumi National Park** (p259).

3 Relaxing on the tranquil shores of **Lake Nyasa** (p279), with its verdant mountains cascading down to quiet coves.

4 Getting acquainted with local life in and around colourful and bustling **Iringa** (p264).

5 Enjoying lush rolling hill panoramas dotted with orchards and stands of bananas around tiny **Tukuyu** (p278).

6 Hiking past waterfalls and spotting birds and monkeys at **Udzungwa Mountains National Park** (p261).

7 Exploring off the beaten track in **Kitulo National Park** (p272), with its orchids, wildflowers and wide vistas.

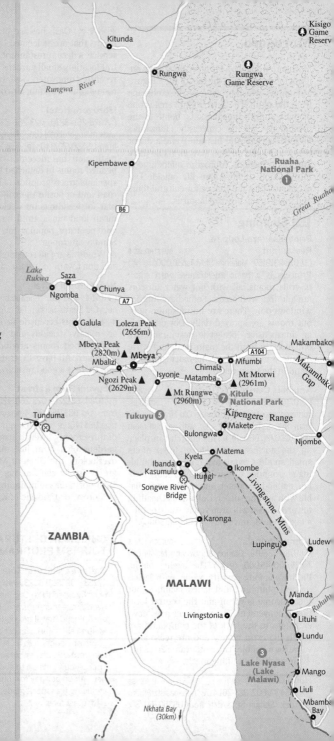

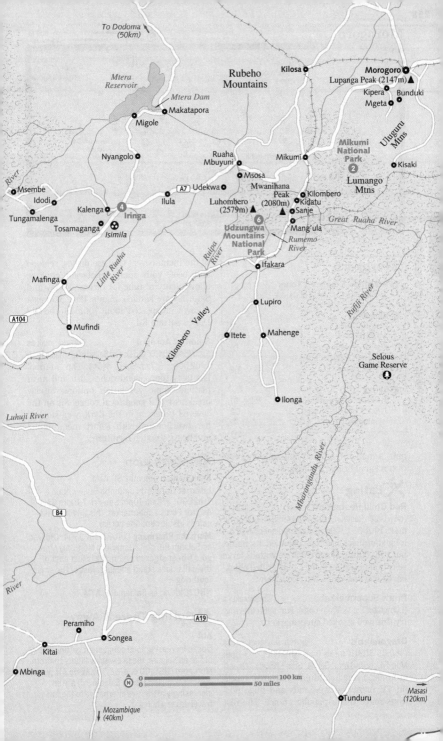

Morogoro

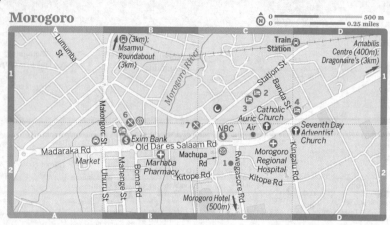

Morogoro

onto a mango-tree-lined lane and continue over a small bridge to the farm.

✗ Eating

Red Chilli Restaurant   INDIAN $
(New Green Restaurant; ☏ 0784 498874; Station St; meals Tsh7000-10,000; ☺ lunch & dinner; ✍) This long-standing place has changed its name, but still retains a loyal clientele with its large selection of Indian dishes, plus grilled chicken, or fish and chips. Service is slow.

Pira's Supermarket   SUPERMARKET $
(Lumumba St; ☺ 10am-6pm) For self-catering, try this well-stocked supermarket.

Dragonaire's   CHINESE, INTERNATIONAL $$
(☏ 0715 311311; meals from Tsh11,000; ☺ 3-11pm Mon-Fri, noon-11pm Sat & Sun; ☎✍) Green grounds, a small children's play area, sports on TV, pizzas on weekends and huge portions make this a popular choice. The rest

of the menu covers Chinese dishes, seafood and beef, with some vegetarian choices; allow plenty of time for orders. Friday and Saturday are karaoke nights. It's 2.5km east of town, signposted about 700m off the Old Dar es Salaam Rd.

Salon at Acropol   INTERNATIONAL $$
(☏ 0754 309410; Old Dar es Salaam Rd; meals from Tsh12,000; ☺ 7am-8pm; ☎✍) The Acropol has tasty soups, sandwiches, fish and meat platters, some vegetarian options, all-day breakfasts and good local coffee. Sit on the covered porch or in the dark, well-stocked bar overflowing with safari memorabilia and heavy wooden furniture.

ⓘ Information

Exim Bank (Lumumba St) ATM.

Internet Cafe (off Lumumba St; per hour Tsh2000; ☺ 8am-10pm Sun-Fri, 7-10pm Sat) Ask for Pira's Supermarket; this tiny internet cafe is just around the corner.

Marhaba Pharmacy (☏ 023-261 3304; Old Dar es Salaam Rd; ☺ 7.30am-5pm Mon-Sat) Morogoro's best-stocked pharmacy is just east of the dalla-dalla stand and just west of the small footbridge.

NBC (Old Dar es Salaam Rd) ATM.

ⓘ Getting There & Away

AIR
Due to increasing road congestion getting out of Dar es Salaam, the five weekly flights to/from Morogoro (US$100 one-way) by **Auric Air** (www.auricair.com; Old Dar es Salaam Rd) are an increasingly attractive alternative to the bus for travellers in a hurry.

HIKING IN THE ULUGURU MOUNTAINS

The verdant Uluguru Mountains – home to the matrilineal Luguru people – rise up majestically from the plains just south of Morogoro, dominating vistas from town. Part of the Eastern Arc chain, the mountains are home to a wealth of birds, plants and insects. These include many unique species, such as the Uluguru bushshrike. The only comparable mountain-forest area in East Africa, as far as age and endemism are concerned, is the Usambara Mountains. Sadly, due to the Uluguru's high population density, most of the original forest cover has been depleted, although small protected patches remain on the upper slopes.

Hiking is the best way to explore and to get acquainted with the life of the local Luguru. A good contact for organising things is Chilunga Cultural Tourism (p255) in Morogoro town. Routes include a half-day return hike (per person US$27) to **Morningside**, an old German mountain hut to the south of town at about 1000m; and a day's return hike (US$40 per person) to **Lupanga Peak** (2147m). Lupanga is the highest point in the immediate vicinity, although views from the top are obscured by the forest. A recommended cultural walk is to **Choma village**, about an hour's walk beyond Morningside, and often included in a two-night, three-day tour (per person US$75).

BUS

The main bus station is 3km north of town on the main Dar es Salaam road, about 300m east of Msamvu roundabout (Tsh5000 in a taxi and Tsh400 in a dalla-dalla; look for vehicles marked 'Kihonda', and confirm that they are going to Msamvu). It's chaotic, with no real order to things; you'll need to ask where to find buses to your destination. Allow at least an hour to catch a dalla-dalla and get yourself sorted at Msamvu. For all destinations, no larger buses originate in Morogoro. It's best to wait for buses from Dar es Salaam (Tsh6000 to Tsh7000, four hours) or Iringa (Tsh13,000 to Tsh15,000, three to four hours), both of which begin passing Morogoro from about 9am. To Tanga, there's a direct bus (Tsh6000, five hours, daily) departing by 8am. Buses also go from Dar via Morogoro to Dodoma (Tsh12,000 to Tsh15,000, four hours). For Kisaki (the closest village to Selous Game Reserve's Matambwe gate), buses go at least once daily from Msamvu (Tsh9000, five to six hours), departing between 9am and 11am.

The main dalla-dalla (minibus) stand is in front of the market, where there is also a taxi rank.

TRAIN

Morogoro is on the Central Line. Service was suspended at the time of research. When functional, arrivals from Dar es Salaam are generally about 10pm.

Mikumi National Park

This is Tanzania's fourth-largest national park, and the most accessible from Dar es Salaam. With almost guaranteed year-round wildlife sightings, Mikumi (Map p294; www.tanzaniaparks.com/mikumi.html; adult/child US$30/10) makes an ideal safari destination for those without much time. Within its 3230 sq km – set between the Uluguru Mountains to the northeast, the Rubeho Mountains to the northwest and the Lumango Mountains to the southeast – Mikumi hosts buffaloes, wildebeest, giraffes, elephants, lions, zebras, leopards, crocodiles and more, and chances are high that you'll see a respectable sampling of these within a short time of entering the park.

The most reliable wildlife watching is around the Mkata floodplain, to the northwest of the main road, with the open vistas of the small but lovely Millennium ('Little Serengeti') area a highlight. This area is especially good for spotting buffaloes – often quite near the roadside – as well as giraffes, elephants and zebras. Another attraction: the Hippo Pools, just northwest of the main entry gate, where you can watch hippos wallowing and snorting at close range, plus do some fine birding.

Mikumi is an important educational and research centre. Among the various projects being carried out is an ongoing field study of yellow baboons, which is one of just a handful of such long-term primate studies on the continent.

To the south, Mikumi is contiguous with Selous Game Reserve.

🛏 Sleeping

Mikumi Park Cottages & Resthouse COTTAGES $$
(📱0767 536135, 0689 062334; mikumi@tanzania parks.com; s/d/tr US$50/75/90; 🅿️❄️) About 3km from the gate, the park cottages and

> ### ⓘ MIKUMI NATIONAL PARK
>
> **Why Go** Easy access from Dar es Salaam; rewarding year-round wildlife watching and birding; giraffes, zebras, buffaloes and sometimes honey badgers
>
> **When to Go** Year-round
>
> **Practicalities** Drive or bus from Dar es Salaam. Entry fees (valid for 24 hours, single entry only) are payable only with Visa or MasterCard. Driving hours inside the park (off the main highway) are 6.30am to 6.30pm.
>
> **Budget Tips** Any bus along the highway will drop you at the park gate. The park doesn't hire vehicles, but staff sometimes rent their own. Arrange at the gate and be prepared to bargain. For sleeping, the park cottages are cheap and pleasant, with a dining room for meals. Post-safari: flag down an Iringa- or Dar-bound bus to continue your travels.
>
> More reliable: hire a safari vehicle through one of the hotels listed under Mikumi town (about US$200 per five-person vehicle for a full-day safari); bring your own lunch and drinks.

resthouse offer rooms in attached brick bungalows, all with bathroom, fan and air-con, and meals on order (Tsh10,000 per plate) at the nearby dining hall. The resthouse, which consists of two double rooms sharing an entrance, also has a kitchen (bring your own gas). Animals frequently wander just in front.

Mikumi Park Campsites CAMPGROUND $
(☏0767 536135, 0689 062334; mikumi@tanzania parks.com; camping public/special US$30/50) The park has four ordinary campsites. The two closest to the park headquarters have toilet facilities and one has a shower. There is a special campsite near Choga Wale in the north of the park.

Mikumi Wildlife Camp LODGE $$$
(Kikoboga; ☏0684 886306, 022-260 0252/3/4; www.mikumiwildlifecamp.com; s/d half board US$218/384; P☷) This camp, about 500m northeast of the park gate, has attractive stone cottages with shaded verandahs and views over a grassy field frequented by grazing zebras and impalas. Given its proximity to the highway, it's not a wilderness experience, but the animals don't seem to mind and you'll probably see plenty from your porch. Vehicle rental is only possible with advance notice.

Vuma Hills Tented Camp TENTED CAMP $$$
(☏0754 237422; www.tanzaniasafaris.info; s/d incl full board & wildlife drives US$365/570; P☷) This pleasant camp is set on a rise about 7km south of the main road, with views over the distant plains. The 16 tented en-suite cottages each have a double and a single bed, the mood is relaxed, the cuisine good and the pool makes a nice post-safari treat. The turn-off is diagonally opposite the park entry gate.

ⓘ Getting There & Around

BUS

All through buses on the Dar es Salaam to Mbeya highway will drop you at the park gate. Pick-ups can also be arranged to continue your journey.

CAR

While vehicle rental can sometimes be arranged privately with park staff, it's better to arrive with your own vehicle or hire one through a Mikumi town hotel.The park gate is about a five-hour drive from Dar es Salaam; speed limits on the section of main highway inside the park are controlled (70km/h during the day and 50km/h at night). A network of generally well-maintained roads in Mikumi's northern section are accessible with a 2WD during most of the year; the south is strictly 4WD, except the road to Vuma Hills Tented Camp. For combining Mikumi NP with Selous GR, the 145km road linking Mikumi's main gate with Kisaki village (21km west of Selous' Matambwe gate) is now open year-round except during the heavy rains, and makes a scenic 4WD alternative; allow about five hours between the two. Alternatively, you can go via Morogoro (140km and five to six hours between Morogoro and Kisaki).

Mikumi

Mikumi is the last of the lowland towns along the Dar es Salaam–Mbeya highway before it starts its climb through the Ruaha River gorge up into the hills of the Southern Highlands. Stretched out along a few kilometres of highway, it has an unmistakable truck-stop feel. It is of interest almost exclusively as a transit point for visits to the Mikumi or Udzungwa Mountains National Parks, although it's possible to visit both without overnighting here.

🛏 Sleeping

Tan-Swiss Hotel & Restaurant LODGE $$
(✆ 0787 191827, 0755 191827; www.tan-swiss.com;
Main Rd; camping US$7, s/d/tr US$55/65/75,
bungalow f US$90; P ❄ 🛜 ⛟) This Swiss- and
Tanzanian-run establishment has a walled-
in camping area with hot-water showers,
plus spacious grounds, comfortable rooms
with private bathroom, and several double
and family bungalows, some with small ter-
races. All are tidy, with fans and surround-
ing greenery. There's a tiny plunge pool and
a good restaurant-bar, also selling takeaway
sandwiches. Vehicle rental to Udzungwa/
Mikumi parks costs US$145/220 per day.

Genesis Motel GUESTHOUSE $$
(✆ 0653 692127, 0716 757707; udzungwamountain
viewhotel@yahoo.com; camping US$5, r per person
with/without air-con US$40/30; P ❄) The func-
tional Genesis, on the highway 2.5km east of
the Ifakara junction, has small, closely spaced
rooms (ask for a newer one), a restaurant and
an attached snake park (admission US$5).
One room has air-con. There's also a small,
walled-in camping area with hot-water showers and nearby kitchen. Vehicle rental costs
US$150/180 per day for Udzungwa/Mikumi
parks; advance notice is required.

Angalia Tented Camp TENTED CAMP $$$
(✆ 0787 518911, 0652 999019; www.angaliacamp.
com; Main Rd; s/d full board US$150/250; P) An-
galia is about 1.5km off the main road, just
west of the Mikumi park boundary, en route
towards Mikumi town. It has five large safari-
style tents set in a patch of forest, alongside
a restaurant and bar. It makes a reasonably
priced alternative to the park-based lodges.

ℹ Getting There & Away

Mikumi's bus stand is at the western end of town
on the main highway. Minibuses go frequently
towards Udzungwa Mountains National Park, but
you'll need to change vehicles at Kilombero. It's
better to wait for one of the larger Dar es Salaam
to Ifakara buses, which begin passing Mikumi
about 11am, going directly to Udzungwa's
Mang'ula headquarters (Tsh6000, two hours)
and on to Ifakara (Tsh13,000, 3½ hours).

Going west, buses from Dar es Salaam begin
passing Mikumi en route to Iringa (Tsh7000,
three hours) from about 9.30am. There's also
a direct bus from Kilombero to Iringa, passing
Mikumi about 5.30am. Going east, there are
large buses to Dar es Salaam (Tsh12,000 to
Tsh13,000, 4½ hours) departing at 6.30am and
7.30am.

Udzungwa Mountains National Park

Towering steeply over the Kilombero Plains
350km southwest of Dar es Salaam are the
wild, lushly forested slopes of the Udzu-
ngwa Mountains, portions of which are
protected as part of the 1900-sq-km **Udzu-
ngwa Mountains National Park** (www.
tanzaniaparks.com/uzdungwa.html; adult/child
US$30/10) – an intriguing offbeat destina-
tion for anyone botanically inclined or in-
terested in hiking away from the crowds. In
addition to an abundance of unique plants,
the park is home to an important popula-
tion of primates (10 species – more than
in any of Tanzania's other parks) as well as
the grey-faced sengi (a species of elephant
shrew). There are also elephants, buffaloes,
leopards, hippos and crocodiles, although
these – particularly hippos and crocodiles –
are primarily in the park's southwest and
seldom seen.

Birding is excellent, especially on the
surrounding Kilombero floodplains. A good
place to start is in the wetlands bordering
the main road about 2km north of Mang'ula
town, just below Hondo Hondo (p263) camp.
Behind here, at the forest's edge, colobus and
other primates are frequently spotted.

🏃 Activities

There are no roads in Udzungwa; instead,
there are about eight major and several lesser
hiking trails winding through various sections
of the park. Most trails are on the eastern side
of the park, although several are now open in
the west as well, including some shorter day
trails in the baobab-studded northwestern

UDZUNGWA MOUNTAINS – A BIODIVERSITY HOTSPOT

The Udzungwas' high degree of ende-
mism and biodiversity is due, in large
part, to the area's constant climate over
millions of years, which has given spe-
cies a chance to evolve. Another factor
is the Udzungwas' altitudinal range.
From the low-lying Kilombero Valley
south of the park (at approximately
200m) to Luhombero Peak (the park's
highest point at 2579m), there is con-
tinuous forest, making this one of the
few places in Africa with uninterrupted
rainforest over such a great span.

corner of the park around Msosa Ranger Post. Bring a water filter for longer hikes.

The going can be tough in parts: the trail network is limited and those trails that do exist are often muddy, steep, humid and densely overgrown. Infrastructure is rudimentary and you'll need to have your own tent and do your hiking accompanied by a guide (US$20 per group per day). In wildlife areas you'll also need to be accompanied by an armed ranger (US$20 per group per day). Porter fees range between Tsh5000 and Tsh15,000 per day, depending on the trail.

But the night-time symphony of forest insects, the rushing of streams and waterfalls and the views down over the plains more than compensate for the logistical challenges. Plus, because the Udzungwas are well off the main road, relatively few travellers come this way and you'll often have trails to yourself.

For supplies there's a tiny market in Mang'ula near the train station, and another small one in town to the north of the station, both with limited selections. Stock up on major items in Dar es Salaam or Morogoro. For longer hikes, bring a supply of dried fruit and nuts to supplement the bland locally available offerings. You can find bottled water near the markets (bring a water filter for longer hikes).

Sanje Falls   HIKING

The most popular route is a short (three to five hours), steep circuit from Sanje village, 10km north of Mang'ula, through the forest to Sanje Falls, where swimming and camping are possible. The park charges a hefty US$20 one-way for transfers between Mang'ula and the Sanje Falls trailhead.

Mwanihana Peak   HIKING

Very satisfying, and a good introduction to the Udzungwas, is the three-day, two-night (or two long days if you're fit) hike up to Mwanihana Peak (2080m), the park's second-highest point.

Luhombero Peak   HIKING

This challenging six-day trail goes from Udekwa (on the park's western side) to Luhombero Peak (2579m), the highest point in the Udzungwas. The trail should be booked well in advance to ensure it is cleared.

Lumemo (Rumemo) Trail   HIKING

A five-day trail from Mang'ula along the Rumemo River to Rumemo Ranger Post, which is connected by a dirt track to Ifakara, about 25km further south.

🛏 Sleeping

🏠 Eastern Udzungwas

Udzungwa Mountain View Hotel   HOTEL **$$**
(📞 0653 692127, 023-262 0218; udzungwamountainviewhotel@yahoo.com; camping US$5, r per person US$30; 🅿) This straightforward hotel, under the same management as Genesis Motel in Mikumi, has simple, somewhat cramped rooms in a shady compound, and a restaurant (meals Tsh12,000 to Tsh20,000). It's about 800m south of the park entrance along the main road.

ℹ UDZUNGWA MOUNTAINS NATIONAL PARK

Why Go Rugged hiking; 10 species of primates (although most are difficult to spot); waterfalls; birding

When to Go Late June through January; avoid the March through May rainy season as many trails are not cleared (and hence not hikeable)

Practicalities Drive or bus from the Tanzam highway to Mang'ula town or take the ordinary train from Dar es Salaam to Mang'ula. Bring in all equipment (including trail snacks and waterproof gear). For now, park fees must be paid at Mang'ula headquarters (currently cash only) unless you make advance arrangements with headquarters for fees to be processed elsewhere.

Budget Tips You'll pay entry and guide fees per 24 hours, whether you take a short stroll or an eight-hour hike. It's best to arrive in Mang'ula, use the afternoon to plan, then set out early the next morning for a full day of hiking. The Udzungwa day trips offered by Mikumi town hotels aren't worth it.

One overnight or multi-night hike in the park is probably enough. Save on fees and spend the rest of your stay exploring the surrounding area. Activities outside park boundaries include village cycling from Hondo Hondo or hiking from Msosa Campsite or Crocodile Camp.

Udzungwa Twiga Hotel
HOTEL **$$**

(☏023-262 0223/4; udzungwatwiga@gmail.com; s/d/tr US$40/60/80; P✷) The Tanapa-run Twiga is set in expansive green grounds surrounded by forest about 700m east of park headquarters. Rooms – overlooking a small courtyard garden – are clean and tidy. All have double bed (married couples only), fan and TV, and there's a restaurant serving local fare.

Udzungwa Mountains Park Campsites
CAMPGROUND **$**

(☏0767 536131, 0689 062291; udzungwa @tanzaniaparks.com; camping US$30) The park has three rudimentary campsites near headquarters, one with a shower and the others near a stream. However, visitors rarely stay at them as prices are high for only the most basic facilities. Bring all supplies. There are also several other similarly priced park-run campsites along the longer trails.

Hondo Hondo
TENTED CAMP **$$$**

(Udzungwa Forest Camp; ☏0758 844228, 0712 304475; www.udzungwaforestcamp.com; s/d/tr hut US$22/44/60, s/d luxury tent US$126/196/252, breakfast extra; P) This camp has several safari-style tents with bathroom, a grassy camping area and two basic mud-and-thatch bungalows sharing ablutions with the campsite. Prices are high for what's on offer, but the tasty cuisine and well-organised excursions compensate, and it's a good base for exploring the Udzungwas. Breakfast/lunch/dinner cost US$10/20/20. It's 2km north of park headquarters on the Mang'ula road.

There's also bike rental and many excursions, including day trips to Kilombero and hiking in nearby forest reserve areas.

🛏 Western Udzungwas

Crocodile Camp
CAMPGROUND, BANDAS **$$**

(☏0784 706835, satellite +882-1645-550267; www.crocodilecamp.de; camping Tsh8000, d/tr/f Tsh70,000/105,000/110,000, d without bathroom Tsh35,000; P) This friendly place is 300m off the main highway 12km east of Ruaha Mbuyuni, with a restaurant, camping and simple bungalows. Staff can organise guides for excursions, including crossing the river running behind the camp via canoe and then hiking a rugged 14km to Msosa village, from where you can explore the western Udzungwas. (Advance notice to park headquarters is essential).

WORTH A TRIP

KILOMBERO VALLEY

The Kilombero Valley's extensive wetlands offer fine birding, wildlife watching, and a glimpse into local life. Hondo Hondo and **Wild Things Safaris** (www.wildthingsafaris.com) organise day canoe trips beginning at the Ifakara ferry. With more time, you can extend your exploration to include Ifakara town, Mahenge (a picturesque mission station) or Itete, another old mission station. There's accommodation in Ifakara at **Mbega Resort** (Ifakara Road; d Tsh40,000; ✷). In Itete, there's a simple mission guesthouse.

Msosa Campsite
CAMPGROUND **$**

(☏0784 414514; camping US$6; P) This bush campsite offers nothing but a shower, toilet, firewood and wilderness walks. It's on the Msosa River, and is a good contact for arranging excursions in the western Udzungwas. Bring food and drink (or rely on the basic provisions available at Msosa village, 2km away), and call in advance to let staff know you're coming.

Take any bus along the highway to Al-Jazeera rest stop, where you can hire a motorcycle (Tsh5000) for the remaining 10km to the campsite; it's down the signposted Udzungwa park road diagonally opposite Al-Jazeera. Sporadic dalla-dallas go from Iringa via Al-Jazeera to Msosa village.

ℹ Information

The closest ATM is in Kilombero, 30km north of Mang'ula en route to Mikumi.

ℹ Getting There & Away

The main entrance gate and park headquarters are in Mang'ula village, 60km south of Mikumi town along the Ifakara road. Entry posts are planned for Msosa, about 10km off the main highway south of Ruaha Mbuyuni, and Udekwa, 60km off the main highway and accessed via a turn-off at Ilula. Once open, these will be useful for those coming from Iringa or wanting to hike in the western Udzungwas.

BUS

Minibuses and pick-ups run daily between Mikumi town (from the dalla-dalla stand on the Ifakara road just south of the main highway) and Kilombero ('Ruaha'), where you'll need to wait for onward transport towards Mang'ula. However, it's faster to wait for one of the larger direct buses coming from Dar es Salaam to Ifakara via Mang'ula. These depart Dar between 6.30am and 10am, and pass Mikumi any time from about 10.30am to 2pm. Going in the other direction, there are several departures each morning from Ifakara, passing Mang'ula between 6am and 10am. The fare between Mang'ula and Mikumi (two hours) is Tsh5000, and the same between Ifakara and Mang'ula (two hours).

From Iringa to Kilombero (Tsh9000, five hours), there are one or two buses daily in each direction, departing by around midday from Iringa and between 5am and 7am from Kilombero.

There are sporadic minibuses between Mang'ula and Sanje (Tsh500), the trailhead for the Sanje Falls hike. Entering the park from the west, there's no reliable public transport to the Msosa or Udekwa entry gates, so you'll need to walk (feasible for Msosa, as it's only 10km off the highway) or hire your own transport.

TRAIN

Tazara ordinary trains stop at Mang'ula (currently arriving from Dar es Salaam at about 3am). The station is about a 30-minute walk from park headquarters; if you make advance arrangements, staff from the hotels will meet you. Express trains stop at Ifakara, 50km further south.

Iringa

POP 151,350

Perched at a cool 1600m on a cliff overlooking the valley of the Little Ruaha River, Iringa was initially built up by the Germans at the turn of the century as a bastion against the local Hehe people. Now it's a district capital, an important agricultural centre and the gateway for visiting Ruaha National Park. Once away from the main street, with its congestion and hustlers, it's also a likeable place, with its bluff-top setting, healthy climate and highland feel, and well worth a stop.

Sights

Market Area MARKET

Iringa's market is piled high with fruits and vegetables, plus other wares, including large-weave, locally made Iringa baskets. On its southern edge, in front of the police station, is a monument honouring Africans who fell during the Maji Maji uprising between 1905 and 1907. West along this same street is the main trading area, dominated by the German-built Ismaili Mosque with its distinctive clock tower.

Commonwealth War Graves Cemetery CEMETERY

At the southeastern edge of town is this cemetery, with graves of the deceased from both world wars.

Iringa Rock Art HISTORIC SITE

This large frieze, similar in style to the Kondoa rock art, is on the edge of town off the Dodoma road. Go with a guide from Neema Crafts.

Neema Crafts CRAFT CENTRE

(☑0783 760945; www.neemacrafts.com; Hakimu St; ☺8.30am-6.30pm Mon-Sat; ☏) ✎ This vocational training centre for young deaf and disabled people is operated by the Anglican church and sells beautiful crafts, handmade paper and cards, jewellery, quilts, clothing, batiks and more. Behind the craft shop is a weaving workshop, and adjoining is a popular cafe (p266). Free tours of the workshops can be arranged. It's just southeast of the Clock Tower roundabout. Highly recommended.

Volunteer opportunities are occasionally available.

Gangilonga Rock HISTORIC SITE

This large rock northeast of town is where Chief Mkwawa meditated and where he learned that the Germans were after him. Its name, *gangilonga*, means 'talking stone' in Hehe. It's an easy climb to the top, with views over town. Iringa Info (p267) or staff at Neema Crafts Centre Internet Cafe (p267) can provide directions and a guide. Don't climb up on your own, as muggings are frequent.

Tours

Warthog Adventures Tanzania TOUR

(☑0688 322888, 0718 467742, 026-270 1988; www.warthogadventures.com; Uhuru Ave) With well-maintained vehicles, this is a good contact for arranging excursions to Ruaha National Park. Safaris cost US$300 per vehicle for the first day, then US$200 for each subsequent day. It's at Iringa Info.

Sleeping

Rivervalley Campsite CAMPGROUND $

(Riverside Campsite; ☑0782 507017, 026-270 1988; www.rivervalleycampsites.com; camping with own/hired tent US$6/10, d tents/cottages US$40/60; ☐) Rivervalley has a lovely setting on the Little Ruaha River, expansive grounds, a large camping area, children's playground, twin-bedded tents, family cottages and tasty

Iringa

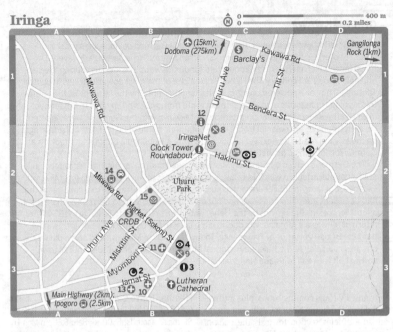

Iringa

meals. It lies 13km northeast of Iringa; take an Ilula dalla-dalla to the signposted right-hand turn-off (Tsh1000), from where it's 1.5km further down a dirt lane. Taxis charge Tsh15,000 to Tsh20,000 from town or Ipogoro bus stand.

The property is wonderfully relaxing, and especially recommended for families. There's also an on-site Swahili language school.

Iringa Lutheran Centre GUESTHOUSE $
(☎0755 517445, 026-270 0722; www.iringa lutherancentre.com; Kawawa Rd; s/d/tr/ste incl full breakfast US$25/45/50/60; P🛜) This long-standing place has clean, quiet and pleasant twin and double-bedded rooms with bathrooms and hot water, and a restaurant. It's on the northeastern edge of town, about 700m southeast of the main road.

Neema Umaki Guest House GUESTHOUSE $
(☎0683 380492, 0786 431274; www. neemacrafts.com; Hakimu St; dm/s/d/f Tsh18,000/25,000/45,000/65,000; 🛜) ✦ This centrally located guesthouse has an array of tidy, comfortable rooms, all with mosquito

CHIEF MKWAWA

Mtwa (Chief) Mkwawa, chief of the Hehe and one of German colonialism's most vociferous resisters, is a legendary figure in Tanzanian history. He is particularly revered in Iringa, near which he had his headquarters. Under Mkwawa's leadership during the second half of the 19th century, the Hehe became one of the most powerful tribes in central Tanzania. They overpowered one group after another until, by the late 1880s, they were threatening trade traffic along the caravan route from western Tanzania to Bagamoyo. In 1891, after several negotiation attempts by Mkwawa with the Germans were rejected, his men trounced the colonial troops in the infamous battle of Lugalo, just outside Iringa on the Mikumi road. The next year, Mkwawa's troops launched a damaging attack on a German fort at Kilosa, further to the east.

The Germans placed a bounty on Mkwawa's head and, once they had regrouped, initiated a counterattack in which Mkwawa's headquarters at Kalenga were taken. Mkwawa escaped, but later, in 1898, committed suicide rather than surrender to a contingent that had been sent after him. His head was cut off and the skull sent to Germany, where it sat almost forgotten (though not by the Hehe) until it was returned to Kalenga in 1954. The return of Mkwawa's remains was due, in large part, to the efforts of Sir Edward Twining, then British governor of Tanganyika. Today, the skull of Mkwawa and some old weapons are on display at the Kalenga Historical Museum (p268), about 13km out of town and just off the road to Ruaha National Park.

nets and TV (fans coming soon), plus a three-bed dorm. It adjoins Neema Crafts, but rooms are in a quieter section towards the back of the complex. Turn east off Uhuru Ave at the Clock Tower and go down about 100m.

Staff can help with information and guides for walking tours of town and excursions, including visits to a local family and homestays. Profits go to support the work of the craft centre.

Mama Iringa B&B
B&B $

(☑0753 757007; mama.iringa@yahoo.com; Don Bosco Area; tw/f Tsh40,000/60,000, s without bathroom Tsh15,000-20,000; ℙ) This quiet place has clean, simple rooms in an old convent. All have nets, and there's a restaurant. It's 3.5km from town, in the Don Bosco area. Follow Mkwawa Rd downhill to the Danish School junction; turn left; take the first (signposted) right. Continue to the end of the graveyards. Turn left. Mama Iringa is 1km further on your right, and poorly signposted.

✖ Eating

Hasty Tasty Too
TANZANIAN, INTERNATIONAL $

(☑026-270 2061; Uhuru Ave; meals from Tsh6000; ⊙7.30am-8pm Mon-Sat, 10am-2pm Sun) This long-standing Iringa classic has good breakfasts, yoghurt, shakes and reasonably priced main dishes, plus an agreeable mix of local and expat clientele. You can get toasted sandwiches packed to go and arrange food for Ruaha camping safaris.

Neema Crafts Centre Cafe
CAFE $

(☑0683 380492; www.neemacrafts.com; Hakimu St; mains about Tsh6500; ⊙8am-6.30pm Mon-Fri; ☎) 🖉 Located upstairs at Neema Crafts, this cafe is justifiably popular, with local coffees and teas, homemade cookies, cakes, soups, and a small selection of sandwiches and light meals. In one corner is a small library where you can read up on development projects in the area.

Ngow'o Supermarket
SUPERMARKET $

(Market St; ⊙8.30am-5.30pm Mon-Sat, 10am-2pm Sun) This well-stocked supermarket is a good bet for self-caterers.

Mama Iringa Pizzeria & Italian Restaurant
ITALIAN $$

(☑0753 757007; mama.iringa@yahoo.com; Don Bosco Area; meals Tsh9000-15,000; ⊙noon-2.30pm & 5-9pm Tue-Sun) Delicious Italian food – pizzas, gnocchi, lasagne and more, plus salads, served in the quiet courtyard of a former convent. It's about 3km from the town centre (Tsh5000 in a taxi). Take Mkwawa Rd to the Danish School junction and follow the signposts.

Sai Villa
INDIAN, INTERNATIONAL $$

(☑0684 062017, 0683 052680; www.saivilla.co.tz; off Kenyatta Dr, Gangilonga Area; mains Tsh9000-20,000; ⊙noon-3.30pm & 7-9pm; ☎☑) A popular spot, especially in the evenings, with a large menu featuring Indian and continental cuisine. Follow Kawawa Rd past the Lutheran guesthouse for about 500m to Mama Siyovelwa pub. Continue past the pub for 300m, taking the second right (just after the road merges with Kenyatta Dr). Sai Villa is the first gate on your right.

ⓘ Information

INTERNET ACCESS

IringaNet (Uhuru Ave; per hour Tsh2000; ⊙8am-6pm Mon-Sat, 10am-1pm Sun)
Neema Crafts Centre Internet Cafe (Hakimu St; per hour Tsh2000; ⊙8.30am-6.30pm Mon-Sat) Wi-fi only.

MEDICAL SERVICES

Aga Khan Health Centre (☑026-270 2277; Jamat St; ⊙8am-6pm Mon-Fri, to 2pm Sat & Sun) Next to the Lutheran cathedral and near the market.
Greenzone Pharmacy (⊙8am-9pm) Opposite the market.
Myomboni Pharmacy (☑026-270 2277, 026-270 2617; ⊙7.30am-7.30pm) Just downhill from the Aga Khan Health Centre.

MONEY

Barclay's Bank (Uhuru Ave) ATM.
CRDB (Uhuru Ave) ATM.

TOURIST INFORMATION

Iringa Info (☑0782 507017, 026-270 1988; info iringa@gmail.com; Uhuru Ave; ⊙9am-5pm Mon-Fri, to 3pm Sat) A recommended first stop and a good place to get information on Ruaha safaris, reliable car rentals, town and village tours and excursions. Also has a cafe and a bookshop.

ⓘ Getting There & Away

AIR

There are almost daily flights on Auric Air (p381) between Iringa and Dar es Salaam (US$160 one-way). Book at Iringa Info. Iringa's Nduli Airfield is about 12km out of town along the Dodoma road.

BUS

To catch any bus not originating in Iringa, you'll need to go to the main bus station at Ipogoro, 3km southeast of town below the escarpment where the Morogoro–Mbeya highway bypasses Iringa (Tsh5000 in a taxi to/from town, though initial quotes are usually much higher). This is also where you'll get dropped off if you're arriving on a bus continuing towards Morogoro or Mbeya. Dalla-dallas to Ipogoro (Tsh400) leave from the Mashine Tatu (M/Tatu) area behind the town bus stand, just off Uhuru Ave. The town bus stand is the place to go for all buses originating in Iringa. These also stop at Ipogoro to pick up additional passengers.

To Dar es Salaam, JM Luxury goes daily, leaving from 7am onwards (Tsh20,000, seven to eight hours) from the town bus stand; book in advance at the JM office behind the bus stand. To Mbeya, Chaula Express departs daily at 7am (Tsh12,000 to Tsh15,000, five hours). Otherwise, you can try to get a seat on one of the through buses from Dar es Salaam that pass Iringa (Ipogoro bus station) from about 1pm. To Njombe (Tsh8000 to Tsh9000, 3½ hours) and Songea (Tsh18,000, eight hours), Super Feo departs at 6am from the town bus station. To Dodoma, Kimotco and several other companies depart daily from 6am (Tsh12,000, four hours), going via Nyangolo and Makatapora on a mostly sealed, mostly good road.

ⓘ Getting Around

The main dalla-dalla stand ('Myomboni') is just down from the market and near the bus station. Taxi ranks include those along the small road between the bus station and the market and at the Ipogoro bus station. Fares from the town bus station to central hotels start at Tsh3000.

Isimila Stone Age Site

Isimila (adult/child Tsh20,000/10,000, plus mandatory guide fee per group Tsh10,000; ⊙8am-6pm) is signposted off the Mbeya road to the left, about 15km west of Iringa. Here, in the late 1950s, amid a landscape of small canyons and eroded sandstone pillars, archaeologists unearthed one of the most significant Stone Age finds ever identified. Tools found at the site are estimated to be between 60,000 and 100,000 years old. There's a museum with small, well-captioned displays highlighting some of the discoveries.

The main pillar area is accessed via a walk down into a steep valley (about one hour round-trip), for which you'll need a guide. Visits are best in the morning or late afternoon, when the sun is not at its zenith. There's also a covered picnic area (bring your own food).

With a bit of endurance for heat and traffic, the site is straightforward to reach by bicycle from Iringa. Via public transport, take an Ifunda or Mafinga dalla-dalla from the Iringa town bus station and ask the driver to drop you at the Isimila junction (Tsh1500), from where it's a 15-minute walk to the site. Taxis charge from about Tsh25,000 for the return trip.

A possible detour on bicycle or with private vehicle is to nearby **Tosamaganga**, a pretty hilltop mission station established by Italian missionaries in the early 20th century. It's reached via the unsignposted 'Njia Panda ya Tosamaganga' turn-off from the main road, 4km northeast of the Kalenga turn-off. Follow the wide, unpaved road for about 5km, first past cornfields and then along a eucalyptus-lined lane to the red-tile roofs and imposing church of the mission.

Kalenga

About 15km from Iringa on the road to Ruaha National Park is the former Hehe capital of Kalenga. It was here that Chief Mkwawa had his headquarters until Kalenga fell to the Germans in the 1890s, and it was here that he committed suicide rather than succumb to the German forces.

⊙ Sights

Kalenga Historical Museum MUSEUM
(adult/child Tsh20,000/10,000; ⊙8am-5.30pm)
This tiny museum contains Mkwawa's skull, personal effects, a python-skin drum and several other relics. The admission price includes a historical explanation by the caretaker, who also appreciates a tip. However, unless you are very interested in Chief Mkwawa or Tanzanian history, or are eligible for the steeply discounted resident rates, it's difficult to recommend this dusty museum at its current price.

It's also possible to arrange with the caretaker to visit other nearby historical sites, including a cemetery with the graves of some of Mkwawa's 62 wives, and the site of part of Kalenga's old defensive wall (the ruins themselves are now nonexistent).

ℹ Getting There & Away

Dalla-dallas go regularly to Kalenga (Tsh500) from Iringa's post office, also stopping at Mlandege bus stand near the roundabout at the start of the Ruaha road. Ask to be dropped at the signposted turn-off, from where it's an 800m walk through the village to the museum.

Ruaha National Park

Together with neighbouring conservation areas, **Ruaha National Park** (www.tanzaniaparks.com/ruaha.html; adult/child US$30/10) forms the core of a wild and extended ecosystem covering about 40,000 sq km and providing home to Tanzania's largest elephant population. In addition to the elephants, which are estimated to number about 12,000, the park (Tanzania's largest, with an area of approximately 22,000 sq km) hosts large herds of buffaloes, as well as greater and lesser kudus, Grant's gazelles, wild dogs, ostriches, cheetahs, roan and sable antelopes, and more than 400 different types of birds.

Ruaha is notable for its wild and striking topography, especially around the Great Ruaha River, which is its heart. Much of this topography is undulating plateau averaging about 900m in height with occasional rocky outcrops and stands of baobabs. Mountains in the south and west reach to about 1600m and 1900m, respectively, and running through the park are several 'sand' rivers, most of which dry up during the dry season, when they are used by wildlife as corridors to reach areas where water remains.

Ruaha is also notable as it straddles a transition zone between East African savannah lands and the *miombo* (moist) woodlands more common further south, thus offering a mix of plant and animal species from both regions.

Although the area around the camps on the eastern side of the park fills up during the August to October high (dry) season, Ruaha receives relatively few visitors in comparison with the northern parks. Large sections are unexplored, and for much of the year, you're likely to have things to yourself. Whenever you visit, set aside as much time as you can spare; it's not a place to be discovered on a quick in-and-out trip.

⊙ Sights & Activities

The best place to experience the park is along the river, especially the circuit that runs northeast, following the riverbanks, before turning inwards towards the area around Mwagusi Safari Camp. Birding here is especially fine and sightings of hippos, crocodiles and elephants are almost guaranteed. Try not to miss sunrise and sunset, when the large rocks dotting the river's channel are illuminated and the bordering vegetation and flatlands come alive. Bat-eared foxes and jackals are common around the Msembe area. Lions aren't as readily seen as in the Serengeti, but they are definitely present, with the area just north of the river towards Mwagusi a good bet.

From June to January, it's possible to organise two- to three-hour **walking safaris** (park walking fee US$20 per group).

❶ RUAHA NATIONAL PARK

Why Go Outstanding dry season wildlife watching, especially elephants, hippos, lions and wild dogs; excellent birding; rugged scenery

When to Go The driest season is between June and November, and this is when it's easiest to spot wildlife along the river beds. During the rainy season, some areas become impassable and wildlife is difficult to locate, but green panoramas, lavender-coloured flowers and rewarding birding compensate.

Practicalities Drive in from Iringa; fly in from Arusha or Dar es Salaam. Entry fees are per 24-hour period, single entry only, and payable with Visa or MasterCard only. The main gate (open 7am to 6pm) is about 8km inside the park boundary on its eastern side, near the park's Msembe headquarters. Driving is permitted within the park from 6am to 6.30pm.

Budget Tips Ruaha has no true budget options. Your best bet: get a group of four or five, hire a vehicle in Iringa for an overnight safari and sleep at the old park *bandas*. Meals are available, but bring your own drinks. It's also possible to take the bus from Iringa to Tungamalenga, and arrange car hire there for a safari (about US$250 per day). But confirm vehicle availability in advance, and remember park fees are single entry only. Car hire from Iringa and sleeping inside the park usually works out at better value.

☞ Tours

Ruaha Cultural Tourism Program

CULTURAL TOUR

(☑ 0757 151349, 0752 142195; www.ruahacultural
tours.com; half-/full-day tour US$20/40, per person full board in Maasai village US$27) Cultural tours of a Maasai *boma* (including the chance to spend the night), traditional cooking lessons, nature walks and more. It's a recommended stop en route to or from Ruaha.

⌂ Sleeping

⌂ Inside the Park

Ruaha Park Bandas & Cottages COTTAGES **$$**

(☑ 0756 144400; ruaha@tanzaniaparks.com; s/d bandas with shared bathroom US$30/60, s/d/f cottages US$50/100/100; **P**) Ruaha's 'old' park *bandas* are twin-bedded metal rondavels in a good setting on the river near park headquarters. Meals are available. Restoration work is underway; soon, all should have private bathroom. About 3km beyond here are the 'new' tidy cement cottages (all with bathroom) on a rise overlooking the river in the distance. There's a dining hall on-site (meals Tsh6000).

Accommodation should be paid for at the entry gate with credit card.

Ruaha Park Campsites CAMPGROUND **$**

(☑ 0756 144400; ruaha@tanzaniaparks.com; camping public/special US$30/50) The park runs several public campsites about 9km

northwest of the Msembe park headquarters, with toilets and showers, and about five special campsites (no facilities) scattered in the bush well away from the Msembe area.

Mwagusi Safari Camp TENTED CAMP **$$$**

(☑ UK +44 18 2261 5721; www.mwagusicamp.com; s/d all-inclusive US$660/1190; ☺ Jun-Mar; **P**) This highly regarded 16-bed owner-managed camp is set in a prime location for wildlife viewing on the Mwagusi Sand River about 20km inside the park gate. The atmosphere is intimate and the guiding is top-notch. In addition to the superb surrounding wildlife, highlights are the spacious tented *bandas*, the rustic, natural feel and the romantic evening ambience.

Ruaha River Lodge LODGE **$$$**

(☑ 0754 237422; www.tanzaniasafaris.info; s/d incl full board & wildlife drives US$405/650; **P**) This unpretentious, beautifully situated 28-room lodge was the first in the park and is the only place on the river. It's divided into two separate sections, each with its own dining area. The stone cottages directly overlook the river – elephants and hippos are frequently spotted here – and there's a treetop-level bar-terrace with stunning riverine panoramas.

It's about 15km inside the gate, southwest of park headquarters.

Mdonya Old River Camp TENTED CAMP **$$$**

(☑ 022-260 1747; www.mdonya.com; per person incl full board & excursions US$390; ☺ Jun-Mar; **P**) The relaxed Mdonya Old River Camp, about 1½ hours' drive from park headquarters, has 12 tents on the banks of the Mdonya Sand River, with elephants occasionally wandering through camp. It's a straightforward, unpretentious place with the necessary comforts tempered by a bush feel. If you take advantage of Coastal Travel's special fly-in offers, it offers good value for a Ruaha safari.

Outside the Park

There are several places just outside the park boundaries along the Tungamalenga village road (take the left fork at the junction when coming from Iringa). If staying here, remember that park entry fees are valid for a single entry only per 24-hour period.

Chogela Campsite CAMPGROUND $

(☎ 0782 032025, 0757 151349; www.chogelasafari camp.wix.com/chogelasafaricamp; camping US$10, s/d safari tents US$30/60; P) Shaded grounds, a large cooking-dining area and hot-water showers make this a popular budget choice. There are also twin-bedded safari-style tents. Vehicle rental can be arranged (US$250 for a full-day safari, advance notice required), as can meals. The camp is about 34km from the park gate along the Tungamalenga road.

Ruaha Cultural Tourism Program (p269) also has a base here, for arranging nature walks, village tours and day or overnight visits to a nearby Maasai community.

Tungamalenga Lodge & Campsite LODGE $

(☎ 026-278 2196, 0787 859369; www.ruahatunga camp.com; Tungamalenga road; camping US$10, r per person with breakfast/full board US$40/65; P) This long-standing place, about 35km from the park gate and close to the bus stand, has a small garden for camping, basic but tidy rooms in double-storey bungalows and a restaurant. Village tours can be arranged. Vehicle rental is possible with advance arrangement only.

Ruaha Hilltop Lodge LODGE $$

(☎ 0784 726709, 026-270 1806; www.ruahahill toplodge.com; r per person full board US$80; P) This friendly no-frills lodge has a fine hilltop perch 1.5km off the Tungamalenga road, with wide views over the plains from the raised restaurant-bar area. Behind these are simple two-person cement *bandas*. During the dry season, it's common to see wildlife passing by down below. Cultural walks in the area can be arranged, as can vehicle rental for Ruaha NP safaris.

Tandala Tented Camp TENTED CAMP $$$

(☎ 0755 680220, 0757 183420; www.tandala camp.com; s/d full board US$250/440; ⊙ Jun–Mar; P ☒) Lovely Tandala is just outside the park boundary, 12km from the gate. Its 11 raised tents are scattered around shaded grounds with a bush feel (elephants and other animals are frequent visitors). Staff can organise vehicle rental to Ruaha NP, and guided walks and night drives in park border areas. The swimming pool and low-key ambience make it a good family choice.

❶ Getting There & Away

AIR

There is an airstrip at Msembe. Coastal Aviation (p381) flies from Dar es Salaam and Zanzibar to Ruaha via Selous Game Reserve (US$350 one-way from Dar es Salaam, from Zanzibar US$390) and between Ruaha and Arusha (US$330). Safari Airlink has similarly priced flights connecting Ruaha with Dar es Salaam, Selous and Arusha, and also with Katavi and Mikumi.

BUS

There's a daily bus between Iringa and Tungamalenga village (Tsh6000, five hours), departing Iringa's Mwangata bus stand (on the south-western edge of town at the start of the Ruaha road) at 1pm. Look for the one marked 'Idodi–Tungamalenga'. Departures from Tungamalenga's village bus stand (along the Tungamalenga road, just before Tungamalenga Camp) are at 6am. From Tungamalenga, there's no onward transport to the park, other than rental vehicles arranged in advance through the Tungamalenga road camps (prices start at US$250 per day). There's no vehicle rental once at Ruaha, except what you've arranged in advance with the lodges.

CAR

Ruaha is 115km from Iringa along an unsealed road. About 58km before the park, the road forks; both sides go to Ruaha and the distance is about the same each way, but it's best to take the more travelled and more populated Tungamalenga road (left fork). The closest petrol is in Iringa. Warthog Adventures (p264) in Iringa offers vehicle rental to Ruaha for US$300 per vehicle for the first day, then US$200 per vehicle for each subsequent day, and is a good contact for finding other travellers interested in joining a group.

Makambako

Makambako (a stop on the Tazara railway line) is a windy, scruffy highland town at the junction where the road from Songea and Njombe meets the Dar es Salaam–Mbeya

WORTH A TRIP

IRINGA TO MAKAMBAKO

From Iringa, the Tanzam highway continues southwest, past dense stands of pine, before reaching the junction town of Makambako. En route are some lovely possibilities for detours.

Kisolanza – The Old Farm House (☑0754 306144; www.kisolanza.com; camping US$7, s/d/tr/f cottages half board from US$110/140/185/170, tw without bathroom US$40; P) This gracious 1930s farm homestead, 50km southwest of Iringa, is fringed by stands of pine and rolling hill country and recommended for its accommodation and its outstanding cuisine. There are two camping grounds (overlanders and private vehicles), twin-bedded rooms, cosy wooden chalets, family cottages with fireplace, and two luxury garden cottages. All are spotless, impeccably furnished and excellent value.

There's also a bar, a shop selling home-grown vegetables and other produce, and many beautiful walks in the area. Buses will drop you at the Kisolanza turn-off, from where it's a 1.5km walk in to the lodge. Advance bookings are advisable for accommodation, but there's always room for campers.

Mufindi Highlands Lodge (☑0754 237422; www.tanzaniasafaris.info; s/d full board US$210/300; P) This lovely lodge, set amid landscaped gardens in the forested hills and tea plantations around Mufindi, offers cool highland air and the chance to recharge, plus walking trails, cycling, horse riding and fishing. The cosy wooden cabins have sunset views and family-style meals are prepared with farm produce. It's 45km south of Mafinga; pick-ups can be arranged.

highway. Geographically, the area marks the end of the Eastern Arc mountain range and the start of the Southern Highlands. While Makambako is also notable for its large market, which includes an extensive used-clothes section, there's no real reason to stop here other than as a lunch stop if you are driving, or to get off the train and onto the bus to head south to Njombe and Songea.

🛏 Sleeping

Shinkansen Lodge HOTEL $
(☑026-273 0029; Njombe Rd; s/d Tsh25,000/35,000; P) A small compound with double- and twin-bedded rooms (some with interior windows only) accessed via an imposing Japanese-style entry gate and a well-fortified parking area. Inside, the rooms are clean, but the overall atmosphere is gloomy. There is no food. It's about 1km south of the main junction, and about 500m north of the bus stand.

Triple J Hotel GUESTHOUSE $
(☑0767 310176, 026-273 0475; kaributriplejhotel@yahoo.com; Njombe Rd; s/d Tsh20,000/25,000; P) Clean, small and somewhat cramped rooms and a restaurant in a tiny compound. The big plus here is the restaurant, which serves filling local-style meals for about Tsh5000, with almost no wait, assuming you order the menu of the day. It's 800m south

of the main junction along the Njombe road, 700m north of the bus stand and signposted.

❶ Getting There & Away

The bus stand is about 1.5km south of the main junction along the Njombe road. The first bus to Mbeya (Tsh8000 to Tsh9500, three hours) leaves at 6am, with another bus at 7am. The first buses (all smaller Coastals) to Njombe (Tsh3000, one hour) and Songea (Tsh12,000, five hours) depart about 6.30am, and there's a larger bus departing at 6.30am for Iringa (Tsh8000, three to four hours) and Dar es Salaam.

Njombe

POP 130,220

Njombe, about 60km south of Makambako and 235km north of Songea, is a district capital, regional agricultural centre and home of the Bena people. It would be unmemorable but for its highly scenic setting on the eastern edge of the Kipengere mountain range at almost 2000m. In addition to giving it the reputation of being Tanzania's coldest town, this perch provides wide vistas over hills that seem to roll endlessly into the horizon. The surrounding area, dotted with tea plantations and fields of wildflowers, is ideal for walking and cycling. As there is no tourism infrastructure, anything you undertake will need to be under your own steam.

🛈 HIKING IN THE SOUTHERN HIGHLANDS

Before visiting Kitulo National Park or hiking elsewhere in the Southern Highlands, get a copy of Liz de Leyser's excellent *A Guide to the Southern Highlands of Tanzania*, available at many bookshops and hotels in and around Mbeya and Iringa. For more on Kitulo's flowers, see *Orchids and Wildflowers of Kitulo Plateau* by Rosalind Salter and Tim Davenport. Greentours (p381) offers upmarket tours combining Kitulo and Udzungwa Mountains parks.

At the northern edge of town, visible from the main road and an easy walk, are the **Luhuji Falls**. It's possible to go from Njombe via public transport or private vehicle along scenic highland backroads to the Kitulo Plateau, and down to the shores of Lake Nyasa.

🛏 Sleeping & Eating

Hill Side Hotel HOTEL $
(Chani Motel; ☏0752 910068, 026-278 2357; chanihotel@yahoo.com; r Tsh30,000-50,000; ℗) This cosy place has modest twin- and double-bedded rooms, hot water (usually), small but lovely poinsettia-studded gardens, and a restaurant with TV and filling meals. There's currently no signpost; turn off the main road onto the dirt lane next to the courthouse (Mahakamani); it's just downhill and diagonally opposite from the police station.

Mwambasa Lodge GUESTHOUSE $
(☏026-278 2301; Main road; r Tsh20,000) Mwambasa is a local-style guesthouse that is slated to be knocked down when the road is expanded. Until this happens (likely not within the lifetime of this book), it remains a reliable shoestring option. It is diagonally opposite (and just north of) the bus stand, on the main road. There's no food.

FM Hotel HOTEL $
(☏0786 513321; Songea Rd; s Tsh30,000-40,000, d Tsh50,000, ste Tsh70,000; ℗) This large, soulless multistorey place bills as Njombe's sleekest place, with modern rooms boasting mosquito nets and TV. Some face the highway, with views over Njombe, others overlook an interior courtyard. There's a restaurant. It's on the main road 1km south of and diagonally opposite the bus stand.

Duka la Maziwa SELF-CATERING $
(Cefa Njombe Milk Factory; ☏026-278 2851; ⊙7am-6pm Mon-Sat, 10am-2pm Sun) Fresh milk, yoghurt and delicious Italian cheeses. It's just off the main road; turn in by the TFA building and go down about two blocks. The shop is to the left.

🛈 Information

NBC and CRDB banks, both along the main road at the southern end of town, have ATMs.

🛈 Getting There & Away

The bus stand is on the west side of the main road, about 600m south of the large grey-water tank.

Buses go daily to Songea (Tsh9000 to Tsh12,000, four hours), Makambako (Tsh3000, one hour), Iringa (Tsh8000, 3½ hours) and Mbeya (Tsh8000 to Tsh9000, four hours), with the first departures at 6.30am.

For hikers, there are daily vehicles to Bulongwa (departing Njombe about 10am) and Ludewa (departing by 8am), from where you can walk down to Matema and Lupingu respectively, both on the Lake Nyasa shoreline. You can also catch transport towards Bulongwa at the start of the Makete Rd at the northern end of town, just downhill from the Chani Motel turn-off. This road, which continues past Kitulo National Park and on to Isyonje and the junction with the Tukuyu road, is easily passable during the dry season, somewhat slower during the rains. A small section near Makete is sealed.

Kitulo National Park

This **national park** (www.tanzaniaparks.com/kitulo.html; adult/child US$30/10) protects the flower-clad Kitulo Plateau, together with sections of the former Livingstone Forest Reserve, which runs south from the plateau paralleling the Lake Nyasa shoreline. The area, much of which lies between 2600m and 3000m in the highlands northeast of Tukuyu, is beautiful, and a paradise for hikers, although tourism infrastructure is almost non-existent. The park reaches its prime during the rainy season from about December until April, when it explodes in a profusion of colour, with orchids (over 40 species have been identified so far), irises, aloes, geraniums and many more flowers carpeting its grassy expanses. Rising up from the plateau is Mt Mtorwi (2961m), which is 1m higher than Mt Rungwe and southern Tanzania's highest peak. The best months for seeing the flowers are December through March, which is also when hiking is at its muddiest. Orchids are at their peak in February.

🛏 Sleeping

The only accommodation inside the park is camping (US$30). At the time of writing, camping is permitted anywhere, although this is likely to change once a planned public camping ground with toilets and showers is opened.

Outside the park there are several basic guesthouses in Matamba village, near park headquarters, and all within less than 10 minutes walk of the bus stand.

Bustani ya Mungu   GUESTHOUSE $
(God's Garden; ☑ 0752 251976; s/d Tsh30,000/35,000) This small place has clean, new rooms overlooking a tiny garden, and meals on order. Take the signposted turn-off for 'Super Eden Motel'; after passing the Super Eden, continue for 150m further down the dirt lane. The unsignposted Bustani ya Mungu will be to your right; look for the red-brick, blue-roofed building.

Super Eden Motel   GUESTHOUSE $
(☑ 0763654441; s/d/f Tsh15,000/15,000/30,000) This local guesthouse has small double-bedded rooms and a larger family room with one double and two twin beds. Meals can be arranged, as can hot water buckets for bathing. It's at the southern end of Matamba village. Go uphill (south) from the bus stand for about 100m to the signposted right-hand turn-off, from where it's 50m further.

ℹ Getting There & Away

The best access is via Mfumbi village, about 90km east of Mbeya along the main highway, from where an all-weather road climbs 32km up to Matamba village and the Tanapa temporary headquarters, with some spectacular views en route. From Matamba, it's about 12km further via 4WD with high clearance (or a couple of hours on foot) along a rough road that is sometimes impassable in the rains up onto the plateau itself.

It's also possible to reach Kitulo via the signposted park turn-off 2km west of Chimala town and about 80km east of Mbeya along the main highway. From here, a rough and rocky road (4WD only) winds its way for 9km up the escarpment via a series of 50-plus hairpin turns, offering wide vistas over the Usangi plains below. From the top, it's a further 12km or so to Matamba, along a wonderfully scenic route across the Chimala River, past fields of sunflowers and the occasional small house. If you use this road, do so with extreme caution, as accidents are frequent.

Another option is via Isyonje village, just east of the Tukuyu road, following a mostly well-maintained dirt track for about 35km to the junction with the park road, from where it is 32km further through the park to Matamba. From Njombe, a good dirt road traverses the 155km to the park via Makete and Bulongwa, joining the route from Isyonje.

Using public transport, a bus goes daily between Mbeya and Matamba via Mfumbi village on the main Tanzam highway, departing Matamba at 6am and Mbeya between noon and 1pm (Tsh30,000, four hours).

Gazelle Safaris (p274) in Mbeya organises Kitulo excursions, as does Kisolanza – The Old Farm House (p271), near Iringa.

ℹ KITULO NATIONAL PARK

Why Go Stunning terrain with flowers and waterfalls; excellent wilderness hiking for well-equipped hikers

When to Go June through October for hiking; December through March for wildflowers

Practicalities Drive in from Mbeya or Iringa; bus from Mbeya. Fees must currently be paid in cash (a card system is planned). Guides are not required, but can be arranged (US$20 per day) at Tanapa's temporary headquarters at Matamba village, which is also where you pay your park fees. For any hiking, you'll need to be self-sufficient, with food, water (bring a filter or purifying tablets) and a GPS (if hiking independently).

Budget Tips There's a daily bus from Mbeya to Matamba village, where you can sleep in a local guesthouse. Next morning, pay park fees, hire a motorbike or pick-up to cover the 12km from town to the park gate, hike southwards through the park, camping overnight, and catch transport the next day along the Makete road on Kitulo's southern boundary to Isyonje village (for Tukuyu) or to Makete (for Njombe). Note: this route is for hardy, fully equipped hikers only. Alternatively, explore Kitulo by vehicle. Rentals from Mbeya are reasonably priced if you are in a group.

Mbeya

POP 385,280

The thriving town of Mbeya sprawls at about 1700m in the shadow of Loleza Peak (2656m), in a gap between the verdant Mbeya mountain range to the north and the Poroto mountains to the southeast. It was founded in 1927 as a supply centre for the gold rush at Lupa, to the north, but today owes its existence to its position on the Tazara railway line and the Tanzam highway, and its status as a major trade and transit junction between Tanzania, Zambia and Malawi.

The surrounding area is lush, mountainous and scenic. It's also a major farming region for coffee, tea, bananas and cocoa. While central Mbeya is on the scruffy side (especially around the bus station), the cool climate, jacaranda trees and views of the hills compensate, and there are many nearby excursions.

Tours

Gazelle Safaris
TOUR, SAFARIS

(☑025-250 2482, 0784 666600; www.gazelle safaris.com; Jacaranda Rd) Arranges guides and transport for day tours around Mbeya, excursions to Kitulo National Park, car rental, and safaris further afield, especially in the southern circuit. It also does domestic and international flight bookings.

Sisi Kwa Sisi
TOUR

(Station Rd) Between the market and the bus station, and unsignposted, this sometimes-on, sometimes-off budget operator can occasionally be useful for arranging a guide to local attractions. The office is often unstaffed (whenever its owner is out leading an excursion), so send a text to the number he leaves on the door.

Sleeping

Karibuni Centre
GUESTHOUSE $

(☑0754 510174, 025-250 3035; www.mec-tanzania.ch/karibuni; camping Tsh5000, s/d Tsh20,000/32,000; P) This quiet mission-run place is in a small, enclosed compound where you can also pitch a tent. Most rooms have bathrooms, and there's a restaurant. Karibuni is 3km southwest of the town centre. Take a taxi from the bus stand (Tsh4000).

If you arc driving, go 1.2km west along the highway from the big town-airport junction at the entrance to Mbeya to the tiny signpost on Lehner St. Turn right, continue 300m to the T-junction, turn right again. The compound is 200m up on the left.

Sombrero Hotel
HOTEL $

(☑0766 755227, 025-250 0663; Post St; s/tw/ste Tsh30,000/40,000/60,000) No-frills rooms in a convenient, central location, and a tiny restaurant downstairs. There are no screens in the windows, but most rooms have nets.

Peace of Mind Rest House
HOTEL $

(☑0754 277410, 025-250 0498; Jamatikhana Rd; r Tsh40,000-60,000; P❄️🛜) The name of this place is as incongruous as its appearance – a columned, lime-coloured multistorey building squeezed into a narrow plot of land – but the modern-ish rooms are decent value for the price. All have one double bed, and meals can be arranged.

Mbeya Hotel
HOTEL $$

(☑025-250 2224/2575; mbeyahotel@hotmail.com; Kaunda Ave; s/d/tr/ste Tsh50,000/70,000/90,000/100,000; P❄️🛜) The former East African Railways & Harbours Hotel has straightforward twins and doubles. The better ones (all doubles) are in an extension attached to the main building. More cramped rooms are in separate bungalows out back. There are also small gardens and a restaurant. It's opposite NBC bank.

New Millennium Inn
GUESTHOUSE $

(☑025-250 0599; Mbalizi Rd; r Tsh17,000-20,000) In a noisy but convenient location directly opposite the bus stand, with good-value 'newer' rooms upstairs and separate from the main building, and smaller, darker rooms near the reception. The more expensive rooms have beds big enough for two, but there's no same-gender sharing.

Ifisi Community Centre
HOTEL, GUESTHOUSE $

(☑0753 011622, 025-256 1021; icc@mec-tanzania.ch; r hotel Tsh50,000-80,000, r guesthouse Tsh25,000-40,000; P) A good option for self-drivers en route to/from the Zambian border. There are small-ish guesthouse rooms plus more spacious rooms in a multistorey 'hotel'. Some hotel rooms have views over an adjoining private wildlife sanctuary, and there's a restaurant. It's on the north side of the main highway, about 20km west of Mbeya.

Utengule Coffee Lodge
LODGE $$

(☑0786 481902, 0753 020901; www.riftvalley-zanzibar.com; camping US$8.50, s US$85-140, d US$100-177, f US$165; P🛜🏊) This lovely

Mbeya

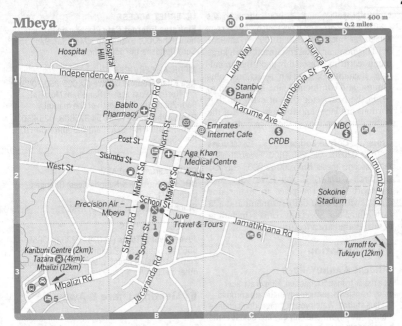

Mbeya

lodge is set in expansive grounds on a working coffee plantation in the hills 20km west of Mbeya. Accommodation includes spacious standard rooms, two-storey balconied suites and a large family room. There are tennis courts and a restaurant. If you want to pamper yourself while in the Mbeya area, this is a good choice. There's also a grassy lawn for campers.

From Mbeya, follow the highway 12km west to Mbalizi junction. Turn right; continue 8.5km to the lodge entry on your right.

Hill View Hotel   HOTEL $$

(☑ 0767 502767, 025-250 2766; www.hillview-hotel. com; Kaunda Ave; r US$77-95, 4- to 6-person ste US$160-237; P❄🛜) This 25-room establishment has a quiet location and modern, comfortable rooms. The more expensive ones have Jacuzzi-style bathtubs, and many are apartment-style with a shared kitchen and TV sitting room. Some 'standard' rooms use the bathroom of the surrounding apartment, meaning you'll have to leave your room to use the toilet or shower, so check when booking. There's a restaurant on-site.

🍴 Eating

Malimbe de Ville   TANZANIAN $

(Jacaranda Rd; meals Tsh5000-12,000; ⊙7am-9pm) Inexpensive snacks and meals, including smoothies and pizza, just opposite Gazelle Safaris.

Sombrero Restaurant   TANZANIAN $

(North St; meals Tsh5000-8000; ⊙breakfast, lunch & dinner) This hotel restaurant serves a small selection of local-style dishes. It's nothing special, but the food is decent and it offers a quiet place to sit in the town centre.

Azra Supermarket   SUPERMARKET $

(School St) Small but well stocked; just up from the Tanesco building.

Mbeya Hotel INDIAN, INTERNATIONAL $
(☑ 025-250 2224/2575; mbeyahotel@hotmail.com;
Kaunda Ave; meals Tsh6000-10,000; ☺ 7am-9pm;
🖉) This popular hotel restaurant has a large
menu featuring reasonably good Indian cuisine, including vegetarian selections, plus
Chinese and continental fare. Meals tend to
be on the heavy side (lots of extra oil), but
portions are large and it remains one of the
better dining options in the town centre.

Utengule Coffee Lodge EUROPEAN $$$
(☑ 0753 020901, 025-256 0100; www.riftvalley-
zanzibar.com; meals Tsh15,000-25,000; ☺ break-
fast, lunch & dinner) If you have your own
transport this is the place to go for fine
dining, with both a daily set menu and à la
carte, and a bar. Speciality coffees (including
to take home) are a feature.

ℹ Information

DANGERS & ANNOYANCES
As a major transport junction, Mbeya attracts
many transients, particularly in the area around
the bus station. Watch your luggage, don't change
money with anyone and only buy bus tickets in the
bus company offices. Also be very wary of anyone
presenting themselves as a tourist guide and
don't make tourist arrangements with anyone
outside of an office. Bus ticketing scams abound,
especially for cross-border connections. Ignore
all touts, no matter how apparently legitimate,
trying to sell you through-tickets to Malawi (espe-
cially) or Zambia. Pay the fare only to the border,
and then arrange onward transport from there.

INTERNET ACCESS
Emirates Internet Cafe (Jacaranda Rd; per
hour Tsh2000; ☺ 8am-8pm Mon-Sat, 9am-3pm
Sun) Opposite the post office.

MEDICAL SERVICES
Aga Khan Medical Centre (☑ 025-250 2043;
cnr North & Post Sts; ☺ 8am-8pm Mon-Sat,
9am-2pm Sun) Just north of the market.
Babito Pharmacy (☑ 0754 376808, 025-250
0965; Station Rd; ☺ 7.30am-6.30pm Mon-Fri,
8am-5pm Sat)

MONEY
CRDB (Karume Ave) ATM.
NBC (cnr Karume & Kaunda Aves) Changes
cash; ATM.
Stanbic Bank (Karume Ave) ATM.

TRAVEL AGENCIES
Juve Travel & Tours (☑ 0767 927627, 0655
656542; School St; ☺ 8am-6pm Mon-Fri, 9am-
2pm Sat) Fastjet agent; also does bookings for
other airlines.

ℹ Getting There & Away

AIR
The opening of Songwe International Airport,
22km outside Mbeya near Mbalizi, has trans-
formed travel to/from Mbeya. Reasonably
priced flights on Auric Air, Air Tanzania, **Preci-
sion Air** (☑ 0686 310228; www.precisionairtz.
com; School St; ☺ 8am-5pm Mon-Fri, to 2pm
Sat & Sun), Fastjet and Flightlink go daily be-
tween Mbeya and Dar es Salaam (Tsh55,000 to
Tsh160,000 one-way), often for not much more
than the cost of a bus fare, and much faster.

THE MBOZI METEORITE

About 65km southwest of Mbeya is the **Mbozi Meteorite** (adult/child Tsh10,000/5000),
one of the largest meteorites in the world. Weighing an estimated 25 metric tonnes, it's
around 3m long and 1m tall. Scientists are unsure when it hit the earth, but it is assumed
to have been many thousands of years ago, since there are no traces of the crater that it
must have made when it fell, nor any local legends regarding its origins.

Although the site was only discovered by outsiders in 1930, it had been known to
locals for centuries, but not reported because of various associated taboos. Like most
meteorites, the one at Mbozi is composed primarily of iron (90%), with about 8% nickel
and traces of phosphorous and other elements. It was declared a protected monument
by the government in 1967 and is now under the jurisdiction of the Department of An-
tiquities. The meteorite's dark colour is due to its high iron content, while its burnished
look comes from the melting and other heating that occurred as the meteorite hurtled
through the atmosphere towards earth.

To reach the site you'll need your own vehicle. From Mbeya, follow the main road to-
wards Tunduma. About 50km from Mbeya there's a signposted turn-off to the left. From
here, it's 13km further down a dirt road (no public transport). During the wet season,
you'll need a 4WD. Otherwise, a 2WD can get through without difficulty, except perhaps
for a tiny stream about 2km before the meteorite.

Auric Air also flies weekly from Mbeya to Ruaha (US$200). In Mbeya, all airlines can be booked through Gazelle Safaris (p274) or Juve Travel & Tours (p276).

BUS

Green Star Express, JM Luxury and other lines depart daily from the main bus station to Dar es Salaam from 6am (Tsh28,000 to Tsh44,000, 12 to 14 hours), going via Iringa (Tsh16,000, five hours) and Morogoro (Tsh30,000, three to four hours).

To Njombe (Tsh8000 to Tsh12,000, four hours) and Songea (Tsh17,000 to Tsh24,000, eight hours), Super Feo departs daily at 6am, with a later departure as well.

To Tukuyu (Tsh3000, one to 1½ hours), Kyela (Tsh5500, two to 2½ hours) and the Malawi border (Tsh5500, two to 2½ hours; take the Kyela bus), there are several smaller Coastal buses daily. It's also possible to get to the Malawi border via dalla-dalla, but you'll need to change vehicles in Tukuyu. For Itungi port, you'll need to change vehicles in Kyela. Note that there are no direct buses from Mbeya into Malawi, though touts at the Mbeya bus station may try to convince you otherwise.

To Matema, there is occasionally one direct bus daily via Kyela, departing Mbeya by about 1pm (Tsh9000 to Tsh10,000, six hours). Usually you'll need to take transport to Kyela, from there to Ipinda, and then Ipinda to Matema.

To Tunduma, on the Zambian border, there are daily minibuses (Tsh5000, two hours). Once across, there's Zambian transport; we recommend doing the journey in this way. There is also a weekly bus between Dar and Lusaka that sometimes takes passengers at Mbeya (Tsh35,000), but ticketing scams are common.

To Sumbawanga, Sumry goes daily at 6am and 8am (Tsh13,000 to Tsh15,000, six hours), with some buses continuing on to Mpanda (Tsh29,000, 14 hours).

To Tabora, there are a few vehicles weekly during the dry season, going via Rungwa. Some, which you can pick up at Mbalizi junction, take the western route via Saza and Makongolosi, while others – catch them along the main Tanzam highway just east of central Mbeya – go via Chunya.

To Moshi (Tsh52,000, 16 hours) and Arusha (Tsh56,000, 18 gruelling hours), Sumry departs daily at 5am.

TRAIN

Book tickets ideally several days in advance (although sometimes cabins are available last minute) at **Tazara train station** (⊘ 8am-noon & 2-5pm Mon-Fri, 10am-2pm Sat).

ⓘ Getting Around

Taxis park at the bus station and near Market Sq. Fares from the bus station to central hotels start at Tsh3000. The Tazara train station is 4km out of town on the Tanzania–Zambia highway (Tsh8000 in a taxi). Dalla-dallas from the road in front of New Millennium Hotel run to the train station and to Mbalizi, but the ones to the train station often don't have room for luggage; taxis are a safer option.

Around Mbeya

Mbeya Peak

Just northwest of Mbeya is **Mbeya Peak** (2820m). It's the highest point in the Mbeya range and makes an enjoyable day hike.

There are several possible routes. One goes from Mbalizi junction, 12km west of town on the Tunduma road. Take a dalla-dalla to Mbalizi, get out at the sign for Utengule Coffee Lodge, head right and follow the dirt road for 1km to a sign for St Mary's Seminary. Turn right here and follow the road up past the seminary to Lunji Farm and then on to the peak. With a vehicle, you can park at Lunji Farm and continue on foot. Allow five hours for the return trip, and only climb accompanied by a guide, which you can arrange at Gazelle Safaris (p274) in Mbeya.

Chunya

This old gold-mining town came to life during the 1920s gold rush, after which it declined to its present status as something of a ghost town. Although Chunya itself has few draws, it's part of an adventurous loop to Lake Rukwa for those with transport. From Mbeya, head northeast along the edge of the Mbeya escarpment, passing **World's End Viewpoint**, with views over the Usangu catchment area (source of the Great Ruaha River). Once in Chunya, where there is a basic guesthouse, it's possible to continue via Saza and Ngomba to the shores of Lake Rukwa; there are no facilities en route. Return the same way, or alternatively, at Saza, head south via Galula and Utengule Coffee Lodge towards Mbeya on a somewhat rougher road.

Pick-ups go daily between Mbeya and Chunya (three hours), but you'll probably need to overnight in Chunya, as return transport departs in the mornings. Departures are from just outside of Mbeya before the Sae area for the northern loop, and from Mbalizi junction for the Galula route. The rough road from Chunya north to Rungwa

Around Mbeya

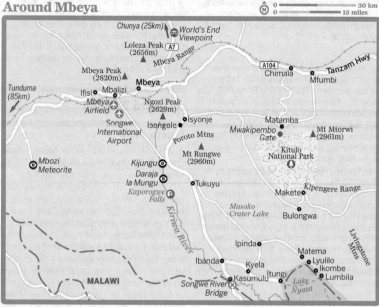

and on to Tabora is traversed by several buses weekly during the dry season.

Lake Rukwa

This large salt lake is notable for its many water birds and its enormous crocodile population. The northern section is part of Rukwa Game Reserve, which is contiguous with Katavi National Park. From Mbeya, the main approaches are via Chunya or Galula, and then on to Saza and the lakeshore. For either route, 4WD is the only realistic way to visit, and even then, access is difficult. It's also possible (and easier via public transport) to access the lake from Sumbawanga.

As the lake has no outlet, its water level varies greatly between the wet and dry seasons. It rarely exceeds about 3m in depth, and sometimes splits into two lakes separated by swamplands.

There are no facilities.

Tukuyu

The small, peppy town of Tukuyu is set in the heart of a beautiful area of hills and orchards near Lake Nyasa. There are many hikes and natural attractions nearby, but only the most basic tourist infrastructure;

for all excursions you'll need to rough it. **NBC bank** (Main Rd) has an ATM. Market days are Mondays and Thursdays.

👁 Sights & Activities

Hiking opportunities abound, with Rungwe Tea & Tours and Bongo Camping the main options for organising something. Afriroots (p53) also does tours here. Expect to pay between Tsh20,000 and Tsh35,000 for most tours.

Daraja la Mungu (Bridge of God) BRIDGE
South of Ngozi Peak and west of the main road, this natural bridge is estimated to have been formed around 1800 million years ago by water flowing through cooling lava that spewed out from the nearby Rungwe volcano. The bridge spans a small waterfall. Further south along the Kiriwa River are the pretty **Kaporogwe Falls**. Also nearby is **Kijungu** (Cooking Pot), where the river tumbles through a rocky gorge.

Mt Rungwe HIKING
(entry per person US$10) This 2960m dormant volcano, much of which is protected as the Rungwe Forest Reserve, rises up to the east of the main road north of Tukuyu, adjoining Kitulo National Park. It marks the point where the eastern and western arms of the

Rift Valley meet, and is an important centre of endemism.

With an early start, you can hike up and down in a day (allow about 10 hours), passing through pristine patches of tropical forest. There are several routes, although not all are always open. Paths are often overgrown and obscure, and it's easy to get lost, so a guide is essential. Before climbing, you need to go first to the Ofisi za Muhifadi ya Milimani Rungwe, in Tukuyu. It's in the Municipality Building (Majengo ya Halmashauri) opposite NMB bank (note: not NBC bank). There, you can pay the required fee and hire a guide (US$15 per group). They will also give you information about which route to use. Both Rungwe Tea & Tours and Bongo Camping can also help you organise a Rungwe climb.

Ngozi Peak & Crater Lake   HIKING
This lushly vegetated 2629m-high volcanic peak has a deep-blue lake – the subject of local legends – about 200m below the crater rim. It is about 7km west of the main road north of Tukuyu. To get here via public transport, take any dalla-dalla travelling between Mbeya and Tukuyu and ask to be dropped off; there's a small sign for Ngozi at the turn-off.

Once at the turn-off, if you haven't come with a guide you'll be approached by locals offering their services; the going rate is about Tsh5000. If you're short on time, you can go about half the distance from the main road to Ngozi by vehicle and then walk the remainder of the way. Once at the base, it's about another steep hour or so on foot up to the crater rim.

🕝 Tours

Rungwe Tea & Tours   HIKING
(☎ 0754 767389, 025-255 2489; rungweteatours@gmail.com) This is a one-man-show type of place where you can organise guides for hikes in the surrounding area. Prices start at about Tsh15,000 per day including a guide and local community fee. It's in the Ujenzi area at the 'Umoja wa Wakulima Wadogo wa Chai Rungwe' building, behind the Landmark Hotel.

Bongo Camping   HIKING
(☎ 0732 951763; www.bongocamping.com) English-speaking guides can be arranged for hikes up Mt Rungwe and for other excursions in the area. There's also a good campsite.

🛏 Sleeping

Landmark Hotel   HOTEL $
(☎ 0782 164160, 025-255 2400; camping US$5, s/d US$40/45; 🅿) Spacious, good-value rooms, all with TV and hot water, a small lawn where it's sometimes permitted to pitch a tent, and a slow but good restaurant. The doubles have two large beds, and the singles have one bed that's big enough for two people. It's the large multistorey building at the main junction just up from NBC bank.

In the off season (April and May), Tanzania's Taifa Stars football team sometimes rent out the entire hotel for their training camp.

DM Motel   HOTEL $
(☎ 0764 061580, 025-255 2332; s/d/ste Tsh15,000/20,000/30,000, s without bathroom Tsh10,000; 🅿) Clean rooms with a large bed (no same-gender sharing permitted) and meals on request. It's just off the main road at the turn-off into Tukuyu town, and signposted.

Bongo Camping   CAMPGROUND $
(☎ 0732 951763; www.bongocamping.com; camping with own/hired tent Tsh6000/8000; 🅿) A backpacker-friendly place with a large, grassy area to pitch your tent, basic cooking facilities, hot-bucket showers, tents for hire and meals on order. It's at Kibisi village, 3.5km north of Tukuyu, and 800m off the main road (Tsh1000 in a taxi from Tukuyu bus stand). They also arrange activities.

ℹ Getting There & Away

Minibuses run several times daily between Tukuyu and both Mbeya (Tsh3000, one to 1½ hours) and Kyela (Tsh2500, one hour).

Two roads connect Tukuyu with the northern end of Lake Nyasa. The main sealed road heads southwest and splits at Ibanda, with the western fork going to Songwe River Bridge and into Malawi, and the eastern fork to Kyela and Itungi port. A secondary dirt road heads southeast from Tukuyu to Ipinda and then east towards Matema.

Lake Nyasa

Lake Nyasa (also known as Lake Malawi) is Africa's third-largest lake after Lake Victoria and Lake Tanganyika. It's more than 550km long, up to 75km wide and as deep as 700m in parts. It also has a high level of biodiversity, containing close to one-third of the world's known cichlid species. The lake is bordered by Tanzania, Malawi and Mozambique. The Tanzanian side is rimmed to the east by the Livingstone mountains, whose green, misty slopes form a stunning backdrop as they cascade down to the sandy shoreline. Few roads reach the towns strung out between the mountains and the shore along the lake's eastern side. To the north and east, the mountains lead on to the Kitulo Plateau.

While the mountains are enticing to hikers, you'll need to be completely self-sufficient (including with tent and water filter) and carry a GPS. One possible route is from the mission station of Bulongwa (reached via bus from Njombe) to Matema, which offers superb views as you make your way down to the lakeshore. Allow about 14 hours for the trip and start out at daybreak. There are inexpensive guesthouses in Bulongwa where you can spend the previous night. A longer version of this hike is also possible, starting near the Kitulo National Park gate. Another possibility is to take a dalla-dalla from Njombe to Ludewa, from where you could make your way down to Lupingu and wait for the MV *Iringa* or MV *Songea*. Once at the shoreline, note that both crocodiles (near river mouths) and malaria-carrying *falciparum* mosquitoes are real hazards, so take the appropriate precautions.

Other places of interest around the Tanzanian side of the lake include (from north to south) Kyela, Itungi, Matema, Ikombe, Liuli and Mbamba Bay.

Kyela

Kyela is the closest town to Itungi – the port 11km to the south where the Lake Nyasa ferries begin and end their journey along the Tanzanian lakeshore. It's a scruffy, nondescript transit town, and there's no reason to linger unless your boat arrives late at Itungi and you need somewhere to spend the night. Photography is prohibited in most areas. The surrounding region, much of which is wetlands dotted with rice paddies, is more appealing.

For updated information on the sailing schedules for the ferries, ask at Kyela Commercial, situated just around the corner from New Steak Inn Restaurant. There are no ATMs; the best bet for changing money is with a local hotel proprietor or shop owner.

🛏 Sleeping

Kyela Beach Resort HOTEL $
(☎ 0784 232650, 025-254 0152; kyelaresort@ya-hoo.com; camping US$3, s/d US$20/30; P ※) If

you have your own transport, this is a good bet, with simple but pleasant, well-ventilated rooms (windows on both walls) set around a garden compound and a restaurant. It's about 1.5km north of town, signposted just off the Tukuyu road.

New Livingstone Cottage GUESTHOUSE $
(r Tsh15,000-25,000) This cheap but clean local-style guesthouse is on the main road just north of the town centre, and about 10 minutes on foot from the bus stand. There is no food.

❶ Getting There & Away

Minibuses go several times daily from Kyela to Tukuyu (Tsh2000, one hour) and Mbeya (Tsh3500, two to 2½ hours) from the minibus stand in the town centre, many stopping also at the Malawi border. Pick-ups run daily between Kyela and Itungi port (Tsh500) in rough coordination with boat arrivals and departures.

Itungi

Itungi, about 11km southeast of Kyela, is the main port for the Tanzanian Lake Nyasa ferry service. There is no accommodation, and photography is forbidden. Pick-ups run sporadically, in rough coordination with boat arrivals and departures, to and from Kyela (Tsh500).

Matema

This quiet lakeside settlement is the only spot on northern Lake Nyasa that has any sort of tourist infrastructure, and with its stunning beachside setting backed by the Livingstone mountains rising steeply up from the water, it makes an ideal spot to relax for a few days. You can arrange walks and dugout canoe rides or lounge on the beach. On Saturdays there's a **pottery market** at Lyulilo village, about 2km east of Matema village centre along the lakeshore and just before Ikombe, where Kisi pots from Ikombe are sold. There's nowhere in Matema to change money, so bring enough shillings with you.

🛏 Sleeping

★ **Blue Canoe Safari** CAMPGROUND, COTTAGES $$
(☎ 0783 575451; www.bluecanoelodge.com; camping US$7, s/d bungalows US$70/90, bandas from US$20/35; P @) ✎ This lovely beachfront place has camping with spotless ablution blocks, plus four 'luxury bungalows' with

verandahs overlooking the lake, polished wood floors and comfortable beds with spacious mosquito netting. Nearby are simple budget *bandas*. The bar is well stocked and the cuisine delicious. Snorkelling and excursions can be arranged. It's 3.5km from Matema's main junction; pick-ups are possible with advance notice.

The owners have made many efforts to integrate their lodge with the local community, training local staff and using traditional building styles and materials from the area. The results are impressive.

Matema Lake Shore Resort　　COTTAGES $
(✆0782 179444, 0754 487267; www.mec-tanzania.ch/matema; camping Tsh6000, d/tr/f Tsh50,000/50,000/60,000, d without bathroom Tsh25,000; P) This recommended Swiss-built place has several spacious, breezy, comfortable two-storey beachfront family chalets, some smaller, equally nice double and triple cottages and a quad. All rooms front directly onto the lake – with lovely views – except the doubles sharing bathrooms. Breakfast is not included in room prices, but the restaurant serves tasty, reasonably priced meals.

It's an ideal choice for families. All self-contained rooms have mini-fridge and fan. Bookings can also be arranged through Karibuni Centre (p274) in Mbeya.

Matema Beach View Lutheran Centre　　COTTAGES $
(✆0684 991030; www.matemabeachview.com; camping Tsh3000, s/d/tr from Tsh35,000/35,000/45,000, tw/q without bathroom Tsh25,000/50,000; P) Rooms at this place – in brick *bandas* on or just back from the beach – are no frills and rather run down, although the local ambience is agreeable. Renovation work is ongoing, and soon several newer rooms should also be open. Prices for rooms without bathrooms don't include breakfast. It's 700m west of Matema hospital and the village centre.

❶ Getting There & Away

BOAT
Schedules are highly variable these days, but there is usually at least one boat weekly – either the **MV Iringa** (1st/economy class Tsh22,000/15,000) or the **MV Songea** (1st/economy class Tsh25,100/16,100) (currently it's the MV *Songea*, on Thursday afternoons) – which stops at Matema on its way from Itungi port down the eastern lakeshore to Mbamba Bay. The boat stop for Matema is actually at Lyulilo village, about 25 minutes on foot from the main Matema junction. Just follow the main 'road' going southeast from the junction, paralleling the lakeshore, and ask for the *bandari* (harbour).

BUS
From Tukuyu, pick-ups to Ipinda leave around 8am most mornings from the roundabout by NBC bank (Tsh2500, two hours). Although drivers sometimes say they are going all the way to Matema, generally they go only as far as Ipinda. Once in Ipinda, pick-ups run sporadically to Matema (Tsh3000 to Tsh3500, 35km, one to two hours), departing around 2pm, which means you'll need to wait around in Ipinda for a while. Returning from Matema, departures are in the morning. If you get stuck in Ipinda, there are several basic guesthouses.

From Kyela, there are several vehicles daily from about 1pm onwards to Ipinda (Tsh1500), a few of which continue on to Matema (Tsh3500 three hours). Departures from Matema back to Kyela run in the morning. From Kyela, it's also fairly easy to hire a vehicle to drop you off at Matema (from about Tsh60,000).

Occasionally, there is also a direct bus between Mbeya and Matema, departing Mbeya by about 1pm and Matema at 5am (Tsh9000, five hours). All transport in Matema departs from the main junction near the hospital.

CAR & MOTORCYCLE
From Kyela, the signposted turn-off to Ipinda and Matema is about 3km north of the town centre. From here, it's about 14km to Ipinda, and another 25km to Matema along a readily passable but rough road. Allow one to 1½ hours for the 40km stretch. There's also a shorter, scenic, slightly less rough route directly from Tukuyu to Ipinda. About 20km out of Tukuyu en route to Ipinda off this road is Masoko Crater Lake, into which fleeing Germans allegedly dumped a small fortune of gold pieces and coins during WWI.

Ikombe

The village of Ikombe is notable for its clay pots, which are made by the local Kisi women and sold at markets in Mbeya and elsewhere in the region. It's just southeast of Matema along the lakeshore and reached via dugout canoe (1½ hours), or walking (about 45 minutes). There are no tourist facilities.

Liuli

Liuli is the site of an old and still-active Anglican mission and the small St Anne's mission hospital, the major health facility on the eastern lakeshore. It's also notable for

SOUTHERN HIGHLANDS LAKE NYASA

a (with some imagination) sphinxlike rock lying just offshore, which earned the settlement the name of Sphinxhafen during the German era. There's no accommodation.

Mbamba Bay

The relaxing outpost of Mbamba Bay is the southernmost Tanzanian port on Lake Nyasa. With its low-key ambience and attractive beach fringed by palm, banana and mango trees, it makes a good spot to spend a few days waiting for a cargo boat across Lake Nyasa or as a change of pace if you've been travelling inland around Songea or Tunduru. En route between Mbamba Bay and Songea, in the heart of a major coffee-producing area, is the small, prosperous town of **Mbinga**. Travelling to/from Mbamba Bay via public transport, you'll probably need to change vehicles here.

🛏 Sleeping

Mbamba Bay Bio Camp   BANDA, CAMPGROUND **$**
(📞0765 925255; info@bushkomba.de; d tent/banda Tsh30,000/70,000) 🏝 Comfortable stone and thatch bungalows with bathrooms, plus some tents on the beach, under *makuti* (thatched roof of palm leaves). Local-style meals are available. It's on the beach about 5km north of Mbamba Bay. Walk, or hire a motorbike at the Mbamba Bay bus stand to bring you there. Snorkelling around nearby islands can be arranged.

St Benadetta Guest House   HOSTEL **$**
(r Tsh15,000) This church-run place near the water has simple, clean rooms and meals on order.

Neema Lodge   GUESTHOUSE **$**
(Mama Simba's; r without bathroom Tsh10,000) Basic rooms, basic meals and a pleasant setting overlooking the lake. Turn left just before the bridge as you enter town.

ℹ Getting There & Away

There's one direct vehicle daily from Songea (Tsh9000, five to six hours). Otherwise you will need to change vehicles at Mbinga.

From Mbamba Bay northbound, there are occasional 4WDs to Liuli mission station. Between Liuli and Lituhi there is no public transport and little traffic, and from Lituhi northwards, there is no road along the lake, only a footpath. There's also a rough track leading from Lituhi southeast towards Kitai and Songea, which opens the possibility for an interesting loop.

Entering or leaving Tanzania via Mbamba Bay, you'll need to stop at the immigration office/police station near the boat landing to take care of passport formalities.

Songea
POP 203,300

The sprawling town of Songea, just over 1000m in altitude, is capital of the surrounding Ruvuma region and will probably seem like a major metropolis if you've just come from Tunduru or Mbamba Bay. Away from the scruffy and crowded central market and bus stand area, it's a pleasant, attractive place, with shaded leafy streets, surrounded by rolling hill country dotted with yellow sunflowers and grazing cattle.

The main tribal group here is the Ngoni, who migrated into the area from South Africa during the 19th century, subduing many smaller tribes along the way. Songea takes its name from one of their greatest chiefs, who was killed following the Maji Maji rebellion and is buried about 1km from town near the Maji Maji Museum.

Songea's colourful **market** (Soko Kuu) along the main road is worth a visit. The impressive carved wooden doors on the **Catholic cathedral** diagonally opposite the bus stand are also worth a look, as are the wall paintings inside. About 30km west of town, in Peramiho, is a large **Benedictine monastery** with an affiliated hospital, should you fall ill.

◎ Sights

Maji Maji Museum   MUSEUM
(admission Tsh10,000; ⊘8am-4pm) About 1km from the town centre, off the Njombe road, is this small museum commemorating the Maji Maji uprising. Behind it is Chief Songea's tomb. From town, take the first sealed road to the right after passing CRDB bank and continue about 200m. The museum entrance is on the left with a pale-blue archway.

🛏 Sleeping & Eating

Anglican Church Hostel   HOSTEL **$**
(d Tsh10,000, without bathroom Tsh5000) This long-standing hostel has no-frills rooms set around a courtyard in a quiet area just northwest of the main road. Food is usually available with advance order. To get to the hostel, head uphill from the bus stand, past the market to the Tanesco building. Go left and wind your way back about 400m to the Anglican church compound.

OK Hotels 92   GUESTHOUSE $

(d Tsh15,000-20,000) Small but decent rooms. From the bus stand, head uphill 400m past the market, take the second right (watch for the sign for the Lutheran church). After about 200m go right again, and look for the apricot-coloured house in a fenced compound to your left. Meals are available at Krista Park across the street.

Heritage Cottage   HOTEL $$

(☑0754 355306, 025-260 0888; www.heritage-cottage.com; Njombe Rd; s/d Tsh75,000/90,000; P✳) This good hotel has modern, clean rooms with TV (some with mini-fridge), a popular bar-restaurant, a large lawn area behind and a playground for children. It's located 3km north of town along the Njombe Rd.

Seed Farm Villa   B&B $$

(☑0752 842086, 025-260 2500; www.seedfarm villa.com; s Tsh75,000-90,000, d Tsh85,000-105,000; P✳) This place has eight modern, quiet rooms with TV set in tranquil garden surroundings away from the town centre in the Seed Farm area. There's a sitting room with TV, and a restaurant (advance order necessary). Head out of town along the Tun-duru Rd for 2.5km to the signposted turn-off, from where it's 200m further.

Agape Cafe   TANZANIAN $

(Main Rd; snacks from Tsh2000; ◷8am-5.30pm) Just uphill from the Catholic church, with pastries and inexpensive meals.

Krista Park Fast Food   TANZANIAN $

(meals Tsh5000; ◷6.30am-6.30pm Mon-Sat) Snacks and local-style meals, plus a small bakery. From the market, go uphill for about 400m, take the second right (there's a sign for the Lutheran church). After about 200m go right again; Krista Park is on your right.

Heritage Cottage   INTERNATIONAL, INDIAN $$

(☑0754 355306, 025-260 0888; Njombe Rd; meals from Tsh10,000; ◷7am-10pm) This hotel restaurant has slow service but tasty continental and Indian cuisine.

ℹ Information

CRDB (Njombe Rd) ATM.

Immigration (Uhamiaji; Tunduru Rd) At the beginning of the Tunduru Rd. Get your passport stamped here if you are travelling to/from Mozambique.

THE MAJI MAJI REBELLION

The Maji Maji rebellion, which was the strongest local revolt against the colonial government in German East Africa, is considered to contain some of the earliest seeds of Tanzanian nationalism. It began around the turn of the 20th century when colonial administrators set about establishing enormous cotton plantations in the southeast and along the railway line running from Dar es Salaam towards Morogoro. These plantations required large numbers of workers, most of whom were recruited as forced labour and required to work under miserable salary and living conditions. Anger at this harsh treatment and long-simmering resentment of the colonial government combined to ignite a powerful rebellion. The first outbreak was in 1905 in the area around Kilwa, on the coast. Soon all of southern Tanzania was involved, from Kilwa and Lindi in the southeast to Songea in the southwest. In addition to deaths on the battlefield, thousands died of hunger brought about by the Germans' scorched-earth policy, in which fields and grain silos in many villages were set on fire. Fatalities were undoubtedly exacerbated by a widespread belief among the Africans that enemy bullets would turn to water before reaching them, and so their warriors would not be harmed – hence the name Maji Maji (maji means 'water' in Swahili).

By 1907, when the rebellion was finally suppressed, close to 100,000 people had lost their lives. In addition, large areas of the south were left devastated and barren, and malnutrition was widespread. The Ngoni, a tribe of warriors much feared by their neighbours, put up the strongest resistance to the Germans. Following the end of the rebellion, they continued to wage guerrilla-style war until 1908, when the last shreds of their military-based society were destroyed. In order to quell Ngoni resistance once and for all, German troops hanged about 100 of their leaders and beheaded their most famous chief, Songea.

Among the effects of the Maji Maji uprising were a temporary liberalisation of colonial rule and replacement of the military administration with a civilian government. More significantly, the uprising promoted development of a national identity among many tribal groups and intensified anti-colonial sentiment, kindling the movement for independence.

SELOUS-NIASSA WILDLIFE CORRIDOR

The Selous-Niassa Wildlife Corridor (www.selous-niassa-corridor.org) – 'Ushoroba' in Swahili – joins the Selous Game Reserve with Mozambique's Niassa Reserve, forming a vast conservation area of about 120,000 sq km, and ensuring protection of one of the world's largest elephant ranges. In addition to the elephants, estimated to number about 85,000, the area is home to one of the continent's largest buffalo herds, and more than half of its remaining wild dog population, and it is an important resting and nesting area for migratory birds.

The area also encompasses large areas of both the Rufiji and Ruvuma river basins, with the watershed running roughly parallel to the Songea–Tunduru road. Local communities in the area are the Undendeule, the Ngoni and the Yao, who have formed various village-based wildlife management areas to support the corridor. Several of these communities have started small ecotourism ventures, including Marumba, southwest of Tunduru. Guides can be arranged at the Chingoli Society office in the village centre to visit Jiwe La Bwana (with views across the border into Mozambique) and Chingoli Table Mountain and caves, used by locals as a hiding place during the Maji Maji rebellion, as well as for village tours. Tourist infrastructure ranges from basic to non-existent, with a no-frills campsite just outside the village.

NBC Behind the market; ATM.

❶ Getting There & Away

Super Feo departs daily from 5am to Iringa (Tsh18,000, eight hours) and Dar es Salaam (Tsh40,000, 13 hours), and at 6am to Mbeya (Tsh18,000 to Tsh24,000, eight hours) via Njombe (Tsh9000 to Tsh12,000, four hours). There are also departures to Njombe at 9.30am and 11am.

For Mbamba Bay, there's one direct vehicle departing daily by 7am (Tsh9000, five to six hours). Otherwise, get transport to Mbinga and from there on to Mbamba Bay.

To Tunduru, there's a daily bus in the dry season departing by 7am (Tsh15,000, seven to eight hours). There's also one bus daily direct to Masasi (Tsh25,000, 13 hours), departing by 6am.

Transport to Mozambique departs from the Majengo C area, southwest of the bus stand and about 600m in from the main road; ask locals to point out the way through the back streets. If you're driving, head west 18km from Songea along the Mbinga road to the signposted turn-off, from where it's 120km further on an unpaved but decent road to the Mozambique border.

Tunduru

Tunduru, halfway between Masasi and Songea, is in the centre of an important gemstone-mining region, with a bit of a Wild West feel. The town is also a truck and transit stop, and you're likely to need to spend the night here if travelling between Masasi and Songea.

🛏 Sleeping

Namwinyu Guest House   GUESTHOUSE $
(☎ 0655 447225, 0786 447225; Songea Rd; r Tsh30,000; 🅿❄) This is Tunduru's newest and best accommodation, with clean, pleasant double-bedded rooms (no same-gender sharing) and tasty, inexpensive meals on order. It's along the north side of the main road at the western edge of town, and an easy 10-minute walk from the bus stand.

❶ Getting There & Away

BUS

There's at least one bus daily between Tunduru and Masasi, departing by 6am (Tsh10,000, five hours) and, in the dry season, between Tunduru and Songea (Tsh15,000, seven to eight hours). In both directions from Tunduru, there is little en route, so bring food and water.

CAR & MOTORCYCLE

The road from Tunduru in either direction is unpaved but easily passable in the dry season, somewhat more challenging (especially between Tunduru and Songea) during the rains. Currently, the most difficult section is between Namtumbo (about 70km east of Songea) and Tunduru; a 4WD is essential here during the rains. Ask locally for an update. Heading east from Tunduru, the sealed road currently starts about 60km before Masasi. En route between Songea and Tunduru, you'll pass through the Selous-Niassa Wildlife Corridor, with wide views over the Ruvuma River basin. About 65km east of Songea is the turn-off for Mbarang'andu Wildlife Management Area, an extension of the Selous ecosystem.

Southeastern Tanzania

Why Go?

Time seems to have stood still in Tanzania's sparsely populated southeast. It lacks the development and bustle of the north and tourist numbers are a relative trickle. Yet, for safari enthusiasts and divers, and for adventurous travellers seeking to learn about traditional local life, the southeast makes an ideal destination. But, get here soon: the region's easy pace is already starting to show signs of strain from recent discoveries of offshore gas reserves.

Among the southeast's highlights: Selous Game Reserve, with its top-notch wildlife watching; white-sand beaches and stunning corals around Mafia island; and the Kilwa Kisiwani ruins, harking back to days when the East African coast was the centre of trading networks stretching to the Far East.

Mafia and the Selous offer comfortable accommodation and Western amenities. Elsewhere, infrastructure is undeveloped, and road journeys can be long and rugged.

Best for Nature

➡ Selous Game Reserve (p292)

➡ Mafia Island Marine Park (p290)

➡ Fanjove Private Island (p301)

Best for Culture

➡ Kilwa Kisiwani Ruins (p298)

➡ Mafia Archipelago (p287)

➡ Mikindani (p308)

When to Go
Mtwara

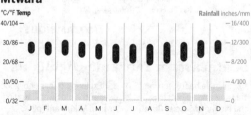

Mar–May Many Selous camps are closed; for those still open, birding is excellent.	Oct This is the prime time for diving and snorkelling around the Mafia area.	Nov–Feb See whale sharks swimming offshore from Kilindoni (Mafia).

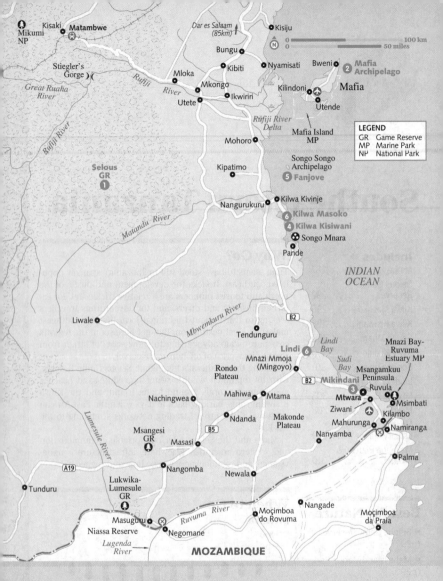

Southeastern Tanzania Highlights

① Taking a boat safari, and enjoying wildlife watching and birding in **Selous Game Reserve** (p292).

② Diving or relaxing in the **Mafia Archipelago** (p287).

③ Exploring traces of bygone days at the old Swahili trading town of **Mikindani** (p308).

④ Visiting the ruins of the famed medieval city-state of **Kilwa Kisiwani** (p298).

⑤ Relaxing on your own private island at **Fanjove** (p301) in the Songo Songo archipelago.

⑥ Immersing yourself in local life in **Kilwa Masoko** (p296), **Lindi** (p301) and other southeastern Tanzanian towns.

Mafia

POP 45,000

Stroll along sandy lanes through the coco-nut palms. Explore a coastline alternating between dense mangrove stands and white-sand beaches. Get to know traditional Swahili culture. If these appeal, you're likely to love Mafia.

This green wedge of land surrounded by turquoise waters, pristine islets and glinting white sandbanks remained off the beaten track for years, undiscovered by all except deep-sea fishing aficionados and a trickle of visitors. Now, this is changing fast, with the island's tourist accommodation growing from one to nearly a dozen hotels over the past decade. Yet Mafia remains refreshingly free of the mass tourism that is overwhelming Zanzibar. It makes an amenable post-safari respite and is a rewarding destination in its own right.

Among Mafia's attractions are its tranquil pace, underwater life, upmarket lodges, strong traditional culture and long history. Green and hawksbill turtles have breeding sites along the island's eastern shores and on the nearby islands of Juani and Jibondo. To protect these and other local ecosystems, the southeastern part of the island, together with offshore islets and waters, has been gazetted as a national marine park. Whale sharks (*potwe* in Swahili) visit Mafia between about November and February, and are best seen offshore near Kilindoni.

History

In addition to Mafia island, the **Mafia archipelago** includes Juani (southeast of Mafia), Chole (between Mafia and Juani), Jibondo (south of Juani) and at least a dozen other islets and sandbars. The archipelago first rose to prominence between the 11th and 13th centuries in the days when the Shirazis controlled much of the East African shoreline. Thanks to its central buffer position between the Rufiji River delta and the high seas of the Indian Ocean, it made an amenable trading base, and the local economy soon began to thrive. One of the first settlements was built during this era at Ras Kisimani, on Mafia's southwestern corner, followed by another at Kua on Juani.

By the time the Portuguese arrived in the early 16th century, Mafia had lost much of its significance and had come under the sway of the Sultan of Kilwa. In the early 18th century, the island's fortunes revived, and by the mid-19th century it had fallen within the domain of the powerful Omani sultanate, under which it flourished as a trade centre linking Kilwa to the south and Zanzibar to the north. It was during this era that the coconut palm and cashew plantations that now cover much of the island were established.

Following an attack by the Sakalava people from Madagascar, Mafia's capital was moved from Kua to the nearby tiny island of Chole. Chole's star ascended to the point where it became known as Chole Mjini (Chole City), while the now-main island of Mafia was referred to as Chole Shamba (the Chole hinterlands). Mafia's administrative seat continued on Chole throughout the German colonial era. It was moved to Kilindoni on the main island by the British, who used Mafia as a naval and air base.

Today, farming and fishing are the main sources of livelihood for Mafia's approximately 45,000 residents, most of whom live on the main island. While shopping in the markets, you'll find cassavas, cashews and coconuts in abundance.

☉ Sights

It doesn't take too much imagination to step back in time in the Mafia archipelago, with village life here much the same as during the island's Shirazi-era heyday. On Mafia island itself, there are small **beaches** interspersed with the mangroves around Chole Bay, and some idyllic nearby sandbanks; all the lodges arrange excursions. One of the closest is **Mange**, with beautiful white

---

ⓘ MAFIA ORIENTATION

Kilindoni, where all boats and planes arrive, is Mafia's hub. Here you'll find the bank (but no ATM), port, market, small shops and several budget guesthouses. The only other settlement of any size is Utende, 15km southeast of Kilindoni on Chole Bay, where most upmarket lodges are located. The Utende–Chole Bay area is also the main divers' base. Mafia's western side is dotted with small villages, offshore islands and sandbanks, and stands of mangrove interspersed with patches of beach. Many lodges are closed in April and May. July and August can be very windy on the eastern side of the island.

Mafia

INDIAN OCEAN
Nyamisati (30km)
Nyororo
Ras Mkumbi
Bweni
Shungumbili
Mbarakuni
Kirongwe
Ras Mbisi
Mafia
Baleni
Kilindoni
Chole Bay
Bwejuu
Mange
Ras Kisimani
Chole
Kitoni
Utende
Kua
Juani
Mrima Reef
Mange Reef
Jibondo
Mafia Island Marine Park
Kitutia Reef
Boundary of Mafia Island Marine Park

sand populated only by sand crabs and sea birds, and surrounded by crystal-clear aqua waters. At **Ras Mkumbi**, Mafia's windswept northernmost point, there's a lighthouse dating to 1892, as well as **Kanga beach**, and a forest that's home to monkeys, blue duikers and many birds.

Chole Island
HISTORIC SITE

(day visit per person US$5) This is a good place to start exploring, especially around its crumbling but atmospheric ruins, dating from the 19th century. Also on Chole is what is probably East Africa's only **Fruit Bat Sanctuary** (Comoros lesser fruit bat). This is thanks to the efforts of a local women's group who bought the area where an important nesting tree is located.

Juani
HISTORIC SITE

The large and heavily vegetated island of Juani, southeast of Mafia, has overgrown but evocative ruins at Kua. This includes the remains of several mosques dating from a Shirazi settlement during the 18th and 19th centuries, and crumbling palace walls. Also note the ablutions area just to the right of the main entrance to the settlement. Access to the ruins is only possible at high tide. South of here is a channel and a nearby lagoon for birding and swimming.

Jibondo
ISLAND

Sparsely vegetated Jibondo is less aesthetically appealing than Mafia's other islands, and its inhabitants are traditionally unwelcoming towards visitors. However, it is intriguing that it supports a population of about 3000 people despite having no natural water sources. Jibondo is renowned as a boat-building centre, with much of the wood coming from forests around mainland Kilwa. In Jibondo's village centre, look for the carved door frame on the mosque, said to come from the old settlement at Kua on Juani.

Except during the peak rainy season (when rainwater is collected on the island from run-off), boats ply daily between Jibondo and Mafia island transporting large yellow containers filled with water. The best time to watch all the activity is just after sunrise, at the Chole Bay beach near Kinasi Lodge (p290).

🏃 Activities

Diving & Snorkelling

Mafia offers divers fine corals, a variety of fish, including numerous pelagics, and relaxing, uncrowded diving, often done from motorised dhows (ancient Arabic sailing vessels). You can dive year-round in Chole Bay at various sites for all levels, plus there is seasonal diving (October to February) outside the bay for experienced divers. The best month is generally October, and the least favourable months are April, May and June, when everything shuts down with the rains. Kinasi Lodge (p290) and Shamba Kilole (p290) offer diving and instruction for their guests.

Big Blu
DIVING

(📞0784 474108; www.bigblumafia.com/blog; Chole Bay) Next to Mafia Island Lodge (p290), and under the direction of Moez, a veteran diver with long experience on Mafia. Offers diving, dive-certification courses, snorkelling, excursions around Mafia and reasonably priced accommodation.

Mafia Island Diving
DIVING

(📞0688 218569; www.mafiadiving.com; Mafia Island Lodge, Chole Bay) Offers snorkelling, diving, dive-certification courses and excursions.

Fishing

Long popular in deep-sea fishing circles, Mafia is known especially for its marlin, sailfish, tuna and other big-game fish. Conditions are best between September and March, with June and July the least-appealing months due to strong winds. Contact Big Blu or Kinasi Lodge (p290). Licences can be arranged through Marine Park Headquarters (p290) in Utende.

Sleeping & Eating

Mafia Island

For all Chole Bay accommodation (including the Utende budget hotels located after entering the park gate and all accommodation on Chole island), you need to pay daily marine-park entry fees, whether you go diving or not. These fees are not included in accommodation rates.

Kilindoni Area

Whale Shark Lodge   GUESTHOUSE $
(Sunset Camp; ☑ 0755 696067, 023-201 0201; carpho2003@yahoo.co.uk; Kilindoni; s/d US$25/50; @) This backpacker-friendly budget place, in a quiet, clifftop setting overlooking a prime whale-shark viewing area, is good value, with six simple, pleasant cottages with fan, mosquito net and bathroom. There's a large, lovely dining terrace with sunset views and local-style meals (US$7) on order. A short walk down the cliffside is a small beach with high-tide swimming.

It's 1.5km from Kilindoni town centre, behind the hospital and Tsh1500 in a *bajaji* (tuk tuk).

New Lizu Hotel   GUESTHOUSE $
(☑ 023-201 0180; Kilindoni; s/d Tsh15,000/20,000; @) This long-standing local guesthouse has spartan, scruffy rooms with fan, cheap food on order and a noisy, central location at Kilindoni's main junction, less than a 10-minute walk from both the airfield and the harbour.

★ Butiama Beach   LODGE $$$
(☑ 0784 474084; www.butiamabeach.com; s/d half board US$180/300; @) This lovely 15-room place is spread out in palm-tree-studded grounds on a fine stretch of beach near Kilindoni, about 2km south of the small harbour. Accommodation is in spacious, breezy, appealingly decorated cottages. It has delicious Italian-style dining, sea kayaks for exploring the birdlife in nearby creeks,

magnificent sunset views and a warm, classy ambience. Very good value for money.

The lodge is well positioned for seeing whale sharks from November to March, as they pass in front. Also, as it is just outside the marine-park boundary, marine-park fees are payable only if you enter the park area on an excursion.

Utende & Chole Bay Area

Big Blu   GUESTHOUSE $
(☑ 0784 474108; www.bigblumafia.com/blog; Chole Bay; r per person US$45, s/d tent US$20/30; ☺ Jul–mid-Apr; @) This friendly dive outfitter on the beach at Chole Bay has several simple, good-value beachside rooms, plus a few tents set back from the beach. It's primarily for divers with Big Blu, although anyone is welcome. Special dive-accommodation packages are available. There's also a good beachside restaurant serving sandwiches, salads and other light meals.

Meremeta Guest House & Apartment   GUESTHOUSE $
(☑ 0787 345460, 0715 345460; www.meremeta lodge.com; s/d/tr US$30/50/75) On the main road about 800m before the marine-park entry gate, this tidy place has unadorned but clean and pleasant budget rooms with fan, meals (US$10 to US$15), and free coffee and tea. It also offers bicycle rental and can help arrange excursions around the island. Look for the pink building and local artwork display.

Mafia Beach Bungalows   COTTAGES $
(☑ 0653 327656, 0654 326404; s/d US$30/50) On a steep hill overlooking the water at Chole Bay, Mafia Beach Bungalows offers several tiny, no-frills bungalows, and meals on order. During high season (July to January), prices sometimes double, depending on occupancy, so confirm before booking.

Didimiza   COTTAGES $
(☑ 0787 071543, 0784 303554; alawia75@yahoo. com; s/d/q US$30/40/70) This very basic place located about 1km before the marine-park entry gate has three simple, OK rooms and a small eating area; local-style meals and excursions can be arranged. It's inland, in rather overgrown grounds reached via a rickety footbridge. The sea is a 10-minute walk away through the mangroves. Transfers from Kilindoni cost US$15 per person.

MAFIA ISLAND MARINE PARK

At around 822 sq km, Mafia Island Marine Park (adult/child US$20/10) is the largest marine protected area in the Indian Ocean – it shelters a unique complex of estuarine, mangrove, coral reef and marine channel ecosystems. These include the only natural forest on the island and almost 400 fish species. There are also about 10 villages within the park's boundaries with an estimated 15,000 to 17,000 inhabitants, all of whom depend on its natural resources for their livelihoods.

The park has been classified as a multiuse area to assist local communities in developing sustainable practices so that conservation and resource use can coexist. Entry fees are payable by everyone, whether you dive or not. They are collected at a barrier gate across the main road about 1km before Utende, and can be paid in any major currency, cash only. Save your receipt, as it will be checked again when you leave. Park Headquarters (☑ 023-240 2690; www.marineparktz.com) are in Utende.

The main way to visit is on a diving excursion with one of the Chole Bay dive operators.

Mafia Island Lodge   LODGE $$

(☑ 0786 303049, 022-260 1530; www.mafialodge. com; Chole Bay; per person US$115-135; ⊘ Jun-Apr; ❄@) This former government hotel is set on a long lawn sloping down to a small beach. There's a mix of 'standard' and nicer 'superior' rooms and two family suites. The main restaurant, under a soaring thatched roof, overlooks Chole Bay. There's a beachside bar and an attached diving and watersports centre. Half-board and full-board options only.

Shamba Kilole Eco Lodge   LODGE $$

(☑ 0753 903752, 0786 903752; www.shamba kilolelodge.com; per person full board in chalet/ste from US$140/180; ☎❄) ✐ Shamba Kilole is set in tranquil grounds on a little escarpment overlooking Kilole Bay, just southwest of Chole Bay. Its chalets are individually themed, all have been tastefully decorated and the Italian owners – long-time Mafia residents – have strived to make the lodge a true ecolodge, with local sourcing and organic foods. There's a PADI dive instructor on-site.

Kinasi Lodge   LODGE $$$

(☑ 0777 424588; www.kinasilodge.com; Chole Bay; s/d full board from US$200/360; @❄) ✐ A lovely, genteel choice, with 14 stone-and-thatch cottages set on a long, green, palm-shaded hillside sloping down to Chole Bay. The Moroccan-influenced decor is at its most attractive in the evening, when the grounds are lit by lanterns. There's an open lounge area with satellite TV, a small beach, a spa, a dive centre and a quiet, welcoming ambience.

Kinasi also runs a luxury bush camp at Mafia's northern tip.

Pole Pole Bungalow Resort   LODGE $$$

(☑ 022-260 1530; www.polepole.com; Chole Bay; s/d full board plus daily excursion US$387/595; @❄) ✐ This luxury hideaway is set amid palm trees and tropical vegetation on a long hillside overlooking Chole Bay. It can be visually underwhelming at first glance. But its quiet style, impeccable service, excellent cuisine, the lack of TVs and the comfort of its bungalows strike a good balance between luxury and lack of pretension. Children under 10 years old are not allowed.

🛏 Chole Island

Chole Foxes Guesthouse   GUESTHOUSE $

(☑ 0787 877393, 0715 877393; www.cholefoxes lodge.webs.com; Chole island; s/d US$30/50) Chole's only budget accommodation, this local guesthouse has a prime location on the southwestern edge of the island overlooking Chole Bay and Mafia island. Rooms are simple, but adequate, and meals are available on order for about US$10.

It's in the Kilimani area of Chole, about 2.5km from the ruins. Wind your way through the palm trees and villages, and ask locals to point out the way, as there are many twists and turns in the road. If you book in advance (which you should do anyway), they will come and collect you with their boat at Utende.

Chole Mjini   TREEHOUSE $$$

(☑ 0787 712427, 0784 520799; www.cholemjini. com; Chole island; s/d full board US$265/420; ⊘ Jun-Easter) ✐ Chole Mjini is unique: an upmarket bush adventure in synchrony with the local community and environment. Sleep in spacious, rustic and fantastic tree-houses, eat fresh seafood, experience the real darkness of an African night without electricity, and take advantage of diving excursions, all while supporting Chole Mjini's work with the local community.

The concept of Chole Mjini grew out of the founders' commitment to the local community, and community development is still at the heart of the undertaking. A portion of earnings are channelled back into health and education projects, and over the almost two decades of the project's life, a health clinic, kindergarten and primary school have been established.

ℹ Information

INTERNET ACCESS
Internet Café (Kilindoni; per hour Tsh3000; ◷8am-6pm) At New Lizu Hotel (p289).

MEDICAL SERVICES
For malaria tests, there's a village clinic on Chole island. For treatment or anything serious, go to Dar es Salaam.

MONEY
National Microfinance Bank Just off the airport road, and near the main junction in Kilindoni; changes cash only (dollars, euros and pounds). There are no ATMs on Mafia.

TELEPHONE
Telephone calls can be made at New Lizu Hotel (p289) in Kilindoni.

ℹ Getting There & Away

AIR
Coastal Aviation (☑ 022-284 2700, 0767 404350, 0654 404350) flies daily between Mafia and Dar es Salaam (US$120), Songo Songo (US$120), Zanzibar (US$160) and Kilwa Masoko (US$190, minimum five passengers), with connections also to Selous Game Reserve and Arusha. **Tropical Air** (☑ 024-223 2511; www.tropicalair.co.tz) has a similarly priced daily flight between Mafia and Dar es Salaam with connections to Zanzibar.

All the Chole Bay hotels arrange airfield transfers for their guests (included in the room price at some, otherwise about US$15 to US$30 per person; inquire when booking).

BOAT
When it's not grounded (a frequent occurence) for repairs or weather, the **MV Baccara** (☑ 0686 649616; www.mafiarufijiexpress.com) sails daily in each direction between Mafia (Kilindoni port) and Nyamisati village on the mainland south of Dar es Salaam, and is the most reliable of the various boat options. Departures from Kilindoni are at 8am and from Nyamisati at 1pm (three to four hours). The one-way fare is Tsh15,000. In Kilindoni, the main ticketing office is next to the big mosque, with another office in the red-roofed building at the port; buy tickets the afternoon before. In Nyamisati, buy tickets at the port.

Otherwise, you'll need to rely on the small motorised boats that ply the Nyamisati–Kilindoni route daily, weather permitting (one way Tsh12,500, about four hours). While a trickle of budget travellers reach Mafia this way, remember that there is no safety equipment on any of these smaller boats. They are often crowded, there is little shade and the ride can be very windy and choppy in the middle of the channel. Departure times depend on the weather and tides, but are usually at around 6am from Kilindoni (departure times from Nyamisati are irregular.)

To reach Nyamisati, get a southbound dalla-dalla (minibus) from Mbagala Rangi Tatu, which is along the Kilwa road and reached via dalla-dalla from Dar es Salaam's Posta (Tsh6000); allow up to four hours from central Dar to Nyamisati. For evening arrivals on Mafia, unless you've made arrangements with the lodges for a pick-up, you will need to sleep in Kilindoni. To get to Kilindoni's town centre, head straight up the hill for about 300m. When arriving at Nyamisati, it's easy to find dalla-dallas north to Mbagala and central Dar es Salaam. If you get stuck overnight in Nyamisati, there's basic accommodation at the old Swedish mission.

ℹ Getting Around

Dalla-dallas connect Kilindoni with Utende (Tsh1500, 45 minutes) several times daily, and at least once daily with Bweni (Tsh4000, four to five hours). On the Kilindoni–Utende route, vehicles depart Kilindoni at about 1pm and Utende at about 7am; the last departure from Utende is about 4.30pm. Departures from Kilindoni to Bweni are at about 1pm, and from Bweni at about 7am. In Kilindoni, the transport stand is in the central 'plaza' near the market. In Utende, the start and end of the dalla-dalla route is at the tiny loading jetty between Mafia Island Lodge (p290) and Big Blu (p289). Work is underway to pave the Kilindoni–Utende road; when completed, this transport information is likely to change.

It's also possible to hire taxis or *bajaji* in Kilindoni to take you around the island. Bargain hard, and expect to pay from Tsh15,000 between

---

DEVELOPMENTS ON CHOLE

Read *Where Spirits Fly* by Jackie Barbour for the story of community-development initiatives on Chole island.

Kilindoni and Utende for a vehicle (Tsh10,000 for a *bajaji*).

The other option is bicycle, either your own (bring a mountain bike) or a rental (from about Tsh500 per hour for a heavy single-speed; ask around at the Kilindoni market).

Between Utende and Chole island, most of the Chole Bay hotels provide boat transport for their guests, and transfers can be arranged with Mafia Island Diving (p288) and with Big Blu (p289). Otherwise, local boats sail throughout the day from the beach in front of Mafia Island Lodge (p290) (Tsh400). Boats also leave from here to Juani, and from Chole it's possible to walk to Juani at low tide. To Jibondo, you can usually catch a lift on one of the water transport boats leaving from the beach near Pole Pole Bungalow Resort (p290).

Selous Game Reserve

At the heart of southern Tanzania is **Selous Game Reserve** (adult/child US$50/30 plus daily conservation fee US$15-25), a vast 48,000-sq-km wilderness area stretching over more than 5% of mainland Tanzania. It is Africa's largest wildlife reserve, and Tanzania's most extensive protected area, although the extended ecosystems of Ruaha National Park and the Serengeti come close. It's also home to large herds of elephants, plus buffaloes, crocodiles, hippos, wild dogs, many bird species and some of Tanzania's last remaining black rhinos. Bisecting it is the Rufiji River, which winds its way more than 250km from its source in the highlands through the Selous to the sea, and boasts one of the largest water-catchment areas in East Africa. En route, it cuts a path past woodlands, grasslands and stands of borassus palm, and provides some unparalleled water-based wildlife watching. In the river's delta area, which lies outside the reserve opposite Mafia island, the reddish-brown freshwater of the river mixes with the blue salt water of the sea, forming striking patterns and providing habitats for dozens of bird species and passing dolphins.

In the northwestern part of the reserve is **Stiegler's Gorge**, which averages 100m in depth, and is named after a Swiss explorer who was killed here by an elephant in 1907.

Although the number of tourists visiting the Selous has increased markedly over the past decade, as have the number of lodges in the central wildlife-viewing sector along and near the Rufiji River, congestion remains low in comparison with Tanzania's northern parks. Other advantages include the Selous' wilderness backdrop and its fine collection of small, atmospheric safari camps. From the moment of arrival, the Selous' wealth of wildlife and its stunning riverine scenery rarely fail to impress.

Only the section of the reserve north from the Rufiji River is open for tourism; large areas of the south have been zoned as hunting concessions.

History

Parts of the reserve were set aside as early as 1896. However, it was not until 1922 that it was expanded and given its present name (after Frederick Courteney Selous, the British explorer who was killed and buried in the reserve during WWI; it is possible to visit his **grave**). The area continued to be extended until 1975 when it assumed its current boundaries. In more recent years, there has been ongoing work to link Selous Game Reserve with the Niassa Reserve in Mozambique, with the first stages of the project – including establishment of a wildlife corridor – already underway.

🏃 Activities

Boat safaris down the Rufiji River or on the reserve's lakes are offered by most camps and lodges. Most also organise **walking safaris**, usually three-hour hikes near the camps, or further afield, with the night spent at a fly camp. Both the boat and foot safaris, as well as the chance to explore in open safari vehicles on **wildlife drives**, can come as a welcome change of pace from Tanzania's northern safari circuit.

🛏 Sleeping

🛏 Inside the Selous

All public campsites can be booked and paid for on arrival at the gates. You'll need to bring a large container to fill up for bathing and cleaning water at one of the entry gates, and then refill as needed closer to the campsites. Bring all food and drink.

Beho Beho
Public Campsite CAMPGROUND $
(camping US$30) Located at Beho Beho bridge, about 12km southeast of Matambwe, this public campsite has only basic facilities, such as a pit toilet.

Lake Tagalala
Public Campsite   CAMPGROUND $
(camping US$30) Lake Tagalala campsite has only basic facilities. It is located roughly midway between Mtemere and Matambwe.

Special Campsites   CAMPGROUND $
(mtbutalii@gmail.com; camping US$50) Special campsites can be arranged in the area between Mtemere gate and Lake Manze (northeast of Lake Tagalala).

For all camping, you'll need to bring a large container to fill up for bathing and cleaning water at one of the entry gates, and then refill as needed closer to the campsites. Bring all food and drink.

★Selous Impala Camp   TENTED CAMP $$$
(☑0753 115908, 0787 817591; www.adventure camps.co.tz; s/d full board plus excursions US$690/1200; ☉Jun-Mar; P☎) Impala Camp has eight well-spaced, nicely appointed tents in a prime setting on the river near Lake Mzizimia. Its restaurant overlooks the river and has an adjoining bar area on a deck jutting out towards the water, and the surrounding area is rich in wildlife.

The camp is especially good value if you take advantage of the flight-accommodation deals of Coastal Travels (p67) in Dar es Salaam.

Lake Manze Tented Camp   TENTED CAMP $$$
(☑0753 115908, 0787 817591; www.adventure camps.co.tz; s/d full board plus excursions US$520/900; ☉Jun-Mar; P) The rustic but comfortable Lake Manze campsite is favourably situated, with 12 simple but pleasant tents in a good location along an arm of Lake Manze. The ambience is low-key with a bush feel, and the camp is recommended for those on tighter budgets, especially as part of Coastal Travels' flight-accommodation deals.

Rufiji River Camp   TENTED CAMP $$$
(☑0784 237422; www.rufijirivercamp.com; s/d per person all inclusive US$465/730; P☎) This long-standing, unpretentious camp is run by the Fox family who own camps throughout southern Tanzania. It has a fine location on a wide bend in the Rufiji River about 1km inside Mtemere gate, tents with river views and a sunset terrace. Activities include boat safaris and overnight walking safaris. Overall good value for those on more limited budgets.

Siwandu   TENTED CAMP $$$
(Selous Safari Camp; ☑022-212 8485; www.selous.com; per person full board plus excursions from US$650; ☉Jun-Mar; P☎) This upmarket camp is set on a side arm of the Rufiji River in a lush, beautiful setting overlooking Lake Nzelekela. It is divided into two separate camps, each with a half dozen spacious tents, giving it a more intimate, exclusive feel. There's a raised dining and lounge area on one side, and impeccable service throughout. No children under six years of age are allowed.

If you can afford the price tag, it's a fine base for a Selous safari.

Beho Beho   LODGE $$$
(☑UK +44 19 3226 0618; www.behobeho.com; per person all inclusive from US$920; P☎) On a hillside northwest of Lake Tagalala, away from the river, Beho Beho is recommended for repeat safari-goers who have already experienced the riverside camps and want to get to know Selous in more depth. The spacious stone and thatch cottages have commanding views over the plains, guiding is excellent and there's the chance for a night in a private treehouse.

Boat safaris are done on Lake Tagalala, which is notable for its birdlife, as well as its hippos and crocodiles.

---

❶ SELOUS GAME RESERVE

Why Go Rewarding wildlife watching against a backdrop of stunning riverine scenery; wonderful, small camps; excellent boat safaris and the chance for walking safaris.

When to Go June through December; many camps close from March through May, during the heavy rains.

Practicalities Fly or drive in from Dar es Salaam; drive in from Morogoro or Mikumi. Both Mtemere and Matambwe gates are open from 6.30am to 6pm.

Reserve Headquarters (mtbutalii@gmail.com) are at Matambwe on the Selous' northwestern edge.

Budget Tips Travel by bus from Dar es Salaam to Mloka village, and base yourself outside Selous' boundaries, paying park fees only when you enter the reserve.

Selous Game Reserve (Northern Section)

Selous Game Reserve (Northern Section)

◉ Sights
1	Mikumi National Park	A2
2	Selous Game Reserve	A3
3	Selous Grave	C2
4	Stiegler's Gorge	B3

🛏 Sleeping
5	Beho Beho	B2
6	Beho Beho Public Campsite	B2
7	Lake Manze Tented Camp	C2
8	Lake Tagalala Public Campsite	C2
9	Rufiji River Camp	D2
10	Sable Mountain Lodge	A2
11	Selous Impala Camp	C2
12	Selous Mbega Camp	D3
13	Selous Mbega Kisaki Annex	A1
14	Selous River Camp	D3
15	Siwandu	C2

🛏 Outside the Selous

Most lodges outside Mtemere gate can arrange boat safaris on the Rufiji River east of the reserve boundaries, walking tours outside the reserve and wildlife drives inside Selous. Reserve fees are payable only for the days you enter within the Selous' boundaries. It's 75km through the Selous between Mtemere and Matambwe gates. Spending a few days on each side, linked by a full day's wildlife drive in between, is a rewarding option, although wildlife concentrations in the Matambwe area cannot compare with those deeper inside the reserve towards Mtemere.

Selous River Camp   COTTAGES $$
(☏ 0784 237525; www.selousrivercamp.com; camping US$5, s/d tent full board US$105/155, s/d mud hut full board US$235/285; ℗) This friendly place is the closest camp to Mtemere gate. It has cosy, river-facing 'mud huts' with bathrooms, plus small standing tents with cots and shared facilities surrounded by forest. The bar-restaurant area is lovely, directly overlooking the river at a particularly scenic spot. Overall, it's a fine choice for budget travellers.

Boat safaris, wildlife drives and village tours can be arranged.

Selous Mbega Camp   TENTED CAMP $$
(☏ 0784624664, 0784748888; www.selous-mbega-camp.com; s/d full board US$140/200, s/d back-

packers' special full board US$95/140) This laid-back, family-friendly camp is located about 1km outside the eastern boundary of the Selous near Mtemere gate and just west of Mloka village. It has raised, no-frills tents set in the foliage directly overlooking the river, and reasonably priced boat safaris and vehicle safaris. Pick-ups and drop-offs to and from Mloka are free. It is very good budget value.

The 'backpackers' special' rate is for travellers arriving in either Mloka or Kisaki villages by bus.

Selous Mbega Kisaki Annex TENTED CAMP **$$**
(☑0784 748888, 0784 624664; www.selous-mbega-camp.com; camping US$10, s/d full board US$140/200, s/d backpackers' special with full board US$95/140; ℗) Near Kisaki village and the train line, and 17km from Selous' Matambwe gate. Run by the same people who manage the similar Selous Mbega Camp. Along with rooms, it also offers camping, for which you'll need to be self-sufficient with food. The 'backpackers' rate is for travellers who arrive in either Mloka or Kisaki by bus.

Sable Mountain Lodge LODGE **$$$**
(☑0713 323318, 022-211 0507; www.selouslodge.com; s/d full board from US$230/350, all inclusive US$410/530; ℗ ☒) Friendly and relaxed, Sable Mountain is about halfway between Matambwe gate and Kisaki village on the northwestern boundary of the reserve. There are cosy stone cottages, tented *bandas* (thatched-roof huts), a snug for stargazing, walking safaris, wildlife drives and night drives outside the reserve.

❶ Getting There & Away

AIR

Coastal Aviation (p291) has daily flights linking Selous Game Reserve with Dar es Salaam (US$185 one way), Zanzibar (US$220 one way), Mafia (via Dar, US$280 one way) and Arusha (via Dar, US$525 one way), with connections to other northern-circuit airstrips. Coastal also flies between Selous and Ruaha National Park (US$320 one way). Other airlines flying these routes for similar prices include ZanAir (p68) and Safari Airlink (p382). Flights into the Selous are generally suspended during the March to May wet season. All lodges provide airfield transfers.

BUS

There is a daily bus from Temeke's Sudan Market (Majaribiwa area) and Mloka village, which is about 10km east of Mtemere gate (Tsh11,000, six to nine hours). Departures in both directions are at 5am. From Mloka, you'll need to arrange a pick-up in advance with one of the camps. Hitching within the Selous isn't permitted, and there are no vehicles to rent in Mloka.

If you are continuing from the Selous to Kilwa, Lindi or Mtwara, there's a daily dalla-dalla from Mloka to Kibiti junction, on the main road. It departs Mloka anywhere between 3am and 5am (three to four hours). Once at Kibiti, you'll need to flag down one of the passing buses coming from Dar es Salaam to take you to Nangurukuru junction (for Kilwa) or on to Lindi or Mtwara.

Coming from Morogoro: Tokyo Bus Line goes at least once daily between Morogoro's Msamvu transport stand and Kisaki village, departing in each direction between about 9am and 11am (Tsh9000, seven hours). From Kisaki, you'll need to arrange a pick-up in advance with the lodges to reach Matambwe gate, 21km further on.

SELOUS GAME RESERVE FEES

All fees are per 24-hour period and currently payable in US dollars cash only. At the time of research, multiple entries within a 24-hour period are permitted, although this may soon change.

Admission US$50 per adult (US$30 per child aged five to 17 years of age)

Conservation fee US$25 per person for those staying at camps inside the Selous; US$15 per person for those staying at camps outside the Selous' boundaries.

Vehicle fee Tsh20,000 for Tanzania-registered vehicles

Camping at ordinary campsite US$30 per adult (US$20 per child)

Camping at special campsite US$50 per adult (US$30 per child)

Wildlife guard (mandatory in camping areas) US$25

Guide US$40 (US$25 for walking- or boat-safari guides)

CAR

You'll need a 4WD in the Selous. There's no vehicle rental at the reserve and motorcycles aren't permitted.

To get here via road, there are two options. The first: take the main sealed road from Dar es Salaam to Kibiti, where you then branch southwestwards on a mostly decent dirt and sand track to Mkongo, Mloka and on to Mtemere gate (250km). The road is in reasonable to good shape as far as Mkongo. Mkongo to Mtemere (75km) is sometimes impassable during heavy rains. Allow six hours from Dar es Salaam.

Alternatively, you can go from Dar es Salaam to Kisaki via Morogoro and then on to Matambwe gate (about 350km) via a scenic but rough route through the Uluguru Mountains. It's 141km from Morogoro to Kisaki and 21km from Kisaki on to Matambwe gate. This route has improved considerably in recent times, but is still adventurous. From Dar es Salaam, the road is good tarmac as far as Morogoro. Once in Morogoro, take the Old Dar es Salaam road towards Bigwa. About 3km or 4km from the centre of town, past the Teachers' College Morogoro and before reaching Bigwa, you will come to a fork in the road, where you bear right. From here, the road becomes steep and scenic as it winds its way through the dense forests of the Uluguru Mountains onto a flat plain. Allow five to six hours for the stretch from Morogoro to Matambwe, depending on the season. If you are coming from Dar es Salaam and want to bypass Morogoro, take the unsignposted left-hand turn-off via Mikese, about 25km east of Morogoro on the main Dar es Salaam road that meets up with the Kisaki road at Msumbisi.

Driving from Dar es Salaam, the last petrol station is at Kibiti (about 100km northeast of Mtemere gate), although supplies aren't reliable. Otherwise, try Ikwiriri; there is no fuel thereafter. Coming from the other direction, the last reliable petrol station is at Morogoro (about 160km from the Matambwe Ranger Post). Occasionally, you may find both petrol and diesel sold on the roadside at Matombo, 50km south of Morogoro, and at several other villages, although quality isn't reliable. If you plan to drive around the Selous, bring sufficient petrol supplies with you as there is none available at any of the lodges, nor anywhere close to the reserve.

Expect to pay about US$250 per vehicle for a one-way transfer from Dar es Salaam via Mloka.

TRAIN

Train is an option for the adventurous, especially if you're staying on the northwestern side of the reserve. With luck, you may even get a preview of the wildlife from the train window. All Tazara trains stop at Kisaki, which is about five to six hours from Dar es Salaam, the first stop for the express train, and the main station of interest.

Ordinary trains also stop at Matambwe, near Selous headquarters, as well as at Kinyanguru and Fuga stations, although these latter two are seldom used these days.

It works best to take the train from Dar es Salaam to Selous, though be sure you have a pick-up confirmed in advance, as the train usually arrives after nightfall (between 7pm and 8pm for both ordinary and express, if on time). Going the other way around, be prepared for delays of up to 20 hours. For this reason, many lodges are unwilling to collect travellers coming from the Mbeya side. There are several basic, local guesthouses (none that we recommend) in Kisaki, should you get stuck.

Kilwa Masoko

Kilwa Masoko (Kilwa of the Market) is a sleepy coastal town nestled amid dense vegetation and several fine stretches of beach about halfway between Dar es Salaam and Mtwara. It's the springboard for visiting the ruins of the 15th-century Arab settlements at Kilwa Kisiwani (p298) and Songo Mnara (p300), and as such, is the gateway into one of the most significant eras in East African coastal history. The town itself is a relatively modern creation, with minimal historical appeal.

⊙ Sights & Activities

On the eastern edge of town is Jimbizi Beach, a short stretch of sand in a partially sheltered cove dotted with the occasional baobab tree. The best coastline is the long, idyllic palm-fringed open-ocean beach at Masoko Pwani, 5km northeast of town, and best reached by bicycle or *bajaji* (Tsh5000 one way). This is also where Kilwa Masoko gets its fish, and the colourful harbour area is worth a look, especially in the late afternoon.

Dhow excursions through the mangrove swamps on the outskirts of Kilwa – interesting for their birdlife and resident hippos – can be arranged with the hotels and with the Kilwa Islands Tour Guides Association (p298), as can excursions to see the hippos at Mto Nyange. About 85km northwest of Kilwa at Kipatimo are extensive limestone caves.

🛏 Sleeping

Kilwa Bandari Lodge GUESTHOUSE $
(☑ 0713 850745; s/d/tw Tsh39,000/49,000/49,000; meals Tsh7000; P) Six tidy, modern rooms with fan, mosquito net, win-

dow screens and Zanzibar-style beds make this one of the best budget bets in town. Local-style meals are available on order. It's about 1.5km south of the bus stand (Tsh1000 in a *bajaji*), along the main road and shortly before the port gates.

Kimbilio Lodge
LODGE **$$**

(☑0656 022166; www.kimbiliolodges.com; s/d/tr/q US$90/130/150/170; ℗) This pleasant place has a good beachside setting on the best section of Jimbizi Beach. Accommodation is in six, spacious, tastefully decorated rondavels (circular African buildings) with *makutis* (thatched roof of palm leaves) directly on the sand. It's warmly recommended. There's good Italian cuisine and (with advance notice) diving. Snorkelling excursions and visits to the hippos and mangrove swamps can be arranged.

Kilwa Seaview Resort
LODGE **$$**

(☑0784 613335, 023-201 3064; www.kilwa.net; Jimbizi Beach; camping US$10, s/d/tr/q half board US$100/130/160/190; ℗⊛) This family-friendly place has spacious A-frame cottages perched along a rocky escarpment overlooking the eastern end of Jimbizi Beach. There's a restaurant built around a huge baobab tree with tasty meals, and the swimming beach is just a short walk away.

Driving, the access turn-off is signposted from the main road. By foot from the bus stand: head south along the main road towards the port, then turn left near the police station, making your way past the police barracks down the hill by Kilwa Ruins to Jimbizi Beach. At the northeastern end of the beach is a small path leading up to the cottages. Transfers from Dar es Salaam or to Selous GR cost from US$250 per vehicle one way.

Kilwa Dreams
COTTAGES **$$**

(☑0784 585330; www.kilwadreams.com; Masoko Pwani; camping US$10, d/f bungalow US$70/95; meals Tsh25,000-35,000; ℗) This is an ideal spot for getting away from just about everything, with a handful of bright blue, spartan but well-tended bungalows with cold water and no electricity in an idyllic setting directly on the long, wonderful beach at Masoko Pwani. There's also a beachside bar-restaurant. Take the airport turn-off and follow the signs along sandy tracks for about 4km to the beach. *Bajaji* charge Tsh5000 from town.

Kilwa Masoko

Kilwa Masoko

◉ Sights

| 1 Jimbizi Beach | B2 |

🛏 Sleeping

2 Kilwa Bandari Lodge	A3
3 Kilwa Pakaya Oceanic Resort	B2
4 Kimbilio Lodge	B2

🍴 Eating

| 5 Mopei Fast Food | B1 |
| 6 Night Market | B1 |

ℹ Transport

7 Buses to Dar es Salaam & Lindi	A1
8 Coastal Aviation Booking Office	A1
9 Transport to Kilwa Kivinje & Nangurukuru	A1

Kilwa Pakaya Oceanic Resort
HOTEL **$$**

(☑0776 570425, 023-201 3253; www.kilwapakayahotel.co.tz; s/d Tsh152,000/184,000; ℗⊛⊜) Well-situated in the centre of Jimbizi Beach, Kilwa Pakaya has a very pleasant beachside dining area, beach volleyball and small, comfortable rooms in a multistorey block to the back. All have sea views plus fan and minifridge.

Mwangaza Hideaway   LODGE **$$**

(📞 0784 637026, 0687 848927; www.fishing-tanzania.com; per person half board US$140; 🅿 🏊) This is Kilwa's main angling destination, with fully equipped fishing and accommodation in four rustic bungalows. Book well in advance for the late October peak fishing season. It's on the western side of the peninsula, reached via a signposted turn-off from the main road just before town.

🍴 Eating

For inexpensive fish or chicken and chips, try **Mopei Fast Food** (meals from Tsh3000) near the market. The lively **night market**, between the main street and the market, has cheap fish and street snacks from dusk onwards.

ⓘ Information

MONEY

National Microfinance Bank (Main Rd) Changes cash. There's no ATM in Kilwa.

TOURIST INFORMATION

Kilwa Islands Tour Guides Association (Main Rd) This small office provides information. It is where you need to go to get guides for visiting Kilwa Kisiwani, Songo Mnara and other local excursions, including to the caves near Kipatimo, the Mto Nyange hippo pools and Kilwa Kivinje. It also rents bicycles. Prices for most excursions start at about US$25 per person for guide and transport (less with larger groups). **District Commissioner's Office** (Halmashauri ya Wilaya ya Kilwa; ⊘7.30am-3.30pm Mon-Fri) This is where you get permits to visit Kilwa Kisiwani and Songo Mnara. Ask for the 'Mambo ya Kale' (Antiquities) office.

ⓘ Getting There & Away

AIR

Coastal Aviation flies daily on demand between Dar es Salaam and Kilwa (US$250 one way), Kilwa and Zanzibar (US$300 one way) and between Kilwa and Mafia (US$190, minimum two passengers). Book through the Dar es Salaam office (p67), or in Kilwa through the **Coastal Aviation Booking Office** (Sudi Travel) north of the petrol station and just north of the transport stand. The airstrip is about 2km north of town along the main road.

BOAT

Dhows are best arranged in Kilwa Kivinje. Boats to Kilwa Kisiwani, Songo Mnara and Songo Songo depart from the jetty at the southern end of town.

BUS

To Dar es Salaam, there are usually two buses daily, usually stopping also in Kilwa Kivinje. Departures in each direction are at 5.30am and 8am (Tsh12,000, four to five hours). Book your tickets the day before. All Kilwa departures are from the transport stand just off the main road near the market. Departures in Dar es Salaam are from 'Mbagala Rangi Tatu', along the Kilwa road, which is also the end terminus for this bus on its run up from Kilwa. Coming from Dar es Salaam it's also possible to get a Mtwara-bound bus and get out at Nangurukuru junction, from where you can get local transport to Kilwa Kivinje (Tsh1000, 11km) or Kilwa Masoko (Tsh2000, 35km), although you'll be charged the full Dar–Mtwara fare. This doesn't work as well leaving Kilwa, as buses are usually full when they pass Nangurukuru (from about 11am). The best place to wait is at the large Kivinje Restaurant rest stop, along the main road about 50m north of Nangurukuru junction; most through buses stop here.

To Lindi, there's at least one direct bus daily (Tsh7000, four hours), departing Kilwa about 6am from the market just south of the Dar es Salaam bus booking offices; book a day in advance. There are no direct connections to Mtwara. Either get a shared taxi to Nangurukuru junction, and then try your luck catching a Mtwara-bound bus from there for the full Dar–Mtwara fare. Otherwise, go first to Lindi, and take a Hiace minivan from there.

TAXI

To Nangurukuru (the junction with the Dar–Mtwara road; Tsh2000, one hour) and Kilwa Kivinje (Tsh2000, 45 minutes), shared taxis depart several times daily from the transport stand on the main road just north of the market. The transport stand is also the place to hire taxis or *bajaji* for local excursions.

Kilwa Kisiwani

A quiet fishing village baking in the sun, **Kilwa Kisiwani** (Kilwa on the Island; adult/student Tsh27,000/13,000) is just off shore from Kilwa Masoko. In its heyday it was the seat of sultans and centre of a vast trading network linking the old Shona kingdoms and the gold fields of Zimbabwe with Persia, India and China. Ibn Battuta, the famed traveller and chronicler of the ancient world, visited Kilwa in the early 14th century and described the town as being exceptionally beautiful and well constructed. At its height, Kilwa's influence extended north past the Zanzibar Archipelago and south as far as Sofala on the central Mozambican coast.

While these glory days are now well in the past, the ruins of the settlement – together with the ruins on nearby Songo Mnara island – are among the most significant groups of Swahili buildings on the East African coast and a Unesco World Heritage site. Thanks to funding from the French and Japanese governments, significant sections of the ruins have been restored, and are now easily accessible, with informative signboards in English and Swahili.

History

The coast near Kilwa Kisiwani has been inhabited for several thousand years, and artefacts from the late and middle Stone Ages have been found on the island. Although the first settlements in the area date to around AD 800, Kilwa remained a relatively undistinguished place until the early 13th century. At this time, trade links developed with Sofala, 1500km to the south in present-day Mozambique. Kilwa came to control Sofala and to dominate its lucrative gold trade, and before long it had become the most powerful trade centre along the Swahili coast.

In the late 15th century, Kilwa's fortunes began to turn. Sofala freed itself from the island's dominance, and in the early 16th century Kilwa came under the control of the Portuguese. It wasn't until more than 200 years later that Kilwa regained its independence and once again became a significant trading centre, this time as an entrepôt for slaves being shipped from the mainland to the islands of Mauritius, Réunion and Comoros. In the 1780s, Kilwa came under the control of the Sultan of Oman. By the mid-19th century, the local ruler had succumbed to the Sultan of Zanzibar, the focus of regional trade shifted to Kilwa Kivinje on the mainland, and the island town entered a decline from which it never recovered.

The Ruins

The ruins at Kilwa Kisiwani are in two groups. When approaching Kilwa Kisiwani, the first building you'll find is the **Arabic Fort** (*gereza*). It was built in the early 19th century by the Omani Arabs, on the site of a Portuguese fort dating from the early 16th century. To the southwest of the fort are the ruins of the beautiful **Great Mosque**, with its columns and graceful vaulted roofing, much of which has been impressively restored. Some sections of the mosque date to the late 13th century, although most are from additions made to the building in the 15th century. In its day, this was the largest

mosque on the East African coast. Further southwest and behind the Great Mosque is a smaller **mosque** dating from the early 15th century. This is considered to be the best preserved of the buildings at Kilwa and has also been impressively restored. To the west of the small mosque, with large, green lawns and placid views over the water, are the crumbling remains of the **Makutani**. Inside this large, walled enclosure is where some of the sultans of Kilwa lived. It is estimated to date from the mid-18th century.

Almost 1.5km from the fort along the coast is **Husuni Kubwa**, once a massive complex of buildings covering almost a hectare and, together with nearby **Husuni Ndogo**, the oldest of Kilwa's ruins. The complex, which is estimated to date from the 12th century or earlier, is set on a hill and must have once commanded great views over the bay. Watch in particular for the octagonal bathing pool. Husuni Ndogo is smaller than Husuni Kubwa and is thought to date from about the same time, although archaeologists are not yet sure of its original function. To reach these ruins, you can walk along the beach at low tide or follow the slightly longer inland route.

☞ Tours

To visit the ruins, you'll need to be accompanied by a guide onto the island, arranged through the Kilwa Islands Tour Guides Association, along the main road in Kilwa Masoko. The District Commissioner's Office, also in Kilwa Masoko (diagonally opposite the post office), is where you must pay for and acquire the mandatory permit. Ask for the Ofisi ya Mambo ya Kale (Antiquities Office); the permit is issued without fuss while you wait. The Antiquities Officer is more likely to be there in the morning. On weekends, telephone numbers of duty officers are posted on the door, and officials are quite gracious about issuing permits outside working hours.

ℹ Information

For detailed information in English about the ruins, look for a copy of HN Chittick's informative manuscript *A Guide to the Ruins of Kilwa with Some Notes on the Other Antiquities of the Region*. The National Museum (p52) in Dar es Salaam also has a small display on Kilwa Kisiwani.

There are no restaurants or hotels on the island.

ℹ Getting There & Away

Local boats go from the port at Kilwa Masoko to Kilwa Kisiwani (Tsh200) whenever there are enough passengers – usually only in the early morning, about 7am. However, as you are required to go with a guide to the islands, you'll generally need to pay their prices. Guides from the Kilwa Islands Tour Guides Association (p298) charge US$25 per person for a guide; this includes dhow transport (US$30 for a boat with motor, less with larger groups). With a good wind, the trip in a sailing dhow takes about 20 minutes. Excursions arranged through the hotels cost about the same or more.

Songo Mnara

Tiny **Songo Mnara** (per adult/student Tsh27,000/13,000), about 8km south of Kilwa Kisiwani, contains ruins at its northern end – including a palace, several mosques and numerous houses – that are believed to date from the 14th and 15th centuries. They are considered in some respects to be more significant architecturally than those at Kilwa Kisiwani, with one of the most complete town layouts along the coast, although they're less visually impressive. Just off the island's western side is **Sanje Majoma**, with additional ruins dating from the same period. The small island of **Sanje ya Kati**, between Songo Mnara and Kilwa Masoko, has some lesser ruins of a third settlement in the area, also believed to date from the same era.

A permit for Songo Mnara costs Tsh27,000 (Tsh13,000 for students under 16 years of age). There's no accommodation or food on the island.

The best way to get to Songo Mnara is via motorboat from Kilwa Masoko, arranged through the Kilwa Islands Tour Guides Association (p298) or one of the hotels. Expect to pay about US$50 per person for a sailing dhow including guide (US$70 with motor). Dhows between Kilwa Masoko and Songo Mnara take about two to three hours with a decent wind (1½ hours with motor). For combined full-day trips including both Songo Mnara and Kilwa Kisiwani, a guide plus motorised boat transport costs US$80 per person.

After landing at Songo Mnara, be prepared to wade a bit through mangrove swamps before reaching the island proper.

Kilwa Kivinje

Kilwa Kivinje (Kilwa of the Casuarina Trees) owes its existence to Omani Arabs from Kilwa Kisiwani who set up a base here in the early 19th century following the fall of the Kilwa sultanate. By the mid-19th century the settlement had become the hub of the regional slave-trading network, and by the late 19th century, a German administrative centre. With the abolishment of the slave trade, and German wartime defeats, Kilwa Kivinje's brief period in the spotlight came to an end. Today, it's a crumbling, moss-covered and atmospheric relic of the past with a Swahili small-town feel and an intriguing mixture of German colonial and Omani Arab architecture.

The most interesting section of town is around the old **German boma** (administrative office). The street behind the *boma* is lined with small houses, many with carved Zanzibar-style doorways. Nearby is a **mosque**, which locals claim has been in continuous use since the 14th century, and a warren of back streets where you can absorb a slice of coastal life, with children playing on the streets and women sorting huge trays of *dagga* (tiny sardines) for drying in the sun. Just in from here on the water is the bustling **dhow port**, where brightly painted vessels set off regularly for Songo Songo, Mafia and other coastal ports.

The best way to visit Kilwa Kivinje is as an easy half-day or day trip from Kilwa Masoko. The Kilwa Islands Tour Guides Association (p298) organises day cycling trips from Kilwa Masoko for about US$25 per person. Overnight options are limited to a clutch of nondescript guesthouses near the market, all with rooms for about Tsh10,000, and each rivalling the others in grubbiness.

ℹ Getting There & Away

Kilwa Kivinje is reached by heading about 25km north of Kilwa Masoko (or 5km south of Nangurukuru junction) along a sealed road and then turning in at the signposted turn-off and continuing for about 5km further down a sandy track. Shared taxis travel several times daily to and from Kilwa Masoko (Tsh2000), and the bus between Dar es Salaam and Kilwa Masoko also usually stops at Kilwa Kivinje. Chartering a private taxi from Kilwa Masoko will cost from around Tsh25,000.

Dhows sail regularly from Kilwa Kivinje to Songo Songo (about Tsh2000, three to five hours; motorised boat Tsh7000, two to three hours). Departures for the motorised boats are usually about 11am. For Mafia, take a bus up the coast towards Dar es Salaam and get a boat at Nyamisati.

Songo Songo

Coconut palms, low shrub vegetation, about 3500 locals, lots of birds, a beach and a major natural-gas field that is being exploited as part of the Songo Songo Gas to Electricity Project are the main attractions on this 4-sq-km island. Together with **Fanjove** and several other surrounding islets, it forms the Songo Songo archipelago, an ecologically important area for nesting sea turtles and marine birds. The surrounding waters also host an impressive collection of hard and soft corals. The archipelago, together with the nearby Rufiji River delta, the Mafia archipelago and the coastline around Kilwa Masoko have been declared a Wetland of International Importance under the Ramsar Convention. The best beach is in Songo Songo's southeastern corner, reached through a coconut plantation. There are no tourist facilities on the island.

Songo Songo lies about 30km northeast of Kilwa Kivinje, from where it can be reached by dhow in about 3½ hours with favourable winds. Coastal Aviation (p291) flies daily to Songo Songo from Dar es Salaam, Kilwa Masoko and Mafia.

🛏 Sleeping

★ **Fanjove Private Island** LODGE $$$
(☑022-260 1747; www.ed.co.tz; per person full board US$350) 🌀 This small, private island has six rustic but comfortable eco-*bandas* directly on a lovely beach, showers open to the stars, and kayaking, snorkelling and other excursions. Everything is low key, with the emphasis on minimising environmental impact. It's unique, and highly recommended, especially in combination with Kilwa and Mafia, for anyone seeking an introduction to life on the Swahili coast.

February to June is green-turtle nesting time.

🌐 Getting There & Away

AIR
Coastal Aviation (p291) flies between Songo Songo main island and Dar es Salaam (US$220 one way), Kilwa Masoko (US$100) and Mafia (US$120). Once on Songo Songo, you'll need to take a short boat ride over to Fanjove; this should be booked in advance when making your Fanjove reservation (US$40 per person round-trip).

BOAT
For something more adventurous, motorised dhows depart most days at about 11am from the Kilwa Kivinje dhow port for Songo Songo (Tsh7000), from where you will need to continue over to Fanjove via boat transfer arranged with Fanjove Private Island. More comfortably and reliably: it's also possible to arrange charter-boat transfer from Kilwa Masoko to Songo Songo through Kimbilio Lodge (p297), opening up the possibility for some very appealing circuit itineraries.

Lindi

POP 78,840
In its early days, Lindi was part of the Sultan of Zanzibar's domain, a terminus of the slave-caravan route from Lake Nyasa, regional colonial capital, and the main town in southeastern Tanzania. The abolishment of the slave trade and the rise of Mtwara as a local hub sent Lindi into a slow decline, from which it has yet to recover, although it again moved briefly into the limelight in the early 20th century when dinosaur bones were discovered nearby.

Today, Lindi is a lively, pleasant place and worth wandering around for a day or so to get a taste of life on the coast. Its small dhow port bustles with local coastal traffic, a smattering of carved doorways and crumbling ruins line the dusty streets, and a Hindu temple and Indian merchants serve as a reminder of once-prosperous trade routes to the east.

Salt production is the main local industry, announced by the salt flats lining the road into town. There's also a sisal plantation in Kikwetu, near the airfield. The coral reef running from south of Lindi to Sudi Bay hosts abundant marine life, and the site has been proposed as a possible protected marine area.

Lindi

to **Kitunda Peninsula** – ask locals to point you in the direction of Mtanda, Wailes ('Wire-less') or Mtuleni neighbourhoods. On Kitunda itself, which was formerly a sisal estate, there's nothing much now other than a sleepy village, but it's a pleasant destination for walking and offers a glimpse of local life. At the end of the peninsula behind the hill is a good beach (hire a local boat to get there).

About 6km north of town off the airfield road is **Mtema Beach**, which is usually empty except for weekends and holidays. Take care with your valuables.

🛏 Sleeping

White Pearl Hotel GUESTHOUSE $
(☑ 0713 766584; s/d Tsh50,000/70,000) This new, local-style guesthouse has clean, modern rooms and meals on order.

Vision Hotel GUESTHOUSE $
(Makonde St; r Tsh35,000; ❄) This place, opposite Brigita Dispensary, has clean rooms, all with fan, TV and one double bed, and meals on order.

Malaika Guest House GUESTHOUSE $
(☑ 023-220 2880; Market St; r Tsh18,000) Malaika, one block east of the market, is worth a look if the other budget places are full. Rooms are very basic but reasonably clean, with fan. Meals can be arranged.

Lindi Beach Resort HOTEL $$
(☑ 0656 032044, 023-220 2829; Waterfront Rd; s/d/ste Tsh60,000/70,000/120,000; Ⓟ❄) This hotel has a prime waterfront location just down from the harbour, decent, sea-facing rooms that are reasonable value for money and a restaurant. The suites have small balconies.

Mtuleni Hills GUESTHOUSE $$
(☑ 0784 782497, 0713 782497; giuseppetrupia@hotmail.com; r Tsh70,000-90,000) This guesthouse, located in the grounds of an Italian restaurant, has a few blocks of modest rooms, most sharing bathrooms. It's about 3km from town in the Mtuleni area beyond Tanesco, and mainly an option for those with their own transport.

🍴 Eating & Drinking

Lindi isn't distinguished for its dining options, but you can get some delicious grilled fish. The best street food is at the bus stand.

◉ Sights & Activities

The old, historical part of town is the section along the waterfront, though you'll have to really hunt for the few still-standing remnants of the town's more glorious past. Watch for the remains of the old **German boma**, ruins of an **Arab tower** and the occasional **carved doorway**. The small **Dhow Port** on palm-fringed Lindi Bay is lively and colourful and worth a stroll. From some of the hills on the edge of town there are good views over large stands of palm trees and Lindi Bay, and across the Lukeludi River

BRACHIOSAURUS BRANCAI

Tendunguru, about 100km northwest of Lindi, is the site of one of the most significant palaeontological finds in history. From 1909 to 1912, a team of German palaeontologists unearthed the remains of more than a dozen different dinosaur species, including the skeleton of *Brachiosaurus brancai*, the largest known dinosaur in the world. The Brachiosaurus skeleton is now on display at the Museum of Natural History in Berlin. Scientists are unsure why so many dinosaur fossils were discovered in the region, although it is thought that flooding or some other natural catastrophe was the cause of the dinosaurs' demise.

Today, Tendunguru is of interest mainly to hardcore palaeontologists. For visitors, there is little to see and access to the site is difficult, even with your own vehicle.

Himo-One TANZANIAN $
(Jamhuri St; meals Tsh4000) This longstanding local favourite is on the scruffy side, but meals – chicken or fish and rice or chips – are quick and reliable. There's no alcohol. It's several blocks south of the market.

La Dolce Vita ITALIAN $$$
(Mtuleni Hills; 0784 782497, 0713 782497; giuseppetrupia@hotmail.com; meals Tsh10,000-32,000; 1-2.30pm & 6.30-10pm; call first) Tasty pizzas, pastas and other Italian cuisine, authentically prepared. It's about 3km from the town centre in the Mtuleni neighbourhood (Tsh3000 in a *bajaji*), past the Tanesco office. Call first to be sure they are open before venturing up.

Santorini TANZANIAN
(Santolin; Waterfront Rd; meals from Tsh5000) This place behind the stadium in the Mikumbi area near the water is a good place for a drink. There's also food, but service is slow.

ℹ Information

MEDICAL SERVICES
Brigita Dispensary (023-220 2679; brigita_dispensary@yahoo.de; Makonde St) This Western-run clinic is the best place for medical emergencies. It's several blocks east of the market; anyone should be able to point you in the right direction.

MONEY
CRDB (Main roundabout) ATM.
NBC (Lumumba St) On the waterfront; changes cash and has an ATM.

ℹ Getting There & Away

BOAT
Cargo boats along the coast, including to Dar es Salaam, call at the port near the NBC bank, although they generally don't take passengers. The dhow port is about 800m further up the coast.

Boats across the Lukeludi River to Kitunda sail throughout the day from in front of NBC.

BUS
All transport departs from the main bus and taxi stand on Uhuru St. Minibuses to Mtwara (Tsh4000) depart daily between about 5.30am and 11am. Otherwise, there are minibuses throughout the day to Mingoyo junction (Mnazi Mmoja; Tsh2000), where you can wait for a Masasi–Mtwara bus.

To Masasi (Tsh3500), there are two or three direct buses daily, departing about 5am and noon. Alternatively, go to Mingoyo and wait for onward transport there. The last Mtwara–Masasi bus passes Mingoyo about 2pm.

To Dar es Salaam, there are direct buses daily, departing Lindi at about 5am (Tsh22,000, eight to 10 hours), and terminating at Mbagala Rangi Tatu transport stand in Dar es Salaam, which is also where you need to go to catch transport heading to Lindi.

To Kilwa Masoko, there's a direct bus leaving Lindi daily by 6am (Tsh7000, four hours).

Mtwara

POP 108,300

Sprawling Mtwara is southeastern Tanzania's major town. It was first developed after WWII by the British as part of the failed East African Groundnut Scheme to alleviate a postwar shortage of plant oils. Grand plans were made to expand Mtwara, then an obscure fishing village, into an urban centre of about 200,000 inhabitants. An international airport and Tanzania's first deepwater harbour were built and the regional colonial administration was relocated here from Lindi. Yet, no sooner had this been done than the groundnut scheme – plagued

Mtwara

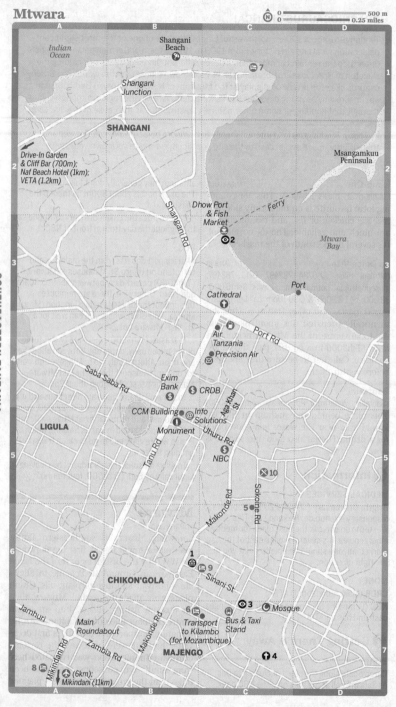

Indian Ocean

Shangani Beach

7

Shangani Junction

SHANGANI

Drive-In Garden
& Cliff Bar (700m);
Naf Beach Hotel (1km);
VETA (1.2km)

Shangani Rd

Dhow Port
& Fish Market

Ferry

Msangamkuu Peninsula

2

Mtwara Bay

Cathedral

Port

Port Rd

Air Tanzania

Precision Air

Saba Saba Rd

Exim Bank

CRDB

CCM Building

Info Solutions

Aga Khan St

Monument

Uhuru Rd

NBC

LIGULA

Tanu Rd

10

Makonde Rd

Sokoine Rd

5

1

9

Sihani St

CHIKON'GOLA

Jamburi

Main Roundabout

Makonde Rd

6

Transport to Kilambo
(for Mozambique)

3

Mosque

Bus & Taxi Stand

Zambia Rd

MAJENGO

Mikindani Rd

8

(6km);
Mikindani (11km)

4

0 — 500 m
0 — 0.25 miles

Mtwara

by conceptional difficulties and an uncooperative local climate – collapsed and everything came to an abrupt halt. While Mtwara's port continued to play a significant role in the region over the next few decades as an export channel for cashews, sisal and other products, development of the town came to a standstill and for years it resembled little more than an oversized shell.

In recent times Mtwara has experienced a major boom, with the discovery of offshore natural gas reserves. Gone is the somnolent, sunbaked atmosphere that characterised the city for so long. Whether recent developments will ultimately be to the benefit of local residents remains to be seen, but for now, Mtwara is hopping. Mtwara lacks the historical appeal of nearby Mikindani and other places along the coast, and has little to recommend it as a tourist destination. Yet, with its decent infrastructure and easy access, it makes a convenient entry or exit point for those travelling between Tanzania and Mozambique.

Mtwara is loosely located between a business and banking area to the northwest, near Uhuru Rd and Aga Khan St, and the market and bus stand about 1.5km away to the southeast. The main north–south street is Tanu Rd. In the far northwest on the sea, and 30 to 40 minutes on foot from the bus stand, is the Shangani quarter, with a small beach. In Mtwara's far southeastern corner, just past the market, are the lively areas of Majengo and Chikon'gola.

◉ Sights & Activities

In town, there's a lively **market** with a small traditional-medicine section next to the main building. **Aga Khan St** is lined with old Indian trading houses dating from the late 1950s and 1960s. Much of Mtwara's fish comes from Msangamkuu on the other side of Mtwara Bay, and the small **dhow port** and adjoining **fish market** are particularly colourful in the early morning and late afternoon. The **beach** in Shangani is popular for swimming (high tide only); its gentle currents and general absence of sea urchins and other hazards make it ideal for children. For views over the bay and the white sands of Msangamkuu Peninsula, look for the tiny footpath leading to a viewpoint near Msemo Hotel (p307).

Centre for African Development Through Economics & the Arts   MUSEUM
(ADEA; Sinani St; entry by donation; ⊙9am-5pm Tue-Sat) This excellent little museum is full of masks, spears, tools and other cultural items from the Makonde, Makua and Yao tribes. All displays are labelled in English and Swahili. This is also the best place to get information on the annual **Makuya Festival** (makuyafestival@gmail.com). From the small roundabout on Makonde Rd, go one block north, then turn right. It's the second building on the left.

Ayayoru Carvings & Tours   GUIDED TOUR
(☑0787 194196; www.mtwaratours.com; Sokoine Rd) Guided tours in and around Mtwara, including village visits with traditional dancing and drumming.

🛌 Sleeping

Drive-In Garden & Cliff Bar   GUESTHOUSE $
(☑0784 503007; Shangani Rd; camping Tsh5000, r Tsh20,000) This friendly place allows campers to pitch their tent in the garden. There are also several simple, good-value rooms, plus a restaurant. Breakfast is not included in the price. It's just across the road from the beach, although for swimming you'll need to walk up to the main Shangani Beach near Shangani junction.

Go left at the main Shangani junction and continue, parallel to the beach, for 1.2km to the small signpost on your left.

VETA   HOSTEL $
(☑023-233 4094; Shangani; s/ste Tsh35,000/ 60,000; ℗❄⊠) This large compound has clean rooms, all with one large twin bed,

SOUTHEASTERN TANZANIA MTWARA

ST PAUL'S CHURCH

If you happen to be in the Majengo area of Mtwara, it's worth stopping in at St Paul's Church to view its remarkable artwork. The entire front and side walls are covered with richly coloured biblical scenes painted by a German Benedictine priest, Polycarp Uehlein, in the mid-1970s. The paintings, which took about two years to complete, are part of a series by the same artist decorating churches throughout southern Tanzania and in a few other areas of the country, including churches in Nyangao, Lindi, Malolo, Ngapa and Dar es Salaam. In addition to their style and distinctive use of colour, the paintings are notable for their universalised portrayal of common biblical themes. The themes were chosen to assist churchgoers to understand the sermons and to relate the biblical lessons to their everyday lives.

During the years he has worked in Tanzania, Father Polycarp has taught several African students. The best known of these is Henry Likonde from Mtwara, who has taken biblical scenes and 'Africanised' them. You can see examples of Likonde's work in the small church at the top of the hill in Mahurunga, south of Mtwara near the Mozambican border, and in the cathedral in Songea.

fan, TV and views towards the water, plus a restaurant. It's in Shangani, about 200m back from the water (though there's no swimming beach here). From the T-junction in Shangani, go left and continue for about 2km. There's no public transport; *bajaji* charge around Tsh3000 from town.

The swimming pool costs Tsh5000 for nonguests.

Naf Blue View Hotel
GUESTHOUSE $

(☑ 023-233 4465; Sinani St; s/d from Tsh70,000/80,000; ✲@🛜) About 400m up (west) from the bus stand, this place is one of the better bets in the busy market area, with small, modern rooms with running hot water, satellite TV and meals on order. There are no mosquito nets. Single rooms come with breakfast; for doubles, you'll need to pay Tsh7000 more so both can eat.

Mtwara Lutheran Centre
HOSTEL $

(☑ 0686 049999, 0754 255576; Mikindani Rd; r Tsh10,000-30,000; 🅿) Clean-ish, no-frills rooms, some with private bathrooms and all with fans. Meals can be arranged with advance notice. It's on the southern edge of town, just off the main roundabout along the road heading to Mikindani (Tsh2000 with a *bajaji* from the bus stand). Arriving by bus, ask the driver to drop you at the roundabout.

FL High Class Hotel
GUESTHOUSE $

(r Tsh50,000) This is a decent budget option near the bus stand. All rooms have a small double bed. Transport to Mozambique departs from next door. It's one block south of the bus stand.

Naf Beach Hotel
HOTEL $$

(☑ 0687 703042, 023-233 4706; www.nafbeach hotels.com; s/d from US$100/130; 🅿✲🛜) This hotel is probably Mtwara's closest to a Western-style business hotel. All rooms have one double bed, minifridge and satellite TV, some have sea views and there's a restaurant. It's just opposite the sea, but for swimming you'll need to go about 1.5km east to Shangani Beach. Visa and MasterCard are accepted.

It's about 1.8km west of the Shangani junction.

Msemo Hotel
HOTEL $$

(Southern Cross Hotel; ☑ 0786 678283, 023-233 3206; www.msemoproject.com; Shangani; r US$80, bungalows US$100; 🅿🛜) This place is popular with the oil and gas workers currently flooding Mtwara. Choose between smaller garden rooms set slightly back from the water, larger waterfront rooms or seafront bungalows. All have fan, TV and Zanzibari-style double bed. There's also a waterside restaurant.

It's on a small, rocky outcrop overlooking the sea in Shangani, with the Shangani swimming beach just a short walk away.

🍴 Eating & Drinking

Drive-In Garden & Cliff Bar
TANZANIAN $

(☑ 0784 503007; meals Tsh6000-12,000; ⊗ lunch & dinner) Simple, delicious and generously portioned meals of grilled fish, prawns or chicken, and chips, plus cold drinks. It is in a peaceful garden setting just back from the water. Call in advance to place your order to minimise waiting time.

Himo 2 Restaurant
TANZANIAN $

(Sokoine Rd; meals Tsh5000; ⊙lunch & dinner)
This popular local-style eatery serves chicken, *mishikaki* (marinated, grilled meat kebabs) and other standard local fare with rice, ugali (a staple made from maize or cassava flour, or both) or chips, as well as fruit juice. Coming from town, take the first right after NBC bank. Himo 2 is a few doors up to the left.

Msemo Hotel
TANZANIAN, EUROPEAN $$

(Southern Cross Hotel; Shangani; meals Tsh12,000-20,000) This hotel restaurant, on a terrace overlooking the water, is popular for sundowners and has tasty meals.

❶ Information

INTERNET ACCESS

Info Solutions (Uhuru Rd; per hour Tsh2000; ⊙8am-6pm Mon-Sat) On the side of the CCM building.

MONEY

CRDB (Tanu Rd) ATM. Other CRDB ATMs are at St Augustine's University, next to the cathedral on Port Rd, and opposite the bus stand. Accepts Visa and MasterCard.

Exim Bank (Tanu Rd) ATM. This is also the best place to change cash. Accepts Visa and MasterCard.

NBC (Uhuru Rd) ATM. Accepts Visa and MasterCard.

❶ Getting There & Away

AIR

There are daily flights between Mtwara and Dar es Salaam (Tsh180,000 to Tsh230,000 one way) on **Precision Air** (www.precisionairtz.com; Tanu Rd) and, less reliably **Air Tanzania** (☑ 0713 506959, 0713 766230; www.airtanzania.co.tz; Tanu Rd) (four times weekly).

BUS

All long-distance buses depart between about 5am and noon from the main bus stand just off Sokoine Rd near the market.

To Masasi, there are roughly hourly departures between about 6am and 2pm (Tsh7500, five hours); once in Masasi you'll need to change vehicles for Tunduru and Songea.

To Lindi (Tsh4000, three hours), there are several direct minibuses daily, departing in both directions in the morning.

To Kilwa Masoko, there's currently no direct bus. You'll need to go first to Lindi and get onward transport from there, or take any Dar es Salaam–bound bus to Nangurukuru junction.

For the latter option, you'll have to pay the full Dar price.

Direct buses to Newala (Tsh7500, six to eight hours) use the southern route via Nanyamba. Departures from Mtwara are between about 6am and 8am daily, except during the wet season when services are more sporadic. It's also possible to reach Newala via Masasi.

To Dar es Salaam, there are daily buses (Tsh26,000, eight hours to Temeke, another hour or two to Ubungo), departing in each direction at 6am, 8am, 10am and noon. Book in advance. The best lines currently are Machinga (departs in each direction at 6.30am, starts and terminates at Temeke) and JM Luxury (departs in each direction at 7.30am). In Dar es Salaam, departures are from Ubungo, or – better and more frequently – from Temeke's Sudan Market area, where all the southbound bus lines also have booking offices.

To Mozambique, there are several pick-ups and at least one minivan daily to Mahurunga and the Tanzanian immigration post at Kilambo (Tsh5000), departing Mtwara between about 5am and 10am. Departures are from in front of Chilindima Guesthouse, one block south of the main transport stand.

CAR & MOTORCYCLE

If you're driving to or from Dar es Salaam, there are petrol stations in Kibiti (unreliable), Ikwiriri (unreliable), Nangurukuru, Kilwa Masoko, Lindi and Mtwara. The road is currently all paved except for about 11km.

For self-drivers between Mtwara and the Mozambique border at Kilambo, the best places for updated information on the Rovuma River crossing are the Old Boma (p308) and Ten Degrees South (p308), both in Mikindani. Note that Mozambican visas are not issued at this border and there is no Mozambique consulate in Mtwara (the closest one is in Dar es Salaam).

❶ Getting Around

Taxis can be difficult to find in Mtwara; you'll mostly need to rely on *bajaji*, which are everywhere. *Bajaji* 'stands' are at the bus stand, and near the CCM building at the intersection of Tanu and Uhuru roads. To and from the airport (6km southeast of the main roundabout) expect to pay about Tsh10,000 for a taxi and about half this for a *bajaji*. The cost for town trips in a *bajaji* is Tsh1000 to Tsh2000 (Tsh3000 from the centre to Shangani).

There are a few dalla-dallas running along Tanu Rd to and from the bus stand, although none to Shangani. To arrange bicycle rental, ask at the market or at one of the nearby bicycle shops.

Mikindani

Mikindani – set on a picturesque bay surrounded by coconut groves – is a quiet, charming Swahili town with a long history. Although easily visited as a day trip from Mtwara, many travellers prefer it to its larger neighbour as a base for exploring the surrounding area.

History

Mikindani gained prominence early on as a major dhow port and terminus for trade caravans from Lake Nyasa. By the late 15th century, these networks extended across southern Tanzania as far as Zambia and present-day Democratic Republic of the Congo (formerly Zaïre). Following a brief downturn in fortunes, trade – primarily in slaves, ivory and copper – again increased in the mid-16th century as Mikindani came under the domain of the Sultan of Zanzibar. In the 19th century, following the ban on the slave trade, Mikindani fell into decline until the late 1880s when the German colonial government made the town its regional headquarters and began large-scale sisal, coconut, rubber and oilseed production in the area. However, the boom was not to last. With the arrival of the British and the advent of larger ocean-going vessels, Mikindani was abandoned in favour of Mtwara's superior harbour, and now, almost a century later, seems not to have advanced much beyond this era. Much of the town has been designated as a conservation zone, and life today centres on the small dhow port, which is still a hub for local coastal traffic.

For David Livingstone fans, the famous explorer spent a few weeks in the area in 1866 before setting out on his last journey.

◉ Sights & Activities

Apart from the various historical buildings, it's well worth just strolling through town to soak up the atmosphere and see the numerous carved Zanzibari-style doors. With more time, make your way up **Bismarck Hill**, rising up behind the Old Boma, for some views.

Boma   HISTORIC BUILDING
The imposing German *boma,* built in 1895 as a fort and administrative centre, has been beautifully renovated as a hotel. Even if you're not staying here, it's worth taking a look and climbing the tower for views over the town.

Slave Market   HISTORIC BUILDING
Downhill from the *boma* is the old Slave Market building, which now houses several craft shops. Unfortunately, it was much less accurately restored than the *boma* and lost much of its architectural interest when its open arches were filled in. The original design is now preserved only on one of Tanzania's postage stamps.

Prison Ruins   RUINS
These ruins are opposite the jetty. Nearby is a large, hollow baobab tree that was once used to keep unruly prisoners in solitary confinement.

ECO2   DIVING
(☑ 0784 855833; www.eco2tz.com; Main Rd) This good outfit offers PADI instruction and diving in both Mikindani Bay and at Mnazi Bay-Ruvuma Estuary Marine Park.

🛏 Sleeping & Eating

Ten Degrees South   LODGE $
(ECO2; ☑ 0766 059380, 0684 059381; www.tendegreessouth.com; Mikindani; d without/with bathroom US$20/60) This good budget travellers' base has four refurbished rooms, all with large double beds and shared bathrooms, plus bay views and deck chairs up on the roof. Next door are a handful of newer, self-contained double-bedded rooms with hot-water showers. There's also an outdoor restaurant-bar with delicious wraps, pancakes, curries and other meals for about Tsh17,000.

ECO2 is based here and is the best contact for arranging diving in Mikindani Bay and Mnazi Bay-Ruvuma Estuary Marine Park.

Samwange Beach Campsite   CAMPGROUND $
(☑ 0784 360774; camping US$20) This beachside camping ground is about 7km north of Mikindani, around the bay in Naumbe village just north of Pemba village. There are basic ablutions, and meals can be arranged with a day's advance notice.

From Mikindani, head towards Lindi. Just after crossing the small bridge on the outskirts of Mikindani, there's a dirt track branching off to the right; follow this north and west around Mikindani Bay until you see the Samwange signpost. Call first.

★ Old Boma at Mikindani   HISTORIC HOTEL $$
(☑ 0756 455978, 023-233 3875; www.mikindani.com; s US$77, r with/without balcony from US$188/120, ste US$223; P @ ☎ 🕸) ☞ This beautifully restored building is on a breezy

hilltop overlooking the town and Mikindani Bay. It offers spacious, atmospheric, high-ceilinged doubles and the closest to top-end standards that you'll find in these parts. Rooms vary, so check out a few before choosing. There's a sunset terrace overlooking the bay, a pool surrounded by bougainvillea bushes and lush gardens, and a restaurant.

It's run by Trade Aid (www.tradeaiduk. org), a nonprofit group committed to improving employment and educational opportunities for the local community. A stay at the Old Boma supports its work; check its website if you want to get involved.

ℹ Information

The closest banking facilities are in Mtwara.

The Old Boma has a tourist information office and an internet connection. Walking tours of towns and local excursions can be organised here and at Ten Degrees South.

ℹ Getting There & Away

Mikindani is 10km from Mtwara along a sealed road. Minibuses (Tsh500) run between the two towns throughout the day. *Bajaji* from Mtwara charge about Tsh10,000 (Tsh20,000 for a taxi).

Mnazi Bay-Ruvuma Estuary Marine Park

This marine park (adult/child US$20/10) encompasses a narrow sliver of coastline extending from Msangamkuu Peninsula (just north and east of Mtwara) in the north to the Mozambique border in the south. In addition to about 5000 people, it provides home to more than 400 marine species. The plan is for the struggling park to become the core of a conservation area extending as far south as Pemba (Mozambique), although conservation and enforcement measures are currently sadly lacking.

The heart of the planned conservation area is the Msimbati Peninsula, together with the bordering Mnazi Bay. Most visitors head straight to the tiny village of Ruvula, which is about 7km beyond Msimbati village along a sandy track (or along the beach at low tide) with a lovely stretch of sand and fine snorkelling. In addition to its beach (one of the few on the mainland offering sunset views), Ruvula is notable as the spot where British eccentric Latham Leslie-Moore built his house and lived until 1967 when he was deported after agi-

tating for independence for the Msimbati Peninsula. His story is chronicled in John Heminway's *No Man's Land* and in *Africa Passion,* a documentary film. Today, Leslie-Moore's house stands in ruins; the property is privately owned.

Msangamkuu Peninsula, at the northern edge of the marine park, is best visited from Mtwara. There's a small beach, and an upmarket hotel is planned.

Most diving in the marine park is done in the waters near Msimbati. The best contact is ECO2 in Mikindani.

🛏 Sleeping & Eating

Ruvula Sea Safari BANDAS $

(☑0788 808004, 0652 320183; camping Tsh20,000, d bandas Tsh50,000; 🅿) This is the only place to stay, with tatty beach-front *bandas* sharing equally tatty facilities, all redeemed, however, by a prime location directly on the sand. Tasty grilled-fish meals are available with advance notice (Tsh15,000). A few basic supplies are available in Msimbati village, but if you're camping, stock up in Mtwara and bring a torch.

Local boats can be arranged to Bird Island, directly opposite, and for exploring nearby mangrove channels. For the best snorkelling, walk left along the beach. The further you go, the better it gets.

Watch for the tiny sign marking the turn-off from the Msimbati–Ruvula road. Day visitors are charged Tsh5000 per person for beach use (the fee is waived if you eat a meal).

ℹ Information

Marine-park entry fees (payable in cash) are collected at the marine-park gate at the entrance to Msimbati village.

ℹ Getting There & Away

There is at least one pick-up daily in each direction between Mtwara and Msimbati (Tsh2500, two hours), departing Mtwara's main transport stand around 10.30am. Departures from Msimbati are around 5.30am from the police post near the park gate.

Driving from Mtwara, take the main road from the roundabout south for 4km to the village of Mangamba, branch left at the signpost onto the Mahurunga road and continue about 18km to Madimba. At Madimba, turn left again and continue for 20km to Msimbati; the road is unpaved, but in good condition. If you are cycling, the major village en route is Ziwani, which has a decent market.

Note that there is no public transport between Msimbati and Ruvula. On weekends, it's sometimes possible to hitch a lift. Otherwise, arrange a lift on a motorbike (about Tsh5000) with one of the locals or walk along the beach at low tide (one hour or more). Although sandy, the road is in reasonably good condition thanks to maintenance work by the gas company, and Ruvula Sea Safari (p309) can generally be reached in a regular 2WD taxi from Mtwara (around Tsh60,000 round-trip).

Small boats travel between the Shangani dhow port dock in Mtwara and Msangamkuu Peninsula throughout the day (Tsh100, about 15 minutes). At the time of research, a vehicle ferry was planned. Once in place, it will be possible to drive via Msangamkuu to Ziwani village, where the route joins the main route from Mtwara (though the latter is faster).

Makonde Plateau & Around

This cool and scenic plateau, much of which lies between 700m and 900m above sea level, is home to the Makonde people, famed throughout East Africa for their exotic woodcarvings. With its comparative isolation, scattered settlements and seeming obliviousness to developments elsewhere in the country, it in many ways epitomises inland areas of southeastern Tanzania, and is worth a detour if you're in the area.

Newala

Bustling Newala is the major settlement on the plateau. Thanks to its perch at 780m altitude, it offers a pleasantly brisk climate, and views over the Ruvuma River valley and into Mozambique. At the edge of the escarpment on the southwestern side of town is the old German *boma* (now the police station) and, nearby, the Shimo la Mungu (Hole of God) viewpoint. There are numerous paths from the edge of town leading down to the river. For any excursions, it's a good idea to carry a copy of your passport and visa (which you should carry around anyway in Newala, given its proximity to the border) and arrange a local guide. Bicycles can be rented near the market.

🛏 Sleeping & Eating

Country Lodge Bed & Breakfast　　GUESTHOUSE $

(Sollo's; ☑0784 950235, 023-241 0355; www. countrylodgetz.com; Masasi Rd; s/d/ste Tsh30,000/ 35,000/50,000; ℗☒) This long-standing place is the best choice in town. Rooms have bathrooms and the doubles have two large beds. There's also a decent restaurant with the usual array of standard dishes. It's just outside town, along the road to Masasi.

ℹ Getting There & Away

Daily buses run from Newala to Mtwara (via Nanyamba; Tsh7000) and to Masasi (Tsh5000, 1½ hours). There is usually also at least one vehicle daily between Newala and Mtama, east of Masasi on the road to Mtwara. The journeys to Masasi and Mtama offer beautiful views as you wind down the side of the plateau.

Masasi

Masasi, a scruffy district centre and the birthplace of former Tanzanian President Benjamin Mkapa, stretches out along the main road off the edge of the Makonde Plateau against a backdrop of granite hills. It's a potentially useful stop if you are travelling to or from Mozambique via the Unity Bridge. The history of the modern settlement dates to the late 19th century, when the Anglican Universities' Mission to Central Africa (UMCA) came from Zanzibar to establish a settlement of former slaves here. Today, it's notable primarily as a transport hub for onward travel along the wild road west towards Tunduru, or north to Nachingwea and Liwale. About 70km east of Masasi along the Mtwara road is Mahiwa, the site of one of WWI's bloodiest battles in Africa, in which German and British Imperial forces (consisting of primarily Nigerian and South African troops) fought and more than 2000 people lost their lives.

🛏 Sleeping & Eating

Sechele Lodge　　GUESTHOUSE $

(☑0784 534438; Newala Rd; r Tsh20,000-35,000; ℗) About 800m from the bus stand along the Newala road, this place has a handful of clean, decent rooms – some with bathrooms, others with a bathroom just outside – and is quieter than the more central guesthouses. Meals are available on order.

Holiday Hotel   MOTEL **$**
(Tunduru Rd; r Tsh35,000) Clean-ish, straight-forward rooms with fan in a noisy but convenient location about 100m east of the bus stand.

ℹ Information

MONEY

NBC Bank ATM; it's on the main road at the eastern end of town.

TOURIST INFORMATION

Masasi Reserve Warden's Office (☑ 0713 311129, 0784 634972, 023-251 0364) It's essential to stop here first to arrange permits if you're planning to visit Lukwika-Lumesule Game Reserve. The office is currently on the Newala road, just south of the Mtwara road and near the immigration office. However, there are plans for it to be moved to Migongo Area, about 1km north of the main road en route to Nachingwea, on the left side. Ask for Mali Asili (Natural Resources).

ℹ Getting There & Away

The bus stand is at the western edge of Masasi at the intersection of the Tunduru, Nachingwea and Newala roads.

The road between Masasi and Mtwara is in generally good condition. Buses travel between the two towns approximately hourly between 6am and 2pm daily (Tsh7500, five hours).

Transport leaves several times daily to Newala (Tsh5000, 1½ hours).

Ndanda

Ndanda, about 40km northeast of Masasi off the edge of the Makonde plateau, is dominated by a large Benedictine monastery founded by German missionaries in 1906. Adjoining is a hospital, which serves as the major health clinic for the surrounding region.

Apart from the monastery guesthouse (reserved for monastery guests), the only accommodation is in a few unappealing budget guesthouses along the main road at the bus stand, and diagonally opposite the hospital.

Buses run daily between Masasi and Ndanda, and any vehicle along the main road will drop you.

THE MAKONDE

The Makonde, known throughout East Africa for their woodcarvings, are one of Tanzania's largest ethnic groups. They originated in northern Mozambique, where many still live, and began to make their way northwards during the 18th and 19th centuries. The Mozambican war sparked another large influx into Tanzania, with up to 15,000 Makonde crossing the border during the 1970s and 1980s in search of a safe haven and employment. Today, although the Makonde on both sides of the Ruvuma River are considered to be a single ethnic entity, there are numerous cultural and linguistic differences between the two groups.

Like many tribes in this part of Tanzania, the Makonde are matrilineal. Children and inheritances normally belong to the woman, and it's common for husbands to move to the village of their wives after marriage. Settlements are widely scattered – possibly a remnant of the days when the Makonde sought to evade slave raids – and there is no tradition of a unified political system. Each village is governed by a hereditary chief and a council of elders.

Due to their isolated location, the Makonde have remained insulated from colonial and post-colonial influences, and are considered to be one of Tanzania's most traditional groups. Even today, most Makonde still adhere to traditional religions, with the complex spirit world given its fullest expression in their carvings.

Traditionally, the Makonde practised body scarring and while it's seldom done today, you may see older people with markings on their face and bodies. It's also fairly common to see elderly Makonde women wearing a wooden plug in their upper lip, or to see this depicted in Makonde artwork.

Most Makonde are subsistence farmers, and there is speculation as to why they chose to establish themselves on a waterless plateau. Possible factors include the relative safety that the area offered from outside intervention (especially during slave-trading days), and the absence of the tsetse fly.

Lukwika-Lumesule Game Reserve

Tiny Lukwika-Lumesule Game Reserve (US$30) is hidden away in the hinterlands southwest and west of Masasi. It's officially off limits during the July to December hunting season, and unofficially off limits during much of the rest of the year due to the rains. According to reserve officials, late June is the best time to visit.

Lukwika-Lumesule is separated from Mozambique's Niassa Reserve by the Ruvuma River, and animals frequently wade across the border. There are no real roads in the reserve, just overgrown bush paths. With great luck you may see elephants, elands, crocodiles and hippos, though it's more likely you'll return having seen none of these. The main challenge, apart from getting around the reserve, is spotting the animals through the often dense vegetation and dealing with the voracious tsetse flies.

Before visiting, it's essential to stop by the Reserve Warden's Office (p311) in Masasi to get an entry permit.

🛏 Sleeping & Eating

Camping is permitted with your own tent; there's currently no charge. Bring everything with you, including drinking water. Water for bathing is normally available.

❶ Getting There & Away

The entry point into Lukwika-Lumesule is about 2.5km southwest of Mpombe village on the northeastern edge of the reserve, and reached via Nangomba village, 40km west of Masasi.

There is no regular public transport, although you may occasionally be able to get a lift with a vehicle from the Reserve Warden's Office in Masasi. Otherwise, you'll need your own 4WD transport. During the dry season, it's possible to drive around Lukwika-Lumesule, following a 'road' running along its periphery.

Understand
Tanzania

Tanzania Today

Tanzania today is moving fast and looking forward. It is one of Africa's top tourist destinations, and seeking to capitalise on the fact that its national parks are at the peak of their popularity. It is also sitting on a potential goldmine in the form of newly discovered natural gas reserves. Politically, the country is inching towards a multiparty system. If corruption, a weak educational system and other hurdles can be overcome, Tanzania will celebrate its centennial on top of the pack.

Best in Print & Film

The Tree Where Man Was Born (Peter Matthiessen, 1972) Lyrical account of northern Tanzania and Kenya's people, wildlife and landscapes.

The Gunny Sack (MG Vassanji, 1989) Memoir of family and growing up told through the contents of a gunny sack.

Tumaini (2005) The devastation of AIDS in a Tanzanian family.

As Old as My Tongue (2006) Story of legendary Zanzibari singer Bi Kidude.

Memoirs of an Arabian Princess from Zanzibar (Emily Ruete, 1888) Autobiography of a 19th-century Zanzibari princess.

Paradise (Abdulrazak Gurnah, 1994) An East African coming-of age tale.

Etiquette

Greetings Take time for greetings.

Dining Don't eat or pass things with the left hand.

Dealing with authority Respect authority, avoid impatience; let deference and good humour see you through.

Visits Before entering someone's house, call out *Hodi* (May I enter?), then wait for the inevitable *Karibu* (Welcome).

Gifts Receive gifts with both hands, or with the right hand while touching the left hand to your right elbow.

Nyerere's Legacy

Just past its half-century mark, Tanzania is still indebted to Julius Nyerere, who was at the country's helm for the first 25 years of its existence. Impelled by an egalitarian social vision, Nyerere introduced Swahili as a unifying national language, instilled ideals of *ujamaa* (familyhood) and initiated a tradition of regional political engagement. Thanks to this vision, Tanzania today is one of East Africa's most stable countries, and religious and ethnic conflicts are minimal.

Economic Challenges

On the economic front, the news is mostly good. Tanzania has been enjoying steady economic growth in recent years, and large natural gas reserves along the southeastern coast hold the potential for transforming its economy over the coming decades. However, major challenges remain. Tanzania is ranked near the bottom on the United Nations Development Programme (UNDP) Human Development Index (152nd out of 186 countries in a recent listing), and daily life for many remains a struggle. Unemployment averages about 12% and underemployment is widespread.

Shadow of Corruption

A major impediment to real progress is corruption. In an effort to combat it, there are signs in banks, immigration offices and elsewhere advertising that you're in a corruption-free zone. Yet its stench permeates every aspect of business and officialdom, stymieing investment and growth. If corruption can be reined in, and economic potential properly developed, Tanzania's future will be bright.

Family Squabbles

In the political sphere, attention is focused on keeping family ties happy between the mainland and proudly independent Zanzibar. While an amicable path for co-existence has been forged, the task requires on-going attention. It is made more challenging by the continued dominance of the Chama Cha Mapinduzi (CCM) party. In the most recent national elections, the opposition made a surprisingly strong showing, with a total of 91 non-CCM seats out of 357 total and 37.2% of the presidential vote. This has given some observers hope that inroads are being made against the CCM monolith and towards the emergence of genuine multiparty democracy. In typical Tanzanian fashion, however, major upsets are unlikely, at least in the short term.

A Lively Media
Tanzania's lively media plays an important role in political debate. While most of the main dailies are aligned to some degree with CCM, the mainland lo-cal press is relatively independent and Tanzania is ranked ahead of its neighbours in press freedom by Reporters Without Borders.

That said, distribution difficulties in rural areas and a countrywide illiteracy rate of 32% mean that the influence of newspapers is limited to urban centres.

Education for the Future
Perhaps the most significant determinant of Tanza-nia's future will be its educational system. Over the past decade, the government has elevated educa-tion to greater prominence on the national agenda, and Nyerere's goal of universal primary education is close to being realised. However, in many parts of the country, quality and standards are low and drop-out rates high. Nationwide, the primary stu-dent-to-teacher ratio is about 54 to 1. At the second-ary level, there is a shortage of secondary schools, and drop-out rates are even higher, with less than 15% of youth finishing secondary school and less than 2% enrolled in university.

POPULATION: **49.6 MILLION (26% URBAN DWELLING)**

PER CAPITA GDP: **US$1700**

INFLATION: **7.8%**

ECONOMIC GROWTH RATE: **7%**

LIFE EXPECTANCY: **61 YEARS**

MOBILE PHONES PER 100 PEOPLE: **56**

belief systems
(% of population)

35 34

Muslim   Indigenous belief

30   1

Christian   Other

if Tanzania were 100 people

74 would be Rural
26 would be Urban

population per sq km

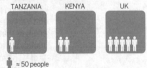

TANZANIA   KENYA   UK

≈ 50 people

History

Tanzania's history begins with the dawn of humankind. Over the millennia, it expands to encompass the great African population migrations, Arabic and European settlement, colonialism and the growth of a strong independence movement before giving way to the modern-day United Republic of Tanzania.

Early Beginnings

About 3.6 million years ago, East Africa's earliest inhabitants trekked across the plains at Laetoli near Oldupai (Olduvai) Gorge in northern Tanzania, leaving their footprints in volcanic ash. The prints were discovered in 1978 by archaeologist Mary Leakey, who identified them as the steps of our earliest known ancestors, hominids known as *Australopithecines*.

About two million years ago, the human family tree split, giving rise to *homo habilis,* a meat-eating creature with a larger brain who used crude stone tools. His traces have been found around Oldupai (Olduvai) Gorge. By 1.8 million years ago, *homo erectus* had evolved, leaving bones and axes for archaeologists to find at ancient lakeside sites throughout East Africa.

What is today Tanzania was peopled by waves of migration. Rock paintings possibly dating back 6000 years have been found around Kondoa. These are believed to have been made by clans of nomadic hunter-gatherers who spoke a language similar to that of southern Africa's Khoisan. Between 3000 and 5000 years ago, they were joined by small bands of Cushitic-speaking farmers and cattle-herders moving down from what is today Ethiopia. The Iraqw who live around Lake Manyara trace their ancestry to this group of arrivals. The majority of modern Tanzanians are descendants of Bantu-speaking settlers who began a gradual, centuries-long shift from the Niger delta around 1000 BC, arriving in East Africa in the 1st century AD. The most recent influx of migrants occurred between the 15th and 18th centuries when Nilotic-speaking pastoralists from southern Sudan moved into northern Tanzania and the Rift Valley. Most of these Nilotic peoples – ancestors of the Maasai – were pastoralists, and many settled in the less fertile areas of north-central Tanzania where their large herds could have grazing space.

Swahili Ruins

Kilwa Kisiwani Unesco World Heritage site

Kaole Ruins, Bagamoyo

Tongoni Ruins, north of Pangani

Juani and Chole Ruins, Mafia

TIMELINE	c 25 million BC	3.6 million BC	10,000–3000 BC
	Tectonic plates collide and the East African plains buckle. Formation of the Great Rift Valley begins, as do changes that result ultimately in the formation of Mt Kilimanjaro and other volcanoes.	Our earliest ancestors amble across the plain at Laetoli in northern Tanzania, leaving their footprints for modern-day archaeologists to find.	Scattered clans of hunter-gatherers, followed by farmers and cattle herders, settle the East African plains, the well-watered highlands and the lakeshores of what is modern-day Tanzania.

Monsoon Winds

As these migrations were taking place in the interior, coastal areas were being shaped by far different influences. Azania, as the East African coast was known to the ancient Greeks, was an important trading post as early as 400 BC. By the early part of the first millennium AD, thriving settlements had been established as traders, first from the Mediterranean and later from Arabia and Persia, came ashore on the winds of the monsoon and began to intermix with the indigenous Bantu speakers, giving rise to Swahili language and culture. The traders from Arabia also brought Islam, which by the 11th century had become entrenched. Over the next few centuries, the Arabic traders established outposts along the coast, including on the Zanzibar Archipelago and Kilwa Kisiwani. These settlements flourished, reaching their pinnacle between the 13th and 15th centuries, and trade in ivory, gold and other goods extended as far away as India and China.

Arrival of the Europeans

The first European to set foot in Tanzania was Portuguese sailor Vasco da Gama, who made his way along the coast in 1498 in search of the Orient. Portuguese traders kept to the coast until the early 18th century, when they were driven out by Omani Arabs. The Omanis took control of Kilwa and Zanzibar and set up governors in coastal towns on the mainland. Traders from the coast plied the caravan routes through the interior to the Great Lakes. They bought ivory and slaves in exchange for cheap cloth and firearms. The traders carried with them virulent strains of smallpox and cholera as well as guns. By the late 19th century, when Europe cast a covetous eye on Africa, East Africa was weakened by disease and violence.

European Control

The romantic reports of early-19th-century European travellers to East Africa such as Richard Burton, John Speke, David Livingstone and Henry Morton Stanley caught the attention of a young German adventurer in the late 19th century. In 1885, without obtaining his government's endorsement, Carl Peters set up a Company for German Colonization. From Zanzibar, he travelled into the mainland, collecting enroute the signatures of African chiefs on a stack of blank treaty forms he had brought with him. In Berlin, Chancellor Bismarck approved the acquisition of African territory after the fact, much to the consternation of the British, who by now had established informal rule over Zanzibar.

In 1886 East Africa was sliced into 'spheres of influence' by the British and the Germans. The frontier ran west from the coast to Lake Victoria along the modern Kenya–Tanzania border. Needless to say, the Africans

The first travel guide to the Tanzanian coast was *Periplus of the Erythraean Sea*, written for sailors by a Greek merchant around AD 60. Third-century AD coins from Persia and North Africa have been found along the Tanzanian coast – proof of a long trading history with Arabia and the Mediterranean.

1st century AD	1331	1498	c 1400–1700
Monsoon winds push Arab trading ships to the East African coast. They are followed later by Islamic settlers who mix with the local population to create Swahili language and culture.	Moroccan traveller Ibn Battuta visits Kilwa, finding a flourishing town of 10,000 to 20,000 residents, with a grand palace, a mosque, an inn and a slave market.	Searching for a route to the Orient, Portuguese sailors arrive on the East African coast and establish a coastal trade in slaves and ivory that lasts for 200 years.	In several waves, small bands of nomadic cattle herders migrate south from the Sudan into the Rift Valley – ancestors of today's Maasai.

weren't consulted on the agreement. Nor was the Sultan of Zanzibar. The Germans parked a gunboat in Zanzibar harbour until he signed over his claim to the mainland.

The Colonial Era

Portuguese influence is still seen in Tanzania's architecture, language and customs (such as bull fighting on Pemba). The Swahili *gereza* (jail), from Portuguese *igreja* (church), dates to the days when Portuguese forts contained both edifices in the same compound.

Colonialism brought western education and healthcare to German East Africa, as well as road and rail networks. However, these developments benefited relatively few Africans, and the German administration was widely unpopular. Harsh labour policies, the imposition of a hut tax and numerous other measures contributed to the discontent. Local opposition began in earnest with the Abushiri Revolt in 1888 (see p135), and culminated in the Maji Maji rebellion of 1905 to 1907 (see p283), which decimated much of southern Tanzania and is considered to contain the first seeds of Tanzanian nationalism.

The German era lasted until the end of WWI, when German East Africa came under British administration as a League of Nations mandate and was renamed Tanganyika. This arrangement lasted until WWII, after which the area became a United Nations trust territory, again under British administration. To assist in its own postwar economic recovery effort, Britain maintained compulsory cultivation and enforced settlement policies. The development of a manufacturing sector was actively discouraged by Britain, which wanted to maintain the Tanzanian market for its own goods. Likewise, very few Africans were hired into the civil service.

The Birth of TANU

In 1948 a group of young Africans formed the Tanganyika African Association to protest colonial policies. By 1953 the organisation was renamed the Tanganyika African National Union (TANU), led by a young teacher named Julius Kambarage Nyerere. Its objective became national liberation. In the end, the British decamped from Tanganyika and Zanzibar rather abruptly in 1961 and 1963, respectively. This was due at least as

SWAHILI

Although Swahili culture began to develop in the early part of the first millennium AD, it was not until the 18th century, with the ascendancy of the Omani Arabs on Zanzibar, that it came into its own. Swahili's role as a *lingua franca* was solidified as it spread throughout East and Central Africa along the great trade caravan routes. European missionaries and explorers soon adopted the language as their main means of communicating with locals. In the second half of the 19th century, missionaries, notably Johann Ludwig Krapf, also began applying the Roman alphabet. Prior to this, Swahili had been written exclusively in Arabic script.

19th century	1840	1840s–60s	1856
Zanzibari slave trader Tippu Tip, tapping into the export slave trade that had thrived since the 9th century, controls a commercial empire stretching from the coast west to the Congo River.	The Sultan of Oman sets up court in a grand palace facing the lagoon on Zanzibar, from where he exerts his authority over coastal mainland Tanganyika.	The first Christian missionaries arrive from Europe. In 1868 the first mainland mission was established at Bagamoyo as a station for ransomed slaves seeking to buy their own freedom.	British explorers Richard Francis Burton and John Hanning Speke venture inland from Zanzibar, searching for the source of the Nile and finding Lake Tanganyika and Lake Victoria.

much to a growing European sentiment that empires were too expensive to maintain as to recognition of the fundamental right of Africans to freedom from subjugation.

Independence

Tanganyikans embraced independence optimistically. However, Tanganyika embarked on the project of nation-building with few of the resources necessary for the task. The national treasury was depleted. The economy was weak and undeveloped, with virtually no industry. In 1961 there were a total of 120 African university graduates in the country.

Faced with this set of circumstances, the first autonomous government of Tanganyika, led by the 39-year-old Julius Nyerere, chose continuity over radical transformation of the economic or political structure. TANU accepted the Westminster-style parliament proposed by the British. It committed to investing in education and a gradual Africanisation of the civil service. In the meantime, expatriates (often former British colonial officers) would be used to staff the government bureaucracy.

As detailed by political scientist Cranford Pratt, the Nyerere government's early plans were drawn up on the assumption that substantial foreign assistance would be forthcoming, particularly from Britain. Yet, this was not the case, and the new country was left scrambling for funds to stay afloat during the first rocky years of liberation. While grappling with fixing roads, running hospitals and educating the country's youth, the government managed to diffuse an army mutiny over wages in 1964. When Zanzibar erupted in violent revolution in January 1964, just weeks after achieving independence from Britain, Nyerere skilfully co-opted its potentially destabilising forces by giving island politicians a prominent role in a newly proclaimed United Republic of Tanzania, created from the union of Tanganyika with Zanzibar in April 1964.

Ujamaa – Tanzania's Grand Experiment

The events of the first few years following independence – the lack of assistance from abroad, rumblings of civil strife at home and the nascent development of a privileged class amid continuing mass poverty – led Nyerere to re-evaluate the course his government had charted for the nation.

Since his student days, Nyerere had pondered the meaning of democracy for Africa. In 1962 he published an essay entitled *Ujamaa [familyhood]: The Basis of African Socialism*. In it he set out his belief that the personal accumulation of wealth in the face of widespread poverty was antisocial. Africa should strive to create a society based on mutual assistance and economic as well as political equality, such as he claimed had existed for centuries before European colonisation.

Historical Hotspots

Oldupai (Olduvai) Gorge Museum

Kondoa Rock-Art Sites

Natural History Museum, Arusha

National Museum, Dar es Salaam

Arusha Declaration Museum, Arusha

Nyerere Museum, Musoma

HISTORY INDEPENDENCE

The word 'Swahili' ('of the coast', from the Arabic word *sahil*) refers both to the Swahili language, and to the Islamic culture of the peoples inhabiting the East African coast from Mogadishu (Somalia) down to Mozambique. Both language and culture are a mixture of Bantu, Arabic, Persian and Asian influences.

1873	1885	5 October 1889	1890
Under pressure from the British Consul, the Sultan of Zanzibar agrees to abolish the Zanzibar slave market and the mainland trade in human beings.	German adventurer Carl Peters beats Henry Morton Stanley in a race to win the allegiance of the inland Kingdom of Buganda, claiming the territory of Tanganyika for Germany en route.	Mt Kilimanjaro is scaled by Yohani Kinyala Lauwo and Hans Meyer. Lauwo spent the remainder of his long life guiding trekkers up the mountain and training new guides.	Britain trades Heligoland in the North Sea to Germany for recognition of British control of Zanzibar. Between them, they divide up East Africa, with Tanganyika allocated to Germany.

The Arusha Declaration

Nyerere's political philosophy is set out in two collections of his major speeches and essays: *Freedom and Unity* (1967) and *Freedom and Socialism* (1968).

In 1967 the TANU leadership met in the northern town of Arusha, where they approved a radical new plan for Tanzania, drafted by Nyerere. What became known as the *Arusha Declaration* outlined the Tanzanian government's commitment to a socialist approach to development, further articulated in a series of subsequent policy papers. The government vowed to reduce its dependence on foreign aid and instead foster an ethos of self-reliance in Tanzanian society. To prevent government becoming a trough where bureaucrats and party members could amass personal wealth, Nyerere passed a Leadership Code. Among other things, it prohibited government officials from holding shares in a private company, employing domestic staff or buying real estate to rent out for profit.

The *Arusha Declaration* also announced the government takeover of industry and banking. It curtailed foreign direct investment and stated that the government would itself invest in manufacturing enterprises that could produce substitutes for imported goods. All land was hence-

JULIUS KAMBARAGE NYERERE

Julius Kambarage Nyerere, known as both Baba wa Taifa ('Father of the Nation') and simply as Mwalimu ('teacher'), rose from humble beginnings to become one of Africa's most renowned statesmen. He was born in 1922 in Butiama, near Lake Victoria, son of a chief of the small Zanaki tribe. After finishing his education, including graduate studies in Scotland, he embarked on a teaching career. In 1953 he joined with a band of like-minded nationalists to form the Tanganyika African National Union (TANU), which he led to the successful liberation of Tanganyika from Britain and through its first two decades of government.

Nyerere gained widespread respect for his idealism, for his success in shaping a society which was politically stable and free of divisive tribal rivalries, and for his contributions towards raising Tanzania's literacy rate, which during his tenure became one of the highest in Africa. He also earned international acclaim for his commitment to pan-Africanism and for his regional engagement – an area where he was active until his death in October 1999.

Despite criticisms of his authoritarian style and economic policies, Nyerere was indisputably one of Africa's most influential leaders, and the person almost single-handedly responsible for putting Tanzania on the world stage. He was widely acclaimed for his long-standing opposition to South Africa's apartheid system, and for his 1979 invasion of Uganda, which resulted in the deposition of the dictator Idi Amin Dada.

In his later years Nyerere assumed the role of elder statesman, serving as chief mediator in the Burundi conflict of 1996. He died in 1999 and was buried in his home village of Butiama, where many of his manuscripts, photos and other memorabilia are on display at the Nyerere Museum.

1905–07	1909–12	1919	1953
In the Matumbi Hills near Kilwa, a mystic called Kinjikitile stirs African labourers to rise up against their German overlords in what becomes known as the Maji Maji rebellion.	A team of German palaeontologists unearths the remains of various dinosaur species near Tendunguru, Lindi region. These include the skeleton of *Brachiosaurus brancai*, the world's largest known dinosaur.	At the end of WWI, Tanganyika is placed under the 'protection' of the British acting on behalf first of the League of Nations and then its successor, the UN.	A charismatic young school teacher named Julius Nyerere is elected President of the Tanganyika African National Union, an organisation dedicated to the liberation of Tanganyika from colonial rule.

forth to be common property, managed by the state. The government strove to provide free education for every child. School children were taught to identify themselves as proud Tanzanians with a shared language – Swahili – rather than just members of one of over 100 ethnic groups residing within the country's borders.

Socialist Leanings?

Nyerere himself was fascinated by Chinese economic development strategies, but dismissed Western fears that Tanzania was toying with doctrinaire Marxism, either Chinese- or Soviet-style. He argued in *Freedom and Unity – Essays on Socialism* (1967) that Tanzanians 'have no more need of being "converted" to socialism than we have of being "taught" democracy. Both are rooted in our own past – in the traditional society that produced us.' Nyerere's vision was enthusiastically embraced not only by the Tanzanian public, but by a body of Western academics and by aid donors from both East and West. Several of his policies nonetheless provoked the consternation of even his most ardent supporters abroad. In 1965 TANU voted to scrap the multiparty model of democracy bequeathed to it by Britain. As a consequence, Tanzania became a one-party state. Nyerere argued that democracy was not synonymous with multiparty politics and that the new country's challenges were so great that everyone had to work together. He advocated freedom of speech and the discussion of ideas, but banned opposition parties. Voters were given a choice of candidates, but they were all TANU party members. Furthermore, Nyerere authorised the detention of some individuals judged to be agitating against the best interests of the state. His defenders say he did his best to hold together a sometimes unruly cabinet and a country at a time when all over Africa newly independent states were succumbing to civil war and dictatorships. Critics say he turned a blind eye to violations of fundamental civil liberties.

'Villagisation'

Perhaps the most controversial of all government policies adopted post-Arusha was 'villagisation'. The vast majority of Tanzanians lived in the countryside, and the *Arusha Declaration* envisioned agriculture as the engine of economic growth. A massive increase in production was to be accomplished through communal farming, such as Nyerere argued was the practice in the old days. Beginning in 1967, Tanzanians were encouraged to reorganise themselves into communal villages where they would work the fields together for the good of the nation. Some did, but only a handful of cooperative communities were established voluntarily.

Exhorting his compatriots to work hard, Nyerere quoted a Swahili proverb: 'Treat your guest as a guest for two days; on the third day, give him a hoe!'

HISTORY SOCIALIST LEANINGS?

Throughout the country, in the wake of the *Arusha Declaration*, people turned out to help their neighbours build new schools, repair roads and plant and harvest food to sell for medical supplies. Nyerere and his ministers made a regular practice of grabbing a shovel and pitching in.

9 December 1961	1964	1967	1978–79
Tanganyika gains independence from British colonial rule, with Nyerere as president. Zanzibar follows suit in December 1963, establishing a constitutional monarchy under the Sultan.	Following a bloody coup on Zanzibar in which several thousand Zanzibaris were killed, Tanganyika and Zanzibar are united to form the United Republic of Tanzania.	At a gathering of TANU party faithful in Arusha, Julius Nyerere garners enthusiastic support for the *Arusha Declaration*, which sets out Tanzania's path to African socialism.	Ugandan dictator Idi Amin Dada invades Tanzania, burning villages along the Kagera River believed to harbour Ugandan rebels. Tanzania's army marches to topple Amin and restore Milton Obote to power.

In 1974 the government commenced the forcible relocation of 80% of the population, creating massive disruptions in national agricultural production. The scheme itself, however, suffered from a multiplicity of problems. The new land was often infertile. Necessary equipment was unavailable. People didn't want to work communally; they wanted to provide for their own families first. Government prices for crops were set too low. To paraphrase analyst Goran Hyden, the peasantry responded by retreating into subsistence farming – just growing their own food. National agricultural production and revenue from cash crop exports plummeted.

Summing up the results of the *Arusha Declaration* policies, Nyerere candidly admitted that the government had made some mistakes. However, he also noted progress towards social equality: the ratio between the highest salaries and the lowest paid narrowed from 50:1 in 1961 to around 9:1 in 1976. Despite a meagre colonial inheritance, Tanzania made great strides in education and healthcare. Under Nyerere's leadership it forged a cohesive national identity. With the exception of occasional isolated eruptions of civil strife on Zanzibar, it has also enjoyed internal peace and stability throughout its existence.

The East African Community – originally formed in 1967 by Tanzania, Kenya and Uganda and later revived after its 1977 collapse – now also includes Rwanda and Burundi. There has been some progress towards economic cooperation, but political federation is still far in the future.

Aid Darling to Delinquent

Post–*Arusha Declaration* Tanzania was the darling of the aid donor community. It was the largest recipient of foreign aid in sub-Saharan Africa throughout the 1970s and was the testing ground for every newfangled development theory that came along.

As the economy spiralled downward in the late 1970s and early '80s, the World Bank, International Monetary Fund (IMF) and a growing chorus of exasperated aid donors called for stringent economic reform – a dramatic structural adjustment of the economic system. Overlooking their own failing projects, they pointed to a bloated civil service and moribund productive sector, preaching that both needed to be exposed to the fresh, cleansing breezes of the open market. Nyerere resisted the IMF cure. As economic conditions continued to deteriorate, dissension grew within government ranks. In 1985 Nyerere resigned. In 1986 the Tanzanian government submitted to the IMF terms. The grand Tanzanian experiment with African socialism was over.

Structural Adjustment

As elsewhere on the continent, structural adjustment was a shock treatment that left the nation gasping for air. The civil service was slashed by over a third. Some of the deadwood was gone, but so were thousands of teachers, healthcare workers and the money for textbooks and chalk and teacher training. Economic growth rates slipped into the negative

Tanzania is ranked 69th worldwide, ahead of its East African neighbours, in press freedom by Reporters Without Borders (www.rsf.org).

1985	1986	1992	7 August 1998
Julius Nyerere voluntarily steps down as president after five terms. This paves the way for a peaceful transition to his elected successor.	After resisting for several years, but with the economy in a downward spiral, Tanzania accepts stringent IMF terms for a structural adjustment program loan.	Opposition parties are legalised under pressure from the international donor community. The first multiparty elections are held in Tanzania in 1995 with 13 political parties on the ballot.	Within minutes of one another, Al Qaeda truck bombs explode at the American embassies in Nairobi and Dar es Salaam. Eleven Tanzanians die in the attack, with dozens more injured.

TANZANIA ON THE WORLD STAGE

Throughout the 1960s to the 1980s, Julius Nyerere, representing Tanzania, was a voice of moral authority in global forums such as the UN, the Organization of African Unity and the Commonwealth. He asserted the autonomy of 'Third World' states, and pressed for a fairer global economic structure.

Nyerere's government was also a vocal advocate for the liberation of southern Africa from white minority rule. From 1963 Tanzania provided a base for the South African, Zimbabwean and Mozambican liberation movements within its territory as well as military support, at great cost – both human and material – to itself.

While accepting Chinese assistance to build the Tazara Railway from Zambia to Dar es Salaam in the 1970s, throughout the Cold War Tanzania remained staunchly nonaligned, resisting the machinations and blandishments of both East and West.

Tanzania's lower profile on the world stage in recent years can be attributed to the passing of the charismatic and revered Nyerere as well as the circumscribed room to manoeuvre afforded the government because of its economic woes and aid dependency. Nevertheless, Tanzania has always opened its doors to civilians fleeing violence in the countries that surround it – Uganda, Burundi, Congo and Mozambique. It still hosts over 100,000 refugees, mainly from Burundi and the Democratic Republic of the Congo (DRC; formerly Zaïre), and living in camps along Tanzania's western borders.

around 1974, where they languished for the next 25 years. In 1997 Tanzania was spending four times as much servicing its external debt than on healthcare, a situation that has improved only slightly in the past two decades.

Multiparty Democracy

Part of the structural adjustment aid program was the re-introduction of Western-style multiparty democracy, and in 1992 the constitution was amended to legalise opposition parties. Since then, four national elections have been held, generally proceeding relatively smoothly on the mainland, less so on the Zanzibar Archipelago, where tensions between the Chama Cha Mapinduzi (CCM) and the opposition Civic United Front (CUF) are strong.

In elections in 2010, Jakaya Mrisho Kikwete was elected president for a second term with 62% of the vote. His main opposition was candidate Willibrod Slaa of the Party for Democracy and Progress, who garnered 27% of the vote – the most decisive opposition showing to date in Tanzania's history. The next elections are scheduled for October 2015. As of this writing, the field of potential candidates is still wide open.

Almost one-third (102) of members of Tanzania's outgoing National Assembly are women, making the country one of a relative handful worldwide that meet the UN target for female political representation set in 1995.

2000	2005	2010	October 2015
Contentious elections for the Zanzibari Legislature boil over into street violence and 22 people are shot by police during mass demonstrations protesting the results.	Chama Cha Mapinduzi (CCM), the party created from the union of TANU and the Zanzibari Afro Shirazi Party in 1977, maintains its hold on government by winning a majority.	Jakaya Mrisho Kikwete is re-elected president with about 62% of the votes in a closely contested election with a surprisingly strong showing by opposition candidates.	National elections are scheduled to elect a successor to President Jakaya Kikwete.

People & Daily Life

A highlight of travelling in Tanzania is getting to know the people and becoming acquainted with the country's many cultures, as well as with the unique traits that set Tanzanians apart from their neighbours. Thanks to relatively widespread knowledge of English, plus a strong tradition of hospitality, local customs and culture in Tanzania are generally quite accessible.

Tanzania's People

Tanzania is home to about 120 tribal groups, plus relatively small but economically significant numbers of Asians and Arabs, and a tiny European community. Most tribes are very small; almost 100 of them combined account for only one-third of the total population. As a result, none has succeeded in dominating politically or culturally, although groups such as the Chagga and the Haya, who have a long tradition of education, are disproportionately well represented in government and business circles.

About 95% of Tanzanians are of Bantu origin. These include the Sukuma (who live around Mwanza and southern Lake Victoria, and constitute about 16% of the overall population), the Nyamwezi (around Tabora), the Makonde (Southeastern Tanzania), the Haya (around Bukoba) and the Chagga (around Mt Kilimanjaro). The Maasai and several smaller groups including the Arusha and the Samburu (all in northern Tanzania) are of Nilo-Hamitic or Nilotic origin. The Iraqw, around Karatu and northwest of Lake Manyara, are Cushitic, as are the northern-central tribes of Gorowa and Burungi. The Sandawe and, more distantly, the seminomadic Hadzabe (around Lake Eyasi), belong to the Khoisan ethnolinguistic family.

Tribal structures, however, range from weak to nonexistent – a legacy of Julius Nyerere's abolishment of local chieftaincies following independence.

About 3% of Tanzania's population lives on the Zanzibar Archipelago, with about one-third of these on Pemba. Most African Zanzibaris belong to one of three groups: the Hadimu, the Tumbatu and the Pemba. Members of the non-African Zanzibari population are primarily Shirazi and consider themselves descendants of immigrants from Shiraz in Persia (Iran).

Tanzania is the only African country boasting indigenous inhabitants from all of the continent's main ethnolinguistic families (Bantu, Nilo-Hamitic, Cushitic, Khoisan). They live in closest proximity around Lakes Eyasi and Babati.

The National Psyche

Partly as a result of the large number of smaller tribes in Tanzania, and partly as a result of the *ujamaa* (familyhood) ideals of Julius Nyerere, which still permeate society, tribal rivalries are almost nonexistent. Religious frictions are also minimal, with Christians and Muslims living side by side in a relatively easy coexistence. Although political differences flare, especially on the Zanzibar Archipelago, they rarely come to the forefront in interpersonal dealings.

Tanzanians place a premium on politeness and courtesy. Greetings are essential, and you'll probably be given a gentle reminder should you forget this and launch straight into a question without first inquiring as to the well-being of your listener and their family. Tanzanian children are trained to greet their elders with a respectful *shikamoo* (literally, 'I hold your feet'), often accompanied in rural areas by a slight curtsy, and strangers are frequently addressed as *dada* (sister) or *mama*, in the case of an older woman; *kaka* (brother); or *ndugu* (relative or comrade).

Daily Life

Family life is central, with weddings, funerals and other events holding centre stage. Celebrations are generally splashed-out affairs aimed at demonstrating status, and frequently go well beyond the means of the host family. It's expected that family members who have jobs will share what they have, and the extended family (which also encompasses the community) forms an essential support network in the absence of a government social security system.

Invisible social hierarchies lend life a sense of order. In the family, the man rules the roost, with the children at the bottom and women just above them. In the larger community, it's not much different. Child-raising is the expected occupation for women, and bread-winning for men, although a small but steadily growing cadre of professional women is becoming increasingly more visible. Village administrators (called *shehe* on Zanzibar) oversee things, and make important decisions in consultation with other senior community members.

The HIV/AIDS infection rate is about 5.1%. Public awareness has increased, with AIDS-related billboards throughout major cities. However, real public discussion remains limited, and in many circles, AIDS deaths are still often explained away as 'tuberculosis'.

Religion

All but the smallest villages have a mosque, a church or both; religious festivals are generally celebrated with fervour, at least as far as singing, dancing and family gatherings are concerned; and almost every Tanzanian identifies with some religion.

Muslims, who account for about 35% of the population, have traditionally been concentrated along the coast, as well as in the inland towns that lined the old caravan routes. There are several sects represented, notably the Sunni (Shafi school). The population of the Zanzibar Archipelago is almost exclusively Sunni Muslim.

About 35% to 40% of Tanzanians are Christians. Major denominations include Roman Catholic, Lutheran and Anglican, with a small percentage of Tanzanians being adherents of other Christian denominations,

In Tanzania, it's sometimes hard to know where the family ends and the community begins. Doors are always open, helping out others in the *jamaa* (clan, community) is expected and celebrations involve everyone.

TANZANIAN STYLE

Tanzanians are conservative, and while they are likely to be too polite to tell you so directly, they'll be privately shaking their head about travellers doing things such as not wearing enough clothing, sporting tatty clothes, or indulging in public displays of affection. Especially along the Muslim coast, cover up the shoulders and legs, and avoid plunging necklines, skin-tight fits and the like.

Another thing to remember is the great importance placed on greetings and pleasantries. Even if just asking directions, Tanzanians always take time to greet the other person and inquire about their well-being and that of their families, and they expect visitors to do the same. Tanzanians often continue to hold hands for several minutes after meeting, or even throughout an entire conversation. Especially in the south, a handshake may be accompanied by touching the left hand to the right elbow as a sign of respect.

BACK TO BASICS?

For a country that was founded by a teacher (Julius Nyerere is still referred to as Mwalimu, or 'teacher'), Tanzania ranks near the bottom of the heap when it comes to education. It wasn't always like this. Nyerere was convinced that success for his philosophy of socialism and self-reliance depended on having an educated populace. He made primary education compulsory and offered government assistance to villagers to build their own schools. By the 1980s the country's literacy rate had become one of the highest in Africa.

Later, much of the initial momentum was lost. Although 94% of children enrol at the primary level, about 30% of these drop out before finishing, and less than 15% complete secondary school. The reasons include not enough trained teachers, not enough schools and not enough money. At the secondary level, school fees are a problem, as is language. Primary school instruction is in Swahili, and many students lack sufficient knowledge of English to carry out their secondary level studies.

including Baptist and Pentecostal. One of the areas of highest Christian concentration is in the northeast around Moshi, which has been a centre of missionary activity since the mid-19th century.

The remainder of the population follows traditional religions centred on ancestor worship, the land and various ritual objects. There are also small but active communities of Hindus, Sikhs and Ismailis.

Historically, the main area of friction has been between Tanzania's Muslim and Christian populations. Today, tensions, while still simmering, are at a relatively low level, and religion is not a major factor in contemporary Tanzanian politics. An exception to this is on the Zanzibar Archipelago, where increasing incidents of interreligious violence in recent years have cast a shadow.

The Role of Women

Women form the backbone of the economy, with most juggling child-rearing plus work on the family *shamba* (small plot), or in an office. However, they are near the bottom of the social hierarchy, and are frequently marginalised, especially in education and politics. Only about 5% of girls complete secondary school, and of these, only a handful goes on to complete university. While secondary school enrolment levels are low across the board, girls in particular are frequently kept home due to a lack of finances, to help with chores, or because of pregnancy.

On the positive side, the situation is improving. Since 1996 the government has guaranteed 20% of parliamentary seats for women, and almost one-third of members of the current National Assembly are women. In education, the 'gender gap' has been essentially eliminated at the primary level.

Arts

Music & Dance

Tanzania has an outstanding music and dance scene, mixing influences from its 100-plus tribal groups, from coastal and inland areas and from traditional and modern. Dar es Salaam is the hub, with the greatest variety of groups and styles, but search around anywhere in the country (asking locals is the best bet) to discover some real gems.

Especially in rural areas, it's common for a woman to drop her own name, and become known as *Mama* followed by the name of her oldest son (or daughter, if she has no sons).

Traditional

Tanzanian traditional dance *(ngoma)* creates a living picture, encompassing the entire community in its message and serving as a channel for expressing sentiments such as thanks and praise, and for communicating with the ancestors.

The main place for masked dance is in the southeast, where it plays an important role in the initiation ceremonies of the Makonde (who are famous for their *mapiko* masks) and the Makua.

Modern

The greatest influence on Tanzania's modern music scene has been the Congolese bands that began playing in Dar es Salaam in the early 1960s, which brought the styles of rumba and soukous (*lingala* music) into the East African context. Among the best known is Orchestre Super Matimila, which was propelled to fame by the late Remmy Ongala (Dr Remmy), who was born in the Democratic Republic of Congo (Zaïre), but gained his fame in Tanzania. Many of his songs (most are in Swahili) are commentaries on contemporary themes such as AIDS, poverty and hunger, and Ongala was a major force in popularising music from the region beyond Africa's borders.

Also popular are Swahili rap artists, a vibrant hip-hop scene and the hip-hop influenced and popular Bongo Flava. The easiest music to find is church choir music (*kwaya*).

On Zanzibar, the music scene has long been dominated by *taarab*. Rivalling *taarab* for attention is the similar *kidumbak,* distinguished by its defined rhythms and drumming, and its hard-hitting lyrics.

Wedding Music

During the colonial days, German and British military brass bands spurred the development of *beni ngoma* (brass *ngoma*), dance and music societies combining Western-style brass instruments with African drums and other traditional instruments. Variants of these are still de rigueur at weddings. Stand at the junction of Moshi and Old Moshi Rds in Arusha any weekend afternoon, and watch the wedding processions come by, all accompanied by a small band riding in the back of a pickup truck.

Visual Arts

Painting

The most popular style of painting is Tingatinga, which takes its name from painter Edward Saidi Tingatinga, who began it in the 1960s in response to demands from the European market. Tingatinga paintings are traditionally composed in a square, with brightly coloured animal motifs

Tanzania's literary scene is dominated by the renowned poet and writer Shaaban Robert (1909–62). Robert, who is considered the country's national poet, was almost single-handedly responsible for the development of a modern Swahili prose style. An English-language introduction to his work is *The Poetry of Shaaban Robert*, translated by Clement Ndulute.

NGOMA

The drum is the most essential element in Tanzania's traditional music. The same word (*ngoma*) is used for both dance and drumming, illustrating the intimate relationship between the two, and many dances can only be performed to the beat of a particular type of drum. Some dances, notably those of the Sukuma, also make use of other accessories, including live snakes and other animals. The Maasai leave everything behind in their famous dancing, which is accompanied only by chants and often also by jumping.

Other traditional musical instruments include the *kayamba* (shakers made with grain kernels); rattles and bells made of wood or iron; xylophones (also sometimes referred to as *marimbas*); *siwa* (horns); and *tari* (tambourines).

set against a monochrome background, and use diluted and often unmixed enamel paints for a characteristic glossy appearance.

Sculpture & Woodcarving

Tanzania's Makonde, together with their Mozambican counterparts, are renowned throughout East Africa for their original and highly fanciful carvings. Although originally from the southeast around the Makonde Plateau, commercial realities lured many Makonde north. Today, the country's main carving centre is at Mwenge in Dar es Salaam, where blocks of hard African blackwood (Dalbergia melanoxylon or, in Swahili, mpingo) come to life under the hands of skilled artists.

Ujamaa carvings are designed as a totem pole or 'tree of life' containing interlaced human and animal figures around a common ancestor. Each generation is connected to those that preceded it, and gives support to those that follow. Tree of life carvings often reach several metres in height, and are almost always made from a single piece of wood. Shetani carvings, which embody images from the spirit world, are more abstract, and even grotesque. The emphasis is on challenging viewers to new interpretations while giving the carver's imagination free rein.

Tanzanians are famous for their proverbs. They're used for everything from instructing children to letting one's spouse know that you are annoyed with them. Many are printed around the edges of kangas (cotton wraparound). For a sampling, see www.glcom.com/hassan/kanga.html and www.mwambao.com/methali.htm

DIRK FREDER/GETTY IMAGES ©

Zebras

Wildlife & Habitat

Think of East Africa and the word 'safari' comes to mind – and Tanzania offers the finest safari experiences and wildlife spectacles found anywhere on the planet. This is a land where predators and prey still live in timeless rhythm. You will never forget the shimmering carpets of wildebeest and zebras, the explosion of cheetahs springing from cover, or the spine-tingling roars of lions at night when you visit the Serengeti or Ngorongoro Crater. With more than 40 national parks and game reserves, there is plenty of room to get off the beaten path and craft the safari of your dreams.

– David Lukas

1. Lioness 2. Lion 3. Leopards 4. Cheetahs

DAVID LAZAR/GETTY IMAGES ©

Big Cats

The three big cats – leopard, lion and cheetah – provide the high point for so many memorable safaris. The presence of these apex predators, even the mere suggestion that they may be nearby, is enough to draw the savannah taut with attention. It's the lion's gravitas, roaring at night, stalking at sunset. It's the elusive leopard that remains hidden while in plain view. And it's the cheetah in a fluid blur of hunting perfection.

Lion

Weight 120-150kg (female), 150-225kg (male); length 210-275cm (female), 240-350cm (male) Those lions sprawled out lazily in the shade are actually Africa's most feared predators. Equipped with teeth that tear effortlessly through bone and tendon they can take down an animal as large as a bull giraffe. Each group of adults (a pride) is based around generations of females that do the majority of the hunting; swaggering males typically fight among themselves and eat what the females catch. Best seen in Serengeti NP and Ngorongoro Crater.

Leopard

Weight 30-60kg (female), 40-90kg (male); length 170-300cm More common than you realise, the leopard relies on expert camouflage to stay hidden. During the day you might only spot one reclining in a tree after it twitches its tail, but at night there is no mistaking their bone-chilling groans. Best seen in Serengeti, Ruaha and Tarangire NPs.

Cheetah

Weight 40-60kg; length 200-220cm Less cat than greyhound, the cheetah is a world-class sprinter. Although it reaches speeds of 112km/h, the cheetah runs out of steam after 300m and must cool down for 30 minutes before hunting again. This speed comes at another cost – the cheetah is so well adapted for running that it lacks the strength and teeth to defend its food or cubs from attack by other large predators. Best seen in Serengeti NP.

1. Serval 2. Caracal 3. Wildcat

Small Cats

While big cats get the lion's share of attention from tourists, Tanzania's small cats are equally interesting though much harder to spot. You won't find these cats chasing down gazelles or wildebeest, instead look for them slinking around in search of rodents or making incredible leaps to snatch birds out of the air.

Caracal

Weight 8-19kg; length 80-120cm The caracal is a gorgeous tawny cat with extremely long, pointy ears. This African version of the northern lynx has jacked-up hind legs like a feline dragster. These beanpole kickers enable this slender cat to make vertical leaps of 3m and swat birds out of the air. Widespread in Tanzania's parks, although difficult to spot.

Serval

Weight 6-18kg; length 90-130cm Twice as large as a house cat, but with towering legs and very large ears, the beautifully spotted serval is highly adapted for walking in tall grass and making prodigious leaps to catch rodents and birds. More diurnal than most cats, it may be seen tossing food in the air and playing with it. Best seen in Serengeti NP.

Wildcat

Weight 3-6.5kg; length 65-100cm If you see what looks like a tabby wandering the plains of Tanzania you're probably seeing a wildcat, the direct ancestor of our domesticated house cats. Occurring wherever there are abundant mice and rats, the wildcat is readily found on the outskirts of villages, where it can be identified by its unmarked rufous ears and longish legs.

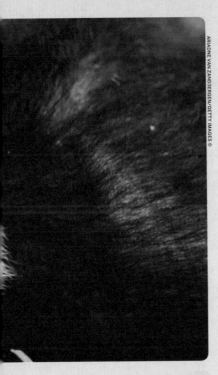

ARIADNE VAN ZANDBERGEN/GETTY IMAGES ©

1. Chimpanzee 2. Olive baboons 3. Vervet monkey

Ground Primates

East Africa is the evolutionary cradle of primate diversity, giving rise to more than 30 species of monkeys, apes and prosimians (the 'primitive' ancestors of modern primates), all of which have dextrous hands and feet. If you think primates hang out in trees, you'll be surprised to see several species that have evolved to ground-living where they are vulnerable to predators.

Chimpanzee

Weight 25-40kg; length 60-90cm Like humans, chimpanzees live in highly social groups built around complex hierarchies with mutually understood rules. It doesn't take a brain surgeon to perceive the deep intelligence and emotion lurking behind such eerily familiar deep-set eyes, and researchers at Gombe Stream and Mahale Mountains National Parks are making startling discoveries about chimp behaviour – you deserve to see it for yourself. Best seen in Gombe Stream and Mahale Mountains NPs.

Olive Baboon

Weight 11-30kg (female), 22-50kg (male); length 95-180cm Although the olive baboon has 5cm-long fangs and can kill a leopard, its best defence consists of running up trees and showering intruders with liquid excrement. Intelligent and opportunistic, troops of these greenish baboons are becoming increasingly abundant over northern Tanzania, while the much paler yellow baboon ranges over the rest of the country. Best seen in Lake Manyara NP.

Vervet Monkey

Weight 4-8kg; length 90-140cm If any monkey epitomised East Africa, it would be the vervet monkey, found almost everywhere. Each troop of vervets is composed of females that defend a home range passed down from generation to generation, while males fight each other for bragging rights and access to females. If you think their appearance drab, check out the extraordinary blue and scarlet colours of their sexual organs when aroused.

Arboreal Primates

Forest primates are a diverse group that live entirely in trees. These agile, long-limbed primates generally stay in the upper canopy where they are well-hidden as they climb and swing among branches in search of leaves and arboreal fruits. It might take the expert eyes of a professional guide to help you find some of these species.

Black-and-White Colobus

Weight 10-23kg; length 115-165cm The black-and-white colobus is one of about seven colobus species found in Tanzania, but it's the mantled colobus that gets the lion's share of attention due to its flowing white frills. Like all colobus, this agile primate has a hook-shaped hand so it can swing through the trees with the greatest of ease. When two troops run into each other, it's a real show. This black-and-white beauty is best seen in Arusha NP.

1. Mantled colobus 2. Blue monkey 3. Greater galago

Blue Monkey

Weight 4-12kg; length 100-170cm These long-tailed monkeys are widespread primates that have adapted to many forested habitats throughout sub-Saharan Africa, including some of the forested parks in Tanzania where they are among the easiest monkeys to spot. These versatile monkeys live in large social groups that spend their entire lives among trees. Best seen in Arusha and Lake Manyara NPs.

Greater & Lesser Galago

Weight 70-2000g; length 30-100cm A nocturnal creature with a dog-like face, greater and lesser galagos belong to a group of prosimians that have changed little in 60 million years. Best known for its frequent bawling cries (hence the common name 'bushbaby'), the galago would be rarely seen except that it readily visits feeding stations at many popular safari lodges. Living in a world of darkness, galagos communicate with each other through scent and sound. Widespread throughout Tanzania.

1. Gerenuk 2. Wildebeest 3. African buffalo 4. Greater kudu

DAVID LAZAR/GETTY IMAGES ©

NIGEL PAVITT/GETTY IMAGES ©

Cud-Chewing Mammals

Hoofed mammals often live in immense herds to protect themselves from predators. Among this family, antelope are particularly numerous, with 40 species in East Africa alone.

Greater Kudu

Weight 120-315kg; length 215-300cm The kudu's white pinstripes conceal it in brushy thickets, while the long spiralling horns of the male are used in ritualised combat. Best seen in Ruaha NP.

Wildebeest

Weight 140-290kg; length 230-340cm On the Serengeti, wildebeest form vast, constantly moving herds accompanied by predators and 4WDs of wide-eyed spectators. Best seen in Serengeti NP, Ngorongoro Crater and Tarangire NP.

Thomson's Gazelle

Weight 15-35kg; length 95-150cm Lanky and exceptionally alert, Thomson's gazelle are built for speed. They migrate in great herds with zebras and wildebeest. Best seen in Serengeti NP and Ngorongoro Crater.

African Buffalo

Weight 250-850kg; length 220-420cm Imagine a big cow with curling horns, and you have the African buffalo (Cape Buffalo). Fortunately they're usually docile, because an angry or injured buffalo is extremely dangerous. Best seen in Katavi NP and Ngorongoro Crater.

Gerenuk

Weight 30-50kg; length 160-200cm Adapted for life in the semi-arid brush of northeastern Tanzania, the gerenuk stands on its hind legs to reach 2m-high branches. Best seen in Tarangire NP.

Waterbuck

Weight 160-300kg; length 210-275cm If you see any antelope it's likely to be the big, shaggy waterbuck. Dependent on waterside vegetation, numbers fluctuate dramatically between wet and dry years. Best seen in Selous GR and Lake Manyara NP.

Hoofed Mammals

A full stable of Africa's most charismatic animals can be found in this group of ungulates. Other than the giraffe, these ungulates are not cud-chewers and can be found over a much broader range of habitats than the cud-chewing animals. They have made their home in Africa for millions of years and are among the most successful mammals to have ever wandered the continent. Without human intervention, Africa would be ruled by elephants, zebras, hippos and warthogs.

Giraffe

Weight 450-1200kg (female), 1800-2000kg (male) The 5m-tall giraffe does such a good job with upward activity – towering above the competition and reaching up to grab mouthfuls of leaves on high branches – that stretching down to get a simple drink of water is a difficult task. Though giraffes usually stroll along casually, they can outrun most predators. Widely sighted, especially in northern safari circuit parks.

African Elephant

Weight 2200-3500kg (female), 4000-6300kg (male); height 2.4-3.4m (female), 3-4m (male) No one, not even a human or lion, stands around to argue when a towering bull elephant rumbles out of the brush. Commonly referred to as 'the king of beasts', elephant society is actually ruled by a lineage of elder females who lead each group along traditional migration routes. Best seen in Ruaha NP, Selous GR, Ngorongoro Crater and Tarangire NP.

Plains Zebra

Weight 175-320kg; length 260-300cm My oh my, those zebras sure have some wicked stripes. Scientists first thought the stripes, each distinct as a human fingerprint, were to confuse predators by making it difficult to distinguish the outline of individual zebras in a herd. However, new studies suggest the stripes help combat disease-carrying horseflies. Best seen in Serengeti and Tarangire NPs.

1. Giraffe **2.** African elephants **3.** Plains zebras

DARYL BALFOUR/GETTY IMAGES ©

1. Black rhinoceros **2.** Rock hyrax **3.** Warthog **4.** Hippopotamus

More Hoofed Mammals

This sampling of miscellaneous hoofed animals highlights the astonishing diversity in this major group of African wildlife. Every visitor wants to see elephants and giraffes, but don't pass up a chance to watch hippos or warthogs.

Black Rhinoceros

Weight 700-1400kg; length 350-450cm
Pity the black rhinoceros for having a horn that is worth more than gold. Once widespread and abundant south of the Sahara, the rhino has been poached to the brink of extinction. Unfortunately, females may only give birth every five years. Best seen in Ngorongoro Crater.

Rock Hyrax

Weight 1.8-5.5kg; length 40-60cm It doesn't seem like it, but those funny tail-less squirrels you see lounging around on rocks are actually an ancient cousin to the elephant. Look for their tiny tusks when one yawns. Best seen in Serengeti NP.

Warthog

Weight 45-75kg (female), 60-150kg (male); length 140-200cm Despite their fearsome appearance and sinister tusks, only the big males are safe from lions, cheetahs and hyenas. To protect themselves when attacked, warthogs run for burrows and reverse in while slashing wildly with their tusks. Easily spotted in many of Tanzania's parks.

Hippopotamus

Weight 510-3200kg; length 320-400cm The hippopotamus is one strange creature. Designed like a floating beanbag with tiny legs, the 3000kg hippo spends its time in or very near water chowing down on aquatic plants. Placid? No way! Hippos have tremendous ferocity and strength when provoked. Best seen in Selous GR and Katavi NP.

JASON EDWARDS/GETTY IMAGES ©

1. Golden jackal **2.** Spotted hyena
3. Banded mongoose **4.** Wild dog

MARC GUITARD/GETTY IMAGES ©

Carnivores

It is a sign of Africa's ecological richness that the continent supports a remarkable variety of predators. When it comes to predators, expect the unexpected and you'll return home with a lifetime of memories!

Banded Mongoose

Weight 1.5-2kg; length 45-75cm Bounding across the savannah on their morning foraging excursions, family groups seek out delicious snacks like toads, scorpions, and slugs. Widespread in Tanzania.

Wild Dog

Weight 20-35kg; length 100-150cm Organised in complex hierarchies maintained by rules of conduct, packs of these efficient hunters (also known as the hunting dog) chase down antelope and other animals. Best seen in Selous GR and Ruaha NP.

Honey Badger

Weight 7-16kg; length 75-100cm Some Africans say they would rather face a lion than a honey badger, and even lions relinquish their kill when one shows up. It finds its favourite food by following honey guide birds to bee hives. It's also known as a 'ratel'. Best seen in Mikumi NP.

Spotted Hyena

Weight 40-90kg; length 125-215cm Living in groups that are ruled by females (who grow penis-like sexual organs), hyenas use bone-crushing jaws to disembowel terrified prey on the run. Best seen in Ngorongoro Crater.

Golden Jackal

Weight 6-15kg; length 85-130cm Through a combination of sheer fierceness and bluff the trim little jackal manages to fill its belly while holding hungry vultures and much stronger hyenas at bay. Best seen in Serengeti NP and Ngorongoro Crater.

1. African fish eagle **2.** Secretary birds
3. White-backed vultures and Rüppell's vulture **4.** Bateleur

2

DANITA DELIMONT/GETTY IMAGES ©

Birds of Prey

Tanzania has nearly 100 species of hawks, eagles, vultures and owls. More than 40 have been seen at Lake Manyara National Park alone, making this one of the best places in the world to see an incredible variety of birds of prey.

Secretary Bird

Length 100cm With the body of an eagle and legs of a crane, the bizarre secretary bird towers 1.3m-tall and walks up to 20km a day in search of vipers, cobras and other snakes. Best seen in Serengeti NP.

Bateleur

Length 60cm French for 'tightrope-walker', bateleur refers to this bird's distinctive low-flying aerial acrobatics. At close hand, look for its bold colour pattern and scarlet face. Best seen in Katavi and Tarangire NPs.

African Fish Eagle

Length 75cm This replica of the American bald eagle presents an imposing appearance, but it is most familiar for its loud, ringing vocalisations that have become known as 'the voice of Africa'. Best seen in Rubondo Island NP.

Augur Buzzard

Length 55cm Perhaps Tanzania's commonest raptor, the augur buzzard occupies a wide range of wild and cultivated habitats, where they hunt by floating motionlessly in the air then stooping down to catch unwary critters.

White-Backed Vulture

Length 80cm Mingling with lions, hyenas and jackals around carcasses, vultures use their sheer numbers to compete for scraps of flesh and bone. Easily spotted in most of Tanzania's parks.

4

1. Superb starling 2. Lesser flamingos
3. Lilac-breasted roller 4. Ostrich

ARIADNE VAN ZANDBERGEN/GETTY IMAGES ©

Other Birds

Birdwatchers from all over the world travel to Tanzania in search of the country's 1100 species of birds – an astounding number by any measure – including birds of every shape and in every colour imaginable.

Saddle-Billed Stork

Height 150cm; wingspan 270cm The saddle-billed stork is the most stunning of Tanzania's eight stork species. As if a 2.7m wingspan wasn't impressive enough, check out its brilliant-red-coloured kneecaps and bill. Best seen in Serengeti NP.

Lesser Flamingo

Length 100cm When they gather by the hundreds of thousands on shimmering salt lakes, lesser flamingos create unforgettable wildlife images. Best seen in Lake Manyara NP.

Lilac-Breasted Roller

Length 40cm Nearly everyone on safari gets to know the gorgeous lilac-breasted roller. Rollers get their name from the tendency to 'roll' from side to side in flight as a way of showing off their iridescent blues, purples and greens. Easily spotted in many of Tanzania's parks.

Ostrich

Height 200-270cm Standing 2.7m high and weighing upwards of 130kg, these ancient birds escape predators by running away at 70km/h or lying flat on the ground to resemble a pile of dirt. Best seen in Serengeti NP.

Superb Starling

Length 18cm With a black face, yellow eyes, and metallic blue-green upperparts that contrast sharply with their red-orange belly, superb starlings seem like a rare find, but are actually surprisingly abundant. Best seen in Tanzania's northern safari circuit parks.

Habitats

Nearly all of Tanzania's birds and animals spend most of their lives in specific types of habitat, and you will hear rangers and fellow travellers refer to these habitats repeatedly as if they were code words. If this is your first time in East Africa, some of these habitats and their seasonal rhythms take some getting used to, but your wildlife-viewing experiences will be greatly enhanced when you learn how to recognise these habitats and which animals you might expect in each one.

for wildlife, but the patient observer will be richly rewarded. While it's true that the lack of water restricts larger animals such as zebras, gazelles and antelope to areas around waterholes, this habitat explodes with plant and animal life whenever it rains. During the dry season, many plants shed their leaves to conserve water and grazing animals move on in search of food and water. Mkomazi National Park is one of the best places in Tanzania to experience this unique habitat.

Semi-Arid Desert

Parts of northeastern Tanzania see so little rainfall that shrubs and hardy grasses, rather than trees, are the dominant vegetation. This is not the Tanzania that many visitors come to see and it doesn't seem like a great place

Savannah

Savannah is the classic East African landscape – broad rolling grasslands dotted with lone acacia trees. The openness and vastness of this landscape make it a perfect home for large herds of grazing zebras and wildebeest, in

1. Serengeti National Park (p189) **2.** Baobab trees, Ruaha National Park (p268)

addition to fast-sprinting predators such as cheetahs, and it's a perfect place for seeing large numbers of animals. Savannah develops in areas where there are long wet seasons alternating with long dry seasons, creating ideal conditions for the growth of dense, nutritious grasses. Shaped by fire and grazing animals, savannah is a dynamic habitat in constant flux with its adjacent woodlands. One of the best places in the world for exploring the African savannah is found at Serengeti National Park.

Woodland

Tanzania is the only place in East Africa to find the woodland habitat, locally known as *miombo* (moist woodland), which is more characteristic of south-central Africa. Here the trees form a continuous canopy cover that offers shelter from predators and shade from the harsh sunlight. This important habitat provides homes for many birds, small mammals and insects, and is a fantastic place to search for wildlife. In places where fingers of woodland mingle with savannah, animals such as leopards and antelope often gather to find shade or places to rest during the day. During the dry season, fires and elephants can wreak havoc on these woodlands, fragmenting large tracts of forest habitat into fragments. Ruaha National Park is a fantastic place to see both pure *miombo* forests and the ecological mix of savannah and *miombo*.

Lionesses, Ngorongoro Conservation Area

Environment & National Parks

At over 943,000 sq km, or almost four times the size of the UK, Tanzania is East Africa's largest country. It encompasses a diversity of landscapes – forested mountains, open savannah lands, several major lakes and rivers and a long coastline. It also hosts a wealth of animal and plant life, and has an exceptional collection of national parks.

Topography

Tanzania is bordered to the east by the Indian Ocean, with its wealth of corals, fish and sea turtles. To the west are the deep lakes of the Western Rift Valley, Lake Tanganyika and Lake Nyasa (Lake Malawi). Both have lush mountains rising up from their shores. Much of central Tanzania is an arid highland plateau averaging 900m to 1800m in altitude and nestled between the eastern and western branches of the Great Rift Valley. Savannah landscapes are best seen in the north, in Serengeti National Park.

Tanzania's mountain ranges are grouped into a sharply rising northeastern section, known as the Eastern Arc, and an open, rolling central and southern section known as the Southern Highlands or Southern Arc. A range of volcanoes and extinct volcanoes known as the Crater Highlands rises from the side of the Great Rift Valley in northern Tanzania.

The country's largest river is the Rufiji, which drains the Southern Highlands en route to the coast. Other major rivers include the Ruvu, Wami, Pangani and Ruvuma.

Wildlife

Zebras, elephants, wildebeest, buffaloes, hippos, giraffes, antelope, dik-diks, gazelles, elands and both greater and lesser kudus – these are just some of the 430 species and subspecies that make up Tanzania's four-million-plus wild animal population. The country is famed in particular for its predators, with Serengeti National Park one of the best places for spotting lions, cheetahs and leopards. There are also hyenas and wild dogs (the latter in Ruaha National Park and in Selous Game Reserve), and in Gombe Stream and Mahale Mountains National Parks, chimpanzees.

Tanzania is notable for lying in a transition zone between the savannah lands of East Africa and the *miombo* (brachystegia) woodland habitats of southern Africa, and hosts species common to each area. This transition is best seen in Ruaha National Park, where East African highlights such as Grant's gazelle are found alongside more southerly ones such as Lichtenstein's hartebeest and greater kudu.

Complementing the country's wealth of large animals are over 1000 bird species, making Tanzania an ornithologist's dream. Commonly sighted birds include kingfishers, hornbills (around Amani in the eastern Usambaras), bee-eaters (along the Rufiji and Wami Rivers), fish eagles (Lake Victoria) and flamingos (Lakes Manyara and Natron). There are also many birds that are unique to Tanzania, including the Udzungwa

Best Places to Spot...

Black Rhino
Ngorongoro Crater

Uluguru Bushshrike
Uluguru Mountains

Red Colobus Monkey Jozani
Forest, Zanzibar

Wild Dogs Selous
GR, Ruaha NP

Pemba Flying Fox
Pemba

SAVING THE SEA TURTLES

Tanzania's sea turtle population is critically endangered, due to nest poaching, subsistence hunting and turtles getting caught in fishing nets. Sea Sense (www.seasense.org) has been working with coastal communities to protect sea turtles, as well as dugongs, whale sharks and other endangered marine species. It has made considerable progress, especially with its community nest protection program, in which locally trained conservation officers assume responsibility for monitoring sea turtle nesting activity, and protecting eggs from poachers and other dangers.

As part of this initiative, local community members are trained as 'turtle tour guides' to take visitors to nesting sites to watch hatchlings emerge and make their way to the sea. Places where this is possible include Dar es Salaam's South Beach, Ushongo beach (south of Pangani) and Mafia island. The modest fee is split between Sea Sense, to support its nest protection program, and local village environment funds. In this way, community members are able to benefit directly from their conservation efforts. If you'd like to watch a sea turtle nest hatching, contact Sea Sense (info@seasense.org).

Top Spots for Botanists

Kitulo National Park

Amani Nature Reserve

Udzungwa Mountains National Park

forest partridge, the Pemba green pigeon, the Usambara weaver and the Usambara eagle owl.

In addition, Tanzania has over 60,000 insect species, about 25 types of reptiles or amphibians, 100 species of snakes and numerous fish species.

Endangered Species

Endangered species include the black rhino; Uluguru bushshrike; hawksbill, green, olive ridley and leatherback turtle; red colobus monkey; wild dog; and Pemba flying fox.

Plants

Patches of tropical rainforest in Tanzania's Eastern Arc mountains provide a home to a rich assortment of plants, many found nowhere else in the world. These include the Usambara or African violet (*Saintpaulia*) and impatiens, which are sold as house plants in grocery stores throughout the West. Similar forest patches – remnants of the much larger tropical forest that once extended across the continent – are also found in the Udzungwas, Ulugurus and several other areas. South and west of the Eastern Arc range are stands of baobab.

Away from the mountain ranges, much of the country is covered by *miombo* ('moist' woodland), where the main vegetation is various types of brachystegia tree. Much of the dry central plateau is covered with savannah, bushland and thickets, while grasslands cover the Serengeti Plains and other areas that lack good drainage.

Amani Nature Reserve and Kitulo National Park are among the country's botanical highlights, and Kitulo is one of Africa's few parks with wildflowers as its focal point.

National Parks & Reserves

About 6% (59,000 sq km) of mainland Tanzania is covered by inland lakes. The deepest is Lake Tanganyika, while the largest (and one of the shallowest) is Lake Victoria.

Tanzania has 15 mainland national parks, 14 wildlife reserves, the Ngorongoro Conservation Area, three marine parks and several protected marine reserves. Until relatively recently, development and tourism were focused almost exclusively on the northern parks (Serengeti, Lake Manyara, Tarangire and Arusha National Parks), plus Kilimanjaro National Park for trekkers, and the Ngorongoro Conservation Area. All of these places are easily reached by road or air, and heavily visited, with a range of facilities. Apart from the evocative landscapes, the main attractions are the high concentrations, diversity and accessibility of the wildlife.

The southern protected areas (Ruaha National Park and Selous Game Reserve, plus Mikumi and Udzungwa Mountains parks) are receiving increasing attention, but still don't see the number of visitors that the north does and most areas tend to have more of a wilderness feel. Except for Mikumi, they also tend to be more time-consuming to reach by road. The wildlife, however, is just as impressive, although it's often spread out over larger areas.

In the west are Mahale Mountains and Gombe Stream National Parks, where the main draws are the chimpanzees and (for Mahale) the remoteness. Katavi is also remote, and the closest to experiencing the pristine wild. Rubondo Island National Park is set on its own in Lake Victoria, and is of particular interest for birding. Saadani, just north of Dar es Salaam, is the only terrestrial national park along the coast. Mkomazi, just off the Arusha–Tanga highway near Same, is a private sanctuary for black rhinos.

Tanzania's montane forests contain 7% of Africa's endemic plant species on only 0.05% of the continent's total area. Check the Tanzania Conservation Group website (www.tfcg.org) for an introduction to the country's forests and the conservation of their exceptional biodiversity.

National Parks

Tanzania's national parks are managed by the **Tanzania National Parks Authority** (Tanapa; www.tanzaniaparks.com; Dodoma Rd, Arusha).

Park entry fees, which are posted on the Tanapa website, range from US$30 to US$100 per adult per day, depending on the park (US$10 to US$20 per child per day for children between five and 16 years of age), with Serengeti, Kilimanjaro, Mahale Mountains and Gombe Stream parks the most expensive, and Mkomazi, Saadani, Mikumi, Udzungwa Mountains, Kitulo, Katavi and Rubondo Island parks the least expensive. Park camping fees are US$30 per adult (US$5 per child) in public campsites and US$50 per adult (US$10 per child) in special campsites. Other costs include guide fees of US$20 to US$25 per group for walking safaris, plus vehicle fees (US$40 per foreign-registered vehicle and Tsh20,000 for Tanzania-registered vehicles). Except at some of the less-visited parks, where credit card machines are planned, but not yet installed, park entry fees and all other park fees must be paid electronically with a Visa card or MasterCard. It is also possible to pay using a 'smart card', available for purchase

ENVIRONMENT & NATIONAL PARKS **NATIONAL PARKS & RESERVES**

THE GREAT RIFT VALLEY

The Great Rift Valley is part of the East African rift system – a massive geological fault stretching 6500km across the African continent, from the Dead Sea in the north to Beira (Mozambique) in the south. The rift system was formed over 30 million years ago when the tectonic plates comprising the African and Eurasian landmasses collided and then diverged. As the plates separated, large chunks of the earth's crust dropped down between them, resulting over millennia in the escarpments, ravines, flatlands and lakes that characterise East Africa's topography today.

The rift system is notable for its calderas and volcanoes (including Mt Kilimanjaro, Mt Meru and the calderas of the Crater Highlands) and for its lakes, which are often very deep, with floors well below sea level although their surfaces may be several hundred metres above sea level.

The Tanzanian Rift Valley consists of two branches formed where the main rift system divides north of Kenya's Lake Turkana. The Western Rift Valley extends past Lake Albert (Uganda) through Rwanda and Burundi to Lakes Tanganyika and Nyasa, while the eastern branch (Eastern or Gregory Rift) runs south from Lake Turkana, past Lakes Natron and Manyara, before joining again with the Western Rift by Lake Nyasa. The lakes of the Eastern Rift are smaller than those in the western branch, with some only waterless salt beds. The largest are Lakes Natron and Manyara. Lake Eyasi is in a side branch off the main rift.

The escarpments of Tanzania's portion of the Rift Valley are most impressive in and around the Ngorongoro Conservation Area and Lake Manyara National Park.

from CRDB and Exim banks. In any case, it is advisable to always bring both Visa or MasterCard as well as US dollars cash or the equivalent in Tanzanian shillings (the latter to cover cases where the card machines are nonexistent or not working) whenever visiting Tanzania's parks.

Wildlife Reserves

Wildlife reserves are administered by the **Wildlife Division of the Ministry of Natural Resources & Tourism** (☎022-286 6064, 022-286 6376; scp@africaonline.co.tz; cnr Nyerere & Changombe Rds, Dar es Salaam). Fees currently must be paid in US dollars cash. Selous is the only reserve with tourist infrastructure. Large areas of most others have been leased as hunting concessions, as has the southern Selous.

Marine Parks & Reserves

Mafia Island Marine Park, Mnazi Bay-Ruvuma Estuary Marine Park, Tanga Coelacanth Marine Park, Maziwe Marine Reserve and the Dar es Salaam Marine Reserves (Mbudya, Bongoyo, Pangavini and Fungu Yasini islands) are under the jurisdiction of the Ministry of Natural Resources & Tourism's **Marine Parks & Reserves Unit** (Map p56; www.marineparks. go.tz; Olympio St, Upanga, Dar es Salaam). Entry fees for marine parks (US$20 per day per adult, US$10 per child) and marine reserves (US$10 per adult, US$5 per child) are payable in cash only.

Ngorongoro Conservation Area

The Ngorongoro Conservation Area was established as a multiple-use area to protect wildlife and the pastoralist lifestyle of the Maasai, who had lost other large areas of their traditional territory with the formation of Serengeti National Park. It is administered by the **Ngorongoro Conservation Area Authority** (www.ngorongorocrater.org). It is notable both for its superlative wildlife watching in the Ngorongoro Crater and for its rugged hiking in the surrounding highlands. Payment for entering the Conservation Area (US$50 per adult per day and US$10 per child entry, plus vehicle and crater service fees) is made via credit card when the machine is working, and via cash when it's not; bring both.

Environmental Issues

Although Tanzania has one of the highest proportions of protected land of any African country (about 40% is protected in some form), limited resources and corruption hamper conservation efforts, and poaching,

THE EASTERN ARC MOUNTAINS

The ancient Eastern Arc mountains (which include the Usambara, Pare, Udzungwa and Uluguru ranges) stretch in a broken crescent from southern Kenya's Taita Hills down to Morogoro and the Southern Highlands. They are estimated to be at least 100 million years old, with the stones forming them as much as 600 million years old. Their climatic isolation and stability has offered plant species a chance to develop, and today these mountains are highly biodiverse and home to an exceptional assortment of plants and birds. Plant and bird numbers in the mountain ranges total about one-third of Tanzania's flora and fauna species, and include many unique species plus a wealth of medicinal plants.

In the late 19th century, population growth and expansion of the local logging industry began to cause depletion of the Eastern Arc's original forest cover, and erosion became a serious problem. It became so bad in parts of the western Usambaras that in the early 1990s entire villages had to be shifted to lower areas. It has now somewhat stabilised, with a reduction in logging and the initiation of several tree planting projects. However, it remains a serious concern.

MAJOR NATIONAL PARKS & RESERVES

PARK	FEATURES	ACTIVITIES	BEST TIME TO VISIT
Arusha National Park	Mt Meru, lakes & crater: zebras, giraffes, elephants	trekking, canoe & vehicle safaris, walking; cultural activities nearby	year-round
Gombe Stream National Park	lake shore, forest: chimpanzees	chimp tracking	Jun-Oct
Katavi National Park	flood plains, lakes & woodland: buffaloes, hippos, antelope	vehicle & walking safaris	Jun-Oct
Kilimanjaro National Park	Mt Kilimanjaro	trekking, cultural activities on lower slopes	Jun-Oct, Dec-Feb
Kitulo National Park	highland plateau: wildflowers & wilderness	hiking	Dec-Apr (for wildflowers), Sep-Nov (for hiking)
Lake Manyara National Park	Lake Manyara: hippos, water birds, elephants	vehicle safaris, walking, cycling & cultural activities; night drives	Jun-Feb (Dec-Apr for birding)
Mahale Mountains National Park	remote lake shore & mountains: chimpanzees	chimp tracking	Jun-Oct, Dec-Feb
Mikumi National Park	Mkata flood plains: lions, buffaloes, giraffes, elephants	vehicle safaris, short walks	year-round
Mkomazi National Park	semi-arid savannah: black rhinos & wild dogs (neither viewable by the general public), birds	vehicle safaris, short walks	Jun-Mar
Ngorongoro Conservation Area	Ngorongoro Crater: black rhinos, lions, elephants, zebras, flamingos	vehicle safaris, hiking	Jun-Feb
Ruaha National Park	Ruaha River, sand rivers: elephants, hippos, kudus, antelope, birds	vehicle & walking safaris	Jun-Oct for wildlife, Dec-Apr for birding
Rubondo Island National Park	Lake Victoria: bird life, sitatungas, chimps	short walks, boating, fishing	Jun-Feb
Saadani National Park	Wami River, beach: birds, hippos, crocodiles, elephants	vehicle safaris, short boat trips, short walks	Jun-Feb
Selous Game Reserve	Rufiji River, lakes, woodland: elephants, hippos, wild dogs, black rhinos, birds	boat, walking & vehicle safaris	Jun-Dec
Serengeti National Park	plains & grasslands, Grumeti River: wildebeest, zebras, lions, cheetahs, giraffes	vehicle, walking & balloon safaris; walks & cultural activities in border areas	year-round
Tarangire National Park	Tarangire River, woodland, baobabs: elephants, zebras, wildebeest, birds	vehicle safaris; walks, night drives & cultural activities in border areas	Jun-Oct
Udzungwa Mountains National Park	Udzungwa Mountains, forest: primates, birds	hiking	Jun-Oct

RESPONSIBLE TRAVEL IN TANZANIA

Tourism is big business in Tanzania. Here are a few guidelines for minimising strain on the local environment:

➡ Support local enterprise.

➡ Buy souvenirs directly from those who make them.

➡ Choose safari or trek operators that treat local communities as equal partners and that are committed to protecting local ecosystems.

➡ For cultural attractions, try to pay fees directly to the locals involved, rather than to tour-company guides or other intermediaries.

➡ Ask permission before photographing people.

➡ Avoid indiscriminate gift-giving; donations to recognised projects are more sustainable and have a better chance of reaching those who need them most.

➡ Don't buy items made from ivory, skin, shells etc.

➡ Save natural resources.

➡ Respect local culture and customs.

The Mpingo Conservation & Development Initiative (www.mpingoconservation.org) and the African Blackwood Conservation Project (www.blackwoodconservation.org) are working to conserve *mpingo* (East African blackwood) – Tanzania's national tree, and one of the main woods used in carvings.

erosion, soil degradation, desertification and deforestation whittle away at the natural wealth. According to some estimates, Tanzania loses 3500 sq km of forest land annually as a result of agricultural and commercial clearing, and about 95% of the tropical high forest that once covered Zanzibar and Pemba is now gone. Poaching has increased markedly in both the northern circuit parks and in Selous Game Reserve due to corruption, increased demand and insufficient enforcement. This, combined with inappropriate visitor use, especially in the northern circuit, is a serious threat to wildlife and ecosystems.

Urban pollution is another serious concern, as the populations of major cities continue to expand without proper sewage treatment plants and air pollution controls. In Dar es Salaam, where it is estimated that close to 70% of households use pit latrines, the ageing sewerage and sanitation systems are inadequate to cope with demand. Although rehabilitation is underway, significant amounts of sewage still flow directly into the ocean, and overflow of raw sewage into stormwater drains is commonplace. Air pollution, too, is a concern, with ever-increasing vehicle numbers, often poor-quality fuel and no adequate emissions controls.

In coastal areas, dynamite fishing remains a problem, although progress has been made in some areas in halting this practice. Mafia Island Marine Park, for example, was created in major part to curb dynamite fishing and other unsustainable fishing practices. In the decade since its creation, dynamite fishing in the area has been largely eliminated, and the park has achieved considerable progress in promoting conservation measures alongside sustainable resource use by local communities.

On the positive side, progress has been made to involve communities directly in conservation, and local communities are now stakeholders in a number of lodges and other tourist developments. Zanzibar's Chumbe Island Coral Park is a good example, illustrating what long-term collaboration with local fishing communities can achieve in terms of conservation and environmental education. Manyara Ranch Conservancy and the Kilimanjaro Conservancy are two other examples. In both of these private conservancy models, a collaborative relationship has been established in which local communities are both involved in and benefit from wildlife conservation.

Tanzanian Cuisine

It's easy to travel through Tanzania thinking that the country subsists on ugali (the main maize and cassava flour staple) and sauce. But there are some treats to be found. The Zanzibar Archipelago is one of East Africa's culinary highlights. Here, scents of coriander and coconut recall the days when the coast was a port of call on the spice route from the Orient. Elsewhere, lively local atmosphere and Tanzanian hospitality compensate for what can otherwise be a rather bland diet.

Tanzanian Specialities

Ugali is the Tanzanian national dish. This thick, doughlike mass – which is somewhat of an acquired taste for many foreigners – varies in flavour and consistency depending on the flours used and the cooking. In general, good ugali should be neither too dry nor too sticky. It's usually served with a sauce containing meat, fish, beans or greens. Rice and *ndizi* (cooked plantains) are other staples, and chips are ubiquitous.

Mishikaki (marinated, grilled meat kebabs) and *nyama choma* (seasoned roasted meat) are widely available. Along the coast and near lakes, there's plenty of seafood, often grilled or (along the coast) cooked in coconut milk or curry-style.

Some Tanzanians start their day with *uji,* a thin, sweet porridge made from bean, millet or other flour. Watch for ladies stirring bubbling pots of it on street corners in the early morning. *Vitambua* – small rice cakes resembling tiny, thick pancakes – are another morning treat, especially in the southeast. On Zanzibar, try *mkate wa kumimina,* a bread made from a batter similar to that used for making *vitambua.* Another Zanzibari treat (you'll also find it in Dar es Salaam) is *urojo,* a filling, delicious soup with *kachori* (spicy potatoes), mango, limes, coconut, cassava chips, salad and sometimes *pili-pili* (hot pepper).

Three meals a day is usual, although breakfast is frequently nothing more than *kahawa* (coffee) or chai (tea) and *mkate* (bread). The main meal is eaten at midday.

> **Good Coffee**
>
> Zanzibar Coffee House, Zanzibar Town
>
> Utengule Coffee Lodge, Mbeya
>
> Union Cafe, Moshi

DOS & DON'TS

For Tanzanians, a shared meal and eating out of a communal dish are expressions of solidarity between hosts and guests.

➡ If you're invited to eat and aren't hungry, it's OK to say that you've just eaten, but try to share a few bites of the meal in recognition of the bond with your hosts.

➡ Leave a small amount on your plate to show your hosts that you've been satisfied.

➡ Don't take the last bit of food from the communal bowl, as your hosts may worry that they haven't provided enough.

➡ Never handle food with the left hand.

➡ If others are eating with their hands, do the same, even if cutlery is provided.

➡ Defer to your host for customs that you aren't sure about.

Drinks

Apart from the ubiquitous Fanta and Coca-Cola, the main soft drink is Tangawizi, a local version of ginger ale. Fresh juices are widely available, although check first to see whether they have been mixed with unsafe water or ice. Tap water is best avoided. Bottled water is widely available, except in remote areas, where it's worth carrying a filter or purification tablets.

In the Tanga area and around Lake Victoria watch for *mtindi* and *mgando*, cultured milk products similar to yoghurt, and usually drunk with a straw out of plastic bags.

Tanzania's array of beers includes the local Safari and Kilimanjaro labels, plus Castle Lager and various Kenyan and German beers. Finding a beer is usually no problem, but finding a cold one can be a challenge.

Local brews fall under the catch-all term *konyagi*. Around Kilimanjaro, watch for *mbege* (banana beer). *Gongo* (also called *nipa*) is an illegal distilled cashew drink, but the brewed version, *uraka,* is legal. Local brews made from papaw are also common.

Tanzania has a small wine industry based in Dodoma.

Dining Tanzanian-Style

You'll likely find yourself dining in a variety of venues, from simple sidewalk stalls ('*Mama Lishe*'), where the local 'mama' prepares a plate of the day, to European-style restaurants.

Hotelis, Night Markets & Tearooms

For dining local style, sit down in a *hoteli* – a small, informal restaurant – and watch life pass by. Many *hoteli* have the day's menu written on a blackboard, and a TV in the corner. Rivalling *hoteli* for local atmosphere are the bustling night markets found in many towns, where vendors set up grills along the roadside and sell *nyama choma,* grilled *pweza* (octopus) and other street food. Especially in small towns and along the coast, you'll find 'tearooms' – great places to get snacks or light meals.

Restaurants

For Western-style meals, stick to cities or main towns, where there's a reasonable to good array of restaurants, most moderately priced compared with their European equivalents.

Lunch is served between about noon and 2.30pm, and dinner from about 7pm to 10pm. The smaller the town, the earlier its restaurants are

---

KARIBU CHAKULA

If you're invited to join in a meal – *karibu chakula* – the first step is hand washing. Your host will bring around a bowl and water jug; hold your hands over the bowl while your host pours water over them. Sometimes soap is provided, and a towel for drying off.

The meal itself inevitably centres around ugali or rice and sauce. Take some with the right hand from the communal pot, roll it into a small ball with the fingers, making an indentation with your thumb, and dip it into the accompanying sauce. Eating with your hand is a bit of an art, but after a few tries it starts to feel natural. Don't soak the ugali too long (to avoid it breaking up in the sauce), and keep your hand lower than your elbow (except when actually eating) so the sauce doesn't drip down your forearm.

Except for fruit, desserts are rarely served; meals conclude with another round of hand washing. Thank your host by saying *chakula kizuri* or *chakula kitamu* – both local ways of saying that the food was tasty and delicious.

GOURMET TREATS

Staying at upmarket safari camps and hotels, you'll dine well. But for independent travellers or those on a limited budget, a diet of rice and sauce quickly gets tiresome. Following are some suggestions for treating yourself if you're craving something tasty and wholesome while travelling away from major centres:

Lushoto Homemade jam, wholegrain bread and cheese from Irente Farm and St Eugene's Lodge

Njombe Italian cheeses and fresh yoghurt at the Duka la Maziwa

Iringa to Makambako Gourmet cuisine and fresh farm produce at Kisolanza – The Old Farmhouse

Iringa Authentic Italian cuisine at Mama Iringa; banana milkshakes and pancakes at Hasty Tasty Too

Pemba Fresh, warm bread from street vendors mornings and evenings in Chake Chake, plus Pemba honey (*asali*) from the market to spread on top

Tanga Fresh yoghurt and cheeses at Tanga Fresh

Tanzanian coast Fresh seafood everywhere

likely to close; after about 7pm in rural areas it can be difficult to find anything other than street food.

Most main towns have at least one supermarket selling various imported products such as canned meat, fish and cheese (but not specialty items such as trail food or energy bars). In coastal areas you can always find a fresh catch of fish and someone to prepare it for you; the best time to look is early morning.

Local Traditions

Tanzanian style is to eat with the hand from communal dishes in the centre of the table. There will always be somewhere to wash your hands – either a bowl and jug of water that are passed around, or a sink in the corner. Although food is shared, it is not customary to share drinks. Sodas are the usual accompaniment, and there will also usually be a pitcher of water, though this may be unpurified. Children generally eat separately. If there's a toast, the common salutation is *afya!* – (to your) health!

Street snacks and meals on the run are common. European-style restaurant dining, while readily available in major cities, is not part of local culture. More common are large gatherings at home, or at a rented hall, to celebrate special occasions, with the meal as the focal point.

In restaurants catering to tourists, tip about 10%, assuming service warrants it. Tipping isn't expected in small, local establishments, though rounding up the bill is always appreciated.

Vegetarian Cuisine

There isn't much in Tanzania that is specifically billed as 'vegetarian', but there are many vegetarian options and you can find *wali* (cooked rice) and *maharagwe* (beans) everywhere. The main challenges are keeping variety and balance in your diet, and getting enough protein, especially if you don't eat eggs or seafood. In larger towns, Indian restaurants are the best places to try for vegetarian meals. Elsewhere, ask Indian shop owners if they have any suggestions; many will also be able to help you find fresh yoghurt. Peanuts (*karanga*) and cashews (*korosho*) are widely available, as are fresh fruits and vegetables.

With fruits and vegetables, it's best to follow the adage: 'Cook it, peel it, boil it or forget it.'

Food Glossary

For a full list of terms and phrases, see p395.

MENU DECODER

biryani	casserole of spices and rice with meat or seafood
chipsi mayai	omelette with chips inside
kiti moto	literally 'hot seat'; fried pork bits
kuku/samaki/nyama na wali/ugali/chips/ndizi	chicken/fish/beef and rice/ugali/chips/cooked plantains
mchuzi	sauce, sometimes with bits of beef and very well cooked vegetables
mishikaki	marinated, grilled meat kebabs
nyama choma	grilled meat
pilau	spiced rice cooked in broth with seafood or meat and vegetables
supu	soup; usually somewhat greasy, and served with a piece of beef, pork or meat fat in it
ugali	staple made from maize and/or cassava flour
uji	porridge
urojo	Zanzibari soup

STAPLES

maharagwe	beans
mkate	bread
matoke	cooked and mashed plantains
ndizi ya kupika	plantains
viazi	potatoes
wali	rice (cooked)

OTHER DISHES & CONDIMENTS

chumvi	salt
mayai (yaliyochemshwa)	eggs (boiled)
maziwa mgando	yoghurt
sukari	sugar

DRINKS

bia	beer
chai	tea
kahawa	coffee
maji (ya kuchemsha/ya kunywa/ya chupa)	water (boiled/drinking/bottled)
maji ya machungwa	orange juice

Survival Guide

Directory A–Z

Accommodation

➡ Accommodation ranges from dingy rooms with communal bucket baths to luxurious safari and island lodges. Choice is good in tourist areas and limited off the beaten track.

➡ Most upmarket hotels consider July, August and the Christmas and New Year holidays to be high season. A peak-season surcharge is sometimes levied on top of regular high-season rates from late December through early January.

➡ During the March to early June low season, it's often possible to negotiate significant discounts (up to 50%) on room rates.

➡ A residence permit entitles you to discounts at many lodges and hotels, including in the national parks.

Camping

Carry a tent to save money and for flexibility off the beaten track. Note that camping in most national parks costs at least US$30 per person per night – as much as

sleeping in park-run accommodation.

Camping prices quoted in this book are per person per night, except as noted.

NATIONAL PARKS

All parks have campsites, designated as either 'public' ('ordinary') or 'special'. Most parks also have simple huts or cottages (sometimes called 'bandas'), several have basic resthouses and some northern circuit parks have hostels (for student groups, or for overflow, if the resthouses or cottages are full).

Public campsites These have toilets (usually pit latrines) and, sometimes, a water source, but plan on being self-sufficient. Most sites are in reasonable condition and some are quite pleasant. No booking required.

Special campsites These are smaller, more remote and more expensive than public sites, with no facilities. The idea is that the area remains as close to pristine as possible. Advance booking required; once you make a booking, the special campsite is reserved exclusively for your group.

ELSEWHERE

➡ There are campsites situated in or near most major towns, near many of the national parks and in some scenic locations along a few of the main highways (eg Dar es Salaam–Mbeya, and Tanga–Moshi).

➡ Prices average from US$7 per person per night to more than double this for campsites near national parks.

➡ Camping away from established sites is generally not advisable. In rural areas, seek permission first from the village head or elders before pitching your tent.

➡ Camping is not permitted on Zanzibar.

Guesthouses

Almost every town has at least one basic guesthouse. At the bottom end of the scale, expect a cement-block room, often small and poorly ventilated, and not always very clean, with a foam mattress, shared bathroom facilities (often long-drop toilets and bucket showers), a mosquito net and sometimes a fan. Rates average Tsh10,000 to Tsh15,000 per room per night.

The next level up gets you a cleaner, decent room, often with a bathroom (although not always with running or hot water). Prices for a double room with bathroom average from about

BOOK YOUR STAY ONLINE

For more accommodation reviews by Lonely Planet authors, check out http://lonelyplanet.com/hotels/. You'll find independent reviews, as well as recommendations on the best places to stay. Best of all, you can book online.

Tsh20,000 (from Tsh15,000 for a single).

Some tips:

➡ For peace and quiet, guesthouses without bars are the best choice.

➡ In many towns, water is a problem during the dry season, so don't be surprised if your only choice at budget places is a bucket bath. Many of the cheaper places don't have hot water. This is a consideration in cooler areas, especially during winter, although staff will almost always arrange a hot bucket if you ask.

➡ In Swahili, the word *hotel* or *hoteli* does not mean accommodation, but rather a place for food and drink. The more common term used for accommodation is *guesti* (guesthouse) or, more formally, *nyumba ya kulala wageni*.

➡ There are many mission hostels and guesthouses, primarily for missionaries and aid-organisation staff, though some are willing to accommodate travellers, space permitting.

➡ In coastal areas, you'll find bungalows or *bandas* (small thatched-roof cottages with wooden or stone walls) ranging from simple huts on the sand to luxurious ensuite affairs.

Hotels & Lodges

Larger towns offer from one to several midrange hotels with ensuite rooms (widely referred to in Tanzania as 'self-contained' or 'self-containers'), hot water, and a fan and/or an air-conditioner. Facilities range from not so great to quite reasonable value, with prices averaging from US$25 to US$100 per person.

At the top end of the spectrum, there's an array of fine hotels and lodges with all the amenities you would expect at this price level (from US$100 or more per person per night). Especially on the safari circuits there are some

---

> **SLEEPING PRICE RANGES**
>
> The following price ranges refer to a standard double room.
>
> **$** less than US$50
>
> **$$** US$50–200
>
> **$$$** more than US$200
>
> ➡ Except for low-budget local guesthouses (where you get a room only), prices include bathroom and continental breakfast (coffee/tea, bread, jam and sometimes an egg). For midrange and top-end hotels, full breakfast is usually included.
>
> ➡ Many lodges and luxury camps around the parks quote all-inclusive prices, which means accommodation and full board plus excursions such as wildlife drives, short guided walks or boat safaris. Park entry fees are generally excluded.
>
> ➡ All rooms come with mosquito nets, except as noted.

---

wonderful and very luxurious lodges costing from US$150 to US$500 or more per person per night, although at the high end of the spectrum, prices are usually all-inclusive. Some park lodges offer discounted drive-in rates for those arriving with their own vehicles.

Tented Camps & Fly Camps

TENTED CAMPS

'Permanent tented camps' or 'luxury tented camps' stay in the same place from season to season. They offer comfortable beds in spacious canvas tents, with screened windows and most of the comforts of a hotel room, but with a wilderness feel. Most such tents also have private bathrooms with hot running water, as well as generator-provided electricity for at least part of the evening.

FLY CAMPS

'Mobile' or 'fly' camps are temporary camps set up for one or several nights, or perhaps just for one season. In the Tanzanian context, fly camps are used for walking safaris away from the main tented camp or lodge, or to offer the chance for a closer,

---

more intimate bush experience. Although fly camps are more rugged than permanent luxury tented camps (ie they may not have running water or similar features), they fully cater to their guests, including with bush-style showers (where an elevated bag or drum is filled with solar-heated water). They are also usually more expensive than regular tented camps or lodges, since provisions must be carried to the site.

Climate

Tanzania has a generally comfortable, tropical climate year-round, although there are significant regional variations. Along the warmer and humid coast, the climate is determined in large part by the monsoon winds, which bring rains in two major periods. During the *masika* (long rains), from mid-March to May, it rains heavily almost every day, although seldom for the whole day, and the air can get unpleasantly sticky. The lighter *mvuli* (short rains) fall during November, December and sometimes into January. Inland, altitude is a major determinant of conditions; you'll need a jacket early morning and evening, especially in highland areas.

Customs Regulations

Exporting seashells, coral, ivory and turtle shells is illegal. You can export a maximum of Tsh160,000 without a permit. There's no limit on the importation or exportation of foreign currency, but amounts over US$10,000 must be declared.

Discount Cards

A student ID gets you a 50% discount on train fares, and often on museum entry fees.

Electricity

220-250V/50Hz

Embassies & Consulates

Embassies and consulates in Dar es Salaam include the following. Most are open from 8.30am to 3pm Monday to Friday, often with a midday break. Visa applications for all countries neighbouring

Tanzania should be made in the morning.

British High Commission (Map p56; ☎022-229 0000; http://ukintanzania.fco.gov.uk; Umoja House, cnr Mirambo St & Garden Ave)

Burundian Embassy (Map p54; ☎022-212 7008; Lugalo St, Upanga) Just up from the Italian Embassy, opposite the army compound and near Palm Beach Hotel. One-month single-entry visas cost US$90 plus one photo. The consulate in Kigoma also issues single- and multiple-entry visas.

Canadian High Commission (Map p56; ☎022-216 3300; www.canadainternational.gc.ca/tanzania-tanzanie/index.aspx; Umoja House, cnr Mirambo St & Garden Ave)

Democratic Republic of the Congo Embassy (Formerly Zaïre) (Map p54; 435 Maliki Rd, Upanga) Visas are only issued to Tanzania residents. Any Congolese visa issued in Tanzania will not be honoured on entry in the DRC unless you have a Tanzania residence permit.

French Embassy (Map p54; ☎022-219 8800; www.ambafrance-tz.org; 7 Ali Hassan Mwinyi Rd)

German Embassy (Map p56; ☎022-211 7409-15; www.daressalaam.diplo.de; Umoja House, cnr Mirambo St & Garden Ave)

Indian High Commission (Map p54; ☎022-266 9040; www.hcindiatz.org; 82 Kinondoni Rd)

Irish Embassy (Map p54; ☎022-260 0629, 022-260 2355; www.embassyofireland.or.tz; 353 Toure Dr) Diagonally opposite Golden Tulip Hotel.

Italian Embassy (Map p54; ☎022-211 5935; www.ambdaressalaam.esteri.it; 316 Lugalo St, Upanga)

Kenyan High Commission (Map p54; ☎022-266 8285/6; www.kenyahighcomtz.org; cnr Ali Hassan Mwinyi Rd & Kaunda Dr, Oyster Bay)

Malawian High Commission (Map p56; ☎022-277 4308, 022-277 4220; mmhcr dar@yahoo.co.uk; Rose Garden Rd, Mikocheni B) Many nationalities, including USA, UK and various European countries, do not require visas.

Mozambique High Commission (Map p56; ☎022-212 4673; 25 Garden Ave) One-month single-entry visas cost US$50 plus two photos, and are issued within five days (US$100 for 24-hour service).

Netherlands Embassy (Map p56; ☎022-211 0000; http://tanzania.nlembassy.org; Umoja House, cnr Mirambo St & Garden Ave)

Rwandan Embassy (Map p54; ☎0754 787835, 022-260 0500; www.tanzania.embassy.gov.rw; 32 Ali Hassan Mwinyi Rd) Three-month single-entry visas cost US$50 plus two photos, and are issued within four days. Citizens of the USA, Germany, South Africa, Canada and various other countries do not require visas.

Ugandan Embassy (Map p54; ☎022-266 7391; info@ughc.co.tz; 25 Msasani Rd) One-month single-entry visas cost US$50 plus two photos and are issued within 24 hours. Located opposite Oyster Bay Secondary School.

US Embassy (Map p54; ☎022-229 4000; http://tanzania.usembassy.gov; Old Bagamoyo & Kawawa Rds)

Zambian High Commission (Map p56; ☎022-212 5529; ground fl, Zambia House, cnr Ohio St & Sokoine Dr) One-month single-entry visas cost US$50 plus two photos, and are issued within two days.

Food

For information on Tanzanian cuisine, see p359.

Gay & Lesbian Travellers

Homosexuality is officially illegal in Tanzania, including

WAYS TO SAVE MONEY WHILE TRAVELLING

⇒ Travel in the low season, and always ask about discounted room and safari prices.

⇒ Families: ask about children's discounts at parks and hotels.

⇒ Travel in a group (four is ideal) for organised treks and safaris.

⇒ Watch for last-minute deals.

⇒ Stay outside park boundaries at those parks and reserves where you can do wildlife excursions in border areas.

⇒ Enter parks around midday: as fees are calculated on a 24-hour basis, you'll be able to enjoy prime evening and morning wildlife viewing hours for just one day's payment.

⇒ Camp when possible.

⇒ Focus on easily accessed parks and reserves to minimise transportation costs.

⇒ Use public transport where possible.

⇒ Do Cultural Tourism Programs rather than wildlife safaris.

⇒ Eat local food.

⇒ Stock up on food and drink in major towns to avoid expensive hotel fare and pricey tourist-area shops.

⇒ Focus on off-the-beaten-track areas, where prices are usually considerably lower than in the northern safari circuit.

Zanzibar, incurring penalties of up to 14 years imprisonment. Prosecutions are rare, but public displays of affection, whether between people of the same or opposite sex, are frowned upon, and homosexuality is culturally taboo.

Insurance

Travel insurance covering theft, loss and medical problems is highly recommended. Some tips:

⇒ Before choosing a policy, shop around; those designed for short package tours in Europe may not be suitable for the wilds of Tanzania.

⇒ Read the fine print, as some policies specifically exclude 'dangerous activities', which can mean scuba diving, motorcycling and even trekking. A locally acquired motorcycle licence isn't valid under some policies.

⇒ Most policies for Tanzania require you to pay on the spot and claim later, so keep all documentation.

⇒ Most importantly, check that the policy covers an emergency flight home. Before heading to Tanzania, also consider taking out a membership with one of the following, both of which operate 24-hour air ambulance services and offer emergency medical evacuation within Tanzania:

⇒ **African Medical & Research Foundation Flying Doctors** (Amref; www.flydoc.org) East Africa memberships available from US$16 per person per month.

⇒ **First Air Responder** (www.firstairresponder.com) East Africa memberships from US$10 per week.

Worldwide travel insurance is available at www.lonelyplanet.com/travel-insurance. You can buy, extend and claim online anytime, even if you're already on the road.

Internet Access

There are many internet cafes in Dar es Salaam, Arusha and Zanzibar, and even smaller towns often have a connection. Prices average Tsh1000 to Tsh2000 per hour. Speed varies greatly; truly fast connections are rare. Most business-class hotels and cafes and some safari lodges have wireless access points, although these can be expensive (from Tsh5000 per hour up

EATING PRICE RANGES

The following price ranges refer to a standard single-course meal with beverage:

$ less than Tsh10,000

$$ Tsh10,000–20,000

$$$ more than Tsh20,000

PRACTICALITIES

➡ **Newspapers** Dailies include the *Guardian* and *Daily News*; *East African* is a weekly.

➡ **Radio** Radio Tanzania (government-aligned); BBC World Service; Deutsche Welle.

➡ **Weights & Measures** Tanzania uses the metric system.

to Tsh15,000 per day for some safari lodge satellite connections. Connections are possible at some, but not all, safari camps. If you will be in Tanzania for a while, consider buying a USB stick from one of the main mobile providers (US$30 to US$75), which you can then load with airtime and plug into your laptop. Various packages are available, averaging about Tsh7000 to Tsh15,000 for 1GB, valid for seven days.

Language Courses

Tanzania is the best place in East Africa to learn Swahili. Some schools can arrange homestays.

ELCT Language & Orientation School (www.study swahili.com; Lutheran Junior Seminary, Morogoro) This is a well-respected mission-run language school on the outskirts of Morogoro town.

Institute of Swahili & Foreign Languages (Map p84; 024-223 0724, 024-223 3337; www.suza.ac.tz; Vuga Rd; per hour/week US$10/200) Zanzibar is regarded as the home of Swahili, making this a great place to take some lessons. Experienced teachers and structured courses are offered by the institute along with homestay hook-ups (full board US$20 per person per night) and cultural excursions accompanied by a teacher. Discounts apply to group lessons.

KIU Ltd (0754 271263; www.swahilicourses.com) At various locations in Dar es Salaam, plus branches in Iringa and Zanzibar.

Makoko Language School (028-264 2518; swahili musoma@juasun.net) This long-standing church-run school is in Makoko neighbourhood, on the outskirts of Musoma.

Meeting Point Tanga (www.meetingpointtanga.net) Just south of Tanga.

MS Training Centre for Development Cooperation (0754 651715, 027-254 1044; www.mstcdc.or.tz) About 15km outside Arusha, near Usa River.

Rivervalley Campsite (026-270 1988; www.rivervalleycampsites.com) Near Iringa.

Legal Matters

➡ Apart from traffic offences such as speeding and driving without a seatbelt (mandatory for driver and front-seat passengers), the main area to watch out for is drug use and possession. Marijuana (*bangi* or *ganja*) is readily available in some areas and is frequently offered to tourists on the street in places like Zanzibar and Dar es Salaam, almost always as part of a set-up involving the police or fake police. If you're caught, expect to pay a large bribe to avoid arrest or imprisonment.

➡ In Dar es Salaam, the typical scam is that you'll be approached by a couple of men who walk along with you, strike up a conversation and try to sell you drugs. Before you've had a chance to shake them loose, policemen (sometimes legitimate, sometimes not) suddenly appear and insist that you pay a huge

fine for being involved in the purchase of illegal drugs. Protestations to the contrary are generally futile and there's often little you can do other than instantly hightailing it in the opposite direction if you smell this scam coming. If you are caught, insist on going to the nearest police station before paying anything and whittle the bribe down as far as you can. Initial demands may be as high as US$300, but savvy travellers should be able to get away with under US$50.

Maps

➡ Good country maps include those published by Nelles and Harms-ic, both available in Tanzania and elsewhere, and both also including Rwanda and Burundi. Harms-ic also publishes maps for Lake Manyara National Park, the Ngorongoro Conservation Area and Zanzibar.

➡ The **Surveys and Mapping Division's Map Sales Office** (Map p56; cnr Kivukoni Front & Luthuli St; ⏰8am-2pm Mon-Fri) in Dar es Salaam sells dated topographical maps (1:50,000) for mainland Tanzania. Topographical maps for Zanzibar and Pemba are available in Stone Town.

➡ Hand-drawn 'MaCo' maps cover Zanzibar, Arusha and the northern parks. They're sold in bookshops in Dar es Salaam, Arusha and Zanzibar Town.

Money

The money situation in Tanzania at a glance:

➡ Tanzania's currency is the Tanzanian shilling (Tsh). There are bills of Tsh10,000, 5000, 1000 and 500, and coins of Tsh200, 100, 50, 20, 10, five and one shilling(s) (the latter three coins are rarely encountered).

➡ Bill design has recently been changed for all amounts, with both the old and new styles currently accepted and in circulation.

➡ A Visa or MasterCard is essential for accessing money from ATMs and for paying entry fees at most national parks.

➡ Credit cards are not widely accepted for hotel payment. Where they are accepted, it's often only with commissions. As a result, you will need to rely heavily on cash and ATMs.

➡ US dollar bills dated prior to 2006 are not accepted anywhere.

ATMs

ATMs are widespread in major towns, and all are open 24 hours. But they are often temporarily out of service or out of cash, so have back-up funds. All internationally linked machines allow you to withdraw shillings with a Visa or MasterCard. Withdrawals are usually to a maximum of Tsh300,000 or Tsh400,000 per transaction (ATMs in small towns often have a limit of Tsh200,000 per transaction) and with a daily limit of Tsh1.2 million (less in small towns). Some machines also accept other cards linked to the Cirrus/Maestro/Plus networks.

The main operators:

Barclays Dar es Salaam, Arusha, Moshi, Zanzibar, Tanga

CRDB Major towns

Exim Arusha, Moshi, Mwanza, Tanga, Dar es Salaam, Morogoro

National Bank of Commerce Major towns

Stanbic Dar es Salaam, Arusha, Moshi, Mbeya

Standard Chartered Dar es Salaam, Arusha, Moshi, Mwanza

In large cities, lines at ATM machines on Friday afternoons are notoriously long; take care of your banking before then.

If your ATM withdrawal request is rejected (no matter what reason the machine gives), it could be for something as simple as requesting above the allowed transaction amount for that particular machine; it's always worth trying again. Entering your PIN number erroneously three times results in a captured card.

Black Market

There's essentially no black market for foreign currency. You can assume that the frequent offers you'll receive on the street to change at high rates are a set-up.

Cash

US dollars, followed by euros, are the most convenient foreign currencies and get the best rates, although other major currencies are readily accepted in major centres. Bring a mix of large and small denominations, but note that US$50 and US$100 bills get better rates of exchange than smaller denominations. Old-style (small head) US bills and US bills dated prior to 2006 are not accepted anywhere.

Credit Cards

Bring a Visa card or MasterCard. These are essential for withdrawing money at ATMs; Visa is most widely accepted. A Visa or MasterCard is also required for paying park fees at most national parks. Some upmarket hotels and tour operators accept credit cards for payment, often with a commission averaging from 5% to 10%. However, many don't; always confirm in advance.

Exchanging Money

➡ Change cash at banks or foreign exchange (forex) bureaus in major towns and cities; rates and commissions vary, so shop around.

➡ Forex bureaus are usually quicker, less bureaucratic and open longer hours than banks, although most smaller towns don't have them. They also tend to accept a wider range of currencies than banks.

➡ The most useful bank for foreign exchange is NBC, with branches throughout the country. Countrywide, banks and forex bureaus are closed from noon on

TO BARGAIN OR NOT...

Bargaining is expected by vendors in tourist areas, particularly souvenir vendors, except in a limited number of fixed-price shops. However, at markets and non-tourist venues, the price quoted to you will often be the 'real' price, so in these situations don't immediately assume that the quote you've been given is too high.

There are no set rules, other than that bargaining should always be conducted in a friendly and spirited manner. Before starting, shop around to get a feel for the 'value' of the item you want. Asking others what they have paid can be helpful. Once you start negotiating, if things seem like a waste of time, politely take your leave. Sometimes sellers will call you back if they think their stubbornness has been counterproductive. Very few will pass up the chance of making a sale, however thin the profit. If the vendor won't come down to a price you feel is fair, it means that they aren't making a profit, or that too many high-rolling foreigners have passed through already.

Saturday until Monday morning.

➡ To reconvert Tanzanian shillings to hard currency, save at least some of your exchange receipts, although they are seldom checked. The easiest places to reconvert currency are at the airports in Dar es Salaam and Kilimanjaro, or try at forex shops or banks in major towns.

➡ For after-hours exchange and exchanging in small towns, as well as for reconverting back to dollars or euros, many Indian-owned businesses will change money, although often at bad rates.

➡ In theory, it's required that foreigners pay for accommodation, park fees, organised tours, upscale hotels and the Zanzibar ferries in US dollars, although (with the exception of some parks, where credit card or US dollars are required) shillings are accepted almost everywhere at the going rate.

Taxes

Tanzania has an 18% value-added tax (VAT) that's usually included in quoted prices.

Tipping

➡ Tipping is generally not practised in small, local establishments, especially in rural areas. In major towns and in places frequented by tourists, tips are expected.

➡ Some top-end places include a service charge in the bill. Usually, however, either rounding out the bill or adding from about 10% to 15% is standard practice, assuming that the service warrants it.

➡ On treks and safaris, it's common practice to tip drivers, guides, porters and other staff.

Travellers Cheques

Travellers cheques can no longer be changed anywhere in Tanzania.

Opening Hours

Opening hours are generally as follows.

Banks and Government Offices 8am to 3pm Monday to Friday

Restaurants 7am to 9am, noon to 2.30pm and 6.30pm to 9.30pm; reduced hours low season

Shops 8.30am to 6pm Monday to Friday, 9am to 1pm Saturday, often closed Friday afternoon for mosque services

Supermarkets 9am to 6pm Monday to Friday, 9am to 4pm Saturday, 10am to 2pm Sunday

Photography

➡ Always ask permission first before photographing people and always respect their wishes. In many places, locals will ask for a fee (usually from Tsh1000 to Tsh5000 and up) before allowing you to photograph them, which is fair enough.

➡ Don't take photos of anything connected with the government and the military, including army barracks, and landscapes and people anywhere close to army barracks. Government offices, post offices, banks, ports, train stations and airports are also officially off limits.

Post

Post is reasonably reliable for letters, but don't send items of value. Sending packages is at your own risk. We've known many success stories of travellers mailing their curios home, but have also heard of packages going missing.

Public Holidays

New Year's Day 1 January

Zanzibar Revolution Day 12 January

Easter March/April – Good Friday, Holy Saturday and Easter Monday

Union Day 26 April

Labour Day 1 May

Saba Saba (Peasants' Day) 7 July

Nane Nane (Farmers' Day) 8 August

Independence Day 9 December

Christmas Day 25 December

Boxing Day 26 December

The dates of Islamic holidays depend on the moon and are known for certain only a few days in advance. They fall about 11 days earlier each year and include the following:

ISLAMIC HOLIDAYS

Following are approximate dates for celebration of Islamic holidays in Tanzania.

Event	2015	2016	2017
Ramadan begins	18 June	6 June	27 May
Eid al-Fitr (end of Ramadan, two-day holiday)	17 July	5 July	25 June
Eid al-Kebir (Eid al-Haji)	23 Sep	11 Sep	1 Sep
Eid al-Moulid	21 Dec	11 Dec	1 Dec

Eid al-Kebir (Eid al-Hajj) Commemorates the moment when Abraham was about to sacrifice his son in obedience to God's command, only to have God intercede at the last moment and substitute a ram. It coincides with the end of the pilgrimage (hajj) to Mecca.

Eid al-Fitr The end of Ramadan, and East Africa's most important Islamic celebration; celebrated as a two-day holiday in many areas.

Eid al-Moulid (Maulidi) Birthday of the Prophet Mohammed.

Ramadan The annual 30-day fast when adherents do not eat or drink from sunrise to sunset. Although Ramadan is not a public holiday, restaurants are often closed during this time on Zanzibar and in other coastal areas.

Safe Travel

Tanzania is in general a safe, hassle-free country and can be a relief if you've recently been somewhere like Nairobi (Kenya). That said, you do need to take the usual precautions and keep up with government travel advisories.

➡ Avoid isolated areas, especially isolated stretches of beach.

➡ In cities and tourist areas take a taxi at night.

➡ Only take taxis from established taxi ranks or hotels. Never enter a taxi that already has someone else in it other than the driver.

➡ When using public transport, don't accept drinks or food from someone you don't know.

➡ Be sceptical of anyone who comes up to you on the street asking whether you remember them from the airport, your hotel or wherever.

➡ Be very wary of anyone who approaches you on the street, at the bus station or in your hotel offering safari deals or claiming to know you.

GOVERNMENT TRAVEL ADVISORIES

Government travel advisories can be good sources of updated security information:

Australia www.smarttraveller.gov.au

Canada www.travel.gc.ca

UK www.gov.uk/government/organisations/foreign-commonwealth-office

US www.travel.state.gov

➡ Never pay any money for a safari or trek in advance until you've thoroughly checked out the company, and never pay any money at all outside the company's office.

➡ In western Tanzania, especially along the Burundi border, there are sporadic outbursts of banditry and political unrest. Things are currently quiet, with better roads and armed guards on buses, but it's worth getting an update locally.

In tourist areas, especially Arusha, Moshi and Zanzibar, touts and flycatchers can be quite pushy, especially around bus stations and budget tourist hotels. Do everything you can to minimise the impression that you're a newly arrived tourist:

➡ Walk with purpose. Duck into a shop if you need to get your bearings or look at a map.

➡ Don't walk around any more than necessary with your luggage.

➡ While looking for a room, leave your bag with a friend or reliable hotel rather than walking around town with it.

➡ Buy your bus tickets a day in advance (without your luggage).

➡ When arriving in a new city, take a taxi from the bus station to your hotel, rather than walking.
A few more tips:

➡ Avoid external money pouches, dangling backpacks and camera bags, and be discreet with jewellery, fancy watches or phones and the like. Carry your passport, money and other documents in a pouch against your skin, hidden under loose-fitting clothing. Or, better, store valuables in a hotel safe, if there's a reliable one, ideally inside a pouch with a lockable zip to prevent tampering.

➡ Arriving for the first time at major bus stations can be a fairly traumatic experience, as you'll probably be besieged by touts as you get off the bus, all reaching to help you with your pack and trying to sell you a safari. Have your luggage as consolidated as possible, with your valuables well hidden under your clothes. Try to spot the taxi area before disembarking and make a beeline for it. It's well worth a few extra dollars for the fare, rather than attempting to walk to your hotel with your luggage.

➡ Take requests for donations from 'refugees', 'students' or others with a grain of salt. Contributions to humanitarian causes are best done through an established agency or project.

➡ Keep the side windows up in vehicles when stopped in traffic and keep your bags out of sight (eg on the floor behind your legs).

➡ When bargaining or discussing prices, don't do so with your money or wallet in your hand.

Telephone

The fast-fading Tanzania Telecom (TTCL) usually has its offices at the post office. TTCL ('land line') numbers are seven digits, preceded by a three-digit mandatory area code.

Mobile Phones

The mobile network covers major towns throughout the country, plus most rural areas, though signal availability can be erratic. Mobile phone numbers are six digits, preceded by 07XX or 06XX; the major companies are currently Vodacom, Airtel, Tigo and (on Zanzibar) Zantel. To reach a mobile telephone number from outside Tanzania, dial the country code, then the mobile phone code without the initial 0, and then the six-digit number. From within Tanzania, keep the initial 0 and don't use any other area code. Dialling from your own mobile is generally the cheapest way to call internationally.

All the companies sell pre-paid starter packages for about US$1.50, and top-up cards are widely available at shops throughout the country.

Phone Codes

Tanzania's country code is ☏255. To make an international call, dial ☏000, followed by the country code, local area code (without the initial '0') and telephone number.

Time

Tanzania time is GMT/UTC plus three hours. There is no daylight saving.

Toilets

Toilets vary from standard long-drops to full-flush luxury conveniences. Most non-budget hotels sport flushable sit-down types. Budget guesthouses often have squat-style toilets, sometimes equipped with a flush mechanism, otherwise with a scoop and a bucket of water for flushing things down. Paper (you'll often need to supply your own) should be deposited in the can that's usually in the corner.

Many upmarket bush camps have 'dry' toilets – a fancy version of the long drop with a Western-style seat perched on top.

Tourist Information

The **Tanzania Tourist Board** (TTB; www.tanzania-touristboard.com) is the official tourism entity.

Travellers with Disabilities

While there are few facilities for the disabled, Tanzanians are generally quite accommodating and willing to offer whatever assistance they can. Some considerations:

➤ A small number of lodges have wheelchair accessible rooms. But, few hotels have lifts (elevators) and many have narrow stairwells, especially in Stone Town on Zanzibar, where stairwells are often steep and narrow. Grips or railings in the bathrooms are rare.

➤ Many park lodges and camps are built on ground level. However, in an attempt to maintain a natural environment, access paths are sometimes rough or rocky, and rooms or tents raised. Inquire about access before booking.

➤ As far as we know, there are no Braille signboards at any parks or museums, nor any facilities for deaf travellers.

➤ Minibuses are widely available on Zanzibar and on the mainland and can be chartered for transport and for customised safaris. Large or wide-door vehicles can also be arranged through car-rental agencies in Dar es Salaam and with Arusha-based tour operators. Taxis countrywide are usually small sedans and buses are not wheelchair equipped. Lonely Planet's **Travel for All** community on Google+ is a helpful initial contact. Other contacts:

Accessible Journeys (www.disabilitytravel.com)

Access-Able Travel (www.access-able.com)

Disability Horizons (www.disabilityhorizons.com)

Mobility International (www.miusa.org)

Naenda Safaris (☏0756 038703; www.naendasafaris.com) Northern circuit safaris for travellers with disabilities.

National Information Communication Awareness Network (www.nican.com.au)

Tourism for All (www.tourismforall.org.uk)

SWAHILI TIME

Tanzanians use the Swahili system of telling time, in which the first hour is *saa moja (asubuhi)*, corresponding with 7am. Counting begins again with *saa moja (jioni)* (the first hour, evening, corresponding with 7pm). Although most will switch to the international clock when speaking English with foreigners, confusion sometimes occurs, so ask people to confirm whether they are using *saa za kizungu* (international time) or *saa za kiswahili* (Swahili time). Signboards with opening hours are often posted in Swahili time.

Visas

Almost everyone needs a visa, which costs US$50 for most nationalities (US$100 for citizens of the USA) for a single-entry visa valid for up to three months. Officially, visas must be obtained in advance by all travellers who come from a country with Tanzania diplomatic representation. One-month single-entry visas (but not multiple-entry visas) are also currently issued on arrival (no matter your provenance) at both Dar es Salaam and Kilimanjaro International Airports, at the Namanga border post between Tanzania and Kenya, and at Tunduma border (between Tanzania and Zambia). This is the situation in theory. In practice, visas are currently also readily issued at most other major land borders and ports (US dollars cash only, single-entry only) with a minimum of hassle. Our advice: get your visa in advance if possible. If not possible, don't despair; it's well worth giving it a try at the border.

Visa Extensions

One month is the normal visa validity and three months the maximum. For extensions within the three-month limit, there are immigration offices in all major towns; the process is free and generally straightforward. Extensions after three months are difficult; you usually need to leave the country and apply for a new visa.

Volunteering

Volunteering opportunities (generally teaching, or in environmental or health work) are usually best arranged prior to arriving in Tanzania. Note that the Tanzanian government has recently changed the cost of volunteer (Class C) resident permits to US$200 for three months. Some places to start include the following:

Frontier (www.frontier.ac.uk) Marine conservation work on Mafia island.

Indigenous Education Foundation of Tanzania (www.ieftz.org) Education work in Maasai areas of northern Tanzania.

Kigamboni Community Centre (www.kccdar.com) Teaching and other opportunities in a rural community on the outskirts of Dar es Salaam.

Peace Corps (www.peacecorps.gov) USA voluntary organisation.

Responsible Travel.com (www.responsibletravel.com) Matches you up with ecologically and culturally responsible tour operators to plan an itinerary.

Trade Aid (www.tradeaiduk.org/volunteer.html) Skills training work in Mikindani village in southern Tanzania.

Ujamaa Hostel (www.ujamaahostel.com) Tutoring, skills training and health work in and around Arusha.

Voluntary Service Overseas (VSO; www.vso.org.uk) British voluntary organisation.

EAST AFRICA TOURIST VISA

In November 2014 Tanzania announced its intention to join the East Africa Tourist Visa (EATV), but did not set a timeline on its entry. The scheme, started in early 2014 by the governments of Kenya, Uganda and Rwanda, allows visitors to purchase a 90-day, multiple-entry visa that covers travel in and out of these three countries for a single fee of US$100.

Check the latest before your departure. If Tanzania is now part of the scheme, the EATV should be available upon arrival at major airports and land crossings. It can also be applied for in advance, though your first port-of-call must be the country through which you applied for the visa.

For more information and links to online application forms, visit www.visiteastafrica.org/visa/.

Women Travellers

Women travellers are not likely to encounter many specifically gender-related problems. More often than not, you will meet only warmth, hospitality and sisterly regard, and find that you receive special treatment that you probably wouldn't be shown if you were a male traveller. That said, you'll inevitably attract some attention, especially if you're travelling alone, and there are some areas where caution is essential. A few tips:

➡ Dress modestly: trousers or a long skirt, and a conservative top with sleeves. Tucking your hair under a cap or scarf, or tying it back, also helps.

➡ Wearing sunglasses can help minimise hassles, as it's hard for hustlers to gauge your reactions and their level of success when they can't make eye contact. That said, keep in mind that wearing sunglasses when trying to chat or make friends with locals can be perceived as rude.

➡ Use common sense, trust your instincts and take the usual precautions when out and about. Avoid walking alone at night. Avoid isolated

SOLO TRAVEL IN TANZANIA

While solo travellers may be a minor curiosity in rural areas, especially solo women travellers, there are no particular problems with travelling solo in Tanzania, whether you're male or female. The times when it's advantageous to join a group are for safaris and treks (when going in a group can be a significant cost-saver) and when going out at night. If you go out alone at night, take taxis and use extra caution, especially in urban and tourist areas. Whatever the time of day, avoid isolating situations, including lonely stretches of beach.

areas at any time and be particularly cautious on beaches, many of which can become quickly deserted.

➡ If you find yourself with an unwanted suitor, creative approaches are usually effective. For example, explain that your husband (real or fictitious) or a large group of friends will be arriving imminently at that very place. Similar tactics are also usually effective in dealing with the inevitable curiosity that you'll meet as to why you might not have children and a husband, or if you do have them, why they aren't with you. The easiest response to the question of why you aren't married is to explain that you are still young (bado kijana), which whether you are or not will at least have some

humour value. Just saying bado ('not yet') to questions about marriage or children should also do the trick. As for why your family isn't currently with you, you can always explain that you'll be meeting them later.

➡ Seek out local women, as this can enrich your trip tremendously. Places to try include tourist offices, government departments or even your hotel, where at least some of the staff are likely to be formally educated young to middle-aged women. In rural areas, starting points include women teachers at a local school, or staff at a health centre.

On a practical level, while tampons and the like are available in major cities,

women will likely come to appreciate the benefits of Western-style consumer testing when using local sanitary products.

Work

Unemployment is high, and unless you have unique skills, the chances of lining up something are small.

➡ The most likely areas for employment are the safari industry, tourism, dive masters and teaching; in all areas, competition is stiff and the pay is low.

➡ The best way to land something is to get to know someone already working in the business. Also check safari operator and lodge websites, some of which advertise vacant positions.

➡ Work and residency permits should be arranged through the potential employer or sponsoring organisation; residency permits normally need to be applied for from outside Tanzania. Be prepared for lots of bureaucracy.

➡ Most teaching positions are voluntary and best arranged through voluntary agencies or mission organisations at home.

Transport

GETTING THERE & AWAY

Flights, cars and tours can be booked online at www.lonely planet.com/bookings.

Entering the Country

➡ Provided you have a visa, Tanzania is straightforward to enter.

➡ Yellow fever vaccination is required if you are arriving from an endemic area (which includes many of Tanzania's neighbours).

Air

Airports

Julius Nyerere International Airport (DAR; Map p72; ☎022-284 2402; www.taa. go.tz) Dar es Salaam; Tanzania's air hub.

Kilimanjaro International Airport (JRO; ☎027-255

4707, 027-255 4252; www.kili manjaroairport.co.tz) Between Arusha and Moshi, and the best option for itineraries in Arusha and the northern safari circuit. Note: not to be confused with the smaller Arusha Airport (ARK), 8km west of Arusha, which handles domestic flights only.

Other airports handling international or regional flights:

Kigoma Airport (TKQ) Occasional regional flights.

Mtwara Airport (MYW) Regional flights.

Mwanza Airport (MWZ) Regional flights.

Songwe Airport Regional flights.

Zanzibar International Airport (ZNZ) International and regional flights.

Airlines

Regional and international carriers include the following (all servicing Dar es Salaam, except as noted):

Air Kenya (www.airkenya.com) Nairobi to Kilimanjaro International Airport (KIA)

Air Tanzania (www.airtanzania. co.tz) Bujumbura (Burundi) to Dar es Salaam

Air Uganda (www.air-uganda. com) Entebbe (Uganda) to KIA and Dar es Salaam

Auric Air (www.auricair.com) Mwanza and Bukoba to Entebbe (Uganda)

British Airways (www.british airways.com)

Egyptair (www.egyptair.com)

Emirates Airlines (www. emirates.com)

Ethiopian Airlines (www.ethiop ianairlines.com) Also KIA

Fastjet (www.fastjet.com) Johannesburg (South Africa) to Dar es Salaam

Fly540.com (www.fly540.com) Nairobi (Kenya) to Zanzibar

Kenya Airways (www.kenya-airways.com)

KLM (www.klm.com) Also KIA

CLIMATE CHANGE & TRAVEL

Every form of transport that relies on carbon-based fuel generates CO_2, the main cause of human-induced climate change. Modern travel is dependent on aeroplanes, which might use less fuel per kilometre per person than most cars but travel much greater distances. The altitude at which aircraft emit gases (including CO_2) and particles also contributes to their climate change impact. Many websites offer 'carbon calculators' that allow people to estimate the carbon emissions generated by their journey and, for those who wish to do so, to offset the impact of the greenhouse gases emitted with contributions to portfolios of climate-friendly initiatives throughout the world. Lonely Planet offsets the carbon footprint of all staff and author travel.

Linhas Aéreas de Moçambique (www.lam.co.mz)

Precision Air (www.precision airtz.com) Dar es Salaam to Entebbe (Uganda), Kigali (Rwanda), Nairobi (Kenya), Pemba (Mozambique), Lubumbashi (DRC) and Lusaka (Zambia); also Mwanza and KIA to Nairobi.

Qatar Airways (www.qatarairways.com) Also KIA

South African Airways (www.flysaa.com)

Swiss International Airlines (www.swiss.com)

Turkish Airlines (www.turkishairlines.com) Also KIA

ZanAir (www.zanair.com) Mombasa to Arusha Airport

Land

Bus

➡ Buses cross Tanzania's borders with Kenya, Uganda, Rwanda, Burundi and Zambia. At the border, you'll need to disembark on each side to take care of visa formalities, then reboard and continue on. Visa fees aren't included in bus ticket prices for trans-border routes.

➡ For crossings with other countries, you'll need to take one vehicle to the border and board a different vehicle on the other side.

Car & Motorcycle

To enter Tanzania with your own vehicle you'll need:

➡ the vehicle's registration papers

➡ your driving licence

➡ temporary import permit (Tsh20,000 for one month, purchased at the border) or a *carnet de passage en douane*, which acts as a temporary waiver of import duty. The *carnet* (arranged in advance through your local automobile association) should also specify any expensive spare parts that you are carrying.

➡ third-party insurance (Tsh50,000 for one year, purchased at the border

or at the local insurance headquarters in the nearest large town)

➡ one-time fuel levy (Tsh5000)

Most rental companies don't permit their vehicles to cross international borders; if you find one that does, arrange the necessary paperwork with it in advance.

Most border posts don't have petrol stations or repair shops; you'll need to head to the nearest large town.

Burundi
BORDER CROSSINGS

The main crossings are at Kobero Bridge between Ngara (Tanzania) and Muyinga (Burundi); and, at Manyovu (north of Kigoma).

BUS

For Kobero Bridge: from Mwanza, Zuberly and Nyehunge lines have buses daily at 5.30am to Ngara (Tsh17,000, seven to eight hours). Also, shared taxis run all day from Nyakanazi to Ngara (Tsh9500, two hours). Once in Ngara, there is onward transport to the Tanzanian border post at Kabanga.

For Manyovu: Hamza Transport and Burugo Travel (both with ticket offices at Kigoma's Bero bus stand) have direct service between Kigoma and Bujumbura (Burundi; Tsh15,000, seven hours) at 7am several times weekly. Otherwise, take a dalla-dalla (minibus) from Kigoma to Manyovu (Tsh5000, one to two hours), walk through immigration and find onward transport. There's always something going to Mabanda (Burundi), where you can find minibuses to Bujumbura, three to four hours away.

Kenya
BORDER CROSSINGS

The main route to/from Kenya is the good sealed road connecting Arusha (Tanzania) and Nairobi (Kenya) via

Namanga border post (open 24 hours). There are also border crossings at Horohoro (Tanzania), north of Tanga; at Holili (Tanzania), east of Moshi; at Loitokitok (Kenya), northeast of Moshi; and at Sirari (Tanzania), northeast of Musoma. With the exception of the Serengeti–Masai Mara crossing (which is currently closed), there is public transport across all Tanzania–Kenya border posts.

TO & FROM MOMBASA

Modern Coast Express (www.moderncoastexpress. com) runs daily between Dar es Salaam and Mombasa via Tanga, departing in the morning in each direction, and departing around noon from Tanga (Tsh15,000, four to five hours Tanga to Mombasa; Tsh25,000, 10 to 11 hours Dar to Mombasa). There's nowhere official to change money at the border. Touts here charge extortionate rates, and it's difficult to get rid of Kenyan shillings once in Tanga, so plan accordingly.

TO & FROM NAIROBI

BUS

Dar Express goes daily between Dar es Salaam and Nairobi (14 to 15 hours, Tsh57,000), departing about 6am in each direction. You can also board in Arusha (Tsh23,000, five hours), if seats are available. Dar Express also has Nairobi-bound buses that begin in Arusha, leaving at 2pm.

DALLA-DALLA

Comfortable nine-seater minivans (Tsh7500, two hours) and decrepit, overcrowded full-sized vans (which stop frequently along the way) go between Arusha's central bus station (they park at the northernmost end) and the Namanga border frequently throughout the day from 6am. At Namanga, you'll have to walk a few hundred metres across the border and then catch one of the frequent matatus (Kenyan minibuses) or shared taxis to Nairobi (KSh500). From Nairobi, the matatu and share-taxi depots are on Ronald Ngala St, near the River Rd junction.

SHUTTLE

The most convenient and comfortable option between Moshi or Arusha and Nairobi are the shuttle buses. They depart daily from Arusha and Nairobi at 8am and 2pm (five hours) and from Moshi (seven hours) at 6am and 11am. The non-resident rate is US$25/30 one way from Arusha/Moshi, but with a little prodding it's usually possible to get the resident price (Tsh25,000/30,000). Pick-ups and drop-offs are at their offices and centrally located hotels. Depending on the timing, they may pick you up or drop you off at Kilimanjaro International Airport. Confirm locations when booking.

Recommended companies:

Impala Shuttle (Map p156; ☏027-250 7197, 027-250 8451; Impala Hotel, Simeon Rd; per person US$25; ⏱8am & 2pm) Leaves from the car park of the Impala Hotel.

Jamii Shuttle (Map p156; off Simeon Rd; per person US$25; ⏱8am & 2pm) Departs/arrives from just off Simeon Rd in eastern Arusha.

Rainbow Shuttle (Map p156; India St; per person US$25; ⏱8am & 2pm) Booking office and departure point on India St.

TO & FROM VOI

Raqib Coach's daily 8.30am bus from Moshi to Mombasa travels via Voi (Tsh16,000, four hours). Also, dalla-dallas go frequently between Moshi and the border town of Holili (Tsh2000, one hour). At the border (6am to 8pm), you'll need to hire a piki-piki (motorbike; Tsh1000) or bicycle to cross 3km of no-man's land before arriving at the Kenyan immigration post at Taveta. From Taveta, sporadic

minibuses go to Voi along a rough road, where you can then find onward transport to Nairobi and Mombasa. If you're arriving/departing with a foreign-registered vehicle, the necessary paperwork is only done during working hours (8am to 1pm and 2pm to 5pm daily).

TO & FROM KISII

BUS

There are currently no direct buses over the border. You'll need to take one of the many daily buses between Mwanza and the Sirari–Isebania border post (Tsh12,000, five hours), and then get Kenyan transport on the other side to Kisii. Dalla-dallas also go daily from Musoma to the border (Tsh6000, one hour).

Malawi

BORDER CROSSINGS

The only crossing is at Kasumulu (Songwe River Bridge; 7am to 7pm Tanzanian time, 6am to 6pm Malawi time), which is southeast of Mbeya (Tanzania).

BUS

From Mbeya, there are daily minibuses and 30-seater buses (known as 'coastals' or thelathini) to the border (Tsh5500, two hours). Once through the Tanzanian border post, there's a 300m walk to the Malawian side, and minibuses to Karonga. There's also one Malawian bus daily from the Malawi side of the border and Mzuzu (Malawi), departing the bor-

der by mid-afternoon and arriving in Mzuzu by evening.

Some tips:

➡ Look for buses going to Kyela (these detour to the border) and verify that your vehicle is really going all the way to the border, as some that say they are actually stop at Tukuyu (40km north) or at Ibanda (7km before the border). Asking several passengers (rather than the minibus company touts) should get you the straight answer.

➡ Your chances of getting a direct vehicle are better in the larger thelathini, which depart from Mbeya two or three times daily and usually go where they say they are going.

➡ The border buses stop at the Kasumulu (Songwe River) transport stand, about a seven-minute walk from the actual border; there's no real need for the bicycle taxis that will approach you.

➡ There are currently no cross-border vehicles from Mbeya into Malawi, although touts at Mbeya bus station may try to convince you otherwise. Going in both directions, plan on overnighting in Mbeya or Tukuyu; buses from Mbeya to Dar es Salaam depart between 6am and 7am.

➡ If you get stuck at the Kasumulu border, there are basic bungalows, camping and meals at **MG Campsite Park** (☏0732 950054; malagcamp@yahoo.com; camping US$5, r US$10-20) and basic rooms (but no food) at **Lug Lodge** (☏0754

630531, 0758 913383; Main Rd; r Tsh20,000-25,000).

Mozambique
BORDER CROSSINGS

The main vehicle crossing is via Unity Bridge over the Ruvuma River at Negomano, reached via Masasi. There is also the Unity 2 bridge across the Ruvuma at Mtomoni village, 120km south of Songea. It's also possible to cross at Kilambo (south of Mtwara) via vehicle ferry. For those travelling along the coast by boat, there are immigration officials at Msimbati (Tanzania) and at Palma and Moçimboa da Praia (Mozambique). Mozambique visas are not issued anywhere along the Tanzania border, so arrange one in advance.

BUS

Buses depart daily from Mtwara between 5am and 10am to the Kilambo border post (Tsh5000, one hour) and on to the Ruvuma River, which is crossed via dugout canoe and other small boats ('fibers'; Tsh5000 to Tsh10,000, depending on your negotiating skills; 10 minutes to over an hour, depending on water levels; and dangerous during heavy rains). Note that it's common for captains on the small boats to stop mid-river and demand higher fees from foreigners. There's also the **MV Kilambo** (per person/vehicle Tsh500/30,000) ferry, which is the best option when it's running.

Once at the Mozambique side, there are usually two pick-ups daily to the Mozambique border post (4km further) and on to Moçimboa da Praia (US$13), with the last one departing by about noon. The Ruvuma crossing is notorious for pickpockets. Watch your belongings, especially when getting into and out of the boats, and keep up with the crowd when walking to/from the river bank.

Further west, one or two vehicles daily depart from Songea's Majengo C area by around 11am (Tsh12,000, three to four hours) to Mtomoni village and the Unity 2 bridge. Once across, you can get Mozambique transport on to Lichinga (Tsh25,000 to Tsh30,000, five hours). It's best to pay in stages, rather than paying the entire Tsh35,000 to Tsh40,000 Songea–Lichinga fare in Songea, as is sometimes requested. With an early departure, the entire Songea–Lichinga trip is very doable in one day via public transport.

CAR

The main vehicle crossing is via the Unity Bridge at Negomano, southwest of Kilambo, near the confluence of the Lugenda River. From Masasi, go about 35km southwest along the Tunduru road to Nangomba village, from where a 68km good-condition track leads southwest down to Masuguru village. The bridge is 10km further at Mtambaswala. On the other side, there is a decent-in-the-dry-season 160km dirt road to Mueda. There are immigration facilities on both sides of the bridge (although you will need to get your Mozambique visa in advance). Entering Tanzania, take care of customs formalities for your vehicle in Mtwara.

The Unity 2 bridge south of Songea is another option. With a private vehicle the Songea to Lichinga stretch should not take more than about eight or nine hours.

At Kilambo, the **MV Kilambo** (per person/vehicle Tsh500/30,000) ferry operates most days around high tide. Inquire at **ECO2** (☏0784 855833; www.eco2tz.com; Main Rd) or **The Old Boma** (☏0756 455978, 023-233 3875; www.mikindani.com; s US$77, r with/without balcony from US$188/120, ste US$223; P@🛜🐾🏊) 🛥 in Mikindani to confirm that the ferry is running.

Rwanda
BORDER CROSSINGS

The main crossing is at Rusumu Falls, southwest of Bukoba (Tanzania).

BUS

At the time of research, there were no direct buses to Kigali. From Mwanza, you will need to go in stages; reckon on about 12 to 14 hours and Tsh25,000 for the journey.

Uganda
BORDER CROSSINGS

The main post is at Mutukula (Tanzania), northwest of Bukoba, with good sealed roads on both sides. There's another crossing further west at Nkurungu (Tanzania), but the road is bad and sparsely travelled. From Arusha or Moshi, travel to Uganda is via Kenya.

BUS

Kampala Coach's air-con buses to Nairobi from both Dar es Salaam and Arusha continue to Kampala (Tsh105,000, 30 hours from Dar es Salaam to Kampala; Tsh66,000, 20 hours from Arusha to Kampala). The cost to Jinja is the same as Kampala.

Several companies (Friends Safari is best) leave Bukoba at 6am for Kampala (Tsh15,000 to Tsh17,000, six hours). Departures from Kampala are at 7am and usually again at 11am.

From Mwanza, there are currently no direct buses. You will need to travel in stages; allow about 16 to 18 hours for the journey.

Zambia
BORDER CROSSINGS

The main border crossing (7.30am to 6pm Tanzania time, 6.30am to 5pm Zambia time) is at Tunduma (Tanzania), southwest of Mbeya. There's also a crossing at Kasesya (Tanzania), between Sumbawanga (Tanzania) and Mbala (Zambia).

BUS

Minibuses go several times daily between Mbeya and Tunduma (Tsh3000 to Tsh4000, two hours), where you walk across the border for Zambian transport to Lusaka (about US$20, 18 hours).

The Kasesya crossing is seldom travelled, and in the rainy season the road can be extremely bad. There's no direct transport; at least one truck daily goes to the border from each side (Tsh10,000, four to five hours from Sumbawanga to Kasesya). With luck you can make the full journey in a day, but since departures from both Sumbawanga and Mbala are in the afternoon, and departures from the borders are in the early morning, you'll likely need to sleep in one of the (rough) border villages.

TRAIN

The Tazara (www.tazarasite. com) train line links Dar es Salaam with Kapiri Mposhi in Zambia twice weekly via Mbeya and Tunduma. 'Express' service departs Dar es Salaam at 3.50pm Tuesday (1st/2nd/economy class Tsh104,000/84,600/72,600, about 40 hours). Ordinary service departs Dar es Salaam at 1.50pm on Friday (Tsh86,500/70,600/60,500, about 48 hours). Delays of up to 24 hours on both express and ordinary services are the rule. Departures from Mbeya to Zambia (Tsh58,000/46,000/40,200 for express 1st/2nd/economy class) are at 1.30pm Wednesday and 2.40pm Saturday. Students with ID get a 50% discount. From Kapiri Mposhi to Lusaka, you'll need to continue by bus. Departures from New Kapiri Mposhi are at 4pm Tuesday (express) and 2pm Friday (ordinary). Visas are currently available at the border in both directions.

CAR

If driving from Zambia into Tanzania, note that vehicle insurance isn't available at the Kasesya border, but must be purchased 120km further on in Sumbawanga.

Sea & Lake

There's a US$5 port tax for travel on all boats and ferries from Tanzanian ports.

Burundi

Regular passenger ferry service between Kigoma and Bujumbura is suspended. Inquire at the passenger port in Kigoma for an update. However, it's possible to travel on cargo ships between Kigoma's Ami port and Bujumbura (Tsh10,000, 18 hours). Sailings are erratic. They average three times weekly, although expect to hear that ships are sailing 'tomorrow' for several days in a row. Lake taxis go once or twice weekly from Kibirizi (just north of Kigoma) to Bujumbura, but are not recommended as they take a full day and are occasionally robbed. However, you could use the afternoon lake taxis to Kagunga (the Tanzanian border post, where there's a simple guesthouse), cross the border in the morning, take a motorcycle-taxi to Nyanza-Lac (Burundi) and then a minibus to Bujumbura.

Democratic Republic of the Congo (DRC; formerly Zaïre)

Cargo boats go roughly once weekly from Kigoma's Ami port to Kalemie (US$10, deck class only, seven hours) or Uvira. When running, the MV *Liemba* also sometimes travels to Kalemie during its off week. Inquire at Ami port, or check with the Congolese embassy in Kigoma about sailing days and times. Bring food and drink with you, and something to spread on the deck for sleeping.

Kenya
DHOW

Dhows sail sporadically between Pemba, Tanga and Mombasa (Tsh15,000 to Tsh20,000 between Tanga and Mombasa); the journey can be long and rough, and is not recommended. Ask at the ports in Tanga, or in Mkoani or Wete on Pemba for information on sailings. In Kenya, ask at the port in Mombasa, or better, at Shimoni, and get an update from informed locals and government travel advisories about piracy-related safety issues on the seas.

FERRY

There's currently no passenger ferry service on Lake Victoria between Tanzania and Kenya, but cargo boats sail about twice weekly between Mwanza and Kisumu, occasionally stopping in Musoma. With luck, you may find a captain willing to take passengers, although most will not. Inquire at the Mwanza South port about sailings.

Malawi

There are currently no passenger ferries operating between Tanzania's Mbamba Bay and Malawi's Nkhata Bay. Cargo boats (Tsh10,000, six hours) accept passengers, but safety standards are minimal; departures are often in the middle of the night to take advantage of calmer waters. There are no fixed schedules; ask at immigration for information on the next sailing.

Mozambique
DHOW

Dhows between Mozambique and Tanzania (12 to 30 or more hours) are best arranged at Msimbati and Moçimboa da Praia (Mozambique).

FERRY

There is currently no official ferry service between southwestern Tanzania and Mozambique. The main option is taking a cargo boat between Mbamba Bay and Nkhata Bay, and then the MV *Chambo* on its weekly run from Nkhata Bay on to Likoma Island (Malawi), Cóbuè (Mozambique) and Metangula (Mozambique); currently departures are from Nkhata Bay on Thursday and from Metangula on Wednesday. There are also small boats that sail along the eastern shore of Lake Nyasa between Tanzania and Mozambique. However, Lake Nyasa is notorious for its severe and sudden squalls, and going this way is risky and not recommended.

There's an immigration officer at Mbamba Bay, Mozambique immigration posts in Cóbuè and in Metangula and Malawi immigration officers on Likoma Island and in Nkhata Bay. Get your Mozambique visa in advance.

Uganda

There's no passenger-ferry service, but it's sometimes possible to arrange passage between Mwanza and Kampala's Port Bell on cargo ships (about 16 hours). Boats sail about three times weekly. On the Ugandan side, you'll need a letter of permission from the train station director (free). Ask for the managing director's office, on the 2nd floor of the building next to Kampala's train station. In Mwanza a letter isn't required, but check in with the immigration officer at the South Port. Expect to pay about US$20, including port fees. Crew are sometimes willing to rent out their cabins for a negotiable extra fee.

Zambia

The venerable MV *Liemba* has been plying the waters of Lake Tanganyika for the better part of a century on one of Africa's classic adventure journeys. It connects Kigoma with Mpulungu in Zambia every other week, with prices for 1st/2nd/economy class costing US$100/90/70 (payment must be in US dollars cash only). The trip takes at least 40 hours and stops en route at various lakeshore villages, including Lagosa (for Mahale Mountains National Park; US$35 for 1st class from Kigoma), Kalema (southwest of Mpanda; US$50), Kipili (US$70) and Kasanga (southwest of Sumbawanga; US$95). In theory, departures from Kigoma are on Wednesday at 4pm, reaching Mpulungu Friday morning. Departures from Mpulungu are (again, in theory) on Friday afternoon at about 2pm, arriving back in Kigoma on Sunday afternoon.

Delays are common and it has often been out of service, though hopefully things will be better after the substantial overhaul it received in 2014. Food, soda, beer and bottled water are sold on board, but it's a good idea to bring supplements. First class is surprisingly comfortable, with two clean bunks, a window and a fan. Second-class cabins (four bunks) are poorly ventilated and uncomfortable. There are seats for third (economy)

DHOW TRAVEL

With their billowing sails and graceful forms, dhows have become a symbol of East Africa for adventure travellers. Yet, despite their romantic reputation, the realities can be quite different. Before undertaking a longer journey, test things out with a short sunset or afternoon sail. Coastal hotels are good contacts for arranging reliable dhow travel. If you decide to give a local dhow a try:

➡ Be prepared for rough conditions. There are no facilities on board, except possibly a toilet hanging off the stern. Sailings are wind and tide dependent, and departures are often predawn.

➡ Journeys often take much longer than anticipated; bring extra water and sufficient food.

➡ Sun block, a hat and a covering are essential, as is waterproofing for your luggage and a rain jacket.

➡ Boats capsize and people are killed each year. Avoid overloaded boats and don't set sail in bad weather.

➡ Travel with the winds, which blow from south to north from approximately July to September and north to south from approximately November to late February.

Note that what Westerners refer to as dhows are called either *jahazi* or *mashua* by Tanzanians. *Jahazi* are large, lateen-sailed boats. *Mashua* are smaller, and often with proportionately wider hulls and a motor. The *dau* has a sloped stem and stern. On lakes and inland waterways, the *mokoro* (dugout canoe) is in common use. Coastal areas, especially Zanzibar's east-coast beaches, are good places to see *ngalawa* (outrigger canoes).

class passengers, but it's more comfortable to find deck space for sleeping. Keep watch over your luggage. Booking (for inquiries ☎028-280 2811) early is advisable, but not always necessary, as 1st-class cabins are usually available.

There are docks at Kigoma, Kasanga and Mpulungu, but at all other stops you'll need to disembark in the middle of the lake, exiting from a door in the side of the boat into small boats that take you to shore. While it may sound adventurous, it can be rather nerve-wracking at night, and if the lake is rough.

Tours

Australia & New Zealand

African Wildlife Safaris (www.africanwildlifesafaris. com.au) Customised trips to the northern circuit parks and Zanzibar.

Classic Safari Company (www.classicsafaricompany. com.au) Upmarket customised itineraries, including to the south and west.

Intrepid Travel (www. intrepidtravel.com) Socially and environmentally responsible tours focusing on the northern circuit, Selous GR and Zanzibar.

Peregrine Travel (www. peregrineadventures.com) Northern circuit treks and safaris for all budgets; also family itineraries.

South Africa

Africa Travel Co (www. africatravelco.co.za) Northern circuit and southern/East Africa combination itineraries.

Wild Frontiers (www.wild frontiers.com) A range of East Africa itineraries.

UK

Africa-in-Focus (www. africa-in-focus.com) Overland tours.

African Initiatives (www. african-initiatives.org.uk) Fair-traded safaris in northern Tanzania.

Baobab Travel (www. baobabtravel.com) A culturally responsible operator with itineraries countrywide.

Camps International (www. campsinternational.com) Community-focused budget itineraries in the northern circuit and on Zanzibar.

Expert Africa (www.expert africa.com) A long-standing, experienced operator with a wide selection of itineraries.

Greentours (www.greentours. co.uk) This UK-based operator offers upmarket, botanically focused tours combining Kitulo and Udzungwa Mountains National Parks.

Responsible Travel.com (www.responsibletravel.com) Matches you up with ecologically and culturally responsible tour operators to plan an itinerary.

Tribes Travel (www.tribes. co.uk) Fair-traded safaris and treks, including in the south and west.

USA & Canada

Abercrombie & Kent (www. abercrombiekent.com) Customised tours and safaris.

Africa Adventure Company (www.africa-adventure. com) Upscale specialist safaris, including in southern and western Tanzania, and Mt Kilimanjaro treks.

African Environments (www.africanenvironments. com) Top-end treks organised by one of the pioneering companies on Mt Kilimanjaro. Also luxury northern circuit vehicle safaris, and walking safaris in Ngorongoro Conservation Area and in Serengeti border areas.

African Horizons (www. africanhorizons.com) A small operator offering various packages, including in the south and west.

Deeper Africa (www.deeper africa.com) Socially responsible, upmarket northern circuit safaris and treks.

Eco-Resorts (www.eco-resorts.com) Socially responsible itineraries in the north, south and west.

Explorateur Voyages (www. explorateur.qc.ca) Northern circuit treks and safaris.

Good Earth (www.goodearth tours.com) Northern circuit safaris.

International Expeditions (www.ietravel.com) Naturalist-oriented northern circuit safaris.

Mountain Madness (www. mountainmadness.com) Upmarket Mt Kilimanjaro treks.

Thomson Family Adventures (www.familyadventures. com) Northern circuit itineraries, including family safaris.

GETTING AROUND

Air

Airlines in Tanzania

There is a good flight network – much of it on small planes – connecting Dar es Salaam, Arusha, Zanzibar and other major centres with each other, and with major national parks. Internal flights are expensive. Always reconfirm your bookings at least once, and expect delays.

Auric Air (☎0783 233334; www.auricair.com) Bukoba, Mwanza, Zanzibar, Dar es Salaam and other towns, plus Katavi and Rubondo Island National Parks.

Air Excel (☎027-254 8429; www.airexcelonline.com) Arusha, Serengeti NP, Lake Manyara NP, Dar es Salaam, Zanzibar.

Air Tanzania (☎022-211 8411; www.airtanzania.co.tz) Dar es Salaam, Mwanza, Kigoma, Tabora, Mtwara, Kilimanjaro, Mbeya, plus Bujumbura (Burundi).

Coastal Aviation (☎022-284 2700; www.coastal.co.tz) Flights to many major towns and national parks, including Arusha, Dar es Salaam, Dodoma, Kilwa Masoko, Lake Manyara NP, Mafia, Mwanza, Pemba, Ruaha NP,

Rubondo Island NP, Saadani NP, Selous GR, Serengeti NP, Tanga, Tarangire NP and Zanzibar.

Flightlink (☏0782 354448, 0782 354449; www.flightlink aircharters.com) Flights connecting Dar es Salaam with the Zanzibar Archipelago, Selous, Dodoma, Serengeti and Lake Manyara.

Precision Air (☏0787 888407, 022-216 8000; www. precisionairtz.com) Flies from Dar es Salaam to many major towns including Bukoba, Kilimanjaro, Mbeya, Mtwara, Mwanza and Zanzibar. Also Dar es Salaam to Entebbe (Uganda), Kigali (Rwanda), Nairobi (Kenya), Pemba (Mozambique), Lubumbashi (DRC) and Lusaka (Zambia).

Regional Air Services (☏027-250 4477, 027-250 2541; www.regionaltanzania. com) Arusha, Dar es Salaam, Kilimanjaro, Lake Manyara NP, Ndutu, Serengeti NP and Zanzibar.

Safari Airlink (☏0777 723274; www.safariaviation. info) Dar es Salaam, Arusha, Katavi NP, Mahale Mountains NP, Pangani, Ruaha NP, Selous GR and Zanzibar.

Tropical Air (☏0777 431431, 024-223 2511; www.tropicalair. co.tz) Zanzibar, Dar es Salaam, Mbeya, Pemba, Mafia and Arusha.

ZanAir (☏024-223 3670, 024-223 3678; www.zanair. com) Flights link Arusha, Dar es Salaam, Pemba, Saadani NP, Selous GR and Zanzibar. Also flies between Zanzibar, Mombasa (Kenya) and Arusha.

Zantas Air (☏0688 434343, 0713 409412; www.zantasair. com) Arusha, Katavi NP, Mahale Mountains NP, Kigoma, Lake Manyara NP and Serengeti NP.

Boat

Dhow

Main routes connect Zanzibar and Pemba with Dar es Salaam, Tanga, Bagamoyo and Mombasa; Kilwa Kivinje, Lindi, Mikindani, Mtwara and Msimbati with other coastal towns; and, Mafia and the mainland. However, foreigners are officially prohibited on nonmotorised dhows, and on any dhows between Zanzibar and Dar es Salaam; captains are subject to fines if they're caught, and may be

unwilling to take you. Safety is also a concern. A better option is to arrange a charter with a coastal hotel (many have their own dhows) or with Safari Blue (p115).

Ferry

Ferries operate on Lake Victoria, Lake Tanganyika and Lake Nyasa, and between Dar es Salaam, Zanzibar and Pemba. There's a US$5 port tax per trip.

LAKE VICTORIA

The MV *Victoria* departs from Mwanza at 9pm on Tuesday, Thursday and Sunday; departures from Bukoba are at 9pm Monday, Wednesday and Friday (1st-class/2nd-class sleeping/2nd-class sitting/3rd-class Tsh36,000/27,600/24,000/17,500). First class has two-bed cabins and 2nd-class sleeping has six-bed cabins. Second-class sitting isn't comfortable, so if you can't get a spot in 1st class or 2nd-class sleeping, the best bet is to buy a 3rd-class ticket. With luck, you may then be able to find a comfortable spot in the 1st-class lounge. First- and 2nd-class

TANZANIA FERRY TRAVEL

Tanzania's ferries can be a pleasant and wonderfully scenic way to travel. Taking the MV *Liemba* down Lake Tanganyika is one of Africa's classic journeys. The Lake Nyasa (Lake Malawi) ferry routes are beautiful, sliding slowly past mountains and lakeshore villages. The sight of Stone Town's skyline coming into view as the Dar es Salaam ferry approaches Zanzibar island is etched into the memories of countless travellers.

Yet, anyone considering ferry travel in this part of the world should also be aware of the risks involved. Most of Tanzania's ferries are ageing, and many are in a dubious state of repair. Many are also the only means of travel for local residents. Most double as cargo boats, and they often travel fully loaded or overloaded with both passengers and cargo. There have been several major ferry tragedies in recent times, including the sinking of the MV *Bukoba* on Lake Victoria in 1996 and the 2011 sinking of the *Spice Islander* en route between Zanzibar and Pemba. Except for the occasional 1st-class cabin, conditions are general extremely basic, with seating only on the overcrowded deck. More significantly, many of the ferries sail with minimal or no safety equipment. Most have life jackets and at least some lifeboats, but rarely enough for the number of passengers on board. An exception are the daytime 'fast ferries' between Dar es Salaam and Zanzibar, which are generally better maintained, and with somewhat better oversight.

If you plan to travel by ferry, choose day boats where possible. Don't get on a boat that appears overloaded, don't set off in bad weather, and poke around on deck to try and find a life jacket.

cabins fill up quickly in both directions, so book as soon as you know your plans. Food is available on board. Note that there's a risk of theft for all deck and seating passengers. The journey takes approximately nine hours.

LAKE NYASA

In theory, the MV *Songea* departs from Itungi port about noon on Thursday and makes its way down the coast via Matema, Lupingu, Manda, Lundu, Mango and Liuli to Mbamba Bay (1st/economy class Tsh25,100/16,100, 18 to 24 hours between Itungi and Mbamba Bay). It then turns around again, reaching Matema and Itungi port on Sunday.

The smaller MV *Iringa*, which also services lakeside villages between Itungi and Manda (about halfway down the Tanzanian lakeshore), was not operating at the time of research. When it is, it usually alternates with the MV *Songea*.

Schedules for both boats change frequently. For an update, ask in Kyela, or at one of the Matema hotels.

Bus

Bus travel is an inevitable part of the Tanzania experience for many travellers. Prices are reasonable for the distances covered, and there's often no other way to reach many destinations.

➡ On major long-distance routes, there's a choice of express and ordinary buses; price is usually a good indicator of which is which. Express buses make fewer stops, are less crowded and depart on schedule. Some have toilets and air-conditioning, and the nicest ones are called 'luxury' buses. On secondary routes, the only option is ordinary buses, which are often packed to overflowing, stop often and run to a less-rigorous schedule (and often

not to any recognisable schedule at all).

➡ For popular routes, book in advance. You can sometimes get a place by arriving at the bus station an hour prior to departure. Each bus line has its own booking office, at or near the bus station.

➡ Express buses have a compartment below for luggage. However, it's best to keep your bag with you. Never put it up on the roof.

➡ Prices are basically fixed, although overcharging happens. Most bus stations are chaotic, and at the ones in Arusha and other tourist areas you'll be incessantly hounded by touts. Buy your tickets at the office and not from the touts, and don't believe anyone who tries to tell you there's a luggage fee, unless you are carrying an excessively large pack.

➡ For short stretches along main routes, express buses will drop you on request, though you'll often need to pay the full fare to the next major destination.

➡ On long routes, expect to sleep either on the bus, pulled off to the side of the road, or at a grubby guesthouse.

Minibus & Shared Taxi

For shorter trips away from the main routes, the choice is often between 30-seater buses ('coastals' or *thelathi-ni*) and dalla-dallas or Hiace minivans. Both options come complete with chickens on the roof, bags of produce under the seats, no leg room and schedules only in the most general sense of the word. Dalla-dallas, especially, are invariably filled to overflowing. Shared taxis are rare, except around Arusha, at Dar es Salaam's Ubungo bus station and several other locations. Like ordinary buses, dalla-dallas and shared taxis leave when full, and are the least safe transport option.

Truck

In remote areas, including much of western Tanzania, trucks operate as buses (for a roughly similar fare) with passengers sitting or standing in the back. Even on routes that have daily bus service, many people still use trucks.

Car & Motorcycle

Unless you have your own vehicle and are familiar with driving in East Africa, it's relatively unusual for fly-in travellers to tour mainland Tanzania by car. More common is to focus on a region and arrange local transport through a tour or safari operator. On Zanzibar, however, it's easy to hire a car or motorcycle for touring, and self-drive is permitted.

Driving Licence

On the mainland you'll need your home driving licence or (preferable) an International Driving Permit (IDP) together with your home licence. On Zanzibar you'll need an IDP plus your home licence, or a permit from Zanzibar, Kenya, Uganda or South Africa.

Fuel & Spare Parts

Petrol and diesel cost about Tsh2200 per litre. Filling and repair stations are found in all major towns, but are scarce elsewhere, so tank up whenever you get the opportunity and carry a range of spares for your vehicle. In remote areas and for longer stays in national parks, it's essential to carry jerry cans with extra fuel. It happens, including at major roadside filling stations, that petrol or diesel may be diluted with kerosene or water. Check with local residents or business owners before tanking up. It's also common for car parts to be switched in garages (substituting inferior versions for the originals). Staying with your car while it's being repaired helps minimise this problem. Always also note your odometer and gas gauge readings before having your car serviced.

Hire

In Dar es Salaam, daily rates for 2WD start at about US$70, excluding fuel, plus from US$30 for insurance and tax. Prices for 4WD are US$100 to US$250 per day plus insurance (US$30 to US$40 per day), fuel and driver (US$20 to US$50 per day). There's also a 20% value added tax.

Outside the city, most companies require 4WD. Also, most will not permit self-drive outside of Dar es Salaam, and few offer unlimited kilometres. Charges per kilometre are around US$0.50 to US$1. Clarify what the company's policy is in the event of a breakdown.

Elsewhere in Tanzania, you can hire 4WD vehicles in Arusha, Karatu, Mwanza, Mbeya, Zanzibar Town and other centres through travel agencies, tour operators and hotels. Except on Zanzibar, most come with driver. Rates average US$100 to US$200 per day plus fuel, less on Zanzibar.

For motorcycle hire, try the Arusha-based **Dustbusters** (www.dustbusters-tz.com). For vehicle hire with driver, contact the Dar es Salaam-based **Jumanne Mastoka** (☑0784 339735; mjumanne@yahoo.com).

Insurance

Unless you're covered from other sources, such as your credit card, it's advisable to take the full coverage offered by hire companies.

Road Conditions & Hazards

Around one-third of Tanzania's road network is sealed. Secondary roads range from good to impassable, depending on the season. For most trips outside major towns you'll need 4WD.

If you aren't used to driving in East Africa, watch out for pedestrians, children and animals on the road or running into the road. Especially in rural areas, many people have not driven themselves and aren't aware of necessary braking distances and similar

concepts. Never drive at night, and be particularly alert for vehicles overtaking blind on curves. Tree branches on the road are the local version of flares or hazard lights and mean there's a stopped vehicle, crater-sized pothole or similar calamity ahead.

Road Rules

Driving is on the left (in theory), and traffic already on roundabouts has the right of way. Unless otherwise posted, the speed limit is 80km/hr; on some routes, including Dar es Salaam to Arusha, police have radar. Tanzania has a seat-belt law for drivers and front-seat passengers. The standard traffic-fine penalty is Tsh20,000.

Motorcycles aren't permitted in national parks except for the section of the Dar es Salaam to Mbeya highway passing through Mikumi National Park and on the road between Sumbawanga and Mpanda via Katavi National Park.

Hitching

Hitching is generally slow going. It's prohibited inside national parks, and is usually fruitless around them. That said, in remote areas, hitching a lift with truck drivers may be your only option. Expect to pay about the same or a bit less than the bus fare for the same route, with a place in the cab costing about twice that for a place on top of the load. To flag down a vehicle, hold out your hand at about waist level, palm to the ground, and wave it up and down.

Expat workers or well-off locals may also offer you a ride. Payment is usually not expected, but still offer some token of thanks, such as a petrol contribution for longer journeys.

As elsewhere in the world, hitching is never entirely safe, and we don't recommend it. Travellers who hitch should understand that they are

---

PERILS OF THE ROAD

Road accidents are probably your biggest safety risk while travelling in Tanzania, with speeding buses being among the worst offenders. Road conditions are poor and driving standards leave much to be desired. Overtaking blind is a problem, as are high speeds. Your bus driver may, in fact, be at the wheel of an ageing, rickety vehicle with a cracked windshield and marginal brakes on a winding, potholed road. However, he'll invariably be driving as if he were piloting a sleek racing machine coming down the straight – nerve-wracking to say the least. Impassioned pleas from passengers to slow down usually have little effect, and pretending you're sick is often counterproductive. Many vehicles have painted slogans such as *Mungu Atubariki* (God Bless Us) or 'In God we Trust' in the hope that a bit of extra help from above will see them safely through the day's runs.

To maximise your chances of a safe arrival, avoid night travel, and ask locals for recommendations of reputable companies. If you have a choice, it's usually better to go with a full-sized bus than a minibus (the worst option) or a 30-seater bus.

taking a potentially serious risk. If you do hitch, it's safer doing so in pairs and letting someone know your plans.

Local Transport

Dalla-Dalla

Local routes are serviced by dalla-dallas and, in rural areas, pick-up trucks or old 4WDs. Prices are fixed and inexpensive (Tsh100 to Tsh400 for town runs). The vehicles make many stops and are extremely crowded. Accidents are frequent, particularly in minibuses. Many accidents are caused when the drivers race each other to an upcoming station in order to collect new passengers. Destinations are either posted on a board in the front window, or called out by the driver's assistant, who also collects fares. If you have a large backpack, think twice about getting on a dalla-dalla, especially at rush hour, when it will make the already crowded conditions even more uncomfortable for the other passengers.

Taxi

Taxis, which have white plates on the mainland and a 'gari la abiria' (passenger vehicle) sign on Zanzibar, can be hired in all major towns. None have meters, so agree on the fare with the driver before getting in. Fares for short town trips start at Tsh2000. In major centres, many drivers have an 'official' price list, although rates shown on it (often calculated on the basis of Tsh1000 per 1km) are generally significantly higher than what is normally paid. If you're unsure of the price, ask locals what it should be and then use this as a base for negotiations. For longer trips away from town, negotiate the fare based on distance, petrol costs and road conditions, plus a fair profit for the driver. Only use taxis from reliable hotels

or established taxi stands. Avoid hailing taxis cruising the streets, and never get in a taxi that has a 'friend' of the driver or anyone else already in it.

Train

For those with plenty of time, Tanzania train travel offers a fine view of the countryside and local life. There are two lines: **Tazara** (Tanzanian Zambia Railway Authority; ☎0713 225292, 022-286 5187; www.tazara.co.tz; cnr Nyerere & Nelson Mandela Rds; ⊗ticket office 7.30am-12.30pm & 2-4.30pm Mon-Fri, 9am-12.30pm Sat), linking Dar es Salaam with Kapiri Mposhi in Zambia via Mbeya and Tunduma; and Tanzanian Railway Corporation's **Central Line** (☎022-211 7833; cnr Railway St & Sokoine Dr, Dar es Salaam; 1st/2nd/economy class Dar es Salaam to Kigoma Tsh75,700/55,400/27,700), linking Dar es Salaam with Kigoma and Mwanza. A Central Line branch also links Tabora with Mpanda. The Central Line spur connecting Singida and Dodoma has been closed, now that the road is fully paved.

In general, Tazara is considerably more comfortable and efficient than the Central Line, but on both lines, breakdowns and long delays (up to 24 hours or more) are common. If you want to try the train, consider shorter stretches, eg from Dar es Salaam into the Selous GR, or between Tabora and Kigoma. For longer stretches, bring extra food and drinks to supplement the basic meals that are available on both lines.

Classes

Tazara has four classes: 1st class (four-bed compartments), 2nd class (six-bed compartments), 2nd-class sitting (also called 'super seater') and economy (3rd) class (benches, usually very

crowded). Men and women can only travel together in the sleeping sections by booking the entire compartment. At night, secure your window with a stick, and don't leave your luggage unattended, even for a moment. Central Line has 1st class (four-bed compartments), 2nd class (six-bed compartments) and economy.

Reservations

Tickets for 1st and 2nd class should be reserved at least several days in advance, although occasionally you'll be able to get a seat on the day of travel. Economy-class tickets can be bought on the spot.

TAZARA

Tazara runs two trains weekly between Dar es Salaam and Kapiri Mposhi in Zambia via Mbeya, departing Dar es Salaam at 3.50pm Tuesday (express) and 1.50pm Friday (ordinary). Express-train fares between Dar es Salaam and Mbeya are Tsh46,000/38,600/32,400 for 1st/2nd/economy class (slightly less for ordinary trains). Departures from Mbeya are at 2.30pm Wednesday (express) and 3pm Saturday (ordinary). Linens are provided for sleeper cars.

CENTRAL LINE

Central Line trains depart Dar es Salaam for Kigoma at 5pm Tuesday and Friday (Tsh75,700/55,400/27,700 for 1st/2nd/economy class, approximately 40 hours). Departures from Kigoma are at 6pm Sunday and Thursday; departures from Mwanza are at 5pm Sunday and Thursday. Sleeper cars are mattresses only (no linens).

Trains between Tabora and Mpanda (Tsh17,800 economy class only, about 14 hours) depart from Tabora at 9pm Wednesday and Saturday and Mpanda at 1pm Thursday and Sunday.

Health

As long as you stay up-to-date with your vaccinations and take basic preventive measures, you're unlikely to succumb to most of the possible health hazards. While Tanzania has an impressive selection of tropical diseases on offer, it's more likely you'll get a bout of diarrhoea or a cold than a more exotic malady. The main exception to this is malaria, which is a real risk throughout most of the country. Road accidents are the other main threat to your health. Never travel at night, and choose buses or private transport over dalla-dallas (minibuses) to minimise the risk.

BEFORE YOU GO

➡ Get a check-up from your dentist and your doctor if you have any regular medication or chronic illness, such as high blood pressure or asthma.

➡ Organise spare contact lenses and glasses.

➡ Get a first-aid and medical kit together; arrange necessary vaccinations.

➡ Consider registering with the International Association for Medical Advice to Travellers (www.iamat.org), which provides directories of certified doctors.

➡ If you'll be spending much time in remote areas, consider doing a first-aid course (contact the Red Cross or St John Ambulance) or attending a remote medicine first-aid course, such as that offered by the Royal Geographical Society (www.wildernessmedicaltraining.co.uk).

➡ Carry medications in their original (labelled) containers.

➡ If carrying syringes or needles, have a physician's letter documenting their medical necessity.

Insurance

Check in advance if your insurance plan will make payments directly to providers or reimburse you later for overseas health expenditures. Most doctors in Tanzania expect payment in cash.

Ensure that your travel insurance will cover any emergency transport required

RECOMMENDED VACCINATIONS

Regardless of your destination, the World Health Organization (www.who.int/en) recommends that all travellers be covered for the following:

➡ diphtheria

➡ tetanus

➡ measles

➡ mumps

➡ rubella

➡ polio

➡ hepatitis B

According to the Centers for Disease Control and Prevention (www.cdc.gov), the following vaccinations are (also) recommended for Tanzania:

➡ hepatitis A

➡ hepatitis B

➡ rabies

➡ typhoid

➡ boosters for tetanus, diphtheria and measles

While a yellow fever vaccination certificate is not officially required to enter Tanzania unless you're coming from an infected area, carrying one is advised.

to get you at least as far as Nairobi (Kenya), or (preferably) all the way home, by air and with a medical attendant if necessary. It's worth taking out a temporary membership with the African Medical & Research Foundation (www.amref. org) or First Air Responder (www.firstairresponder. com).

Medical Checklist

Carry a medical and first-aid kit with you, to help yourself in case of minor illness or injury. Following is a list of items to include:

➡ acetaminophen (paracetamol) or aspirin

➡ adhesive tape

➡ antibacterial ointment for cuts and abrasions

➡ antibiotics eg ciprofloxacin (Ciproxin) or norfloxacin (Utinor)

➡ antidiarrhoeal drugs (eg loperamide)

➡ antihistamines (for hay fever and allergic reactions)

➡ anti-inflammatory drugs (eg ibuprofen)

➡ antimalaria pills

➡ bandages, gauze, gauze rolls and tape

➡ DEET-containing insect repellent

➡ digital thermometer

➡ oral rehydration salts

➡ Permethrin-containing insect spray for clothing, tents and bed nets

➡ pocket knife

➡ scissors, safety pins, tweezers

➡ self-diagnostic kit to identify from a finger prick if malaria is in the blood

➡ sterile needles, syringes and fluids if travelling to remote areas

➡ sun block (SPF 30+)

➡ water purification tablets

Websites

General information:

➡ Lonely Planet (www. lonelyplanet.com)

➡ MD Travel Health (www. mdtravelhealth.com)

➡ Fit for Travel (www. fitfortravel.nhs.uk)

➡ *International Travel and Health* (www.who.int/ith), a free, online publication of the World Health Organization

Government travel-health websites:

➡ Australia: www. smartraveller.gov.au

➡ Canada: www.phac-aspc. gc.ca

➡ UK: www.nhs.uk/nhs england/healthcareabroad/ pages/healthcareabroad. aspx

➡ USA: www.cdc.gov/travel

Further Reading

➡ *Wilderness and Travel Medicine* by Eric A Weiss (2012)

➡ *Essential Guide to Travel Health* by Jane Wilson-Howarth (2009)

➡ *Africa – Healthy Travel Guide* by Isabelle Young and Tony Gherardin (2008)

IN TANZANIA

Availability & Cost of Health Care

Good medical care is available in Dar es Salaam, and reasonable-to-good care is available in Arusha and in some mission stations. Otherwise, you'll need to go to Nairobi (Kenya), which is the main destination for medical evacuations from Tanzania, or return home. If you have a choice, try to find a private or mission-run clinic, as these are generally better equipped than government ones. If you

fall ill in an unfamiliar area, ask staff at your hotel or resident expatriates where the best nearby medical facilities are; in an emergency contact your embassy. Larger towns have at least one clinic where you can get an inexpensive malaria test and, if necessary, treatment.

Pharmacies in major towns are generally well stocked for commonly used items, and rarely require prescriptions; always check expiry dates. Antimalarials are relatively easy to obtain in larger towns. However, it's recommended to bring antimalarials, as well as drugs for chronic diseases, from home. Some drugs for sale in Tanzania might be ineffective: they might be counterfeit (especially antimalarial tablets and antibiotics) or might not have been stored under the right conditions. The availability and efficacy of condoms also cannot be relied upon; they might not be of the same quality as in Europe or Australia and might have been incorrectly stored.

There is a high risk of contracting HIV from infected blood transfusions. The BloodCare Foundation (www. bloodcare.org.uk) is a good source of safe blood, which can be transported to any part of the world within 24 hours.

Infectious Diseases

Following are some of the diseases found in Tanzania. With basic preventive measures, it's unlikely that you'll succumb to any.

Cholera

Cholera is usually only a problem during natural or artificial disasters, such as war, floods or earthquakes, although outbreaks can also occur at other times. Travellers are rarely affected. It's caused by a bacteria and spread via contaminated drinking water. The main symptom is profuse watery diarrhoea, which causes debilitation if fluids are not replaced quickly. An oral cholera vaccine is available in the USA, but is not particularly effective. Most cases of cholera could be avoided by close attention to good drinking water and by avoiding potentially contaminated food. Treatment is by fluid replacement (orally or via a drip), but sometimes antibiotics are needed. Self-treatment is not advised.

Dengue Fever

Mini-epidemics of this mosquito-borne disease crop up with some regularity in Tanzania, notably in Dar es Salaam. Symptoms include high fever, severe headache and body ache (dengue used to be known as breakbone fever). Some people develop a rash and experience diarrhoea. There is no vaccine, only prevention. The dengue-carrying *Aedes aegypti* mosquito is active at day and night, so use DEET-mosquito repellent periodically throughout the day. See a doctor to be diagnosed and monitored (dengue testing is available in Dar es Salaam). There is no specific treatment, just rest and paracetamol – do not take aspirin as it increases the likelihood of haemorrhaging. Severe dengue is a potentially fatal complication.

Diphtheria

Diphtheria is spread through close respiratory contact. It usually causes a temperature and a severe sore throat. Sometimes a membrane forms across the throat and a tracheotomy is needed to prevent suffocation. Vaccination is recommended for those likely to be in close contact with the local population in infected areas, but is more important for long stays than for short-term trips. The vaccine is given as an injection, alone or with

tetanus, and lasts 10 years. Self-treatment: none.

Filariasis

Filariasis is caused by tiny worms migrating in the lymphatic system and is spread by a bite from an infected mosquito. Symptoms include localised itching and swelling of the legs and/or genitalia. Treatment is available. Self-treatment: none.

Hepatitis A

Hepatitis A is spread through contaminated food (particularly shellfish) and water. It causes jaundice and, although it is rarely fatal, it can cause prolonged lethargy and delayed recovery. If you've had hepatitis A, you shouldn't drink alcohol for up to six months afterwards, but once you've recovered, there won't be any long-term problems. The first symptoms include dark urine and a yellow colour to the whites of the eyes. Sometimes a fever and abdominal pain are present. Hepatitis A vaccine (Avaxim, VAQTA, Havrix) is given as an injection: a single dose will give protection for up to a year, and a booster after a year gives 10-year protection. Hepatitis A and typhoid vaccines can also be given as a single-dose vaccine, hepatyrix or viatim. Self-treatment: none.

Hepatitis B

Hepatitis B is spread through sexual intercourse, infected blood and contaminated needles. It can also be spread from an infected mother to her baby during childbirth. It affects the liver, causing jaundice and sometimes liver failure. Most people recover completely, but some people might be chronic carriers of the virus, which could lead eventually to cirrhosis or liver cancer. Those visiting high-risk areas for long periods, or those with increased social or occupational risk, should be immunised. Many countries now routinely give hep-

atitis B as part of childhood vaccination. It is given singly or can be given at the same time as hepatitis A.

A course will give protection for at least five years. It can be given over four weeks or six months. Self-treatment: none.

HIV

Human immunodeficiency virus (HIV), the virus that causes acquired immune deficiency syndrome (AIDS), is a major problem in Tanzania, with infection rates averaging about 5.1%, and much higher in some areas. The virus is spread through infected blood and blood products, by sexual intercourse with an infected partner and from an infected mother to her baby during childbirth and breastfeeding. It can be spread through 'blood to blood' contact, such as with contaminated instruments during medical, dental, acupuncture and other body-piercing procedures, and through sharing used intravenous needles. At present there is no cure; medication that might keep the disease under control is available, but these drugs are too expensive, or unavailable, for many Tanzanians. If you think you might have been infected with HIV, a blood test is necessary; a three-month gap after exposure and before testing is required to allow antibodies to appear in the blood. Self-treatment: none.

Malaria

Malaria is endemic throughout most of Tanzania and is a major health scourge (except at altitudes higher than 2000m, where the risk of transmission is low, and on Zanzibar island, where it has been eradicated). Infection rates are higher during the rainy season, but the risk exists year-round and it is extremely important to take preventive measures, even if you will be in the country for just a short time.

Malaria is caused by a parasite in the bloodstream spread via the bite of the female *Anopheles* mosquito. There are several types, falciparum malaria being the most dangerous and the predominant form in Tanzania. Unlike most other diseases regularly encountered by travellers, there is no vaccination against malaria (yet). However, several different drugs are used to prevent malaria and new ones are in the pipeline. Up-to-date advice from a travel-health clinic is essential, as some medication is more suitable for some travellers than others. The pattern of drug-resistant malaria is changing rapidly, so what was advised several years ago might no longer be the case.

SYMPTOMS

The early stages of malaria include headaches, fevers, generalised aches and pains, and malaise, which could be mistaken for flu. Other symptoms can include abdominal pain, diarrhoea and a cough. Anyone who develops a fever in Tanzania or within two weeks after departure should assume malarial infection until blood tests prove negative, even if you have been taking antimalarial medication. If not treated, the next stage could develop within 24 hours, particularly if falciparum malaria is the parasite: jaundice, then reduced consciousness and coma (also known as cerebral malaria) followed by death. Treatment in hospital is essential, and the death rate might still be as high as 10% even in the best intensive-care facilities.

SIDE EFFECTS & RISKS

Many travellers are under the impression that malaria is a mild illness, that treatment is always easy and successful and that taking antimalarial drugs causes more illness through side effects than actually getting malaria. Unfortunately, this is not true. Side effects of the medication depend on the drug being taken. Doxycycline can cause heartburn and indigestion; mefloquine (Lariam) can cause anxiety attacks, insomnia and nightmares and (rarely) severe psychiatric disorders; chloroquine can cause nausea and hair loss; and proguanil can cause mouth ulcers. These side effects are not universal and can be minimised by taking medication correctly, eg with food. Also, some people should not take a particular antimalarial drug, eg people with epilepsy should avoid mefloquine, and doxycycline should not be taken by pregnant women or children younger than 12.

If you decide that you really don't want to take antimalarial drugs, you must understand the risks and be obsessive about avoiding mosquito bites. Use nets and insect repellent, and report any fever or flu-like symptoms to a doctor as soon as possible. Some people advocate homeopathic preparations against malaria, such as Demal200, but as yet there is no conclusive evidence that this is effective, and many homeopaths do not recommend their use. Malaria in

TRADITIONAL MEDICINE

According to some estimates, at least 80% of Tanzanians rely in part or in whole on traditional medicine, and close to two-thirds of the population have traditional healers as their first point of contact in case of illness. The *mganga* (traditional healer) holds a revered position in many communities, and traditional-medicinal products are widely available in local markets. In part, the heavy reliance on traditional medicine is because of comparatively higher costs of conventional Western-style medicine, and because of prevailing cultural attitudes and beliefs, but also because it sometimes works. Often, though, it's because there is no other choice. In northeastern Tanzania, for example, it is estimated that while there is only one medical doctor to over 30,000 people, there is a traditional healer for approximately every 150 people. Countrywide, hospitals and health clinics are concentrated in urban areas, and most are limited in their effectiveness because of insufficient resources and chronic shortages of equipment and medicines.

While some traditional remedies seem to work on malaria, sickle-cell anaemia, high blood pressure and other ailments, most traditional healers learn their art by apprenticeship, so education (and consequently application of knowledge) is often inconsistent and unregulated. At the centre of efforts to correct these problems is the **Institute of Traditional Medicine** (www.muchs.ac.tz; Muhimbili Medical Centre, Dar es Salaam). Among other things, the institute is studying the efficacy of various traditional cures, and promoting those that are found to be successful. There are also local efforts to create healers' associations, and to train traditional practitioners in sanitation and other topics.

pregnancy frequently results in miscarriage or premature labour and the risks to both mother and foetus during pregnancy are considerable. Travel in Tanzania when pregnant should be carefully considered.

STAND-BY TREATMENT

If you will be away from major towns, carrying emergency stand-by treatment is highly recommended, and essential for travel in remote areas. Be sure to seek your doctor's advice before setting off as to recommended medicines and dosages. However, this should be viewed as emergency treatment only and not as routine self-medication, and should only be used if you will be far from medical facilities and have been advised about the symptoms of malaria and how to use the medication. If you do resort to emergency self-treatment, seek medical advice as soon as possible to confirm whether the treatment has been successful. In particular, you want to avoid contracting cerebral malaria, which can be fatal within 24 hours. Self-diagnostic kits, which can identify malaria in the blood from a finger prick, are available in the West and are worth buying.

Meningococcal Meningitis

Meningococcal infection is spread through close respiratory contact and is more likely in crowded places, such as dormitories, buses and clubs. While the disease is present in Tanzania, infection is uncommon in travellers. Vaccination is recommended for long stays and is especially important towards the end of the dry season. Symptoms include a fever, severe headache, neck stiffness and a red rash. Immediate medical treatment is necessary.

The ACWY vaccine is recommended for all travellers in sub-Saharan Africa. This vaccine is different from the meningococcal meningitis C vaccine given to children and adolescents in some countries; it is safe to be given both types of vaccine. Self-treatment: none.

Onchocerciasis (River Blindness)

This disease is caused by the larvae of a tiny worm, which is spread by the bite of a small fly. The earliest sign of infection is intensely itchy, red, sore eyes. It's rare for travellers to be severely affected. Treatment undertaken in a specialised clinic is curative. Self-treatment: none.

Poliomyelitis

This disease is generally spread through contaminated food and water. It is one of the vaccines given in childhood and should be boosted every 10 years, either orally (a drop on the tongue) or else as an injection. Polio can be carried asymptomatically (ie showing no symptoms) and could cause a transient fever. In rare cases it causes weakness or paralysis of one or more muscles, which might be permanent. Self-treatment: none.

Rabies

Rabies is spread via the bite or lick of an infected animal on broken skin. It is always fatal once the clinical symptoms start (which might be up to several months after an infected bite), so post-bite vaccination should be given as soon as possible. Post-bite vaccination (whether or not you've been vaccinated before the bite) prevents the virus from spreading to the central nervous system. Consider vaccination if you'll be travelling away from major centres (ie anywhere where a reliable source of post-bite vaccine is not available within 24 hours). Three preventive injections are needed over a month. If you have not been vaccinated you'll need a course of five injections starting 24 hours, or as soon as possible, after the injury. If you have been vaccinated, you'll need fewer post-bite injections, and have more time to seek medical help. Self-treatment: none.

Schistosomiasis (Bilharzia)

This disease is a risk throughout Tanzania. It's spread by flukes (parasitic flatworm) that are carried by a species of freshwater snail, which then sheds them into slow-moving or still water. The parasites penetrate human skin during swimming and then migrate to the bladder or bowel. They are excreted via stool or urine and could contaminate fresh water, where the cycle starts again. Swimming in suspect freshwater lakes (including Lake Victoria) or slow-running rivers should be avoided. Symptoms range from none to transient fever and rash, and advanced cases might have blood in the stool or in the urine. A blood test can detect antibodies if you might have been exposed, and treatment is readily available. If not treated, the infection can cause kidney failure or permanent bowel damage. It's not possible for you to infect others. Self-treatment: none.

Trypanosomiasis (Sleeping Sickness)

This disease is spread via the bite of the tsetse fly. It causes headache, fever and eventually coma. If you have these symptoms and have negative malaria tests, have yourself evaluated by a reputable clinic in Dar es Salaam, where you should also be able to obtain treatment for trypanosomiasis. There is an effective treatment. Self-treatment: none.

Tuberculosis (TB)

TB is spread through close respiratory contact and occasionally through infected milk or milk products. BCG vaccination is recommended if you'll be mixing closely with the local population, especially on long-term stays, although it gives only moderate protection against TB. TB can be asymptomatic, only being picked up on a routine chest X-ray. Alternatively, it can cause a cough, weight loss or fever, sometimes months or even years after exposure. Self-treatment: none.

Typhoid

This is spread through food or water contaminated by infected human faeces. The first symptom is usually a fever or a pink rash on the abdomen. Septicaemia (blood poisoning) can sometimes occur. A typhoid vaccine (typhim Vi, typherix) will give protection for three years. In some countries, the oral vaccine Vivotif is also available. Antibiotics are usually given as treatment, and death is rare unless septicaemia occurs. Self-treatment: none.

Yellow Fever

Tanzania (including Zanzibar) requires you to carry a certificate of yellow-fever vaccination only if you are arriving from an infected area (which includes Kenya). However, it is a requirement in some neighbouring countries (eg Rwanda, Burundi). Yellow fever is spread by infected mosquitoes. Symptoms range from a flu-like illness to severe hepatitis (liver inflam-

mation), jaundice and death. The yellow-fever vaccination must be given at a designated clinic and is valid for 10 years. It is a live vaccine and must not be given to immunocompromised or pregnant travellers. Self-treatment: none.

Travellers' Diarrhoea

It's not inevitable that you'll get diarrhoea while travelling in Tanzania, but it's likely. Diarrhoea is the most common travel-related illness, and sometimes can be triggered simply by dietary changes. To help prevent diarrhoea, avoid tap water, only eat fresh fruits or vegetables if cooked or peeled and be wary of dairy products that might contain unpasteurised milk. Although freshly cooked food can be a safe option, plates or serving utensils might be dirty, so be selective when eating from street vendors (make sure that cooked food is piping hot all the way through). If you develop diarrhoea, be sure to drink plenty of fluids, preferably an oral rehydration solution. A few loose stools don't require treatment, but if you start having more than four or five stools a day you should start taking an antibiotic (usually a quinoline drug, such as ciprofloxacin or norfloxacin) and an antidiarrhoeal agent (such as loperamide) if you

are not within easy reach of a toilet. If diarrhoea is bloody, persists for more than 72 hours or is accompanied by fever, shaking chills or severe abdominal pain, seek medical attention.

Amoebic Dysentery

Contracted by eating contaminated food and water, amoebic dysentery causes blood and mucus in the faeces. It can be relatively mild and tends to come on gradually, but seek medical advice if you think you have the illness as it won't clear up without treatment with specific antibiotics.

Giardiasis

This is caused by ingesting contaminated food or water. The illness usually appears a week or more after you have been exposed to the offending parasite. Giardiasis might cause only a short-lived bout of typical travellers' diarrhoea, but it can also cause persistent diarrhoea. Seek medical advice if you suspect you have giardiasis. If you are in a remote area you could start a course of antibiotics, with medical follow-up when feasible.

Environmental Hazards

Altitude Sickness

Reduced oxygen levels at altitudes above 2500m affects most people. The effect may be mild or severe and occurs because less oxygen reaches the muscles and the brain at high altitudes, requiring the heart and lungs to compensate by working harder. Symptoms of Acute Mountain Sickness (AMS) usually develop during the first 24 hours at altitude but may be delayed for up to three weeks. Mild symptoms include headache, lethargy, dizziness, sleeping difficulties and loss of appetite. AMS may become more severe without warning and can be

DRINKING WATER

Unless your intestines are well accustomed to Tanzania, don't drink tap water that hasn't been boiled, filtered or chemically disinfected (eg with iodine tablets) and be wary of ice and fruit juices diluted with unpurified water. Avoid drinking from streams, rivers and lakes unless you've purified the water first. The same goes for drinking from pumps and wells; some bring pure water to the surface, but the presence of animals can contaminate supplies. Bottled water is widely available, except in very remote areas, where you should carry a filter or purification tablets.

fatal. It is a significant risk for anyone, no matter what their fitness level, who tries to ascend Mt Kilimanjaro or Mt Meru too rapidly. Severe symptoms include breathlessness; a dry, irritative cough (which may progress to the production of pink, frothy sputum); severe headache; lack of coordination and balance; confusion; irrational behaviour; vomiting; drowsiness; and unconsciousness. There is no hard-and-fast rule as to what is too high: AMS has been fatal at 3000m, although 3500m to 4500m is the usual range.

Treat mild symptoms of AMS by resting at the same altitude until recovery, which usually takes a day or two. Paracetamol or aspirin can be taken for headaches. If symptoms persist or become worse, however, immediate descent is necessary; even descending just 500m can help. Drug treatments should never be used to avoid descent or to enable further ascent.

The drugs acetazolamide and dexamethasone are recommended by some doctors for the prevention of AMS; however, their use is controversial. They can reduce the symptoms, but they may also mask warning signs and cause severe dehydration; severe and fatal AMS has occurred in people taking these drugs. In general, we do not recommend them for travellers.

To prevent AMS, try the following:

➡ Ascend slowly. On Mt Kilimanjaro, this means choosing one of the longer routes that allow for a more gradual ascent. Whatever route you choose, opt to take an additional rest day on the mountain, sleeping two nights at the same location, and using the day for short hikes. All operators can arrange this, and the extra money (a relative pittance in comparison with the overall costs of a Kili trek) will be money well spent.

➡ It's always wise to sleep at a lower altitude than the greatest height reached during the day ('climb high, sleep low').

➡ Drink lots of fluids. Mountain air is dry and cold and moisture is lost as you breathe. Evaporation of sweat may occur unnoticed and result in dehydration.

➡ Eat light, high carbohydrate meals for more energy.

➡ Avoid alcohol as it increases risk of dehydration.

➡ Avoid sedatives.

Heat Exhaustion

This condition occurs after heavy sweating and excessive fluid loss with inadequate replacement of fluids and salt, and is primarily a risk in hot climates when taking part in unaccustomed exercise before full acclimatisation. Symptoms include headache, dizziness and tiredness. Dehydration is already happening by the time you feel thirsty; aim to drink sufficient water to produce pale, diluted urine. Self-treatment: fluid replacement with water and/or fruit juice, and cooling the body with cold water and fans. The treatment of the salt-loss component consists of consuming salty fluids (as in soup) and adding a little more table salt to foods than usual.

Heatstroke

Heat exhaustion is a precursor to the much more serious condition of heatstroke. In this case there is damage to the sweating mechanism, with an excessive rise in body temperature; irrational and hyperactive behaviour; and, eventually, loss of consciousness and death. Rapid cooling by spraying the body with water and fanning is ideal. Emergency fluid and electrolyte replacement is usually also required by intravenous drip.

Hypothermia

If you are trekking at high altitudes, such as on Mt Kilimanjaro or Mt Meru, you'll need to have appropriate clothing and be prepared for cold, wet conditions. Even in lower areas, such as the Usambara Mountains, the rim of Ngorongoro Crater or the Ulugurus, conditions can be wet and quite chilly.

Symptoms of hypothermia are exhaustion, numb skin (particularly of the toes and fingers), shivering, slurred speech, irrational or violent behaviour, lethargy, stumbling, dizzy spells, muscle cramps and violent bursts of energy. Irrationality may take the form of sufferers claiming they are warm and trying to take off their clothes.

To treat mild hypothermia, first get the person out of the wind and/or rain, remove their clothing if it's wet and replace it with dry, warm clothing. Give them hot liquids – not alcohol – and high-kilojoule, easily digestible food. Do not rub victims: allow them to slowly warm themselves instead. This should be enough to treat the early stages of hypothermia. The early recognition and treatment of mild hypothermia is the only way to prevent severe hypothermia, which is a critical condition.

Insect Bites & Stings

Bites from mosquitoes and other insects can cause irritation and infected bites. To avoid these, take the same precautions as you would for avoiding malaria. Bee and wasp stings cause real problems only to those who have a severe allergy to the stings (anaphylaxis), in which case, carry an adrenaline (epinephrine) injection.

Scorpions are found in arid areas. They can cause a painful bite that is sometimes life-threatening. If bitten by a scorpion, seek immediate medical assistance.

Bed bugs are often found in hostels and cheap hotels. They lead to very itchy, lumpy bites. Spraying the mattress with crawling insect killer after changing the bedding will get rid of them.

Scabies is also frequently found in cheap accommodation. These tiny mites live in the skin, particularly between the fingers. They cause an intensely itchy rash. The itch is easily treated with Malathion and permethrin lotion from a pharmacy; other members of the household also need to be treated to avoid spreading scabies, even if they do not show any symptoms.

Snake Bites

Avoid getting bitten! Don't walk barefoot or stick your hand into holes or cracks. However, 50% of those bitten by venomous snakes are not actually injected with poison (envenomed). If bitten by a snake, do not panic. Immobilise the bitten limb with a splint (such as a stick) and apply a bandage over the site with firm pressure, similar to bandaging a sprain. Do not apply a tourniquet, or cut or suck the bite. Get medical help as soon as possible so an antivenin can be given if needed. Try to note the snake's appearance to help in treatment.

HEALTH ENVIRONMENTAL HAZARDS

Language

Swahili is the national language of Tanzania (as well as Kenya). It's also the key language of communication in the wider East African region. This makes it one of the most widely spoken African languages. Although the number of speakers of Swahili throughout East Africa is estimated to be well over 50 million, it's the mother tongue of only about 5 million people, and is predominantly used as a second language or a *lingua franca* by speakers of other African languages. Swahili belongs to the Bantu group of languages from the Niger-Congo family and can be traced back to the first millenium AD. It's hardly surprising that in an area as vast as East Africa many different dialects of Swahili can be found, but you shouldn't have problems being understood in Tanzania (or in the wider region) if you stick to the standard coastal form, as used in this book.

Most sounds in Swahili have equivalents in English. In our coloured pronunciation guides, ay should be read as in 'say', oh as the 'o' in 'role', dh as the 'th' in 'this' and th as in 'thing'. Note also that the sound ng can be found at the start of words in Swahili, and that Swahili speakers make only a slight distinction between r and l – instead of the hard 'r', try pronouncing a light 'd'. In Swahili, words are almost always stressed on the second-last syllable. In our pronunciation guides, the stressed syllables are in italics.

WANT MORE?

For in-depth language information and handy phrases, check out Lonely Planet's Swahili Phrasebook. You'll find it at shop.lonelyplanet.com

BASICS

Jambo is a pidgin Swahili word, used to greet tourists who are presumed not to understand the language. If people assume you can speak a little Swahili, they might use the following greetings:

Hello. (general)	*Habari*	ha·*ba*·ree
Hello. (respectful)	*Shikamoo.*	shee·ka·*moh*
Goodbye.	*Tutaonana.*	too·ta·oh·*na*·na

Good ...	*Habari za ...*	ha·*ba*·ree za ...
morning	*asubuhi*	a·soo·*boo*·hee
afternoon	*mchana*	m·*cha*·na
evening	*jioni*	jee·*oh*·nee

Yes.	*Ndiyo.*	n·*dee*·yoh
No.	*Hapana.*	ha·*pa*·na
Please.	*Tafadhali.*	ta·fa·*dha*·lee
Thank you (very much).	*Asante (sana).*	a·*san*·tay (*sa*·na)
You're welcome.	*Karibu.*	ka·*ree*·boo
Excuse me.	*Samahani.*	sa·ma·*ha*·nee
Sorry.	*Pole.*	*poh*·lay

How are you?
Habari? · ha·*ba*·ree

I'm fine.
Nzuri./Salama./Safi. n·*zoo*·ree/sa·la·ma/*sa*·fee

If things are just OK, add *tu* too (only) after any of the above replies. If things are really good, add *sana sa*·na (very) or *kabisa* ka·*bee*·sa (totally) instead of *tu*.

What's your name?
Jina lako nani? jee·na la·koh *na*·nee

My name is ...
Jina langu ni ... jee·na *lan*·goo nee ...

KEY PATTERNS

To get by in Swahili, mix and match these patterns with words of your choice:

When's (the next bus)?
(Basi ijayo) (ba·see ee·ja·yoh)
itaondoka lini? ee·ta·ohn·doh·ka lee·nee

Where's (the station)?
(Stesheni) iko (stay·shay·nee) ee·koh
wapi? wa·pee

How much is (a room)?
(Chumba) ni (choom·ba) nee
bei gani? bay ga·nee

I'm looking for (a hotel).
Natafuta (hoteli). na·ta·foo·ta (hoh·tay·lee)

Do you have (a map)?
Una (ramani)? oo·na (ra·ma·nee)

Please bring (the bill).
Lete (bili). lay·tay (bee·lee)

I'd like (the menu).
Nataka (menyu). na·ta·ka (may·nyoo)

I have (a reservation).
Nina (buking). nee·na (boo·keeng)

Do you speak English?
Unasema oo·na·say·ma
Kiingereza? kee·een·gay·ray·za

I don't understand.
Sielewi. see·ay·lay·wee

ACCOMMODATION

Where's a ...?	... iko wapi?	... ee·koh wa·pee
campsite	Uwanja wa kambi	oo·wan·ja wa kam·bee
guesthouse	Gesti	gay·stee
hotel	Hoteli	hoh·tay·lee
youth hostel	Hosteli ya vijana	hoh·stay·lee ya vee·ja·na

Do you have a ... room?	Kuna chumba kwa ...?	koo·na choom·ba kwa ...
double (one bed)	watu wawili, kitanda kimoja	wa·too wa·wee·lee, kee·tan·da kee·moh·ja
single	mtu mmoja	m·too m·moh·ja
twin (two beds)	watu wawili, vitanda viwili	wa·too wa·wee·lee, vee·tan·da vee·wee·lee

How much is it per ...?	Ni bei gani kwa ...?	nee bay ga·ne kwa ...
day	siku	see·koo
person	mtu	m·too

air-con	a/c	ay·see
bathroom	bafuni	ba·foo·nee
key	ufunguo	oo·foon·goo·oh
toilet	choo	choh
window	dirisha	dee·ree·sha

DIRECTIONS

Where's the ...?
... iko wapi? ... ee·koh wa·pee

What's the address?
Anwani ni nini? an·wa·nee nee nee·nee

How do I get there?
Nifikaje? nee·fee·ka·jay

How far is it?
Ni umbali gani? nee oom·ba·lee ga·nee

Can you show me (on the map)?
Unaweza oo·na·way·za
kunionyesha koo·nee·oh·nyay·sha
(katika ramani)? (ka·tee·ka ra·ma·nee)

It's ...	Iko ...	ee·koh ...
behind ...	nyuma ya ...	nyoo·ma ya ...
in front of ...	mbele ya ...	m·bay·lay ya ...
near ...	karibu na ...	ka·ree·boo na ...
next to ...	jirani ya ...	jee·ra·nee ya ...
on the corner	pembeni	paym·bay·nee
opposite ...	ng'ambo ya ...	ng·am·boh ya ...
straight ahead	moja kwa moja	moh·ja kwa moh·ja

Turn ...	Geuza ...	gay·oo·za ...
at the corner	kwenye kona	kway·nyay koh·na
at the traffic lights	kwenye taa za barabarani	kway·nyay ta za ba·ra·ba·ra·nee
left	kushoto	koo·shoh·toh
right	kulia	koo·lee·a

EATING & DRINKING

I'd like to reserve a table for ...
Nataka na·ta·ka
kuhifadhi koo·hee·fa·dhee
meza kwa ... may·za kwa ...

(two) people	(wawili)	(wa·wee·lee)
(eight) o'clock	saa (mbili)	sa (m·bee·lee)

I'd like the menu.
Naomba menyu. na·ohm·ba may·nyoo

What would you recommend?
Chakula gani ni cha·koo·la ga·nee nee
kizuri? kee·zoo·ree

Do you have vegetarian food?
Mna chakula	m·na cha·koo·la
bila nyama?	bee·la nya·ma

I'll have that.
Nataka hicho.	na·ta·ka hee·choh

Cheers!
Heri!	hay·ree

That was delicious!
Chakula kitamu sana!	cha·koo·la kee·ta·moo sa·na

Please bring the bill.
Lete hili	lay·tay bee·loo

I don't eat ...	*Sili ...*	see·lee ...
butter	*siagi*	see·a·gee
eggs	*mayai*	ma·ya·ee
red meat	*nyama*	nya·ma

Key Words

bottle	*chupa*	choo·pa
bowl	*bakuli*	ba·koo·lee
breakfast	*chai ya asubuhi*	cha·ee ya a·soo·boo·hee
cold	*baridi*	ba·ree·dee
dinner	*chakula cha jioni*	cha·koo·la cha jee·oh·nee
dish	*chakula*	cha·koo·la
fork	*uma*	oo·ma
glass	*glesi*	glay·see
halal	*halali*	ha·la·lee
hot	*joto*	joh·toh
knife	*kisu*	kee·soo
kosher	*halali*	ha·la·lee
lunch	*chakula cha mchana*	cha·koo·la·cha m·cha·na
market	*soko*	soh·koh
plate	*sahani*	sa·ha·nee
restaurant	*mgahawa*	m·ga·ha·wa
snack	*kumbwe*	koom·bway
spicy	*chenye viungo*	chay·nyay vee·oon·goh
spoon	*kijiko*	kee·jee·koh
with	*na*	na
without	*bila*	bee·la

Meat & Fish

beef	*nyama ng'ombe*	nya·ma ng·ohm·bay
chicken	*kuku*	koo·koo
crab	*kaa*	ka
fish	*samaki*	sa·ma·kee
hering	*heringi*	hay·reen·gee
lamb	*mwanakondoo*	mwa·na·kohn·doh
meat	*nyama*	nya·ma
mutton	*nyama mbuzi*	nya·ma m·boo·zee
oyster	*chaza*	cha·za
pork	*nyama nguruwe*	nya·ma n·goo·roo·way
seafood	*chakula kutoka bahari*	cha·koo·la kuo·toh·ka ba·ha·ree
squid	*ngisi*	n·gee·see
tuna	*jodari*	joh·da·ree
veal	*nyama ya ndama*	nya·ma ya n·da·ma

Fruit & Vegetables

apple	*tofaa*	toh·fa
banana	*ndizi*	n·dee·zee
cabbage	*kabichi*	ka·bee·chee
carrot	*karoti*	ka·roh·tee
eggplant	*biringani*	bee·reen·ga·nee
fruit	*tunda*	toon·da
grapefruit	*balungi*	ba·loon·gee
grapes	*zabibu*	za·bee·boo
guava	*pera*	pay·ra
lemon	*limau*	lee·ma·oo
lentils	*dengu*	dayn·goo
mango	*embe*	aym·bay
onion	*kitunguu*	kee·toon·goo
orange	*chungwa*	choon·gwa
peanut	*karanga*	ka·ran·ga
pineapple	*nanasi*	na·na·see
potato	*kiazi*	kee·a·zee
spinach	*mchicha*	m·chee·cha
tomato	*nyanya*	nya·nya
vegetable	*mboga*	m·boh·ga

Signs

Mahali Pa Kuingia	Entrance
Mahali Pa Kutoka	Exit
Imefunguliwa	Open
Imefungwa	Closed
Maelezo	Information
Ni Marufuku	Prohibited
Choo/Msalani	Toilets
Wanaume	Men
Wanawake	Women

Other

bread	mkate	m·ka·tay
butter	siagi	see·a·gee
cheese	jibini	jee·bee·nee
egg	yai	ya·ee
honey	asali	a·sa·lee
jam	jamu	ja·moo
pasta	tambi	tam·bee
pepper	pilipili	pee·lee·pee·lee
rice (cooked)	wali	wa·lee
salt	chumvi	choom·vee
sugar	sukari	soo·ka·ree

Drinks

beer	bia	bee·a
coffee	kahawa	ka·ha·wa
juice	jusi	joo·see
milk	maziwa	ma·zee·wa
mineral water	maji ya madini	ma·jee ya ma·dee·nee
orange juice	maji ya machungwa	ma·jee ya ma·choon·gwa
red wine	mvinyo mwekundu	m·vee·nyoh mway·koon·doo
soft drink	soda	soh·da
sparkling wine	mvinyo yenye mapovu	m·vee·nyoh yay·nyay ma·poh·voo
tea	chai	cha·ee
water	maji	ma·jee
white wine	mvinyo mweupe	m·vee·nyoh mway·oo·pay

EMERGENCIES

Help!	Saidia!	sa·ee·dee·a
Go away!	Toka!	toh·ka

I'm lost.
Nimejipotea. — nee·may·jee·poh·tay·a

Call the police.
Waite polisi. — wa·ee·tay poh·lee·see

Call a doctor.
Mwite daktari. — m·wee·tay dak·ta·ree

I'm sick.
Mimi ni mgonjwa. — mee·mee nee m·gohn·jwa

It hurts here.
Inauma hapa. — ee·na·oo·ma ha·pa

I'm allergic to (antibiotics).
Nina mzio wa (viuavijasumu). — nee·na m·zee·oh wa (vee·oo·a·vee·ja·soo·moo)

Where's the toilet?
Choo kiko wapi? — choh kee·koh wa·pee

SHOPPING & SERVICES

I'd like to buy ...
Nataka kununua ... — na·ta·ka koo·noo·noo·a ...

I'm just looking.
Naangalia tu. — na·an·ga·lee·a too

Can I look at it?
Naomba nione? — na·ohm·ba nee·oh·nay

I don't like it.
Sipendi. — see·payn·dee

How much is it?
Ni bei gani? — ni bay ga·nee

That's too expensive.
Ni ghali mno. — nee ga·lee m·noh

Please lower the price.
Punguza bei. — poon·goo·za·bay

There's a mistake in the bill.
Kuna kosa kwenye bili. — koo·na koh·sa kwayn·yay bee·lee

ATM	mashine ya kutolea pesa	ma·shee·nay ya koo·toh·lay·a pay·sa
post office	posta	poh·sta
public phone	simu ya mtaani	see·moo ya m·ta·nee
tourist office	ofisi ya watalii	o·fee·see ya wa·ta·lee

TIME & DATES

Keep in mind that the Swahili time system starts six hours later than the international one – it begins at sunrise which occurs at about 6am year-round. Therefore, saa mbili sa m·bee·lee (lit: clocks two) means '2 o'clock Swahili time' and '8 o'clock international time'.

What time is it?
Ni saa ngapi? — nee sa n·ga·pee

It's (10) o'clock.
Ni saa (nne). — nee sa (n·nay)

Half past (10).
Ni saa (nne) na nusu. — nee sa (n·nay) na noo·soo

morning	asubuhi	a·soo·boo·hee
afternoon	mchana	m·cha·na
evening	jioni	jee·oh·nee
yesterday	jana	ja·na
today	leo	lay·oh
tomorrow	kesho	kay·shoh
Monday	Jumatatu	joo·ma·ta·too
Tuesday	Jumanne	joo·ma·n·nay
Wednesday	Jumatano	joo·ma·ta·noh
Thursday	Alhamisi	al·ha·mee·see
Friday	Ijumaa	ee·joo·ma
Saturday	Jumamosi	joo·ma·moh·see
Sunday	Jumapili	joo·ma·pee·lee

TRANSPORT

Public Transport

Which ...	... ipi	... ee·pee
goes to (Mbeya)?	huenda (Mbeya)?	hoo·ayn·da (m·bay·a)
bus	Basi	ba·see
ferry	Kivuko	kee·voo·koh
minibus	Daladala	da·la·da·la
train	Treni	tray·nee

When's the ... bus?	Basi ... itaondoka lini?	ba·see ... ee·ta·ohn·doh·ka lee·nee
first	ya kwanza	ya kwan·za
last	ya mwisho	ya mwee·shoh
next	ijayo	ee·ja·yoh

A ... ticket to (Iringa).	Tiketi moja ya ... kwenda (Iringa).	tee·kay·tee moh·ja ya ... kwayn·da (ee·reen·ga)
1st-class	daraja la kwanza	da·ra·ja la kwan·za
2nd-class	daraja la pili	da·ra·ja la pee·lee
one-way	kwenda tu	kwayn·da too
return	kwenda na kurudi	kwayn·da na koo·roo·dee

What time does it get to (Kisumu)?
Itafika (Kisumu) saa ngapi? · ee·ta·fee·ka (kee·soo·moo) sa n·ga·pee

Does it stop at (Tanga)?
Linasimama (Tanga)? · lee·na·see·ma·ma (tan·ga)

I'd like to get off at (Bagamoyo).
Nataka kushusha (Bagamoyo). · na·ta·ka koo·shoo·sha (ba·ga·moh·yoh)

Numbers

1	moja	moh·ja
2	mbili	m·bee·lee
3	tatu	ta·too
4	nne	n·nay
5	tano	ta·noh
6	sita	see·ta
7	saba	sa·ba
8	nane	na·nay
9	tisa	tee·sa
10	kumi	koo·mee
20	ishirini	ee·shee·ree·nee
30	thelathini	thay·la·thee·nee
40	arobaini	a·roh·ba·ee·nee
50	hamsini	ham·see·nee
60	sitini	see·tee·nee
70	sabini	sa·bee·nee
80	themanini	thay·ma·nee·nee
90	tisini	tee·see·nee
100	mia moja	mee·a moh·ja
1000	elfu	ayl·foo

Driving & Cycling

I'd like to hire a ...	Nataka kukodi ...	na·ta·ka koo·koh·dee ...
4WD	forbaifor	fohr·ba·ee·fohr
bicycle	baisikeli	ba·ee·see·kay·lee
car	gari	ga·ree
motorbike	pikipiki	pee·kee·pee·kee

diesel	dizeli	dee·zay·lee
regular	kawaida	ka·wa·ee·da
unleaded	isiyo na risasi	ee·see·yoh na ree·sa·see

Is this the road to (Embu)?
Hii ni barabara kwenda (Embu)? · hee nee ba·ra·ba·ra kwayn·da (aym·boo)

Where's a petrol station?
Kituo cha mafuta kiko wapi? · kee·too·oh cha ma·foo·ta kee·ko wa·pee

(How long) Can I park here?
Naweza kuegesha hapa (kwa muda gani)? · na·way·za koo·ay·gay·sha ha·pa (kwa moo·da ga·ni)

I need a mechanic.
Nahitaji fundi. · na·hee·ta·jee foon·dee

I have a flat tyre.
Nina pancha. · nee·na pan·cha

I've run out of petrol.
Mafuta yamekwisha. · ma·foo·ta ya·may·kwee·sha

GLOSSARY

(m) indicates masculine gender, (f) feminine gender and (pl) plural

ASP – Afro-Shirazi Party

bajaji – tuk-tuk

banda – thatched-roof hut with wooden or earthen walls; the term is also used to refer to any simple bungalow- or cottage-style accommodation

bangi – marijuana

bao – a board game widely played in East Africa, especially on Zanzibar

baraza – the stone seats seen along the outside walls of houses in Zanzibar's Stone Town, used for chatting and relaxing

boda-boda – motorcycle taxi (from 'border-border', as they are commonly used transport for bridging the no-man's land between country borders)

boma – a fortified living compound; colonial-era administrative offices

bui-bui – black cover-all worn by some Islamic women outside the home

Bunge – Tanzanian Parliament

chai – tea

chakula – food

Chama Cha Mapinduzi (CCM) – Party of the Revolution (governing party)

choo – toilet

Cites – UN Convention on International Trade in Endangered Species

Civic United Front (CUF) – main opposition party

Coastal ('thelathini') – 30-seater buses, commonly used on some routes instead of large, full-size buses; also known as coasters

dada – sister; often used as a form of address

dalla-dalla – minibus

Deutsch-Ostafrikanische Gesellschaft (DOAG) – German East Africa Company

dhow – ancient Arabic sailing vessel

duka – small shop or kiosk

fly camp – a camp away from the main tented camps or lodges, for the purpose of enjoying a more authentic bush experience

flycatcher – used mainly in Arusha and Moshi to mean a tout working to get you to go on safari with an operator from whom he knows he can get a commission. We assume the name comes from a comparison with the sticky-sweet paper used to lure flies to land (and then get irretrievably stuck) – similar to the plight of a hapless traveller who succumbs to a flycatcher's promises and then is 'stuck' (ie with their money and time lost in a fraudulent safari deal).

forex – foreign exchange (bureau)

ganja – see *bangi*

gongo – distilled cashew drink

hodi – called out prior to entering someone's house; roughly meaning 'may I enter?'

hotel/hoteli – basic local eatery

jamaa – clan, community

kahawa – coffee

kaka – brother; used as a form of address, and to call the waiter in restaurants

kanga – printed cotton wrap-around worn by many Tanzanian women; Swahili proverbs are printed along the edge of the cloth

kanzu – white robe-like outer garment worn by men, often for prayer, on the Zanzibar Archipelago and in other Swahili areas

karanga – peanuts

karibu – Swahili for 'welcome'; heard throughout Tanzania

kidumbak – an offshoot of *taarab* music, distinguished by its defined rhythms and drumming, and hard-hitting lyrics

kikoi – cotton linen wrap-around traditionally worn by men in coastal areas

kitenge – similar to a *kanga*, but larger, heavier and without a Swahili proverb

kofia – a cap, usually of embroidered white linen, worn by men on the Zanzibar Archipelago and in other Swahili areas

kopje – rocky outcrop or hill

kwaya – church choir music

maandazi – doughnut

makuti – thatch

marimba – musical instrument played with the thumb

mashua – motorised dhow

masika – long rains

matatu – Kenyan minivan

matoke – cooked plantains

mbege – banana beer

mgando – see *mtindi*

mihrab – the prayer niche in a mosque showing the direction to Mecca

mishikaki – meat kebabs

mnada – auction, usually held once or twice monthly on a regular basis

moran – Maasai warrior

mpingo – African blackwood

mtepe – a traditional Swahili sailing vessel made without nails, the planks held together with only coconut fibres and wooden pegs

mtindi – cultured milk product similar to yogurt

mvuli – short rains

Mwalimu – teacher; used to refer to Julius Nyerere

mzungu – white person, foreigner (pl *wazungu*)

nazi – fermented coconut wine

NCA – Ngorongoro Conservation Area

NCAA – Ngorongoro Conservation Area Authority

ndugu – brother, comrade

ngoma – dance and drumming

northern circuit – the northern safari route, including Serengeti, Tarangire and Lake Manyara National Parks and the Ngorongoro Conservation Area

nyika – bush or hinterland

orpul – Maasai camp where men go to eat meat

papasi – literally 'tick'; used on Zanzibar to refer to street touts

piki-piki – motorbike

potwe – whale shark

pweza – octopus, usually served grilled, at night markets and street stalls

public (ordinary) campsite – type of national park campsite, with basic facilities, generally including latrines and a water source

shamba – small farm plot

shehe – village chief

shetani – literally, demon or something supernatural; in art, a style of carving embodying images from the spirit world

shikamoo – Swahili greeting of respect, used for elders or anyone in a position of authority; the response is '*marahaba*'

special campsite – type of national park campsite, more remote than *public campsites*, and without facilities

TAA – Tanganyika Africa Association, successor of the African Association and predecessor of TANU

taarab – Zanzibari music combining African, Arabic and Indian influences

Tanapa – Tanzania National Parks Authority

TANU – Tanganyika (later, Tanzania) African National Union

TATO – Tanzanian Association of Tour Operators

Tazara – Tanzania–Zambia Railway

tea room – a small shop, usually with a few tables, serving snacks and light meals

tilapia – a cichlid fish very

common around Lake Victoria

Tingatinga – Tanzania's best-known style of painting, developed in the 1960s by Edward Saidi Tingatinga; traditionally in a square format with colourful animal motifs against a monochrome background

TTB – Tanzania Tourist Board

ugali – a staple made from maize and/or cassava flour

uhuru – freedom; also the name of Mt Kilimanjaro's highest peak

ujamaa – familyhood, togetherness

umoja – unity

Unguja – Swahili name for Zanzibar island

vitambua – rice cakes

wali – cooked rice

ZIFF – Zanzibar International Film Festival

ZNP – Zanzibar Nationalist Party

ZPPP – Zanzibar & Pemba People's Party

ZTC – Zanzibar Tourist Corporation

Behind the Scenes

SEND US YOUR FEEDBACK

We love to hear from travellers – your comments keep us on our toes and help make our books better. Our well-travelled team reads every word on what you loved or loathed about this book. Although we cannot reply individually to your submissions, we always guarantee that your feedback goes straight to the appropriate authors, in time for the next edition. Each person who sends us information is thanked in the next edition – the most useful submissions are rewarded with a selection of digital PDF chapters.

Visit **lonelyplanet.com/contact** to submit your updates and suggestions or to ask for help. Our award-winning website also features inspirational travel stories, news and discussions.

Note: We may edit, reproduce and incorporate your comments in Lonely Planet products such as guidebooks, websites and digital products, so let us know if you don't want your comments reproduced or your name acknowledged. For a copy of our privacy policy visit lonelyplanet.com/privacy.

OUR READERS

Many thanks to the travellers who used the last edition and wrote to us with helpful hints, useful advice and interesting anecdotes:

Anneke Valk, Annika Goorsenberg, Annika Gunnarsson, Astrid Naundorf, Aurelie Cloix, Bob Demyan, Bruce Becker, Chris Hughes, Darren Keogh, Eduardo Fajer, Eleanor Kirby, Elizabeth Greive, Friederike Haberstroh, Gianluca Valenti, Hervé Palanchon, Hilbert Weemstra, Isabel Vorrath, Jan Gorter, Johann Schelesnak, Jonas Kronqvist, Jose Rocha, Julian Hercun, Katarina Forsström, Katerina Sourouni, Lena Leuthold, Lisa Henry, Maaike Bouma, Marc Eichen, Marco van Zwetselaar, Marijke Bakker, Mbaraka Kilopola, Neil Bennett, Neil Cook, Nicolas Combremont, Panagiota Fatourou, Patricia Moreira, Renate Hellerud, Rouna Ali, Steph Lewis, Steve Conway, Tajan Tober, Terry Noctor, Thomas Mayes, Vince Calderhead

AUTHOR THANKS

Mary Fitzpatrick

Many thanks to the inimitable J4 in Dar es Salaam, to the Mtemere entry gate rangers at Selous Game Reserve, to Matt Phillips for all the assistance, wise perspectives and patience, to my co-authors for their professionalism and their help with so many extra bits and pieces of information, and – most of all – to Rick, Christopher, Dominic and Gabriel for the companionship and humour on this and all our journeys.

Stuart Butler

Researching sections of the *Tanzania*, *Kenya* and *East Africa* guidebooks on one trip meant I was away from home for a long time, so I must first and foremost thank my wife for holding things together at home – again – and my children for once again going without their daddy for so long. In Tanzania I would like to thank Rama for driving, William at Kiroyera Tours, Louise and Chris at Lakeshore Lodge, Canon Shaban, Mercedes Bailey, Michelle Attala, Nick Greaves in Katavi, Des and Kim in Mahale Mountains and all the wildlife guides I had who never failed to amaze me with their knowledge.

Anthony Ham

Heartfelt thanks to Matt Phillips and Mary Fitzpatrick, two wise companions of the Africa road of long-standing. Thanks also to Sandy Evans, (Manyara Ranch Conservancy), Ingela Jansson (Ngorongoro Lion Project), Daniel Rosengren and Craig Packer (Serengeti Lion project) and Peter Ndirangu. To Marina, Carlota and Valentina – next time with you.

BEHIND THE SCENES

Paula Hardy

Doors opened in Dar es Salaam, Zanzibar and beyond thanks to the generosity of Mohammed Abdul Samad, Stefanie Schoetz, Suzanne Degeling, Said el-Gheity, Martin Mhando, Bobby McKenna, Simai Mohammed Said, Christian and Tammy Moorhouse-Chilcott, Hafsa Mbamba, Nassor Haji, Eliakira Pallangyo, David Bega, Russell Bridgewood, Julie Lawrence, Mohammed Okala and Kelly Atkins. The biggest thank you of all, though, goes to Nasir Mussa, for so many laughs along the way, and Harold Webb and David Hardy for their endless adventuring in East Africa.

ACKNOWLEDGMENTS

Climate map data adapted from Peel MC, Finlayson BL & McMahon TA (2007) 'Updated World Map of the Köppen-Geiger Climate Classification', Hydrology and Earth System Sciences, 11, 163344.

Cover photograph: Cheetahs, Serengeti National Park. © Mitsuaki Iwago/Corbis.

THIS BOOK

This 6th edition of Lonely Planet's *Tanzania* guidebook was researched and written by Mary Fitzpatrick, Stuart Butler, Anthony Ham and Paula Hardy. This guidebook was produced by the following:

Destination Editor Matt Phillips

Product Editors Briohny Hooper, Luna Soo

Senior Cartographer Corey Hutchison

Book Designer Mazzy Prinsep

Assisting Editors Kate Chapman, Melanie Dankel, Andrea Dobbin, Paul Harding, Victoria Harrison, Andi Jones, Kellie Langdon, Jenna Myers, Saralinda Turner

Assisting Cartographer Mick Garrett

Cover Researcher Naomi Parker

Thanks to Sasha Baskett, Ryan Evans, Campbell McKenzie, Claire Naylor, Martine Power, Diana Saengkham, Samantha Tyson, Tracy Whitney, Amanda Williamson

Index

NOTES

Map Legend

Sights

- Beach
- Bird Sanctuary
- Buddhist
- Castle/Palace
- Christian
- Confucian
- Hindu
- Islamic
- Jain
- Jewish
- Monument
- Museum/Gallery/Historic Building
- Ruin
- Shinto
- Sikh
- Taoist
- Winery/Vineyard
- Zoo/Wildlife Sanctuary
- Other Sight

Activities, Courses & Tours

- Bodysurfing
- Diving
- Canoeing/Kayaking
- Course/Tour
- Sento Hot Baths/Onsen
- Skiing
- Snorkelling
- Surfing
- Swimming/Pool
- Walking
- Windsurfing
- Other Activity

Sleeping

- Sleeping
- Camping

Eating

- Eating

Drinking & Nightlife

- Drinking & Nightlife
- Cafe

Entertainment

- Entertainment

Shopping

- Shopping

Information

- Bank
- Embassy/Consulate
- Hospital/Medical
- Internet
- Police
- Post Office
- Telephone
- Toilet
- Tourist Information
- Other Information

Geographic

- Beach
- Hut/Shelter
- Lighthouse
- Lookout
- Mountain/Volcano
- Oasis
- Park
- Pass
- Picnic Area
- Waterfall

Population

- Capital (National)
- Capital (State/Province)
- City/Large Town
- Town/Village

Transport

- Airport
- Border crossing
- Bus
- Cable car/Funicular
- Cycling
- Ferry
- Metro station
- Monorail
- Parking
- Petrol station
- Subway station
- Taxi
- Train station/Railway
- Tram
- Underground station
- Other Transport

Routes

- Tollway
- Freeway
- Primary
- Secondary
- Tertiary
- Lane
- Unsealed road
- Road under construction
- Plaza/Mall
- Steps
- Tunnel
- Pedestrian overpass
- Walking Tour
- Walking Tour detour
- Path/Walking Trail

Boundaries

- International
- State/Province
- Disputed
- Regional/Suburb
- Marine Park
- Cliff
- Wall

Hydrography

- River, Creek
- Intermittent River
- Canal
- Water
- Dry/Salt/Intermittent Lake
- Reef

Areas

- Airport/Runway
- Beach/Desert
- Cemetery (Christian)
- Cemetery (Other)
- Glacier
- Mudflat
- Park/Forest
- Sight (Building)
- Sportsground
- Swamp/Mangrove

Note: Not all symbols displayed above appear on the maps in this book